GREAT
QUOTATIONS
THAT SHAPED THE WESTERN WORLD

GREAT
QUOTATIONS
THAT SHAPED THE WESTERN WORLD

COMPILED AND WRITTEN BY CARL H. MIDDLETON

PARAGON HOUSE
St. Paul, Minnesota

First Edition 2008

Published in the United States by
Paragon House
1925 Oakcrest Ave, Suite 7
St. Paul, MN 55113
www.paragonhouse.com

Middleton, Carl H., 1938 –
Great Quotations that Shaped the Western World
ISBN: 978-1-55778-864-1

Selection of quotes were at the discretion of the compiler and do not necessarily
reflect the opinion of the publisher.

Library of Congress Cataloging-in-Publication Data

Great quotations that shaped the western world / compiled and written by
Carl H. Middleton.
    p. cm.
  Includes index.
  Summary: "This large collection of quotations from Ancient Greece to the
present day emphasizes the development of the ideas that shaped the freedom
and character of Western Civilization"--Provided by publisher.
  ISBN-13: 978-1-55778-864-1 (pbk. : alk. paper)
  1. Quotations, English. I. Middleton, Carl H.
  PN6081.G6353 2008
  082--dc22
                          2007041182

The paper used in this publication meets the minimum requirements of American National Standard for Information Sciences—Permanence of Paper for Printed Library Materials, ANSIZ39.48-1984.

Manufactured in the United States of America
10 9 8 7 6 5 4 3 2

For current information about all releases from Paragon House, visit the website at
http://www.paragonhouse.com

DEDICATION

You are both angels with only one wing.
You can only soar while embracing each other.

Luciana de Crescenzo

A turtle can't get on top of a fence post by itself. My trophy-wife, the lovely and resourceful Genevieve (Ginny) Campbell Middleton, mother of our three sons, did the heavy lifting in putting *Great Quotations* on top of a post. She pulled the family's financial wagon by herself for ten years as a I scribbled on the book. Curiously, our local board of education helped this "A" college graduate to become a super breadwinner by telling her she was unqualified to teach calculus, chemistry, or biology in high school because she had had "too much math and science." She needed two years worth of education courses "to learn how to communicate." But when a disappointed Ginny entered her second choice, real estate sales, she became a top producer overnight. She even won the coveted Pink Bear by selling a house her first week. Only a Scotch-Irish lassie from Mobile, Alabama could be both Melanie and Scarlet.

Ginny Campbell, my Jo, Ginnny,
We clamb the hill thegither;
And monie a canty day, Ginny,
We've had wi'ane anither;
Now we maun totter down, Ginny,
But hand in hand we'll go,
And sleep thegither at the foot,
Ginny Campbell, my Jo.

Adapted from Robert Burns,
"John Anderson, My Jo."

ACKNOWLEDGEMENTS

Writers need friends to critique their drafts. I am indebted to Neal Petersen, a Princeton classmate and historian for the Department of State and Central Intelligence Agency; Peter Hays, F-15 fighter pilot; English Professor John H. Pritchard Jr.; and Professor of Philosophy John Brough. At EEI Communications, Inc. in Alexandria, Virginia, Jane H. Ray, Manager of Editorial Services, and Susan Becelia did an outstanding job of copyediting the manuscript. Any inadequacies, errors, and misjudgments in *Great Quotations* are mine.

Great Quotations is not a scholarly book. It was written for a broad audience, especially for students in high school to graduate school, to give them an overview of Western thought.

Great Quotations includes many quotations without citations because the "authoritative" quotation reference books with citations lacked those quotations, and I did not have platoons of scholars to research the citations. Also, most citations include only the name of the book and author without the name of the publisher and page number. But it is better to include great quotations without citations or full citations than to omit the quotations.

CONTENTS

PART 1
CHRONOLOGICAL QUOTATIONS

PART 2
QUOTATIONS ORGANIZED THEMATICALLY

LIST OF TOPICS

BOUNTIFUL BARONS

MODERNISM TO POSTMODERNISM (1900–1980)

MANAGEMENT IN THE INFORMATION AGE

TURBO SCIENCE IN HYPER-DRIVE

PREFACE

In high school and college during the 1950s, I read *Bartlett's Familiar Quotations* to improve my writing skills, just as Winston Churchill had done as a youth. Quotations added wisdom and wit to my papers in high school, college, and law school, and later to my work as lawyer, CEO, civil servant, and international consultant. When our son Austin was struggling as a freshman in high school with his history and literature papers, I decided that he, too, could both gain insights from wise quotations and use them to add punch to his papers. As Isaac Newton said, "If I have seen further, it is by standing on the shoulders of giants." And if you can aptly quote authorities, people will think you are better read than you are.

Austin did not have time to read the massive quotation tomes, so I cherry-picked from 1,200 authorities some 8,000 penetrating expressions. I added value by subtraction—by mining through mountains of chaff in a heap of quotation books to select prize nuggets. A book of 3,500 epigrams yielded only nine for this one. The wisdom of ancient writing remains fresh because human nature has not changed. When Heraclitus wrote 2,600 years ago, "Character is destiny," he wrote to us today. Owen Meredith put it this way, "The classics are always modern."

Great Quotations that Shaped the Western World is chronologically organized as a history of Western civilization. 60 percent of it consists of quotations, and forty percent is author biographies, annotations of the quotations, and commentaries on Western history and culture.

The Western canon of books consists of more than beautiful poetry and literature on the human condition. It comprises the philosophical, religious, political, economic, and scientific precepts that gave rise to the West's liberty and prosperity.

Great Quotations that Shaped the Western World serves four purposes. It helps improve one's writing by featuring beautiful and insightful language. It helps readers achieve "cultural literacy," to wit, an understanding of the background information that a writer or speaker assumes an audience already has. It adds to the cohesion of a common Western culture by promoting the shared reading of its great works. Last, it identifies the core precepts that enabled the West to forge a modern world of liberty, democracy, and capitalism. This book is for students and educated laymen, not the literati.

Its selection criteria were: (1) uniqueness, perceptiveness, beauty, and historical criticality; (2) an emphasis on liberty and meritocracy; (3) opposition to nonjudgmental multiculturalism; and (4) exclusion of clichés, the false, cynical, fatalistic, and commonplace. For example, Balzac's false "Behind every great fortune there is a crime" is omitted. But Peter Drucker's true insight into wealth creation is included:

"Where there is a successful business, someone once made a courageous decision." The selection criteria also follow Robert Conquest's insight:

> Literature exists for the ordinary educated man, and any literature that actively requires enormous training can be at best of only peripheral value. Such a mood in literature produces the specialist who only knows about literature. The man who only knows about literature does not know even about literature. The more incomprehensible the poem, the worse it must be.

Great Quotations that Shaped the Western World focuses on Western civilization because, as Peter Drucker said, "The future may be post-Western or even anti-Western, but it cannot be non-Western." And as T. S. Eliot said, a good artist knows his own culture. So must anyone who aspires to become an architect in his chosen profession rather than a mere mechanic.

To highlight the West's uniqueness, this book synopsizes the Confucian, Buddhist, and Hindu civilizations. To be educated, Westerners must appreciate the contributions of foreign cultures because Western civilization is the most mongrelized civilization. But, not every foreign culture is praiseworthy.

Today many teachers are multiculturalists who want the West to lose its cultural identity. But the West must pass on to the next generation its canonical works, its shared values, and pride in its achievements. Robert Hutchins said, "To destroy the Western tradition of independent thought, it is not necessary to burn the books. All we have to do is to leave them unread for a couple of generations." The

historian David McCullough agreed, saying, America's "historical amnesia" threatens her "liberty."

The traditional standard for teaching the humanities was given by the venerable Dr. Johnson. He said, "The first requisite is the religious and moral knowledge of right and wrong; the next is an acquaintance with the history of mankind. Those authors, therefore, are to be read at schools that supply most axioms of prudence, most principles of moral truth." Because most public schools now abjure traditional moral lessons, parents should give their children private reading assignments, and especially stories of the West's heroes and the virtues that led them to liberty and prosperity.

Great Quotations that Shaped the Western World differs from most anthologies for having been compiled by a conservative. Conservatism confers no magic divining rod for finding the truth, but it adds value by complementing the overwhelmingly liberal perspectives of almost all other compilers. For example: *Bartlett's Familiar Quotations*, 16th edition, features 37 quotations from Franklin Roosevelt, 28 from John Kennedy, and only three from Ronald Reagan. When its editor Justin Kaplan was told that the three quotations he had selected for Reagan made Reagan look ridiculous, he replied, "I'm not going to disguise the fact that I despise Ronald Reagan."

You will find herein the quotes from a diversity of professionals, including chief executives of corporations and coaches, not just poets, politicians, playwrights, and professors. Its mission is to celebrate liberty, which is sustained by virtue, which is sustained by religion and to glory in the wonderful words of free men and women.

Great Quotations that Shaped the Western World also examines the pleasures of living a life of the mind. Ralph Waldo Emerson said, "Great men are they who see that the spiritual is stronger than any material force, that thoughts rule the world." William Faulkner said:

> It is [the writer's] privilege to help man endure by lifting his heart, by reminding him of the courage and pity and sacrifice, which have been the glory of his past. The poet's voice can be one of the props, the pillars to help him endure and prevail.

INTRODUCTION

WHY READ *GREAT QUOTATIONS THAT SHAPED THE WESTERN WORLD*?

Great Quotations that Shaped the Western World highlights both Western history's great moments and its greatest written passages about the human condition. It sides with Emerson "that thoughts rule the world," and against Marx's belief that "material life conditions the social, political and intellectual life processes." The primary importance of ideas was evidenced early on by the ancient Greeks, whose epic literature inspired them to seek truth, to excel, and to cherish liberty. The West was jump-started into forging the modern world by the combination of Greek liberty and openness to truth with Judeo-Christianity's belief in each human's dignity. The Western canon of philosophy, history, and economics led the world to liberty and prosperity.

Robert Frost said, only "virtuous founding fathers" could "usher in a new order of the ages." Yet Russell Kirk saw that post–World War II America was "using up her moral and intellectual traditions," and Will Herberg sees Europe as "a cut flower culture" severed from its Judeo-Christian roots. The West cannot survive a revised canon that lacks fixed verities, that subordinates the rule of law to quotas, and that tolerates a stigma-free society vacillating between timidity and authoritarianism. Multiculturalists are wrong to call for a "new revolution to emancipate America from its European civilization and its Anglo-Protestant values," and Walt Whitman was right to say: "The United States itself is essentially the greatest poem."

Arthur M. Schlesinger Jr. in *The Disunity of America* (1994), wrote, "Europe is the unique source of the ideas of individual liberty, political democracy, the rule of law, human rights, and cultural freedom. These are European ideas, not Asian, nor African, nor Middle Eastern ideas. The Multiculturalists are very often ethnocentric separatists who see little in the Western heritage other than Western crimes." Samuel P. Huntington in *The Clash of Civilizations* (1996) concludes that the West must preserve, protect, and renew these unique Western ideas, and that means "rejecting the siren calls of multiculturalism."

One reason to read *Great Quotations that Shaped the Western World* is to enjoy some of the best that the West has written. As Chesterton observed, so long as there are civilized men, they will be talking of Troy. One should also read it to arm oneself to defend the West. William F. Buckley Jr. said, "The survival of everything we cherish depends on the survival of the culture of liberty; and that this hangs on our willingness to defend this extraordinary country of ours, so awfully mixed up so much of the time [and] to defend it at all costs."

> There is no use in excellent laws, if the citizens have not been educated in the city's way of life.
>
> Aristotle, *Politics* 5.9

PART 1
CHRONOLOGICAL QUOTATIONS

Part 1 of *Great Quotations that Shaped the Western World* is organized chronologically by the year of the author's birth. Authors born in the same year are arranged alphabetically. Events are listed chronologically, so there are often many pages separating descriptions of events from the authors made famous by those events. Words within brackets are the compiler's, except if in quotation marks.

Most quotation books are organized thematically, but some are organized chronologically, like *Bartlett's Familiar Quotations*. Part 1, which is 88 percent of the book, is organized chronologically to cover the development of Western civilization's main ideas. Part 2 of *Great Quotations* is organized thematically as a "catchall" of a variety of topics that do not fit easily into a chronology of civilization, such as aphorisms, ironic humor, and self-improvement wisdom.

1

GREEK KNOWLEDGE EXPLOSION

Although Greek civilization was late in coming, after the Greeks added vowels to the Phoenician alphabet around 800 B.C., they authored the greatest written explosion of science, philosophy, and literature in history. Greeks replaced myth with rationality by discovering: that the physical world conforms to a rational scheme and is intelligible; that one can organize knowledge in curricula; and the basics of science, to wit, questioning all things and proving solutions. Greek science often missed the mark, but the Greeks' openness to explore ideas and their relatively tolerant institutions set them apart from all other ancient civilizations.

Greek openness to cross-fertilization from other cultures came from its littoral civilization. Greek cities hugged the narrow coastal regions between the mountains and the sea. Indeed, Greek colonies were scattered around the Mediterranean, as Plato said, "Like frogs around a pond." The Greek-speaking peoples called themselves "Hellenes," and "Europe" was their word for the lands to their west.

The Greeks distinguished themselves from other ancient civilizations by their passion for liberty and by their meritocratic culture, symbolized by their motto: "Always to be the best." Generally, Greek governments were democratic or aristocratic, albeit occasional tyrants gained power. Sparta was an oligarchic republic—power lay in an assembly of its oldest citizens, male and female. Greek individualism is evidenced in the Olympics beginning in 776 B.C. that featured only individual contests—no team contests. Greece's individualism may have been caused by its rocky soil, which required the Greeks to import grain, so they exported wine, oils, and pottery. Merchants, artisans, traders, and pirates tend to be individualistic. Athens organized its economy around private property that generated the surplus to support its arts and sciences. In other ancient civilizations, property was owned either communally or by the ruler as God's vicar. The despotic Middle Eastern and Eastern cultures valued obedience above all—Egypt's Instruction of Ptahhotep (c. 2350 B.C.) read, "To resist him who is set in authority is evil."

Civilizations in the river valleys of the Tigris and Euphrates, the Nile, the Indus, and the Yellow River predated the Greeks in literacy by up to two thousand years. The first civilization arose in southern Mesopotamia, present-day Iraq, where it domesticated animals and built cities forty-five centuries before they arose in the world's second civilization, China. By 6000 B.C., Sumerians had invented agriculture, the wheel, writing, bronze, glass, and a complete pantheon of gods. They wrote the oldest story in 2000 B.C., the *Epic of Gilgamesh*, who built an ark to survive a great flood. By 3200 B.C., Egyptians united the Nile Valley with the Nile Delta in one kingdom and built the Great Pyramids (2700 to 2300 B.C.). They invented papyrus, a quasi-paper, and they first established a calendar year of 365 and one-quarter days (by measuring the Nile's flooding). But all of these non-Greek civilizations stalled out at a low level of development because their kings and mandarins suppressed liberty. Jacob Bronowski wrote in *The Ascent of Man* (1973) in chapter 13:

> Who am I to belittle the civilizations of Egypt, of China, of India…? And yet by one test they all fail: they limit the freedom of imagination….

Greeks called their neighbors "barbarians" (for making sounds like "bar-bar") who lived without reason and liberty. Valuing reason and liberty, the Greeks produced the first rational philosophies, sciences, complete body of literary forms, and democratic government. Other than machinery, there is little that is secular in Western culture not traceable to Greek antecedents. Washington, D.C., features Greek Revivalist architecture, from the Jefferson Memorial to the Supreme Court. Greece in its architecture and democracy was the model for the new republic. Robert M. Hutchins said, "No dialogue in any other civilization can compare with that of the West in the number of great works of the mind that have contributed to this dialogue." The Greeks started this tradition. Their first heavy hitter was the blind poet, Homer, who recorded the oral history of the siege of Troy in 1250 B.C.

HOMER
C. 750 B.C.

Greek, blind poet who set the literary standard for understanding human nature. His epic poems, *The Iliad* and *The Odyssey*, demonstrate *arete*, or "excellence," Greek qualities that make a perfect character, from battle prowess to courtly manners. The courage of Achilles, the cleverness of Odysseus, the moral strength and cunning of Penelope, the wisdom of Mentor, and the nobility and strength of Ajax illustrate *arete*. Greeks read these epics as part of their character-shaping curriculum, as the Bible was read in our culture. The Homeric ideal is to compete for the foremost place by striving for perfection, an aristocratic code of *arete*. Homer's emphasis on striving for place conflicted with Plato's striving for truth.

Other epics include the following: *Gilgamesh* (Assyrian), *Exodus* (Hebrew), *Ramayana* (Indian), *Chanson de Roland* (French), *El Cid* (Spanish), *Nibelungenlied* (German), *Beowulf* (English), Vergil's *Aeneid* (Roman), Dante's *Divine Comedy* (Italian), and Milton's *Paradise Lost* (English).

> Murderous, doomed.
> *Iliad,* opening, tr. Robert Eagel

> You talk of food?
> I have no taste for food—what I really crave is slaughter and blood and the choking groans of men! (Achilles)
> Ibid., l. 254

> Ajax the great, himself a host.
> Ibid., bk. III, l. 293, tr. F. Max Müller

> Without a sign, his sword the brave man draws,

And asks no omen but his country's cause.

Ibid., bk. XII, l. 283

The best of things, beyond their measure, cloy.

Ibid., bk. XIII, l. 795

I loathe like Hell's Gates the man who thinks one thing and says another.

Ibid., bk. IX, l. 312

To be both a speaker of words and a doer of deeds.

Ibid., l. 443

No season now for calm, familiar talk, Like youths and maidens on an evening walk.

Ibid., bk. XVII, l. 169

Not even Achilles will bring all his words to fulfillment.

Ibid., bk XX, l. 369

Achilles absent was Achilles still.

Ibid., bk. XXII, l. 418

It is not strength, but art, obtains the prize
And to be swift is less than to be wise.
It's more by art, than force of num'rous strokes.

Ibid., bk. XXIII, l. 383

The Iliad honors the "city sacking Achilles" and shows a Bronze Age warrior culture where life is noble or ignoble, powerful or weak. No Greek or Trojan shows any pity or is concerned about the "just" or the "good." The Iliad's merciless savagery exposes the West's primitive roots. It is the tragedy of an individual warrior undone by his rage and his preference to die young for fame. It is also the tragedy of the fall of Troy, the "civilized city," whose men are slaughtered and women enslaved.

The Iliad recounts a war in 1250 B.C. between the Greeks (Achaians) and the Trojans, who lived on the Asian shore of the Hellespont. Priam was the king of the Trojans, Hecuba was his wife, and his children included Paris, Cassandra, and Hector. The war was fought over the daughter of Zeus and the mortal Leda, the beautiful Helen, who was the wife of Menelaus, King of Sparta.

The story begins when all the goddesses, except Eris (Discord), were invited to the wedding of Thesis. In revenge, Eris dropped a golden apple inscribed "Property of the Fairest" among the guests. When the apple was claimed by Hera, Athena, and Aphrodite, Paris, a Trojan prince, was asked to award it. He chose Aphrodite, who had promised him Helen. The enraged Hera stirred up the Greek king Agamemnon, brother of Menelaus, to attack Troy (Ilium in Greek, whence The Iliad).

The Iliad is the story of the wrath of Achilles, a Greek hero warrior, during three days of the ten-year siege of Troy. Achilles, who was invulnerable except in the heel by which his mother had held him while she dipped him in the River Styx, sulked in his tent after Agamemnon took his captive girl, Briseis. When the Trojans forced the Greeks back to their ships, Achilles' closest friend, Patroclus, borrowed Achilles' armor to frighten the Trojans but was slain by the Trojan hero Hector. That snapped Achilles out of his funk. Despite a prophecy that he would die if he returned to the fight, Achilles strode to his death, preferring honor to a long ignominious life. Achilles slew Hector and bound twelve Trojan captives to Patroclus's funeral pyre. Achilles felt no sense of guilt or pity. In turn he was slain by Paris, who shot a poisoned arrow into his vulnerable heel. Achilles asserted his individualism against the needs of his warrior clan just as Helen asserted her lust for Paris against the interests of her family, her home, and also Troy.

Odysseus persuaded Agamemnon to build a great hollow horse to leave to the Trojans, as the Greeks appeared to sail away. Greek soldiers hidden inside the horse came out at night and opened Troy's gate to the Greek army, which had returned during the night. The Greeks sacked Troy, killed the men and children, and enslaved the women. Of the House of Priam, only Aeneas escaped. Andromache, the wife of Hector and the ideal of the loyal wife and mother, is slaughtered, and her son Astyanax is hurled off the battlements.

Achilles, who personified the Greek aristocratic code of manliness, took his father's (Peleus's) advice:

> Always be the best and fight among the champions in the front ranks."
>
> Iliad, bk. VI, l. 208

Omitted by Homer, but included by others, is the warning of Laocoon about the wooden horse: "I fear the Greeks, even when bringing gifts."

> How prone to doubt, how cautious are the wise!
>
> *Odyssey*

> Ever to excel and to surpass other men.
>
> Ibid.

Homer's *Odyssey* describes the trip home from the Trojan War of Odysseus (*Ulysses* in Latin), the Greek king of Ithaca. He had tried to avoid being drafted into the war by

hitching a horse and ox together to plow salt into the ground, but once he enlisted, he became a stalwart commander and won the war by devising the wooden horse. Odysseus had discovered Achilles trying to avoid the war by dressing as a woman. Odysseus and his crew encountered perilous adventures, like the Sirens, whose songs caused sailors to crash their ships on the rocks trying to reach them. Odysseus had his crew fill their ears with wax, and he had himself lashed to the mast so he could hear the songs but be restrained from jumping ship. On the island of the "lotus eaters," those who ate the lotus blossoms forgot their wives, their homes, and their duty; all they desired was to eat lotus and to live in ease.

On an island inhabited by three cyclops, giants with one large eye, Odysseus and his crew were trapped in the cave of one cyclop, Polyphemus, who began to eat the Greeks. Odysseus did not kill Polyphemus because only he was large enough to roll away the stone from the cave entrance. Odysseus told Polyphemus his name was "Noman," and when Polyphemus went to sleep, Odysseus stuck a stake through his eye. Polyphemus cried for help, but the other cyclops did not come to his aid because when they asked who had hurt him, Polyphemus said, "Noman," so they thought a god was punishing Polyphemus.

Odysseus and his crew escaped by hanging under Polyphemus's large sheep, which he let out of the cave daily to graze. Odysseus boasted as he sailed away, alerting Polyphemus's father Poseidon, god of the sea, who pursued and stirred up trouble for Odysseus. Odysseus visited Phaeacia, a utopia where all are rich and happy, and he encountered the enchantress Circe, who turned his crew into swine. Odysseus passed through the straits of Messina between Italy and Sicily, guarded on one side by Scylla, a six-headed sea monster, and on the other side by Charybdis, a whirlpool that sucked water three times daily. Odysseus sacrificed six crewmen to Scylla rather than risk the ship.

Returning home after twenty years, Odysseus discovered suitors demanding that his wife, Penelope, reconcile herself to Odysseus's death and marry one of them. Penelope delayed them by saying she must weave a funeral cloth for Odysseus's elderly father, Laertes. Each night she unwound her work of the day. When discovered, she was forced to choose, so she said she would marry the one who could string Odysseus's bow and shoot an arrow through the openings of twelve axes ranged in line. They all failed except Odysseus, who had returned disguised as a beggar. Odysseus killed the suitors and all his maids who had served them. Athena delayed sunrise so they could make love for a longer time.

The *Odyssey* teaches that we can achieve nothing significant without struggle, and life's agony and ecstasy are one. Penelope, the paragon of marital fidelity, preferred to die rather than to "please the mind of an inferior husband."

> A great deal my dear Liege, depends
> On having clever bards for friends
> What had Achilles been without his
> Homer?
>
> John Wolcot (1738–1819)

GREEK AND ROMAN MYTHOLOGY

Myths are stories about gods and heroes that describe creation, explain natural phenomena, and allow men to ascribe their failures to the gods' capriciousness. They also provide moral lessons: Achilles' striving for glory inspired all Greeks to seek excellence. Competition for fame among the Greeks mirrored their gods' quarrelsome natures. See C. K. Hillegass, *Mythology* (1991):

The Creation: Chaos gave birth to Gaea (female earth) and Tartarus (underworld); then Gaea gave birth to Uranus (male sky). Gaea and Uranus gave birth to twelve Titans and three cyclops. Due to Uranus's severity, Cronus, leader of the Titans, cut off his father's genitals. Blood from them formed the Furies, who punish crimes, the Giants, and Aphrodite, the goddess of love who rose from the sea.

Cronus became Lord of the Titans and married his sister, Rhea. Hearing he would be deposed by one of his children, Cronus swallowed at birth the gods Hestia, Demeter, Hera, Hades, and Poseidon. Rhea saved their sixth child, Zeus, by giving Cronus a rock wrapped in swaddling clothes to swallow. When Zeus was grown, he made Cronus throw up the swallowed children (gods), who helped Zeus bind Cronus and the other Titans in Tartarus, except for Prometheus and Epimetheus, who supported the gods. The Titan Atlas was made to bear the world on his shoulders. It is possible that the Titans were the gods of the original inhabitants of Greece and that the Olympians were the gods of the Dorian invaders.

Prometheus made man out of clay after his brother, Epimetheus, had made all the animals and given them such attributes as swiftness and strength. All that was left for man was an upright posture, like the gods. Prometheus stole fire from Olympus to give to man. An angry Zeus retaliated by having Hephaestus create a woman, Pandora, who was given to Epimetheus, along with a box that Pandora was instructed not to open. But she opened it and released all the evils of mankind. However, the box also released hope. To punish Prometheus's disobedience, Zeus chained him to a rock in the Caucasus. Each day an eagle pecked out his liver, which grew back at night. Later Heracles (*Hercules* in Latin) killed the eagle and unbound Prometheus.

THE GREEK–ROMAN OLYMPIANS

Zeus—Jupiter or Jove: the supreme deity who wielded a thunderbolt. He often broke his duty to make the gods leave men's fate up to Destiny.

Hera—Juno: jealous wife and sister of Zeus, the protector of marriages.

Poseidon—Neptune: lord of the sea who carried a trident.

Demeter—Ceres: Zeus's sister and goddess of vegetation and fertility. Her daughter by Zeus, Persephone, was taken to Hades but allowed to return to earth for six months (spring and summer).

Apollo: the Bright One, god of intelligence, prophecy, healing, and the arts (Delphi Shrine). Chided for falling in love, he replied, "I teach moderation in all things—including moderation."

Artemis—Diana: Apollo's twin sister, goddess of chastity, the virgin huntress.

Aphrodite—Venus: goddess of love and beauty who sprung from the foam of the sea. Hesphaestus was her husband, Ares her lover, and Eros her son. Her liaison with a Trojan prince gave birth to Aeneas, whose descendants founded Rome.

Athena—Minerva: virgin goddess of wisdom, war, and the arts, and guardian of Athens. To reward Athena for protecting Perseus, Zeus gave her the Aegis to wear on her breastplate.

Hestia—Vesta: virgin goddess of the hearth, the family, and peace, whose fire in Rome was attended by six virgins.

Ares—Mars: the Greeks' brutal god of war and a coward. Romans saw Mars as stern and stalwart in battle rather than as evil, cowardly, and feckless.

Hephaestus—Vulcan: ugly, master craftsman, forgeman, and lame god of artisans.

Hermes—Mercury: the cleverest god, patron of travel and commerce, and herald of the gods who wore winged shoes and carried a special staff, the caduceus, a stick encircled by twin snakes interlacing good and evil.

Hades—Pluto: god of the underworld.

Lesser gods included: the Three Graces, who brought cheer to banquets and beauty to young girls; the Nine Muses, goddesses of the arts led by Calliope, queen of Muses and Muse of epic poetry and, Clio, Muse of history; Dionysus—Bacchus, god of wine and the arts; and the Fates, who determined the lives of men (Clotho wove the thread of life, Lachesis measured it out, and Atropos cut it).

Greek gods could be vengeful. For example, Nemesis, goddess of divine retribution, punished those who violated the moral code or who were guilty of hubris.

SOME MYTHS

1. Under the Aegis of: to be protected by someone of great power. The Aegis was Zeus's shield, which had imprinted on it the head of Medusa that terrified all who saw it. Zeus gave the Aegis to Athena to wear on her breastplate.

2. Antaeus: a giant who killed his enemies by wrestling. When thrown to the earth, his strength would double. Hercules beat Antaeus by strangling him while holding him aloft.

3. Atalanta: abandoned as a child, she was raised by a bear. Her beauty attracted many suitors, but she would marry only the man who could outrun her, and those who failed were killed. Hippomenes won by tossing three golden apples to the side during the race to delay her.

4. Augean task: a seemingly impossible task, especially in cleaning up corruption. King Augeas required Hercules to clean, in one day, a stable for 3,000 oxen, which had not been cleaned in thirty years. Hercules diverted two rivers through it.

5. Cassandra: Trojan princess given the power of prophecy by Apollo in exchange for her love. When she reneged, he punished her by allowing her to continue to prophesy the truth about impending danger, but no one would ever heed her.

6. Cerberus: a three-headed dog guarding the Underworld's exit. Aeneas passed by Cerberus by giving him a drugged honey cake. A gift to keep someone quiet is "giving a sop to Cerberus." Hercules throttled Cerberus, and Orpheus lulled Cerberus's three heads to sleep with music.

7. Daedalus: the architect directed by King Minos of Crete to build the Labyrinth, a vast maze from which none could escape from the monstrous Minotaur, half man, half bull. Daedalus built wings for his son, Icarus, and himself so they could escape the maze by flying. Icarus ignored his father's warning not to fly too close to the sun; his wings melted so he fell into the sea and was drowned.

8. Echo: a nymph who always tried to get in the last word. After Echo had annoyed her, Hera punished Echo by allowing her to have the last word, but she could never speak first or differently.

9. Europa: a Phoenician woman beguiled by Zeus in the guise of a snow-white bull. Her brother, Cadmus, brought writing to Greece from Phoenicia. Europa rode in the path of the sun from east to west, so "Europe" was the name for the land to the west.

10. Harpies: monsters, part woman and part bird, which snatched the souls of the dying. In modern parlance, Harpies are greedy women who will do anything for wealth.

11. Hero and Leander: lived on either side of the Hellespont. Whenever Hero shone a light at night, Leander swam the Hellespont to make love to her. One night during a storm, Hero lit her signal lamp and Leander drowned in the turbulence. When Hero saw his body in the rocks the next morning, she jumped to her death to be with him.

12. Jason and the Argonauts: found the Golden Fleece with the help of the sorceress Medea, who deceived her father, king of Colchis, and killed her brother. Medea also killed King Pelias to get Jason a throne. Jason had two children by Medea, but left her to marry a princess of Corinth. For revenge, Medea gave the princess a robe that consumed her in fire, and then Medea killed her own two children. The

disconsolate Jason returned to his ship, the *Argo*, whose falling prow killed him.

13. Leda and the Swan: Zeus, who had taken the form of a swan, raped Leda, queen of Sparta. That union conceived Helen of Troy.

14. The Minotaur: a monstrous offspring of the queen of Crete and a bull—the queen had had a hollow wooden cow built with a hole in it so she could be impregnated. The Minotaur devoured the young men and women who were put into King Minos's Labyrinth. Thus, a ruler who sacrifices young people for his ambitions "feeds a Minotaur."

15. Narcissus: a lad who fell so in love with his reflection in water that he died pining away over it. A purple flower grew in place of his body.

16. Niobe: queen of Thebes, who sought to be worshiped. To punish her arrogance, the gods tortured her fourteen children to death. Niobe was metamorphosed into a waterfall, where her tears cascade down.

17. Orpheus: son of Calliope. When he played the lyre, trees uprooted themselves to hear, and the stones wept with joy. He assisted Jason in his quest for the Golden Fleece. When his wife, the nymph Eurydice, died, he went to the Underworld, where he charmed Hades into freeing her on the condition that he not look at her until he returned to earth. Orpheus disobeyed, so Eurydice was held in the Underworld.

18. Palladium: a protector. The statue of Pallas Athena protected Troy, until Odysseus stole it.

19. Perseus: a demigod, son of Zeus and Danaë (Zeus visited her in the form of a shower of gold), slew Medusa, one of the three Gorgons, to save Andromeda from the sea monster. Medusa's head, which had snakes for hair, was so ugly that whoever saw it turned into stone, including the sea monster. Perseus and Andromeda were Hercules' ancestors.

20. Phoenix: Egyptian bird that every five hundred years would be consumed by fire, after which it would rise from the ashes youthful again.

21. Procrustes: who made travelers who slept in his home fit exactly into his bed, by either being stretched to fill it or having their feet cut off. He is the quintessence of inflexibility.

22. Pygmalion: a sculptor who hated women, but he fell in love with an ivory statue he made. He asked Venus to find him a woman like the statue. Instead she made the statue, Galatea, come to life.

23. Pyramus and Thisbe: two young lovers whose parents refused permission to marry, met on either side of a wall and talked through a chink in it. When Pyramus mistakenly believed a lion had devoured Thisbe, he killed himself. When Thisbe discovered his body, she killed herself. Shakespeare used this story in *Midsummer's Night Dream* and as the theme of *Romeo and Juliet*.

24. Satyrs: hairy men with two legs like horses' haunches and tails. They drank wine and chased nymphs. Fauns were little men with goat ears, legs, and tails (Pan was a Faun), and Centaurs were savage beasts, half horse and half man.

25. Silenus: a jolly, fat, old man and companion of Dionysus, and also famous for his wisdom.

26. Sisyphus: king of Corinth who tricked his way out of the Underworld and was punished by having to perpetually roll a stone up a mountain, only to have it roll back when it nears the top.

27. Stygian darkness: the impenetrably gloomy River Styx flowing around the Underworld. The ferryman Charon transported dead souls across the Styx to a final judgment. The wicked are led across a river of fire to the tortures of Tartarus, while the virtuous are lifted to the Elysian Fields in heaven.

28. Tantalus: a king punished by the gods for killing and serving his son to them. He was grounded in water up to his chin. When he bent over to drink, the water subsided, and when he lifted his hand to grab the fruit above him, it rose beyond his reach. Whence the word "tantalizing."

29. Theseus: son of King Aegeus of Athens, slew the Minotaur in the Cretan labyrinth after Princess Ariadne gave him a ball of string to find his way out. Returning to Athens, Theseus forgot to change the color of his sails to signal his survival; King Aegeus drowned himself in the Aegean Sea.

30. The Tenderest Tale: Philemon and Baucis: shared their meager dinner with Hermes, who was posing as a beggar. He asked what they most desired, believing it would be long life or gold. But they wished to die together so neither would face the world without the other. Where they stood, two trees arose with their branches intertwined.

31. Tithonus: Trojan prince who asked the goddess Eos for eternal life, but forgot to ask for eternal youth. Later he chose to become a mortal grasshopper rather than live as an insensate human.

> They that change old love for new,
> Pray God they change for worse.
> "Cupid's Curse"

TEUTONIC GODS

The principal Scandinavian God, Odin (*Woden* to the Germans), and his brothers Vili and Ve, were created by the evil frost giants. Odin and brothers live in Asgard, and they created humans and other creatures such as the Valkyries, who are Amazon-like females that wear breastplates and carry spears and shields. The Valkyries choose which warriors will go to Valhalla and then serve them there. Valhalla is a hall in Asgard with five hundred doors, each one large enough for eight hundred warriors to walk in abreast.

Odin, the god of war and intelligence, is pictured as a warrior with a golden helmet and a spear on a horse. Odin sacrificed himself for humanity by allowing himself to be fastened for nine days by spears to the tree of knowledge, Yggdrasil, so he could learn the secrets of the runes.

Odin and the warriors at Valhalla must prepare to fight the frost giants at the final battle of Ragnarok. But it is fated that all the gods and humans will perish at Ragnarok at the hands of the frost giants.

HERCULES' LABORS

Hercules, son of Zeus and a mortal, helped the gods defeat the Giants, rescued Prometheus, and instituted the Olympic Games. Juno tried to kill him at birth out of jealousy of Zeus's philandering, but Hercules strangled the serpents Juno put into his crib. Due to his unfaithfulness, his wife, Deianeira, gave him a shirt dipped in the blood of Nessus, which slowly killed him. But Zeus raised Hercules from the dead and made him a god. Hercules,

Greece's most glorious hero, was admired for his strength, attention to duty, and self-reliance.

Juno obligated Hercules to perform twelve labors. In his first labor Hercules strangled the Nemean lion and wore its hide, which was too tough to be pierced by an arrow. He killed the nine-headed hydra, which grew two heads when one was cut off. He seared the neck to prevent it from growing more heads. He beat the Erymanthian boar, the stag with golden antlers, the Stymphalian birds, the mares of Diomedes, and Geryoneus, and returned King Minos's sacred bull. By diverting two rivers, he cleaned in one day the stables of Augeas that housed three thousand oxen and had not been cleaned for thirty years. He seized the girdle of the Amazon queen, Hippolyta, after killing her, and he retrieved the golden apples of Hesperides by holding earth while Atlas fetched the apples. Last, he brought back the three-headed dog, Cerberus, from the underworld.

GILGAMESH
C. 2000 B.C.

Assyrian, epic figure that was part god and part man and king of Uruk. Gilgamesh went on a terrifying journey to find Utnapishtim, who knew the secret of life. Utnapishtim told him about the Great Flood and landing on Mount Nisser in an ark with pairs of all the animals. The secret of life is that death is inevitable. Not even demigods can find immortality, so all should accept death and their allotted role, no matter how lowly, and meanwhile enjoy life:

Make every day a day of joy.
Dance, play, day and night
Cherish the child who grasps our hand.
Let your wife rejoice in your bosom
For this is the fate of man.

I CHING
C. 1100 B.C.

I Ching [The Book of Changes], Chinese.

The superior man acquaints himself with many sayings of antiquity and many deeds of the past in order to strengthen his character.

ARCHILOCHUS
714?–676 B.C.

Greek, poet.

Old women should not seek to be perfumed.
Fragment 27

The fox knows many things, but the hedgehog knows one big thing.
Fragment 103

HESIOD
C. 700 B.C.

Greek, father of didactic poetry and the *Theogony (Birth of the Gods)*, which detailed the genealogy of the gods and the myth of creation. Greeks thought man was godlike.

Money is life to us wretched mortals.
Theogony

Potter bears a grudge against potter, and craftsman against craftsman, and beggar is envious of beggar, and bard of bard.

Theogony l. 25

And I would not myself be just, nor have
    my son
Be just among bad men: for it is bad
To be an honest man where felons rule;
I trust wise Zeus to save me from this pass.

"Works and Days," 264, tr. D. Wender, in
A. Gottlied, *The Dream Of Reason* (2001)

SEVEN SAGES
C. 650–550 B.C.

Scholars dispute who were the Seven Sages and their sayings. On Mount Parnassus, home of the Muses, lies the Temple of Apollo (Delphic Oracle), on which is inscribed two of the sayings: "Know Thyself" and "Nothing to Excess." A person who knows himself knows his potentialities. A person not knowing himself will try the wrong things or too much or too little. "Nothing to excess" is found in Aristotle's "moderation in all things," Horace's "Golden Mean," and Confucius's "Middle Way." The most frequent other five sayings are:

Know the right moment.
Most men are bad.
Practice is everything.
Consider the end.
Nothing is impossible to industry.

SEVEN WONDERS OF THE ANCIENT WORLD

These Seven Wonders were listed by Antipater of Sidon in the second-century B.C.: the Colossus of Rhodes, the Hanging Gardens of Semiramis at Babylon, the Pharos (Lighthouse of Alexandria), the Pyramids of Egypt, the Statue of Zeus at Olympia by Phidias, the Temple of Artemis (Diana) at Ephesus, and the Tomb of Mausolus at Halicarnassus. Only the pyramids remain.

Herostratus burned down the Temple of Artemis so his name would be immortal. The Greeks tried but failed to strike it from the record.

THALES
640?–546? B.C.

Greek, the first scientist. He replaced Hesiod's gods with the impersonal power of nature. He discovered many of the theorems Euclid later collected, and he predicted an eclipse of the sun in 585 B.C., proving gods did not run heaven. He taught how to navigate by the stars, and he used the length of his shadow to measure the height of the pyramids. He theorized that all matter was composed of an underlying substance, water. Today, we guess it might be strings of energy. Aristotle called him a "physicist" for asking, "What is the world made of?" Thales was not a materialist. He thought matter and life were inseparable.

Thales, who was taunted for being poor despite his knowledge, speculated in olives on the basis of his weather forecasts. After making a fortune, he gave it away and returned to contemplation. Thales' pupil, Anaximander, thought the world an infinite inchoate mass that had been made physical by the revolving of a world-mind that he called a "nous."

To the question, "What is most difficult?" Thales replied, "To know thyself." To the question, "What is divinity?" Thales answered, "That which has neither beginning nor end."

SOLON
638–559 B.C.

Greek, statesman who ruled Athens after Draco, famous for his "draconian code." When asked why he made death the penalty for most offenses, Draco replied, "The lesser ones deserve it and for the greater ones no heavier sentence could be found." Solon rewrote Athens' constitution to reduce the power of the aristocrats by giving to the Ecclesia, the assembly of all citizens, legislative and judicial powers. Solon's taxes were graduated—those with the lowest incomes paid no tax, but were ineligible for public office. The poor hoped Solon would be a tyrant and redistribute property. Solon prohibited debtor slavery, introduced coinage, and encouraged the emigration of skilled artisans. Asked if he had given the Athenians the best laws, he responded, "No, but the best that they could receive." Asked what was a well-ordered state, he said, "When people obey the rulers, and rulers obey the laws."

After Solon retired, Peisistratus seized power as a tyrant through a bodyguard the assembly had granted to him. He confiscated land to redistribute to the poor. In a subsequent rebellion Leaena, a courtesan, was tortured to elicit the names of the conspirators. She bit off her own tongue and

spit it out to prevent herself from telling. Cleisthenes restored democracy and completed Solon's work. From Cleisthenes' time on, Athens led Greece economically and culturally.

[When asked how to reduce crime, Solon replied:]
Wrongdoing can only be avoided if those who are not wronged feel the same indignation as those who are.

[Anacharsis laughed at Solon for imagining the dishonesty and covetousness of his countrymen could be restrained by written laws, which were "like spiders' webs, and would catch, it is true, the weak and poor, but easily be broken by the mighty and rich."]
    In Plutarch, *Lives*, "Life of Solon"

Poets tell many lies.
    Fragment 21

Reprove thy friend privately, commend him publicly.

Sir, if any other comes that hath better iron than you, he will be master of all this gold.
[To the wealthy King Croesus of Lydia, whose army was small and weak.]

LAO-TZU
604–531 B.C.

Chinese, "the Old Master." He wrote *Tao Te Ching (The Way)* and founded Taoism, which revered nature but did not believe in God. Taoism, like Confucianism, believed in the opposing forces "yin" (feminine, passive qualities) and "yang" (male, aggressive qualities). The interaction between these forces leads to endless cycles.

Lao-Tzu feared an intellectual king because he would try to reconstruct society "like a geometry design," and thereby destroy life-giving freedom.

> The softest things in the universe over-
> come the hardest things.

> A journey of a thousand miles must
> begin with a single step.

> He who knows much about others may
> be learned,
> but he who understands himself is more
> intelligent.
> He who controls others may be powerful,
> but he who has mastered himself is
> mightier still.

> Birth is not a beginning; death is not
> an end.

> Govern a large country as you would
> cook a small fish—lightly.

> The best way to manage anything is by
> making use of its own nature.

> When opposites supplement each other,
> everything is harmonious.

> When men do not have a sense of awe,
> there will be disaster.

> Take care of what is difficult while it
> is still easy, and deal with what will
> become big while it is yet small.

> Truth is always paradoxical.

> The wise are not learned; the learned are
> not wise.

> When the best leader's work is done,
> the people say, "We did it ourselves."

> The more prohibitions there are,
> The poorer people will be.
> The more laws are promulgated,
> The more thieves and bandits there
> will be.
> Therefore the sage says:
> So long as I do nothing, the people will
> of themselves be transformed.
> So long as I love quietude, the people
> will of themselves go straight.
> So long as I act only by inactivity, the
> people will of themselves become
> prosperous.
> No. 57, *Tao Te Ching (The Way)* (1972) tr.
> Gia-fu Feng and Jane English

Taoism's principle of *wu-wei* (nonaction) rules by "noninterference," that is, by letting people work things out their own way. Laissez-faire is inherent to the Taoist vision of a self-regulating order.

After Lao-tzu, the next greatest Taoist was Chuang-tzu, c. fourth century, who wrote the text *Chuang Tzu*. In it, Chuang-tzu awakes from a dream and for a moment does not know if he is Chuang-tzu dreaming he is a butterfly, or if he is a butterfly dreaming he is Chuang-tzu. He said, "A well-frog cannot imagine the ocean, nor can a summer insect conceive of ice. How then can a scholar understand the Tao? He is restricted by his own learning." Chuang-tzu told the story of the man who complained the tree in his yard was too gnarled to be valuable as lumber. Chuang-tzu replied, "But you could make use of the shade it provides. It is useless to you because you want to make it into something else and do not use it in its proper way."

CHINESE STORIES

The Chinese painting of *The Vinegar Tasters* shows the three masters around a vinegar vat, each having tasted it—one with a sour look, another with a bitter look, and the third smiling. Confucius sees life as sour because man is out of step with the past, not having perfectly shown respect for his ancestors nor carried out the emperor's prescribed rituals. To Buddha, life is bitter—it is filled with desires that lead man to suffering on a revolving wheel of pain. But Lao-tzu smiles because everyone can find The Way of the Universe, though it cannot be described in words because it transcends human intelligence. It is to be learned from everyday life by discarding arrogance and enjoying the simple, the natural, the plain, and the quiet.

A stonecutter was envious of a wealthy merchant. He became that merchant, but remained dissatisfied because he had to bow to a high government official. He became that official, but was unhappy because the sun made him hot, so he wished to become the sun. A cloud trumped his power as the sun, so he became the cloud, yet he was pushed around by the wind. Becoming the wind, he noticed he could not budge a large stone. He wished to become the stone, and then he realized that the stonecutter controlled him.

"The Circle of Chalk" (Yuan dynasty, 1259–1368). When a wife and concubine argued over to whom a baby belonged, Judge Pao placed the baby in a circle of chalk and offered it to whomever could pull the baby to her side. When the concubine did not pull hard, Judge Pao awarded her the baby.

CHINESE HISTORY

For almost a thousand years until the eighth century B.C., China was a feudal system of some eighteen hundred warlords under the loose suzerainty of the Zhou royal house. In 770 B.C., the Zhou capital was sacked by barbarians, after which the feudal lords warred amongst themselves until the fifth century B.C. when there were only seven major powers and six minor ones. From 475 B.C. to 221 B.C., the period of the Warring States *(Chan-kuo)*, China's art, philosophy, and genius for technology bloomed.

Eventually there were only three powers: Ch'u in the south, Ch'in in the west, and Ch'i in the east. In 223 B.C., Ch'in (China) conquered its rivals and established China's first unified state. But due to the Ch'in emperor's adoption of legalism, an inflexible bureaucratic system, a revolt in 206 B.C. replaced the Ch'in with the Han dynasty. It reigned four hundred years, but the Confucian ethical and social system the Han adopted has lasted until today.

Succeeding the Han were the T'ang and Song dynasties, which ended in 1268 with the invasion of the Mongols under Kublai Khan, who established the Yuan dynasty. The Yuan instituted a highly centralized government that stopped virtually all technological progress. Equally oppressive was the Black Death, which by 1370 reduced the population in half. A peasant rebel, who took the name Ming, overthrew the Yuan in 1368. The Ming dynasty was replaced in 1644 by the Ch'ing Manchu dynasty that reigned until 1912.

In 223 B.C. China held a gargantuan lead in technology over the West, and it was still a substantial lead in A.D. 1268. Why did China lose this lead? The answer is centralization of power. Confucianism, which emphasized stability above all, formed merchant cartels for all industries under tight government control. The Mongol invasion substituted an even more autocratic imperial system, compared to the relatively relaxed governance of the T'ang and Song Dynasties. After the Mongols were expelled, the Ming dynasty was afraid to loosen controls for fear that weakness would tempt the barbarians. Most of all, unlike Europe, China was one giant centralized empire. Without free competition, progress froze in place.

INDIAN STORY

Sage: When does the night end and the dawn begin?
Disciple: When the first rays of the sun rise over the ocean and hit the tops of the palm trees?
Sage: No. That is not it.
Disciple: When the sun first reflects off the snow on the mountaintop?
Sage: No. That is not it.
Disciple: Please tell me master, when does the night end and the dawn begin?
Sage: When men from the ends of the earth realize that they are brothers.

PYTHAGORAS
c. 582–500 B.C.

Greek, philosopher and mathematician. His "Pythagorean theorem" demonstrated mathematics was useful in the real world—

a powerful idea. He discovered that dividing instrumental strings in simple ratios, like 1:2, 2:3, and 3:4, produced harmonious sounds—a sign of an order in nature that made investigating it worthwhile. He believed the world was round because eclipses made a curved line on the moon. A religious dissenter, he believed in the transmigration of souls between humans and animals and thus he refused to eat meat, or beans, the pathway of souls to Hades.

> Everything is numbers.
> From Diogenes Laertius,
> *Lives of Eminent Philosophers*

> Reason is immortal, all else mortal.
> Ibid.

> Life…is like a festival; just as some come to the festival to compete, some to ply their trade, but the best people come as spectators, so in life the slavish men go hunting for fame or gain, the philosophers for truth.
> Ibid.

> *Omnia mutantur nihil interit.*
> Everything changes; nothing dies.

XENOPHANES
c. 570–c. 475 B.C.

Greek, monotheist who tried to displace the Olympian pantheon and the Delphic Oracle. He believed God and matter had always existed because it was impossible for something to be made out of nothing or for something to become nothing. He anticipated the Law of the Conservation of Energy.

One god, greatest among gods and men, similar to mortals, neither in shape nor even in thought.

Diogenes Laertius, Lives of Eminent Philosophers, "Xenophanes," IX

It takes a wise man to recognize a wise man.

Ibid.

JUDAISM

The Hebrews ("wanderers") were first to think of God as spirit and to forbid God's representation in images. God, who is benevolent, omnipotent, and omniscient, created man as a companion to love. God chose the Jews as His special people through whom to work His will on earth. A problem for Jews and Christians is reconciling man's free will with God's omniscience.

The Old Testament of the Bible, written between 900 B.C. and 300 B.C., projects an end to history in a final day of judgment. Jews, Christians, and Muslims see history as a movement toward a goal, not as meaningless cycles, as do the Eastern religions. Because of God's covenant with the Jews, they became His agents. Later, Christians saw themselves as the new chosen people responsible for implementing God's will. The West's view of history as progress toward a goal is one of its most distinctive and energizing features.

Jewish rabbis during the Babylonian Captivity walled out Jewish life from the secular through the Talmud's voluminous proscriptions that regulated the minutiae of life, which resulted in Jews living together in tightly knit communities. Later, the church and the guilds forced Jews out of land-owning and the trades. Money-lending and speculating were considered sins, but since Christians considered Jews damned anyway, the church encouraged them to enter those fields. That made Jews useful for the authorities even though Christians treated them as second-class citizens.

Judaism's strain of antiauthoritarianism comes from its prophets, like Amos, Isaiah, and Jeremiah, who condemned both kings and chief priests for falling away from the Covenant. They said all men were equal before God, and that kings and priests should be disobeyed when in error. Hebrews invented the concept of natural law: the tradition that rulers cannot do anything they want, because the moral law applies to everyone. The prophets became role models for Protestant dissenters, who prevented Catholicism from becoming unified and reactionary, as did Islam and Confucianism.

Jews were part of the Canaanite society, which was a part of the larger Semitic society. Canaanite culture extended from the Levant across North Africa, including Carthage. Canaanites/Phoenicians invented the first alphabet. They worshiped various "Baals," including Moloch, who required the throwing of infants into his fire. Solomon built an altar to him.

After King Solomon's death in 935 B.C., Jews split into two kingdoms: Israel consisted of ten tribes whose capital in the north was Samaria, and Judah consisted of the tribes of Benjamin and Judah whose capital, Jerusalem, was in the south. The Assyrians extinguished Israel in 722 B.C., deporting all. In 587 B.C., the Babylonians razed the Temple in Jerusalem and deported its leading citizens after a Jewish revolt. After Persia overthrew Babylon in 438 B.C., many Jews returned to Jerusalem to rebuild the Temple. Jews lost their independent state for two thousand years when Rome asserted its control in 63 B.C. Rome destroyed the Temple and dispersed Jerusalem's Jews after the Zealot revolt at Masada in A.D. 73.

Few societies have valued education with the intensity of the Jews. The Talmud dictates: "If your teacher and your father have need of your assistance, help your teacher before helping your father, for the latter has given you only the life of this world, while the former has secured for you the life of the world to come."

SIDDHARTHA GAUTAMA BUDDHA
563?–483? B.C.

Nepalese, warrior prince, not a Brahman (priest). "Gautama" was his name; "Buddha," a title meaning "Enlightened One," and "Siddhartha," a title meaning "He Who Has Reached His Goal." At twenty-nine, Gautama left his wife, child, and palace for six years to ponder death. His asceticism produced no answers. So he sat for a day and a night under a banyan tree and thereafter taught what he had discovered, the Middle Way, a life between hedonism and self-denial. The Four Noble Truths: (1) life is suffering; (2) suffering comes from desiring pleasure, power, and continued life; (3) to end suffering, one must stop desiring; and, (4) you stop desiring by following the Noble Eightfold Path: right views, aspirations, speech, conduct, livelihood, effort, mindfulness, and contemplation. Doing all

that, you reach Nirvana or self-annihilation, that is, freedom from rebirth and transmigration. Man's goal is to become nothing.

The Creation was beyond comprehension. The Silence of the Buddha comes from refusing to entertain the Fourteen Questions, such as, "If God is ever perfect and complete, how could the will to create have arisen in Him?" Buddhism virtually disappeared in its homeland, but thrived elsewhere.

BUDDHISM

Buddhism, like Confucianism and Taoism, is a philosophy. Buddhism does not worship deities as does Hinduism and some other religions. Yet all four see life as endless cycles based on the two universal forces: the passive, negative, female yin and the active, positive, male yang. Daniel J. Boorstin wrote in *The Creators* (1992): "Buddha's aim was not to know the world or to improve it, but to escape its suffering." Nirvana was attained by ceasing all cravings. Or, as Lugwig von Mises said in *Human Action* (1946): "The essence of the Indian and Buddhist philosophies is to become perfectly passive, indifferent, and inert like the plants, to abandon thinking and acting." Boorstin wrote it this way in *The Discoverers* (1983):

> While Hindus and Buddhists sought ways out of history, Christianity and Islam sought ways into history. Instead of promising escape from experience, they sought meaning in experience. Christianity and Islam were both rooted in Judaism, and all three revealed a dramatic shift from a world of cycles to a world of history.

Buddhism seeks to escape material attachments, focusing rather on acheiving *nirvana*, which is a form of spiritual bliss. It values nonviolence more than Christianity, Islam, or Judaism do. Like Islam, Buddhism emphasizes justice rather than liberty and economic competition, which explains why they have been lacking in material production. The Japanese, in Zen Buddhism, allowed for material development because of the emphasis on action and perfection.

Buddhists and Hindus believe in "karma," the sum of one's acts in this and previous incarnations. Karma shapes one's destiny—a notion of fatality with a hint of freedom of action. Suffering is just punishment for misdeeds in prior incarnations.

In contrast to the East, the West is optimistic because God called the material world "good." Christian optimism comes from viewing the physical world as good and comprehensible and the spiritual world as even better. All souls are fit for salvation, so there is a hopeful external reality. This view rejects despair. But the Eastern religions view the material world as corrupt, so one must shun it to achieve spirituality.

The Reformation opened Christianity to new ideas. It broke away from the medieval worldview held by traditional Catholicism and Islam. The New Testament did not cancel the Old Testament, but supplemented it, and even the New Testament is not the final statement. Rather, truth unfolds over time. Calvinism made economic success a religious virtue, Max Weber analyzed the impact of the Protestant mentality on economic development, and R. H. Tawney established (in *Religion in the Rise of Capitalism*, 1926) the relationship of the Protestant work ethic to material progress.

HINDUISM

The oldest Hindu texts are the Vedas (1500 to 900 B.C.), which tell about the "deva" or the many lesser gods and goddesses that surround Brahmä (the impersonal supreme being), Vishnu (the Preserver), Shiva (the Destroyer), and his wife Kali (the four-armed goddess of death). Most sects are polytheistic with vast pantheons of gods. *The Upanishads* (700 B.C.) are commentaries on the Vedas. They that teach all souls will be reunited in a universal soul after Maya (the end of the illusion of time and space). Two epic poems are sacred literature that teach the values of Hinduism: the Mahabharata (fifth century B.C., which contains the *Bhagavad Gita,* or *Song of God*, the core Hindu beliefs) and the Ramayana (fourth century B.C.).

Baffling to Westerners is that the gods came after the Creation, whose origin is never explained. The Creation was a shattering of the unity of nature so that the great object is to be "uncreated" or to "get off the wheel," back into "the oneness." The *samsara*, or transmigration of souls from one life to the next, allows one to pay for the misdeeds of the earlier life. The objective is to lead an exemplary life so you can reach Nirvana, that is, where you will be extinguished. Essential to Hinduism is the soul's pathway to Nirvana through the four castes: Shudra (untouchables), Vaishiva (merchants), Kshatriya (warriors), and Brahmin (priests).

Vardhamana, called Mahavira (Great Hero), founded the Jain sect of Hinduism.

An extreme ascetic, he did not even wear a loincloth. Because all animal life is reincarnated, he brushed the dirt before him as he walked so he would not step on a flea. The Jains destroyed animal husbandry in India. They are famous for their story of six blind men who each felt different parts of an elephant and thus described it differently.

A polytheistic Hinduism and a monotheistic Islam both exist on the Indian subcontinent causing significant religious tension. Few innovations since medieval times have been developed in the Islamic, Hindu, Confucian, or Buddhist cultures.

MAHABHARATA

Mahabharata, fifth century B.C., epic poem about the descendants of King Bharata (India's formal name is Bharata-varsha) who war over a kingdom split between five brothers, the Pandavas, led by Yudhishthira, against a hundred cousins, the Kauravas. Krishna, an ally of the Pandavas, sings the divine song, the *Bhagavad-Gita*, which tells the precepts of Brahma's theology. The war, which is of *Iliad* proportions, is won by the Pandavas, but they learn there is nothing to earthly glory. So with their joint wife, Draupadi, and their dog, they journey to Mount Meru, home of the gods. All die on the way except Yudhishthira and the dog. At heaven, Yudhishthira was offered admission, but not the dog. Yudhishthira refused to enter—a good thing because the dog was the god of justice. In time, Yudhishthira became lonely for his brothers and their wife, so he went to the Underworld to suffer with them. The gods took pity and brought them all to heaven.

RAMAYANA

Ramayana, fourth century B.C., epic poem. Rama was a partial incarnation of Vishnu and the favorite son of King Dasa-ratha. He won the hand of Sita, daughter of King Janak. Queen Kaikeyi made King Dasa-ratha grant her two boons, which were that Rama would go into harsh exile for fourteen years and that her son, Bharat, be regent. In exile, Rama and Sita hear that the king died the day after their departure and that Bharat offered to give the kingdom to Rama. But Rama remained in exile as he had vowed to his father. In exile, a demon maiden solicited Rama's company, which he denied. She got her brother, Ravan, demon king of Lanka (Sri Lanka), to abduct Sita. Then Rama made an alliance with Hanuman, king of the monkey people, to war with Ravan. Winning the war, Rama returned to his kingdom with Sita, but suspicious of her virtue, he set out trials for her. Mother Earth protected her. The epic emphasizes everyone acknowledging their proper places, telling the truth, and doing their duty.

SIMONIDES OF CEOS
556–468? B.C.

Greek, poet who composed epitaphs and dirges for fallen Greek heroes.

The city is the teacher of the man.
Fragment 53

[When asked whether it was better to be wise or rich, Simonides replied:]
Rich, for we see the wise spending their time at the doors of the rich.

Go tell the Spartans, thou that passeth by,
That here, obedient to their laws, we lie.

Herodotus, Histories

Confucius
c. 551–479 b.c.

China's ethical teacher claimed he was restating traditional family wisdom. His teachings were compiled posthumously as *The Analects* that emphasized the Middle Way, the avoidance of extremes. His Golden Rule was to treat inferiors as you would have your superiors treat you. He advocated everyone knowing his place and doing his duty — like Plato's definition of justice as "everyman in his right place." He had no interest in science, math, history, or the individual.

Confucius promoted disinterested government service by an absolute ruler whose responsibility, like that of a father, was to rule benevolently. The subject's responsibility, like that of a son, was to obey cheerfully. Confucius said, "Let the prince be a prince, the minister a minister, the father a father, and the son a son." Scholars, selected by merit examinations, ruled as "mandarins." He objected to publishing the law because a ruler's dictate superseded prior law. Confucians supported state-owned monopolies of all industries, redistribution of estates, and the prevention of speculation. Confucians inspired "society above self," conflict avoidance, consensus building, and obedience to authority, all of which reinforced a rigid hierarchy.

When walking through a wild region, Confucius and his disciples came to a woman weeping at the grave of her son.

She said her son, like her husband and father, had been killed by a tiger. When Confucius asked why she lived in such a remote place, she replied, "Because there is no oppressive government here." Confucius said, "My children, remember oppressive government is worse than a tiger."

The Little, Brown Book of
Anecdotes, Clifton Fadiman (1985)

When you know a thing, to hold that you know it; and when you do not know a thing, to allow that you do not know it—that is knowledge.

The Confucian Analects, bk. 2, ch. 17, tr.
James Legge (1930)

We do not yet know how to serve man, how can we know about serving the spirits? We don't know yet about life, how can we know about death?

Ibid., 11:11

What is called a great minister is one who serves his prince according to what is right; and when he finds he cannot do so, retires.

Ibid., 11: 23

Behave toward everyone as if receiving a great guest.

Ibid., 12:2

Govern for the benefit of the people, reduce taxes, and recruit superior men of any origin.

Learning without thought is labor lost; thought without learning is perilous.

What has one who is not able to govern himself to do with governing others?

A King asked, "Is there one word which may serve as a rule of practice for all one's life?" The Master said, "Is not reciprocity such a word? What you do not want done to yourself, do not do to others."

The wise man resembles an archer, who when he misses the bull's-eye, turns and seeks the reason for failure in himself.

To put the world right in order, we must first put the nation in order; to put the nation in order, we must first put the family in order; to put the family in order, we must first set our hearts right.

Our greatest glory is not in never falling, but in rising every time we fall.

The way of a superior man is threefold. Virtuous, he is free from anxieties; wise, he is free from perplexities; bold, he is free from fear.

Study the past if you would divine the future.

When words lose their meaning, people will lose their liberty.

The aim of the superior man is truth.

AESOP
C. 620–560 B.C.

Greek, slave who wrote/compiled fables—tales with a moral involving animals, men, and gods. Slaves were usually war captives, a better fate than being killed. Greeks used slaves for household help, but seldom for plantations/mines like the Romans.

You have put your head inside a wolf's mouth and taken it out again in safety. That ought to be reward enough for you.
> "The Wolf and the Crane"

Better beans in peace than cakes and ale in fear.
> "The Town Mouse and the Country Mouse"

Thinking to get at once all the gold the Goose could give, the farmer killed it and opened it only to find—nothing.
> "The Goose with the Golden Eggs"

He that is neither one thing nor the other has no friends.
> "The Bat, the Birds and the Beasts"

Our insignificance is often the cause of our safety.
> "The Great and the Little Fishes"

Be content with your lot; one cannot be first in everything.
> [When the Peacock asked Hera to be given the voice of a Nightingale.]
> "The Peacock and Juno"

A young shepherd cried, "Wolf!" to trick the villagers. Later, when a wolf came and the boy cried, "Wolf," the villagers stayed home and the sheep were eaten.
> "The Boy Who Cried Wolf"

It is not only fine feathers that make fine birds.... Borrowed plumes.
> [The Jay tied peacock feathers to its tail.]
> "The Jay and the Peacock"

You thought I was too small to help, but you owe your life to a mouse.
> [Because the lion had spared the mouse, the mouse bit though a net trapping the lion.]
>> "The Lion and the Mouse"

Little by little does the trick.
> [The thirsty crow dropped pebbles into the pitcher until its water rose to the top.]
>> "The Crow and the Pitcher"

Slow and steady wins the race.
> [The tortoise beat the hare in a race when the hare fell asleep after it stopped to rest.]
>> "The Hare and the Tortoise"

Who is to bell the Cat? It is easy to propose impossible remedies.
> [Tie a bell to its tail.]
>> "Belling the Cat"

A crow in a tree held in her beak a tasty bit of cheese. A fox complimented her on her beautiful voice and asked her to sing. The cheese dropped into the fox's mouth as the crow began to croak.
>> "The Fox and the Crow"

A stag looking into a clear spring admired his large, beautiful antlers, but was ashamed of his spindly legs. Later when chased by a huntsman and pack of hounds, his horns got entangled in a thicket. Realizing he would be torn to pieces by the hounds, he lamented that what he had prided himself in was the cause of his undoing and that he had disliked his legs, which could have saved him.
>> "The Stag Looking Into the Water"

When an ailing lion invited a fox into his den, the fox said, "I would come inside if I hadn't seen a lot of footprints are pointing inwards toward your cave but none are pointing out."
>> "The Aging Lion and the Fox"

An olive tree boasting of its steadfastness and strength taunted the reed about his pliancy in the wind. When a strong wind came up, the reed leaned with the gusts and survived, but the tree was torn up by its roots as it stood firm.
>> "The Reed and the Olive Tree"

A fly sat sitting on the axle of a moving chariot wheel said, "What a dust I do raise."

HERACLITUS
c. 540–480 B.C.

Greek, philosopher called the "obscure." He held that the world is balanced between opposing dynamic principles, for example, the path up the hill is the path down the hill; goodness and badness; birth and death—all opposites are aspects of the same thing. Birth and death are both beginnings and both endings. A dialectic between opposites drives change. Everything is fleeting because everything is mutable and constantly changing. He thought all matter was made of fire, which always changes. Thales thought it was water and Pythagoras thought it was numbers. If you substitute "energy" for "fire," many moderns believe Heraclitus was right.

Nothing endures but change.
> In Diogenes Laertius, *Lives of Eminent Philosophers*, bk. IX, sec. 1

Character is destiny.

> Fragment 12

All is flux, nothing is stationary; everything gives way and nothing stays fixed. You can't twice step into the same river.

> Fragment 41

Nature is wont to hide herself.

> *On the Universe*, Fragment

The mixture not shaken decomposes.

THEMISTOCLES
C. 528–462 B.C.

Greek, Athenian statesman who built a strong navy to cut the lines of supply of the gigantic Persian army. The Oracle at Delphi had prophesied: "Safe shall the wooden wall continue for thee and thy children." Wise Athenians fled to the nearby island of Salamis, where the wooden walls of the Athenian navy saved Greece in the naval battle of Salamis. When Themistocles heard the Greek fleet might flee, he goaded the Persians into attacking before the Greeks could escape.

He who commands the sea commands everything.

> Quoted in Cicero, *Epistulae Ad Atticum*, bk. X, l. 8

I can't fiddle, but I can make a large state out of a small city.

AESCHYLUS
525–456 B.C.

Greek, tragic playwright who introduced a second actor, which permitted dialogue other than with a chorus. He won thirteen of the Athenian dramatic contests. He wrote about conflict between heroes, and conflict between man and God. In *Prometheus Bound*, the Titan Prometheus disobeyed Zeus by giving man fire, for which Zeus bound him to a rocky cliff. Prometheus remains defiant because he has foreknowledge that a descendent of Io, Herakles, will release him, and he knows Zeus is not all-powerful—only Fate is. Aeschylus does not tell us if Prometheus is prideful or if he is just a rebel. Io, whom Zeus had turned into a heifer for resisting his advances, is tormented by a stinging gadfly sent by the jealous Hera.

Aeschylus's masterpiece was the *Oresteia* trilogy (*Agamemnon*, *The Libation Bearers*, and *The Eumenides*), the supreme achievement of Greek culture. It is not merely a tale of revenge and lust for power, but a search for the cause of evil and the reason why humans suffer. Aeschylus gave his characters freedom of choice so they were responsible, but their personalities directed their deeds, so Fate was also involved. After earlier rounds of revenge killings in the bloody dynasty of Atreus, King Agamemnon of Argos sacrificed his daughter, Iphigenia, for a fair wind to sail to Troy. This infuriated her mother, Queen Clytemnestra, who took Aegisthus as a lover. For revenge, they murdered Agamemnon on his return from Troy, which, to satisfy his pride, he had turned to rubble. Agamemnon's captive and mistress, Cassandra, had forecast that they would be murdered in Argos, but Cassandra had been cursed always to prophesy the truth but never to be heeded. Agamemnon's son, Orestes, and his sister, Electra, killed Clytemnestra and Aegisthus for revenge, not for the throne, which he renounced. The Furies pursued Orestes for revenge, but a divided Athenian jury freed him.

Orestes broke the chain of crime and retribution because he felt remorse and did not assume the throne. Apollo argued at the trial that Orestes was not guilty of shedding family blood because mothers only nourish in their wombs the seed of the father; that is mothers are not related to their children. With the acquittal the feud ended, and Athena turned the Furies into Eumenides, or "gracious ones." We have risen from Homer's pitiless warrior society of 1200 B.C. to a compassionate fifth-century B.C. Athens.

> For he wishes not to seem, but to be, the best.
> *The Seven against Thebes*, ch. 1, l. 592

> Helen brought to Ilium her dowry, destruction.
> *Agamemnon*, ch. 1, l. 406

> For only Zeus is free.
> Prometheus Bound

> Tyranny's disease is to trust no friends.
> Ibid., ch. 1, l. 224

> Once an eagle, stricken with a dart,
> Said, when he saw the fashion of the shaft,
> "With our own feathers, not by others' hands,
> Are we now smitten."
> In Norman Augustine, *Augustine's Laws* (1986)

> It is not the oath that makes us believe the man, but the man the oath.

GREEK DRAMA

Greek drama developed from religious festivals that originally featured only a chorus, to which Thespis in 535 B.C. added an actor (hero or god) who conversed with the chorus. Aeschylus added more actors, who played different parts by wearing masks. Aeschylus, Sophocles, and Euripides were Greece's star tragedians, and Aristophanes was the star comedian. Tragedy is always man-made. Death from natural causes may be awful, but it is never a tragedy. In Greek tragedy, the hero always had a *hamartia*, or fatal flaw, which Aristotle argued was necessary because there would be no point in a completely virtuous or completely evil person being destroyed. Often, the *harmatia* was the hero's "hubris," or arrogance, which was punished by Nemesis, the goddess guardian of the moral code. Tragedy produces a "catharsis," a purgation of one's emotions.

PINDAR
c. 518–438 B.C.

Greek, lyric poet. Lyric poetry was meant to be performed, i.e., to be accompanied by the lyre.

> O my soul, do not aspire to immortal life,
> But exhaust the limits of the possible.
> *Pythian Odes*, ch. 3, l. 109

> Words have a longer life than deeds.
> *Nemean Odes*, IV, l. 1

> Custom, Lord of all mortals and immortals.
> Fragment 169

ANAXAGORAS
500–428 B.C.

Greece's Copernicus and Darwin. He believed in a dualistic universe composed of tiny particles of matter and a force, or mind, called "nous," which brought order to chaos and transformed inorganic matter into organic forms. He also claimed that organic life reforms itself from lower into higher orders, such as humans; and humans also live on other planets revolving around other suns. The sun and stars are huge fiery masses, and the moon reflects the sun's light. He fled after being convicted of impiety for denying that the stars were divinities. When told Athens had condemned him to death, he replied, "Nature has long since condemned both them and me."

HORATIUS COCLES
C. 500 B.C.

Roman, soldier. Horatius single-handedly held one end of the Sublician Bridge against the Etruscan army while his comrades destroyed the bridge behind him. He swam the Tiber and was given the land he could plow around in a day. See poem of Thomas Macaulay (1800).

CINCINNATUS
C. 500–440 B.C.

Roman who dropped his plow when appointed dictator of Rome in order to go rescue a Roman army. Despite his victory and a grateful republic, he resigned the dictatorship and returned to plowing his farm. He epitomizes the "citizen soldier."

SOPHOCLES
496–406 B.C.

Greek, tragic playwright, pessimist, and Athenian general. In his *Oedipus* trilogy—*Oedipus the King, Oedipus at Colonus*, and *Antigone*, he focused on character and the theme that man suffers because of ignorance. In *Oedipus*, an oracle tells the king of Thebes, Laius, and his queen, Jocasta, that their son will kill him and sleep with her. So they expose their infant son, Oedipus, on a hill, but a shepherd rescues him. On achieving manhood, Oedipus unknowingly kills a man (his father). He then encounters the Sphinx (a lion with a woman's head), who kills travelers who fail to answer her riddle: "What walks in the morning on four feet, at noon upon two and at evening upon three?" Oedipus guesses "man" because as a babe he crawls, at mid-age walks on two feet, and in old age uses a cane. Upon hearing the correct answer, the Sphinx kills herself. The grateful Thebans make Oedipus their king, because Laius had disappeared. Oedipus marries the queen, his mother, and they have four children, Antigone, Polynices, Eteocles, and Ismene. Thebes is struck by plague, which an oracle says will be relieved only when the murderer of Laius leaves the city. When Oedipus discovers that he is the murderer, he blinds himself and goes into exile.

In *Oedipus at Colonus*, the blind Oedipus, led about by Antigone, decries the baseness of life. In *Antigone*, the brothers Polynices and Eteocles fight for the kingdom and are both killed. Creon, an ally of Eteocles, becomes king and refuses to bury Polynices. Because Greeks thought that the spirits of the unburied lived in torment, Antigone buries Polynices, which forces King Creon to decide whether to enforce his decree. He entombs Antigone alive. Creon's son, Haemon, whose pleas for mercy are ignored, enters Antigone's tomb and falls on his sword to lie next to her.

Antigone reflects on the conflict between a citizen's obligation to natural law and to commands of the sovereign. Natural law, a theory widely accepted by America's Founding Fathers and Dr. Martin Luther King Jr., holds that basic moral principles are inherent in human consciousness and are discernible through reason. In contrast is Justice O. W. Holmes Jr.'s Positive Law, that is a citizen should obey whatever law the sovereign commands, even genocide.

> Nobly to live, or else nobly to die,
> Befits proud birth.
>> *Ajax*, l. 480

> How dreadful knowledge of the truth
>> can be
> When there's no help in truth.
>> *Oedipus Rex*, l. 316

> Let every man in mankind's frailty
> Consider his last day; and let none
> Presume on his good fortune until he find
> Life, at his death, a memory without pain.
>> Ibid., l. 1529

> Not to be born is, past all prizing, best.
>> *Oedipus at Colonus*, l. 1224

> Dreadful is the mysterious power of Fate; there is no escape from it by wealth or war, by walled city, or dark, sea-beaten ships.
>> *Antigone*

> Your edict, King, was strong.
> But all your strength is weakness itself
>> against
> The immortal unrecorded laws of God.
> They are not merely now: they were, and
>> shall be
> Operative forever, beyond man utterly.
>> Ibid.
>> [Idea of a higher, natural law that compels Antigone to defy the king.]

> Numberless are the world's wonders,
>> but none
> More wonderful than man....
>> Ibid., l. 133

> Our ship of state, which recent storms
>> have threatened to destroy, has come
>> safely to harbor at last.
>> Ibid., l. 442

> No enemy is worse than bad advice.
>> Electra

> Death is not the greatest of evils: it is worse
>> to want to die, and not be able to.
>> Ibid., l. 1008

> It is hope that maintains most of mankind.
>> Fragment

> A woman's vows I write upon the wave.
>> Fragment

> It is terrible to speak well and be wrong.

PERICLES
C. 495–429 B.C.

Greek, statesman who democratized Athens by stripping the aristocratic Aeropagus Council of its veto. That made the citizen assembly supreme. He built the

Acropolis and Parthenon and led Athens to empire. During the Peloponnesian War, his "Funeral Oration" praised the Athenians for their openness to the world and their willingness to assume great risks. He believed a free people would prevail against a militaristic society. The Periclean Age was the Golden Age of Athens.

> We throw open our city to the world, and never by alien acts exclude foreigners from any opportunity of learning or observing, although the eyes of an enemy may occasionally profit by our liberality....
>
> "Funeral Oration for Fallen Athenian Warriors," in Thucydides, *The Peloponnesian War*, tr. Richard Crawley and T. E. Wick (1982)

> When it is a question of settling disputes, everyone is equal before the law. When it is a question of putting one person before another in positions of public responsibility, what counts is not membership in a particular class, but the actual ability that the man possesses.
>
> Ibid.

> We are lovers of the beautiful, yet simple in taste; and we cultivate the mind without loss of manliness.
>
> Ibid.

> We regard wealth as something to be properly used...and place the real disgrace of poverty not in owning to the fact but in declining to struggle against it.
>
> Ibid.

> The man who can most truly be accounted brave is he who best knows the meaning of what is sweet in life and what is terrible, and then goes out undeterred to meet what is to come.
>
> Ibid.

> Men naturally despise those who court them, but respect those who do not give way to them.
>
> Ibid.

> The secret of happiness is freedom, and the secret of freedom, courage.
>
> Ibid.

> Wait for the wisest of all counselors, Time.
>
> Ibid.

> In short, I say not only that as a city we are the school of Hellas, but also in my opinion there is no other place where the individual can develop independence and self-reliance so easily, so gracefully, and in so many directions.
>
> Ibid.

GREEK AND ROMAN PHILOSOPHY

The following is synopsized from Anthony Gottlieb's *The Dream of Reason: A History of Western Philosophy from the Greeks to the Renaissance* (2001) and from William and Mabel Sahakian's *Ideas of the Great Philosophers* (1996):

Aristotle divided pre-Socratic Greek thinkers into the *theologi*, who believed in supernatural beings, and the *physici*, who explained the world in natural principles. The Milesians, the earliest *physici*, sought to learn what constituted the *arche*, or basic stuff of the universe. Thales (c. 640–

c. 546 B.C.) believed it to be water because it is found in all three states: liquid, solid, and gas. The Milesians advanced the practical arts as geographers, surveyors, navigators, and mathematicians.

Pythagoras (582–500 B.C.) added to the Milesians' naturalism the notion that nature should be investigated for the sake of knowledge alone, that is, for philosophy (love of wisdom). He made strides in mathematics by devising useful applications, and he said that the *arche* was mathematics, that is, the ultimate, permanent, unchanging reality was numbers, which give shape or form to corporal bodies.

Four philosophers from Elea (Eleatic School) concluded that "all is one; change is nonexistent." Parmenides (b. 515 B.C.), leader of the school, argued that change is illusion because there is no empty space, so motion cannot exist. Zeno of Elea (490–430 B.C.), whom Aristotle credited with being the inventor of the dialectic method of reasoning (the refutation of arguments by reducing them to absurdities or contradictions), argued that at any moment of time a flying arrow is at rest in one piece of space, so it never moves.

Heraclitus of Ephesus (540–480 B.C.) argued the opposite of the Eleatics, that is, that nothing abides, all things are in ceaseless change. His three fundamental beliefs were as follows: everything is in perpetual turmoil and change ("War is father of all and king of all"); all opposites are part of the same; and the *arche* is "fire" because it is ever moving and changing. He also said, "Nature loves to hide," that is, nothing is as it seems.

To jump ahead, Plato adopted the Heraclitean doctrine that the physical world is in flux, so there is no sure knowledge of it.

But like Parmenides, Plato held that part of the world is eternal and unchanging; it can be understood only by reason.

Empedocles (c. 495–c. 435 B.C.), the first Pluralist, argued that the four elements (fire, air, water, and earth) are unchanging, so nothing is ever created or destroyed. But by changing their combinations, the elements become different things. He also believed, as Darwin later proved, in the evolution of life forms through natural selection.

Democritus (c. 460–c. 370 B.C.), the most eminent Pluralist and the "father of materialism," argued that all matter is formed of tiny, moving atoms that are eternal and unchanging, albeit they combine to create new things in the "void." He anticipated two modern principles of physics, that is, the indestructibility of matter and the conservation of energy. Early Christians condemned "atomism" because it explained the world without a deity and because Democritus held there was no soul independent of a material structure. The Latin poet Lucretius's *De Rerum Natura* attacked religion on the basis of atomism. Atomism's concept of a "void" contended against Parmenides, who had argued that there is no motion because there is no empty space. Democritus argued that because our senses cannot detect atoms, we only have subjective impressions of reality, which by convention we describe by color, hardness, taste, and other perceptions.

Protagoras (485–410 B.C.) was the most famous Sophist, one who taught for pay how to achieve power through debating by developing skills in grammar, rhetoric, politics, ethics, and law. Protagoras held that there is no universal truth—what each person perceives is true for him, or in other words, relativism. His famous expression was, "Man is the measure of all things." There is no objective truth because all we know comes from our senses, which are so flawed that we know nothing for sure; we can only have opinions. There is no knowledge and no truth; there are only opinions. The Sophist Gorgias carried relativism to its ultimate conclusion, that is, nihilism: There is no ultimate reality to perceive even if we had perfect senses.

Nihilism and skepticism are each self-contradictory. If there is no truth (nihilism), then the posited truth of nihilism cannot be true. If there is no knowledge (skepticism), how can we come to know that? See *Ideas of the Great Philosophers*:

> The Relativist is expressing an absolute truth when he asserts that truth is not absolute, for he sincerely believes that the real truth is that truth is relative. Hence he necessarily contradicts himself and implicitly admits that truth is objective, not relative.

To look ahead, relativism in its nihilistic and skeptical forms was anathema to Plato, whose philosophy restored validity to the concepts of knowledge and reality.

Socrates (469–399 B.C.) held that the soul, which exists prior to birth and after death, is "mutilated by wrong actions and benefited by right actions." If people knew the spiritual degradation caused by stealing, lying, and other vices, they would avoid those evils. Protecting the soul is paramount, so the search for virtue is paramount. No rational man would do wrong intentionally. Thus, wisdom and virtue are the same, and ignorance is the fount of evil.

Antisthenes (445–360 B.C.) formed the cynic school, an ascetic philosophy which believed that only virtue and nature mattered, so conventional values should be disregarded. The cynic's embrace of poverty appeared to ape Socrates, but Socrates had nothing against wealth per se—he was just preoccupied with other things. Plato described the cynic, Diogenes (400–335 B.C.), as "a Socrates gone mad." Diogenes lived in a tub, ate raw meat, and advocated free love and suicide. Yet the cynic's worldly detachment was a foundation of stoicism.

Plato's dualism posits an unchanging reality of forms and absolute ethical standards combined with Heraclitus's physical world, which is in constant flux. Plato (427–347 B.C.) repudiated the Sophists, whose relativism saw no right or wrong, but accepted all beliefs, lifestyles, and moral systems. To Plato in his *Timaeus*, God was an intelligent being, the "master craftsman," who used the rules of the Forms to shape earth to further His purposes for mankind. Unlike the *theologi*, Plato did not see God intervening in the world he had set in motion.

Aristotle (384–322 B.C.) invented formal logic and biology, and developed political theory, literary criticism, theology, zoology, meteorology, physics, astronomy, chemistry, anatomy, mathematics, and psychology, albeit his conclusions were usually wrong. He rejected Plato's forms and Parmenides' denial of change. Aristotle saw change as a passage from potentiality to actuality—a seed is a potential tree. He was a materialist in that life was organized matter, so life disappeared when its matter became disorganized. But, life had a purpose, or "telos"—a seed to become a tree. Aristotle believed a prime mover had given the universe a first push, and afterward God just let His physical laws work. Aristotle believed that virtue and vice are not innate, but that they result from personal decisions that develop into habits, for which each person is responsible. Vice is either doing too little or too much; for example, bravery is a virtue, while cowardice and rashness are the vices on either side of bravery.

After Aristotle, three Greek philosophies (epicureanism, stoicism, and skepticism) gave practical relevance to philosophy and dominated Western thinking until the Christian era.

Hedonism is the school advocating the pursuit of pleasure and avoidance of pain. The Cyrenaic branch of Hedonism (Aristippus of Cyrene, 435–355 B.C.) sought immediate physical pleasures.

The Epicurean branch of Hedonism (Epicurus, 342–270 B.C.) held that the greatest good (*summum bonum*) is to be found through prudence, not drunkenness, gluttony, and so forth. The epicurean ideal was tranquility, which results from dispelling fear of death by realizing there is no hell because life is a mere organization of atoms. Epicurus was a materialist who believed that a sober life gave the greatest tranquility. The epicurean drive to avoid pain and seek pleasure found expression in the utilitarianism of Jeremy Bentham (1748–1832) and John Stuart Mill (1806–73). Epicureans focused on relieving personal anxiety, while utilitarians focused on material welfare for the greatest number. Epicureanism is a form of radical individualism.

Stoicism was developed by Zeno of Citium (335–264 B.C.) and the Romans:

Seneca, Epictetus, and Marcus Aurelius. Zeno took from the cynics the idea that virtue and nature are supreme, so one should not be impressed with society. He took from Plato the idea that the universe was created by a beneficent, but noninterfering, Providence. Zeno took from Heraclitus the idea that learning to live with the inevitable is the key to happiness. The ideal is a tranquil indifference to life's vicissitudes. As a Roman stoic put it, "Do not seek to have everything that happens happen as you wish, but wish for everything to happen as it does happen, and your life will be serene." Stoics are disciplined, public-spirited types, but intolerant of frailty in themselves and others. Fatalism is their weakness. Their opposites are epicureans, who are tolerant types, but with no sense of duty to any person or thing.

The Skeptic school began with Pyrrho of Elis (360–270 B.C.) whose extreme skepticism made him impassive. Because one could learn nothing from untrustworthy senses, one should hold no opinions. Extreme skeptics do not know whether to eat an apple or a rock. Less extreme skeptics "act on appearances" — apples seem edible, even if one is not sure. Less extreme skeptics are open-minded people who admit that someday we may know the truth, but now we must suspend judgment on controversial matters.

Sextus Empiricus, a second-century A.D. Roman physician, coined the word skeptic, meaning "searcher." Skepticism evolved into empiricism, which makes only limited claims about the appearance of things based on observation, but nothing is ever considered to be proved finally.

ZENO OF ELEA
490–430 B.C.

Greek, pupil of Parmenides. Zeno propounded paradoxes to prove motion and change are illusory, including "Achilles' paradox," illustrated as follows: Achilles can never catch a turtle which has a head start, because every time he reaches the spot where the turtle had been, it would have gone a little further. In another example, Zeno picked grains of sand from a sand heap, but said he could never identify that grain whose removal changed the heap into a nonheap. Such "fuzzy thinking" runs counter to Aristotle's belief that something was either "A" or "not-A," which is the basis of Western science. This Aristotelian faith in "bivalence" may be supplanted by fuzzy thinking, or "multivalence," just as Newtonian physics fell to Einstein's relativity. Bart Kosko's *Fuzzy Thinking* (1993), like Zeno, argues that our science establishment thinks in terms of black and white, while the real world is gray. The "fuzzy principle" holds that up close everything is a matter of degree.

PERSIAN WARS
490 B.C.

The Persian emperor Darius I set out in 490 B.C. to punish Athens for aiding rebellious Greek cities in Asia in 499 B.C. Eleven thousand Athenians at Marathon defeated Persia's thirty thousand soldiers because the Persians were lightly armed and fought as individuals, while the Greeks were heavily armed and fought as a team. Pheidippides ran twenty-two miles to Athens to say, just before he died, "Rejoice, we conquer." Today a marathon is 26 miles, 385 yards.

Darius's son, Xerxes, began the second invasion in 480 B.C. when Leonidas's 300 Spartans delayed 250,000 Persians for three days at a mountain pass at Thermopylae, which gave Themistocles time to prepare his 300 triremes at Salamis to destroy Persia's 400 triremes. Xerxes could not resupply his army, so he retreated to Asia except for a 50,000-man army left in central Greece. In 479 B.C. at Platea, 5,000 Spartans routed the 50,000 Persians.

The Greek victory at Salamis ranks as one of the most consequential battles in history, along with the Romans beating the Huns at Chalons, the Franks beating the Saracens at Tours, and, the Spanish and Italians beating the Turks at Lepanto. Because Western armies had heavily armed and highly drilled warriors, they generally prevailed against the Eastern preference for cavalry, numbers, and missile troops. All of these victories prevented Eastern despotism from suffocating the West.

PROTAGORAS
485–410 B.C.

Greek, philosopher, the most renowned Sophist, or teacher of wisdom and political skills, who accepted pay for classes. Unlike Parmenides, who rejected sensation as the way to truth, Protagoras held sensation to be the only means of finding truth. He believed that nothing exists beyond the senses; if anything did, it would be unknowable; and if knowable, it could not be communicated other than by the senses. His belief that the external world had no reality outside of how man perceived it was anathema to Socrates and Plato. Sophists, who doubted the gods and elevated man, are heroes to today's secular humanists.

> Man is the measure of all things.
> > In Plato, *Theaetetus*, tr. Benjamin Jowett (1894)

EURIPEDES
484–406 B.C.

Greek, tragic playwright who attacked slavery, war, oracles, and polytheism, albeit he covered his tracks with pious and patriotic passages. *Medea* is his most famous play. Goethe thought Euripedes was the greatest Greek dramatist. His skepticism made him a hero of the French Enlightenment.

Euripedes' *The Trojan Women* may be the most powerful indictment of war ever written. While it records the Greek slaughter of the Trojan men and the enslavement of their women and children, it targets the Athenian massacre at Melos for being neutral in the Peloponnesian War. Euripides shows that moral evil is not caused externally by the gods, but it is an aspect of our human nature.

> Whoso neglects learning in his youth, loses the past and is dead for the future.
> > *Phrixus*, Fragment 927

> A second wife is hateful to the children of the first; a viper is not more hateful.
> > *Alcestis*, l. 238

> Humility, a sense of reverence...of all the prizes that a mortal man might win, these, I say, are wisest; these are best.
> > *The Bacchae*, l. 1150

> But this is slavery, not to speak one's thought.
> > *The Phoenician Women*

> The God of war hates those who hesitate.

> Zeus, if there be a Zeus,
> For I know of him only by report—
> > *Melanippe*

> But now everything has turned to hatred and where love was once deepest, a cancer spreads.
> > *Medea*

> Venus thy eternal sway
> All the race of men obey.

HERODOTUS
C. 480–425 B.C.

Greek, called the "father of history" by Cicero. History means "search for the truth." The English poet A. E. Housman said, "A historian is not like a scientist examining a specimen under a microscope. He is more like a dog searching for fleas." Better is John Lukacs's, "History is a certain kind of memory, organized and supported by evidence." Believing in oracles and gods, Herodotus recorded legend, lore, and fact, and let the reader separate them. In order to sell his history lectures, he tried to be entertaining. In the tradition of Homer, he wrote history to celebrate the deeds of great men, and he commented widely on Greek customs.

He recorded the history of Greece and the eastern Mediterranean in narrative form from 560 B.C. through the final attempt of the Persians under Xerxes in 480 B.C. to invade Greece. The first muckraker, he exposed the Delphic Oracle for accepting bribes to predict favorable outcomes to pending battles. He differed from the earlier chroniclers in that he evaluated history, revealed the roots of the Persian wars, and derived useful lessons from history. Also, he was the first significant Greek writer to eschew poetry for prose.

> Men trust their ears less than their eyes.
>
> *Histories*, bk. 1

> No one is fool enough to choose war instead of peace. For in peace sons bury fathers, but war violates the order of nature, and fathers bury sons.
>
> Ibid., ch. 87

> Chances rule men and not men chances.
>
> Ibid., bk. VII, ch. 49

> Not snow, nor rain, nor heat, nor night keeps them from accomplishing their appointed courses with all speed.
> [The U. S. Postal Service motto is, "Neither snow, nor rain, nor gloom of night stays these couriers from the swift completion of their appointed rounds."]
>
> Ibid., bk. VIII, ch. 98

> This is the greatest pain among men, to have much knowledge but no power.
>
> Ibid., bk. IX, ch. 16

Herodotus told the story of the proverbially wealthy Croesus, king of Lydia. Croesus asked Solon, "Who is the world's happiest man?" Solon named a poor man whose sons had grown to great stature before he died. Croesus objected that Solon had not named him. Solon replied: "No man can say whether you are happy or not

until you die. For no man knows what misfortunes may overtake you, or what misery may be yours in place of all this splendor." Later the Persian king Cyrus overran Lydia and ordered Croesus to be burned at the stake. Croesus moaned "Solon, oh Solon." Cyrus had Croesus explain why he had called on Solon. Moved by his answer, Cyrus freed Croesus.

Croesus had initiated the war with the Persians after the Delphic Oracle had prophesied, "If Croesus should make war on the Persians, he would destroy a mighty empire." The Oracle had not said which empire.

Midas, king of Phrygia, accepted a stranger's offer of the power to turn everything he touched into gold. But afterward, Midas could not eat because his food turned into gold, and his touch turned his daughter into a golden statue. Midas accepted the stranger's offer to take back his power.

Herodotus also wrote of El Dorado, a place where large "ants" bigger than foxes dug flakes of gold from the sand. In 1996 a place in Pakistan was found where marmots the size of foxes burrow into sand mixed with gold flakes. The Greek words for "ant" and "marmot" are virtually identical.

BATTLE OF THERMOPYLAE
480 B.C.

The Spartan king Leonidas made a brilliant decision to delay the Persian army of 250,000 men at the narrow pass of Thermopylae. Knowing it was a suicide mission, he required that all his volunteers have sons. The Oracle at Delphi had prophesied that either the Persians would lay waste to Sparta or a Spartan king would die. On leaving home, his wife asked what she should do. Leonidas replied, "Marry a good man and bear good sons."

The 300 Spartans and 7,000 other Greeks held the pass for three days, killing some 20,000 Persians, including most of Xerxes' "ten thousand immortals." When Leonidas heard that the Persians would shoot so many arrows as to darken the sky, he replied, "Good, we prefer fighting in the shade." The Spartans fell after a traitor showed the Persians a secret path across the mountain to the rear of Leonidas's position. Seeing the betrayal, Leonidas told his men, "Eat a good breakfast, for tonight we will all eat in hell." Only the 300 Spartans and 1,000 Thesians stayed to fight to the death.

Great wars involving millions of men can turn on the grit of a few. Three hundred Spartans saved Greece; seven hundred Royal Air Force (RAF) pilots saved the world from Nazism. Reginald Mitchell was ordered both by the RAF and his company to design a biplane for maneuverability. He refused to obey. He designed a single-wing fighter for speed, the Spitfire.

SOCRATES
469–399 B.C.

Greek, philosopher, warrior, and Athens' most loved and hated citizen. Because he felt ignorance prevented him from addressing theology, physics, and metaphysics, he confined himself to ethics and politics, using logic and the "Socratic method" of asking questions to strip away the false and to lead the student to a certain conclusion, but never giving his opinion. He called himself a "mid-wife of truth" who asks "questions of others and have not the wit to answer them myself." He claimed to be a "gad fly" sent to arouse the slumbering horse, Athens. The words of Socrates have been passed down principally through Plato's dialogues, but also through Xenophon, Aristophanes, and Aristotle.

Socrates asked the key question in ethics: Can a secular moral code work? He thought so; he believed that virtue is knowledge—to know the good is to do the good. He said, "No one does evil voluntarily." Socrates believed that if we were wise enough to understand our own best interest, we would choose to do the good. He spoke of the shepherd Gyges, who found a golden ring that made its bearer invisible and thus able to steal with impunity. Socrates said that if Gyges were wise, he would not steal because he can be happy only if he is just.

Few moderns accept Socrates' philosophy that to know the good is to do the good. Most claim that man's instincts override his rationality. Moreover, in the name of rationality, Robespierre, Stalin, Hitler, and the like committed unspeakable crimes. Indeed, Socrates' prize students, Critias, Alcibiades, and Charmides, were profoundly evil men.

Believing that knowledge is the key to excellence, Socrates claimed that government by aristocracy was best. For example, one goes to a physician for advice, not to the whole citizenry. However, complexity theory supports democracy: Flocks of birds locate new food sources and identify dangers via the senses of every member of the flock.

History's most famous trial was that of Socrates in 399 B.C. for "impiety and corrupting the youth." Due to a decree prohibiting retribution for the reign of terror under the "rule of the thirty," Socrates could not be tried for his real offense, that is, that his students had led a bloody antidemocrat revolt. The jury offered to spare him if he stopped teaching. He said that "the unexamined life" would not be worth living. When asked to propose an alternative to execution, he proposed that he be given free meals. After being convicted by a margin of 60 votes out of 501, he refused to escape, believing that a citizen must obey the law. Socrates can be seen as a martyr for reason. But his peers saw him as World War II Americans saw Ezra Pound, an apologist for Hitler. In any case, Socrates was old, ailing, and had a witch for a wife. He said he "relinquished only the most burdensome part of life, in which all feel their powers of intellect diminished."

Virtue does not come from money, but from virtue comes money and all other good things to man, both to the individual and to the state.

"Plato's Apology," in *Diogenes Laertius, Lives of Eminent Philosophers*, tr. R. D. Hicks (1925), 30b

There is only one good, namely, knowledge; and only one evil, namely, ignorance.

Ibid., 31

All I know is that I know nothing.

Ibid., 32

The unexamined life is not worth living.

Ibid., 38 a

The hour of departure has arrived and we go our ways; I to die, and you to live. Which is better? Only God knows.

Ibid., 42 a

I am not an Athenian, nor a Greek, but a citizen of the world.

In Plutarch, *Of Banishment*

Some things I have said of which I am not altogether confident. But that we shall be better and braver and less helpless if we think we ought to inquire than we should have been if we had indulged in the idle fancy that there was no knowing and no use seeking to know what we do not know—that is a theme on which I am ready to fight, in word and deed, to the utmost of my power.

Socrates in the Meno

Philosophy begins in wonder.

In Plato, *Theaetetus*, ch. 21, tr. Benjamin Jowett (1894)

Man is a prisoner who has no right to open the door of his prison and run away....

Ibid.

Either death is a state of nothingness and utter unconsciousness, or, as men say, there is a change and migration of the soul from this world to another.... Now if death be of such a nature, I say that to die is to gain; for eternity is then only a single night.

Ibid.

Crito, I owe a cock to Asclepius; will you remember to pay the debt?
[Last words.]

Ibid.

Our prayers should be for blessings in general, for God knows best what is good for us.

What a disgrace it is for a man to grow old without ever seeing the beauty and the strength of which his body is capable!

What mean ye, fellow citizens, that ye turn every stone to scrape wealth together, and take so little care of your children, to whom ye must one day relinquish all?

Let him that would move the world, first move himself.

By all means marry. If you get a good wife, you'll be happy. If you get a bad one, you'll become a philosopher.
> [Socrates' wife, Xanthippe, was a most troublesome woman.]

DEMOCRITUS
C. 460–370 B.C.

Greek, philosopher, "father of materialism," whom Francis Bacon called the greatest ancient philosopher. Democritus said matter was made of tiny, irreducible, and indestructible particles (*atomos*, or indivisible) within an infinite void of space. Moreover, atoms are never created or destroyed, and mind, soul, and matter are all mere atoms. More profoundly, atoms are in continuous motion—the notion of inertial mass. There is no chance; there is only our ignorance. Because the world consists of atoms working mechanically according to underlying laws, we can learn how the world works. Here Democritus derived the gospel of human progress.

None of his seventy books survived, but his reputation as "the laughing philosopher" did. He believed stars, like our sun, are born and die, and that there are an infinite number of worlds.

The first principles of the universe are atoms and empty space; everything else is merely thought to exist.
> Quoted in Diogenes Laertius,
> "Democritus"

I would rather discover a single demonstration [in geometry] than win the throne of Persia.
> G. Grote, *Plato and the Other Companions of Socrates* (1875), pt. 1

HIPPOCRATES
460–377 B.C.

Greek, physician who saw that ailments have natural causes and are not punishments by the gods. His theory of disease, that the body remains healthy when its four humors—blood, phlegm, yellow bile, and black bile—are kept in proportion, survived until the nineteenth century. While the humors are in proportion, there is no need to bleed excess blood. The discovery of bacteria awaited Louis Pasteur. Greek medicine relied on diet and exercise. By 1970, no U.S. medical school still used the Hippocratic Oath because of its prohibitions against abortion and assisted suicide.

I will use treatment to help the sick according to my ability and judgment but never with a view of injury or wrongdoing. Neither will I administer a poison to anybody when asked to do so, nor will

I suggest such a course. Similarly I will not give to a woman a pessary to cause abortion....

The Hippocratic Oath for Physicians

Extreme remedies are very appropriate for extreme diseases.

Aphorisms, Sec. 1, tr. W. H. S. Jones (1923)

Life is short, the art long, opportunity fleeting, experience treacherous, and judgment difficult.

Ibid.

As to diseases make a habit of two things— to help, or at least, to do no harm.

Epidemics, bk. 1, ch. 11

The art of medicine consists in three things: the disease, the patient, and the physician. The patient must combat the disease along with the physician.

THUCYDIDES
460–400 B.C.

Greek, Athenian general, and historian who began compiling the *History of the Peloponnesian War* when it started. He was the first to write history as "an aid to the interpretation of the future" by distilling general truths to guide statesmen to wise governance. For example, we learn from the Athenian slaughter of the Melian men after they surrendered their city that advanced cultures can be barbaric—witness, inter alia, Hitler's Germany and the Allies' carpet bombing of German and Japanese cities. While Herodotus had regarded pride and impiety as the sources of disasters, Thucydides ascribed them to lack of forethought. Although an Athenian,

he is objective about Sparta and Athens. Like Machiavelli, he makes no moral judgments. Unfortunately, he focuses only on political-military history with few asides on Greek culture.

We must remember that one man is much the same as another; and that he is best who is trained in the severest school.

History of the Peloponnesian War to 411 B.C.

I shall be content if those shall pronounce my *History* useful who desire to have a view of events as they did really happen, and as are very likely, in accordance with human nature, to repeat themselves at some future time, if not exactly the same, yet very similar.

Ibid., bk. 1

War is an evil thing; but to submit to the dictation of other states is worse.... Freedom, if we hold fast to it, will ultimately restore our losses, but submission will mean permanent loss of all that we value....

Ibid., bk. 4

To you who call yourselves men of peace, I say: You are not safe unless you have men of action on your side.

Ibid.

For of the gods we believe, and of men we know, that by a necessity of their nature wherever they have power they always rule. And so in our case since we neither enacted this law nor when it was enacted were the first to use it, but found it in existence and expect to leave it in existence for all time, so we make use of it, well aware that both you and others, if clothed with the same power as we are, would do the same thing.... You know as well as we do that right, as the world goes, is only in question between equals in power, while the strong do what they can and the weak suffer what they must.

[Here, the Athenians demanded tribute solely because they were more powerful. When the Melians refused, every man was slaughtered and the women and children were enslaved.]

Ibid., "Speech of the Athenians to the Melians"

Without commerce, without freedom of communication either by land or sea, cultivating no more of their territory than the exigencies of life required, [people] could never rise above nomadic life and consequently neither build large cities nor attend to any other form of greatness.

Ibid.

The Peloponnesus and Athens were both full of young men whose inexperience made them eager to take up arms.

Of all manifestations of power, restraint impresses men most.

Men secure peace by using their power justly and by making it clear that they will not allow others to wrong them.

Neither excited by success nor despairing in misfortune.

[The nature of the Spartans.]

SPARTA

Sparta was a Greek city in the Peloponnesus that contended against Athens for Greek hegemony. Sparta ("the scattered") consisted of five towns without walls populated by about seventy thousand people who lived on a narrow plain surrounded by high mountains—a natural citadel. The Dorian conquerors living in Sparta enslaved the Ionian people in the Peloponnesus known as the Helots (serfs), who outnumbered the Spartans ten to one. Lycurgus (born between 900 and 600 B.C.) authored the Spartan code, the antithesis of Athenian governance. When a friend pleaded for a democracy, Lycurgus responded, "Begin by setting it up in your own family." He forbade all industry, insisting that Spartans concentrate on the martial arts and overseeing the Helot's farms. Sparta's emphasis on brevity in speech made philosophy and other higher-order thinking impossible.

Sparta was an oligarchic republic ruled by a council of five "Ephors" elected for one-year terms by an Assembly of the oldest citizens (male and female), who had to be tough to have survived. The younger adults also had an assembly, but it had no power. At the end of their terms, the Assembly tried each Ephor for corruption. The two Spartan kings were military commanders subject to the Ephors' command. The purpose of Sparta's constitution was to prevent change; it worked.

Sparta was organized for war. Each male Spartiate was liable for military service until age sixty, and each mother's farewell to her son going into battle was "Return with your shield or on it." Defective infants were thrown off a cliff. Young men impregnated the wives of impotent husbands. Celibacy was a crime. At age seven, males were put in military barracks where adults stirred up quarrels to encourage fighting. Young women had to play naked in public games to encourage them to keep trim. Women and men who had not picked mates by the age of twenty and thirty respectively were huddled naked together in a dark room and forced to emerge with a mate. Husbands were allowed to leave their regiments only to go home at night to procreate. All meals were eaten in a common room; all wore the same dress without ornaments. In Sparta, women could vote, inherit, and hold property, none of which were possible in Athens. In Athens, a woman could not contract for any item more highly valued than a bushel of corn.

Although Sparta was more democratic than Athens in the sense of allowing all citizens to vote, Sparta went to extremes in limiting the freedom of its citizens. Equality was absolute; all owned equal amounts of land; all did the same type of work, dressed the same, lived in the same style house, ate the same, and so forth.

One did not trifle with Spartans. After Philip II of Macedon (382–336 B.C.) conquered the rest of Greece, he told Sparta: "You are advised to submit without further delay, for if I bring my army into your land, I will destroy your farms, slay your people, and raze your city." The Spartans replied with one word: "If." Philip left Sparta alone. Spartans were called the "Lacons," thus "laconic."

PELOPONNESIAN WAR
431–404 B.C.

The Peloponnesian War was started by Pericles and other Athenian democrats seeking hegemony over Hellas. The war pitted Athens and her allies, the Delian coastal city-states around the Aegean, which were democratic, commercial, and industrial, against Sparta and her allies in the Peloponnesian League, which were agricultural. Athens had organized the Delian Confederacy to resist Persia, but it devolved into an empire during the Golden Age of Pericles. Some Delian cities turned to Sparta rather than pay tribute to Athens. Sparta won the war by promising Persia control over Greek cities on Anatolia in return for Persian assistance. The fall of Athens cleared the way for Rome to dominate Greece and the Mediterranean.

Athens later reestablished a second empire but lost it through internecine class warfare. A new one-man-one-vote law gave control of government to the poor, who then raised taxes so high that Athens' wealth melted away. The robbed middle class preferred to be conquered by foreigners rather than be expropriated by its poor citizens. Isocrates said:

> When I was a boy, wealth was regarded as a thing so secure as well as admirable that almost everyone affected to own more property than he actually possessed…. Now a man has to be ready to defend himself against being rich as if it were the worst of crimes.

Thucydides, *History of the Peloponnesian War*, VIII, bk. 24, l. 18

ARISTOPHANES
c. 450–385 B.C.

Greek, comic playwright, and champion of religion and aristocracy who was the Rabelais of antiquity. The most conservative of Greek dramatists, he abhorred the corruption of post-Periclean democracy and the interminable war with Sparta. Twenty years into the Peloponnesian War, his *Lysistrata* (*Dismisser of Armies*, today's most frequently produced Greek drama), anticipated Herbert Marcuse's slogan, "Make love, not war." Lysistrata leads the Athenian wives in a sex strike until their husbands end the war with Sparta.

> These impossible women! How they do get around us!
>> *Lysistrata*, l. 1038 (411 b.c.)

> The poet was right: can't live with them, or without them.
>> Ibid., Male Chorus

> The wise learn many things from their enemies.
>> *The Birds*, 1. 375

> By words the mind is winged.
>> Ibid., 1. 1447

> You should not decide until you have heard what both have to say.
>> *The Wasps*

> You get too much at last of everything: Of sunsets, of cabbages, of love.

SUN-TZU
430?–381? B.C.

Chinese, military strategist, and author of *The Art of War,* which was translated by Lionel Giles in 1910 and excerpted in *Roots of Strategy* (1940). He was profoundly anti-Clausewitzian, he sought to win without fighting by maneuvering and avoiding battle until victory was assured. Mao Tse-tung and Ho Chi-minh exploited Sun-Tzu's strategies to wear down larger armed forces.

> The art of war is of vital importance to the state. It is a matter of life and death, a road either to safety or to ruin. Hence under no circumstances can it be neglected.

> There is no instance of a country having been benefited from prolonged warfare.

> Know yourself, know your opponent; in a hundred battles, win a hundred victories.

> All warfare is based on deception. Hence when able to attack, we must seem unable; when using our forces, we must seem inactive; when we are near, we must make the enemy believe that we are far away; when far away, we must make him believe we are near.

> There are roads that must not be followed, armies that must not be attacked, towns that must not be besieged, positions that must not be contested, commands of the sovereign that must not be obeyed.

> In all fighting the direct method may be used for joining battle, but indirect methods will be needed to secure victory.

The victorious strategist seeks battle after the victory has been won.

An army avoids strength and strikes weakness.

Speed is the essence of war.

To fight and conquer in all your battles is not supreme excellence; supreme excellence consists in breaking the enemy's resistance without fighting.

The good fighters of old, first put themselves beyond the possibility of defeat, and then waited for an opportunity of defeating the enemy. To secure ourselves against defeat lies in our own hands, but the opportunity of defeating the enemy is provided by the enemy.

If we wish to fight, the enemy can be forced to an engagement even though he is sheltered behind a high rampart and a deep ditch. All we need to do is to attack some other place that he is obliged to relieve.

Water shapes its course according to the ground over which it flows; the soldier works out his victory in relation to the foe whom he is facing. Therefore, just as water retains no constant shape, so in warfare there are no constant conditions.

When you surround an army leave an outlet free. Do not press a desperate foe too hard.

The art of war teaches us to rely not on the likelihood of the enemy's not coming, but on our own readiness to receive him. There are five essentials for victory: (1) He will win who knows when to fight and when not to fight. (2) He will win who knows how to handle both superior and inferior forces. (3) He will win whose army is animated by the same spirit throughout the ranks. (4) He will win who, prepared himself, waits to take the enemy unprepared. (5) He will win who has military capacity and is not interfered with by his sovereign.

The general who advances without coveting fame and retreats without fearing disgrace, whose only thought is to protect his country and do good service for his sovereign, is the jewel of the kingdom.

Hostile armies may face each other for years, striving for victory that is decided in a single day.

We shall be unable to turn natural advantages to account unless we make use of local guides.

What enables a good general to strike and conquer, and achieve things beyond the reach of ordinary men, is foreknowledge, which can only be obtained from the use of spies....

PLATO
427–347 B.C.

Greek, the most celebrated philosopher. He founded his Academy in the groves of Academos and inscribed on its entrance: "Let no one ignorant of geometry enter here." Emerson said

Out of Plato came all things that are still written and debated among men of thought. Great havoc makes he among our originalities. We have reached the mountain from which all these drift boulders were detached.

Plato saw truth as being dual realities: a reality of nature, which is transitory, and a higher reality of ideas, spirit, soul, and God, which is permanent. This "idealism" held that truth in this higher reality was absolute and could be found only through reason, and not through the senses; truth can come only from logical deductions from premises. Plato's idealism was opposed by Aristotle's one reality called realism, materialism, or naturalism. Plato also opposed Protagoras's relativism, which held that there was no right or wrong, so that all beliefs, lifestyles, and moral systems should be accepted.

Plato's "theory of forms" held that there are pure forms that are not shapes but combinations of properties belonging to any idea and discoverable only by reason. Knowledge is possible only through generalized images, for example, the concept of a table. This concept would remain real even if the physical world disappeared. Thought would be impossible if we could only think of individual things and could not generalize. Plato's championing of transcendent ideas and spirit over the material world made him a favorite philosopher of Christian theologians.

"Plato's Cave": Man cannot trust his senses because they do not directly connect with reality. It is like a man chained to a floor in a cave with a passage behind him leading to the sunlight. The chains prevent him from looking at himself or behind him, so he only sees shadows on the cave wall. He can never see reality directly with his senses; thus he must seek truth through reason.

Plato's ethics or moral philosophy held that justice for individuals was the balanced fulfillment of human nature, which consists of a hierarchy of reason (which should be in control), which leads to wisdom; spirit (the desire for honor and success), which leads to courage; and the bodily appetites, whose virtue is temperance. Similarly, in *The Republic* (443-D & E), Plato defines justice for the state as every man in his right place: the wise as Guardians (rulers), who are led by reason; the courageous as Auxiliaries (soldiers); and the Workers, whose goods satisfy the appetites. Plato says justice "is the having and doing what is one's own." Will Durant defined Plato's justice thusly: "Justice may be defined as the cooperation of the parts in a whole...or of the people in a state, each part performing its fittest function properly." (*The Life of Greece*, 1939).

The second central issue of *The Republic* was the question "Why be moral?" Glaucon argues that people are moral solely because they fear punishment. Glaucon gives the example of Gyges, a shepherd who finds a magic ring that makes the wearer invisible. He uses the ring to slay the king and become king himself. Anyone will succumb to the absolute power of the ring and use it for selfish reasons. Socrates rejects this cynical conclusion and argues that if Gyges is wise, he will not use the ring. An immoral life corrupts the soul and leads to the loss of loved ones and to psychological emptiness. Power without love, friendship, and the joy of using one's talents causes unhappiness. Note the similar temptation to power and resulting corruption from Gyges's ring and J. R. R. Tolkien's ring.

Socrates is a doer of evil, who corrupts the youth; and who does not believe in the gods of the state, but has other new divinities of his own. Such is the charge.

[Plato wrote thirty surviving dialogues, often with Socrates as one of the speakers.]

Dialogues, "Apology," 24

What I say is that "just" or "right" means nothing but what is in the interest of the stronger party.

[This dialogue by Thrasymachus is Plato's masterpiece, containing his principal ideas, like the concept of justice and the theory of forms.]

The Republic tr. Benjamin Jowett (1894), bk. 1, 338C

When there is an income tax, the just man will pay more and the unjust less on the same amount of income.

Ibid., bk. 1, 343D

Wealth is the parent of luxury and indolence, and poverty of meanness and viciousness, and both of discontent.

Ibid., bk. 4, 422A

Until philosophers are kings, or the kings and princes of this world have the spirit and power of philosophy...cities will never have rest from their evils....

Ibid., bk. 5, 473C

Solon was under a delusion when he said that a man when he grows old may learn many things—for he can no more learn much than he can run much; youth is the time for any extraordinary toil.

Ibid., bk. 7. 536D

Democracy, which is a charming form of government full of variety and disorder,

dispenses a sort of equality to equals and unequals alike.

Ibid., bk. 8, 558C

The people have always some champion whom they set over them and nurse into greatness. This and no other is the root from which a tyrant springs; when he first appears he is a protector.

Ibid., 565C

When the tyrant has disposed of foreign enemies by conquest or treaty, and there is nothing to fear from them, then he is always stirring up some war or other, in order that the people may require a leader.

Ibid., 566D

The soul of man is immortal and imperishable.

Ibid., 608D

The best of either sex should be united with the best as often, and the inferior with the inferior, as seldom as possible; and that they should rear the offspring of the one sort of union, but not of the other, if the flock is to be maintained in first-rate condition.

Education should begin before birth.

[Supporting eugenics.]

Plato's Republic was to be ruled by Guardians, a self-perpetuating elite, as in the Communist Party. The guardians would have absolute power but no possessions or wives; they would live in a common barracks sharing concubines. Women would be equal to men and allowed to perform any function for which they were physically qualified.

In Plato's *Laws*, the state would be limited to 5,040 citizens who would farm; there would be no trade, coinage, or banking; and the richest could not have more than four times as much as the poorest. In contrast, Aristotle praised private property. He saw Plato's utopia as inefficient economically and destructive of the human spirit. Plato would also ban discussion of competing theories of how to run a state, and he would ban poets. He wanted to excise Homer's aesthetics and myths because they conflicted with the search for pure truth.

The Republic embodies Plato's ideal form of rule, an aristocracy of philosopher kings who value reason most. Next to aristocracy, the most desirable form of rule is a timocracy, an aristocracy of those who value honor most. (The modern meaning of timocracy is rule by the propertied class). Next is rule by oligarchs. Then comes rule by democrats—the undisciplined, chaotic people. And the worst is rule by tyrants, who disregard the rule of law. To Plato, a democracy undermines the whole culture:

> [In democracies]
> The teacher...fears and fawns upon the pupils...while the old...imitate the young for fear they may be thought disagreeable and authoritarian.
> In A. Gottlied, *The Dream of Reason* (2001), from *The Republic*

Of all the animals, the boy is the most unmanageable.

Laws, 808

The worst of all deceptions is self-deception.

Cratylus

[Plato referred to his young pupil Aristotle] as a foal that kicks its mother after draining her dry.

Democracy does not contain any force that will check the constant tendency to put more and more on the public payroll. The state is like a hive of bees in which the drones display, multiply and starve the workers so the idlers will consume the food and the workers will perish.

...in all of us, even in good men, there is a lawless wild-beast nature.

Every king springs from a race of slaves, and every slave has had kings among his ancestors.

Man—a being in search of meaning.

What is honored in a country will be cultivated there.

Poets utter great and wise things that they do not themselves understand.

I thank God that I was born Greek and not barbarian, freeman and not slave, man and not woman, but above all that I was born in the Age of Socrates.

PLATO'S DIALOGUES

Republic:	Theory of forms and nature of justice and good government.
Charmides:	The virtues, like temperance and courage, involve knowledge.
Ion:	Poetry is a sort of divine madness.
Protagoras:	No one chooses evil except through ignorance, i.e., virtue is knowledge.

Euthydemus:	Attack on Sophists for fighting with words.
Meno:	Virtue is right opinion, but cannot be taught—ideas are implanted in the soul.
Euthyphro:	Piety is not whatever is pleasing to the gods.
Apology:	Praise of Socrates as a gadfly who is unfairly condemned.
Crito:	Socrates respects the law by refusing to escape.
Phaedo:	The soul is immortal: Opposites generate opposites, so death generates life.
Greater Hippias:	Does not define beauty but concludes, "All that is beautiful is difficult."
Symposium:	The highest love is love of the good, the beautiful, and the true.
Gorgias:	About rhetoric, and that it is better to suffer evil and to do evil.
Parmenides:	Critiques Plato's theory of ideas, etc.
Cratylus:	The relation of language to understanding reality.
Phaedrus:	Another examination of love.
Theaetetus:	Rejects idea that knowledge is sense perception.
Sophist:	Examination of the methods of Sophists.
Statesman:	Idea (for states and individuals) that virtue is a mean (Aristotle elaborated this).
Philebus:	The highest good is a combination of pleasure and wisdom.
Timaeus:	Examination of physics, i.e., the elements, gravity, soul, god, etc.
Critias:	Story of the ancient war between Athens and Atlantis.
Laws:	Longest dialogue, which that surveys many issues, including the soul.

DIOGENES THE CYNIC
C. 400–323 B.C.

Greek, a former banker turned philosopher and contemplative beggar who walked through Corinth in the daytime carrying a lantern "looking for an honest man." His cynic philosophy held worldly goods in contempt—he ate only raw meat because cooking was unnatural. Happiness meant satisfying only basic physical needs, so he threw away his cup when he saw a child drinking with his cupped hands, saying: "In the practice of moderation a child has become my master." Like Rousseau, Diogenes thought civilization was a mistake; unlike Rousseau, Diogenes was no hypocrite. When he cleaned his feet on the carpet in Plato's home, saying, "I trample on Plato's pride," Plato rejoined, "Yes, Diogenes, with pride of another sort."

> Plato defined man as a "two-legged animal without feathers." Diogenes plucked a chicken and said, "This is Plato's man." Plato then added, "With broad flat nails."
>
> Diogenes Laertius, *Lives of Eminent Philosophers*, "Diogenes," sec. 6

> When asked what wine he liked to drink, he replied, "That which belongs to another."
>
> Ibid.

> The sun too penetrates into privies but is not polluted by them.
>
> Ibid.

A man once asked Diogenes what was the proper time for supper, and he made answer, "If you are a rich man, whenever you please; and if you are a poor man, whenever you can."

Ibid.

[Diogenes struck the father of a son who swore.]

Alexander, finding Diogenes sunbathing, said, "I am Alexander the Great King." "I am Diogenes the dog," was the reply. Alexander offered to grant any favor and Diogenes replied, "Yes, stand out of my light." The two most famous men of their time died on the same day in 323 B.C. The Corinthians placed a marble dog on Diogenes' tomb.

ARISTOTLE
384–322 B.C.

Greek, father of the scientific method and cooperative research. He attended Plato's Academy for twenty years but founded its rival, the Lyceum, because he rejected Plato's "eternal ideas," separate from the sensible world. Aristotle reasoned by induction (posteriori) rather than by deduction from general principles (priori). He codified knowledge about plants, animals, the stars, and so forth. He erred in most things; for example, he thought that stars rotated around the earth. The Platonic method usually got closer to the truth; for example, Democritus expounded an atomic theory, and Empedocles believed in evolution based on survival of the fittest. Aristotle took science as far as it could go without measuring instruments. Aristotle's great contribution was his attitude

that nature was worthy of analysis because nature was not run by gods but by physical laws that could be discovered.

Aristotle was not a relativist, but a different type of absolutist than Plato. Everything seeks to become what it can be. The "telos" of an acorn is to become a tree. A girl's telos is to become a mother. Aristotle believed that man had only limited control over his destiny. Destiny is controlled by the physical laws the Prime Mover has set in motion.

Anticipating Edmund Burke, Aristotle distrusted theories on ethical questions not rooted in custom, tradition, and common sense. For example, he preferred the judgments of grandmothers on how to raise children to that of philosophers. While there can be exact logical truths for math and science, in the fuzzier disciplines of ethics and politics, we must be content with approximations and partial insights. Thus, Aristotle would repudiate modern political and ethical theories based on a priori principles, like those of Descartes, Kant, Mill, and Marx.

Aristotle's *Nicomachean Ethics* holds that one becomes virtuous by doing virtuous acts. The key is to discover and emulate good role models. One does this by becoming a *phronemos*, or "person of practical wisdom."

Aristotle held that the best government is a timocracy, in which only property owners can vote; otherwise the poor will rob the rich. The poor rebel when inequality is too great, and the rich rebel when the state compels equality. The middle class is the flywheel that prevents exploitation of the few rich by the numerous poor and vice versa. Each form of government has a degenerative analog: monarchy to tyranny, aristocracy to oligarchy, and timocracy to democracy. Note: "democracy" was a pejorative word in George Washington's time.

Man is by nature a political animal.
Politics. bk. 1, ch. 2., tr. Benjamin Jowett
(1885)

States are likely to be well administered in which the middle class is large.
Ibid., bk. 4, ch. 4

Inferiors revolt in order that they may be equal, and equals that they may be superior. Such is the state of mind that creates revolutions.
Ibid., bk. 5, ch. 1

No government can stand which is not founded upon justice.
Ibid., bk. 7, ch. 14. in L. R. Frank,
Quotationary (1999)

Laws, properly enacted, should define the issue of all cases as far as possible, and leave as little as possible to the discretion of the judges....
Rhetoric i, 1.7

It is better that law should rule than any individual.... He who entrusts any man with the supreme power gives it to a wild beast, for such his appetites sometimes make him; passion influences those who are in power, even the very best of men; but law is reason without desire.
Politics, 1287a

Educated men are as much superior to uneducated men as the living are to the dead.
Diogenes Laertius, *Lives of Imminent Philosophers*, bk. V, 17

It is not always the same thing to be a good man and a good citizen.
Ibid., bk. V, ch. 2. tr. J. A. K. Thompson
(1953)

Without friends no one would choose to live, though he had all other goods.
Ibid., bk. VIII

The most fortunate of men is he who combines a measure of prosperity with scholarship, research, or contemplation; such a man comes closest to the life of the gods.
Ibid., 1178b

Youth is easily deceived because it is quick to hope.
Rhetoric, bk. I, ch. 11, sec. 25

I count him braver who overcomes his desires than him who conquers his enemies; for the hardest victory is the victory over self.
Quoted in Stobaeus, *Floritegium*

Aristotle's *Poetics* argues that the essence of art is "imitation of life," which helps us understand reality. Comedy presents inferior persons who make us laugh. Tragedy arouses our emotions by presenting superior persons who suffer a reversal of fortune due to the hero's tragic flaw—a flaw to which all men are vulnerable, so pity and fear well up in us and are purged in a catharsis. Also, art must exhibit "unity of action"; any part that does not make a difference should not be in the work of art. The beginning need not follow from what has gone before, but it must give rise to the middle, which flows from the beginning and leads to the ending, which should not present new problems.

The aim of art is to represent not the outward appearance of things, but their inward significance.

He is by nature a slave who is capable of belonging to another.

We become just by performing just actions, temperate by performing temperate actions, brave by performing brave actions.
    [This was the great "discovery" of William James.]

We are what we habitually do.

There are plenty of instances of a constitution that according to its law is not democratic, but which owing to custom and way of upbringing is democratic in its workings; there are likewise others which according to the law incline towards democracy, but by reason of custom and upbringing operate more like oligarchies.

But to die to escape from poverty or love or anything is not the mark of a brave man, but rather of a coward; for it is softness to fly from what is troublesome, and such a man endures death not because it is noble but to fly from evil.

That which is common to the greatest number has the least attention bestowed upon it. Everyone thinks chiefly of his own, hardly ever of the public interest.

The only stable state is the one in which all men are equal before the law.

It is more difficult to organize peace than to win a war; but the fruits of victory will be lost if the peace is not well organized.

The worst form of inequality is to try to make unequal things equal.

The fate of empires depends on the education of youth.

Meanness is incurable; it cannot be cured by old age, or by anything else.

Persuasion is achieved by the speaker's personal character when the speech is so spoken as to make us think him credible. His character may almost be called the most effective means of persuasion.

Aristotle said that good speakers have ethos (moral character, an essential ingredient in persuasion), pathos (the ability to move emotionally), and logos (rational arguments that move intellectually).

DEMOSTHENES
384–322 B.C.

Greek, the most celebrated ancient orator. To overcome a speech impediment, he shaved half his head so he would not go into the public until he learned to speak clearly by speaking with pebbles in his mouth. He was famed for his "Philippics," his speeches against Philip of Macedon. Because Demosthenes spoke well only after preparation, Pytheas accused his speeches of "smelling of the lamp," meaning they were being composed at night.

The easiest thing of all is to deceive oneself; for what a man wishes he generally believes is true.
Third Olynthiac, sec. 19

When Demosthenes was asked what was the first part of Oratory, he answered,

"Action," and which was the second, he replied, "Action," and which was the third, he still answered "Action."

Plutarch, Lives

I do not purchase regret at such a price.
[Reply to a courtesan's solicitation.]

MENCIUS
372–289 B.C.

Chinese philosopher, called the "Second Sage," after Confucius. He believed that man innately does good when he has sufficient material goods for peace of mind. *The Book of Mencius* is the classic commentary on Confucius. It advises rulers to be philosopher kings and redistribute wealth periodically. Government should own all industries—early socialism. Chinese Communism is merely an updated form of Mencian-Confucianism.

The tendency of man's nature is to do good, like the tendency of water is to flow downwards.

Works, bk. 6, 1: 2.2

Correct what is wrong in the prince's mind. Once rectify the prince, and the kingdom will be settled.
[Intellectuals prefer authoritarians because it is easier to manipulate one man than a congress.]

Mencius, Yang Chu

[A ruler who arouses the enmity of the people may be deposed for:] losing the Mandate of Heaven.
[This introduced the radical idea of the right of oppressed subjects to rebel.]

A woman is subject to the rule of the three obediences. When young she has to obey her parents; when married she has to obey her husband; when a widow she has to obey her son.

PYRRHO OF ELIS
c. 360–270 B.C.

Greek, philosopher and "father of skepticism" who suspended judgment on everything due to the unreliability of the senses. On his deathbed, he said he did not know if he were alive. His ideas infected Plato's Academy, which fell into permanent decline from its inability to stand for anything thereafter.

ALEXANDER THE GREAT
356–323 B.C.

Conqueror of the known world, a student of Aristotle, and son of King Philip II of Macedonia, who had conquered northern Greece. A Persian agent boasted that he had had Philip II assassinated and that Persia had nothing to fear from Philip's son, who was only twenty years old. But Alexander assembled a congress of the Greek city-states to appoint himself captain general of the Greeks and provision him to invade Persia. He thought that he was a new Achilles invading Asia. According to legend, whoever untied the Gordian Knot would rule Asia. Alexander cut the knot, invaded Asia in 334 B.C., defeated the Persians, and campaigned in India. He died of an illness in Babylon while he was contemplating invading Europe to the Pillars of Hercules (Straits of Gibraltar).

Alexander showed that the age of autonomous city-states was past; they could no longer contend with organized empires. He increased the cross-pollination of Greek and Middle Eastern cultures, enriching both. Last, he proved what a leader of indomitable will could achieve. When in an Indian desert, one of his soldiers offered him a helmet full of water. Alexander poured it out, saying there wasn't enough for all his soldiers—that is leadership.

> Here is a man preparing to cross from Europe into Asia, who cannot step surely from one couch to another. [His father was too drunk to strike Alexander with a sword at a dinner party.]

> [When Alexander tamed the giant horse, Bucephalus, Philip II perceptively said] My son, Macedonia is too small for you; seek out a larger empire worthier of you.

> Fortunate youth, who found a Homer to proclaim thy valor.
>   [On visiting Achilles' tomb.]
> Cicero, Pro Archia, 24

> If I were not Alexander, I should wish to be Diogenes.
> Plutarch, Lives, "Alexander"

> The end and perfection of our victories is to avoid the vices and infirmities of those whom we subdue.
> Ibid.

> I am dying with the help of too many physicians.
> Ibid.

Alexander's strategic concept when fighting the far larger armies of Darius at Issus and Gaugameta was to hold the line with his infantry. When the moment was right, he broke through the enemy line with his cavalry and charged right at Darius, who fled both times, thereby prompting his army to flee. Ardant du Picq's *Battle Studies* argued that most battle wounds are in the back because armies fight only until it becomes apparent which is superior. Then the weaker flees, so most of the battle's casualties are incurred during the pursuit. Most panic flights by armies begin in the rear echelons, not on the front line.

On his deathbed, Alexander was asked to whom he willed his empire. He replied, "To the strongest." The empire was split into three parts controlled by three generals, who then warred with each other.

EPICURUS
341–270 B.C.

Greek, philosopher who rejected God and metaphysics, believing we can never know about the suprasensual. Philosophy cannot explain the world, but it can guide us in how to live. The ideal life is to seek pleasure and avoid pain.

For Epicurus the ideal pleasures were simple, natural ones, like time with family and friends, watching sunsets, and walking in the woods. He spoke against gluttony and drunkenness because they caused more pain than pleasure. But many followers were easily corrupted into seeking only physical pleasures. Epicureanism is silent on man's duties, if any, to family and nation.

> Pleasure is the beginning and the end of living happily.
> From Diogenes Laertius, Lives

When we say that pleasure is the end [goal of life], we do not mean the pleasures of the dissipated...but freedom from pain in the body and from disturbance in the soul. For what produces the pleasant life is not continuous drinking and parties or pederasty or womanizing or..., but sober reasoning which...banishes the opinions that beset the soul with the greatest confusion.

"Letter to Menoeceus"

The gods can either take away evil from the world and will not, or, being willing to do so cannot.... If they have the will to remove evil and cannot, then they are not omnipotent. If they can, but will not, then they are not benevolent.

Aphorisms

ZENO OF CITIUM
C. 335–264 B.C.

Greek/Phoenician, philosopher who founded stoicism, the deepest principle of which is self-mastery. Stoics believe the good is obeying nature's laws and being indifferent to pleasure and pain. Man is responsible for what he does and fails to do and should be hard on himself and his charges. But man must accept his fate and not be agitated by things he cannot change. Stoicism was a noble philosophy that attracted high achievers, aristocrats, and the strongest-willed people. Stoicism's virtues are courage, justice, and discipline; its downside is fatalism. Most proletarians embrace epicureanism.

The goal of life is living in agreement with nature.

From Diogenes Laertius, *Lives*, bk. VII

When Zeno beat his slave for stealing, the slave, having learned something of philosophy, argued, "But it was fated that I should steal." Zeno retorted, "And that I should beat you." The moral: Fate does not relieve one of responsibility.

PYRRHUS
C. 319–272 B.C.

King of Epicurus, who failed to forestall Roman hegemony. Knowing that the Greeks called all foreigners barbarians, King Pyrrhus remarked that while the Romans might be barbarians, their troop formations were not.

In 216 B.C., after Hannibal defeated the Romans at Cannae, Greece allied with Carthage against Rome in the two Macedonian Wars. In 196 B.C., Rome conquered Greece.

Another such victory over the Romans, and we are undone.
[On defeating the Romans at Asculum in 279 B.C., where most of his army was decimated. Hence, a "Pyrrhic victory."]

Plutarch, *Lives*, sec. 21

EUCLID
C. 300 B.C.

Greek, mathematical synthesizer who compiled all the proofs of geometry made by others into a book, *The Elements of Geometry*, of which more copies have been made than any other book, save the Bible. When someone asked the use of a theorem, Euclid said, "He wants to profit from learning—give him a penny."

There is no royal road to geometry.
[Told to King Ptolemy.]
Proclus, *Commentary on Euclid*, Prologue

ARCHIMEDES
287–212 B.C.

Greek (Syracuse), mathematician and scientist second only to Newton. He discovered the value of "pi" so that he could compute the area of a circle. He invented a water drawing screw and antisiege machines that could lift attacking vessels out of the water, and his large lens set Roman ships on fire. A Roman soldier killed Archimedes for not responding to an order to stand up. The absentminded Archimedes had been engrossed in drawing a design in the sand. Losing Syracuse in that war tipped the balance of power from the Carthaginian-Greek alliance to the Romans.

He realized when stepping into a public bath that he could determine whether King Heiro's crown was made of pure gold. Pure gold weighing the same as the crown would displace the same amount of water in a filled vase as the crown itself. He exclaimed "Eureka!" [I've got it!] as he ran home naked to perform the experiment.

Give me a place to stand and I will move the world.
[Referring to using a long enough lever.]
Pappus, *Synagogue*, VIII, 10

RISE AND FALL OF ROME

Rome was founded as a kingdom in 753 B.C., around the time of the founding of many Greek city-states. In 509 B.C.,

Sextus Tarquinius, son of Rome's tyrant, raped Lucretia, who then extracted oaths of revenge from her husband and father before stabbing herself to death. They assisted Lucius Brutus (later the first consul) to kill Sextus and found a government ruled for one-year periods by two equal consuls with the advice and consent of a Senate chosen from the patrician class. The two consuls ruled in alternate months, and a consul had to wait ten years to stand for reelection.

Rome became quasi-democratic in 451 B.C., when Rome's laws (the Twelve Tables) were written. Voting in the Military Assembly was weighted by wealth according to Rome's progressive tax rate, that is, a timocracy. It elected the two consuls, eight *praetors* (magistrates), four *aediles* (responsible for public works and games) and twenty *questors* (treasury officials). Censors were former consuls elected to bring charges against corrupt senators. The two consuls could appoint a dictator to rule for six months under martial law, if the Senate issued a *senatus consultum ultimum* "that the consuls should see to it that no harm should come to the state."

The Tribal Assembly or General Assembly of all citizens was based on one citizen, one vote, and was thus controlled by the plebeians. However, the franchise extended only to citizen soldiers, which excluded the *proletarri*, who paid no taxes and could not serve in the army. In 287 B.C., Rome became more democratic when the Lex Hortensia provided that the General Assembly could veto Senate decisions. Also, it gained the power to appoint eight tribunes who became ex-officio members of the Senate; each tribune could veto Senate and magistrate decisions, and veto the vetoes of other tribunes, a formula for deadlock.

Rome avoided the danger of a Praetorian Guard by not allowing police or soldiers in Rome. Julius Caesar recognized the potential of controlling the streets with a private army of thugs run by Publius Clodius—they murdered Caesar's opponents.

Politics was partly based on the loyalty of *clientela* to patrons. More generally, there was a division between the *optimates*, or conservatives, including patricians, *equites* (bourgeoisie and rural gentry), and successful plebeians (artisans and small holders) versus the *populares*, low-class plebeians led by aristocratic opportunists. The *optimates* sought to maintain the constitution. The *populares*, especially after the *proletarri* gained the vote in the General Assembly following the rule of Marius around 100 B.C., sought to abolish the Senate, redistribute wealth, cancel debts, and provide free food and games. Eventually free food and games filled Rome with so many alien *proletarri* that the Latins became a racial minority in Rome.

Rome, like Hellas, protected private property, contrary to the rule in most ancient civilizations where the state or ruler owned the land. However, Roman property rights were not totally secure; they were better only relative to most other civilizations.

Property rights became tenuous after the Gracchi brothers and Marius confiscated estates to redistribute them, just as Catilina, Caesar, Anthony, and Octavius later promised redistributions of land in order to gain political power. Eventually the republic fell to an alliance between *proletarri* and plutocratic aristocrats, such as Caesar and Crassus, who joined with the *proletarri* to confiscate the property of the middle and upper classes.

Rome was a republic when she became master of the Mediterranean, developed her legal system, and built engineering marvels. She flowered during her republican years and thereafter coasted on her dominant position. The consul Marius sounded the death knell of the republic when around 100 B.C. he changed the composition of the army from taxpayers, who served out of duty, into *proletarri*, who served for pay, booty, and donations.

The republic entered her final crisis when three warlords, Caesar, Pompey, and Crassus, formed a triumvirate to trump the Senate. Recognizing that a corrupt Senate had undermined the rule of law, the great republican general Lucullus retired from the Senate rather than defend it. The death-blow came when Julius Caesar crossed the Rubicon in 49 B.C. to defeat Pompey and become dictator-for-life. Caesar put Rome on a path of permanent decline by setting the precedent of a general initiating a civil war to become dictator-for-life.

The Roman Imperium coasted on the old republican virtues through the age of the Antonine emperors: Trajan, Hadrian, Antonius Pius, and Marcus Aurelius, until A.D. 180. Eighty different emperors, mostly military usurpers, ruled for the next ninety years by bribing the mob with the doles and the army with donations. To fund the dole and the shows at the 87,000-seat Colosseum and the 385,000-seat Circus Maximus, confiscatory taxes were levied. The state nationalized all mines, mills, forges, shipping fleets, and banks. Emperor Diocletian (284–305) decreed universal wage and price controls after Rome's currency fell 98 percent in the third century.

A contemporary wrote, "People brought provisions no more to markets." The economy imploded, civil wars raged, and the empire's population fell 40 percent. "Eternal Rome" passed in A.D. 330, when the empire's capital was transferred to Byzantium, 1,083 years after its founding. In a.d. 332, Emperor Constantine declared all peasants had to remain on the land as *coloni* (serfs) to prevent their fleeing to avoid taxes. Most people became serfs who were bound to the land until medieval times.

The most important result of centralizing power in government, according to F. A. Hayek, is "a change in the character of the people." The yeoman felt it was not his duty to defend one usurper against another—that was for mercenaries. The old self-reliant stoicism gave way to extreme cynicism about a corrupt, debauched, and thieving state.

Rome, like Hellas, died from class warfare that expropriated its productive citizens to subsidize the alien *proletarri,* who were allied with the dictators. After generations of expropriations, a depopulated Rome was sacked by the Visigoths in A.D. 410, threatened by Attila the Hun in 451, sacked by the Vandals in 455, and ruled after 493 by the Ostrogoths. Many Romans welcomed the barbarians for tax relief. The historian Gibbon confused cause and effect when he concluded that Christianity crippled Rome. Christianity became dominant only after the Edict of Milan in 313, well after the end of republican virtues. Will Durant's *Epilogue to Caesar and Christ* (1944) reads:

> A great civilization is not conquered from without until it has destroyed itself

within. The essential causes of Rome's decline lay in her morals, her class struggle, her failing trade, her bureaucratic despotism, her stifling taxes, her consuming wars.

OTHER FACTS

Julius Caesar was the first dictator appointed since Hannibal had threatened Italy 167 years earlier. When Julius Caesar became dictator-for-life in 48 B.C., someone wrote on the statue of Lucius Brutus, "If only you were living!"

Other than the censors who prosecuted senators, there were no public prosecutors. Individuals brought criminal charges. Lawyers did not accept pay for services but did accept bequests on the death of their clients. There were no jails: The convicted were executed, exiled, or "proscribed." Anyone could collect a reward by bringing the head of a proscribed person to Rome.

In 168 B.C. a Roman ambassador told a Persian king to abandon his invasion of Egypt or fight Rome. When the king said he needed time to think about it, the ambassador drew a circle around the king and told him to decide before he stepped out of the circle. The king abandoned his invasion.

Rome's motto was Senatus Populusque Romanus, or SPQR: The Roman Senate and People.

One *sesterce* was worth about $1.50 in 2004, and a talent was worth 24,000 sesterces.

For fascinating details on Roman life and politics, read Anthony Everitt, *Cicero*, (2001).

QUINTUS FABIUS MAXIMUS
C.275–203 B.C.

Roman, general. In the Second Punic War he chose to follow a "waiting" strategy rather than engage Hannibal. Rome replaced him, and his successor's army was annihilated at Cannae. Reinstated, Maximus scorched the earth, which forced Hannibal to return to Zama, Africa, where he was defeated in 202 B.C. Maximus's epithet was "Cunctator," or "the delayer." A "Fabian strategy" is a delaying strategy. Russian general Kutuzov followed a Fabian strategy in 1812 by allowing Napoleon to occupy an abandoned Moscow.

To be turned from one's course by men's opinions, by blame, and by misrepresentation show a man unfit to hold an office.
Plutarch, *Lives*, "Fabius Maximus"

PLAUTUS
254–184 B.C.

Roman, dramatist who wrote about lower-class characters.

No man is wise enough himself.
Miles Gloriosus, Act III, sc. 1

The gods confound the man who first found out
How to distinguish hours! Confound him, too,
Who in this place set up a sundial,
To cut and hack my days so wretchedly
Into small portions.

Homo homini lupus.
Man is a wolf to man.

MARCUS REGULUS
C. 250 B.C.

Roman, general. Captured during the First Punic War, he promised to return to Carthage if he was allowed to go to Rome and was unable to persuade Rome to stop the war. In Rome, he counseled continuing the war. He returned to Carthage, where he was executed.

Shall a Roman not keep his word? I shall return as I promised.

HANNIBAL
247–182 B.C.

Carthaginian, general who crossed the Alps with 26,000 troops in 217 B.C. and gained Italian allies to win a series of battles against Roman armies. He failed to conquer Rome because he stuck with his original plan of not attacking Rome but attacking its alliance system. Rome countered by making its allies Roman citizens. He lost to Scipio in the battle of Zama near Carthage in 203 B.C.

You know how to gain a victory, Hannibal; you know not how to use one.
[Said by Marhabal at Cannae in 216 b.c.]
In Livy, *Ab Urbe Condita*, bk. 22

CATO (THE ELDER)
234–149 B.C.

Roman, statesman known as "Cato the Censor" or "Cato the Elder" to distinguish him from his grandson, the Stoic philosopher. Cato embodied the Roman republic's ideal of incorruptibility and discipline. Cato instigated the Third Punic War that eliminated Carthage by plowing salt into its land. "Punic" means "Phoenician" in Latin.

> *Delenda est Carthago.*
> Carthage must be destroyed.
>   In Pliny, *Naturalis Historia*, bk. 15, ch. 74

> [No matter the subject matter of any of his speeches, they all ended with the sentence]
> For the rest, I am of the opinion Carthage must be destroyed.

> Cato the Elder wondered how that city was preserved wherein a fish was sold for more than an ox.
>   Plutarch, *Lives*, "Cato the Elder"

> It is difficult to argue with a belly, for it has no ears.
>   Ibid., sec. 8

> Wise men profit more from fools than fools from wise men; for the wise men shun the mistakes of fools, but fools do not imitate the successes of the wise.
>   Ibid., 9

> I would rather men asked why I have no statue, than why I have one.
>   Ibid., 19

> The wise man does no wrong in changing his habits with the times.
>   [When asked why he started to learn Greek at eighty, he replied that was the youngest age he had left.]

Scipio Africanus (the Younger) *184–129 b.c.*

Roman, general who won the Third Punic War (149–146 b.c.), and he destroyed Carthage. Amid the destruction he cried, "It is glorious, but I have a dread foreboding that sometime the same doom will be pronounced upon my own country."

Cornelia's Jewels and the Gracchi c. 150 b.c.

Romans. When a friend asked to see Cornelia's jewels, she called her sons, Tiberius Sempronius and Gaius, and said, "These are my jewels, in which alone I delight." In 133 b.c., her sons passed the Sempronian Law, which expropriated farms larger than 333 acres and redistributed them in 20-acre lots. This confiscation reduced farm productivity because Italy's mountainous terrain was best suited for pasturage requiring large holdings. To prevent reassembly into large estates, the law prohibited the sale of redistributed land, which caused many smallholdings to lie fallow. In the twentieth century, Communists formed collectives because they knew that redistributions provided equal ownership only briefly. Tiberius was killed in an election riot when seeking a second consecutive term as tribune, a violation of Rome's constitution.

Gaius Gracchi introduced the "dole," subsidized food. According to Will Durant's *Caesar and Christ* (1944), the dole attracted to Rome a polyglot of Oriental loafers who became an indigent mob supporting Julius Caesar against the republic. The dole made the Latins a racial minority in Rome.

LUCIUS SULLA
138–78 B.C.

Roman, statesman born noble but poor. He protected the republic against Marius, a rich aristocrat who had the Assembly elect him consul in 104–100 B.C., violating the constitution's prohibition of successive one-year consulships. Marius increased the dole's subsidy from 50 percent to 95 percent and transformed the army from citizens fighting for the republic to *proletarri* fighting for booty. Because enfranchisement was tied to army service, this shifted control of the assemblies from yeomen to *proletarri*, whose allegiance was to their army commander and whose demands included redistribution of wealth. These proletarian armies led to incessant civil wars among generals. When Sulla was in Syria, Marius captured Rome with a slave army and slaughtered the republican senators. Sulla returned to defeat Marius and restore the constitution. Sulla resigned all his powers, dismissed his bodyguards, retired to private life, and walked unarmed in the Forum.

No friend ever served me, and no enemy ever wronged me, whom I have not repaid in full.

[Speaking of Julius Caesar]
...be aware that the man you so desired to save, believing him to be attached to the aristocratic cause for which you have fought alongside me, will be its downfall. For in Caesar there are many Mariuses.

Suetonius, *Lives of The Caesars*, ch. 1

CICERO
106–43 B.C.

Roman, statesman, Stoic, orator, and the best writer of Latin prose. He favored a pre-Gracchian constitution with checks and balances, so that consuls could not become despots, aristocrats could not become oligarchs, and democrats could not rule by mob violence. He sought a *concordia ordinum* (concord of the classes). His mixed constitution influenced the European Enlightenment and the American Constitution: the president is like a monarch; the house is democratic; and the Senate is aristocratic (elected by state legislators).

Cicero was honored as father of his country for organizing the defeat of Catilina's rebellion, which sought to cancel all debts, redistribute land, and abolish the Senate. However, Cicero was exiled for executing some Catiline rebels without a trial. He felt it necessary to thwart Catilina's four hundred armed men in Rome poised to murder the senators. Cicero later defended the republic against Julius Caesar, but was pardoned by Caesar. After Caesar's assassination, in which he took no part, Cicero gave fourteen speeches (Philippics) against Marc Antony and organized the war against him. Cicero won the war, but the republican consuls died, which gave Antony time to regroup. Antony, a bisexual, nailed Cicero's head and right hand to the Forum's rostrum.

Cicero's *De Officiis (On Duties)* has been used for centuries as a text on ethics in great universities. Cicero transmitted to Locke, Montesquieu, and Schiller the stoic notion of a higher, natural law:

The supreme law, which existed through the ages, before the mention of any written law or established state...Nor may any other law override it, nor may it be repealed as a whole or in part, nor have we power through Senate or people to free ourselves from it.... Nor is it one thing at Rome and another at Athens, one thing today and another tomorrow, but one eternal and unalterable law that binds all nations forever. It is the one universal lord and ruler of all, and God himself is its author, promulgator and enforcer.

De Legibus (On the Laws)

...the unscrupulous Gaius Caesar who disregarded all divine and human law for the sake of the preeminence of which he had deludedly set his heart.... If a man insists on outcompeting everyone else, then it is hard for him to respect the most important aspect of justice: equality under the law. Men of this type put up with no restraint by way of debate or due process; they emerge as spendthrift faction leaders, because they wish to acquire as much power as possible.

De Officiis (On Duties), tr.
Walter Miller (1913)

For the chief purpose in the establishment of constitutional state and municipal governments was that individual property rights might be secured.

Ibid., bk. 2

Out of an ungoverned populace, one is usually chosen as leader...someone bold and unscrupulous...who curries favor with the people by giving them other men's property.... He surrounds himself with an armed guard, and emerges as a tyrant over the very people who raised him to power.

De re Publica, ch. I

O tempora, O mores!
Oh, the times, the customs!

In *Catilinam*, ch. 1

Cui bono?
Who stood to gain?

Pro Milone, IV, 32

When arms speak, the laws are silent.

In L. R. Frank, *Quotationary*, (1999)

There is nothing so absurd but some philosopher has said it.

De Divinatione, II, 119

The more laws, the less justice.

De Officiis, 44 B.C.

Salus populi suprema est lex.
The safety of the people shall be their highest law.

De Legibus, 3, 3., tr. Clinton
Walker Keyes (1928)

There is no better way to convince others than first to convince oneself.

In L. R. Frank, *Quotationary* (1999)

It is the judge's responsibility always to seek the truth in trials; while it is the advocate's to make out a case for what is probable, even if it doesn't precisely correspond to the truth.

In Anthony Everitt, *Cicero* (2001)

No king remains, no tribe, no nation who can cause you any alarm. No external or foreign threat can infiltrate our Republic. If you wish Rome to live forever and our empire to be without end, if you wish that our glory never fade, we must be on our guard against our own passion, against men of violence, against the enemy within, against domestic plots.

Ibid.

I wish I could punish him. But his own character will do that.

Ibid.

I only supply the words, and I have plenty of those.

[Cicero was a great synthesizer and popularizer, not a great original thinker.]

Ibid.

I do not reject peace, but I am afraid of war disguised as peace. [7th Philippic.]

Ibid.

The sinews of war are infinite money.

Philippics, V, 2:5

Cato wondered how two soothsayers could be able to look at each another without laughing.

We are in bondage to the law in order that we may be free.

A room without books is a body without a soul.

To know nothing of what happened before you were born is to remain ever a child.

The aim of justice is to give everyone his due.

[Cicero asked the Oracle of Delphi how to achieve the greatest fame. The Oracle replied:]

Make your own nature, not the opinion of the multitude, the guide of your life.

DAMON, PYTHIAS, AND DAMOCLES

Cicero told the story of Damon and Pythias in Syracuse. Dionysius condemned Pythias to death for advocating democracy, but agreed to let Pythias journey home to take leave of his family before his execution, on condition that Damon agree to be executed if Pythias failed to return. Damon was about to be executed when Pythias returned. Seeing such friendship, Dionysius freed both of them.

Cicero also told of Damocles, who envied King Dionysius. Dionysius traded places with Damocles for a day. When Damocles sat at the head of the banquet table, he saw a sword held by a single hair hanging above him. Dionysius explained that a king was always subject to assassination. Damocles pleaded to return to his former status forthwith.

GAIUS JULIUS CAESAR
100–44 B.C.

Roman, general and dictator. He conquered Gaul and Britain, where he killed a million Celts. He enslaved another million—40 percent of Rome's population became slaves. Caesar became Rome's richest man and head of the popular party, while Pompey represented the conservative party. Caesar cowed the Senate by bribery and bringing false charges against opponents, resulting in their executions. The Senate ordered him to give up his legions and return to Rome. Instead, in 49 B.C., he crossed the Rubicon River to start a civil war. He defeated Pompey at Pharsalus in 48 b.c. and went to Egypt, where he had an affair with Cleopatra. To secure his power as dictator-for-life, Caesar doubled the pay of the soldiers and used Publius Clodius to organize the Roman mob. Brutus, Cassius, Casca, and Cimber assassinated Caesar on the steps of the Senate. Octavius (Caesar's heir), Antony, and Lepidus formed the Second Triumvirate and defeated the republicans at Philippi, Macedonia, in 42 B.C. In 32 B.C., Octavius defeated Antony at Actium. This completed Plato's political cycle: monarchy to aristocracy to timocracy to democracy to chaos to tyranny.

Curio termed Caesar "a man to every woman and a woman to every man." Suetonius's *Lives of the Caesars* covers the first twelve Caesars, most of whom were bisexuals, like Julius, or homosexuals. Excepting Titus, the first twelve Caesars were cruel; many enjoyed watching women being raped and strangled as live entertainment at dinner parties. Most Caesars began their administrations restrained, but over time became totally debauched and cruel.

> I had rather be first in a village than second at Rome.
>> Plutarch, *Parallel Lives*

> I wished my wife to be not so much as suspected.
>> [Why he divorced Pompeia, who was suspected of having an affair with Clodius.]
>>> Ibid.

> Iacta alea est.
> The die is cast.
>> [Said when his army crossed the Rubicon River, the boundary between Cisalpine Gaul and Italy.]
>>> Suetonius, *Lives of the Caesars*, ch. 1

> The republic is nothing—just a name, without substance or form…. Men should now have more consideration in

speaking with me and regard what I say as law.
>> Ibid.

> All men who deliberate upon difficult questions ought to be free from hatred and friendship, anger and pity.
>> In Crispus G. Sallustius, *The War with Catiline*, tr. J.C. Rolphe

Spurinna, a soothsayer, had warned Caesar to beware the Ides of March (March 15). On that day, Caesar chided him: "The Ides of March is come." Spurinna replied, "So it is, but it is not past." Hours later, Caesar was assassinated. One assassin was Brutus, his adopted son (and perhaps his real son, because Caesar was having an affair with Brutus's mother when she became pregnant with Brutus). As he was dying, Caesar reportedly said, "Et tu Brute?—You too Brutus?" Shakespeare called the republican Brutus "the noblest Roman of them all."

> Veni, vidi, vici.
> I came, I saw, I conquered.
>> [After his victory at Pharnaces.]
>>> Plutarch, *Caesar* 50, 3–4

> In war, trivial causes produce momentous events.

> No one is so brave as not to be disconcerted by unforeseen circumstances.

Julius Caesar could have been stopped easily early on by Senate impeachment for his perjuries, subornation of perjuries, and his false indictments of the innocent. The Roman republic died because the senators in Caesar's party (Populares) turned a blind eye to Caesar's crimes in order to further their own political ambitions. As James Madison said, [Without virtue], "no theoretical checks—no form of government, can render us secure."

Caesar's tyranny could have ended with his death but for Brutus' failure to assassinate Caesar's henchman, Marc Antony. Brutus reasoned that it was constitutional to kill a tyrant but not a consul. Brutus's delicate scruples doomed the republic.

LUCRETIUS
C. 98–52 B.C.

Roman, philosophical poet. His *De Rerum Natura (On the Nature of Things)* outlines his epicurean philosophy of a world composed of atoms in infinite space. Men should understand the material world, pursue pleasure, and not fear death because there is no soul and no god. With Lucretius and Cicero, leadership in letters passed from Greece to Rome.

> Life is one long struggle in the dark.
> *De Rerum Natura*, bk. II, l. 54

> And life is given to none freehold, but it is leasehold for all.
> Ibid., bk. III, l. 97

> By protracting life, we do not deduct one jot from the duration of death.
> Ibid., bk. III, l. 1087

CATO (THE YOUNGER)
95–46 B.C.

Roman, great grandson of Cato the Elder and a stoic republican who fought against Caesar. After Pompey's defeat at Pharsalus

in 48 B.C., he retreated to Africa, the last republican stronghold. Upon Caesar's approach, Cato fell on his sword. When his doctor tried to sew up the wound, Cato pulled out his own intestines.

DIODORUS SICULUS
C. 1ST CENTURY

Greek, historian.

> Over the door of a library in Thebes is the inscription, "Medicine for the soul."

PUBLILIUS SYRUS
85–42 B.C.

Roman (Syrian-born), slave, and poet.
> A god could hardly love and be wise.
> *Moral Sayings*, tr. Darius Lyman, Jr. (1862),
> maxim 25

> To spare the guilty is to injure the innocent.
> Ibid., maxim 113

> He gives twice who gives soon.
> Ibid., maxim 274

> A cock has great influence on his own dunghill.
> Ibid., maxim 357

> Anyone can hold the helm when the sea is calm.
> Ibid., maxim 358

> Necessity knows no law except to conquer.
> Ibid., maxim 553

No man is happy who does not think himself so.

Ibid., maxim 584

Look for a tough wedge for a tough log.

Ibid., maxim 584

Let a fool hold his tongue and he will pass for a sage.

Ibid., maxim 723

He is much to be dreaded who stands in dread of poverty.

Ibid., maxim 914

No one reaches a high position without daring.

Ibid., maxim 933

Do not despise the bottom rungs in the ascent to greatness.

VIRGIL
70–19 B.C.

Roman, among the greatest of Latin writers. He wrote the national epic, *The Aeneid*. Augustus loved Virgil's *Georgics*, which argued that the old Roman virtues came from tilling the soil, so Augustus commissioned the writing of the heroic epic poem, *The Aeneid*, as a sacred scripture of the Romans. Virgil wrote and polished it for ten years, even though on his deathbed he pleaded to his friends to burn it as unworthy.

In *The Aeneid*, Aeneas exemplifies *pietas*, the Roman virtue of faithful service to one's parents, the gods, and Rome. Aeneas sacrifices his love for Dido and fights not for fame or wealth, but from his promise to start a new city that in the distant future will be a monument to the gods. Voltaire

considered *The Aeneid* to be the best work of antiquity.

Non omnia possumus omnes.
We are not all capable of everything.

Eclogues (Bucolics) (37 b.c.), bk. VIII, l. 63

Carpent tua poma nepotes.
Your descendants shall gather your fruits.

Ibid., bk. IX, l. 50

Omnia fert aetas, animum quoque.
Time bears away all things, even the memory.

Ibid., bk. IX, l. 51

Omnia vincit amor, et nos ceda mus.
Love conquers all things. Let us too give in to love.

Ibid., bk. X, l. 69

Tempus fugit.
Time flies.

Georgics

Happy is he who has been able to know the causes of things.

Ibid.

I sing of arms and the man who, fated to be an exile, was the first to come from the coasts of Troy to Italy and its shores near Lavinium, a man who was much harassed on land and sea by divine power on account of the relentless anger of savage Juno.

Aeneid, c. 19 b.c., bk. I, l. I

Fury provides arms.

Ibid., l. 150

Perhaps someday it will be pleasant to remember even this.

Ibid., l. 203

Do not trust the horse, Trojans. Beware of Greeks bearing gifts.

Ibid., bk. II, l. 48

The only safe course for the defeated is to expect no safety.

Ibid., l. 354

Audenetes Fortuna juvat.
Fortune favors the bold.

Ibid., bk. X, l. 284

But yours, my Roman, is the gift of
    government,
That is your bent—to impose upon the
    nations
The code of peace; to be clement to the
    conquered,
But utterly to crush the intransigent!
    [Charge to Aeneas by his father,
    Anchises. It is also Rome's mission
    statement.]

Through chances various,
Through all vicissitudes
We make our way....

They conquer who believe they can.

The Aeneid recounts the exploits of the Trojan hero Aeneas, son of a mortal, Anchises, and Venus. Anchises charged Aeneas to escape the siege of Troy and sail to Italy to rebuild Troy. He accepts this mission, knowing that civilization's future depends on his fulfilling his duty. Duty is hard on the individual, who must sacrifice his individual arete to serve the community. Aeneas is like Hector, who represented not only Troy, but also the idea of the city. Aeneas, in order to found a city, has to slay Turnus, a brave chieftain like Achilles. Earlier, in furtherance of his duty, Aeneas spurned the lovely Dido, the Phoenician queen who founded Carthage. In *The Aeneid*, there is a sea journey followed by a war, the reverse of *The Iliad* and *The Odyssey*. *The Aeneid* associates Rome with the antiquity and cultural prestige of Greece.

Aeneas's descendant, Rhea Silvia, a vestal virgin, gave birth to two sons, Romulus and Remus, whose father she claimed to be Mars. The king had her put to death and ordered her sons to be drowned, but they survived and were raised by a she-wolf. They overthrew the king, and Romulus slew Remus. Romulus removed his kingdom to the Seven Hills of the Latins and named it "Rome."

In 700 B.C., lacking young women, Rome invited the citizens of Sabine to a party. Roman boys carried off the Sabine maids. According to legend, they were all married and the cities were reconciled. Today Romans still cry out "Thalassio" when the groom carries the bride over the threshold, in tribute to Livy's story of Thalassio, who carried off the most beautiful of the Sabine maidens.

HORACE
65–8 B.C.

Roman, greatest Latin lyrical poet, who fought in Brutus's army at Philippi to save the republic. His eclectic philosophy contains stoic and epicurean strains. His Golden Mean, or moderation in all things, endorses Aristotle's theory of the trade-offs to happiness. His ethics influenced the Renaissance via Petrarch. Defending the simple life, he wrote, "The chief pleasure lies not in the costly savor, but in yourself. So earn your sauce with hard exercise." In *The Odes* he wrote, "To those who seek for much, much is ever lacking; blest is he to whom the god with chary hand has given just enough."

The man is either mad or he is making verses.

Satires

We rarely find anyone who can say he has lived a happy life, and who, content with his life, can retire from the world like a satisfied guest.

Ibid., bk. 1, l. 117

You that intend to write what is worthy to be read more than once, blot frequently.

Ibid., l. 174

Carpe diem, quam minimum credula postero.
Seize the day, put no trust in the future.
    [Horace is counseling a friend to give up his ambition for a great career and to tend his own vineyard.]

Odes, bk. 1, ode ix, last line

A grudging and infrequent worshiper of the gods.

Ibid., ode xxxiv, l. 1

Nunc est bibendum!
Now is the time to drink!

Ibid., ode xxxvii, l. 1

The people are a many-headed beast.

Epistles, bk. 1, i, l. 14

You will find me in a fine state, fat and sleek, a true hog of Epicurus' herd.

Ibid., iv, l. 13

No poems can live for long that are written by water drinkers.

Ibid., xix, l. 2

I have raised a monument more lasting
    than bronze,
Loftier than the royal peak of pyramids;
No biting storm can bring it down,
No impotent north wind, nor the
    unnumbered series
Of the years, nor the swift course of time.
I shall not wholly die.

Ars Poetica

Of good writing, the source and fount is wisdom.

Ibid.

In laboring to be concise, I become obscure.

Ibid., l. 25

The mountains will be in labor and a ridiculous mouse will be brought forth.
    [He is advising writers to choose subjects suited to their powers—do not overreach.]

Ibid., l. 139

He wins every hand who mingles profit with pleasure, by delighting and instructing the reader at the same time.

Ibid., l. 343

Even the worthy Homer sometimes nods.

Ibid., l. 359

If a man is just and resolute, the whole world may break and fall upon him and find him, in the ruins, undismayed.

Ibid., bk. 3, l. 3

Who has self-confidence will lead the rest.

Everyone has his own way of enjoying himself. Mine is to put words into meter. No use talking about it. Whether peaceful old age awaits me or death, rich or poor, in Rome or, if chance so bids, in exile, whatever my life shall be, bright or dark, I will write.

Those unacquainted with the world take pleasure in intimacy with great men; those who are wiser fear the consequences.

Dulce et decorum est pro patria mori.
It is sweet and fitting to die for one's country.
    [Wilfred Owen called this "The old Lie."]

Seek for truth even in the groves of academe.

What the wary fox said to the lion, "Those footprints scare me, all directed your way and none coming back."
    [Why he did not follow popular opinion.]

AUGUSTUS CAESAR (OCTAVIUS)
63 B.C.–A.D. 14

Roman, the first emperor, adopted son of Julius Caesar. He formed the Second Triumvirate with Mark Antony and Lepidus to defeat the republicans (Brutus and Cassius) at Philippi in 42 B.C., and he defeated Antony at Actium in 31 B.C. He declined the honors of being king and adopted the title of *princeps senatus* (first senator) and initiated the Principate, a disguised monarchy that accepted the old conventions — consuls, tribunes, magistrates, elections, and the like. Unlike Julius Caesar, he went out of the way to consult the Senate. However, he assumed proconsular authority over most provinces, giving him control of most legions, the real power.

Augustus initiated 210 years of stability under a centralized Roman Empire. Yet, to prosper during the empire, it became increasingly more necessary to be political than to be productive, that is, to become a confiscator rather than a confiscatee. The economy collapsed as gangster patricians stole the wealth of the productive to pay off their proletarian supporters.

Quintilius Varus, give me back my legions.
    In Suetonius, *Augustus*, Sec. 23

The Germans in A.D. 9 under Arminius, chief of the Cherusci, annihilated three legions (fifteen thousand men) in their march north of the Rhine. Thereafter, Rome stayed on the defensive south of the Rhine.

Festina lente.
Hasten slowly.
    [His motto.]
        Ibid., Sec. 25

I found Rome a city of bricks and left it a city of marble.
    [Republican Romans had denounced marble as an effeminate luxury.]
        Ibid., Sec. 28

Have I played my part in the farce of life well enough? If it was any good, please applaud for the play, and send us with pleasure on our way. The play is over.
    [Last words.]
        Ibid., Sec. 99

LIVY
59 B.C.–A.D. 17

Roman, historian, who ascribed Rome's triumph over Carthage to republican virtues, which were lost under the Caesars. Livy's anecdotes include Horatius; Cincinnatus; the Tarpeian Rock, from which traitors were thrown; Coriolanus, the turncoat general who led the Volsci to Rome's walls only to be stopped by his mother; and Gaius Scaevola, a general who held his hand in a fire to show the Etruscans he would bear any pain to defeat them.

We can endure neither our evils nor their cures.

History of Rome, Prologue

Vae victis!
Woe to the conquered.
[Livy's catchphrase.]

OVID
43 B.C.–A.D. 18

Roman, erotic poet famous for his *Ars Amatoria (The Art of Love)*, a how-to seduction book, and *Metamorphoses*, which narrates all Greek and Roman mythology. G. B. Shaw made into a play Ovid's myth about the sculptor, Pygmalion, who falls in love with his beautiful statue, Galatea, which the goddess Venus brings to life.

Ovid was banished for knowing about the sexual escapades of Augustus's granddaughter, Julia.

To be loved, be lovable.

Ars Amatoria, II, 107

Love yields to business. If you seek a way out of love, be busy; you'll be safe then.

Remedia Amoris, 143

I see the better things, and approve; I follow the worse.

Metamorphoses VII, 1.20, tr. Peter Green

Tempus edax rerum.
Time, the devourer of everything.

Nothing is more useful to man than those arts that have no utility.

The good of other times let people state;
I think it lucky I was born so late.

HILLEL
C. 30 B.C.–A.D. 10

Hebrew, rabbi and Patriarch in Jerusalem.

If I am not for myself, who is for me; but if I am for myself only, what am I? And if not now, when? If not us, Who?

Sayings of the Fathers

What is hateful to you do not do to your neighbor. That is the whole Torah. The rest is commentary.

From Talmud, Shabbath

More flesh, more worms; more wealth, more care;…more Torah, more life; more assiduity, more wisdom; more counsel, more understanding; more charity, more peace…. He who has acquired words of Torah has acquired for himself the life of the world to come.

In Harold Bloom, *Where Shall Wisdom Be Found?* (2004)

SENECA (THE YOUNGER)
C. 4 B.C.–A.D. 65

Roman, Stoic philosopher, politician, and advocate of the traditional Roman virtues: *pietas* (mutual devotion of parents and children), *gravitas* (responsibility), and *simplicitas* (avoidance of extravagance). Stoicism was self-mastery. His *Epistulae Morales (Moral Letters)* expressed his stoicism: happiness is the goal, but virtue is the way. Implicated in Piso's conspiracy to assassinate Nero, Seneca was ordered to commit suicide. He knew decadence and absolute power was killing Rome, but there was nothing he could do about it.

His play, *Thyestes*, recounts the legend of how Thyestes, Atreus's brother, seduced Atreus's wife and started a civil war. Atreus won, but invited Thyestes to return with his family to share in the kingdom. At a banquet, Thyestes was fed parts of the bodies of his three sons. Seneca wrote this fiendish play to show the helplessness of citizens before an absolute ruler driven to bestiality by having godlike powers.

The "Silver Age" of Latin letters (A.D. 14–117) includes the writings of Seneca, Lucan, Petronius, the elder Pliny, Martial, Quintilian, Tacitus, Juvenal, Pliny the Younger, and Epictetus.

> Love of bustle is not industry.
> *Epistulae Morales*, tr. Richard M. Gummere, (1918)

> It is part of the cure to wish to be cured.
> Ibid.

> Living is not the good, but living well. The wise man therefore lives as long as he should, not as long as he can.
> Ibid.

This is the reason we cannot complain of life: It keeps no one against his will.
> Ibid.

Let us train our minds to desire what the situation demands.
> Ibid.

We break up life into little bits and fritter it away.
> Ibid.

To be able to endure odium is the first art to be learned by those who aspire to power.
> Ibid.

Sometimes it is an act of bravery even to live.
> Ibid.

…the lofty utterance that rises above the attempts of others is impossible unless the mind is excited.
> *On Tranquility of the Mind*, XVII

True happiness is founded on virtue.
> In L. R. Frank, *Quotationary* (1999)

Qui timide rogat, docet negare.
Who makes timid requests, invites denial.
> *Phaedra* 593-94, tr. F. J. Miller

However many you put to death, you will never kill your successor.
[To Nero.]

What does reason demand of a man? A very easy thing: to live in accord with his nature.

The artist finds a greater pleasure in painting than in having a completed painting.

Precepts or maxims are of great weight; and a few useful ones at hand do more toward a happy life than whole volumes that we know not where to find.

VESPASIAN
9–79

Roman general and emperor (69–79) who won a civil war against Emperor Vitellius, who had won a civil war against Emperor Otho, who had won a civil war against Emperor Galba, who had won a civil war against Emperor Nero. Vespasian built the Colosseum and the Athenaeum, a great library.

> Money does not smell.
> [Vespasian's reply to his son for objecting to his new tax on urinals.]
> In Suetonius, *Vespasian*, 23

> Dear me, I must be turning into a god.
> [Last words.]
> [Romans deified dead emperors.]
> Ibid.

CALIGULA
12–41

Roman, emperor (37–41), a spendthrift for gladiatorial games for the mob. He appointed his horse consul, dressed in women's clothes, and committed incest with his sisters and sodomy with many men. He was assassinated after he forced the senators' wives and sons into prostitution. Claudius, his successor, was more bloodthirsty. Then came Nero, a homosexual who castrated and married a boy. Nero murdered his mother and most of his rela-

tives, but was loved by the plebeian mob for his circuses. He sang "The Fall of Troy" and fiddled as Rome burned, which fire he may have set. Galba's rebellion against Nero set a precedent for military coups d'etat and civil wars. Committing suicide, Nero wept, "What an artist dies in me!"

> Remember that I can do anything to anybody.
> Suetonius, *Lives of the Caesars*, "Gaius Caligula"

> Would that the Roman people had one neck.
> Ibid.

> Do you think you can take a remedy against Caesar?
> [Said before killing his brother.]
> Ibid.

MARTIAL
c. 40–104

Roman (Spanish-born), writer of 1,561 insouciant epigrams. He advised using epigrams only in small portions, like hors d'oeuvres.

> I do not love you, Sabidius, the reason I cannot tell;
> This only I can say—I dislike you very well.
> *Epigrams*, bk. 1, no. 32

> Conceal a flaw and the world will imagine the worst.
> Ibid., III, 42

> Virtue extends our days: he lives two lives who relives his past with pleasure.
> Ibid., X, 23

PLUTARCH
46–120

Greek, historian and "physician of the soul." His *Parallel Lives* emphasized the impact of virtue and vice on destiny by portraying forty-six pairs of Romans and Greeks, such as Theseus and Romulus, founders of Athens and Rome, and the traitors Alcibiades and Coriolanus. Only twenty-two pairs survive. His greatest studies were on Themistocles, Pericles, Aristides, Alexander, Sulla, Julius Caesar, Cicero, and Cato the Younger. His sixty essays on ethics, *The Moralia*, influenced Montaigne. Plutarch said Romulus and Remus were suckled by a prostitute, not a she-wolf. In Latin, she-wolf and prostitute are both called lupa.

There is no doubt that the real destroyer of the liberties of any people is he who spreads among them donations and largesse.

Parallel Lives

Nor are we to use living creatures like old shoes or dishes and throw them away when they are worn out or broken with service.

Ibid., "Marcus Cato"

Agesilaus being invited once to hear a man who admirably imitated the nightingale, he declined saying he had heard the nightingale itself.

Ibid., "Agesilaus"

Medicine, to produce health, has to examine disease, and music, to create harmony, must investigate discord.

Ibid., "Demetrius"

To Harmodius, descended from the ancient Harmodius, when he reviled Iphicrates [a shoemaker's son] for his mean birth, "My nobility," said Iphicrates, "begins with me, but yours ends in you."

Ibid., "Iphicrates"

King Agis said, "The Lacedaemonians are not wont to ask how many, but where are the enemy."

Ibid., "Phocion"

Once when Phocion had delivered an opinion, which pleased the people... he turned to his friend and said, "Have I not unawares spoken some mischievous thing or other?"

Ibid.

Of one who promised to give him hardy cocks that would die fighting, "Prithee," said Cleomenes, "give me cocks that will kill fighting."

Ibid., "Cleomenes"

A soldier told Pelopidas, "We are fallen among the enemy." Said he, "How are we fallen among them more than they among us?"

Ibid., "Pelopidas"

When the candles are out all women are fair.

Ibid., "Conjugal Precepts"

Pythagoras, when he was asked what time was, answered that it was the soul of this world.

Ibid., "Platonic Questions"

Even a nod from a person who is esteemed is of more force than a thousand arguments or studied sentences from others.

In L. R. Frank, Quotationary (1999)

Lampis the ship owner, on being asked how he acquired his great wealth, replied, "My great wealth was acquired with no difficulty, but my small wealth, my first gains, with much labor."

EPICTETUS
c. 55–135

Roman (Greek slave), Stoic, and godly man who believed in a divine birthright of free will that sets noble humans free from pain, sorrow, and fear. The Stoic lays no blame on God or man and thus suffers no negative emotions because "To a good man there is no evil, either in life or death." He said, "Never say of anything that I have lost it but that I have given it back." (Man holds only by leasehold.) He sought tranquility because nothing was worth getting disturbed about. Those who make you angry are your masters. Stoicism teaches both resignation to what cannot be changed and an unconquerable will. As Epictetus said, "Anytus and Meletus have power to put me to death, but not to harm me." Or as he said, "The essence of philosophy is that a man should so live that his happiness shall depend as little as possible on external things."

When Domitian decreed that philosophers had to cut off their long beards or be beheaded, Epictetus refused. Domitian, afraid to decapitate him, exiled him to Greece where Epictetus founded a school that influenced Emperor Marcus Aurelius.

What were you taught to call exile, slander, prison, and death?
Externals, indifferent things.
How do you define indifferent things?
Those that are not dependent upon our Will.
What is the inference from that statement?
Things independent of our Will are nothing to us.
Upon what does the good of Man depend?
Upon the rectitude of his Will and an understanding of those things are that are external to us.
What is your goal in life?
To follow God.

In Jacques Barzun, From Dawn to
Decadence (2000)

Show me a man who is sick—and happy; in danger—and happy; on his death-bed—and happy; an exile—and happy; in evil report—and happy! I long to see one Stoic.

Discourses

The man of noble nature does not become noble all of a sudden; he must train through the winter and make ready....

Ibid.

No great thing is created suddenly, any more than a bunch of grapes or a fig. If you tell me that you desire a fig, I answer you that there must be time. Let it first blossom, then bear fruit, then ripen.

Ibid.

What is the first business of one who studies philosophy? To part with self-conceit. For it is impossible for anyone to begin to learn what he thinks that he already knows.

Ibid.

JUVENAL
c. 55–130

Roman, poet, Stoic, and most famous social critic of the vice, perversion, and tyranny of the Roman Empire. His ferocious descriptions of the debauchery of the leading men and women of his times cost him twenty-eight years in exile to Egypt by Emperor Domitian. He wrote about the eunuchs, sadists, and whores who frequented the houses of the great. Like Tacitus, he feared that Rome might not endure given its moral decay. He scorned: plebeians who could be bought with circuses, immigrants from the East who undermined Rome's traditional virtues and culture, and Roman women, who were "shrewish, extravagant, quarrelsome, vain, adulterous, athletic, and worse, readers of literature."

> *Quis custodiet ipso custodes?*
> Who shall guard the guardians?
> > [He was concerned about finding a guard to watch his philandering wife.]
> > *Satires*, tr. Peter Green (1967)

> *Mens sana in corpore sano.*
> A healthy mind in a healthy body.
> > Ibid., ch. 10

> The people long for only two things: bread and circuses.
> > Ibid.

TACITUS
c. 56–120

Rome's greatest historian who wrote about the forces that he forecast would destroy Roman civilization. He contrasted the noble republican Romans with the early corrupt dictators and their proletarian mobs. Censorship prevented him from condemning his real target, the corrupt imperial government and social decay of his own time.

> The desire for safety stands against every great desire and noble enterprise.
> > *Annales*, c. 90

> The chief duty of the historian is to judge the actions of men, so that the good may meet with the reward due to virtue, and pernicious citizens may be deterred by the condemnation that awaits evil deeds at the tribunal of posterity.
> > Ibid., bk. 3, ch. 65

> Christus…suffered the extreme penalty during the reign of Tiberius at the hands of one of our procurators, Pontius Pilatus.
> > [The first historical reference to Christ.]
> > Ibid., bk. 15, ch. 44

> The gods are on the side of the stronger.
> > *Histories*

> Otho would hold out his hands, bow to the mob and throw them kisses, in everything aping the slave in order to become the master.
> > Ibid., bk. 1, ch. 2

> The mutiny followed the classical pattern of all mutinies: the view of the majority was suddenly found to be the view of everybody.
> > Ibid., bk. 1, ch. 3

> From time immemorial, man has had an instinctive love of power. With the

growth of our empire, this instinct has become a dominant and uncontrollable force…. Worldwide conquest and the destruction of all rival communities opened the way to the secure enjoyment of wealth and an overriding appetite for it. This was how the smoldering rivalry between Senate and people was first fanned into a blaze. Unruly tribunes alternated with powerful consuls.

Ibid., bk. 2, ch. 2

To robbery, slaughter, plunder they give the lying name of empire, they make a wilderness and call it peace.
  [Said by Calgacus (first century A.D.), chief of the Britons facing Agricula's Roman army.]
The Life of Cnacus Julius Agricola, ch. 30, tr.
Alfred J. Church (1942)

PETRONIUS
D. 66

Roman, satirist, who killed himself at his own dinner party when Nero charged him with treason. Known as Petronius Arbiter, because Nero called him director of elegance (Arbiter Elegantiae). His *Satyricon* was the first novel, a pornographic book with two homosexuals as the protagonists.

Abitt ad plures.
He's gone to join the majority.
[The Dead.]

Satyricon

HADRIAN
76–138

Emperor of Rome who ended the empire's expansion and built walls in Germany and Britain (six feet high, eight feet thick for seventy-three miles across the narrows of Britain). Backing down to Hadrian in a dispute over Greek grammar, a scholar said, "You must allow me to recognize as the most learned of men he who has thirty legions."

MARCUS AURELIUS
121–180

Roman, emperor whose *Meditations* was the last great book of Stoic philosophy, which claimed that man's fate is largely determined, but man is obligated to act as closely as he can in concert with nature. That which departs from nature is evil. Contentment only comes from within; it has nothing to do with things external to man. Stoicism's virtues are attention to duty and courage; its vice fatalism.

A man's worth is no greater than the worth of his ambitions.

Meditations

Our life is what our thoughts make it.
Ibid., vol. 4, pt. 2

Regard the universe as one living being, having one substance and one soul…

The art of living is more like wrestling than dancing.

It is not death that a man should fear, but he should fear never beginning to live.

…our children will see nothing fresh, just as our fathers too never saw anything more than we.

GALEN
129–199

Greek, physician. Just as Ptolemy put astronomy on the wrong track by asserting that the sun revolved around the earth, so Galen put medicine on the wrong track for fifteen hundred years: His treatises on anatomy argued that good health meant keeping four bodily fluids in balance. His errors were gospel until Pasteur discovered bacteria.

MANICHAEUS
c. 242

Persian, teacher who combined Christianity with Zoroastrianism, the Persian religion. The prophet Zoroaster, c. 500 B.C., accounted for life's good and evil as being due to two gods, one good and one evil. He preached about the resurrection of the dead, life everlasting after judgment, a hell of fire with devils, and a heaven with angels. Manichaeus saw the forces of darkness and light struggling for supremacy, the dualistic view of St. Paul. Manichaeus's fierce dualism and asceticism appealed to St. Augustine in his youth.

CONSTANTINE
288–337

Half Serb, half Celt (English), emperor of Rome and Byzantium, later called Constantinople. In a dream he saw a burning cross and was told by an angel: *In hoc signo vinces* or "By this sign shalt thou conquer." The next day he ordered his soldiers to paint crosses on their shields, after which he won the battle of Milvian Bridge, which gave him control of the Roman Empire. Constantine made Christianity Rome's official religion in A.D. 312 when perhaps one-twelfth of the empire's population was Christian. In A.D. 325 he convened the Council of Nicaea, which denounced the Arian heresy that Christ was inspired but not divine. He transferred imperial power in A.D. 330 from Rome to Byzantium, which thereafter protected the West from the Muslims until Byzantium fell to the Turks in 1453. Behind the shield of Constantinople, a fragmented West developed its culture of liberty free from Oriental despotism.

OTHER FACTS

Christians built in Constantinople a church, the Hagia Sofia, or Divine Wisdom, now a mosque, which may be the world's most beautiful building.

Rome's bishops claimed authority over other bishops due to the Donation of Constantine, an alleged grant of supremacy by Constantine to Pope Sylvester I (314–335). Lorenzo Valla (1407–57) demonstrated that the donation was a papal forgery.

"Pope" comes from "father" in Italian.

VEGETIUS
c. 325

Roman, general under Theodosius I "the Great," and author of *De Re Militari*, the bible for generations of European soldiers. He called for the return of the old standards of discipline, but was not heeded.

It is essential to know the character of the

future, such as *aruspex* (the flight of birds), chiromancy (reading palms), necromancy (learning from the dead), tarots (cards), and astrology (stars).

During the tumult of the Dark Ages, little was created, and what was saved of the West's Greek and Latin heritage was largely preserved in monastic scriptoria and in Arab and Jewish libraries. Outside of Plato, the West knew little of Aristotle and Greek science and philosophy until translated from Arabic in the twelfth century. Al-Khwarazmi (c. 780–850) transferred to the West algebra and Hindu numerals, which included the concepts of zero and negative numbers— the keys to constructing cathedrals.

Europe's population began to rise in A.D. 800 after starting to decline precipitously in the second century A.D. Charlemagne's coronation in A.D. 800 not only marked the end of the Dark Ages, but also the shift of the center of gravity in Europe from Italy to northwestern Europe.

After the Dark Ages, Europeans conquered forests and marshes, ended slavery, and gradually reduced serfdom. Trade opened, modern banking techniques were created, Friar Luca Pacioli invented double-entry accounting, the economy was monetized, and the practical arts were improved with inventions, such as cast iron, water and wind mills, annual fairs, and the lateen sail. The cultivation of heavy soils was made possible by five related inventions: the iron plow, the breeding of large horses, the horse collar, horseshoes, and cultivating oats for animal feed. The three-field crop rotation system increased peasant productivity by 50 percent over the two-field system. Eyeglasses doubled the years skilled people could be productive at close work, and clocks regulated work and measured productivity. Clockmakers evolved into manufacturers of precision machinery. Neither eyeglasses nor clocks were available in China or Islam for another five hundred years.

In the eleventh century, a social and economic revolution began with the revival of commerce, town life, and the middle class. Cities incubated democracy by buying charters of self-government or by building fortifications and declaring independence. Western civilization was reinvented in free cities such as Florence, Siena, and Pisa. Most important, the restoration of property rights raised an economic surplus that funded civilization.

As feudal lords acquired ever more territory and as provinces were consolidated into nations, the extreme political decentralization during the Dark Ages was rolled up by about A.D. 1100. "Feudal monarchy" gave way to "dynastic monarchy" by 1500, after the inventions of firearms and cannon gave the military edge to royal armies over the feudal lords' mounted knights and castles.

The critical new technology was movable type. The world has had five transforming technologies: settled farming, around 9000 B.C.; writing, around 3000 B.C.; movable type printing in 1450; the power revolution (steam engine–1769 and electric dynamo–1832); and today's digital and Internet revolution.

Catholicism gave dignity to all men and a sense of a common destiny in "Christendom." But Catholic censorship made medieval writing a wasteland. For a thousand years, little was written worth quoting. Umberto Eco's *The Name of the Rose* (1981) depicts the church's antipathy toward philosophy and humor. The Council at Narbonne (1227) forbade laymen to possess a Bible, fearing it would undermine the church's authority.

The church controlled the economy as well as thought. It seized a third of Europe's land, and its revenues exceeded those of all European states combined. It outlawed lending money at interest at the Second Lateran Council in 1139, and it considered trading goods to be a sin. St. Augustine said, "If one does not lose, the other does not gain" *(Si unus non perdit, alter non acquirit)*. Catholicism thus equated making a profit with sinful avarice. The church's "just price" regulations inhibited stockpiling food, and it was "unjust" to sell goods cheaply or use machines to manufacture because that caused unemployment. Poverty results when labor-saving, borrowing, and investing are condemned.

The Industrial Revolution was impossible until the church's "social justice" regulations were smashed. Toynbee wrote that the essence of the Industrial Revolution was "the substitution of competition for the medieval regulations which had previously controlled the production and distribution of wealth" (*The Industrial Revolution*, 1884.) In Spain, where Catholicism was strongest in Western Europe, the economy progressed the slowest. But Catholicism was not strong enough to shut down all economic progress, which happened under Islamic theocracy, and to a lesser extent under Chinese Confucianism.

In the thirteenth century, the *encyclopédists* awakened pure science from its thousand-year sleep by compiling from Islamic sources the state of the art in each of the sciences. The founding of universities, like Bologna (1158), Paris (1180), and Oxford (1214), reduced the dependency of kings on the church for scribes. By 1400 there were fifty-three additional European universities. By 1500, textile and printing machines formed great industries in France, the Low Countries, Germany, and England; Italy led the artistic Renaissance and modern banking; and Portugal and Spain explored the world.

AUGUSTINE OF HIPPO
354–430

Bishop of Hippo, Algeria, who was the first real autobiographer because he related only those events relevant to his schema and because the important matters in his life were his decisions, not external events. *Confessions* (395) explains his conversion, and *The City of God* (415) absolves Christians from responsibility for the fall of Rome in 410. The *civitas terrena*, or city of man, was unimportant compared to the *civitas caelestis*, or city of God. It did not matter that Rome had fallen; what mattered was keeping spiritual things, or "the mind of God," dominant. Whenever reason and faith clashed, reason had to be repressed, including the classics.

Augustine argued that God revealed part of his nature in the Old Testament and more in the New Testament, and he will reveal more over time through his church, as humanity is able to understand it. The Bible must not be taken literally because it was written to be intelligible to simple people. The collective wisdom of the church must be used to find correct interpretations, as God reveals more over time. Contrariwise, some fundamentalists believe the Bible is literally true and complete (that no more can be learned of God).

Augustine struggled with the theological problem of the existence of evil with an omnipotent and benevolent God. Drawing on Plotinus, he concluded that evil was merely the absence of God's goodness, a necessary condition to free will.

Man is born corrupt—the doctrine of "original sin." Man cannot purify his corrupt nature; he can be saved only by God's grace. This doctrine of the inherent evil in man's nature opposes the later view of the French Enlightenment that evil results from ignorance, so man will be good if well educated. This doctrinal divide separates conservatives and liberals. Conservatives distrust man's nature, while liberals believe that men will be good if their environment and education are structured properly. History shows that many evil people have been highly educated, for example, Lenin and Mao. Augustine argued that God grants earthly boons to the just and the unjust for reasons we cannot understand, although only the just are granted felicity.

Augustine, architect of the Catholic Church, argued that its sacraments were the sole means to God's grace. Martin Luther later argued that man could only be saved by faith, so the sacraments were not critical. Calvin modified Luther by retaining Augustine's notion of predestination, that is, God by his grace gave faith to the "elect," whereas the preterit were damned because God withheld from them the capacity for faith.

> A law which is not just does not seem to be a law.
>
> *The Problem of Free Choice*

> Give me chastity and continence—but not yet.
>
> *Confessions*, A.D. 398

> I had first to believe in order to understand.
>
> Ibid.

> *Extra Ecclesiam Catholicam totum potest praeter salutem.*
> Outside the Catholic Church everything may be had except salvation.

> *Dilige et quod vis fac.*
> Love and do what you want.

> *Cum dilectione hominum et odio vitiorum.*
> Love the sinner and hate the sins.

> *Roma locuta est, causa finita est.*
> Rome has spoken, the case is concluded.
> [Ending for all his sermons.]

> What maketh the heart of the Christian heavy? The fact that he is a pilgrim, and longs for his own country.
> [His epitaph.]

KING ARTHUR
C. SIXTH CENTURY

Historic king of Wales, whose legend was written in Mallory's *Morte D'Arthur* (c. 1470). By the magic of Merlin, Arthur, son of Uther Pendragon and Igraine, was raised by Sir Ector until he pulled the sword, Excalibur, from a boulder, thereby becoming king. He defeated the Saxon invaders and built the Round Table for his knights. After Arthur's wife, Guinevere, committed adultery with his most valiant knight, Lancelot, and after Arthur committed incest with his sister, the kingdom went into decline, culminating in Arthur and his bastard son, Mordred, killing each other. The kingdom is restored when Sir Galahad, son of Lancelot and descendant of Joseph of Arimathea, succeeds in his quest to find the Holy Grail, the chalice from which Christ drank wine at the Last Supper. Joseph of Arimathea had brought the grail to England. Only the purest could find the grail and release the Fisher King who guarded it. That release brought healing and fertility to the kingdom.

SIR GAWAIN AND THE GREEN KNIGHT

A Green Knight on Christmas Eve challenged any knight of the Round Table to trade blows—the Green Knight's blow to come in a year. Gawain accepted and cut off the Green Knight's head. But the Green Knight just picked it up and left.

In a year, Gawain started for his rendezvous and overnighted at the castle of Lord Bercilak, who proposed that he give Gawain the fruits of his hunting for three days and that Gawain give him whatever he acquired. Bercilak's beautiful wife tempted Gawain with adultery, but he resisted. On the third day, she gave Gawain a scarf to protect him from the Green Knight's blow. Gawain kept the scarf when he rode off. The Green Knight, who was also Bercilak, spared Gawain because he did not commit adultery but wounded him for not giving up the green scarf. Gawain wore the scarf the rest of his life to remind himself of his moral weakness.

BEOWULF
c. 700

In this Anglo-Saxon epic poem, the monster Grendel ravages Heorot, the mead hall of Hrothgar, king of the Danes. Beowulf, nephew of the Swedish king, comes with fourteen companions to fight Grendel. Beowulf pulls off one of Grendel's arms. The next night Grendel's mother retrieves the arm. Beowulf tracks her and severs her head and that of Grendel. Decades later when he is king, Beowulf dies battling a dragon, which is evil incarnate. A model of courage and self-sacrifice, Beowulf shows us that peace is fragile and strong armed men are essential to the preservation of civilization.

CHARLEMAGNE
742–814

Charlemagne was king of the Franks (768–814) and emperor of the West (800–814), with his capital in Aachen. His grandfather, Charles Martel, defeated the Moors in 732 at the Battle of Tours. Charlemagne was coroneted Holy Roman Emperor in 800 by Pope Leo III, ending the papal reliance on Byzantium. He conquered Germany, part of Italy, Eastern Europe, and northern Spain. He converted the Saxons by the sword and he chopped down the Irminsul, the pagan Saxons' sacred oak. Although illiterate, his palace school began the Carolingian Renaissance, the beginning of the classical revival.

ROLAND
D. 778

Roland was the French hero of the medieval poetic epic *La Chanson de Roland,* based on the historic ambush by the Basques of the rear guard of Charlemagne's army while it exited Spain. Roland, nephew of Charlemagne, is a chivalrous knight who carried the sword Durandal and his grandfather's horn, which only Roland could blow. In the poem, during a retreat through the Pyrenees, Saracens attack the rear guard. The poem celebrates the loyalty and courage of the French in the face of desperate odds. Roland proudly refuses to call for help with his horn until all in his command are dead but him. He breaks his sword to prevent its capture and blows his horn to alert Charlemagne.

The Song of Roland provides a lifelike panorama of medieval thought. The song, like *Arthur's Round Table,* was called a "romance," a tale of chivalry. The literary usage of "romance" means a story of mystery, like Gothic novels, but the common usage today means a novel about love.

THE VIKINGS

The Vikings (Raiders), with their 793 raid on England's Lindisfarne monastery, inspired the Anglo-Saxon prayer, "From the fury of the Northmen, deliver us, O Lord." Their great technology was their longship, which could traverse oceans and navigate shallow rivers by sail or oar. They rowed up the Seine in 841 to attack Paris. In 911 the French granted land (Normandy) to the Norsemen to deter raiding, and the English paid the Danegeld for pro-

tection as Vikings ruled northern and eastern England for one hundred years, while Alfred the Great (d. 899) ruled southern and western England. Many Viking settlements, such as Dublin, became major cities. Viking raids ended in the eleventh century due to the Vikings' conversion to Christianity in 1030 and a new defensive strategy of garrisoning mounted knights in coastal forts. Viking threats hastened the consolidation of European provinces into nation-states for self-defense.

The Vikings penetrated today's Russia, attacked Constantinople with two thousand ships in 907, and traded furs and slaves with the Arabs for silver. They organized the Slavs into a nation-state under Vladimir, a descendant of the Viking Rurik. Vladimir chose Orthodox Christianity over Islam because Vikings loved to drink alcohol.

In 982, Erik the Red from Iceland discovered Greenland. Around 997, Eric's son Leif discovered Newfoundland, which he named Vinland, but it was not defensible from the Native Americans. Iceland's Vikings developed a representative democracy—they met annually at the "Althing." The West was ignorant of the Viking discoveries because the Vikings abandoned Greenland during the five-hundred-year Little Ice Age that began around 1250.

Also, Vikings never put horns in their helmets—that was a theatrical invention used in operas to identify Norse maidens.

MURASAKI SHIKIBU
978–1031

Japanese novelist and lady-in-waiting to an empress. She wrote *The Tale of the Genji,* the best of Japanese medieval storytelling and perhaps the world's first novel. It describes in detail the life of the Japanese court, which enjoyed nature, the arts, chivalry, and war. No one has excelled Murasaki in explaining why and how great novels are written:

> [The novel] happens because one's own experience of people and things has moved one to an emotion so passionate that it can no longer be shut up in one's own heart. Again and again something in one's own life or in the lives of those around one will seem so important that the thought of letting it pass into oblivion is unbearable. There must never come a time, one feels, when people do not know about it.

KING CANUTE
994?–1035

King Canute was a Danish King of England who ruled 1016–35. Much of England was then part of the Danish empire. Tiring of court flattery, he ordered his throne to be placed at the edge of the seashore, where he shouted at the sea, "I command you to come no further! Do not touch my feet!" When the tide came in, he reminded his courtiers that only God's powers were unlimited. Most Viking raids in Europe were raids by the Danes.

GREGORY VII
c. 1020–1085

Italian (Hildebrand), pope (1073–85) who abolished simony and required celibacy of priests. His *Dictatus Papae* in 1073 held that no church council was canonical with-

out papal approval and that a pope may "depose emperors… and absolve subjects of unjust men from their fealty." Previously the bishop of Rome had only been first among equals.

Hildebrand excommunicated Holy Roman Emperor Henry IV over lay investiture (power to appoint bishops). Henry stood barefoot in the snow for three days at Canossa until forgiven. Henry had to because Hildebrand had released the German princes from their obligations of fealty to Henry. The pope's victory assured that in the West the state could not become all-powerful. Hildebrand later claimed the power to replace misbehaving kings. Henry IV in turn thwarted a theocratic Europe by capturing Rome and exiling Hildebrand. The power struggle ended at the Concordat of Worms in 1122, whereby the German emperor and Gregory's successor as pope agreed to select bishops jointly.

> The Roman church has never erred, nor can it err until the end of time.

Only later, under Pope Pius IX in 1870, did the Vatican General Council pass the dogma *Pastor Aeternus*, declaring the pope to be infallible in defining doctrine on faith and morals.

WILLIAM THE CONQUEROR
1027?–1087

William was a descendant of a Norseman who had been granted Normandy in 911 by Charles II of France. He invaded England in 1066 and defeated with armored cavalry King Harold Godwinson's "shield wall" at the Battle of Hastings. The invaders included the Britons, who had fled

England after the Anglo-Saxons defeated the descendants of King Arthur. William modernized English law (added a jury), warfare (added armored cavalry), and architecture (Norman). He took England's first census, the *Doomsday Book* (1086).

FEUDALISM

Political chaos during the Dark Ages pushed Europe into "feudalism," a contractual social order in which overlords granted the use of land and gave protection to subordinates in return for military and other services. The word "feudal" comes from "fief," an interest in land. Feudalism was based upon the military power of warlords, who controlled castles and mounted armored knights. Kings were able to check feudal barons only after muskets and cannons made armored knights and castles obsolete.

Feudalism contributed many positive values, such as contractual rights, private property, and the rule of law, and it radically decentralized Europe. That increased competition, as contrasted with a monolithic China. Decentralization spurred growth through copying of the best practices. For example, Holland, the first modern state to secure property rights, became Europe's first *Wirtschaftswunder*, or "economic miracle," and its example was copied by many, including Peter the Great of Russia.

The feudal term "gentleman" was not derived from nor had anything to do with "gentleness," but was derived from the French *gens*, or ancestry (genes); that is, good blood's right to knighthood.

LADY GODIVA
c. 1040

The English Lady Godiva asked her husband the Earl of Mercia to repeal his oppressive taxes on Coventry. He would only do so if she rode naked on a horse at midday in the market square. She did.

THE CRUSADES

[Muslims] have occupied more and more of the lands of those Christians... They have killed many and have destroyed the churches and devasted the empire. If you permit them to continue thus for awhile with impunity, the faithful of God will be much more widely attacked by them.

Urban II (Pope 1088 – 1099) called for
the first Crusade to help Byzantium repel
an Islamic invasion (November 26, 1095)

In the four hundred years prior to the Crusades, Muslims conquered two-thirds of Christendom, and might have conquered it all but for Charles Martel, who defeated Gen. ab al-Rahman in central France at Tours in 732. Islam tried to obliterate Christianity as it had obliterated Zoroastrianism. The Crusades were counterattacks after the Muslims defeated Byzantium at Manzikert in 1070, threatening Constantinople, a Christian buffer against Islam. Muslims continued to attack the West, taking Constantinople in 1453 and besieging Vienna in 1529 and in 1683. See *A Concise History of the Crusades* (2003), Thomas F. Madden.

The eight major Crusades preserved the West until its culture of liberty enabled it to develop the technologies to thwart Islam's jihad. Jerusalem was taken in 1099 on the

First Crusade, and a narrow belt of Christian states was established to the Euphrates. The first state fell to Islam in 1144 and Damascus fell in 1154. In the Third Crusade (1189–92), Richard I, king of England, took Acre but could not recapture Jerusalem from Saladin.

Innocent III's Fourth Crusade (1202–4) looted Constantinople, and Crusaders committed many other atrocities, such as massacring 60,000 Muslims in 1099 after taking Jerusalem. But Muslims had often done that to Christians. When Islam took Antioch, 100,000 Christians were sold into slavery, and the 16,000 too old to be enslaved were beheaded. By 1291 the Levant was back in Muslim hands, but the Crusades had kept an expansionist Islam at bay for two hundred years while the West developed its liberal institutions.

OTHER FACTS

The Teutonic Knights, a religious order founded in 1190 to crusade in the Holy Land, was mobilized in 1234 by a Pole to stop Prussian raiding in Poland. But instead, the Knights-Brothers seized Poland and the Baltic states. This first *Drang Nach Osten*, or "drive to the east," inspired Hitler—with consequences reaching down to our own time.

Medieval Christian geographers sought the Garden of Eden and the lands of Gog and Magog, to which the Book of Revelation had prophesied Satan would repair for a thousand years to gather his forces to attack Christendom. Gog and Magog were in the north and Eden in the east. Also sought was the realm of Prester John's forty-two "mighty Christian" kings, whom the West counted on as allies against the impending attack from Gog and Magog under the anti-Christ.

ABELARD
1079–1142

French, theologian and philosopher who advanced Aristotelian reason. This was not easy, because Aristotle posited only a mechanistic God, a Prime Mover. Opposed was Plato's realism, which held that the universal is everything, that is, general concepts, such as "circle" or "tree" have an independent reality that exists before any particular circle or tree. For Plato, reality was not material but was made of ideas or spirit, the universal. The church agreed with Plato that the spirit world behind the material world was most real. Aristotle's view, later called nominalism, held that "circle" and "tree" were abstract words, not realities.

Abelard held that there was no conflict between the material world and faith in Christianity. Abelard was denounced for seeking to understand God with reason, even though his reason drew him to orthodox conclusions, because reason might draw others to different conclusions.

Religion (faith) could either reject materialism or conclude that it was compatible with religion. Christianity and Judaism wrestled with the problem, but Islam flatly rejected materialism and suspended scientific study for eight hundred years, to wit, the "closing of the gate of *ijtihad*," or the abandonment of reason.

Abelard is famous for his love letters to his wife, Héloîse, his 17-year-old pupil whom he married when he was 38 years old. Abelard kept the marriage secret to protect his clerical career, but when Héloîse's uncle, a canon, found out, he had Abelard castrated. After the castration, Abelard and Héloîse became monk and nun. They were buried together, and Parisian lovers still decorate their tomb.

> Against the disease of writing one must take special precautions, since it is a dangerous and contagious disease.
>
> Letter 8 to Héloîse

> By doubting we come to questioning, and by questioning we perceive the truth.
> [A book of 157 sets of contradictory biblical quotations. Abelard argued that the Bible had been corrupted by copying, so reason must resolve the contradictions.]
>
> *Yes and No* (1120)

ABBE SUGER
1081?–1151

French, abbot and architect who built the first Gothic church, St. Denis (1140s), in which France's kings were buried until it was destroyed during the French Revolution. Suger was one of the physically tiny great men, along with Erasmus, Pope, Mozart, and Wesley. He pioneered Gothic architecture, that is, ribbed vaults to support a roof on non–load bearing walls, with large windows admitting copious light. "Gothic" was a pejorative misnomer for the new "open French" architecture.

> It is only through symbols of beauty that our poor spirits can raise themselves from things temporal to things eternal.

EL CID
D. 1099

El Cid was an epic poem written in 1140 by an unknown Castilian bard describing the heroic struggle of the Christian knights led by Rodrigo Díaz de Bivar (El Cid, or the Lord), the prototype noble Castilian warrior, to recover Spain from the Moors. Banished by King Alfonso of Castile, he raises his own armies to defeat and cast out the Moorish kings from Spain. Near death, El Cid's banishment is rescinded and his daughters are married to the kings of Aragón and Navarre—his family had risen from knighthood to royalty.

AVERROËS
1126–98

Arab philosopher and theologian, whom Roger Bacon ranked next to Aristotle. With Avicenna, he transmitted early Greek works via Arabic to a barbarized Europe. Like Aquinas for the Christians and Maimonides for the Jews, Averroës sought to reconcile Islam with science.

HENRY II
1133–89

English, king (the first Plantagenet) whose royal courts eliminated the feudal courts. His Assize of Clarendon (1166) substituted a twelve-man jury for trial by combat or ordeal. His friend, Thomas à Becket, whom he had made Archbishop of Canterbury, resisted the trying of clergy in royal courts. Henry II exclaimed to an assembly of nobles, "Will no one rid me of this turbulent priest?" Four knights then murdered

Thomas in the cathedral, for which Henry did penance. Becket became a martyr and Canterbury a holy shrine.

Under Henry II, the police power, tax collection, and administration of justice were divided between three different people, each of whom came from the local community. This system decentralized power and enhanced local control. In stark contrast, in Continental Europe all three functions were combined in one official, the *bailli*, who was appointed by the king and rarely stationed in his home community.

Henry married Eleanor of Aquitaine. Their combined dominions gave Henry ownership of three-fifths of France, to wit, the "Angevin empire."

MOSES MAIMONIDES
1135–1204

Jewish, philosopher and physician to Saladin. His Mishna Torah compiled the oral law, a vast body of law developed by the Sanhedrin in Jerusalem before the Diaspora and by rabbis thereafter. He saw the Torah as allegory, that is, there was no Garden of Eden. In reconciling the Torah with Greek philosophy, he argued that God had given man reason that could not be contrary to revelation. Maimonides was denounced as a heretic for denying individual souls, saying that at death we become reunited with a universal soul, the theory of Averroës and the American Transcendentalists.

There is one [disease] which is widespread, and from which men rarely escape. This disease varies in degree in different men... I refer to this: that every person thinks his mind... more clever and more learned than it is.... I have

found that this disease has attacked many an intelligent person.... They...express themselves [not only] upon the science with which they are familiar, but upon other sciences about which they know nothing...if met with applause.

"Aphorisms," in *Chambers Dictionary of Quotations* (1996)

INNOCENT III
1160–1216

Italian, one of the most powerful popes, who claimed to be overlord of kings and who levied a general tax on Christians. His Fourth Crusade came home after sacking Constantinople. He started the Inquisition by sending his own legates to torture suspected heretics and burn the unrepentant. His Fourth Lateran Council of 1215 made marriage a sacrament. Few had been married in a church. Controlling weddings gave control over family life.

This [Magna Carta] has been forced from the King. It constitutes an insult to the Holy See, a serious weakening of the royal power, a disgrace to the English nation, a danger to all Christendom.... Therefore...we condemn the charter and forbid the King to keep it.

Papal Bull (August 24, 1215)

...everything in the world is the province of the pope, that St. Peter had been commissioned by Christ to govern not only the universal Church but also the entire secular world.

friends and their nations. At the center is the three-headed Lucifer in ice, who chews on Judas, Cassius, and Brutus—reverse of the Holy Trinity.

The Comedy is a commentary on human nature, a vision of God's order, and beautiful poetry. It was the first wonderful literature to have been written in a derivative language of Latin.

> Abandon all hope, ye that enter.
> [Sign on the gate to Hell.]
> *The Inferno* (1314), Canto III, l. 9

> "Master, what gnaws at them so hideously," their lamentations stun the very air?
> "They have no hope of death," he answered me.
> Ibid., Canto III

> This miserable state is borne by the wretched souls of those who lived without disgrace and without praise.
> Ibid., l. 34

> What sweet thoughts, what longing led them to this woeful pass.
> Ibid., Canto V, l. 113

> But since fraud is the vice of which man alone is capable, God loathes it most. Therefore, the Fraudulent are placed below, and their torment is more painful.
> Ibid., Canto XI

> You were not born to live as brutes,
> But to follow virtue and knowledge.
> Ibid., Canto XVI, l. 118-20

> A mighty flame followeth a tiny spark.
> Ibid., Canto XXXIII, l. 34

> The hottest places in Hell are reserved for those who, in times of great moral crisis, maintain their neutrality.

> [The fate of seers? In Hell, the Beast] twists front to back the heads of each of those whose glance too far before him ranged.

GIOTTO DI BONDONE
1267?–1337

Italian, early Renaissance painter, who broke with the mannerist style with his innovations in realism. Note, it was Paolo Uccello (1396–1475) who invented perspective by drawing parallel lines seeming to converge at a vanishing point, which created a three dimensional flat surface. Realism after Giotto reigned supreme until photography.

Pope Boniface VIII requested samples before giving a commission. Giotto drew a perfect circle on paper and told the courier, "Tis enough and to spare, send it together with the others, and you will see if it will be recognized." It was.

HENRY DE BRACTON
D. 1268

English, jurist and author of *On the Laws and Customs of England*, the leading legal treatise of medieval times.

> …the king must not be subject to any man, but to God and the law; for the law makes him king. Let the king therefore give the law what the law gives to him, dominion and power; for there is no king where will, and not law, bears rule.
> *On the Laws and Customs of England*

Rex non debet esse sub homine, sed sub Deo et lege.
The king should not be under any man, but under God and law.

> [Roman emperors operated on *Quod principi placuit legis habet vigorem,* Whatever pleases the king is the law.]

Ibid.

3

WESTERN RENAISSANCE VERSUS CHINESE ATROPHY

The 1100–1500 Renaissance (rebirth) refers to Europe's return from a God-centered scholasticism to Greek and Roman humanism. People became Europeans rather than citizens of Christendom.

The rediscovery of lost Greek works revived a celebration of human achievement and joy in living rather than concentrating on the afterlife. Europe, unlike Islam, began to formulate its laws based on reason, not Scripture. This was abetted by the diminution of papal power due to the failed Crusades (1095–1291), the Babylonian captivity of the popes in Avignon (1309–78) and the Great Schism (1378–1417), when there were three rival popes.

The Renaissance also declared independence from ancient secular authorities, such as Aristotle, Ptolemy, and Galen. In general, fragmented civil authority fostered independent thought and individualism. John Wycliffe in England and John Hus in Bohemia preached that individuals could find God's truth by reading the Bible themselves.

The Greek and Roman classics inspired confidence that man could master the arts and sciences and become self-governing. Renaissance painters idealized the human body. Paolo Uccello discovered perspective. Renaissance painters and sculptors, such as Leonardo and Michelangelo, have never been surpassed. Clean classical lines replaced ornate Gothic architecture.

Two Florentines, Petrarch and Boccaccio, searched for lost classical works, translated them into the vernacular, and wrote about love and chivalry. Pico Mirandola reflected on man's newfound dignity:

> I have come to understand why man is the most fortunate of creatures and consequently worthy of all admiration and what precisely is that rank which is his lot in the universal chain of Being—a rank to be envied not only by the brutes but even by the stars and by minds beyond this world....

The Renaissance first flourished in Italy's city-states, which invented the joint-stock company that permitted the amassing of large capital from many small investments. Civilization is most indebted to small states, like ancient Israel, Athens, Florence, Holland, and Elizabethan England. For example, Tom Bethell's *The Noblest Triumph* (1998) analyzes how England's common law swept away medieval restrictions on property, such as "just prices" and guild restrictions and prohibitions against charging interest and hoarding. The common law created the sinews of modernity.

When China was made up of one hundred states, it invented most of the basic technologies before Europe, which had a population of equivalent size. The Chinese invented the stirrup, compass, ship's rudder, porcelain, horse collar, and wheelbarrow, spinning and weaving, gunpowder, steel, water mills, map grids, movable type, vaccination, iodine, and the like. But after 221 B.C. when China was united into one state, her inventiveness slowed, albeit Ts'ai Lun invented paper in the second century, and movable type was invented in the ninth century. But, China's inventions did not transform her society.

China's Confucian doctrine had created a rigid hierarchy where everyone accepted his allotted role: "Let the ruler be a ruler and the subject be a subject." A merchant's ambition was for a son to become a mandarin, who would maintain the status quo. Every Chinese industry—iron, salt, tea, trading, printing, banking, education, cloth making, and so forth—was a state monopoly. Lacking private enterprise, China's technical triumphs lay fallow; for example, China used her magnetic compass to lay out temples, not to explore.

China's stifling statism is shown by Su Sung's invention of the first mechanical clock in 1086. But only the royal astrologers were permitted to see it, and the next emperor destroyed it. In the West, private clockmakers became the manufacturers of precision machine tools to make steam engines, and other inventions.

China's statism is also seen in its Great Treasure Fleet of 300 ships and 35,000 men that sailed to South Asia and East Africa from 1405 to 1433 under the eunuch admiral Chêng Ho. The fleets did not trade, but distributed gifts to enhance China's prestige. In 1433 a new emperor scrapped that prodigal practice in the Great Withdrawal. Then the emperors burned China's ocean fleets and outlawed ocean-worthy ships.

Thus, a centralized state of 80 million people was discovered by a joint stock-owned ship from minuscule Portugal.

Mandarin egalitarianism for over two thousand years crowded out China's Taoist libertarian culture. No other society has been so ill run by scholars, becoming in the words of Paul Johnson "a bottomless pit of idle bureaucrats and corruption."

Technology is necessary for prosperity, but not sufficient. Today, technologies can easily be copied, yet many nations remain poor. Each nation's culture largely explains why it is getting richer or poorer.

In 1793, when King George III of England sought to trade with China, the Chinese emperor refused, referring to "the lonely remoteness of your island, cut off from the world by intervening wastes of sea." The emperor did compliment George for his "submissive loyalty in sending this tribute mission" and encouraged him to "show even greater devotion and loyalty in the future."

ROBERT I
1274–1329

Scot, king 1306–29, known as Robert the Bruce. Having lost many engagements against Edward I of England in fighting for Scotland's independence, a dispirited Robert hid in a cave, where he watched a spider repeatedly try to moor its web to another rock. The spider's success inspired Robert to continue his struggle. He won the Battle of Bannockburn in 1314 and independence in 1328.

PETRARCH
1304–74

Italian (Florentine) poet, one of the great humanists, and a devoutly religious man. Out of his love for Laura, he invented the sonnet form of poetry with the command, "Thou shalt stop at fourteen lines." The humanists saw Cicero and Brutus as republican heroes and Caesar as a despotic usurper. Humanism developed first in Italy, which led the Renaissance in the visual arts, literature, business management, science, law, and cookery. Italian was the first pan-European language, superseded by French and then by English in the twentieth century.

> Whenever we wish to leave some memory of ourselves to posterity by thinking or writing something and thus to arrest the flight of days and extend this short span of life, we must flee and spend the little time that is left us in solitude.
> "On the Solitary Life," in Jacques Barzun, *From Dawn to Decadence* (2000)

> To be able to say how much you love is to love but little.
> "To Laura in Death," canzone 137

> If you choose to grant me nothing else, let it be my portion to be a good man.... If learning alone is granted us, it puffs and ruins....

GIOVANNI BOCCACCIO
1313–75

Italian, poet, businessman, storyteller. In his *The Decameron* (1352), each of ten travelers tells a story a day on a ten-day trip as they flee plague-infested Florence in 1348. The first story is about Cepperello of Prato, Italy's worst man, who gave false oaths, stirred up bad blood among relatives, murdered for profit, blasphemed God, gambled with loaded dice, ate and drank to excess, and preferred men to women. He was hired to use his guile to collect a loan from an evil Burgundian, but en route he contracted a fatal disease. Not wanting to lie in a potters' field, he confessed to a local priest that after he fasted three days each week he drank water with the relish of a great imbiber of wine, that he had boasted of his virginity, that he had harshly admonished a neighbor beating his wife, and that as a child he had once yelled at his mother. The priest buried Italy's worst man in a marble tomb and initiated his beatification. Another of Boccaccio's stories concerned a monk who gave a penance that required the confessed to hold a nightly vigil—allowing the monk to bed the penitent's wife.

THE DECLARATION OF ARBROATH
1320

This letter was written by Scottish barons and bishops to argue their case to the pope, who had recognized the English claim to Scotland. It concluded that no matter what the pope did, the Scots would not bow to the English. It declared Scottish independence and said that the Scots were bound to obey their king, Robert Bruce, only so long as he recognized their traditional freedoms:

> For as long as a hundred of us remain alive, never will we bow to the yoke of English dominion. It is not for glory,

THE BLACK DEATH

The Black Death, which had struck Rome in a.d. 165 and Constantinople in 542, entered Europe in 1347 at the Sicilian port of Messina on a ship from the Black Sea. The Mongols had provided a highway for the plague into Europe after it had ravaged China and Japan. Its worst European phase ended in 1350 after killing some thirty million of ninety million Europeans, but it returned periodically, last in 1390. The bacillus, carried by fleas living on rats, caused internal hemorrhaging, turned the skin black, and made it stink. The bubonic strain killed half of those infected. The pneumonic strain was more contagious and fatal—coughing spread it. The deadliest strain, septicemia, killed before any symptoms appeared.

To atone to God, the Flagellants slaughtered Jews, witches, and heretics. Doctors spread the plague, and they warned against bathing, because it opened the skin's pores to the bad vapors—thus the old Western aversion to bathing. Milan, the least plague-affected city, immediately bricked in all inhabitants of every stricken house. Petrarch said, "Happy posterity who will not experience such abysmal woe, will look on our testimony as fable!" The fourteen-century was the "calamitous century" because of its famines, the Black Plague, and the Hundred Year's War (1337–1453). Yet these catastrophes resulted in labor shortages that ended serfdom in Western Europe.

WILLIAM OF OCKHAM
c. 1300-49

English, Franciscan monk whose principle of parsimony (Ockham's Razor) has since guided scientific inquiry: "What can be done with fewer assumptions is done in vain with more," or "When two hypotheses cover the facts, use the simpler of the two." The principle of parsimony attacked Plato's universals; that is, Ockham favored logical realism against nominalism. He denied a reality apprehended solely by the intellect in favor of a reality known through the senses. He said science must accept only observable facts supplemented by logic. God could not be proven by science because God is infinite. Lack of rational proof did not detract from Ockham's belief in God, but it made revelation the sole way to belief. Separating reason from faith laid the foundation for scientific experimentation and modern empiricism.

> If you will defend me with the sword,
> Sire, I shall defend you with the pen.
> To Emperor Lewis of Bavaria, in Norman
> Davies, *Europe: A History* (1996)

THOMAS À KEMPIS
1380–1471

German, monk who compiled a mosaic of Christian writing into *The Imitation of Christ*, one of the most cherished guides to Christian devotion for five hundred years.

> Man proposes, but God disposes.
> *De Imitatione Christi*, tr. Leo Sherley-Price
> (1952)

When the day-of-judgment comes, we shall not be asked what we have read, but what we have done.

Ibid., in "Wisdom," vol. 36 (1961)

All men desire peace but few indeed desire those things which make for peace.

Ibid., in L. R. Frank *Quotationary* (1999)

Whatever you offer to me beside yourself, I account as nothing; I seek not your gift, but yourself.

Ibid., in *Quotationary*

Do not try to find a place free from temptations and troubles. Rather, seek a peace that endures even when you are beset by various temptations and tried by much adversity.

Ibid., in *Quotationary*

Seek not to know who said this or that, but take note of what has been said.

EUGENIUS IV
c. 1383–1447

Italian, pope from 1431.

We decree and order that from now on, and for all time, Christians shall not eat or drink with Jews, nor admit them to feasts, nor cohabit with them, nor bathe with them…. Christians shall not allow Jews to hold civil honors over Christians, or to exercise public offices in the state.

Decree of (1442)

JOHANN GUTENBERG
1397–1468

German, who in 1450–55 invented a stamping mold for precise typecasting, a metal alloy for type, a screw-compressed printing press, and permanent oil ink. This followed the Black Death, which had killed a third of all Europeans, making their clothing available as inexpensive rags for paper.

Gutenberg's movable type printing started the second information revolution—the first had been writing in 3000 B.C. Before Gutenberg, few parish priests even had access to a Bible. Monks in thousands of monasteries had worked six days weekly, copying four pages daily, or two books annually. Monks were sometimes told that for each line they copied, God would forgive one sin. The abbot of St. Evroul (c. 1050) told his brothers that a former brother had escaped hell by a single letter. Twenty-five years after Gutenberg's invention, most scriptoria were closed because one printing worker could produce four hundred books annually!

The impact of Gutenberg's revolution was comparable to the modern Information Revolution. Printing made the Protestant Reformation possible by eliminating the Catholic monopoly on communications, and it hastened development in all fields by driving down the cost of information by 98 percent. At Gutenberg's birth, Europe and China were about equal in technology. Gutenberg's invention allowed Europe's privatized economy to soar.

Gutenberg died in poverty after creditors seized his press. In 1987, one of his three hundred original "Mazarin Bibles" sold for $5.9 million!

JOAN OF ARC
1412–31

French peasant girl, Jeanne D'arc, known as the "Maid of Orléans," whose religious visions inspired her to organize and lead a French army to defeat the English at Orléans in 1429, the turning point in the Hundred Years' War. She opened the way for the coronation of King Charles VII at Reims and restored faith in the Valois dynasty. Tried for sorcery, blasphemy, and wearing men's clothing, she recanted her sins and was given life in prison. But she repudiated her recantation and was burned at the stake by the English. Her martyrdom made her a symbol of French nationalism. She was canonized in 1920.

TORQUEMADA
1420–98

Spanish, Dominican monk appointed inquisitor general of Castile and Aragon in 1478 by Ferdinand and Isabella to test the sincerity of the Jewish *maranos* (pigs) and Moorish *Moriscos* (little Moors). These groups were believed to be secretly worshiping Jehovah and Allah. Ferdinand and Isabella received the pope's permission to launch their own inquisition. Their purpose may have been to expropriate the wealthy *maranos* and *Moriscos*. Torquemada expelled 160,000 Jews in 1492 and most Muslims by 1506. This crippled Spain economically; thereafter Spain excelled only in war and in stealing gold from natives. Many Jews went to Holland, which became a leading trading nation.

The English and French had expelled their Jews centuries earlier. Jews who fled to central Europe were called Ashkenazim

and those who went to Muslim lands were called Sephardim. Jews helped finance Columbus's voyage, hoping to find a refuge from persecution. In *The Story of Philosophy* (1926), the historian Will Durant opined that Christopher Columbus was an Italian Jew.

THE INQUISITION

In 1233, Pope Gregory IX initiated the Inquisition on the basis of Deuteronomy 17:25, and Exodus 22.18, which required heretics and witches to be stoned. He empowered inquisitors to act as investigators, prosecutors, judges, and juries, with the power to torture. Names of accusers were kept secret, and they got one-third of the victim's property—the church and state also each got one-third. Death by burning (auto-da-fe, or "act-of-faith") was preferred since it shed no blood. Particularly heinous heretics were denied the usual courtesy of being garroted before being burned.

In the papal inquisitions, most of the accused only lost their property. Bernard Gui wrote the *Inquisitor's Manual*, c. 1320, which limited the duration of torture and its use as evidence. Pope Innocent VIII's bull, *Summis Desiderantes Affectibus* of 1486, warned that witches gave themselves "to incubi [male demons who have sex with sleeping women] and succubi [female demons who have sex with sleeping men], and by their incantations, spells, conjurations, and other accursed offenses have slain infants yet in the mother's womb...."

The Spanish Inquisition, which was begun by Ferdinand and Isabella in 1480 and lasted until 1808, was more brutal than the papal ones. It executed 31,900 people, and 125,000 victims died in prison. It murdered more Christians than the Roman emperors! Also, inquisitors were thought-police who stifled progress in Spain. England and the Germanic states refused to admit inquisitors.

When Spain expelled its Gypsies, many went to the Low Countries, where they took their Andalusian Gypsy music with its plaintive melodies. It acquired the name Flamenco, for "Flemish."

FRANCOIS VILLON
c. 1431–84

French, poet who oscillated between the ribald and the pious. At the University of Paris he was a member of a gang of thieves and was convicted of murder, but pardoned.

Until the nineteenth century, jails incarcerated prisoners only before their trials. Afterward they were either hung, enslaved, or freed. Why feed, clothe, and house felons for life at public expense?

> Ah God! Had I but studied
> In the days of my foolish youth.
> *Le Grand Testament* (1461)

> But where are the snows of yesteryear?
> Ibid., "Ballad of the Ladies
> of Bygone Times"

> Brothers in humanity who live after us,
> Let not your hearts be hardened against us,
> For, if you take pity on us poor ones,
> God will be more likely to have mercy
>   on you.
> But pray God that he may be willing to
>   absolve us all.
> Ibid., "Ballad of the Lost"

CHRISTOPHER COLUMBUS
1451–1506

Italian and probably Jewish—he shrouded his background in secrecy. He was a merchant sailor who raised money privately (from Jewish merchants?) to finance his first Atlantic crossing. Isabella, the Spanish queen, did not pawn her jewels to finance the voyage, but did provide incentives, such as naming him "admiral of the ocean sea." He discovered San Salvador on October 12, 1492, sailing the *Santa Maria, Pinta,* and *Nina* due west on the trade winds for thirty-three days from the Madeira Islands. His crew of ninety convicts, released to make the voyage, almost mutinied because the winds were so favorable going west that they thought they could not return. The flagship *Santa Maria* was only thirty meters long. Columbus died impoverished after four voyages.

The experts opposing his voyage were the better geographers. All educated people believed that the earth was round; the real questions were the earth's size and the extent of its dry land. Experts figured that the distance from the Canaries to Japan was 10,600 miles, a voyage no ship could survive. Columbus figured it at 2,400 miles based on Book II of Esdra 6:42, which held the earth to be six-sevenths dry land.

Most historians consider modern times to have begun in 1492 with Columbus's voyage, although some favor 1453, when Constantinople fell.

> [Columbus's chart of the Atlantic
>   Ocean was inscribed:]
> "Here be dragons."

AGE OF DISCOVERY

Prince Henry the Navigator (1394–1460) of Portugal designed the caravel—a small, shallow-draft ship with a sternpost rudder and a triangular lateen sail to sail close to the wind. He assembled the best astronomers and cartographers, most being Jews who had fled Spain. In 1488, Bartholomew Diaz rounded the Cape of Good Hope. In 1492, Columbus sailed to the Caribbean. Vasco da Gama in 1502 claimed Goa and shipped spices, which cut the price of pepper in Europe by 90 percent (important in preserving meat). An Italian, Americo Vespucci, sailed down the South American coast, proving it was not Asia. Cortés in 1519 burned his ships on landing on the Mexican coast so there could be no retreat: His 600 men conquered the Aztec empire of 5 million. Ferdinand Magellan, a Portuguese, in 1522 led five ships and 265 men around the world—the *Victoria* and eighteen crew survived. Pope Alexander VI gave Africa and Brazil to Portugal and the rest of the Americas and Asia to Spain by the Treaty of Tordesillas of 1494.

The opening to America and Asia profoundly impacted Europe. The importation of the potato, corn, and tomato enabled Europe's population to quadruple. The potato grows in poor soil and is rich in vitamins and protein. Corn yielded twice the food per acre as English grains. More generally, commerce begets commerce, and specialization of labor is the driver of productivity. International commerce bifurcated Europe; Eastern Europe, lacking access to the water highways, fell behind.

LEONARDO DA VINCI
1452–1519

Italian, painter, architect, sculptor, engineer, and designer of the helicopter, parachute, submarine, elevator, and machine gun. His *Mona Lisa* with her cryptic smile is the world's most popular painting. An ideal Renaissance man, he tried to become an expert in all fields, as Aristotle had been. But few of his architectural, engineering, and other projects were completed, and he produced only seventeen paintings. Other Renaissance men, like Pico Mirandola, also dispersed their energies too widely.

> As a well-spent day brings happy sleep, so life well used brings happy death.
> *The Notebooks* (1508-18) vol. 1, ch. 1

Every now and then go away, have a little relaxation, for when you come back to your work your judgment will be surer, since to remain constantly at work will cause you to lose power of judgment. Go some distance away, because then the work appears smaller, and more of it can be taken in at a glance, and lack of harmony and proportion is more readily seen.

[For good health:]
…you will the better succeed in proportion as you keep clear of physicians.
[Illnesses spread by physicians and hospitals are called "iatrogenic diseases."]

Simplicity is the ultimate sophistication.

Just as courage imperils life, fear protects it.

GIROLAMO SAVONAROLA
1452–98

Italian, Dominican friar, dictator of Florence for four years. In 1494 he drove out the ruler, Piero de' Medici, and ignited the "bonfire of the vanities," burning "decadent" art, dresses, books, and the like. He sought to reform the Catholic Church, led by Pope Alexander VI (Borgia), the most murderous and corrupt of all popes. Borgia poisoned his Curia opponents, showered church money on his nine illegitimate children from three women, including Lucretia and Cesare, Machiavelli's model for *The Prince*. After he wrote that Borgia was going to hell, Savonarola was burned at the stake for heresy. On his way to the stake, Savonarola predicted Borgia would rend the church in two. The Protestant Reformation began nineteen years later.

DESIDERIUS ERASMUS
1466–1536

Dutch, scholar, theologian, and the "prince of humanists," who struggled against the "barbarians of the church" that discouraged classical studies. His principal plea was for tolerance, a unique stand at the time.

His assault against the church, *The Praise of Folly*, preceded Luther's *95 Theses* by eight years. He ridiculed Scholasticism as trivial and criticized the pope for heading an army and a civil state. Although he opposed the Reformation by saying that there was no doctrinal necessity for a schism and criticized Luther's denial of free will, his attacks on the church had weakened it and made it vulnerable to Luther's assault. Erasmus wrote for the "Dutch ear," or common sense, not for the logic-chopping Scholastics. His works were placed on the *Catholic Index of Forbidden Books*. His *Adagia Collectanae* (1509) was a best-seller compiling 818 Latin and Greek proverbs with annotations. The *Adagia's* theme, like *Quotations*, is republican liberty.

> Do we not see that noble cities are erected by the people and destroyed by princes? That a state grows rich by the industry of its citizens and is plundered by the rapacity of its rulers? That good laws are enacted by representatives of the people and violated by kings? That the commons love peace and the monarchs foment war?
>
> *Adages: Collected Works of Erasmus,* Introduction (1982), tr. Margaret M. Phillips

> A knowledge of proverbs contributes to philosophy, persuasiveness, grace and charm in speaking and the understanding of the best authors.
>
> Ibid.

> Immortal God! What a century do I see beginning! If only it were possible to be young again!
> [Comment on Luther's Reformation.]
> Letter to Guillaume Budé (1517)

> It is the chief point of happiness that a man is willing to be what he is.

> When I get a little money, I buy books; if any is left, I buy food and clothes. My home is where I have my library.

> Plato's famous saying is often quoted, "Happy are the states where either philosophers are kings or kings philosophers." But if you look at history you will see that no state has been so plagued by

its rulers as when power has fallen into the hands of some dabbler in philosophy or literary addict.

The most ruthless men have been intellectuals whose uncompromising social engineering schemes prompted them to kill the impediments to their visions. Robert Conquest recommended publishing a book of the poetry of Nero, Stalin, Castro, Mao, and Ho Chi Minh, with illustrations by A. Hitler.

NICOLÒ MACHIAVELLI
1469–1527

Italian, Florentine diplomat whose *The Prince* (1532) was a guide to seizing and holding political power, the essence of which was to be hypocritical, merciless, and to rule by fear. He believed that while republics are superior to princedoms, republics are feasible only if the people are virtuous, which is rare. Detractors say he was unscrupulous and cynical; apologists say he portrayed the world as it is by telling uncomfortable truths, such as one should use violence to minimize violence. Frederick the Great said *The Prince* was useful only for "petty princes."

Men should be either treated generously or destroyed, because they take revenge for slight injuries—for heavy ones they cannot.
The Prince (1513), tr.
Luigi Ricci (1903), ch. 3

A man who wants to act virtuously in every way necessarily comes to grief among so many who are not virtuous.
Ibid., ch. 5

All armed Prophets have been victorious, and all unarmed Prophets have been destroyed.
Ibid., ch. 6

It ought to be remembered that there is nothing more difficult to take in hand, more perilous to conduct, or more uncertain in its success, than to take the lead in the introduction of a new order of things. Because the innovator has for enemies all those who have done well under the old conditions, and lukewarm defenders among those who may do well under the new.
Ibid.

War should be the only study of a prince. He should consider peace only as a breathing time, which gives him leisure to contrive, and furnishes the ability to execute.
Ibid., ch. 14

Among other evils which being unarmed brings you, it causes you to be despised.
Ibid.

It is much safer to be feared than to be loved, when you have to choose between the two.
Ibid., ch. 17

A prince must imitate the fox and the lion, for the lion cannot protect himself from traps, and the fox cannot defend himself from wolves.
Ibid.

But above all, a prince must refrain from taking property, for men forget the death of a father more quickly than the loss of their patrimony.
Ibid.

When neither their property nor their honor is touched, the majority of men live content.

Ibid.

It is necessary that the prince should know how to be a hypocrite and dissembler. For men are so simple, and yield so much to immediate necessity, that the deceiver will never lack dupes.

Ibid., ch. 18

Whoever takes it upon himself to establish a commonwealth and prescribe laws must presuppose all men naturally bad, and that they will yield to their innate evil passions as often as they can do so with safety.

The Discourses (1517), ch. 3.
in L. R. Frank, *Quotationary*

You do not know the unfathomable cowardice of humanity...servile in the face of force, pitiless in the face of weakness, implacable before blunders, indulgent before crimes...and patient to the point of martyrdom before all the violence of bold despotism.

Anyone wishing to see what is to be must consider what has been: all the things of this world in every era have their counterparts in ancient times.

I hold it to be a proof of great prudence for men to abstain from threats and insulting words toward anyone, for neither diminishes the strength of the enemy.

[In Mario Puzo's *Godfather*, the Mafia never threatened the powerful. They only made "offers that could not be refused" to the unarmed.]

Only those cities and countries that are free can achieve greatness.... In free countries we also see wealth increase more rapidly...for everybody gladly multiplies those things and seeks to acquire those goods the possession of which he can tranquilly enjoy.

He who takes no position cannot even get a dog to bark at him.

NICHOLAS COPERNICUS
1473–1543

Polish (German parents), cleric and astronomer whose heliocentric hypothesis dethroned earth in 1510 shortly after Columbus had enlarged it.

Finally we shall place the Sun himself at the center of the Universe. All this is suggested by the systematic procession of events and the harmony of the whole Universe, if only we face the facts, as they say "with both eyes open."

De Revolutionibus Orbium
Coelestium (1543)

He launched the first scientific revolution by denying the Aristotelian and Christian concepts of earth being the center of a universe surrounded by divine spheres. Earth became a mere cog in the universe, which followed mechanical laws. The second scientific revolution came in the twentieth century, with Neils Bohr and quantum mechanics; to wit, matter is subject to uncaused change.

Aristarchus of Samos, a fourth-century B.C. Greek, said that the earth revolved around the sun, a "heliocentric" view. In the second century A.D., Claudius Ptolemy, a Greco-Egyptian astronomer, developed a "geocentric" view, placing the earth at the center of the universe, an erroneous scientific claim that was accepted as truth for 1380 years. Copernicus's heliocentric hypothesis made more accurate predictions, but he erred by assuming that planetary orbits were perfect circles, not ellipses, and he had no proof. Later, Tycho Brahe and Kepler deduced that the planets moved in ellipses, which Galileo's math and telescope proved.

MICHELANGELO
1475–1564

Italian, greatest sculptor of all time (*David, Moses*, and *The Pieta*). For Pope Julius II, from 1508–12 he painted the seventy-foot-high ceiling of the Sistine Chapel. At the age of seventy-two, he became chief architect for rebuilding the Basilica of St. Peter. Michelangelo inscribed his name on only one work, his *Pieta*, a white marble statue of the Virgin Mary holding the crucified Christ—the most beautiful object ever seen by your compiler.

Ancora imparo.
I am still learning.

I've finished that chapel I was painting. The Pope is quite satisfied.
   [Letter in 1512 to his father after completing the Sistine Chapel ceiling.]
                In *Chambers Dictionary of Quotations* (1996)

And further, if I am to do any work for Your Holiness, I beg that none may be set in authority over me in matters touching my art. I beg that full trust may be placed in me and that I may be given a free hand.
                Letter to Pope Julius II (1524)

I have too much of a wife in this art of mine, who has always kept me in tribulation, and my children shall be the works I leave, which, even if they are naught, will live a while.
   In *Chambers Dictionary of Quotations* (1996)

It is with fire that blacksmiths' iron subdue
Unto fair form, the image of their
      thought:
Nor without fire hath any artist wrought
Gold to its utmost purity of hue.
Nay, nor the unmatched phoenix lives
      anew,
Unless she burn.
                Sonnet 59

It is only well with me when I have a chisel in my hand.

If people knew how hard I worked to get my mastery, it wouldn't seem so wonderful.

SIR THOMAS MORE
1478–1535

English, lord chancellor, author of *Utopia* (1516), canonized in 1935. Henry VIII beheaded him for refusing to subscribe to the Act of Supremacy, permitting the king's divorce. A martyr, he was immortalized by Erasmus as "A man for all seasons." Utopia ("no place") is a mythical island where property is held in common and there are no bankers or lawyers. More ominously, in More's *Utopia* "everything's under state control."

They have no lawyers among them, for they consider them as a sort of people whose profession it is to disguise matters.

"Of Law and Magistrates," *Utopia* (1516)

We may not look at our pleasure to go to heaven in featherbeds; it is not the way.

In William Roper, *Life of
Sir Thomas More* (1626)

If the parties will at my hands call for justice, then, all were it my father stood on the one side, and the Devil on the other, his cause being good, the Devil should have right.

Ibid.

I pray you, master Lieutenant, see me safe up, and my coming down let me shift for my self.

[On mounting the scaffold to be beheaded.]

Ibid.

This hath not offended the king.

[Drawing his beard aside on the block.]

MARTIN LUTHER
1483–1546

German, theologian who called himself "the chief of sinners" and who precipitated the Protestant Reformation. Infuriated by the sale of indulgences, he protested by nailing his *95 Theses* on the door of All Saints Church at Wittenberg. The Imperial Diet in Worms in 1521 excommunicated him for challenging the necessity of priests and sacraments for salvation. His revolutionary doctrine of "the priesthood of all believers" was a bolt aimed at the church, a popular stance given the scandalous materialism of the church. His definitive statement was his *To the Christian Nobility of the German Nation* (1520), that is, salvation is achieved through faith. That supports individual responsibility and liberty and is destructive of religious and political hierarchies. His translating the Bible into German broke the church's monopoly over the scriptures and established German as a national language.

Luther and Calvin agreed on the supremacy of the Scriptures, but differed otherwise. Calvin saw God in Hebraic terms as a God of wrath, leading to a more authoritarian church. Luther saw God as love, so Luther was more tolerant of differences.

Lutherans have emphasized training musicians and composers, like Bach. Luther praised hymns: "Next to theology, the Devil hates music because it drives away temptation and evil thoughts."

An indulgence can never remit guilt; the Pope himself cannot do such a thing; God has kept that in His own hand.

From *95 Theses* (1517)

The Roman church, once the holiest of all, has become the most licentious den of thieves, the most shameless of all brothels, the kingdom of sin, death, and hell. It is so bad that even the Antichrist himself, if he should come, could think of nothing to add to its wickedness.

"An Open Letter to Pope Leo X"
(September 6, 1520)

I have such hatred of divorce that I prefer bigamy to divorce.

The Babylonian Captivity of the Church
(1520)

I am overcome by the Scriptures I have quoted; my conscience is captive to God's Word. I cannot and will not recant anything, for to go against conscience is neither right nor safe. Here I stand; I cannot do otherwise. God help me. Amen.

[*Ich kann nicht anders*: I cannot do otherwise.]

"Speech at Diet of Worms"
(April 18, 1521)

God uses lust to impel men to marriage, ambition to office, avarice to earning, and fear to faith.

Quoted in *Time* (March 24, 1967)

Peace if possible, but truth at any rate.

[To the question of what was God doing before he created the universe, Luther replied:]

He sat under a birch tree cutting rods for those who ask nosy questions.

THE PROTESTANT REFORMATION

Martin Luther, in trying to reform the Catholic Church, launched the Protestant Reformation that fostered individualism and nationalism. It held that man was saved by faith alone, not by the sacraments or the church. Each individual must communicate with God through Bible reading. Luther declared everyone to be a priest: "A Christian man is a perfectly free lord, subject to none." Luther added, "A Christian man is a perfectly dutiful servant of all, subject to all."

Catholicism had been weakened by prelates who cared little for souls. For example, Pope Alexander VI (1492–1503) gave prizes at a Vatican banquet for the cardi-

nals who had the most couplings with the fifty naked whores he supplied.

The Reformation's "Protestant ethic" held that, to glorify God, each person should work hard, be frugal and prudential, postpone gratification, revere the family, and serve the community. If each individual is responsible for his or her eternal salvation, how much more is each individual responsible for his or her earthly condition? Protestantism fostered the doctrine of a "sacred calling to work." One no longer worked just to live well, but to accumulate wealth to glorify God by being successful. Prosperity from the "stewardship of talents" witnessed God's grace. This ethic created a middle-class committed to pursuing wealth creation as a sacred duty. The Protestant ethic inspired a democratic rebellion against kings and aristocrats and laid the foundation for the Industrial Revolution.

The downside of Protestantism was noted by Matthew Arnold, who said that individual judgments` could not replace the metaphysics of two millennia of interpreting Scripture. Even the worst popes protected the centuries of work in constructing Catholic dogma.

HENRY VIII
1491–1547

English, king. In 1534, he signed the Act of Supremacy, which made him "Protector and Only Supreme Head of the Church and Clergy of England." This act united the English state and church and freed Henry from Pope Clement VII, which permitted him to divorce Catherine of Aragon, mother of Mary, and marry Anne Boleyn, mother of Elizabeth I. He executed Sir

Thomas More (later canonized as a saint) when More refused to assent to the divorce or to subscribe to the Act of Supremacy. Pope Clement VII refused the divorce to avoid antagonizing Holy Roman Emperor Charles V, Catherine's nephew.

> They sent me a Flanders' mare.
>> [Speaking of Anne Boleyn, who was horribly pocked and smelled awful and who was beheaded for adultery.]

SAINT IGNATIUS OF LOYOLA
1491–1556

Spanish, former soldier who founded the Society of Jesus (Jesuits), whose mission has been education. This largest Catholic order is organized along military lines and consists of scientists, scholars, and the brightest teachers. The Jesuits may have saved Catholicism from being swamped by the Protestant Reformation.

> Teach us, good Lord, to serve Thee as
>   Thou deservest:
> To give and not to count the cost;
> To fight and not to heed the wounds;
> To toil and not to seek for rest;
> To labor and not ask for any reward
> Save that of knowing that we do Thy will.
>> "Prayer for Generosity" (1548)

FRANCOIS RABELAIS
c. 1494–1553

French, defrocked monk, and one of the most learned men of his age. He used earthy humor in his masterpiece, *Gargantua and Pantagruel*, to attack theologians at the Sorbonne University for refusing to use reason ("Reason. We never use it here.") and to attack the asceticism of monks. This "Father of French literature," who wrote in the "vulgar," was Falstaff personified who upheld the dignity of common people and who liked good food, drink, and the pleasure of the opposite sex. He described himself as "hale and cheery, as sound as a bell, and ready to drink if you will." Because life's purpose is to expand the soul through experience, the rule is "Do As Thou Wilt." He used the pseudonym Alcofribas Nasier.

> One falls to the ground in trying to sit on two stools.
>> *To the Readers*, ch. 2

> The Rule of their Order had but one clause: Do What Thou Wilt.
>> *Gargantua and Pantagruel* (1533–35),
>> bk. 1, ch. 57, tr. J. M. Cohen (1955)

> Knowledge without conscience is but the ruin of the soul.
>> Ibid., bk. 2, ch. 8. in L. R. Frank,
>> *Quotationary* (1999)

> [Below, in *Gargantua and Pantagruel*, Rabelais caricatures a fictitious skeptic philosopher, Trouillogan:]
> Are you married?
> I think so.
> You were also married before you had this wife?
> It is possible.
> Had you good luck in your first marriage?
> It is not impossible.
> How thrive you with this second wife of yours?
> Even as it pleaseth my fatal destiny.

But, what in good earnest? Tell me: Do
you prosper well with her?
It is likely.
In the name of God: I vow, by Saint
Christopher, that I had rather
undertake the fetching of a fart
forth of the belly of a dead ass, than
to draw out of you a positive and
determinate resolution.

[Pantagruel said:] "I seem to hear people
talking in the air. But I can't see anything. Listen, listen...." So as to miss
nothing, some of us cupped the palms
of our hands to the backs of our ears.
The more keenly we listened, the more
keenly we made out voices, until in the
end we made out whole words.

He replies in nothing but monosyllables.
I believe he would make three bites of a
cherry.

I owe much. I possess nothing. I give the
rest to the poor.

Last Will

Rabelais' friend and publisher, Etienne
Dolet, also printed works of Plato. That
violated the Counter Reformation being
led by the faculty of the Sorbonne who
considered Greek to be subversive. Dolet
was thus burned at the stake for heresy.
Before dying, Dolet said, "Dolet does not
suffer for himself, but he suffers for the
sake of reason."

EVERYMAN
1508

Everyman was a morality play by
an unknown author. Morality plays
were allegories to teach moral lessons to
the illiterate, much as "mystery plays"
were simple dramas based on Scripture.
In *Everyman,* God orders Death to summon Everyman on a pilgrimage to judgment. Death allows Everyman to take any
willing companions with him. But Goods,
Fellowship, and Kindred decline to go.
Good-Deeds agrees to go, but is too weak.
Fortunately, Knowledge leads Everyman
to Confession, where he finds penance.
This revives Good-Deeds. Then, Beauty,
Strength, and Discretion also agree to
accompany Everyman, but they fall by
the wayside, so only Good-Deeds is with
Everyman at judgment. The moral is that
man at the beginning of life should look
toward its end. While Fellowship, Kindred, and Goods are not sins, they divert
man from God and salvation, and that
Knowledge of the church and Confession
are necessary to Good-Deeds.

JOHN CALVIN
1509–1564

French, theologian whose *Institutes of the
Christian Religion* (1536) laid a firm theological foundation for Luther's Reformation. Calvin made Geneva the "Protestant
Rome." The Bible, not the church, was the
source of religious authority, and each person must read and interpret it. Redemption
is a gift of faith from God for the elect and
cannot be achieved by works. Each con-
gregation chose its own pastor and elected
its elders. Calvinism inspired the Puritans,
the Scottish Covenanters, and the French
Huguenots.

Calvin believed in glorifying God, the
"great taskmaster," through discipline
and hard work. Industriousness and thrift
became Protestant virtues. The Calvinist

strongholds of Scotland, England, Holland, Switzerland, Germany, and America became the citadels of democracy and capitalism.

Laborare est Orare. To work is to pray.

SIR THOMAS GRESHAM
1519–79

English, founder of the Royal Exchange, who persuaded England's Elizabeth I to re-coin currency after Henry VIII had debased it.

> When depreciated, mutilated, or debased coinage is in concurrent circulation with money of high value in terms of precious metals, the good money automatically disappears.
> [Gresham's Law: Bad money drives good money out of circulation.]

PHILIP II
1527–98

Spanish, king who wasted Spain's vast mineral wealth fighting as the champion of the Catholic Counter-Reformation. In 1588 his "invincible armada" of 130 ships, with 8,500 seamen and 19,000 troops, attempted to invade England to restore Catholicism and prevent her from helping the Protestant Netherlands escape Spanish rule. No ship was sunk by gunfire, but England's superior cannons and maneuverable ships kept the armada at bay until high winds sank half of it.

Spain's reach for European dominance ended in 1648 when she lost the Thirty Years' War, during which Spain spent the last of the treasure she had looted from Latin America. Earlier, Spain had lost her commercial and industrial classes when she expelled her Jews in 1492, and her Moors by 1506. Seeking enrichment through expropriation, Catholic zealots condemned Spain to Europe's backwaters, where Spain produced saints but no scientists. However, Spain did perform the inestimable service of cutting the cancer of Muslim despotism out of Western Europe. The militarization of Spain necessary to oust Islam contributed to preventing her from developing an entrepreneurial culture.

Time and myself against any two.

JEAN BODIN
1530–96

French, political philosopher, whose *On the Republic* (1576) surveyed ancient and extant governments and their laws to determine the best structures. He concluded that one should use the experience of each nation to design its government. For some peoples, only a despot can govern.

> It is necessary for the wise government of a people to understand fully its humors and nature before it can expect anything from changes in the state or the laws. For the main foundation of a commonwealth lies in the adaptation of the state to the nature of the citizens, and the edicts and ordinances to the nature of the place, the person, and times.
> On the Republic (1576)

ELIZABETH 1
1533–1603

English, queen, daughter of Henry VIII and Anne Boleyn. As queen she consolidated the power of the Anglican Church, reformed the currency, passed the Poor Laws, stalemated France by diplomacy, stimulated an economic boom with non-intervention, and allowed privateers to loot Spain's treasure ships. Destroying Spain's invincible armada in 1588, she made England sovereign of the oceans until the 1930s. The Elizabethan age of literature was the greatest outpouring of literature in history. Most important, she deferred to the Commons' law-making powers. Elizabeth, England's greatest sovereign, ruled by "inaction." She let the private sector develop the economy under a regime of low taxes and sparse regulation.

Elizabeth's greatest privateer, Francis Drake, was the second person to circumnavigate the globe.

I know I have the body of a weak and feeble woman, but I have the heart and stomach of a king, and of a king of England too.
> Speech awaiting the approach of the
> Spanish Armada in 1588

My dogs wear my collars…
[Elizabeth forbade English diplomats to accept foreign decorations.]

There is no jewel, be it of never so rich a price, which I prefer before…your love. For I do esteem it more than any treasure…. And though God has raised us high, yet this I count the glory of my crown, that I have reigned with your loves…. And though you have had and may have many mightier and wiser princes sitting in this seat, yet you never had, nor shall have, any love you better.
> The Golden Speech, November 20, 1601,
> her last speech to Parliament

[The English Poor Law of 1601 was the mother of all welfare laws. It read in part:]
Be it enacted by the authority of this present parliament, that the church wardens of every parish, to raise by taxation… competent sums of money for and towards the necessary relief of the lame, impotent, old, blind, and such other among them being poor and not able to work.

MICHEL DE MONTAIGNE
1533–92

French, Jewish atheist, secular moralist, nominal Catholic, and a wisdom writer, like Seneca, Goethe, and Emerson. He invented the personal essay, attempting to "spy on himself" as he wrote about life, death, pain, fear, faith, friendship, and so on. Emerson, a disciple of Montaigne, said of the *Essays*, "Cut these words and they would bleed; they are vascular and alive." His creed was: "To compose our character is our duty, not to compose books, and to win, not battles and provinces, but order and tranquility in our conduct."

Nor is there anything more remarkable in Socrates than the fact that in his old age he finds time to take lessons in dancing and playing instruments, and considers it well-spent.
> Essays, (1580), "Of Experience" (1587–88)

They want to get out of themselves and escape from the man. That is madness:

instead of changing into angels, they change into beasts…. There is reason to pity the men who will have to live with and obey a man who exceeds and is not content with a man's proportions.

Ibid.

Sits he on ever so high a throne, a man still sits on his bottom.

They have only stepped back in order to leap farther.

It is very easy to generate in a people a contempt for their ancient observances; no man ever attempted it without succeeding. But many have come to grief in their attempt to establish a better state of things in place of what they have destroyed.

Men are nothing until they are excited.

As for dying, practice can give us no assistance…. we are all apprentices when we come to it.

Since Ptolemy was once mistaken over his basic tenets, would it not be foolish to trust what moderns are saying now?

I hate that accidental repentance that old age brings. I shall never be grateful to impotence for any good it may do me….

MIGUEL DE CERVANTES
1547–1616

Spanish, author of the first novel—a long story about an individual—and "best novel" according to some. Having little education, his style was not cluttered with classical allusions. *Don Quixote*, a sensational hit written at age fifty-seven, fetched him little money because his publisher cheated him. The protagonist, Don Quixote, lost his wits from compulsive reading about the age of chivalry, so he rode off to the plain of La Mancha to become a knight-errant. His aim was to defend the oppressed and right iniquities while riding on his nag Rosinante, a "lean, lank, drooping" cart horse that became a knight-errant's charger, with his squire Sancho Panza astride his donkey. Don Quixote's quest was to free his lady, La Dulcinea del Toboso, from an enchantment that had turned her into his village's goat keeper, Aldonza Lorenzo.

As with Hamlet, there are as many Don Quixotes as readers. To some he is a romantic who always hurts people despite just intentions, while to others he is kind and chivalrous. Sancho Panza, a realist and lovable coward, is interested in creature comforts, but he often prevents Don Quixote from causing even greater havoc. José Ortega y Gasset sees Don Quixote as a hero: "His life is a perpetual resistance to what is habitual and customary." Quixote defends himself in volume 2, chapter 32

> I have set injuries and insults straight, righted wrongs, punished arrogance, conquered giants, and trampled on monsters.

Only the Bible, the Koran, and Euclid have been translated more than *Don Quixote*, the world's best-known literary character. Cervantes was an unrewarded hero of the Battle of Lepanto, a failed playwright, a captive of the Turks, and so on. But he claimed one satisfaction:

> One of the things most pleasant to a virtuous and distinguished man is to

see himself, while he is still alive, go out among the nations and languages of the world, printed and bound, and bearing a good reputation.

By a small sample we may judge of the whole piece.

> *Don Quixote* (1605), tr. Peter Anthony
> Motteux

The famous Don Quixote de la Mancha, otherwise called the Knight of the Woeful Figure.
[Or, Sorrowful Countenance.]

> Ibid.

He preaches well that lives well, quoth Sancho, that's all the divinity I understand.

> Ibid.

He had a face like a benediction.

> Ibid.

Hunger is the best sauce in the world.

> Ibid.

That's the nature of women…not to love when we love them, and to love when we love them not.

> Ibid.

Tell me thy company and I will tell thee what thou art.

> Ibid.

Between a woman's yea and nay I would not engage to put a pin's point, so close they be to one another.

> Ibid.

There are only two families in the world…; the Haves and the Have-nots.

> Ibid.

Everyone is as God made him and often worse.

> Ibid.

Pray look better, sir. Those things yonder are no giants, but windmills.
[Sancho Panza to Don Quixote.]

> Ibid.

Under a bad cloak is often a good drinker.

> Ibid.

A silly remark can be made in Latin as well as in Spanish.

> Ibid.

The road is always better than the inn.

> Ibid.

If I did not accomplish great things, I died in their pursuit.
[Don Quixote's epitaph.]

Cervantes died on the same day as Shakespeare, and *Don Quixote* was published on the opening day of *King Lear* at the Globe.

SIR EDWARD COKE
1552–1634

English, incorruptible jurist, whose name is pronounced "cook." His *Reports and Institutes* held that the law was not the king's instrument, but that it bound the king, and that the king could not create criminal offenses without Parliament's consent. James I put Coke in the Tower of London, and claimed to rule by divine right. He said, "It is sedition in subjects to dispute what a king may do."

Coke created the writ of habeas corpus and as a member of Parliament instigated the Petition of Right in 1628, to which Charles I capitulated: no taxes without Parliament's consent; no imprisonment without cause; no quartering of soldiers on citizens; and no martial law in peacetime. Only after Coke died did Charles I disregard the petition.

Unlike the case in Britain, European monarchs gained total control over taxation so their ancient representative institutions died out. Coke prevented that from happening in England. He also asserted the common law against the rival systems of law in the Crown Chamber and Ecclesiastical Courts.

Coke in Bonham's Case (1610) held that the judiciary could overturn statutes, "When an Act of Parliament is against common right and reason, or repugnant, or impossible to be performed, the common law will control it and adjudge such Act to be void." Judicial review later disappeared in England but took root in America.

Coke attacked government monopolies, "All monopolies are against the great Charter, because they are against the liberty and freedom of the subject, and against the law of the land." Hayek called Coke "the great fountain of Whig principles."

> Reason is the life of the law; nay the common law itself is nothing else but reason.... The law, which is perfection of reason.
>> *First Institute of the Laws of England* (1628), ch. 2, sec. 6

> The house of every one is to him as his castle and fortress, as well for his defense against injury and violence as for his repose.
>> *Seymayne's Case*, 5 Rep. 91

> *Iniquum est aliquem rei sui esse judicem.*
> It is unjust that anyone should be judge in his own cause.

> The law of the realm cannot be changed but by parliament.

SIR WALTER RALEGH
c. 1552–1618

English, explorer who first colonized America. Even though he seduced a maid of honor of Elizabeth I, she favored him for his New World voyages, for throwing his cloak over a puddle, and for introducing potatoes, tomatoes, and maize to Europe. James I executed him in 1618 for disobeying a direct order not to attack the Spanish.

> If all the world and love were young,
> And truth in every shepherd's tongue,
> These pretty pleasures might me move
> To live with thee, and be thy love.
>> *"The Nymph's Reply to the Passionate Shepherd"* (1600)

> The world itself is but a large prison, out of which daily some are led to execution.

> 'Tis a sharp remedy, but a sure one for all ills.
> [Feeling the ax blade before his execution.]

HENRI IV
1553–1610

French, king, the first Bourbon and one of the greatest French kings, known as Henri of Navarre. Having been a Protestant before converting to Catholicism in order to become king, Henry IV gave French Huguenots the same civil rights as French Catholics by his Edict of Nantes in 1598. Louis XIV revoked it in 1685.

> Paris is well worth a mass.
> [He converted to Catholicism to become king.]

> I want there to be no peasant in my kingdom so poor that he is unable to have a chicken in his pot every Sunday.
> *de Prefixe Histoire de Henri le Grand* (1681)

GEORGE CHAPMAN
1559–1634

English, poet, playwright, and the first English translator of Homer.

> An Englishman being flattered is a lamb; threatened, a lion.
> *Alphonsus, Emperor of Germany*
> (1654), act 1

FRANCIS BACON
1561–1626

English, perhaps the greatest man of science, although he was not a scientist. He criticized philosophers for failing to organize "a single experiment which tends to relieve and benefit the condition of man." Bacon had no interest in metaphysics; he was interested only in how to satisfy human needs. He pioneered the scientific method: Use an inductive process to seek patterns in nature, make hypotheses, and test them by experimentation. A

hypothesis becomes a theory if an experiment can be repeated successfully. He despised philosophical speculation. His attacked both Scholasticism and European rationalism. His purpose was to effect "a total reconstruction of sciences, arts, and all human knowledge, raised upon the proper foundations."

Bacon died of a cold after experimenting on refrigeration. He wrote: *Essays* (1597–1625), *The Advancement of Learning* (1605), *Novum Organum* (1620), and *The New Atlantis* (1627).

> There are and can be only two ways of searching into and discovering truth. The one flies…to the most general axioms…this way is now in fashion. The other derives axioms from the senses and particulars, rising by a gradual and unbroken ascent so that it arrives at the most general axioms last of all. This is the true way, but as yet untried.
> *Norum Organum* (1620)

> Nature to be commanded, must be obeyed.
> Ibid., Aphorism 129

> Mathematics is the door and the key to the sciences.
> *Opus Majus*

> Knowledge is power.
> *Meditations Sacrae* (1597), "Of Heresies"

> *Silentium, stultorum virtus.*
> Silence is the virtue of fools.
> *De Dignitate et Augmentis Scientiarum*
> (1640)

> We see, then, how far the monuments of wit and learning are more durable

than the monuments of power or of the hands. For have not the verses of Homer continued twenty-five hundred years or more, without the loss of a syllable or letter; during which time infinite palaces, temples, castles, cities, have been decayed and demolished?

The Advancement of Learning (1605)

If we begin with certainties, we shall end in doubts; but if we begin with doubts, and are patient in them, we shall end in certainties.

Ibid., bk. I, ch. 5, sec. 12

They are ill discoverers that think there is no land, when they can see nothing but sea.

Ibid., bk. VII, ch. 7, Sec. 5

Men must know, that in the theater of life it is reserved only for God and the angels to be lookers-on.

Ibid., ch. 20, Sec. 8

Philosophy directs us first to seek the goods of the mind, and the rest will be supplied, or not much wanted.

Ibid., bk. VIII, ch. 2

Hope is a good breakfast, but a bad supper.

Apothegms (1624), no. 36

The virtue of Prosperity is temperance; the virtue of Adversity is fortitude. …for Prosperity doth best discover vice, but Adversity doth best discover virtue.

The Essays or Counsels, Civill and Morall (1625), "Of Adversity"

A little philosophy inclineth man's mind to atheism, but depth in philosophy bringeth men's minds about to religion.

Ibid., "Of Atheism"

In civil business: What first? Boldness; What second, and third? Boldness.

Ibid., "Of Boldness"

Muhammed called the mountain to come to him again and again; and when the mountain stood still he was never a whit abashed, but said, "If the mountain will not come to Muhammed, Muhammed will go to the mountain.'

Ibid.

A just fear of an imminent danger, though there be no blow given, is a lawful cause of war.

Ibid., "Of Empire"

Judges ought to remember that their office is *jus dicere* and not *jus dare*, to interpret law and not to make law.

Ibid., "Of Judicature"

Nobility of birth commonly abateth industry.

Ibid., "Of Nobility"

Children sweeten labors; but they make misfortunes more bitter. They increase the care of life; but they mitigate the remembrance of death.

Ibid., "Of Parents and Children"

To spend too much time in studies is sloth; to use them too much for ornament, is affectation.

Ibid., "Of Studies"

Some books are to be tasted, others to be swallowed, and some few to be chewed and digested.

Ibid.

Young men are fitter to invent than to judge; fitter for execution than for counsel; and fitter for new projects than for settled business.... Men of age object too much, consult too long, adventure too little, repent too soon, and seldom drive business home to the full period but content themselves with a mediocrity of success.

Ibid., "Of Youth and Age"

He that will not apply new remedies must expect new evils; for time is the greatest innovator; and if time of course alter things to the worse, and wisdom and counsel shall not alter them to the better what shall be the end?

Ibid., "Of Innovations"

A man would do well to carry a pencil in his pocket, and write down the thoughts of the moment. Those that come unsought for are commonly the most valuable, and should be secured, because they seldom return.

In *Wisdom*, vol. 38

He that defers his charity until he is dead is, if a man weights it rightly, rather liberal of another man's goods than his own.

Nothing conduces more to the well-representing of a man's self than not to disarm one's self by too much sweetness and good nature, which exposes a man to injuries and reproaches; but rather...at times to dart out some sparks of a free and generous mind, that have no less of the sting than the honeybee.

The true and lawful end of the sciences is that human life be enriched by new discoveries and powers.

Truth is more likely to arise from error than from confusion.

Acorns were good till bread was found.

GALILEO GALILIE
1564–1642

Italian, mathematician, astronomer, and physicist. His *A Dialogue on the Two Great Systems of the World* (1632) proved Copernicus's heliocentric theory that the earth revolves around the sun. Earth became an insignificant speck in space and understandable without religion. The Holy Office in Rome pronounced this doctrine heretical and Galileo was ordered not to teach it. Galileo wrote, "The Holy Scriptures are inerrant but fallible men interpret them." When Pope John Paul II redressed in the 1990s the censure of Galileo, he repeated the phrase above. Also, after Galileo, scientists could no longer rely on authorities, such as Ptolemy. They had to engage in empirical research to understand the physical world.

[The Inquisition denounced Galileo's theory as heresy in 1616. During his recantation to avoid being burned at the stake, he muttered about earth:]
E pur si muove ("But still, it moves").

The doctrine of the movements of the earth and the fixity of the sun is condemned on the ground that the Scriptures speak in many places of the sun moving and the earth standing still....

The Authority of the Scripture in Philosophical Controversies

In questions of science, the authority of a thousand is not worth that humble reasoning of a single individual.

All truths are easy to understand once they are discovered. The point is to discover them.

Galileo also proved Aristotle wrong in arguing that heavy objects fall faster than light ones, although Galileo did not drop objects off the Leaning Tower of Pisa. He proved the first law of motion: The distance traversed by a falling object is proportional to the square of the number of seconds it has been falling, and he discovered the law of inertia. Previously, people believed that all moving objects naturally slowed to a stop. He increased the Dutch telescope's magnification from 3X to 30X.

CHRISTOPHER MARLOWE
1564–93

English, playwright who laid the foundation for Shakespeare by establishing blank verse for drama. Ben Johnson characterized Marlowe's verse as the "mighty line." Marlowe's Faustus is a scholar and theologian who sells his soul for knowledge and power. The good angel begged him to forsake knowledge: "O Faustus, lay that damned book aside," but Lucifer's agent Mephistopheles promised, "Be thou on Earth as Jove is in the sky, Lord and commander of these elements." For twenty-four years of power and knowledge, Faustus loses his capacity for repentance, which dooms him.

> Was this the face that launched a
>   thousand ships,
> And burnt the topless towers of Ilium?
> Sweet Helen, make me immortal with
>   a kiss!

Her lips suck forth my soul; see, where
    it flies!
> *The Tragical History of Doctor Faustus*,
> act 5, sc. 1

> Now hast thou but one bare hour to live,
> And then thou must be damned
>   perpetually!
> Stand still, you ever-moving spheres of
>   heaven,
> That time may cease, and midnight
>   never come.
> Fair nature's eye, rise, rise, again, and make
> Perpetual day…
> The stars move still, time runs, the clock
>   will strike,
> The devil will come, and Faustus must
>   be damned…
> See, see, where Christ's blood streams in
>   the firmament!
> One drop would save my soul, half a
>   drop, ah, my Christ.
>   [On the last day at midnight, Lucifer
>   dragged Dr. Faustus down into hell.]
> Ibid., act 5, sc. 2

> Hell hath no limits, nor is circumscribed
> In one self place; for where we are is hell,
> And where hell is, there must we ever be.
>   [Mephistopheles' description of hell.]

> Our swords shall play the orators for us.
> *Tarnburlaine the Great* (1587), pt. 1, act 1

> Come live with me, and be my love;
> And we will all the pleasures prove
> That valleys, groves, hills, and fields,
> Woods or sleepy mountain yields.
>   "The Passionate Shepherd to his Love"
>   (1589), T*he Passionate Pilgrim* (1599)

WILLIAM SHAKESPEARE
1564–1616

English, possibly the world's greatest author and most creative person, who wrote 36 plays in 25 years and also collaborated with others in writing plays. Some plays have been panned: *Coriolanus, Pericles, Henry VI, Titus Andronicus*, and *The Rape of Lucrece*, and two are politically incorrect: *The Taming of the Shrew* (wife abuse) and *The Merchant of Venice* (anti-Semitism).

Jacques Barzun said, "Shakespeare's knowledge of life and human beings was not equaled by any other poet or playwright. Next to these powers his faults counted for nothing...." Yet for two centuries after his death, Shakespeare was generally disparaged in England. For example, Garrick thought his work was usable only if cut and doctored. It was the Germans who first recognized his universal genius: Goethe, Schiller, and Herder, and then the French: Stendhal and Hugo, who promoted this "European" writer. Ten plays were sited in England, 26 in Europe. Falstaff was "the most active fellow in Europe" and Petrucchio wooed "the prettiest Kate in Christendom."

Harold Bloom wrote, "If we could conceive of a universal canon multicultural and multivalent, its one essential book would not be a scripture, whether Bible, Koran, or Eastern text, but rather Shakespeare, who is acted and read everywhere, in every language and circumstance." In *The Western Canon* (1994), Bloom noted that Shakespeare excelled equally in comedy and tragedy, a feat never accomplished by any other playwright.

Shakespeare's most opinionated play, *Troilus and Cressida*, shows he was a conservative who hated using violence to redress grievances against the state, according to Paul Johnson's *Creators* (2006). Rather than revolution, he favored making incremental improvements, a practical English tradition as opposed to the abstract-thinking European.

Scholars debate whether "William Shaksper" of Stratford-on-Avon was "Shakespeare." Shaksper did not attend school, travel abroad, speak French, Latin, or Greek, read the law, or associate with aristocrats. His daughters were illiterate and his home lacked bookshelves. Most scholars believe Shakespeare was Shaksper due to contemporary references to him as a playwright. Unbelievers are guilty of "bardolatry" and an intellectual snobbery that great men cannot arise from humble stations.

SHAKESPEARE'S PLAYS

KING HENRY VI, PT. II
1590–91

What stronger breastplate than a heart
    unstained!
Thrice is he armed that hath his quarrel
    just,
And he but naked, though locked up in
    steel,
Whose conscience with injustice is
    corrupted.
    [King]
                    Act III, sc. 2

The first thing we do, let's kill all the
    lawyers.
    [Dick Butcher]
                    Act IV, sc. 2

Ignorance is the curse of God.
Knowledge is the wing wherewith we
    fly to heaven.
    [Saye]

                        Ibid., sc. 7

KING HENRY VI, PT. III

Beggars mounted run their horses to
    death.
    [Richard, Duke of York]

                        Act I, sc. 4

But Hercules himself must yield to
    odds;
And many strokes, though with a
    little ax,
Hew down and fell the hardest tim-
    bered oak.
    [Messenger]

                        Act II, sc. 1

A little fire is quickly trodden out.
Which, being suffered, rivers cannot
    quench.
    [Clarence]

                        Act IV, sc. 8

KING RICHARD III
1592–93

Richard III was defeated by Henry Tudor
(Henry VII), the Lancastrian claimant, at
Bosworth Field in 1485, ending the War of
the Roses (1455–85): Lancaster (white) and
York (red). Henry VII married the daughter of Edward IV, thereby uniting the two
houses. The wars killed the ancient nobility, which increased royal power. Shakespeare's Richard kills his brother, wife,
nephews (the little princes in the Tower),
and his friends as he fights for the crown
with treachery and guile. Richard is pure

evil, who, unlike Macbeth, suffers no inner
conflicts and therefore is only feared and
not pitied.

Now is the winter of our discontent.
    [Richard]

                        Act I, sc. 1

No beast so fierce but knows some
    touch of pity.
    [Richard]

                        Ibid., sc. 2

And thus I clothe my naked villainy
With odd old ends stolen forth of
    holy writ,
And seem a saint when most I play the
    devil.
    [Richard]

                        Ibid., sc. 3

Why, I can smile and murder whiles I
    smile,
And cry, "Content" to that which
    grieves my heart,
And wet my cheeks with artificial tears,
And frame my face to all occasions…
I can add colors to the chameleon,
Change shapes with Proteus for advantages,
And set the murderous Machiavelli to
    school.
Can I do this, and cannot get a crown?
    [Richard]

                        Act III, sc. 2

A horse, a horse, my kingdom for a horse!
    [Richard]

                        Act V, sc. 4

I have set my life upon a cast,
And I will stand the hazard of the die.
    [Richard]

                        Ibid.

THE TAMING OF THE SHREW
1593–94

[In this male chauvinist play, the groom, Petrucchio, tames the spirited Katharina.]

No profit grows where is no pleasure ta'en
In brief, sir, study what you most affect.
   [Trania]
                  Act I, sc. 1

There is small choice in rotten apples.
   [Gremio]
                  Ibid.

Your father hath consented that you
   shall Be my wife, your dowry 'greed on,
And will you, nill you, I will marry you.
   [Petruccio to Kate]
                  Act II, sc. 1

A little pot and soon hot.
   [Grumio]
                  Act IV, sc. 1

Thy husband is thy lord, thy life, thy
   keeper, Thy head, thy sovereign; one
   that cares for thee....
And craves no other tribute at thy hands
But love, fair looks, and true obedience
Too little payment for so great a debt.
Such duty as the subject owes the prince,
Even such a woman oweth to her
   husband....
I am asham'd that women are so simple
To offer war where they should kneel
   for peace;
Or seek for rule, supremacy, and sway
When they are bound to serve, love and
   obey.
   [Katherina]
                  Act V, sc. 2

KING RICHARD II
1595

Lions make leopards tame.
   [Richard]
                  Act I, sc. 1

This royal throne of kings, this sceptered
   isle,
This earth of majesty, this seat of Mars,
This other Eden, demi paradise,
This fortress built by Nature for herself
Against infection and the hand of war,
This happy breed of men, this little world,
This precious stone set in the silver sea,
Which serves it in the office of a wall
Or as a mote defensive to a house,
Against the envy of less happier lands,
This blessed plot, this earth, this realm,
   this England,
This nurse, this teeming womb of royal
   kings,
Fear'd by their breed and famous by
   their birth.
   [John of Gaunt]

[The Gaelic geographer, Paul Vidal de la Blache, rejoined:]
'This paltry little isle with acres few and
   weather vile.'
                  Act II, sc. 1

Let's talk of graves, of worms, and
   epitaphs...
Let's choose executors and talk of wills.
   [King Richard]
                  Act II, sc. 2

ROMEO AND JULIET
1595–96

A pair of star crossed lovers.
                  Prologue

Romeo, Romeo! wherefore art thou
 Romeo?
Deny thy father, and refuse thy name;
Or, if thou wilt not, be but sworn my love,
And I'll no longer be a Capulet.
 [Juliet]

        Act II, sc. 2

What's in a name? That which we call
 a rose
By any other name would smell as sweet.
 [Juliet]

        Ibid.

Good night, good night! parting is such
 sweet sorrow,
That I shall say good night till it be
 morrow.
 [Romeo]

        Ibid.

No, 'tis not so deep as a well, nor so
 wide as a church door, but 'tis
 enough, 'twill serve.
 [Mercutio mortally wounded by
 Tybalt]

        Act III, sc. 1

A plague o' both your houses! They have
made worms' meat of me.
 [Mercutio]

        Ibid.

A MIDSUMMER NIGHT'S DREAM
1595–96

Shakespeare's most famous comedy introduces the Fairy King and Queen, Oberon and Titania, and Puck, Oberon's jester, who is a comical goblin of mischievous pranks. Shakespeare uses the play to demonstrate the shifting and unstable nature of love—the opposite of that portrayed in *Romeo and Juliet*. Lysander describes love as:

Momentary as a sound,
Swift as a shadow, short as any dream,
Brief as the lightning in the collied
 night,

        Act I, sc. 1

To live a barren sister all your life,
Chanting faint hymns to the cold fruit-
 less moon.
 [Theseus, Duke of Athens]

        Ibid.

Shall we their fond pageant see?
 [Puck]
Lord, what fools these mortals be!

        Act III, sc. 2

KING HENRY IV, PT. I
1597

Falstaff sweats to death
 [Prince Henry]
And lards the lean earth as he walks
 along.

        Act II, sc. 2

Constant you are,
 [Hotspur]
But yet a woman; and for secrecy,
No lady closer; for I well believe
Thou wilt not utter what thou dost not
 know
And so far will I trust thee, gentle Kate.

        Ibid., sc. 3

There live not three good men
 unhanged in England, and one of
 them is fat and grows old.
 [Falstaff]

        Ibid., sc. 4

You care not who sees your back;
Call you that backing of your friends?

A plague upon such backing.
[Falstaff]

Ibid.

Give you a reason on compulsion!
If reasons were as plentiful as blackberries,
I would give no man a reason upon
    compulsion, I.
[Falstaff]

Ibid.

I can call spirits from the vasty deep.
[Glendower]
Why, so can I, or so can any man;
but will they come when you do call for
    them?
[Hotspur]

Act III, sc. 1

Honor pricks me on. Yea, but how if
honor prick me off when I come on, how
then? Can honour set to a leg? no; or
an arm? no; or take away the grief of a
wound? no. Honour hath no skill in sur-
gery, then? no. What is honour? a word.
What is in that word honour; what is
that honour? air. A trim reckoning! Who
hath it? he that died o' Wednesday. Doth
he feel it? no. Doth he hear it? no. Why?
detraction will not suffer it. Therefore I'll
none of it. Honour is a mere escutcheon.
And so ends my catechism.
    [Falstaff, the most popular of Shake-
    speare's characters, was introduced in
    Henry IV, pt. I, and he was brought
    back in pt. II and in *The Merry Wives
    of Windsor* at Queen Elizabeth's
    request to see a play with Falstaff in
    love. He was a con man and a hero, a
    fool and a philosopher.]

Act V, sc. 2

THE MERCHANT OF VENICE
1596–1598

My ventures are not in one bottom trust
Nor to one place; nor is my whole estate
Upon the fortune of this present year;
Therefore my merchandise makes me
    not sad.
[Antonio]

Act I, sc. 1

I hold the world but as the world,
    Gratiano—
A stage, where every man must play a part,
And mine a sad one.
[Antonio]

Ibid.

His reasons are as two grains of wheat
hid in two bushels of chaff; you shall
seek all day ere you find them, and when
you have them, they are not worth the
search.
[Bassanio]

Ibid.

If to do were as easy as to know what were
good to do, chapels had been churches,
and poor men's cottages princes' palaces.
[Portia]

Ibid., sc. 2

God made him, and therefore let him
pass for a man.
[Portia]

Ibid.

When he is best, he is a little worse than
a man, and when he is worst, he is little
better than a beast.
[Portia]

Ibid.

I will buy with you, sell with you, talk

with you, walk with you, but I will not
eat with you, drink with you, nor pray
with you. What news on the Rialto?
> [Shylock]

Act II, sc. 3

The devil can cite Scripture for his
purpose.
> [Shylock]

Ibid.

I hate him for he is a Christian;
But more for that in low simplicity
He lends out money gratis, and brings
down
The rate of usance here with us in Venice.
> [Shylock]

Ibid.

I like not fair terms and a villain's mind.
> [Bassanio]

Ibid.

If you prick us, do we not bleed? if you
tickle us do we not laugh? If you poison
us, do we not die? and if you wrong us,
shall we not revenge?
> [Shylock]

Act III, sc. 1

Though justice be thy plea, consider this
That in the course of justice, none of us
Should see salvation. We do pray for mercy.
> [Portia]

Act IV, sc. 1

To do a great right, do a little wrong.
And curb this cruel devil in his will.
> [Bassanio]

Ibid.

Is it so nominated in the bond?
> [Shylock]

Ibid.

You take my house when you do take
the prop
That doth sustain my house; you take
my life,
When you do take the means whereby
I live.
> [Shylock]

Ibid.

The man that hath no music in himself,
Nor is mov'd with concord of sweet sounds,
Is fit for treasons, stratagems, and spoils;
> [Lorenzo]

Act V, sc. 1

KING HENRY IV, PT. II
1598

I am not only witty in myself, but the
cause that wit is in other men.
> [Falstaff]

Act 1, sc. 2

It were better to be eaten to death with
rust than to be scoured to nothing with
perpetual motion.
> [Falstaff]

Ibid.

Uneasy lies the head that wears a crown.
> [King Henry]

Act III, sc. 1

A man can die but once; we owe God
a death.
> [Feeble]

Ibid., sc. 2

Presume not that I am the thing I was,
For God doth know...
That I have turned away my former self.
> [King Henry V]

[Hal, Prince of Wales, who had cavorted as a youth with Sir John Falstaff, rebukes Falstaff for saying, "King Hal, my royal Hal" after he becomes King Henry V. Men are transformed by responsibility.]

Act V, sc. 5

KING HENRY V
1599

Once more unto the breach, dear
　　friends, once more;
Or close the wall up with our English
　　dead!
In peace there's nothing so becomes a
　　man
As modest stillness and humility;
But when the blast of war blows in our
　　ears,
Then imitate the action of the tiger;
Stiffen the sinews, summon up the blood
Disguise fair nature with hard favour'd
　　rage;
Then lend the eye a terrible aspect....
I see you stand like greyhounds in the
　　slips,
Straining upon the start. The game's
　　afoot!
Follow your spirit; and upon this charge
Cry "God for Harry! England and Saint
　　George."
　　[King Henry]

Act III, sc. 1

O that we now had here
　　[Westmoreland]
But one ten thousand of those men in
　　England
That do no work today!
What's he that wishes so?
　　[King Henry]

My cousin Westmoreland? No, my fair
　　cousin.
If we are mark'd to die, we are enow
To do our country loss; and if to live,
The fewer men, the greater share of
　　honour....
O, do not wish one more! Rather pro-
　　claim it,
Westmoreland, through my host,
That he which hath no stomach to this
　　fight,
Let him depart; his passport shall be
　　made
And crowns for convoy put into his purse.
We would not die in that man's
　　company
That fears his fellowship to die with us.
This day is called the feast of Crispian.
He that outlives this day, and comes safe
　　home,
Will stand a tip toe when this day is
　　named....
This story shall the good man teach his
　　son;
And Crispin Crispian shall ne'er go by,
From this day to the ending of the world,
But we in it shall be remembered
We few, we happy few, we band of
　　brothers;
For he today that sheds his blood with me
Shall be my brother; be he never so vile,
This day shall gentle his condition.
And gentlemen in England, now abed,
Shall think themselves accursed they
　　were not here;
And hold their manhood's cheap whiles
　　any speaks
That fought with us upon Saint Crisp-
　　in's day.

Act IV, sc. 3

King Henry at Agincourt in 1415 defeated 20,000 Frenchmen while suffering minimal losses. Of the 7,500 English,

5,500 were longbowmen. Henry's army was arrayed on a hill overlooking an hour-glass-shaped field narrowing into rain-soaked bog into which the French cavalry charged into rows of wooden spikes covered by longbows, whose arrows penetrated steel plate. The English had earlier beaten armored French knights with the longbow in 1346 at Crècy. The longbow (Welsh origin) generated its extraordinary power from its length and yew wood, whose outside (sap wood) was flexible and inside extremely hard. It had the equivalent power of a crossbow (invented c. 850), but a rate of fire six times faster. The triumph of the longbow over aristocratic armored cavalry meant feudalism would fall to the peasant armies of kings.

MUCH ADO ABOUT NOTHING
1598–1600

He wears his faith but as the fashion of
    his hat, it ever changes with the next
    block.
[Beatrice]
                                    Act I, sc. 1

Everyone can master a grief but he that
    has it.
[Benedict]
                                  Act III, sc. 2

The fashion wears out more apparel
    than the man.
[Conrad]
                                   Ibid., sc. 3

If two men ride a horse, one must ride
    behind.
[Dogberry]
                                   Ibid., sc. 5

AS YOU LIKE IT
1599

All the world's a stage,
    [Jaques De Boys]
And all the men and women merely
    players.
They have their exits and their entrances;
And one man in his time plays many
    parts,
His acts being seven ages. At first the
    infant,
Mewling and puking in the nurse's arms.
Then the whining schoolboy, with his
    satchel
And shining morning face, creeping like
    snail
Unwillingly to school. And then the lover,
Sighing like a furnace, with a woeful
    ballad
Made to his mistress's eyebrow. Then a
    soldier,
Full of strange oaths, and bearded like
    the pard,
Jealous in honour, sudden and quick in
    quarrel,
Seeking the bubble reputation
Even in the cannon's mouth....
Last scene of all,
That ends this strange eventful history,
Is second childishness and mere oblivion,
Sans teeth, sans eyes, sans taste, sans
    everything.
                                   Act II, sc. 7

Sell when you can, you are not for all
    markets.
[Rosalind]
                                  Act III, sc. 5

Twelfth Night
1601

If music be the food of love, play on;
Give me excess of it, that, surfeiting;
The appetite may sicken, and so die,
[Orsino, Duke of Illyria]

Act I, sc. 1

Many a good hanging prevents a bad
marriage.
[Clown]

Ibid., sc. 5

Then come kiss me, sweet and twenty,
Youth's a stuff will not endure.
[Clown]

Act II, sc. 3

…but be not afraid of greatness;
some are born great, some achieve
greatness,
and some have greatness thrust upon
them.
[Malvolio]

Act II, sc. 5

This fellow's wise enough to play the fool.
[Viola]

Act III, sc. 1

This is very midsummer madness.
[Olivia]

Act III, sc. 4

If this were played upon a stage now,
I could condemn it as improbable fiction.
[Fabian]

Ibid.

Julius Caesar
1599

This play highlights the difference
between public and private virtue. Brutus
sought "Peace, freedom and liberty," but
he caused a civil war because his private
scruples prevented him from killing Antony when he had him in his power.

Beware the ides of March.
[Soothsayer]

Act I, sc. 1

Why, man, he doth bestride the narrow
world
Like a Colossus; and we petty men
Walk under his huge legs, and peep about
To find ourselves dishonorable graves.
Men at some time are masters of their
fates;
The fault, dear Brutus, is not in our stars,
But in ourselves, that we are underlings….
Upon what meat doth this our Caesar
feed,
That he is grown so great? Age, thou art
shamed
Rome, thou hast lost the breed of noble
bloods!
[Cassius]

Act I, sc. 2

Let me have men about me that are fat;
Sleek-headed men and such as sleep
o'nights;
Yon Cassius has a lean and hungry look;
He thinks too much; such men are
dangerous.
[Caesar]

Ibid.

Cowards die many times before their
death;

The valiant never taste of death but once.
  [Caesar]

Act II, sc. 2

O! Pardon me, thou bleeding piece of
  earth,
That I am meek and gentle with these
  butchers....
Cry "Havoc!" and let slip the dogs of war.
  [Antony]

Act III, sc. 1

Friends, Romans countrymen, lend me
your ears;
  [Antony]
I come to bury Caesar, not to praise him.
The evil that men do lives after them,
The good is oft interred with their bones.

Ibid., sc. 2

I am no orator, as Brutus is;
  [Antony]
But (as you know me all) a plain blunt
  man,
That love my friend....
For I have neither wit, nor words, nor
  worth,
Action, nor utterance, nor the power of
  speech,
To stir men's blood: I only speak right on;
I tell you that which you yourselves do
  know.

Ibid.

For Brutus is an honorable man;
So are they all, all honorable men.
  [Antony]

Ibid.

When the poor have cried, Caesar hath
  wept;
Ambition should be made of sterner stuff.
  [Antony]

Ibid.

There is a tide in the affairs of men
  Which, taken at the flood, leads on
  to fortune;
Omitted, all the voyage of their life
Is bound in shallows and in miseries.
We must take the current when it serves,
Or lose our ventures.
  [Brutus]

Act IV, sc. 3

O, that a man might know
The end of this day's business ere it
  come!
But it sufficeth that the day will end,
And then the end is known.
  [Brutus]

Act V, sc. 5

This was the noblest Roman of them all.
All the conspirators save only he
Did that they did in envy of great
  Caesar;
He, only in a general honest thought
And common good to all, made one of
  them.
His life was gentle, and the elements
So mix'd in him that Nature might
  stand up
And say to all the world, "This was a
  man!"
  [Antony speaking of Brutus.]

Ibid.

HAMLET
1601

Hamlet, which has been performed more
than any other play in history, is the subject of volumes of conflicting interpretations. One view is that he is an indecisive
man swept along by events. Another is
that he is right to doubt the charges of a
ghost and prudently waits to find proof,
after which he moves resolutely toward

revenge. In *Hamlet,* as in the other great tragedies, *Lear, Macbeth,* and *Othello,* the hero is transformed during the play so that we no longer fixate on his plight but marvel at his spirit of triumph in defeat. Hamlet is transformed from a deep depression where the world is "an unweeded garden." He comes to understand man is not a free agent, but that "a divinity shapes our ends" so that success or failure is not as important as that a man strive under the conditions in which he finds himself. In the grave digger's scene, Hamlet faces the worst of the human condition and steels himself. In scene 2 of the last act, Hamlet is finally at peace with himself, spurning his friend Horatio's plea to cancel the fencing match with Laertes by saying:

> Not a whit, we defy augury. There is special providence in the fall of a sparrow. If it be now, 'tis not to come; if it be not to come; it will be now; if it be not now, yet it will come. The readiness is all.

> If thou art privy to thy country's fate, which, happily, foreknowing may avoid, O speak—
> [Horatio]
>
> Act I, sc. 1

> That this too solid flesh would melt, Thaw, and resolve itself into a dew! Or that the Everlasting had not fix'd His canon 'gainst self-slaughter! O God! God! How weary, stale, flat, and unprofitable Seem to me all the uses of this world! Fie on't, ah fie, 'tis an unweeded garden That grows to seed.... Frailty, thy name is woman!
> [Hamlet]
>
> Ibid., sc. 2

Those friends thou hast, and their
   adoption tried,
Grapple them to thy soul with hoops of
   steel.
   [Polonius]

Ibid., sc. 3

Beware of entrance to a quarrel, but
   being in,
Bear't that the opposed may beware of
   thee.
Give every man thy ear, but few thy
   voice;
Take each man's censure, but reserve thy
   judgment.
Costly thy habit as thy purse can buy,
But not express'd in fancy; rich, not gaudy;
For the apparel oft proclaims the man.
   [Polonius]

Ibid.

Neither a borrower, nor a lender be;
For loan oft loses both itself and friend,
And borrowing dulls the edge of
   husbandry.
This above all; to thine own self be true.
And it must follow as the night the day,
Thou canst not then be false to any man.
   [Polonius]

Ibid.

Something is rotten in the state of
   Denmark.
   [Marcellus]

Ibid., sc. 4

There are more things in heaven and
   earth, Horatio,
Than are dreamt of in your philosophy.
   [Hamlet, after seeing his father's
   ghost]

Ibid., sc. 5

The time is out of joint. O cursed spite,
That ever I was born to set it right.
   [Hamlet]
                          Ibid.

By indirections, find directions out.
   [Polonius]
                   Act II, sc. 1

Brevity is the soul of wit.
   [Polonius]
                   Ibid., sc. 2

More matter with less art
   [Gertrude—asking Polonius to
   speak plainly.]
                       Ibid.

"Doubt thou the stars are fire,
Doubt that the sun doth move;
Doubt truth to be a liar,
But never doubt I love."
   [From Hamlet's letter to Ophelia]
                       Ibid.

What do you read, my lord?
   [Polonius]
Words, words, words.
   [Hamlet]
                       Ibid.

Though this be madness, yet there is a
   method in't.
   [Polonius]
                       Ibid.

There is nothing either good or bad but
   thinking makes it so.
   [Hamlet]
                       Ibid.

O God, I could be bounded in a nut-
   shell and count myself a king of

infinite space, were it not that I have
bad dreams.
   [Hamlet]
                       Ibid.

What a piece of work is man! how
   noble in reason! how infinite in
   faculties! in form and moving how
   express and admirable! in action
   how like an angel! in apprehension
   how like a god! the beauty of the
   world! the paragon of animals! And
   yet, to me, what is this quintessence
   of dust? Man delights not me.
   [Hamlet]
                       Ibid.

To be, or not to be: that is the question:
Whether 'tis nobler in the mind to suffer
The slings and arrows of outrageous
   fortune,
Or to take arms against a sea of troubles,
And by opposing end them? To die—to
   sleep
No more; and by a sleep to say we end
The Heartache, and the thousand natu-
   ral shocks
That flesh is heir to. 'Tis a consummation
Devoutly to be wish'd. To die—to sleep.
To sleep: perchance to dream: ay, there's
   the rub!
For in that sleep of death what dreams
   may come
When we have shuffled off this mortal coil,
Must give us pause....
But that the dread of something after
   death
The undiscover'd country, from whose
   bourn
No traveler returns—puzzles the will,
And makes us rather bear those ills we
   have
Than fly to others that we know not of.

Thus conscience does make cowards of
  us all...
And enterprises of great pith and moment
With this regard their currents turn awry
And lose the name of action....
  [Hamlet]
                              Act III, sc. 1

Get thee to a nunnery: why wouldst
  thou be a breeder of sinners?
  [Hamlet]
                                    Ibid.

Be thou as chaste as ice, as pure as snow,
thou shalt not escape calumny.
  [Hamlet]
                                    Ibid.

Madness in great ones must not
  unwatch'd go.
  [King Claudius]
                                    Ibid.

Our wills and fates do so contrary run
That our devices still are overthrown:
Our thoughts are ours, their ends none
  of our own.
  [Player King]
                              Ibid., sc. 2

For 'tis a question left us yet to prove,
Whether love lead fortune, or
    else fortune love.
  [Player King]
                              Ibid., sc. 2

The lady doth protest too much,
  methinks.
  [Queen Gertrude]
                                    Ibid.

It's now the very witching time of night,
When churchyards yawn and hell itself
    breathes out

Contagion to this world: now could I
  drink hot blood,
And do such bitter business as the day
Would quake to look on.
  [Hamlet]
                                    Ibid.

"Forgive me my foul murder?"
That cannot be: since I am still possess'd
Of those effects for which I did the murder.
My crown, mine own ambition, and my
  queen.
May one be pardoned and retain th'
  offense?...
My words fly up, my thoughts remain
  below.
Words without thoughts never to heaven go.
  [King Claudius]
                              Ibid., sc. 3

Hamlet, speak no more:
Thou turn'st mine eyes into my very soul.
  [Queen Gertrude]
                              Ibid., sc. 4

Assume a virtue if you have it not,...
For use can almost change the stamp of
nature.
  [Hamlet]
                                    Ibid.

I must be cruel only to be kind.
  [Hamlet]
                                    Ibid.

Now, Hamlet, where's Polonius?
  [King Claudius]
At supper.
  [Hamlet]
At supper? Where?
  [King Claudius]
Not where he eats, but where'a is eaten.
  A certain convocation of politic
    worms are e'en at him....We fat all

creatures else to fat us, and we fat
ourselves for maggots. Your fat king
and your lean beggar is but variable service—two dishes, but to one
table. That's the end.
[Hamlet]

Act IV, sc. 3

Lord, we know what we are, but know
not what we may be.
[Ophelia]

Ibid., sc. 5

When sorrows come, they come not
single spies,
But in battalions.
[King Claudius]

Ibid.

Alas, poor Yorick! I knew him, Hortio:
a fellow of infinite jest, of most excellent
fancy; he hath borne me on his back a
thousand times;
[Hamlet]

Act V, sc. 1

Let Hercules himself do what he may,
The cat will mew and dog will have his
day.
[Hamlet]

Ibid.

Not awhit, we defy augury; there's a special providence in the fall of a sparrow. If
it be now, 'tis not to come; if it be not to
come, it will be now; if it be not now, yet
it will come; the readiness is all.
[Hamlet]

Act V, sc. 2

The rest is silence.
[Hamlet's last words]

Ibid.

Now cracks a noble heart. Good night
sweet prince,
And flights of angels sing thee to thy rest!
[Horatio]

Ibid.

MEASURE FOR MEASURE
1604

Our doubts are traitors,
And make us lose the good we off
might win
By fearing to attempt.
[Lucio]

Act I, sc. 4

Some rise by sin, and some by virtue fall.
[Escalus]

Act II, sc. 1

Yet show some pity,
[Isabella]
I show it most of all when I show justice,
For then I pity those I do not know.
[Angelo]

Act II, sc. 2

The law hath not been dead, though it
hath slept.
[Angelo]
[Justifying the execution of one for
violating a law that heretofore had
not be enforced.]

Ibid.

Oh, it is excellent
To have a giant's strength, but it is
tyrannous
To use it like a giant.
[Isabella]

Ibid.

But man, proud man,
[Isabella]

Drest in a little brief authority,
Most ignorant of what he's most assured,
His glassy essence, like an angry ape,
Plays such fantastic tricks before high
    heaven
As make the angels weep.

Ibid.

The miserable have no other medicine
But only hope.
    [Claudio]

Act III, sc. 1

Be absolute for death. Either death or life
Shall thereby be sweeter. Reason thus
    with life:
If I do lose thee, I do lose a thing
That none but fools would keep.
    [Duke]

Ibid.

OTHELLO
1602–04

This morality play spotlights three characters. "Honest Iago," an ambitious lieutenant, is the quintessence of evil, who maintains a false image of being a plain-speaking soldier. He prompts Othello to murder his wife, Desdemona, who is moved by unselfish love and is alone what she seems to be. Guileless, she is falsely accused of treachery by Iago. Othello, failing to understand men can be pure evil, is duped by Iago into murdering Desdemona, which leads him to committing suicide.

The Moor is of a free and open nature,
That thinks men honest that but seem
    to be so,
And will as tenderly be led by th' nose

As asses are.
    [Iago]

Act I, sc. 3

Reputation is...oft got without merit,
    and lost without deserving.
    [Iago]

Act II, sc. 3

Who steals my purse steals trash; 'tis
    something, nothing;
'Twas mine, 'tis his, and has been slave
    to thousands;
But he that filches from me my good
    name
Robs me of that which not enriches him,
And makes me poor indeed.
    [Iago]

Act III, sc. 3

I will in Cassio's lodging lose this napkin,
And let him find it. Trifles light as air
Are to the jealous confirmations strong
As proofs of holy writ; this may do
    something.
    [Iago]

Ibid.

Of one that loved not wisely but too well;
Of one not easily jealous, but, being
    wrought,
Perplex'd in the extreme; of one whose
    hand,
Like the base Indian, threw a pearl away
Richer than all his tribe;
    [Othello stabs himself over his loss
    of Desdemona.]

Act V, sc. 2

KING LEAR
1605–06

This play shows Shakespeare's most pessimistic view in two related stories of filial ingratitude. King Lear tests his daughters' love by their praise. His favorite, Cordelia, refuses to participate, so Lear disowns her, the only daughter who loves him. He abdicates his power to his other daughters, Goneril and Regan, who cast him out. Similarly, the Earl of Gloucester disinherits his loyal son, Edgar, and draws near his duplicitous bastard, Edmund, who hangs Cordelia and prompts the murder/suicide of Goneril and Regan. The king sees all in which he believed crumble. The wicked perish, but so do the good, the consequence of the careless loosing of evil. The fool tells Lear: "Thou shouldst not have been old till thou hadst been wise."

> For I want that glib and oily art, To
>   speak and purpose not.
>   [Cordelia]
>
>   Act I, sc. 1

> How sharper than a serpent's tooth it is
>   to have a thankless child!
>   [Lear]
>
>   Ibid., sc. 4

> Blow, winds, and crack your cheeks!
>   rage! blow!
> You cataracts and hurricanes, spout.
>   [Lear]
>
>   Act III, sc. 2

> I am a man
> More sinn'd against than sinning.
>   [Lear]
>
>   Ibid.

> Oh! that way madness lies; let me shun
>   that.
>   [Lear]
>
>   Ibid., sc. 4

> He's mad that trusts in the tameness of
>   a wolf, a horse's health, a boy's love,
>   or a whore's oath.
>   [Fool]
>
>   Ibid. sc. 6

> As flies to wanton boys are we to the gods.
> They kill us for their sport.
>   [Gloucester]
>
>   Act IV, sc. 1

> When we are born, we cry that we are
> come to this great stage of fools.
>   [Lear]
>
>   Ibid., sc. 6

> I am a very foolish, fond old man,
> Fourscore and upward, not an hour
>   more or less;
> And, to deal plainly, I fear I am not in
>   my perfect mind.
>   [Lear]
>
>   Ibid., sc. 7

MACBETH
1606

After the witches tell Macbeth he will be king, Lady Macbeth urges him to murder Duncan, who is king of Scotland and their houseguest. Macbeth understands fully the evil of murdering Duncan and the wife and babes of Macduff, Duncan's successor. Yet the villainy of Macbeth and Lady Macbeth does not rise to the pure evil of Iago and Richard III, because the Macbeths are at least troubled in their consciences.

> When shall we three meet again
>   [First Witch]
> In thunder, lightning, or in rain?
> When the hurly burly's done
>   [Second Witch]

When the battle's lost and won.
                              Act I, sc. 1

Fair is foul, and foul is fair;
     [Witches]
Hover through the fog and filthy air.
                              Ibid.

And oftentimes, to win us to our harm,

The instruments of darkness tell us truths,
Win us with honest trifles, to betray's
In deepest consequence.
     [Banquo]
     [The Devil deceives by statements
     which are true in a certain sense.]
                              Ibid., sc. 3

Nothing in his life
     [Malcolm]
Became him like the leaving it; he died
As one that had been studied in his death
To throw away the dearest thing he owned,
As 'twere a careless trifle.
                              Ibid., sc. 4

Yet do I fear thy nature; It is too full o'
the milk of human kindness.
     [Lady Macbeth]
                              Ibid., sc. 5

If it were done when 'tis done, then
     'twere well
It were done quickly;
     [Macbeth]
                              Ibid., sc. 7

But screw your courage to the sticking
     place,
And we'll not fail.
     [Lady Macbeth]
                              Ibid.

The bell invites me.
Hear it not, Duncan; for it is a knell
That summons thee to heaven or to hell.
     [Macbeth]
                              Act II, sc. 1

The primrose way to the everlasting
     bonfire.
     [Porter]
                              Ibid., sc. 3

But now I am cabin'd, cribb'd, confined,
     bound in
To saucy doubts and fears.
     [Macbeth]
                              Act III, sc. 4

Stand not upon the order of your going,
But go at once.
     [Lady Macbeth]
                              Ibid.

Double, double toil and trouble;
Fire burn and cauldron bubble.
     [Witches]
                              Act IV, sc. 1

Something wicked this way comes.
     [Witch]
                              Ibid.

Be bloody, bold, and resolute, laugh to
     scorn
The power of man, for none of woman
     born
Shall harm Macbeth.
     [Second Apparition]
                              Ibid.

Macbeth shall never vannquish'd be until
Great Birnam wood to high Dunsinane
     hill
Shall come against him.
     [Third Apparition]
                              Ibid.

Out, damned spot! Out I say....
Here's the smell of blood still, and
All the perfumes of Arabia will not
    sweeten this little hand.
    [Lady Macbeth]
                    Act V, sc. 1

Tomorrow, and tomorrow, and tomorrow,
Creeps in this petty pace from day to day,
To the last syllable of recorded time;
And all our yesterdays have lighted fools
The way to dusty death.
Out, out, brief candle!
Life's but a walking shadow, a poor player
That struts and frets his hour upon the
    stage,
And then is heard no more; it is a tale
Told by an idiot, full of sound and fury,
Signifying nothing.
    [Macbeth]
                    Ibid., sc. 5

To doubt th' equivocation of the fiend,
That lies like truth. "Fear not, till Birnam
    wood
Do come to Dunsinane!"
    [Macbeth]
                    Ibid.

I gin to be a-weary of the sun,
    [Macbeth]
And wish th' estate o' th' world were
    now undone.
Ring the alarm bell! Blow wind! come,
    wrack!
At least we'll die with harness on our
    back.
                    Ibid.
Lay on, Macduff
And damn'd be him that first cries,
    "Hold enough!"
    [Macbeth]
                    Ibid., sc. 8

TIMON OF ATHENS
1607

Tis necessary he should die.
Nothing emboldens sin so much as mercy.
    [Senate]
                    Act III, sc. 5

Everyman has his fault, and honesty is his.
    [Lucullus]
                    Act III, sc. 1

CYMBELINE
1609–10

As chaste as unsunn'd snow.
    [Posthumus]
                    Act II, sc. 5

Golden lads and girls all must,
As chimney sweepers, come to dust.
    [Guiderius]
                    Act IV, sc. 2

Fortune brings in some boats that are
    not steered.
    [Pisanio]
                    Act IV, sc. 3

THE WINTER'S TALE
1610

Let me have no Lying; it becomes none
    but tradesmen.
    [Autolycus]
                    Act IV, sc. 4

Although I am not naturally honest, I
    am so sometimes by chance.
    [Autolycus]
                    Ibid.

THE TEMPEST
1611

This was Shakespeare's last play, and many see its protagonist, Prospero, as being Shakespeare himself. Each has traversed a long spiritual journey. The surface of the comedy is light and fantastical, although betrayal and conspiracy underlie it. Prospero, Duke of Milan, is overthrown by his brother, Antonio, aided by Alonso, Duke of Naples. Prospero and his daughter, Miranda, are cast adrift in a small boat. They land on a magical island inhabited by Ariel, a puckish spirit, and Caliban, a misshapen son of a witch.

In the end, love wins out. The tempest that sinks Antonio and Alonso's ship next to the island is more of a baptism than like the deadly storm that broke King Lear—no one dies. Miranda is married to Ferdinand, son of Alonso, after Prospero forgives Alonso, who has been transformed and returned to a "clear life." Prospero declares, "I'll drown my book" referring to his book of magic, as he prepares to join the banquet, which appears to be a holy communion. Yet this remains the real world, for there is no redemption for Antonio or Caliban. Shakespeare's parting vision may have been that while treachery and violence are part of life, its essence remains beauty and wonder.

> My library was dukedom large enough.
>   [Prospero]
> > > Act I, sc. 2

> What is past is prologue.
>   [Antonio]
> > > Act II, sc. 1

> Our revels now are ended. These our
>   actors,

As I foretold you, were all spirits and
Are melted into air, into thin air;
And, like the baseless fabric of this vision,
The cloud capp'd towers, the gorgeous
    palaces,
The solemn temples, the great globe itself,
Yea, all which it inherit shall dissolve
And, like this insubstantial pageant
    faded
Leave not a rack behind. We are such
    stuff
As dreams are made of, and our little life
Is rounded with a sleep.
    [Prospero]
> > > Act IV, sc. 1

O, wonder!
How many goodly creatures are there
    here!
How beauteous mankind is! O brave
    new world
That hath such people in it!
    [Miranda, speaking of young men.]
> > > Act V, sc. 1

As you from crimes would pardon'd be,
Let your indulgence set me free.
> > > Epilogue
    [Shakespeare's own farewell.]

SONNETS

Shall I compare thee to a summer's day?
Thou art more lovely and more temperate.
Rough winds do shake the darling buds
    of May,
And summer's lease hath all too short a
    date:
Sometimes too hot the eye of heaven
    shines,
And often is his gold complexion
    dimmed:
And every fair from fair sometime
    declines,

By chance, or nature's changing course,
    untrimmed:
But thy eternal summer shall not fade
Nor lose possession of that fair thou
    owest;
Nor shall Death brag thou wanderest in
    his shade
When in eternal lines to time thou
    growest,
So long as men can breathe or eyes can
    see
So long lives this, and this gives life to
    thee.

Sonnet 18

Let me not to the marriage of true minds
Admit impediments; love is not love
Which alters when it alteration finds,
Or bends with the remover to remove.
O' no, it is an ever-fixed mark
That looks on tempests and is never
    shaken;
It is the star to every wand'ring bark,
Whose worth's unknown, although his
    height be taken
Love's not Time's fool, though rosy lips
    and cheeks
Within his bending sickle's compass
    come;
Love alters not with his brief hours and
    weeks,
But bears it out even to the edge of doom.
If this be error and upon me proved,
I never writ, nor no man ever loved.

Sonnet 116

Th' expense of spirit in a waste of shame
Is lust in action; and, till action, lust
Is perjured, murd'rous, bloody, full of
    blame,
Savage, extreme, rude, cruel, not to trust;
Enjoyed no sooner but despised straight;
Past reason hunted, and no sonner had,
Past reason hated as a swallowed bait

On purpose laid to make the taker mad;
Mad in pursuit, and in possession so;
Had, having, and in quest to have,
    extreme;
A bliss in proof, and proved a very woe,
Before a joy proposed; behind, a dream.
All this the world well knows, yet none
knows well
To shun the heaven that leads men to
    this hell.

Sonnet 129

JAMES I
1566–1629

Scottish, king of Scotland and Great Britain (1603–25), and son of Mary, Queen of Scots. He claimed to rule by divine right. He said at his coronation, "No bishop, no king."

In 1611, James commissioned fifty-eight scholars to translate a new Bible, the *King James Bible*, which transformed Greek into moving prose. James' Bible and Cranmer's *Book of Common Prayer* (1552) stand at the pinnacle of English literature.

The state of monarchy is the supremest thing upon earth; for kings are not only God's lieutenants upon earth, and sit upon God's throne, but even by God they are called gods.

I can make a Lord, but only God can make a gentleman.

Have you not reason then to be ashamed, and to forbear this filthie noveltie... a custome loathsome to the eye, hateful to the nose, harmful to the brain, dangerous to the lungs, and in the black stinking fume thereof, nearest resembling the horrible Stygian smoke of the pit that is bottomlesse.

[On tobacco.]

SIR HENRY WOTTON
1568–1639

English, diplomat and poet.

This man is free from servile bands,
Of hope to rise, or fear to fall:
Lord of himself, though not of lands;
And having nothing, yet hath all.
  "The Character of a Happy Life" (1641), st. 6

An ambassador is an honest man sent abroad to lie for the good of his country.
  Reliquiae Wottonianae (1651)

JOHANNES KEPLER
1571–1630

German, who discovered that the planetary orbits were elliptical.

I give myself up to divine ecstasy… My book is written. It will be read either by my contemporaries or by posterity—I care not which. It may well wait a hundred years for a reader, as God has waited 6,000 years for someone to understand his work.
  [Referring to Astronomia Nova (1609).]

JOHN DONNE
1572–1631

English, Anglican minister, dean of St. Paul's, and a "metaphysical poet." His

Holy Sonnet XIV welcomed God's harsh action to give him salvation: "That I may rise and stand, o'erthrow me, and bend your force to break, blow, burn and make me new."

New Philosophy calls all in doubt…
The Sun is lost, and th'earth, and no
    man's wit
Can well direct him where to look for it.
…Tis all in pieces, all coherence gone.
All just supply, and all Relation.
Prince, Subject, Father, Son, are things
    forgot.
  [Of Copernicus's cosmology.]
    An Anatomy of the World (1611)

Death, be not proud, though some have
    called thee
Mighty and dreadful, for thou are not so;
For those whom thou think's thou dost
    overthrow
Die not, poor Death, nor yet canst thou
    kill me….
Why swell'st thou then? One short
    sleep past, we wake eternally,
And death shall be no more. Death,
    thou shalt die.
        "Death Be Not Proud" (1612),
          Holy Sonnets (1633)

No man is an island, entire of itself; every man is a piece of the Continent, a part of the maine; if a clod be washed away by the sea, Europe is the less… any man's death diminishes me, because I am involved in mankind; and therefore never send to know for whom the bell tolls; it tolls for thee.
  Devotions upon Emergent Occasions,
    XVII (1624)

BEN JONSON
1572–1637

English, comedic playwright, critic, and poet laureate who was held in higher regard than Shakespeare during his era. He was best known for *The Alchemist* (1610) and *Volpone, or The Fox* (1606). He escaped the death penalty for dueling by claiming "benefit of clergy" (the ancient defense to execution of reading the Latin Bible). Those using this legal defense were branded on the thumb so they could not use the defense twice. Jonson's plays embodied the four medieval humors: blood (temper), melancholy (depression), choler (irascibility), and phlegm (sluggishness).

Apes are apes though clothed in scarlet.
Poetaster (1601), act V, sc. 1

I glory
More in the cunning purchase of my wealth
Than in the glad possession.
[An old man (the fox) feigns illness to get legacy hunters, Voltore (vulture), Corbaccio (crow), and Corvino (raven), to give him substantial gifts, including borrowing Corbaccio's wife for a night.]
Volpone (1606), act I, sc. 1

Come my Celia, let us prove,
While we can, the sports of love;
Time will not be ours forever,
He at length our good will sever.
Spend not then his gifts in vain;
Suns that set may rise again,
But if once we lose this light,
'Tis with us perpetual night.
"Song to Celia" (1607)

Drink to me only with thine eyes,
And I will pledge with mine;
Or leave a kiss but in the cup,
And I'll not look for wine.
The Forest (1616)
"To Celia" st. 1

Thou art a monument without a tomb,
And art alive still, while thy book doth live,
And we have wits to read, and praise to give.
"To the Memory of My Beloved, the Author Mr. William Shakespeare" (1623)

Triumph, my Britain, thou hast one to show
To whom all scenes of Europe homage owe.
He was not of an age but for all time!
Ibid.

O Rare Ben Jonson.
Epitaph at Westminster

ROBERT BURTON
1577–1640

English, clergyman.

They lard their lean books with the fat of others' works.
The Anatomy of Melancholy (1621-51)
"Democritus to the Reader"

A dwarf standing on the shoulders of a giant may see farther than a giant himself.
Ibid.

There is no greater cause of melancholy than idleness.
Ibid.

THOMAS MIDDLETON
1570–1627

English, playwright known for the comic *Women Beware Women* (1631) and the tragedy *The Changeling* (1623).

There's scarce a thing but is both loved and loathed.
> *The Changeling* (1622), act 1, sc. 1

In the election of a wife, as in
A project of war, to err but once is
To be undone forever.
> *Anything for a Quiet Life* (c. 1627)

The slowest kiss makes too much haste.
> *A Chaste Maid in Cheapside* (1607), act 4

PETER MINUIT
1580–1638

Dutch, agent for the Dutch West India Company. He bought Manhattan Island from the Canarsie Indians in 1626 for twenty-four dollars worth of wampum beads, metal knives, and wool blankets, to found New Amsterdam. Had the Canarsie invested that twenty-four dollars at a 10 percent return (the average return on common stocks over the past two hundred years), the principal would have doubled every 7.2 years and now be far more than enough to buy back the island in 2006 with its improvements. The Carnarsie won the trade, but did not invest prudently.

RICHELIEU
1585–1642

French, cardinal (Red Eminence), chief minister under Louis XIII. He made the monarchy master over the nobility and France the leading European power. He persecuted the Huguenots for being "a state within a state." He saved Protestant Germany by allying with it against the Catholic Hapsburgs (Austria, Spain, Italy, and the Netherlands). His centralization of power made France Europe's most statist nation, which continues until today. In 1634 he founded the French Academy for literature.

Richelieu elaborated the principle that foreign affairs are governed by weaker moral principles than domestic affairs. He called it *raison d'état*.

If you give me six lines written by the hand of the most honest of men, I will find something in them which will hang him.

Nothing so upholds the laws as the punishment of persons whose rank is as great as their crime.
> Richelieu, *Oeuvres*

Never write a letter; never destroy one.

THOMAS HOBBES
1588–1679

English, the "gloomy philosopher," who argued that a state receives its legitimacy from the people, not God. People need a sovereign because their highest value is self-preservation, for which they must live in society. Being selfish, the people need an all-powerful sovereign to protect every man from his neighbors. That is, to avoid a "state of nature," man gives up some of his freedom to a common sovereign, the state, or "Leviathan," which must have absolute power. The sovereign could be a king, Parliament, and so on. Each is bound to obey all laws, even those one considers to be "unjust," so that all others will be equally bound to obey all laws. Like the Romans, Hobbes' inalienable rights are natural rights, not ones granted by Providence.

Hobbes' view that man is naturally rapacious is the keystone of the American Constitution. Madison constructed a constitution of checks and balances in order that "ambition must be made to counteract ambition." Hobbes modernized the old idea of Aristotle that the purpose of the state was to defend property from criminals, domestic and foreign. Today's middle-class citizens cosseted in advanced economies often fail to appreciate how violent life would quickly become without the police and army.

> The obligation of the subjects to the sovereign is understood to last as long, but no longer, than the power lasteth by which he is able to protect them.
>
> *Liberty and Necessity*

> When a covenant is made, then to break it is unjust. And the definition of injustice is no other than the nonperformance of a covenant. And whatsoever is not unjust, is just.
>
> *Leviathan* (1651)

> …where no covenant hath preceded… every man has right to every thing; and consequently, no action can be unjust.
>
> Ibid.

> Intemperance is naturally punished with diseases; rashness, with mischance; injustice, with violence of enemies; pride,

with ruin; cowardice, with oppression; and rebellion, with slaughter.
>
> Ibid.

> *Bellum omnium contra omnes.*
> All warring against all.
>
> Ibid.

> A relentless desire of power in all men. So that in the first place, I put for a general inclination of all mankind, a perpetual and restless desire of power after power that ceaseth only in death.
>
> Ibid., ch. 1

> During the time men live without a common power to keep them all in awe, they are in that condition which is called war; and such a war as is of every man against every man…. Force and fraud are in war the cardinal virtues. In such condition there is no place for Industry because the fruit thereof is uncertain; and consequently no culture; no arts; no letters; no society; and which is worst of all, continual fear and danger of violent death, and the life of man, solitary, poor, nasty, brutish and short.
>
> Ibid., ch. 13

> The world is governed by opinion.
>
> *Elements of Law*, ch. 1

> Democracy is no more than an aristocracy of orators.
>
> Ibid., ch. 2

> Covenants without swords are but words.

> I am about to take my last voyage, a great leap in the dark.
>
> Last words

JOHN WINTHROP
1588–1649

American (born-English), governor of Massachusetts Bay Colony who, in 1630, said to fellow pilgrims on the tiny *Arbella* off the coast of New England:

> We shall be as a city upon a hill. The eyes of all the people are upon us so that if we shall deal falsely with our God in this work we have undertaken, and so cause him to withdraw his present help from us, we shall be made a story and a byword throughout all the world.

WILLIAM BRADFORD
1590–1657

American (English-born), governor of Massachusetts, who hired the *Mayflower*, a wine ship, in 1620, to transport English Puritan Nonconformists who refused to submit to the Romish Church of England. The forty-one heads of household who called themselves "pilgrims" signed the Mayflower Compact, their rules of governance. Succeeding Puritans often came as entire congregations led by their ministers. John Winthrop brought a thousand Anglicans to found Boston.

Roger Williams, after being banished from Massachusetts in 1635, secured a royal charter from King Charles II to found Rhode Island, the first colony to grant freedom of religion as distinguished from religious tolerance. The charter specified "no person within the said colony, at any time hereafter, shall be in any wise molested, punished, disquieted or called in question for any difference of opinion in matters of religion." A forerunner of Locke, Milton,

and Cromwell on natural rights, Williams founded a democracy that clashed with traditional Calvinism, which restricted the voting franchise to church members.

The first written democratic constitution of modern times was The Fundamental Orders of Connecticut (1639) of John Hooker, who left Massachusetts to establish a congregational church free of a Presbyterian aristocracy. Note: Pilgrims were often also Puritans, a word connoting their belief that the Bible was the "pure" word of God.

> They knew they were pilgrims.... So they committed themselves to the will of God and resolved to proceed.... Being thus arrived in a good harbor, and brought safe to land, they fell upon their knees and blessed the God of Heaven who had brought them over the vast and furious ocean and delivered them from all the perils and miseries thereof....And for the season it was winter....sharp and violent, and subject to cruel and fierce storms... and the whole country, full of woods and thickets...a desolate wilderness, full of wilde beasts and wilde men.... If they looked behind them, there was a mighty ocean which they had passed, and was now as a main bar or gulph to separate them from all the civil parts of the world.
>
> From William Bradford, of Plymouth Colony (1620–47)

> Thus out of small beginnings greater things have been produced by His hand that made all things of nothing, and gives being to all things that are; and, as one small candle may light a thousand, so the light here kindled hath shone unto many, yea in some sort to our whole nation.
>
> Ibid.

THANKSGIVING

The first Thanksgiving blessed the harvest with a feast of venison, turkey, corn bread, baked oysters, pumpkin, and popcorn, a specialty of the Wampanoag Indians.

But Virginians assert that the first Thanksgiving was in September 1619 on the founding of the Berkeley Hundred settlement on the James River. The directors proclaimed "that the day of our ship's arrival at the place assigned for the plantation in the land of Virginia shall be yearly and perpetually kept holy as a day of Thanksgiving to Almighty God." George Washington proclaimed Thanksgiving to be a national holiday, fixed in 1941 as the fourth Thursday of November.

For the first three years at Plymouth Colony, all land was held in common, resulting in starvation. The commune, Bradford wrote, had proved the "vanity of that conceit of Plato's...that the taking away of property and bringing community into a commonwealth would make them happy and flourishing." Holding property in common "was found to breed much confusion and discontent and retard much employment that would have been to their benefit and comfort." After dividing the land into private family parcels, Bradford noted:

> This had very good success, for it made all hands very industrious, so as much more corn was planted than otherwise would have been by any means the Governor or any other could [have contrived.] The women now went willingly into the field, and took their little ones with them to set corn; which before would allege weakness and inability; whom to have compelled

would have been thought great tyranny.

Ibid.

In the Jamestown Colony (1607) all production went to a common store, resulting in famine. After a new governor instituted private property, the colony flourished. (See Tom Bethell's *The Noblest Triumph*, 1998). Also, Protestant Christianity promoted industry and thrift. As Cotton Mather said, "Religion brought forth Prosperity, and the daughter destroyed the mother...."

Pilgrims/Puritans have been stereotyped by Hawthorne's *Scarlet Letter*, Miller's *The Crucible*, and so on, as drab, glum, narrow-minded prudes and teetotalers. But they consumed huge quantities of rum, beer, and ale, wore colorful clothing, played games, and relished sex in the confines of marriage. The two dozen witches the New England Puritans executed compares favorably to the 50,000 witches executed in Europe by Catholics. Puritans were politically advanced. For example, Puritan women could inherit, run businesses, and vote in the 1630s.

ROBERT HERRICK
1591–1674

English, one of the greatest Cavalier poets. Also known for fanciful love poems were: John Suckling, Richard Lovelace, and Thomas Carew.

> Give me a kiss, and to that kiss a score;
> Then to that twenty, add a hundred more:
> A thousand to that hundred: so kiss on,
> To make that thousand up a million.
> Treble that million, and when that is done,
> Let's kiss afresh, as when we first begun.
> *Hesperides* (1648), "To Anthea:
> Ah, My Anthea"

Gather ye rosebuds while ye may,
Old Time is till a flying,
And this same flower that smiles today
Tomorrow will be dying.
> Ibid., "To the Virgins to Make Much of
> Time" st. 1

Pray love me little, so you will love me
long.
> Ibid., "Love Me Little, Love Me Long"

Wash, dress, be brief in praying;
Few beads are best, when once we go a
   Maying.
> Ibid., "The Vision"

Whenas in silks my Julia goes,
Then, then (methinks) how sweetly flows
That liquefaction of her clothes.
> Ibid., "Upon Julia's Clothes"

For want of a nail the shoe is lost,
For want of a shoe the horse is lost,
For want of a horse the rider is lost.
> Ibid., no. 499

Show me a liar, and I'll show you a thief.
> Ibid., no. 652

One sword keeps another in its sheath.
> Ibid., no. 723

GEORGE HERBERT
1593–1633

English, metaphysical poet and cleric
known for Jacula Prudentum.

He that will learn to pray, let him go to
   sea.
> Jacula Prudentum (1651)

Deceive not thy physician, confessor,
   nor lawyer.
> Ibid., no. 105

Marry your son when you will; your
   daughter when you can.
> Ibid., no. 149

The best mirror is an old friend.
> Ibid., no. 296

4

THE AGE OF SCIENCE

Francis Bacon initiated the "scientific method," which is to seek truth in the material world without bias, emotion, or regard to taboo by (1) framing a tentative hypothesis, (2) gathering all evidence relating to it, (3) framing a hypothesis, (4) testing the hypothesis in a controlled experiment, (5) recording the results so others could repeat the experiment, and (6) treating the resulting theory as tentative, no matter how often tested. There is no final truth; theories are never "proved." Science means reaching successive and closer approximations to the truth.

Science is the "invention of invention." It is not knowledge, but method only—experimentation and verification. It uses Ockham's Razor: A hypothesis explains observations with the fewest assumptions. This is based upon the "uniformity of nature," that is, that the whole universe obeys the same laws.

The scientific method ended dependence on Aristotle, Galen, Ptolemy, and other "authorities." Indeed, the earliest enemies of science were the rationalists, like Pythagoras and Plato, who argued that observing with the human senses misleads and that truth can be found only through reason. Scientists began to observe for themselves, whence came the motto of the Royal Society: *Nullius in Verba* ("Take nobody's word for it"). Paracelsus (1493–1541) even began his lectures on medicine by burning one of Galen's books. Science did not contend so much with ignorance as with false ideas.

Science was born in a culture of a benevolent, noncapricious God whose laws were immutable and were thus worth discovering. Science was not born in China, which lacked a personal God, and Islam expelled it because Islam's theology taught that God does not operate through constant laws. Rodney Stark in *For the Glory of God: How Monotheism Led to Science*...(2003) notes that in science's golden age (1543–1680) that of the 52 leading scientists, 25 were Catholics, 25 were Protestants, and only two were free thinkers.

Science and Christianity did have to take account of each other. For example, Copernicus challenged the Bible as literal truth when he hypothesized that the earth rotated on its axis and revolved around the sun. John Donne wrote, "The sun is lost, and th'Earth, and no man's wit can well direct him where to look for it…. Tis all in pieces, all coherence gone." But Christianity slowly accepted that, as Jesus spoke in Parables, the Bible was metaphor, and that as Thomas Aquinas wrote, God gave man intelligence as a tool to find truth. This came with sacrifices, for example, in 1600, Giordano Bruno was burned for his heretical belief in atoms.

While the scientific method flowered, Europe engaged in bloody religious wars, even though Jesus had exalted toleration. Repelled by religious conflict, the Enlightenment following the Age of Science freed Europe from a potential theocracy, which had stifled Islam. Yet the dark side of the Enlightenment denigrated spiritual life. That invited the horrors of the French Revolution and the twentieth-century's socialist holocausts.

Before the Age of Science, Western and Eastern cultures were different, but their technologies were equivalent. Afterward, Western discoveries came thick and fast while discovery in the East atrophied. Modern science emerged in the West and nowhere else. Critical to Western science was the push given by private corporations that converted discoveries into profits. Science and free markets are the articulated propellers of Western prosperity.

William Whewell coined the word "science" in 1840 to distinguish between investigating nature and speculating on what it meant (philosophy).

RENÉ DESCARTES
1596–1650

French, mathematician, scientist, and "father of modern rationalism." He grounded philosophy in logic and mathematics, that is, in intuition and deduction, and not in experience. In math, intuition discovers self-evident axioms and postulates from which truth is deduced, for example, "A straight line is the shortest distance between two points." Like Plato, Descartes dismissed truth founded upon sensory perception. His proof by logic opposes empiricism, which is based on sensory perception.

Basing his philosophy on pure reason, he extrapolated from the premise, "*Cogito ergo sum,*" or "I think therefore I am," or the existence of the thinking self. The proof of the mind is inherent in its disproof, that is, in the attempt to cast doubt on it: "I doubt that I exist." "But if I do not exist, then who is doing all of this doubting?" He could not doubt that he doubted, so he must exist.

Descartes, a Deist, only allowed for God to set physical laws in motion. He opposed Aristotle's distinction between the methods of exact science and those used to examine the issues of human life. His abstract "moral algebra" was used by Enlightenment intellectuals to promote a materialistic and atheistic view of life. Louis XIV proscribed Descartes' writing, so he fled to Holland.

> The first precept was never to accept a thing as true until I knew it as such without a single doubt.
> *Le Discours de la Methode* (1637), ch. 1, tr.
> Laurence J. Lafleur (1964)

> *Cogito ergo sum.*
> I think, therefore I am.
> Ibid., ch. 4

The reading of good books is like a conversation with the best men of past centuries—in fact like a prepared conversation, in which they reveal their best thoughts.

Truths are more likely to have been discovered by one man than by a nation.

In order to improve the mind, we ought less to learn than to contemplate.

OLIVER CROMWELL
1599–1658

English, Lord Protector of the Common-wealth of England (1653–58.) He led the "Puritan Revolution" (1640). Shunning a crown, he served as the Protectorate's dictator because a Presbyterian Parliament refused to form the constitutional monarchy he favored. Cromwell moved England toward constitutional government at a time when European kings reigned by divine right. After Cromwell, no English king claimed absolute power or ruled by divine right. After the Restoration, Cromwell's body was removed from Westminster Abbey and buried with the criminals at Tyburn.

A few honest men are better than numbers. If you choose godly, honest men to be captains of horse, honest men will follow them.
> Letter in 1643 to Sir William Spring, in Thomas Carlyle, *Letters and Speeches of Oliver Cromwell* (1845)

I beseech you, in the bowels of Christ, think it possible you may be mistaken.
> Letter to the General Assembly of the Kirk of Scotland (August 3, 1650)

You have sat here too long for any good you have been doing lately.... Depart, I say, and let us have done with you. In the name of God, go!
> To the Rump Parliament in 1653

Sir, the state, in choosing men to serve it, takes no notice of their opinions; if they be willing to serve it, that satisfies. I advised you formerly to bear with minds of different men from yourself.

Take heed of being sharp against those to whom you can object little but that they square not with you in matters of religion.
> Letter to Major General Crawford (1643), in Jacques Brazen, *From Dawn to Decadence* (2000)

Mr. Lely, I desire you would use all your skill to paint my picture truly like me, and not flatter me at all, but remark all these roughness, pimples, warts and everything as you see me.
> Remark to the artist, Peter Lely (1657?)

It's a maxim not to be despised: though peace be made, yet it is interest that keeps the peace.

[Being told that many had come to see his triumph, Cromwell replied:] Three times as many would have come to see me hanged.
> Speech (September 4, 1654), in L. R. Frank, *Quotationary* (1999)

A man o' war is the best ambassador.

Rebellion to tyrants is obedience to God. [Thomas Jefferson adopted this as his motto.]

Put your trust in God my boys, and keep your powder dry.
[Attributed to Cromwell and others.]
> In Alison Jones (ed.), *Chambers Dictionary of Quotations* (1998)

PIERRE CORNEILLE
1606–84

French, tragic playwright of noble characters who are caught up in conflicts of duty.

Drawing on historical and mythological themes, his haunting phrases created classical French theater. In his tragedy *The Cid* (1636), honor drives Don Rodriguez (the Cid) to avenge the insult of his father by Don Gomès, the king's champion, by slaying him despite Don Gomès being the father of his beloved, Chimène. Family honor in turn causes Chimène to reject her love of the Cid. Happily, it works out.

> To conquer without risk is to triumph without glory.
>
> Le Cid (1636), act. II, sc. 2

> Do your duty, and leave the rest to heaven.
>
> Horace (1639), act II, sc. 8

> The manner of giving is worth more than the gift.
>
> Le Menteur (1642), act I, sc. 1

JOHN MILTON
1608–74

English, poet, Cromwell's secretary, and republican pamphleteer who was forced into hiding after the Restoration of Charles II in 1660. Blind and with his son dead, his daughters estranged, his friends executed, and his marriage ended, he wrote in blank verse his epic *Paradise Lost* (1667), the stories of Satan's rebellion and Adam and Eve as an attempt to explain evil and "to justify the ways of God to men," where God limited his interference by creating man "sufficient to stand though free to fall."

The indomitable Milton was like his hero in *Samson Agonistes* (1671), who, while chained and besieged, defied his captors by saying, "My heels are fettered, but my fist is free." In *Paradise Regained* (1671) he tells the story of Christ's temptation. His pamphlet *Areopagitica* (1644) is the most eloquent defense of freedom of the press, better than *Locke's Letters on Toleration* (1689) and Mill's *On Liberty* (1859).

Milton is usually considered the second-greatest man of English letters. Harold Bloom said Milton "allows us to see what was and is always there, but which we might never see without him." Yet T. S. Eliot thought him "withered by book learning," and Dr. Johnson said of *Paradise Lost*, "Nobody ever wished it longer."

> Haste thee nymph, and bring with thee
> Jest and youthful jollity,
> Quips and cranks and wanton wiles,
> Nods, and becks, and wreathed smiles
>
> "L'Allegro" (1631), l. 25

> Come, pensive nun, devout and pure,
> Sober, steadfast, and demure.
>
> "Il Penseroso" (1631), l. 32

> Look homeward, Angel, now, and melt with ruth;
> And, O ye Dolphins, waft the hapless youth.
> [Harold Bloom deemed this the best poem of middle length in English! It decries an early death that prevents a poet from completing his great work.]
>
> "Lycidas" (1637), l. 163

> Tomorrow to fresh woods and pastures anew.
>
> Ibid., l. 192

> …who kills a Man kills a reasonable creature, God's Image; but he who destroys a good Book, kills reason itself, kills the Image of God…
>
> Areopagitica (1644)

Though all the winds of doctrine were let loose to play upon the earth, so Truth be in the field, we do injuriously by licensing and prohibiting to misdoubt her strength. Let her and Falsehood grapple: who ever knew Truth put to the worse, in a free and open encounter?

Ibid.

He that can apprehend and consider vice with all her baits and seeming pleasures, and yet abstain…he is the true war faring Christian. I cannot praise a cloistered virtue, unexercised that never sallies out and sees her adversary, but slinks out of the race, where that immortal garland is to be run for, not without dust and heat.

Of Education (1644)

What though the field be lost?
All is not lost; th' unconquerable will,
And study of revenge, immortal hate,
And courage never to submit or yield.

Paradise Lost (1667), bk. 1, l. 105

The mind is its own place and in itself
Can make a heaven of hell,
A hell of heaven.

Ibid., l. 254

Better to reign in hell, than serve in
heaven.
[This is Satan's plea to Beelzebub and other fallen angels after losing the battle with God and being cast out of heaven and into hell. Satan, the former archangel, thinks that at least in hell he will be free. But even in Pandemonium, the capital of hell where all demons reside, Satan becomes an instrument of God.]

Ibid., l. 262

Awake, arise, or be forever fallen!

Ibid., l. 330

To sit in darkness here
Hatching vain empires.

Ibid., bk. 2, l. 377

Long is the way and hard,
That out of hell leads up to light.

Ibid., l. 432

Who overcomes
By force hath overcome but half his foe.

Ibid., l. 648

Live while you may,
Yet happy pair, enjoy, till I return,
Short pleasures, for long woes are to
succeed.
[Satan to Adam and Eve]

Ibid., bk. 4, l. 532-35

Millions of spiritual beings unseen
Walk the earth up and down.

Ibid., bk. 4, l. 677

What boots it at one gate to make defense,
And at another to let in the foe?

Samson Agonistes (1671), l. 560

They also serve who only stand and wait.

"On His Blindness" (1673)

SIR JOHN SUCKLING
1609–42

English, a Cavalier poet and royalist.

Why so pale and wan, fond lover?
Prithee, why so pale?
Will, when looking well can't move her,
Looking ill prevail?

Aglaura (1637), act 4, sc. 1, "Song"

Out upon it, I have loved
Three whole days together;
And am like to love three more,
If it prove fair weather.
    "A Poem with the Answer" (1641), st. 1

FRANCOIS, DUC DE LA ROCHEFOUCAULD
1613–80

French, moralist and cynic.

We are all strong enough to bear the misfortunes of others.
    Reflections; or, Sentences and Moral Maxims
    (1678), tr. Leonard Tancock (1959), no. 19

Philosophy triumphs over past evils and future evils; but not over present evils.
    Ibid., no. 22

Hypocrisy is the homage that vice pays to virtue.
    Ibid., no. 218

The height of cleverness is to be able to conceal it.
    Ibid., no. 245

Absence diminishes commonplace passions and increases great ones, as the wind extinguishes candles and kindles fires.
    Ibid., no. 276

We hardly find any persons of good sense save those who agree with us.
    Ibid., no. 347

There are bad people who would be less dangerous if they had no good in them.

The greatest of all gifts is the power to estimate things at their true worth.

RICHARD LOVELACE
1618–58

English, a Cavalier poet.

I could not love thee, dear, so much
Lov'd I not honour more.
    "To Lucastra: Going to the Wars"
    (1649), st. 3

Stonewalls do not a prison make,
Nor iron bars a cage
    "To Althea: From Prison" (1649), st. 4

JEAN BAPTISTE COLBERT
1619–83

French, finance minister to Louis XIV, and mercantilist who amassed a fortune while retarding France's growth by permitting private monopolies, financing state-owned industries, erecting protective tariffs, and closing France's ports to foreign ships. Businessmen pleaded to "*Laissez nous faire*" or leave us alone. Colbert executed some sixteen thousand smugglers and unlicensed small manufacturers of cotton cloth and condemned a larger number to slavery in galleys for violating his industrial regulations. These outrages, which he organized to benefit unions and other interests, helped to fire inflation and the French Revolution.

The art of taxation consists in so plucking the goose as to obtain the largest possible amount of feathers with the least possible amount of hissing.

ANDREW MARVELL
1621–78

English, metaphysical poet, and John Milton's assistant. His "Coy Mistress" is a carpe diem poem.

> Had we but world enough, and time
> This coyness lady, were no crime….
> But at my back I always hear
> Time's winged chariot hurrying near;
> And yonder, all before us lie
> Deserts of vast eternity….
> Then worms shall try
> That long preserved virginity,
> And your quaint honour turn to dust,
> And into ashes all my lust,
> The grave's a fine and private place
> But none I think do there embrace….
> "To His Coy Mistress" (1650)

MOLIÈRE
1622–73

Great French comic playwright, best known for *Tartuffe* (1664), who, like Chaucer's Pardoner, was a religious hypocrite. He affected piety to defraud the credulous Orgon while bedding his wife. Louis XIV tried to protect Molière, but church authorities banned *Tartuffe*. Some say Molière drew himself as Alceste, the selfish and Falstaff-like hero-villain of *The Misanthrope* (1664). In both plays Molière showed how good manners could mask savage villainy. Molière was never elected to the French Academy because in his youth he had been an actor, a disgraceful profession. His troupe was the Comédie Française.

Molière's protagonists were enemies of society and its norms. Tartuffe is a world-class religious hypocrite who "from motives of self-interest, makes a trade of piety." In *Don Juan*, the protagonist's voracious sexual appetites caricatured the chase that preoccupied the empty lives of most idle aristocrats. *The Misanthrope* features two monsters: Alceste, whose hostility toward society leads to bad consequences, and the utterly cynical Célimène, who uses her beauty and intelligence to dominate a society that she considers to be shallow.

> We die only once, but for such a long time.
> *Le Depit Amoureux* (1656), act 5, sc. 3

> And not this man alone, but all humanity
> Do what they do from interest and
> vanity;
> They prate of honor, truth, and
> righteousness,
> But lie, betray, and swindle nonetheless.
> Come then: man's villainy is too much
> to bear;
> Let's leave this jungle and this jackal's lair.
> Yes! Treacherous and savage race of men,
> You shall not look upon my face again.
> *Le Misanthrope* (1666), tr. Richard Wilbur

> He makes his cook his merit, and the world visits his dinners and not him.
> Ibid., act I, sc. 1

> Good heavens! For more than forty years I have been speaking prose without knowing it.
> [Spoken by M. Jourdain.]
> *Le Bourgeois Gentilhomne* (1671),
> act II, sc. 4

> *Les envieux mourront, mais non jamais l'envie.*
> The envious will die, but envy never.

RICHARD RUMBOLD
1622–58

Scottish, Puritan soldier.

I never would believe that Providence had sent a few men into the world, ready booted and spurred to ride, and millions ready saddled and bridled to be ridden.
[Scaffold speech before being hung.]
In L. R. Frank, *Quotationary*

BLAISE PASCAL
1623–62

French, philosopher and mathematician, who discovered probability theory. He also invented the calculating machine, barometer, omnibus for cities, and so forth. Pascal knew that reason, being based on the senses, was unreliable, so "to make light of philosophy is to be a true philosopher" (*Pensées*, no. 4). Religion could not be based on reason. Our hearts, the truer guides, cannot accept a meaningless life, so we should "place our faith in our feelings" (Pensées no. 24). Will Durant said, "*Pensées* is the most eloquent book of French prose."

However vast a man's spirit, he is only capable of one great passion.
Discourse on the Passions of Love (1653)

I have made this letter longer than usual because I lack the time to make it short.
Letters Provinciales (1656–57), no. 16

All the miseries of mankind come from being unable to sit still in a room.
Pensées (1670), tr. William F. Trotter (1931), in *Bartlett's Familiar Quotations*, 16th ed., Justin Kaplan, ed., no. 139

Cleopatra's nose, had it been shorter, the whole face of the world would have been changed.
Ibid., no. 162

Let us weigh up the gain and loss involved in calling heads that God exists. Let us assess the two cases: if you win you win everything, if you lose you lose nothing. Do not hesitate then; wager that he does exist.
["Pascal's Wager": One cannot know if God exists, but one should act as if he does even if there is only one chance in a trillion, because happiness for eternity depends on it. Also, Pascal thought Christians were happier, so they won the wager anyway.]
Ibid., no. 233

The best function of reason is to recognize that there is an infinity of things which surpass it.
Ibid., no. 267

The heart has reasons which reason knows nothing of.
Ibid., no. 277

Man is neither angel nor beast; and the misfortune is that he who would act the angel acts the beast.
Ibid., no. 358

It is the heart that experiences God, and not reason. This, then, is faith: God felt by the heart, not by reason.
Ibid., no. 424

It is not permitted to the most equitable of men to be a judge in his own cause.

God of Abraham, God of Isaac, God of Jacob, not of the philosophers and

scholars. Certainty. Feeling. Joy.
[Note stitched to his coat at his death.]
Chambers Dictionary of Quotations (1998)

JOHN BUNYAN
1628–88

English. While in prison for unlicensed preaching, he wrote *Pilgrim's Progress From This World to That Which Is to Come* (1678). In the medieval tradition of mystery and morality plays, *Pilgrim's Progress* is an allegory of man seeking God. Christian, the protagonist, travels from the City of Destruction to the Celestial City, traversing deadly obstacles such as the Slough of Despond, Mr. Worldly-Wiseman, the town Vanity Fair, the Giant Despair, and Mr. Timorous. Next to the Bible, it was the most widely read book in England for over two hundred years. Theodore Roosevelt accounted it to be the greatest book ever written because it exuded courage and perseverance.

> And in that town there is a fair called Vanity Fair and in it are all such merchandise sold as places, honours, preferments, titles, lusts, pleasures, and delights of all sorts. It beareth the name of Vanity-Fair, because the town where 'tis kept, is lighter than vanity.
> *Pilgrim's Progress* (1678), pt. 1

> My great-grandfather was but a waterman, looking one way, and rowing another.
> Ibid.

> Now Giant Despair had a wife, and her name was Diffidence.
> Ibid.

> A man that could look no way but downward, with a muck rake in his hand.
> Ibid., pt. 2

> Who would true valor see,
> Let him come hither;
> One here will constant be,
> Come wind, come weather.
> There's no discouragement
> Shall make him once relent
> His first avowed intent
> To be a pilgrim.
> Ibid.

> Man did so manly play the man as to make the fiend fly.
> Ibid.

> A man there was, though some did count him mad,
> The more he cast away, the more he had.
> Ibid.

> My marks and scars I carry with me, to be a witness for me, that I have fought his battles, who will now be my rewarder.... So he passed over, and the trumpets sounded for him on the other side.
> Ibid.

JOHN DRYDEN
1631–1700

English, playwright, critic, and poet laureate in 1668, who so dominated his literary era that it is called the "Age of Dryden." His plays are no longer performed, but his poetry still reigns.

> In friendship false, implacable in hate,
> Resolv'd to ruin or rule the State.
> "Absalom and Achitophel" (1680),
> pt. 1, l. 73

A man so various that he seem'd to be
Not one, but all mankind's epitome:
Stiff in opinions, always in the wrong;
Was everything by starts, and nothing long:
But, in the course of one revolving moon,
Was chemist, fiddler, statesman, and
    buffoon.

> Ibid., l. 545

Beware the fury of a patient man.

> Ibid., l. 1005

Happy the man, and happy he alone,
He who can call today his own;
He who, secure within, can say,
Tomorrow, do thy worst, for I have liv'd
    today.
> *Imitation Horace*, (1685), bk. III, ode 29,
> l. 65

All heiresses are beautiful.
> "King Arthur or the British Worthy"
> (1695), act I, sc. 1

War is the trade of kings, who fight for
    empire.

> Ibid., Act II, sc. 2

Ill habits gather by unseen degrees
As brooks make rivers, rivers run to seas.
> "The Worship of Aesulapius" (1700), l. 155

Oh! Give me liberty
For were ev'n Paradise my prison
Still I should long to leap the crystal walls.

JOHN LOCKE
1632–1704

English, history's most influential political philosopher who, along with Bacon and Hobbes, preferred experience to reason. They pushed the British Enlightenment toward empiricism as Europe slid into the swamp of metaphysical rationalism.

Locke believed in Natural Law, a school beginning with the Platonic, Aristotelian, Stoic, and Thomistic systems that there are objective standards of morality that are inherent in consciousness and discernible through reason. This implies Natural Rights to life, liberty, and property. To Locke, citizens enter a compact to form a government to protect those rights. Not even a majority can legitimately usurp Natural Rights: If it tries to, citizens have a right to rebel.

The Declaration of Independence was based on Natural Law. But, after the French Revolution's "Rights of Man" were used to trample the social and political order, Burke and other conservatives shied away from Natural Law in preference for traditions and customs as the soundest basis of law. Relativist philosophies hold there is no truth outside of science, and thus no Natural Law. Leo Strauss is Natural Law's twentieth-century champion.

Locke's *Essay Concerning Human Understanding* (1690) rejected Descartes' *Innate Ideas*. Rather, knowledge is derived only from experience. At birth, Locke said, the mind is a blank tablet (tabula rasa). [Neuroscience proves a brain is an exposed negative that can be developed well or poorly, but it can differ little from the original film.] Minds as blank slates is a dangerous idea, implying that the state can train humans to become whatever it wants—per Rousseau, Lenin, Hitler, or Stalin.

Locke formulated the theory of the "separation of powers," legislative and executive, which Montesquieu extended by separating the judicial power out of the executive power. Locke favored a constitutional monarchy in which the parliament was supreme, but in which the powers of both were limited by the rule of law and natural rights.

Locke published his *Two Treatises* in 1689 at age fifty-four, after the deposal of James II by the Glorious Revolution of 1688. The Second Treatise's novelty lay in its limitations on the power of government. Locke favored a written constitution, but the English constitution is an "unwritten constitution of custom."

For Locke, "property" included both tangible goods and intangible rights. In the Declaration of Independence, Jefferson's broader term "pursuit of happiness" was used in lieu of "property" to make clear that intangible rights were protected. Locke said, "[Government is instituted] for the mutual preservation of [our] Lives, Liberties, and Estates, which I call by the general name, Property.... The great and chief end, therefore, of men uniting into commonwealths and putting themselves under government, is the preservation of their property." *Second Treatise on Civil Government* (1690).

In asserting the sacredness of property, Locke laid the foundation for free enterprise. He believed that property rights would eliminate economic scarcities. Locke said that lacking property rights, the chief of an Indian tribe "feeds, lodges and is clad worse than a day laborer in England."

> Government has no other end but the preservation of Property.
> *Second Treatise of Government* (1690)

> Where there is no Law, there is no Freedom.... Where Law ends, Tyranny begins.
> Ibid.

> If the innocent honest man must quietly quit all he has, for peace's sake, to him who will lay violent hands on it, I desire it may be considered, what kind of peace there will be in the world, which consists only in violence and rapine, and which is to be maintained only for the benefit of robbers and oppressors.
> Ibid.

> 'Where there is no property, there is no justice ' is a proposition as certain as any demonstration in Euclid...
> *An Essay Concerning Human Understanding* (1690), ed. Alexander Campbell Fraser (1894)

> Let us then suppose the mind to be, as we say, white paper, void of all characters, without any ideas. How comes it to be furnished?...To this I answer, in one word, from experience.
> Ibid., bk. II

BENEDICT SPINOZA
1632–77

Dutch, foremost seventeenth-century rationalist, who attempted to make metaphysics intelligible by setting out a series of theorems deduced from self-evident premises. He is the preeminent modern pantheist, one who believes that the universe and God are the same. His masterpiece, *Ethics,* saw man to be bound by his passions, with reason being his only chance for liberation, albeit, there is no free will. Spinoza was vilified as an atheist, although Novalis called him the "God-intoxicated man."

In his *Tractus Politicus,* he noted Hobbes' failure to appreciate that men have social as well as individual instincts: "Since fear of solitude exists in all men—because no one in solitude is strong enough to defend himself and procure the necessaries of life—it follows that men by nature tend towards social organization." The purpose of the state is liberty. He detested monarchy. He favored democracy with adult males enfranchised and "armed to maintain their spirit."

> To become what we are capable of becoming is the only end of life.

> He whose honor depends on the opinion of the mob must day by day strive with the greatest anxiety, act and scheme in order to retain his reputation. For the mob is varied and inconstant, and therefore if a reputation is not carefully preserved it dies quickly.
>
> *Ethics* (1677), pt. IV, 58

> I have striven not to laugh at human actions, not to weep at them, nor to hate them, but to understand them.
>
> *Tractatus Politicus* (1677), ch. 1, sec. 4

> I do not know how to teach philosophy without becoming a disturber of the peace.
>
> [When offered a professorship in 1670.]

> What Paul says about Peter tells us more about Paul than about Peter.
>
> In L. R. Frank, *Wit and Humor Quotationary*

Louis XIV
1638–1715

French, *Roi Soleil* or Sun King (1643–1715), who was one-quarter French, half Spanish, and one-quarter Italian. He preceded Napoleon and Hitler in seeking to unify Europe by conquest and was opposed by the first Grand Alliance of European states in the Palatinate War (1689–97) and during the War of the Spanish Succession (1701–13). The latter was the first world war. It reduced France's population from 23 million to 19 million due to war-related famines. William of Orange, *stadholder* of Holland (later king of England), cut the dikes to flood Amsterdam to protect it from a French army. John Churchill, the Duke of Marlborough (the Iron Duke, and ancestor to Winston Churchill), defeated Marshal Tallard at the Battle of Blenheim in 1704, preventing the union of the Spanish and French crowns and the French acquiring land to the Rhine.

The five-foot, four-inch, pudgy, pock-faced Louis empowered his chief adviser Colbert to grant monopolies, regulate manufacturing, nationalize industries, embargo imports, and tax agriculture to subsidize loss-making state-owned industries, a system known as *Colbertisme*, or mercantilism. Thousands of laborers died building Versailles, the palace, where Louis required France's highest nobility to live—thus France's farms were managed absentee. Mercantilism and wars bankrupted the world's richest country and fired the inflation that later consumed Louis's Bourbon dynasty.

Louis in 1685 revoked the Edict of Nantes, which had granted religious liberty to French Protestants, the Huguenots. They had to convert to Catholicism or be enslaved in galleys. Perhaps 250,000 of the 1.5 million Huguenots fled, many to Holland, including the leading industrialists in the banking, engineering, silk, textile, paper, and printing industries. French intellectuals supported Louis's "revocation" and slaughter because he was the self-styled "protector of the French Academy," "the forty immortals." French playwrights, such as Molière, Corneille, and Racine performed plays in the gilded halls of Versailles while France's peasants died of starvation by the millions. Carlyle noted in his *History of the French Revolution* (1837), "France was long a despotism tempered by epigrams." Only a dozen courtiers attended Louis's funeral. One said, "Our eyes were too full of tears during his life to leave us any for his death." On his deathbed, leaving an impoverished state after a seventy-two-year reign, Louis said, "I loved war too much."

> Every time I fill a vacant office I make ten malcontents and one ingrate.
> In Voltaire, *Siecle de Louis* XIV
> (1751), ch. 26

> L'état c'est moi.
> (I am the state.)
> DeLaure, *History of Paris* (1853)

> How could God do this to me after all I have done for him?
> [After he lost the Battle of Blenheim.]
> In Agnes Hooper Gottlieb, et. al., *1,000 Years, 1,000 People* (1998)

> Continue to write to me whatever comes into your mind and do not be discouraged though I do not always do what you suggest.
> [To Vauban, greatest master of fortifications and siege operations.]
> J. E. King, *Science and Rationalism in the Government of Louis XIV*

It is legal because I wish it.

[The French writer, Fenelon, wrote in a letter to Louis XIV in 1694:]
Sire: For thirty years your ministers have violated all the ancient laws of the state so as to enhance your power. They have…impoverished all of France for the sake of your luxury at court…[T]hey have made the French nation intolerable to its neighbors by bloody wars…. Meanwhile, your people are starving.

JEAN RACINE
1639–99

French, dramatist known for his tragedies, which explored human emotions, especially those of women. He captured the destructive capacity of love in Theseus's wife Phaèdre, who falls in love with her stepson, Hippolyte, to whom she makes sexual advances when she thinks Theseus is dead. But when Theseus returns, she accuses Hippolyte of raping her. Racine's realism also features men who are often unsure and less than noble. La Bruyère commented that Corneille portrayed men "as they should be" and Racine "as they are."

> I loved him too much not to hate him at all!
> *Andromaque* (1667), act II

> It is no longer a passion hidden in my heart; it is Venus herself fastened to her prey.
> *Phaèdre* (1677), act I, sc. 3

> You think you can be holy and righteous with impunity?
> *Athalie* (1691), act I, sc. 1

PURITAN REVOLUTION
(ENGLISH CIVIL WAR)
1642–49

The English gentry and bourgeoisie flourished during the Elizabethan era of low taxes, as trade expanded ten-fold. The gentry enclosed the commons to raise sheep to supply wool to the bourgeoisie's mills. Because the bourgeoisie ran the economy, they demanded a larger share in the government, which was controlled by the king and aristocrats. Also, the aristocrats were Catholics or Anglicans, who supported the unity of the church and state, while the bourgeoisie were Presbyterian or Puritan, who wanted to separate church and state.

James I (king of England 1603–25), Elizabeth's successor and son of Mary Queen of Scots, thought he ruled by divine right, and his successor, Charles I (1625–49), was even more intractable. Charles signed the "Petition of Right" on May 28, 1628, promising not to levy any taxes without Parliament's consent, but he refused to call Parliament into session for eleven years (1629–40), during which time he levied new taxes, such as the Ship's Tax, which John Hampden refused to pay. In 1640, Charles summoned Parliament due to a Scottish invasion. This "Long Parliament" (1640–49) abolished the Star Chamber and stopped the taxation. Charles agreed, but he refused Parliament's ultimatum that it advise and consent on his choice of counselors. Charles entered Parliament to arrest its five ringleaders, which started the First Civil War (1642–46). Royalists won most battles until Parliament formed a "New Model Army" under Oliver Cromwell, a Puritan member of Parliament. Cromwell's army never lost a battle, and Charles sur-

rendered in 1646. In 1647, Charles I started the Second Civil War, which Cromwell also won.

Cromwell's Puritan army demanded that Charles relinquish his veto power to be reinstated as king. Charles refused and was executed. Previously, Parliament, controlled by Presbyterians, had offered to take Charles's side against the Puritan army if Charles would agree to make Presbyterianism the state church of England. Charles had also refused that deal. The army's radical Independents under John Lilburne wanted universal manhood suffrage, so they expelled the Presbyterian members of Parliament. The remaining fifty-six Puritans, or Rump Parliament, executed Charles I. Cromwell, who favored a constitutional monarchy but refused a crown, ruled as Lord Protector.

A letter from Maj. Gen. Sir William Waller of the Parliamentary army to Sir Ralph Hopton, commander of the Royalist army, prior to the battle of Roundway Down in 1643, read:

> My affections to you are so unchangeable that hostility itself cannot violate my friendship to your person, but I must be true to the cause I serve.... [God knows] with what perfect hatred I look upon this war without an enemy. We are both upon the stage and we must act the parts assigned to us in this tragedy. Let us do it in a way of honour and without personal animosities.
>
> S. R. Gardiner, *History of the Great Civil War*, (164 2–49), (London, 1886-89), I, 168

SIR ISAAC NEWTON
1642–1727

English, one of the world's greatest scientists whose masterpiece was *Principia Mathematica* (1687). He invented integral calculus, the tool used for most subsequent scientific advances, and discovered the mechanical laws of motion, force, and gravity. He was the first to propound a universal law of nature, to wit, gravity is the pull of two objects proportional to the mass of each and varies inversely as the square of the distance between them.

He was most creative during eighteen months when a plague prompted him to stay in his mother's house in Lincolnshire, where his bubble baths gave insights into optics and where the fall of an apple focused his thoughts on gravity. His universal laws of force and motion "freed physics from metaphysics." He also built the first reflecting telescope. Newton proved the world to be a mechanical system explainable by simple principles, which is evidence of science's extreme power. Einstein said Newton's work "determined the course of Western thought, research and practice to an extent that nobody before or since his time can touch." Yet, half of his life was devoted to studying alchemy and religious speculation.

Every body continues in its state of rest, or of uniform motion in a right line, unless it is compelled to change that state by forces impressed thereon.
[First law of motion.]
Philosophiae Naturalis Principia Mathematica, tr. Andrew Motte (1729)

The alteration of motion is ever proportional to the motive force impressed; and is made in the direction of the right line in which that force is impressed.
[Second law of motion.]
Ibid.

To every action there is always opposed an equal reaction: or, the mutual actions of two bodies upon each other are always equal, and directed to contrary parts.
[Third law of motion.]
Ibid.

If I have seen further [than Descartes] it is by standing on the shoulders of giants.
Letter to Robert Hooke
(February 5, 1675)

I don't know what I may seem to the world, but as to myself, I seem to have been only like a boy playing on the sea shore and diverting myself by now and then finding a smoother pebble or a prettier shell than ordinary, whilst the great ocean of truth lay all undiscovered before me.
His last words, in Joseph Spence's
Anecdotes

I can calculate the motions of heavenly bodies, but not the madness of people.
[After losing twenty thousand pounds in the South Sea Bubble.]

WILLIAM PENN
1644–1718

English, founded the state of Pennsylvania as a refuge for persecuted Quakers.

I expect to pass through this world but once; any good thing, therefore, that I can do, or any kindness that I can show

to any fellow creature, let me do it now;
let me not defer or neglect it, for I shall
not pass this way again.

Men are generally more careful of the
breed of their horses and dogs than of
their children.
                Some Fruits of Solitude in Reflections and
                                        Maxims (1693)

He that has more knowledge than judgment, is made for another man's use
more than his own.
                                                Ibid.

Have a care, therefore, where there is
more sail than ballast.

JEAN DE LA BRUYERE
1645–96

French satiric playwright and moralist.

We come too late to say anything that
has not been said already.
        Les Caractères (1688), "Des Ouvrages de
                                        l'Esprit"

Liberality consists less in giving a great
deal than in gifts well timed.
                            Ibid., "Du Coeur"

If life is miserable, it is difficult to endure;
if it is happy, it is horrible to lose.
                    Ibid., "De L'homme" no. 33

Children have neither past nor future.
They live in the present, something that
rarely happens to us.
                                        Ibid., no. 51

Men fall from great fortune because of the
same shortcomings that led to their rise.

The best way to get on in the world is to
make people believe it's to their advantage to help you.

GOTTFRIED VON LEIBNITZ
1646–1716

German, mathematician and philosopher,
who developed calculus independent of
Newton. He believed, given free will, that
this was the best of all possible worlds. Voltaire satirized Leibnitz in the novel, *Candide*.

The present is great with the future.

PIERRE BAYLE
1647–1706

French, skeptic, who fled France to live in
the Dutch Republic after the revocation of
the Edict of Nantes. His *Dictionnaire Histo-
rique et Critique* (1697) alphabetically listed
important people in history, mythology,
theology, literature, and philosophy, and
synopsized their ideas. An eighteenth-cen-
tury survey of French libraries found his
Dictionnaire to be the most popular book.

Bayle was hailed by Diderot as "the
most redoubtable exponent of skepticism
in either ancient or modern times." He
treated God as either a cruel deity or one
of limited powers. He claimed that either
God causes evil or there are two Gods, one
being evil (Manicheanism). Liberals, such
as Bayle, led the West to stop believing in
witches, but they failed to appreciate man's
immense capacity for doing evil. Burners of
witches murdered a tiny fraction of those
liquidated later by "enlightened" socialists
purportedly acting to serve mankind.

THOMAS FULLER
1654–1734

English, physician and author.

A stumble may prevent a fall.
> *Gnomologia: Adages and Proverbs*
> (1732), no. 424

Bacchus hath drowned more men than Neptune.
> Ibid., no. 830

He is poor indeed that can promise nothing.
> Ibid., no. 1941

Security is the mother of danger and the grandmother of destruction.
> Ibid., no. 2195

If an Ass goes a-traveling, he'll not come home a Horse.
> Ibid., no. 2668

Learning makes a man fit company for himself.
> Ibid., no. 3163

Reputation is commonly measur'd by the acre.
> Ibid., no. 4023

Sail, quoth the King; hold, saith the Wind.
> Ibid., no. 4064

Some have been thought brave because they were afraid to run away.
> Ibid., no. 4214

The real difference between men is energy.

A young trooper should have an old horse.

Praise makes good men better and bad men worse.

DANIEL DEFOE
1660-1731

English, novelist, loved by the middle class and hated by the intelligentsia. He is celebrated for *Moll Flanders* (1722) and *Robinson Crusoe* (1719), a fable of a man who survives a shipwreck for twenty-four years on an uninhabited island through intelligence, industry, and faith in God. He accounts himself happy on the island after his conversion compared to his former wicked ways. He rescues a native from cannibals and names him "Man Friday," who asked, "Why God no kill the Devil?" Defoe is no tree-hugging Rousseau; he sides with culture and civilization in opposition to raw nature.

Nature has left this tincture in the blood,
That all men would be tyrants if they could.
> *Addenda to the Kentish Petition* (1713)

[Defoe said that there were thousands ready to fight to the death against popery, without knowing whether popery was a man or a horse.]

THOMAS BROWN
1663–1704

English, satirist.

I do not love thee, Doctor Fell,
The reason why I cannot tell;
But this alone I know full well,
I do not love thee, Doctor Fell.
> [Doctor Fell, a dean at Christ

Church, Oxford, agreed not to expel Brown if he translated the 32nd Epigram of Martial.]

JONATHAN SWIFT
1667–1745

Irish, clergyman, novelist, and foremost British satirist. His "A Modest Proposal for preventing the Children of poor People in Ireland from being a Burden to their Parents or Country; and for making them beneficial to the Publick, 1729" argued the Irish should raise babies to sell as food to the English, who forbade manufacturing in Ireland. A satire is ironic: It means the opposite of what it says. In *Gulliver's Travels* (1726), Swift satirizes the follies and vices of his scientific protagonist, Lemuel Gulliver, a rationalist who notices details exactly, but cannot comprehend their significance.

Harold Bloom says Swift's greatest work is his *A Tale of the Tub*, "the best prose in English." It attacks with cold fury the materialism of Descartes.

When a true genius appears in the world, you may know him by this sign, that the dunces are all in confederacy against him.
Thoughts on Various Subjects (1711)

While some build Castles in the Air, Directors build 'em in the Seas; Subscribers plainly see 'um there, For Fools will see as Wise men please.
"The Bubble" (1720)
[The collapse of the South Sea Company.]

Censure is the tax a man pays to the public for being eminent.
Ibid.

Every man desires to live long; but no man would be old.
Ibid., enlarged ed. (1727)

I have heard of a man who had a mind to sell his house, and therefore carried a piece of brick in his pocket, which he showed as a pattern to encourage purchasers.
The Drapier's Letters (1724), no. 2

There was a society of [lawyers] among us bred up from their youth in the art of proving by their words, multiplied for the purpose, that white is black and black is white, according as they are paid.
Gulliver's Travels (1726)

He replied that I must needs be mistaken, or that I said the thing which was not. (For they have no word in their language to express lying or falsehood.)
Ibid., "A Voyage to the Houyhnhnms," ch. 3

He had been eight years upon a project for extracting sun beams out of cucumbers, which were to be put into vials hermetically sealed, and let out to warm the air in raw inclement summers.
Ibid., "Voyage to Laputa" ch. 5

The man who can make two ears of corn or two blades of grass grow on the spot where only one grew before, would deserve better of mankind and render more essential service to the country than the whole race of politicians put together.
Ibid., "Voyage to Brobdingnag" ch. 7

He [King of Brobdingnag] was perfectly astonished with the historical account I gave him of our affairs during the last century, protesting it was only a heap of conspiracies, rebellions, murders, massacres, revolutions, banishments, the very worst effects that avarice, faction, hypocrisy, perfidiousness, cruelty, rage, madness, hatred, envy, lust, malice, or ambition could produce.

Ibid.

Lemuel Gulliver, a ship's surgeon and modern man, is shipwrecked on fantasy islands during his voyages. This adventurous tale serves as the format for satirizing Deism, rationalism, Whig politics, and England's subjugation of Ireland. While man is capable of reasoning, Swift sees man (per the Christian tradition) as being depraved and using reason to justify doing exactly what he wants to do.

On the island of Lilliput, six-inch-tall, warlike Lilliputians, who obsess with pompous "points of honor," tie Gulliver up with silken threads. Lilliput is divided between orthodox Little-Endians, who break eggs at the little end, and heretic Big-Endians, who break eggs at the big end. Lilliputian children are "wisely" raised by the state. The Laputa live on an island in the air and are all philosophers so absent-minded and impractical that they cannot build a house with a right angle in it. Constant learning made the immortal Struldbrugs senile. Houyhnhnms are so wise and gentle as to need no lawyers or clergy—but they are devoid of any spark of life. The Yahoos are dirty, greedy, and drunken; the Yahoo king "remains in office until a worse can be found." Yahoos are "lumps of deformity smitten with pride." We are the Yahoos.

How haughtily he lifts his nose,
To tell what every schoolboy knows.
"The Journal" (1727), 1.81-2

The best doctors are Doctor Diet, Doctor Quiet, and Doctor Merryman.
Polite Conversations (1738)

She wears her clothes as if they were thrown on her with a pitchfork.
Ibid.

He was a bold man that first ate an oyster.
Ibid.

May you live all the days of your life.
In L. R. Frank, *Wit and Humor Quotationary*

GIOVANNI BATTISTA VICO
1668-1744

Italian, first modern historian and "father of comparative history." His *New Science* (1725) saw a cyclical theory of history: theocracy, aristocracy, and democracy, followed by chaos leading to a new Theocratic Age. Like Jung, Vico examined a culture's mythologies in order to understand it. He believed intuition was the talent most needed by historians, not logical thinking.

Governments must be conformable to the nature of the governed; governments are even a result of that nature.
Scienza Nuova (1725)

WILLIAM CONGREVE
1670–1729

English, playwright of cynical comedies.

Married in haste, we may repent at leisure.
The Old Bachelor (1693), act 5, sc. 8

Music has charms to soothe a savage beast.
To soften rocks, or bend a knotted oak.
The Mourning Bride (1697), act 1, sc. 1

Heaven hath no rage like love to hatred
turned,
Nor hell a fury like a woman scorned.
Ibid., act 3, sc. 8

Women are like tricks by slight of hand,
Which, to admire, we should not
understand.
Love for Love (1695), act 4, sc. 2

JOSEPH ADDISON
1672–1719

English, essayist, poet, MP, and cofounder
with Richard Steele of *The Spectator* in
1711. It was the first opinion journal and
its aim was to bring "philosophy out of
closets and libraries to dwell in clubs and
assemblies." Alexander Hamilton said the
six bound volumes of *The Spectator* was the
best teacher of writing style.

If I can any way contribute to the diversion or improvement of the country in
which I live, I shall leave it, when I am
summoned out of it, with the secret satisfaction of thinking that I have not lived
in vain.
The Spectator, no. 1 (March 1, 1711)

There is not a more unhappy being than
a superannuated idol.
The Spectator, no. 73 (May 24, 1711)

A true critic ought to dwell rather upon
excellencies than imperfections, to discover the concealed beauties of a writer,
and communicate to the world such
things as are worth their observation.
The Spectator, no. 291 (February 2, 1712)

"We are always doing," says he, "some-
thing for Posterity, but I would fain see
Posterity do something for us."
The Spectator, no. 583 (August 20, 1714)

There is no defense against reproach but
obscurity.
In L. R. Frank, *Wit and Humor
Quotationary* (2000)

PETER I "THE GREAT"
1672–1725

Russian, Romanov, tsar from 1689, who
won back from Sweden Russia's territories
on the Baltic and seized lands near the Black
Sea. With a Russian population of 8 million backward folk, he defeated the Poles,
Swedes, Cossacks, Tartars, Ottomans, Persians, and Asiatic states bordering Siberia.
He built a new capital, St. Petersburg, in
a swamp on the Baltic, and canals to connect the Caspian Sea with the Baltic Sea.
In the Great Northern War with Sweden,
Moscow was saved by the severe winter of
1708–9 that also froze the Seine River.
Russia missed the defining events of
Western civilization: Catholicism, feudalism, Renaissance, Reformation, overseas
colonies, and Enlightenment. It was an offspring of the Byzantine civilization, and for

two hundred years (mid-thirteenth to mid-fifteenth centuries) it was under Mongol suzerainty. Its Orthodox Church, the only institution not destroyed by the Mongols, felt encircled by Islam to the south and east, Catholicism to the west, and Lutheranism to the north. This issolation stuck Russia in a medieval time warp. The only distinctive feature of Western civilization shared by Russia was the classical legacy from ancient Greece and Rome.

Peter, a six-foot, seven-inch tsar, abolished primogeniture and liberated women. He imported foreigners to manage the military and government, start private industries, and staff the new colleges, hospitals, and so forth. But he also guarded the Russian culture, saying, "We need Europe for a few decades, but then we must turn our back on it." Peter stripped the old nobility of its privileges; his Table of Ranks allowed citizens to become hereditary noblemen through achievement. Peter tolerated serfdom to supply soldiers and the manpower needed for his grand projects. Catherine reversed Peter's quasi-meritocratic rule.

> Without loss of a single instant, we devote all our energies to work.
>
> Letter to Menshikov, in Robert K. Massie, *Peter the Great* (1980)

RUSSIA IN A CAPSULE

Russians, unlike Americans, built farmhouses in villages to defend against marauding Tartars, Vikings, wolves, and the like—an explanation for Russia's communal spirit. Being mostly Slavic, Russians are tied by blood to Byelorussia, Ukraine, Poland, Bulgaria, Romania, Walachia, and Serbia.

The Orthodox Greek priests, St. Cyril (d. 869) and St. Methodius translated religious texts in the Cyrillic alphabet to form a Slavic culture. Vladimir I, Duke of Kiev, accepted Orthodox Christianity in 986 for the Rus ("rowers" in Swedish). Alexander Nevsky (c.1220–63), Grand Duke of Novgorod, defeated the Swedes on the River Neva in 1240 and the Teutonic Knights on Lake Peipus in 1242.

The first national ruler of Russia was Ivan III, "The Great" (1440–1505), Duke of Muscovy, whose realm initially was less than half the size of the state of Indiana, which he tripled in size. He took the title of tsar ("caesar") after marrying the niece of the last Byzantine emperor. Moscow became the Third Rome and the protector of the Orthodox Church. He also freed Russia from paying tribute to the Tartar Golden Horde. His grandson, Ivan IV, "The Terrible" (1530–84), conquered Kazan and Astrakhan from the Tartars and entered Siberia. He established an autocracy by curbing the power of the Boyars (nobles), and he killed his eldest son in a fit of rage. Boris Godunov (1552–1605) regent for the imbecile Fyodor I, was elected tsar on Fyodor's death. He colonized Siberia and regained land from Sweden.

OTHER FACTS

Ivan IV embraced the title "Terrible" as a laudatory title, meaning that he was a threat to Russia's enemies.

Tamerlane, the Mongol, did more to destroy the Tartars than the Russians.

Catherine II, "The Great" (1729–96), daughter of a German noble, married and murdered a demented tsar. Heroine of the French Enlightenment, she enslaved the serfs and made the nobility partners with the autocracy by exempting them from taxation, a reversal of Peter the Great's meritocratic policies. She waged aggressive wars to include the Balkans in her Orthodox Empire.

Catherine's field marshal and lover, Potemkin, built facades of rich villages along a boat tour of the Dnieper River to deceive Catherine into believing that the Russian people were well off and loved her, thus, "Potemkin villages."

Czar Alexander II in 1861 freed Russia's 20 million serfs, saying, "It is better to abolish serfdom from above than to wait until the serfs begin to liberate themselves from below."

Russia expanded fifty-five square miles daily from 1683 to 1914. The great European problem from the eighteenth century to 1991 was to contain Russia. The Crimean War of 1853–55 was fought by the British and French to prevent Russia from overrunning Istanbul. Similarly, the Russo-Japanese War (1904–5) halted Russia's eastern expansion. Russian expansion since the fifteenth century was achieved by over two hundred Russian acts of aggression, not by defensive responses.

THE AGRICULTURAL REVOLUTION

Charles Townshend ("Turnip Townshend") 1674–1738, English farmer, is representative of the agricultural revolution. He increased yields by 30 percent with a four-year crop rotation system that planted turnips for sheep to graze on in the fourth year, instead of leaving the land fallow every third year, the former practice. Planting leguminous crops injected nitrogen into the soil. Also, Townshend's "fencing in" animals (enclosures) improved their breeding.

Jethro Tull's mechanical seed sowing machine delivered seed to the right depth, correctly spaced in straight lines. This permitted efficient weeding and avoided wasteful scattering by hand. Rotherham's triangular plow enabled a horse to replace a team of oxen. Such inventions increased agricultural production in England tenfold per acre where best practices were used. Also, parliamentary enclosure bills converted 2 million acres of commons into private farms, making them larger, which justified mechanization. Agricultural productivity released its surplus labor to man the factories of the Industrial Revolution.

TAKAFUSA MITSUI
1684–1748

Japanese, third generation of the second largest Japanese trading company.

> Never waste your attention on matters that have nothing to do with your work. Merchants who ape samurai or think that Shinto, Confucianism or Buddhism will preserve their inner heart will find that they will only ruin their houses if they become too deeply engrossed in them. How much more true is this of other arts and entertainments! Remember, it is the family business that must not be neglected for a moment.
>
> Mikiso Hane, *Premodern Japan: A Historical Survey* (1991)

JOHANN SEBASTIAN BACH
1685–1750

German, Lutheran musical director and perhaps the greatest composer due to his immortal harmonies, rhythms, and counterpoint. None of his seventeen hundred compositions were published in his lifetime. He was forgotten until Mendelssohn performed "Saint Matthew's Passion" a hundred years after Bach had performed it. Bach is best known for his *Brandenburg Concertos* and his *Mass in B Minor*. See Paul Johnson, *Creators*, 2006. When old, sick, and blind, Bach wrote the moving "Kǒmm, Susser Tod":

> Come, kindly Death, blessed repose,
> Come, for my life is dreary,
> And I of earth am weary.
> Come, for I wait for thee,
> Come soon and calm thou me;
> Gently mine eyelids close;
> Come, blest repose.

GEORGE BERKELEY
1685–1753

Irish, Anglican bishop, and idealist and empiricist who carried Locke's ideas to their ultimate conclusion. If all knowledge comes from experience, then whatever is incapable of being experienced, cannot exist: "To be is to be experienced." Moreover, the nature of experience is mental or spiritual, not material. Nothing exists but God, finite spirits, and their ideas.

Berkeley did not argue that rocks are not real, but that all qualities exist only in our senses so that when matter is not sensed, it does not exist. The observing mind of God makes possible the existence of matter. This is another way of saying that anything that could be experienced (even though no person is present to experience it) does exist, but that whatever could never be experienced does not exist. Reality is what perceives, that is, spirit.

> All the choir of heaven and furniture of earth in a word, all those bodies which compose the mighty frame of the world—have not any subsistence without a mind.
>
> *A Treatise Concerning the Principles of Human Knowledge* (1710)

> Truth is the cry of all, but the game of the few.
>
> *Siris* (1744), para. 368

> It is impossible that a man who is false to his friends and neighbors should be true to the public.
>
> *Maxims Concerning Patriotism* (1750)

> He who says there is no such thing as an honest man, you may be sure is himself a knave.

GEORG FRIEDRICH HANDEL
1685–1759

English (German-born), composer, who went to London for a visit and stayed for forty-six years. In 1742 he composed his masterpiece, *The Messiah*, in twenty-three days, during which he told a friend, "I did think I did see all Heaven before me, and the great God himself." The king of Great Britain began a royal custom of standing during *The Messiah's* "Hallelujah Chorus."

THE GLORIOUS REVOLUTION
1688

Following Cromwell's death in 1658, the English, tiring of military government, recalled in 1660 the exiled Charles II in a "restoration" of the monarchy. But Charles's brother and successor, James II, plotted to restore the Catholic Church and refused to accept financial dependence on Parliament. Upon the birth of James II's son, Whig and Tory lords invited William III of Orange, Stadholder of Holland, and his Protestant wife, Mary, daughter of James II, to invade England. The invasion was real—Holland's fleet was four times the size of the Spanish Armada. The English army deserted and James II fled.

Parliament offered joint crowns to William and Mary on the condition of accepting the "Bill of Rights," which made Parliament supreme. England became a "limited monarchy." Protestants in Ireland who supported William against a Catholic uprising fomented by James II were called "Orangemen."

ALEXANDER POPE
1688–1744

English, translator of *The Iliad*, biting satirist, and poet renown for his "heroic couplets." He was a four-foot, six-inch hunchback and Catholic, whose *Essay on Man* (1733) contains 652 couplets with more memorable lines than any other work of that length.

Happy the man whose wish and care
A few paternal acres bound,
Content to breathe his native air

In his own ground.
  [Written at age twelve.]
      "Ode on Solitude" (1700), st. 1

Thus let me live, unseen, unknown,
Thus unlamented let me die;
Steal from the world, and not a stone
Tell where I lie.

             Ibid., st. 5

Where'er you walk, cool gales shall fan
  the glade,
Trees where you sit, shall crowd into a
  shade:
Where'er you tread, the blushing flowers
  all rise,
And all things flourish where you turn
  your eyes.
     Pastorals (1704), "Summer," l. 73

A little learning is a dangerous thing;
Drink deep, or taste not the Pierian
  spring;
There shallow draughts intoxicate the
  brain,
And drinking largely sobers us again.
     "Essay on Criticism" (1711), l. 15

Be not the first by whom the new are
  tried,
Nor yet the last to lay the old aside.
          Ibid., l. 135

Some praise at morning what they
  blame at night;
But always think the last opinion right.
          Ibid., l. 230

To err is human, to forgive divine.
          Ibid., l. 325

Fools rush in where angels fear to tread.
          Ibid., III, l. 65

The hungry judges soon the sentence sign,
And wretches hang that jurymen may
    dine.
    The Rape of the Lock (1712), canto III, l. 21

Where order in variety we see,
And where, though all things differ, all
    agree.
    Windsor Forest (1713), l. 11

A man should never be ashamed to own
he has been in the wrong, which is but
saying, in other words, that he is wiser
today than he was yesterday.
    Miscellanies, "Thoughts on Various Sub-
        jects" (1727), vol. 2

Fix'd like a plant on his peculiar spot,
To draw nutrition, propagate and rot.
    "Essay on Man" (1733), epistle, 1, l. 63

The lamb thy feast dooms to bleed today,
Had he thy reason, would he skip and
    play?
Pleased to the last, he crops the flowery
    food,
And licks the hand just raised to shed
    his blood.
    Ibid., l. 81-84

Hope springs eternal in the human breast;
Man never is, but always to be blest.
    Ibid., l. 95

All nature is but art, unknown to thee;
All chance, direction, which thou canst
    not see;
All discord, harmony not understood;
All partial evil, universal good.
    Ibid., l. 289

Know then thyself, presume not God
    to scan;

The proper study of mankind is man.
Placed on this isthmus of a middle state,
A being darkly wise, and rudely great;
With too much knowledge for the
    skeptic side,
With too much weakness for the stoic's
    pride,
He hangs between; in doubt to act, or rest;
In doubt to deem himself a god, or beast;
In doubt his mind or body to prefer;
Born but to die, and reasoning but to
    err....
Created half to rise, and half to fall;
Great Lord of all things, yet a prey to all;
Sole judge of truth, in endless error
    hurled;
The glory, jest, and riddle of the world!
    Ibid., Epistle 2, l. 1

Vice is a monster of so frightful mien,
As, to be hated, needs but to be seen;
Yet seen too oft, familiar with her face,
We first endure, then pity, then embrace.
    Ibid., l. 217

Order is Heaven's first law; and this
    confessed,
Some are, and must be, greater than the
    rest.
    Ibid., Epistle 4, l. 49

A wit's a feather, and a chief a rod;
An honest man's the noblest work of God.
    Ibid., l. 247

Nature and Nature's laws lay hid in night;
God said, Let Newton be! and all was
    light.
    "Epitaph for Sir Isaac Newton" (1730)

Blessed is he who expects nothing;
for he shall never be disappointed.
    "Epistle to Gay" (1732)

Who shall decide when doctors
disagree?
    "Epistle to Lord Bathurst" (1733)

'Tis education forms the common
mind;
Just as the twig is bent the tree's
inclined.
    "Epistle to Lord Cobham" (1734).

Damn with faint praise, assent with civil
leer,
And without sneering teach the rest to
sneer.
    "Epistle to Dr. Arbuthnot" (1735), l. 201

A cherub's face, a reptile all the rest.
    Ibid., l. 331

I am His Highness' dog at Kew.
Pray tell me sir, whose dog are you?
    "Epigram on collar of a dog given to the
King" (1738)

Yes, I am proud; I must be proud to see
Men, not afraid of God, afraid of me.
    Imitations of Horace (1738), Epilogue,
Dialogue 2, l.208

Get place and wealth, if possible, with
grace;
If not, by any means get wealth and
place.
    Imitations of Horace (1738), Epilogue to
the Satires, Epistle 1, bk1, l. 103

And all who told it added something
new, and all who heard it made enlarge-
ments too.

He that would pun would pick a pocket.

CHARLES MONTESQUIEU
1689–1755

French, political philosopher. His *The Spirit of the Laws* (1748) recommended the "separation of powers" between the executive, legislative, and judicial branches. The U. S. Constitution rests on the separation of powers and Locke's denial of government's power to abridge the "natural rights" to life, liberty, and property.

Montesquieu thought liberty could only survive in small republics. James Madison thought that in large republics more countervailing interests would gridlock each other, thereby preventing the coalescing of a "durable tyrannical majority."

Deterioration of a government begins almost always by the decay of its principles.
    The Spirit of the Laws (1748)

Republics end by wealth; monarchies end by poverty.
    Ibid., VII, 4

The Catholic religion is most agreeable to monarchy, and the Protestant to a republic…
    J. Michelet, *Historie de France*

Commerce cures destructive prejudices. It polishes and softens barbarous mores…. The natural effect of commerce is to lead to peace.
    The Spirit of the Laws, Cambridge Univ.
Press (1989)

If triangles had a god, he would have three sides.

Countries are well cultivated, not as they are fertile, but as they are free.

4TH EARL OF CHESTERFIELD
1694–1773

English, also known as Philip Stanhope, remembered for his *Letters to His Son* (1774) as guides to worldly success:

An injury is much sooner forgotten than an insult.
Letters to His Son, October 9, 1746

Advice is seldom welcome; and those who want it the most always like it the least.
Ibid., January 29, 1748

Wear your learning, like your watch, in a private pocket, and do not pull it out and strike it merely to show you have one. If you are asked what o'clock it is, tell it; but do not proclaim it hourly unasked like a watchman.
Ibid., February 22, 1748

Women who are either indisputably beautiful, or indisputably ugly, are best flattered upon the score of their understandings; but those who are in a state of mediocrity are best flattered upon their beauty, or at least their graces; for every woman who is not absolutely ugly thinks herself handsome.
Ibid. September 5, 1748

People hate those who make them feel their own inferiority.
Ibid. April 30, 1750

The greatest favors may be done so awkwardly and bunglingly as to offend; and disagreeable things may be done so agreeably as almost to oblige.
Ibid. April 7, 1751

Firmness of purpose is one of the most necessary sinews of character and one of the best instruments of success. Without it, genius wastes its efforts in a maze of inconsistencies.

Barbarism begins her reign by banishing the Muses.

Lord Chesterfield is often thought of as a fop preaching stilted etiquette to his nephew. But, he was an astute political analyst. He discerned Britain's folly in imposing a stamp tax on America designed to raise 60,000 pounds a year that would put at risk British exports of 2 million pounds annually. Proponents of the Stamp Act of 1765 knew its prospective revenue would be small, but they wanted to assert the right of Parliament to tax the colonies. Chesterfield said, "It is absurd to assert a right you cannot exert." As he predicted, the Act raised little revenue and it led to a boycott of British goods by all the colonies, known as "Non-Importation." Worse for Britain, Americans began to manufacture their own goods. That struck at the heart of Britain's Navigation Acts, which were intended to prevent any manufacturing in America.

5
ENLIGHTENMENT: THE AGE OF REASON

In the seventeenth century's Age of Science, Britain and Europe took different paths that led to different types of Enlightenments in the eighteenth century. However, both Enlightenments shifted away from the revelation of Jerusalem and toward the cognition of Athens.

In Britain, the "empiricism" of Bacon and Newton, in which truth was provisional, engendered a step-by-step approach to problem solving based on observation and experience. This complemented Britain's case-by-case discovery of the common law and the philosophies of Milton and Locke, which favored reformation over revolution. The same, cautious, reform-oriented approach obtained in British letters with Jonathan Swift, Samuel Johnson, William Blake, and Edmund Burke, who were all fierce critics of Rousseau and revolution.

In Europe's Age of Science, "rationalism" or "reason" held sway. This methodology searched for a theoretical system that could explain everything—that is, it bred new systems out of whole cloth without regard to experience, traditions, or customs. Indeed, Descartes, the supreme rationalist, said of traditional order, "I know no better remedy than absolutely to raze it to the ground, in order to raise a new one in its stead." This favored destruction and utopian transformation, not reform. It followed the Greek rationalist example per W. H. S. Jones, "Greek philosophy sought

for uniformity in the multiplicity of phenomena, and the desire to find this uniformity led to guess-work and neglect of facts in the attempt to frame a comprehensive theory." But Hume observed that there is in man "only a speck of reason on a sea of passion."

Reacting to the British Enlightenment, Voltaire started the rationalist French Enlightenment. French *philosophes* were bookish men seeking to reorder civilization out of reason to achieve their supreme goals of equality for the masses and philosopher kingships for themselves. The *philosophes* thought man could be perfected. To subdue the hated church and nobility, they supported the state and enlightened despots, such as Frederick the Great (so entitled by the *philosophes*). Behind the French trotted the German rationalists: Kant, Humboldt, Schopenhauer, and Hegel. The result of European Enlightenment was to replace Europe's limited monarchies with absolute military dictatorships. French rationalism failed in perfecting man, but succeeding in cultivating ferocious pagan tyrants, like Napoleon, Lenin, and Hitler.

Differences between the two Enlightenments remain today: the "Anglo-American" and "Franco-German" mind-sets. Anglo-Americans emphasize individualism and limitations on majority rule. Karel Čapek wrote, "Wherever on this planet ideals of personal freedom and dignity apply, there you will find the cultural inheritance of England." Franco-Germans prefer popular sovereignty and the state guiding society. In short, Anglo-Americans favor liberty and Franco-Germans favor equality.

America took the British bent for liberty even further in its 1776 libertarian Revolution. Anglo-American free markets now dominate the global economy while many European states are technology free-riders on a glide-path to trailing China and India by the middle of the twenty-first century.

Arthur Herman's *How the Scots Invented the Modern World* (2001) shows the disproportionate Scottish contribution to the Enlightenment and modern capitalism. Scots relied on experience and common sense to know the right. Honor, discipline, risk acceptance, and a sense of duty gave the Scots a hard entrepreneurial edge. According to George Will and Charles Murray, Great Britain has contributed more to civilization, relative to its numbers, than any other people since the Greeks.

VOLTAIRE
1694–1778

French, a freethinker, of whose influence de Tocqueville said caused "the universal discredit into which all religious belief fell at the end of the eighteenth century." From a positive perspective, he was the French champion of tolerance, science, and the Enlightenment. He said, "If there is anything that can stop the frenzy of fanaticism, it is publicity."

Voltaire ended all his correspondence with *"Écrasez l'infâme"* (Crush the infamy). The long form was, "Whatever you do, crush this infamy and love those who love you." The *infâme* was Christianity, against

which he assembled an arsenal of arguments in his *Dictionnaire Philosophique*.

During Voltaire's stay in England (1726-29) he learned about the connection between commerce and toleration. He became a free market economist: Merchants were heroes, and priests and aristocrats were villains. He scorned the Christian and the Spartan hatred of luxury and their virtues of self-denial. He saw that economic self-interest was an antidote to political and religious fanaticism, and the Royal Exchange a tolerant proxy for capitalism:

> The Jew, the Mohametan, and the Christian deal with one another as if they were of the same religion, and reserve the name of infidel for those who go bankrupt.... Commerce established an arena within which people dealt with each other solely for economic benefit and, so, ignored extraneous factors such as the other party's religious practices.... The Presbyterian trusts the Anabaptist, and the Church of England man accepts the promise of the Quaker.

Voltaire anticipated Adam Smith and Hayek by holding that self-interest was the surest basis for social order, not a threat to it per Christianity and the civic moralists (Stoics) and collectivists:

> It is as impossible for a society to be formed and lasting without self-interest as it would be to produce children without carnal desire or to think of eating without appetite. It is love of self that encourages love of others.... That is the foundation of all commerce, the eternal link between men.
> "On the Pensées of Pascale."

After fifteen thousand people perished in 1755 in the Lisbon earthquake, Voltaire was incensed that priests ascribed it to divine retribution. In reaction, Voltaire wrote in three days the novella *Candide, or Optimism,* to attack Leibnitz's view that this was the best of all worlds. Candide, pupil of Dr. Pangloss, professor of metaphyusicotheologiocosmonigology, and friends are swept up in a series of wars, torture, slavery, cannibalism, and the like. The result of a battle between the Bulgars and Abars is described:

> When all was over and the rival kings were celebrating their victory with Te Deums in their respective camps, Candide…picked his way over piles of dead and dying, and reached a neighboring village on the Abar side of the border. It was now no more than a smoking ruin, for the Bulgars had burned it to the ground in accordance with the terms of international law. Old men, crippled with wounds, watched helplessly the death-throes of their butchered women-folk, who still clasped their children to their bloodstained breasts. Girls who had satisfied the appetites of several heroes lay disemboweled in their agonies…. Whichever way he looked, the ground was strewn with the legs, arms, and brains of the dead villagers.

At the end, Candide and friends farm twenty acres in Turkey where Pangloss muses that their suffering brought them this peace in the best of worlds. Note: Voltaire never engaged Leibnitz's argument that evil cannot be excluded where men are free to choose evil or good, and that it is a better world than if there were no free will and no evil or good.

Eternal host of useless sufferings!
Ye silly sages who cry, "All is well,"…
Women and children heaped in common death….
Will you, before this mass of crimes, say,
"God is revenged, their death repays
    their crimes"?…
What must we do, O mortals?
Mortals, we must suffer, submit in
    silence, adore, and die.
    "On the Lisbon Disaster, or An Examination of the Axiom that All Is Well."

The superfluous, a very necessary thing.
    Le Mondain (1736)

He who is merely just is severe, and he who is only wise is sad.
    Letter to Frederick the Great (1740)

The Holy Roman Empire was neither holy, nor Roman, nor an empire.
    Essai sur les Moeurs et L'Esprit des Nations
    (1756)

Dr. Pangloss:… as all things have been created for some end, they must necessarily have been created for the best end. Observe, for instance, the nose is formed for spectacles…. All is for the best in the best of all possible worlds.
    Candide (1759)

In this country [England] it is found good, from time to time, to kill one admiral to encourage the others.
    Ibid.

Candide: "And why was the world created?"
Martin: "To drive us mad, Candide."
    Ibid.

Dr. Pangloss: "There is a concatenation of events in this best of all possible worlds; for if you had not been put into the Inquisition…you would not be here eating preserved citrons and pistachio-nuts."
Candide: "All of that is very well, but let us cultivate our garden."

> Ibid.

No one has ever used so much intelligence to persuade us to be stupid. After reading your book one feels that one ought to walk on all fours. Unfortunately during the last sixty years I have lost the habit.
[Returning his *Discourse on the Origin of Inequality*, which argued that man had been happy until civilization corrupted him.]

> Letter of August 31, 1761 to
> Jean J. Rousseau

[Speaking of Rousseau:]
I am tired of all these people who govern states from the recesses of their garrets…unable to govern their wives or households they take great pleasure in regulating the universe.

Men will always be mad and those who think they can cure them are the maddest of all.

> Letter (1762)

Common sense is not so common.

> *Dictionnaire Philosophique* (1764),
> "Common Sense"

In general, the art of government consists in taking as much money as possible from one class of citizens to give to the other.

> Ibid., "Money"

Very learned women are to be found, in the same manner as female warriors; but they are seldom inventors.

> Ibid., "Women"

The best is the enemy of the good.

> Ibid., "Dramatic Art"

I have always made one prayer to God, a very short one. Here it is: "My God, make our enemies very ridiculous!" God has granted it to me.

> Letter to M. Damilaville (May 16, 1767)

Any one who has the power to make you believe absurdities has the power to make you commit injustices.

> *Collection of Letters on the Miracles* (1767)

If God did not exist it would be necessary to invent Him. But all nature cries aloud that He does exist; that there is a supreme intelligence, an immense power, an admirable order, and everything teaches us our own dependence on it.

> Epître, "A Lauteur de Livere des Trois
> Imposteurs" (November 10, 1770)

I advise you to go on living solely to enrage those who are paying you annuities. It is the only pleasure I have left.

> Letter to Madame du Deffand

He who has not the spirit of his age,
Of his age has all the misery.

> Letter to Madame du Chatelet

I disapprove of what you say, but I will defend to the death your right to say it.

> Apocryphal letter to Helvetius

Froth at the top, dregs at bottom, but the middle excellent.
[Speaking of the English people.]

In the case of news, we should always wait for the sacrament of confirmation.
> Letter to Count d'Argental

To believe in God is impossible; not to believe in Him is absurd.
> In L. R. Frank, *Wit and Humor Quotationary*

Almost nothing great has ever been done in the world except by the genius and firmness of a single man combating the prejudices of the multitude.

The fate of a nation has often depended on the good or bad digestion of a prime minister.

One great use of words is to hide our thoughts.

Marriage is a dull meal, with dessert served first.

Man is free at the moment he wishes to be.

They who say all men are equal speak an undoubted truth, if they mean that all have an equal right to liberty, to their property, and to the protection of the laws. But they are mistaken if they think men are equal in their station or employments, since they are not so by their talents.

Originality is nothing but judicious imitation. The most original writers borrowed one from another.

Every man is the creature of the age in which he lives; very few are able to raise themselves above the ideas of the time.

Books rule the world, or at least those nations which have a written language; the others do not matter.

If you see a Swiss banker jumping out of a window, follow him: There's bound to be money in it.

Judge a man by his questions rather than his answers.

[When Voltaire praised the book of Swiss physiologist von Haller, Casanova noted von Haller had called Voltaire's work nonsense. Voltaire replied:] Perhaps we are both mistaken.

If there were only one religion in England, there would be danger of despotism, if there were two, they would cut each other's throats, but there are thirty, and they live in peace.

The art of medicine consists of amusing the patient while nature cures the disease.

To bore the reader, tell him everything.

My trade is to say what I think.

[On a Catholic abstemious day, Voltaire ordered a beef omelet at an inn. Just as the waiter served the omelet, a bolt of lightning hit the inn. Voltaire threw the omelet out the window, exclaiming, "*Voilà bien du bruit pour une omelette*" or "What a row about an omelet."]

This is no time for making new enemies.
[Deathbed response to renouncing Satan.]

Doubt is not a pleasant state, but certainty is a ridiculous one.

LORD KAMES
1696–1782

Scottish, justice, who believed men form governments to pursue the common good, which chiefly is protecting private property. A threat to the life and property of any citizen threatens the life and property of all. Next comes enforcing contracts and supporting the moral order as it evolves. Law must evolve to keep up with an evolving society.

Kames saw history as a progression toward a greater freedom and morality. He divided history into four stages: (1) hunter-gatherers, (2) pastoral-nomads, (3) agriculture, and (4) commercial. Under barbarism, individual rights must give way to group survival. With civilization, man's moral sense advances, so the harsh necessities for primitive man, such as slavery, are no longer permitted.

> Law ripens gradually with the human faculties, and by ripeness of discernment and delicacy of sentiment, many duties formerly neglected are found to be binding on conscience.
> Arthur Herman, *How the Scots Invented the Modern World* (2001)

> The law of a country is in perfection when it corresponds to the manners of a people, their circumstances, their government. And as these are seldom stationary, the law ought to accompany them in their changes.
> Ibid.

MAURICE DE SAXE
1696–1750

French, Count of Saxony, marshal who wrote *Mes Rêveries* (1732), a book still studied for its insights into military organization.

> It is wearisome to carry a cuirass and trail a pike half a century to use it a single day. But as soon as discipline is neglected in a nation, as soon as comfort becomes an aim, it needs no inspiration to foretell that its ruin is near.

> The first of all qualities is courage. Without this the others are of little value, since they cannot be used. The second is intelligence which must be strong and fertile in expedients. The third is health.

JAMES THOMSON
1700–48

Scot, poet and playwright.

> When Britain first, at Heaven's
>   command,
> Arose from out of the azure main,
> This was the charter of the land,
> And guardian angels sang the strain:
> Rule Britannia, rule the waves
> Britons never will be slaves.
> "Rule Britannia" (1740), st. 1

> The nations not so blest as thee
> Must, in their turns, to tyrants fall,
> Whilst thou shalt flourish, great and free,
> The dread and envy of them all.
> Ibid., st. 2

JONATHAN EDWARDS
1703–58

American, evangelist whose *Treatise Concerning the Religious Affections* (1746) taught free will, thus breaking with Augustine and Calvin. Edwards ended Calvinist supremacy in New England. Belief in the duty to take charge of one's life inspired the American Revolution. Edwards and George Whitefield (1714–70) launched the Great Awakening, the greatest revival of religious faith in history, which inspired a Christianity that was described by Paul Johnson as "undogmatic, moralistic rather than creedal, tolerant, but strong and all-pervasive of society."

> The God that holds you over the pit of hell, much as one holds a spider, or some loathsome insect, over the fire, abhors you and is dreadfully provoked....
> "Sinners in the Hands of an Angry God"
> (1741)

JOHN WESLEY
1703–91

English, possibly the greatest evangelist, who founded Methodism (for methodical Bible reading), a church that brought the working class to religion and infused them with a desire for respectability. A "field preacher" of free will, he rode four thousand miles annually on horseback. He influenced England more in his century than anyone except William Pitt the Elder. Prior to Wesley, religion had been declining in Britain's upper class due to French Deism, and very few working class attended church. He disdained appeals to reason, believing that religion must be based on faith through divine inspiration.

> I look upon the world as my parish.
> *Journal* (June 11, 1739)

> Act as if the whole election depended on your single vote.
> "Word to a Freeholder" (1748), in L. R. Frank, *Quotationary* (1999)

> Religion must necessarily produce both industry and frugality, and these cannot but produce riches.... We ought not to prevent people from being diligent and frugal; we must exhort all Christians to gain all they can, and to save all they can; that is, in effect, to grow rich.
> Southey, *Life of John Wesley*, ch. 29

> Do all the good you can, by all the means you can, in all the ways you can, in all the places you can, at all the times you can, to all the people you can, as long as you ever can.
> In Rick Warren, *The Purpose Driven Life* (2002)

> Best of all, God is with us.
> Last words

BENJAMIN FRANKLIN
1706–90

American, scientist, businessman, inventor, diplomat, and commonsense writer known for industry, thrift, equipoise, and having an open mind. He and Washington were the most famous Americans of their era. He was the only man to have done all of the following: help draft the Articles of Confederation, the Declaration of

Independence, and the Constitution, and sign the Treaty of Alliance with France and Treaty of Paris, granting independence. His British friend Strahan said he was "an honor to his country and an ornament to human nature."

He invented: the Franklin stove, which reduced the wood needed to heat a small house during the winter from five cords to one cord; the lightning rod; bifocal lenses; artificial fertilizer; and the chimney damper; he discovered ocean currents and mapped the Gulf Stream, saving countless sailors and time; and, as a colonel, he organized the first militia in Pennsylvania to fight Indians with the motto "Join or die." He organized the colonies' first lending library, first private secondary school, first public university, first public fire department, first public hospital, first scientific society, and first insurance company; and he proved that lightning is an electrical discharge.

When he was post master general of the colonies, you could post a letter from Philadelphia to New York on one day and receive a reply the next day! His Articles of Confederation and Perpetual Union held the colonies together during the Revolutionary War, and his endorsement won the ratification of the Constitution. His friendship with essentially the first minister of France, Charles Vergennes, led a monarchy to bankrupt itself in order to aid a republican revolution. A Physiocrat in France, he became the first American free-trade economist.

> Most of the statutes…for regulating, directing or restraining of trade, have, we think been either political blunders, or jobs obtained by artful men for private advantage, under pretense of public good. When Colbert assembled some wise old merchants of France, and desired their advice and opinion, how he could best serve and promote commerce, their answer was *Laissez-nous faire*: "Let us alone…." *Pas trop gouverner*: "Not to govern too much." Which, perhaps, would be of more use when applied to trade, than in any other public concern. It were therefore to be wished, that commerce was as free between all the nations of the world, as it is between the several counties of England; so would all, by mutual communication, obtain more enjoyments…. No nation was ever ruined by trade, even seemingly the most disadvantageous.
>
> Works, vol. II

His *Poor Richard's Almanac* (1733) (alias Richard Saunders) contained 1,044 sayings, mostly taken from English maxims. Less than twenty were original to Franklin. It became the most popular book in the colonies next to the Bible due to its leitmotiv of rags-to-riches through self-help and his invention of the "wisecrack," a joke that imparts wisdom, for example, "Neither a fortress nor a maidenhead will hold out long after they begin to parley."

Franklin, like Adams, Jefferson, and Hamilton, was a Deist who relied on reason rather than revelation and did not believe in a God that intervened actively in human affairs. But he accepted Christianity as a just system of morality.

Franklin was not perfect. His detractors said he was a ladies' man and a materialist. Also, he disinherited his son for being a royalist, whereas Robert E. Lee gave his son the freedom to decide whether to support the Confederacy or the Union.

No longer virtuous no longer free, is a maxim as true with regard to a private person as a commonwealth.

Whoever would overthrow the liberty of a nation must begin by subduing the freedom of speech, a thing terrible to traitors.

> By Silence Dogood (Franklin's nom de plume at age seventeen) (1722). In H. W. Brand, *The First American* 2002

Since without virtue man can have no happiness in this world, I firmly believe [God] delights to see me virtuous, because He is pleased when He sees me happy.

> Ibid.

1. It is necessary for me to be extremely frugal for some time, till I have paid what I owe. 2. To endeavor to speak truth in every instance, to give nobody expectations that are not likely to be answered, but aim at sincerity in every word and action, the most amiable excellence in a rational being. 3. To apply myself industriously to whatever business I take in hand, and not divert my mind from my business by any foolish project of growing rich, for industry and patience are the surest means of plenty. 4. I resolve to speak ill of no man whatever.

> [Franklin's Four Principles of Success]
> Ibid.

[Franklin told the story of a father and son going to market with the father riding on an ass. A passerby criticized the father for making the son walk, so the father let the boy ride behind. Another passerby criticized them for overloading the ass, so the father then walked beside the ass that carried the son. The next passerby said what a bad son to so abuse his father so they then both walked beside the ass. A company of passersby laughed at them for walking beside an unloaded ass.]

> Ibid.

It is the man and woman united that make the complete human being. Separate, she wants his force of body and strength of reason; he, her sensibility and acute discernment. Together they are more likely to succeed in the world. A single man has not nearly the value he would have in that state of union. He is an incomplete animal. He resembles the odd half of a pair of scissors.

> Ibid.

Happiness in this life rather depends on internals than externals...there is such a thing as being of a happy or an unhappy constitution.

> Ibid.

One's true happiness depends more upon one's own judgment of one's self, on a consciousness of rectitude in act and intention, and in the approbation of those few who judge impartially, than upon the applause of the unthinking, undiscerning multitude, who are apt to cry Hosanna today, and tomorrow, Crucify him.

> Ibid.

If such a fellow is not damned, it is not worthwhile to keep a Devil.

> [Speaking of one who stole from starving prisoners.]
> Ibid.

This is the time of life in which you are to lay the foundations of your future improvement, and of your importance among men. If this season is neglected, it will be like cutting off the spring from the year.

> [Letter to his son urging him to resume his studies in college.]
>
> Ibid.

Tyranny is so generally established in the rest of the world that the prospect of an asylum in America for those who love liberty gives general joy, and our cause is esteemed the cause of all mankind.

> [Of the American Revolution.]
>
> Ibid.

If the rascals knew the advantage of virtue, they would become honest men out of rascality.

> Ibid.

Only a virtuous people are capable of freedom. As nations become more corrupt and vicious, they have more need of masters.

> Ibid.

> [Although he owned slaves most of his life, in 1790 he forwarded an anti-slavery petition to Congress, writing:]

"Mankind are all formed by the same Almighty Being, alike objects of his care and equally designed for the enjoyment of happiness."

> Ibid.

If honor had to be assigned to families, it ought to be handed up to parents rather than down to children. The parents of a person who did good deeds might logically share some credit for the good deeds of their child, in that they were responsible for the child's education and overall rearing, but the children of the one who did good deeds could not share any such credit.

> Ibid.

So vast is the territory of North America that it will require many ages to settle it fully; and till it is settled, labor will never be cheap here, where no man continues long a laborer for others but gets a plantation of his own, no man continues long a journeyman to a trade, but goes among those new settlers and sets up for himself.

> L. W. Labaree et al., *Papers of Benjamin Franklin*, iv (1959–70)

He founded the University of Pennsylvania, and argued it was anachronistic to teach Latin and Greek. He lampooned Harvard as teaching what could be learned in a dancing school, and that its graduates emerged "as great blockheads as ever, only more proud and conceited."

They that can give up essential liberty to obtain a little temporary safety deserve neither liberty nor safety.

> Reply to Governor Morris (November 11, 1755), *Historical Review of Pennsylvania* (1759)

Our North American colonies are to be considered as the frontier of the British Empire on that side. The frontier of any dominion being attacked, it becomes not merely "the cause" of the people immediately attacked but properly "the cause" of the whole body. It is therefore invidious to represent "the blood and treasure" spend in this war as spent in "the cause of the colonies" only...

In Jacques Barzun, *From Dawn to Decadence* (2000)

We must all hang together, or assuredly we shall all hang separately.
[At the signing of the Declaration of Independence, July 4, 1776. Cromwell had said the same thing 136 years earlier.]

A republic, if you can keep it.
[Response to whether the Constitution gave the country a monarchy or a republic.]

September 18, 1787

Our new Constitution is now established, and has an appearance that promises permanency; but in this world nothing can be said to be certain, except death and taxes.

Letter to Jean Baptiste Leroy (November 13, 1789)

What good is a new born baby?
[Franklin's reply when asked the use of a hot air balloon invented by the Montsolfier brothers. Franklin saw its first flight. When it landed in a field outside of Paris, the surprised peasants attacked it.]

Poor Richard's Almanac
1733–58

To lengthen your life, lessen your meals.
[In 1999: Mice raised on half rations lived twice as long as mice given normal rations.]

Early to bed and early to rise, makes a man healthy, wealthy, and wise.

Beware of little expenses. A small leak will sink a great ship.

A little house well filled, a little field well tilled, and a little wife well willed, are great riches.

Necessity never made a good bargain.

There are three faithful friends: an old wife, an old dog, and ready money.

Laws too gentle are seldom obeyed, too severe, seldom executed.

Experience keeps a dear school, yet fools will learn in no other.

Dost thou love life? Then do not squander time; for that's the stuff life is made of.

Little strokes fell great oaks.

Creditors have better memories than debtors; and creditors are a superstitious sect, great observers of set days and times.

A learned blockhead is a greater blockhead than an ignorant one.

Eat to please thyself, but dress to please others.

Read much, but not many books.

No longer virtuous, no longer free.

Would you persuade, speak of interest, not of reason.

Remember that time is money.
Advice to a Young Tradesman (1748)

Plow deep while sluggards sleep.

Vessels large may venture more,
But little boats should keep near shore.

The way to wealth is as plain as the way to market. It depends, chiefly on two words, industry and frugality.

Where liberty dwells, there is my country.
[*Ubi libertas ibi patria.* A Latin saying.]
Letter to B. Vaughn (March 4, 1783)

I have always thought that one man of tolerable abilities may work great changes, and accomplish great affairs among mankind, if he first forms a good plan, and cutting off all amusements or other employments that would divert his attention, makes the execution of that same plan his sole study and business.
Autobiography (1788)

In the course of my observation, the disputing, contradicting and confuting people are generally unfortunate in their affairs. They get victory sometimes, but they never get good will, which would be of more use to them.
In Peter Baida, *Poor Richard's Legacy: American Business Values from Benjamin Franklin to Michael Milken* (1990), ch. 1

Hereafter, if you should observe an occasion to give your officers and friends a little more praise than is their due, and confess more fault than you can justly be charged with, you will only become the sooner for it, a great captain. Criticizing and censuring almost everyone you have to do with will diminish friends, increase enemies, and thereby hurt your affairs.
Letter to John Paul Jones (1780)

The best investment is in the tools of one's trade.

Freedom is not a gift bestowed upon us by other men, but a right that belongs to us by the laws of God and nature.

A frequent recurrence to fundamental principles… is absolutely necessary to preserve the blessings of liberty and keep a government free.

When the people find that they can vote themselves money, that will herald the end of the republic.

Men will ultimately be governed by God or tyrants.

History affords us many instances of the ruin of states …the ordaining of laws in favor of one part of the nation to the prejudice and oppression of another, is certainly the most erroneous and mistaken policy. …An equal dispensation of protection, rights, privileges, and advantages, is what every part is entitled.

HENRY FIELDING
1707–54

English, novelist. His masterpiece is *Tom Jones* (1743), which reveals truths about human nature through his characters. Tom Jones, a foundling, is wild but honorable and good-hearted, in contrast to his half brother, Master Blifil, a hypocrite with

Iago's mask of sincerity covering a villainous nature. Squire Allworthy, Tom's foster father, is a just but precipitous man, who disinherits Tom.

> Thwackum was for doing justice, and leaving mercy to heaven.
>
> *Tom Jones* (1749), bk. 3, ch. 10

> His designs were strictly honorable, as the phrase is; that is, to rob a lady of her fortune by way of marriage.
>
> Ibid., bk. 11, ch. 4

> Hairbreath missings of happiness look like the insults of Fortune.
>
> Ibid., bk. 13, ch. 2

WILLIAM PITT (THE ELDER)
1708–1778

English, prime minister, known as "the Great Commoner." He expanded the British Empire more than any other statesman. He allied England with Frederick the Great of Prussia in the Seven Years' War (1756–63) against France, Austria, and Russia, during which Prussia battled the Continental powers to a bloody stalemate while England cheaply pocketed Canada and India from France.

He opposed taxing Americans without representation: "The Americans are the sons, not the bastards of England." He also said, "I know I can save this country and that I alone can." Pitt, like Franklin, favored a commonwealth of sovereign states, but Britain wanted to milk the colonies.

> The poorest man may in his cottage bid defiance to all the force of the Crown. It may be frail; its roof may shake; the

wind may blow through it; the storms may enter, the rain may enter, but the King of England cannot enter; all his forces dare not cross the threshold of the ruined tenement.
>
> Speech in the House of Commons
> (March 6, 1741)

DR. SAMUEL JOHNSON
1709–84

English, lexicographer, and great literary critic. A gruff man dubbed Ursus Major (Great Bear) and Great Cham (Khan) of Literature, he was coarse and ill natured, yet charitable. His 42,377-word dictionary was the standard until Webster's 70,000-word dictionary in 1828. Johnson was Britain's national sage and a "wisdom writer." His dictionary was far more than definitions. He gave examples of usage, and they were sentences from moral and political philosophers that mirrored his Tory views, that is, a prescriptive lexicography.

The Lives of the Poets (1781), an anthology of English poets, set the standard for literary criticism. He lauded Dryden, Pope, Swift, and Addison, but not Milton and the "metaphysical" poets due to their obscurities, like Greek myths. He said that in evaluating literature, "Nothing can please many, and please long, but just representations of general nature." He also said, "The only end of writing is to enable the reader better to enjoy life, or better to endure it." Johnson told us why we read literature:

> Works of imagination excel by their allurement and delight; by their power of attracting and detaining the attention. That book is good in vain which the reader throws away. He only is

master who keeps the mind in pleasing captivity; whose pages are perused with eagerness, and in hope of new pleasure perused again….

Comments on Dryden's *Aeneid*

The task of an author is, either to teach what is not known, or to recommend known truths by his manner of adorning them; either to let new light in upon the mind, and open new scenes to the prospect, or to vary the dress and situation of common objects, so as to give them fresh grace…

The Rambler, no. 3

The irregular combinations of fanciful invention may delight awhile, by that novelty of which the common satiety of life sends us all in quest; but the pleasures of sudden wonder are soon exhausted, and the mind can only repose on the stability of truth.

Preface to Shakespeare

…since genius, whatever it be, is like fire in the flint, only to be produced by collision with a proper subject, it is the business of every man to try whether his faculties may not happily cooperate with his desires….

The Rambler, no. 125

There is nothing more dreadful to an author than neglect, compared with which reproach, hatred, and opposition are names of happiness.

Ibid. (March 24, 1750)

Curiosity is one of the permanent and certain characteristics of a vigorous mind.

Ibid. (March 12, 1751)

No man ever yet became great by imitation. [Whoever] hopes for the veneration of mankind must have invention in the design or the execution; either the effect must itself be new, or the means by which it is produced.

Ibid. (September 17, 1751)

The English dictionary was written with little assistance of the learned, and without any patronage of the great; not in the soft obscurities of retirement, or under the shelter of academic bowers, but amidst inconvenience and distraction, in sickness and in sorrow.

A Dictionary of the English Language
(1775), Preface

Change is not made without inconvenience, even from worse to better.

Ibid.

Every quotation contributes something to the stability or enlargement of the language.

Ibid.

Essay: A loose sally of the mind; an irregular undigested piece…

Lexicographer: A writer of dictionaries, a harmless drudge.

Oats: A grain, which in England is generally given to horses, but in Scotland supports the people.

Ibid., "Definitions"

Abstinence is as easy to me, as temperance would be difficult.

William Roberts, ed., *Memoirs of the Life and Correspondence of Mrs. Hannah More*
(1834), vol. 1

Johnson, a devout Christian, wrote *Rasselas* to refute Rousseau's notion that happiness is to be found in a simple return to nature. It begins: "Ye who listen with phantoms of hope, who expect that old age will perform the promises of youth, and that the deficiencies of the present day will be supplied by the morrow; attend to the history of Rasselas." Rasselas vainly travels his kingdom seeking someone who is happy. He concludes he must accept life's trials calmly and trust in the salvation of his soul. Johnson thought philosophy was a trap leading to metaphysical nonsense and atheism.

> Human life is everywhere a condition in which much is to be endured, and little to be enjoyed.
> *The History of Rasselas, Prince of Abyssinia* (1759)

> Example is always more efficacious than precept.
> Ibid.

> Integrity without knowledge is weak and useless, and knowledge without integrity is dangerous.
> Ibid.

> Promise, large promise, is the soul of an advertisement.
> *The Idler*, no. 40 (Janury 20, 1759)

> But what is success to him that has [no one else] to enjoy it? Happiness is not found in self-contemplation; it is perceived only when it is reflected from another.
> *The Idler*, no. 41

> Why is it we hear the loudest yelps for liberty among the drivers of Negroes?
> "Taxation No Tyranny" (1775)

> Those who attain any excellence, commonly spend life in one pursuit; for excellence is not often gained upon easier terms.
> *Lives of the English Poets* (1779–81), "Pope"

> An author places himself uncalled before the tribunal of criticism and solicits fame at the hazard of disgrace.
> Ibid.

> Self-confidence is the first requisite to great undertakings.
> Ibid.

> To judge rightly of an author we must transport ourselves to his time, and examine what were the wants of his contemporaries, and what were his means of supplying them.
> Ibid., "Dryden"

> To be of no church is dangerous. Religion, of which the rewards are distant, and which is animated only by faith and hope, will glide by degrees out of the mind unless it be invigorated and reimpressed by external ordinances, by stated calls to worship, and the salutary influence of example.
> Ibid., "Milton"

At sixty-four years, Johnson and Boswell took a three-month trip by horseback to an island in north Scotland. Recalling the hardships of that trip, Johnson "heartily laughed at the ravings of those absurd visionaries who have attempted to persuade us of the specious advantages of a state of nature."

> I have, all my life long, been lying till noon; yet I tell all young men, and tell them with great sincerity, that nobody who does not

rise early will ever do any good.
Boswell, *Journal of a Tour to the Hebrides*
(1785)

Many things difficult to design prove easy to perform.
Ibid.

[When asked, "if no man was naturally good," he replied:] No, madam, no more than a wolf.
Ibid.

When he rode he had no command or direction of his horse, but was carried as if in a balloon.
[Boswell on Johnson riding a horse.]
Ibid.

Corneille is to Shakespeare as a clipped hedge is to a forest.
In Mrs. Piozz, *Anecdotes of the Late Samuel Johnson* (1786)

Dictionaries are like watches, the worst is better than none, and the best cannot be expected to go quite true.
Ibid.

THE LIFE OF SAMUEL JOHNSON
1791
BY JAMES BOSWELL

VOL. 1

Is not a patron, my lord, one who looks with unconcern on a man struggling for life in the water, and when he has reached ground encumbers him with help?
[A letter to Lord Chesterfield, who did not subscribe to Johnson's dictionary when he was impoverished, but offered help after Johnson became rich and famous.]

They [letters of Lord Chesterfield] teach the morals of a whore, and the manners of a dancing master.

If a man does not make new acquaintances as he advances through life, he will soon find himself left alone. A man, Sir, should keep his friendships in constant repair.

No man will be a sailor who has contrivance enough to get himself into a jail; for being in a ship is being in a jail, with the chance of being drowned.

A decent provision for the poor is the true test of civilization.

I am a great friend to public amusements; for they keep people from vice.

A cow is a very good animal in the field; but we turn her out of a garden.

Much may be made of a Scotsman, if he be caught young.

Rousseau, Sir, is a very bad man. I would sooner sign a sentence for his transportation than that of any felon who has gone from Old Bailey these many years.

[Asked why he had defined "pastern" as the knee of a horse, he replied:] Ignorance madam, pure ignorance.

But if he does really think that there is no distinction between virtue and vice, why, Sir, when he leaves our houses, let us count our spoons.

A man with a good coat upon his back meets with a better reception than he who has a bad one.

Your levellers wish to level down as far as themselves; but they cannot bear levelling up to themselves.

A woman's preaching is like a dog walking on its hind legs. It is not done well; but you are surprised to find it done at all.

Nature has given women so much power that the law has very wisely given them little.

Sir John, Sir, is a very unclubable man. [Sir John Hawkins was expelled from the "Literary Club" for not paying his dues. Members included Burke, Garrick, Reynolds, Dr. Johnson, and Goldsmith.]

We all know our will is free, and there's an end on't.

All theory is against the freedom of the will, all experience for it.

That fellow seems to me to possess but one idea, and that is a wrong one.

You may abuse a tragedy, though you cannot write one. You may scold a carpenter who has made you a bad table, though you cannot make a table. It is not your trade to make tables.

VOL. 2

I do not care to speak ill of any man behind his back, but I believe the gentleman is an attorney.

Read over your compositions, and wherever you meet with a passage which you think is particularly fine, strike it out.

There are few ways in which a man can be more innocently employed than in getting money.

The greatest part of a writer's time is spent in reading, in order to write: a man will turnover half a library to make a book.

Patriotism is the last refuge of a scoundrel.
[Critique of the Boston Tea Party.]

Knowledge is of two kinds: we know a subject ourselves, or we know where we can find information upon it.

In lapidary inscriptions a man is not upon oath.

Every man is, or hopes to be, an idler.

There is nothing which has yet been contrived by man, by which so much happiness is produced as by a good tavern or inn.

The triumph of hope over experience.
[Remarriage after an unhappy marriage.]

Attack is the reaction. I never think I have hit hard unless it rebounds.

VOL. 3

No man but a blockhead ever wrote except for money.
[After the king granted Johnson a pension of three hundred pounds per annum, he ceased writing.]

It is better that some should be unhappy than that none should be happy, which would be the case in a general state of equality.

Depend upon it, Sir, when a man knows he is to be hanged in a fortnight, it concentrates his mind wonderfully.

When a man is tired of London, he is tired of life.

So it is in traveling; a man must carry knowledge with him, if he would bring home knowledge.

Worth seeing? yes; but not worth going to see.

Every man has the right to utter what he thinks truth, and every other man has a right to knock him down for it.

VOL. 4

Classical quotation is the parole of literary men all over the world.

Resolve not to be poor; whatever you have, spend less. Poverty is a great enemy to human happiness; it certainly destroys liberty, and it makes some virtues impracticable, and others extremely difficult.

Sir, there is no settling the point of precedence between a louse and a flea.

As I know more of mankind I expect less of them, and am ready now to call a man a good man, upon easier terms than I was formerly.

Sir, your wife under pretense of keeping a bawdy house, is a receiver of stolen goods.
  [Common exchange of insults while boating on the Thames.]

No man was more foolish when he had not a pen in his hand, or more wise when he had.
  [Of Oliver Goldsmith.]

We are not here to sell a parcel of boilers and vats, but the potentiality of growing rich, beyond the dreams of avarice.
  [Of the sale of Thrale's brewery.]

UNSOURCED QUOTATIONS FROM DR. JOHNSON

All argument is against it, but all belief is for it.
  [Of God.]

Lady: You smell!
Dr. Johnson: No Madame, you smell; I stink.

You will find those very feeling people not very ready to do you good. They pay you by feeling.

Clear your mind of cant.

At 77, it is time to be in Earnest.

[Falstaff manifests] the most pleasing of all qualities, perpetual gaiety.

I look upon it, that he who does not mind his belly will hardly mind anything else.

Boswell was never in any one's company who did not wish to see him again.

Great works are performed not by strength but by perseverance.

Human experience, which is constantly contradicting theory, is the great test of truth. A system built on the discoveries of a great many minds is always of more strength than what is produced by the mere workings of any one mind.

I do not know, Sir, that the fellow is an infidel; but if he be an infidel, he is an infidel as a dog is an infidel, that is to say he has never thought upon the subject.

If a madman were to come into this room with a stick in his hand, no doubt we should pity the state of his mind; but our primary consideration would be to take care of ourselves. We should knock him down first, and pity him afterwards.

The Irish are a fair people—they never speak well of one another.

A horse that can count to ten is a remarkable horse—not a remarkable mathematician.

So far is it from being true that men are naturally equal, that no two people can be half an hour together but one shall acquire an evident superiority over the other.

The art of memory is the art of attention.

[Responding to Rousseau's favoring the life of the noble savage:] Do not allow yourself to be imposed on by such gross absurdity. It is sad stuff. If a bull could speak he might as well exclaim: "Here am I with this cow and this grass; what being can enjoy greater felicity!"

Your manuscript is both good and original, but the part that is good is not original, and the part that is original is not good.

It seems to be the fate of man to seek all his consolations in futurity.

Sorrow is the mere rust of the soul. Activity will cleanse and brighten it.

Such seems to be the disposition of man, that whatever makes a distinction produces rivalry.

You are much surer that you are doing good when you pay money to those who work, as the recompense of their labors, than when you give money merely in charity.

Nothing will ever be attempted if all possible objections must be first overcome.

Every man thinks meanly of himself for not having been a soldier, or not having been at sea. The profession of soldiers and sailors has the dignity of danger. Mankind reveres those who have gotten over fear, which is so general a weakness.

Courage is a quality so necessary for maintaining virtue that it is always respected, even when it is associated with vice.

Gratitude is the fruit of great cultivation; you do not find it among gross people.

A man of genius has seldom been ruined but by himself.

The chief glory of every people arises from its authors.

I will be conquered, I will not capitulate.
    [During his last illness.]

Louis XV
1710–74

French, king (1715–74), who was Louis XIV's great-grandson. Influenced by his concubine, Madame de Pompadour, his reign was noted for its corruption, mismanagement, and senseless wars. Wrongly attributed to Louis, but apt, was the ancient French saying, "After me, the flood." Louis, like Mao Tse-tung, regularly deflowered girls as young as nine years old; he spent 33 million *livres* on Madame de Pompadour, known at court as "Madame Whore"; and he spent a quarter of government revenues on his household. Louis for no good reason joined Austria and Russia in the Seven Years' War (1756–1763) against Prussia, and lost Canada and India to England. While peasants and laborers lived at subsistence and were taxed at 30 percent of income, France's 250,000 noblemen paid no taxes. Compare that to England's mere 200 noblemen due to its rule of primogeniture! Only 2 percent of French farmland was worked by its owners! The Bourbons impoverished France to make Paris the world's cultural capital with *belle lettrès*, Fragonard's frivolities, and Boucher's boudoir embellishments.

Thomas Reid
1710–96

Scottish, philosopher, who refuted the skeptic Hume who had said reality is not knowable. To Reid, reality was illuminated by observation and experience. Humans have innate "common sense," which allows them to make very certain judgments. Progress depends on educating people so that knowledge can make their common sense powerful. Moreover, this common sense leads to the discovery of self-evident moral truths—thus Reid attacked moral relativists as well as the skeptics. Thomas Paine borrowed "common sense" as a title for his pamphlet. In part due to Reid, Scotland became the eighteenth century's most literate nation, more literate than the United States in 2007, and without a single public school in Scotland.

> I despise philosophy and renounce its guidance; let my soul dwell in common sense.
> Arthur Herman, *How the Scots Invented the Modern World* (2001)

David Hume
1711–76

Scottish, skeptic, empiricist philosopher, and political scientist. Hume's theory of knowledge held that there were only two kinds of knowledge: sense impressions, and ideas from sense impressions—thus abstract ideas are impossible. This attacked Plato's theory that reality was ideas and Descartes' rationalism. Arguing that there is no way to bridge the gap between sense impressions and the external world, Hume even questioned the validity of science. He argued that "cause and effect" is merely based on observations that one thing follows another, but human reasoning cannot prove the causation. He also denied the mind, soul, and God because they cannot be proven by the senses.

As an empiricist, he assumes Berkeley's position and goes further. Since matter cannot be perceived, it does not exist, and neither do scientific laws because they cannot be perceived. You cannot see the law of gravity or any law of causation.

Hume's belief that we cannot give good reasons for what we believe did not lead him, like the Greek skeptics, to conclude we can believe nothing. We must believe things for which there is no rational basis: "Nature, by an absolute and uncontrollable necessity, has determined us to judge as well as to breathe and feel...." We must restrict our thinking to the world which is perceptual, that is, that which is subject to observation. Hume is the dominant influence on the dominant philosophy of our era, to wit, Wittgenstein's logical positivism.

Hume is equally as important as a political theorist. We act morally because our social instincts are inherent—the virtues and vices that help or hurt society are apparent. Customs evolve organically, that is, social consensus informs us what is right and wrong, albeit varying from one society to another. Hume's morality was not a relativist one. One can argue empirically that one society's customs are better than those in another.

Hume's notion of the organic growth of custom as the basis of morality anticipates Adam Smith, who saw the organic growth of free markets as creating the most productive economy possible. Organic growth via experimentation is the common denominator in the thinking of Hume, Adam Smith, Edmund Burke, Herbert Spencer, Carl Menger, von Mises, Friedrich Hayek, Lao-tzu, the science of complexity, and so on. This Scottish theory of spontaneous order saw civil society as self-generating and self-regulating. Thus, what is needed of a state is to defend against internal force and fraud and external invasion.

His *Treatise of Human Nature* (1739) attacked a priori principles and natural law. Contrary to Locke and Rousseau, governments were not formed by social contract, but by "usurpation or conquest." Any prosperous society must make contracts binding and protect the ability to transfer property. This theory was based, not on reason, but experience. Justice Holmes said Hume legitimized the common law by legitimizing experience. Justice Holmes later adopted Hume's belief that morality was based in social existence, not in natural law.

[The market economy made it possible] to do a service to another without bearing him a real kindness or even knowing him; or to act to the advantage of the public though it be not intended for that purpose...[or] even of bad men to act for the public good.

A Treatise on Human Nature (1739),
bk. 2, pt. 3

Reason is, and ought only to be the slave of the passions, and can never pretend to any other office than to serve and obey them.

Ibid.

It is not, therefore, reason, which is the guide of life, but custom.

Ibid.

It is seldom that liberty of any kind is lost all at once. Slavery has so frightful an aspect to men accustomed to freedom that it must steal in upon them by degrees and must disguise itself in a thousand shapes in order to be received.

On the Liberty of the Press (1742)

Render possessions ever so equal, men's different degrees of art, care, and industry will immediately break that equality. Or if you check these virtues…the most rigorous inquisition is requisite to watch every inequality on its first appearance, and the most severe jurisdiction to punish and redress it…. So much authority must soon degenerate into tyranny.

Inquiry Concerning Morals
(1750), ii, Sec. 155

The increase of riches and commerce in any one nation, instead of hurting, commonly promotes the riches and commerce of all its neighbors.

Essays Moral, Political and Literary (1752),
"Jealousy of Trade"

The perpetual war among all living creatures must go on.

Philosophical Works, vol. II, "Dialogues
Concerning Natural Religion"

Democracies are turbulent.

Idea of a Perfect Commonwealth (1752)

…liberty is the perfection of civil society [but] authority must be acknowledged essential to its very existence.

In Arthur Herman, *How the Scots Invented
the Modern World* (2001)

Generally speaking, the errors of religion are dangerous; those of philosophy only ridiculous.

PROSPECTUS FOR A SOUTH SEA COMPANY
1711

This fraudulent stock prospectus raised two hundred pounds. After taking subscriptions for just one day, the issuer fled England that evening. It illustrates how investors in euphoric markets will pay wild prices for junk securities. The prospectus was entitled "A Company for carrying on an undertaking of Great Advantage, but no one to know what it is."

FREDERICK II "THE GREAT"
1712–1786

Hohenzollern and Prussian king (1740–86), entitled "the Great" by Voltaire and called "the Great Drill-Sergeant of the Prussian Nation" by Carlyle. Despised by his father as effeminate, he curled his hair; wrote poems in French; composed flute concertos; hated hunting; and lived as a bachelor husband. Yet he led Europe's most feared army. Prussia fielded thirty times more soldiers as a ratio of its population than did Poland-Lithuania.

Frederick expanded Prussia with Silesia and chunks of Poland. During Poland's partition he saw Maria Theresa weeping. He remarked, "She wept, but she took." During the Seven Years' War (1756–1763), with a population of 4 million, he fought Saxony, France, Austria, and Russia (combined population of 60 million) to a standstill, even though deserted by Great Britain. He was saved by the death of Catherine I, whose successor, Tsar Peter III, halted the Russian army outside Berlin.

A brave colonel makes a brave battalion.

In L. R. Frank, *Quotationary* (1999)

[Of Russia, which was called "the gendarme of Europe."] It will need the whole of Europe to keep those gentlemen within bounds.

Norman Davies, *Europe: A History* (1996)

My people and I have come to an agreement that satisfies us both. They are to say what they please, and I am to do what I please.

[Said as he lowered a poster castigating him so the public could read it better.]

Margaret Goldsmith,
Frederick the Great (1929)

Rascals, would you live forever?
[To reluctant soldiers at Kolin 1757.]
Attributed

When I find any officer that answers me with firmness, intelligence, and clearness, I set him down in my list for making use of his service on proper occasions.

In L. R. Frank, *Quotationary* (1999)

It is not necessary that I live, but it is necessary that I perform my duty.

Ibid.

Machiavelli wrote only for petty princes.

Ibid.

Since officers must necessarily lead them into the greatest dangers, the soldiers should fear their officers more than all the dangers to which they are exposed.... Good will can never induce the common soldier to stand up to such dangers; he will only do so through fear.

In Robert Fitton, *Quotations from the World's Greatest Motivators* (1997)

By push of bayonets, no firing till you see the whites of their eyes.

Ibid. (May 6, 1758)

God is always with the strongest battalions.

Ibid. (May 8, 1760)

If I wished to punish a province, I would have it governed by philosophers.

JEAN JACQUES ROUSSEAU
1712–78

Swiss, political theorist. Robespierre said, "Rousseau is the one man who, through the loftiness of his soul and the grandeur of his character, showed himself worthy of the role of teacher of mankind." Edmund Burke called him the "Socrates of the National Assembly" (French Revolution). He reoriented Europe's intelligentsia away from attacking religion and toward expanding the state. An atheist, yet he supported a government religion to control the common people at a low cost, with banishment for those who refused to worship. Morbidly shy, he found relief in the woods, whence his worship of nature. Despite his glamorization of nature, Rousseau preferred to live in large cities.

Rousseau rose from obscurity in 1750 by winning an Academy of Dijon prize for an essay on "Has the restoration of the sciences and the arts contributed to corrupt or to purify morals?" Rejecting the Enlightenment, he argued that man in a state of nature is a "noble savage" who "is by nature good, and only our institutions have made him bad!" A competitive society pushes men to acquire property, resulting in inequality, which creates vice out of envy. Because men are equal, the state should enforce "social justice." His belief in man's natural goodness is the great philosophical divide between liberals, who agree, and conservatives, who see man as naturally self-interested and not to be trusted.

Rousseau championed the collective good found in the volonté générale, or "general will," which cannot be obtained by the deliberations of a representative government, but only by a "legislator" who knows what is best. Rousseau said, "There is often a great deal of difference between the will of all and the General Will; the latter regards only the common interest, while the former has regard to private interests, and is merely a sum of particular wills...." In *The Social Contract,* he is the "legislator" where he writes a constitution for all states, which should only be small city-states.

Rousseau's ideal of concentrating power in an elite justified the French Revolution's Committee for Public Safety. It later justified Napoleon, the Communist Politburo, and the Nazi Führerprinzip. Rousseau, "father of socialism," was hailed by the French Revolutionists in their manifestos as they tried, per Rousseau, "to force man to be free."

Rousseau, a morose masochist and inveterate liar, was described by Voltaire as "a mad dog who bites everybody" and as "a lackey of Diogenes." Grimm called him "a wicked and ferocious man." "He was an interesting madman," said Countess Sophie d'Houdetot, whom Rousseau claimed to be his true love. Like most who love mankind in the abstract, Rousseau abused those around him. A philanderer, he tried to seduce his patrons' wives. Calling his children "inconveniences," he forced his mistress, Thérèse Le Vasseur, to leave their five infants at the foundlings' asylum, where 95 percent of infants died. He believed he was exempt from morality. Like Dostoevsky's Raskolnikov, he thought morals applied only to the little people.

Rousseau and Burke represent the opposite poles of political thought. For liberals: Man is good, but is corrupted by social institutions, especially competition, which creates envy. But, man can be educated to sacrifice for the common good and move toward perfection. For conservatives, man is self-centered, so society must structure incentives (rewards and punishments) to harness his productivity for the group. An intellectual's good intentions are masks that disguise his bid for power, and without wisdom they can spell disaster.

The first person who, having enclosed a plot of land, took it into his head to say this is mine and found people simple enough to believe him, was the true founder of civil society. What crimes, wars, murders, what miseries and horrors would the human race have been spared, had someone pulled up the stakes or filled in the ditch and cried out to his fellow men: "Do not listen to this impostor. You are lost if you forget that the fruits of the earth belong to all and the earth to no one!"
Discourse on the Origin of Inequality (1755), ch. 1

Man is born free, and everywhere he is in chains.
Social Contract (1762), bk. I, ch. 1

The strongest is never strong enough to be always the master, unless he transforms strength into right, and obedience into duty.
Ibid., ch. 3

As soon as public service ceases to be the chief business of the citizens, and they would rather serve with their money than with their persons, the state is not far from its fall.

Ibid., ch. 15

All my assertions are but reasons to doubt me. Seek truth for yourself; for my own part I only promise you sincerity.
[Rousseau's philosophy of education in *Émile* sought a natural unfolding of the student. This technique abjured drilling. His catchphrase was "No books before age twelve."]

Émile (1762), ch. 4, tr. Barbara Foxley (1911). In L. R. Frank, *Quotationary* (1999)

He who wants to defend everything defends nothing, and he who wants to be everyone's friend has no friends in the end.

In Patrick J. Buchanan, *A Republic, Not an Empire* (1999), ch. 2

He who would dare to undertake the political creation of a people ought to believe that he can, in a manner of speaking, transform human nature; transform each individual—who, by himself, is a solitary and perfect whole—into a mere part of a greater whole from which the individual will henceforth receive his life and being. Thus the person who would undertake the political creation of a people should believe in his ability to alter man's constitution; to strengthen it; to substitute for the physical and independent existence received from nature, an existence which is partial and moral. In short, the would-be creator of political man must remove man's own forces and endow him with others that are naturally alien to him.

In Frederic Bastiat, *The Law*

Those who control a people's opinions control its actions.

[Rousseau planned to tell God on Judgment Day:] "I was better than that man over there."
[Referring to Voltaire.]
Norman Davies, *Europe: A History* (1996)

For summaries on Rousseau, see Paul Johnson, *Intellectuals* (1988), and Jacques Barzun, *From Dawn To Decadence* (2000).

DIDEROT
1713–84

French, editor of the *encyclopédie* called *The Revolution before the Revolution*. Diderot intended only to translate *Chambers' Cyclopedia* of 1723, but he mobilized the French rationalists to attack religion and praise science. A Deist, he accepted a mechanical God who made physical laws. The *encyclopédie* attacked intolerance, especially interference with publishing. Pope Clement XII placed it on the *Index of Forbidden Books*. The coeditor was D'Alembert, whose mother was a defrocked nun and the mistress of John Law.

There is only one step from fanaticism to barbarism.
"Essay on the Merits of Virtue" (1745)

I can be expected to look for the truth, but not to find it.
"Pensées Philosophiques" (1746)

The greatest good of the people is liberty. It is to the state what health is to the individual.
"Government"

And his hands would twist the entrails
   of the priest,
For the lack of a rope to strangle the
   kings.
            "The Freedom Maniacs" (1795)

Watch out for the fellow who talks about
putting things in order; this means getting other people under his control.
            Supplement to "Bourgainville's Voyage"
                                    (1796)

We have made a labyrinth and have got
lost in it. We must find our way again.

LAURENCE STERNE
1713–68

English, humorist and Anglican clergyman. His *Tristram Shandy* (1759), a book
without a plot, like Rabelais' *Gargantua* and
Pantagruel, is a series of humorous asides,
a sort of prolonged conversation with the
author. Tristram, the narrator, complains
that his life got off on the wrong foot at his
conception, when his mother interrupted
the action by inquiring if her husband had
set the clock. From there it went downhill.
The whimsical Tristram Shandy is a great
work of literature.

'Tis known by the name of perseverance
in a good cause—and of obstinacy in a
bad one.
            Tristram Shandy (1759), bk. 1, ch. 17

Digressions, incontestably, are the sunshine—they are the life, the soul of
reading; take them out of this book for
instance—you might as well take the
book along with them.
                            Ibid., ch. 22

Science may be learned by rote, but wisdom not.
                            Ibid., bk. 5

MARQUIS DE VAUVENARGUES
1715–47

French, writer.

Men's maxims reveal their characters.
        Reflections and Maxims (1746), no. 107, tr.
                            F. G. Stevens (1940)

The greatest evil which fortune can inflict
on men is to endow them with small talents and great ambition.
                            Ibid., no. 562

The greatest achievement of the human
spirit is to live up to one's opportunities
and make the most of one's resources.

HELVÉTIUS
1715–71

French, tax collector, who made an illicit
fortune and became an *encyclopédist*. He
held that all men are born equally intelligent (applying to individuals and races),
and differing environments shape them
into geniuses or dunces. He formulated
the basic belief of socialism: Man's nature
can be reformed by law—as per the "new
Soviet man."

…it is not on religion, nor on what is
called morality,…but on legislation alone,
that the vices, the virtues, the power and
the felicity of a people depend.
        M. Grossman, *The Philosophy of Helvetius*,
                                    (1926)

Education can change everything.
Treatise on Man, vol. II

[Voltaire retorted:] "What folly to imagine that every man could be a Newton."
Letter to M. Daquir

THOMAS GRAY
1716–71

English, poet.

...where ignorance is bliss, 'Tis folly to
be wise.
"On a Distant Prospect of
Eton College" (1742)

The curfew tolls the knell of parting day,
The lowing herd winds slowly o'er the lea,
The ploughman homeward plods his
weary way,
And leaves the world to darkness and
to me.
"Elegy Written in a Country Churchyard"
(1751), st. 1

The boast of heraldry, the pomp of pow'r
And all that beauty, all that wealth e'er gave,
Await alike the inevitable hour:
The paths of glory lead but to the grave.
Ibid., st. 9

Full many a gem of purest ray serene,
The dark, unfathomed caves of ocean bare;
Full many a flower is born to blush unseen,
And waste its sweetness on the desert air.
Ibid., st. 14

Some village Hampden, that with
dauntless breast
The little tyrant of his fields withstood,
Some mute inglorious Milton here may
rest,

Some Cromwell guiltless of his country's
blood.
[Dr. Johnson said of "Elegy," "Had
Gray written often thus, it had
been in vain to blame, and useless
to praise him." "Elegy" may be the
greatest pastoral poem.]
Ibid., st. 15

HORACE WALPOLE
1717–97

English, statesman and writer of 3,600
moving, delightful letters. His *The Castle of
Otranto* (1764) was the first "gothic novel."
A son of Robert Walpole (1676–1745), Britain's first PM and the person who coined
"the balance of power."

What has one to do, when one grows
tired of the world, as we both do, but to
draw nearer and nearer, and gently waste
the remains of life with friends with
whom one began it?
Letter to George Montagu
(November 21, 1765)

The world is a comedy to those that
think, a tragedy to those that feel.
Letter to Anne, Countess of Upper Ossory
(August 16, 1776)

It was said of old Sarah, Duchess of
Marlborough, that she never put dots
over her i's to save ink.
Letter to Sir Horace Mann (October 4,
1785), in L. R. Frank, *Quotationary* 1999

I am persuaded that foolish writers and
foolish readers are created for reach
other; and that fortune provides readers
as she does mates for ugly women.

SAMUEL ADAMS
1722–1803

American, militant democrat, who attacked royal magistrates who were usurping colonial assemblies. He rebelled in order to transfer power to assemblies from judges. Understanding publicity, his *Sons of Liberty* and *Committees of Correspondence* made "a push for perfect political liberty." As anti-federalists, he and John Hancock conditioned Massachusetts' ratification of the Constitution upon a Bill of Rights.

> Let us contemplate our forefathers, and posterity, and resolve to maintain the rights bequeathed to us from the former, for the sake of the latter.... Let us remember that "if we suffer tamely a lawless attack upon our liberty, we encourage it, and involve others in our doom."...millions yet unborn may be the miserable sharers of the event.
>
> Speech 1771

WILLIAM BLACKSTONE
1723–80

English, jurist. His *Commentaries on the Laws of England* (1765–69), a best-seller in England and America, restated English law and identified three "great and primary rights": "personal security, personal liberty, and private property." He believed the common law was governed by broad principles that could be applied by deductive logic to individual cases. This gave the law predictability, and opposed the chancery principles of equity that gave inordinate power to judges:

> The liberty of considering all cases in an equitable light must not be indulged too far, lest thereby we destroy all law, and leave the decision of every question entirely in the breast of the judge. And law, without equity, though hard and disagreeable, is much more desirable for the public good, than equity without law; which would make every judge a legislator and introduce most infinite confusion.
>
> Commentaries

> Time whereof the memory of man runneth not to the contrary.
>
> Ibid., bk. I, ch. 17

> That the king can do no wrong is a necessary and fundamental principle of the English constitution.
>
> Ibid., bk. III, ch. 17

> The liberty of the press is indeed essential to the nature of a free state, but this consists in laying no previous restraints upon publication, and not in freedom from censure for criminal matter when published.
>
> Ibid., bk. IV

FRIEDRICH M. GRIMM
1723–1807

French (German-born), author of *Nouvelles Littéraires*, a fortnightly newsletter (1747–90) reporting on current events in French literature, philosophy, science, and art. This *Correspondance Littéraire* was subscribed to by Europe's royalty and aristocracy, and it was the principal conveyor of the French Enlightenment throughout Europe.

ADAM SMITH
1723–90

Scottish, "father of political economy." The supreme works of the British Enlightenment were published in 1776: Jefferson's Declaration of Independence, and Smith's *An Inquiry Into the Nature and Causes of The Wealth of Nations*, the Bible for minimalist government. Smith's thesis was: A market economy with little state intervention leads to "general opulence," where luxuries become common to all; and a market economy promotes political liberty and peaceful relations among states. Though seemingly chaotic, a free market is a self-regulating mechanism that produces the goods most desired by most people. Smith set out to smash government overregulation of the market, as where justices of the peace set wages, guilds set prices, and the state regulated international trade by protective tariffs, state monopolies, and other measures.

Smith was first a moral philosopher. He fused Hutcheson's belief in an innate morality that makes man do good with Hume's view that man, being ruled by self-interested passion, would only be fit for a society that rewarded and punished. Smith believed that man has an inborn moral sense growing, not out of religion, but from our identification with humans—we suffer when we see others suffer.

Smith's *The Theory of Moral Sentiments* (1759) established him as a moral philosopher, and its royalties financed sixteen years of writing *The Wealth of Nations*—two closely related books. Smith wrote that we desire "mutual sympathy," that is, the pleasure of finding our sentiments echoed in others. We shade our sentiments toward those we admire. Mutual moderation of sentiments leads to the formation of cultures and subcultures. Moral standards thus arise organically, like an efficient market arises organically from willing exchanges.

The Wealth of Nations (1776) argues that man is selfish: "The desire to improve our lot in life comes to us our of the womb of our mothers and never leaves till the day we die." But, an "invisible hand" leads selfish man to advance social interests. For example, man produces more than he consumes, so society harvests the surplus. And the market's self-interest serves the needs of others, its customers.

The notion of self-interest benefiting society goes back to Bernard Mandeville's *Fable of the Bees,* or *Private Vices, Public Benefits* (1714). Capitalism generates inequality of wealth, but it generates such prodigious wealth that it frees man from the age-old dependence of serfs toiling for their masters, the common fate of the vast majority of people until capitalism. Moreover, unless it is totalitarian, an economic system cannot be founded on benevolence because man resists extending benevolence in exchanges beyond those he loves.

Smith took from Hume the idea that the market is a self-regulating organism that draws investment to where demand is great (high prices) and withdraws it from where demand is slack (low prices). Consumers benefit because shortages are relieved, and workers benefit because the market maximizes productivity, the only possible source of higher wages. Complex social coordination occurs without central planning; for example, without any central planning, millions are fed daily in London.

Nowhere does Smith say that capitalism is perfect, only that it is better than order imposed by politicians. Indeed, the father of capitalism was so critical of businessmen that one cannot find a single favorable reference to them in *The Wealth of Nations*. Also, government is absolutely needed: "It is only under the shelter of the civil magistrate that the owner of that valuable property, which is acquired by the labor of many years, or perhaps of many successive generations, can sleep a single night in security." Smith thought government's role would grow in more advanced economies given their greater infrastructure and defense needs.

Smith thought no economy could prosper in a corrupt culture where the people do not fulfill their moral obligations. Moreover, free markets must be protected against private interests, like unions and corporations, which lobby government to shut out competitors and/or to obtain subsidies, benefits, and coercive powers.

"Division of labor" or "specialization of labor" increases productivity. Smith described the benefit of specialization in the manufacturing of pins—it increased productivity by a factor of 200! Free trade multiplies the opportunities for the division of labor by enlarging the geographic area of exchange.

Smith coined the term "the mercantile system," for the notions that: 1) one nation's gain is another's loss, 2) a nation's objective should be a "favorable balance of trade" (inflows of gold), so government should embargo any imports that can be produced domestically; and 3) government should guide the economy. Mercantilism leads to monopolies and foreign colonies that generate net costs.

Free markets are efficient because the prices negotiated by buyers and sellers signal which goods to produce and the least expensive combinations of inputs by which to produce them. Competition slashes prices and improves quality. In America from 1968 to 1998, after-tax profits averaged 6 percent to 9 percent annually. Profits fund the R&D and investments that create new jobs. As Peter Drucker said, "Profits are the costs of the future." Cuba, whose economy grew 6 percent per annum for a decade before Castro outlawed profits in 1958, has had zero increase in per capita income in the forty-eight years since. Had Cuba's economy continued to grow at 6 percent per annum, per capita income would have quadrupled by 2005!

Smith was not perfect—he believed in the "labor theory of value." The first sentence of *The Wealth of Nations* says: "The annual labor of every nation is the fund which originally supplies it with all the necessaries and conveniences of life which it annually consumes, and which consist always either in the immediate produce of that labour, or in what is purchased with that produce from other nations." Karl Marx later wrecked political havoc with Smith's erroneous labor theory of value by claiming that capitalists stole the "suplus value" created by labor. We now know that neither labor nor any other cost creates "value." It is value that makes purchasers willing to repay the costs of producing. That is, value is "consumer preference."

> Little else is required to carry a state to the highest degree of affluence from the lowest barbarism but peace, easy taxes, and a tolerable administration of justice; all the rest being brought about by the natural course of things. Governments

which thwart this natural course, which force things into another channel, or which endeavor to arrest the progress of society are obliged to be oppressive and tyrannical.

1749 Lecture

[Every individual does not intend] to promote the public interest.... He intends only his own gain, and he is in this, as in many other cases, led by an invisible hand to promote an end which was not part of his intention. Nor is it always the worse for the society that it was no part of it. By pursuing his own interest he frequently promotes that of the society more effectively than when he really intends to promote it. I have never known much good done by those affected to trade for the public good.

The Wealth of Nations (1776)

It is not from the benevolence of the butcher, the brewer, or the baker, that we expect our dinner, but from their regard to their own interest. We address ourselves, not to their humanity but to their self love, and never talk to them of our own necessities but of their advantages. Nobody but a beggar chooses to depend chiefly upon the benevolence of his fellow-citizens.

Ibid.

People of the same trade seldom meet together, even for merriment and diversion, but the conversation ends in a conspiracy against the public, or in some contrivance to raise prices.

Ibid.

...every prodigal [is] a public enemy, and every frugal man a public benefactor.

Ibid.

It is the maxim of every prudent master of a family never to attempt to make at home what it will cost him more to make than to buy. What is prudence in the conduct of every private family can scarce be folly in that of a great kingdom. If a foreign country can supply us with a commodity cheaper than we ourselves can make it, better buy it of them with some part of the produce of our own industry employed in a way in which we have some advantage.

Ibid.

The wealth of a neighboring nation...is certainly advantageous in trade.... Private people who want to make a fortune, never think of retiring to the remote and poor provinces of the country.... A nation that would enrich itself by foreign trade is certainly most likely to do so when its neighbors are all rich, industrious and commercial nations.

Ibid.

Consumption is the sole end and purpose of all production; and the interest of the producer ought to be attended to, only so far as it may be necessary for promoting that of the consumer. The maxim is so perfectly self evident, that it would be absurd to attempt to prove it. But in the mercantile system, the interest of the consumer is almost constantly sacrificed to that of the producer...

Ibid.

[Regarding outsized national debts, inflation] has been the most usual expedient by which a real public bankruptcy has been disguised under the appearance of a pretended payment.

Ibid.

As soon as government management begins, it upsets the natural equilibrium of industrial relations, and each interference only requires further bureaucratic control until the end is the tyranny of the totalitarian state.

Parsimony, and not industry, is the immediate cause of the increase of capital. But whatever industry might acquire, if parsimony did not save and store up, the capital would never be the greater.

That unprosperous race of men commonly called men of letters...

IMMANUEL KANT
1724–1804

German (Scottish parents), five-foot-tall metaphysician who never traveled more than sixty miles from his home.

Many hold Kant's *Critique of Pure Reason* (1787) as the greatest work of modern philosophy. It purports to avoid the unwarranted a priori assumptions of rationalists, who have no footing in experience, and the skepticism of the empiricists. That is, Kant sought to synthesize rationalism and empiricism, the great philosophical divide going back to Plato's idealism and Aristotle's realism.

Kant argues that because of our imperfect senses, we never perceive anything directly, only how it appears. The real world (noumenal), or the "thing-in-itself," exists, but we can only experience the "phenomenal." Thus there are two levels of reality: the way things are and the way we perceive them. While Hume is right that we can never prove cause and effect in the noumenal world, we can prove them in the world of our perceptions by the interaction of our senses and our mind.

His moral code was based on reason leading to rules that are universally binding and absolute. Thus, lying is forbidden regardless of the consequences. One should not lie to a Hitler even though it means thousands of innocents will die horribly. Thus, many ethicists prefer Aristotle's looser moral code, based on using "practical reason." Similarly elastic, Hume's moral code is based on customs.

To Kant, universal laws are those that we want everyone else to abide by. Such laws mean seeing every person as an end in himself. Without such ideals there would be no basis for human rights, as per the Declaration of Independence, whose rights are inalienable because we wish them without contradiction to be universal.

Kant's *Critique of Pure Reason* attacked the rationalist fallacy that reason can comprehend all reality. Much of reality is beyond our five senses. This limit to reason opens the door to faith.

Kant predicted in his *Perpetual Peace* (1795) that a federal world government would initiate a "perpetual peace." But, the First and Second Definitive Articles of that federation requires that every constituent nation must be a "free republic," to wit, a liberal democracy. In 2006, few members of the United Nations qualify as free republics.

> There is... only one categorical imperative and it is this: Act only on that maxim through which you can at the same time will that it should become a universal law.
>
> *The Metaphysic of Morals* (1797), ch. 11

Envy is the vice of mankind.

Dare to know. [*Sapere aude.*] That is the slogan of the Enlightenment.

Kant's motto

GEORGE MASON
1725–92

American, writer of the first draft of the Bill of Rights at the Constitutional Convention. Jefferson copied from Mason's Virginia Bill of Rights much of the Preamble to the Declaration of Independence:

> That all men are by nature equally free and independent, and have certain inherent rights, of which, when they enter into a state of society, they cannot by any compact deprive or divest their posterity; namely the enjoyment of life and liberty, with the means of acquiring and possessing property, and pursuing and obtaining happiness and safety.
>
> Virginia Bill of Rights (June 12, 1776)

ANNE ROBERT JACQUES TURGOT
1727–81

French, a disciple of the physiocrats Gournay, Quesnay, and du Pont, who were the first people to call themselves "political economists." They argued for private property, free trade, and against government interference in the market. Their slogan was *laissez-faire, laissez-passer,* or "Let us work, let the goods pass." Named comptroller-general by Louis XVI in 1774, he slashed spending, cut taxes, eliminated internal tariffs, abolished the guilds that monopolized the trades, and abolished tax exemptions for the nobles and clergy. The economy surged! But Louis dismissed Turgot because Marie Antoinette and all special interests turned against him. Turgot warned Louis XVI that if he reversed his reforms, the economy would collapse, a revolution would follow, and Louis would lose his head. It happened!

> Americans are the hope of this world.
>
> Letter (March 22, 1778)

JAMES COOK
1728–79

Scottish, first scientific explorer to calculate precisely his ship's position in all weather by using James Harrison's chronometer to determine longitude (east-west). He made the first accurate charts. He identified Australia for transporting British felons. He sailed around Antarctica in the *Endeavor*. He failed in his search for a Northwest Passage. Hawaiian natives killed him.

Cook discovered that sauerkraut, which is rich in vitamin C, cured the seaman's curse, scurvy. A Scottish surgeon, James Lind, had earlier written a paper claiming limes prevented scurvy. It lay dormant in the admiralty for decades, an oft-cited example of bureaucratic lethargy. British sailors are called "limeys."

> I…had ambition not only to go farther than any man had ever been before, but as far as it was possible for a man to go.

6
LIBERTY AND DEMOCRACY

Liberty preceded democracy in England by over a millennium. The Magna Carta in 1215 merely restated ancient Teutonic liberties, like the freedom not to be taxed except according to the law. Democracy (majority rule) did not begin until after the Glorious Revolution of 1688, and as of 1800 only 2 percent of the English could vote. Democracy is majority rule, and majorities have butchered minorities, as did the Spartans, who were more democratic than the libertarian Athenians.

Hitler's democratic triumph exposed the true nature of democracy. Democracy has few values of its own: It is as good, or as bad, as the principles of the people who operate it. In the hands of liberal and tolerant people, it will produce a liberal and tolerant government; in the hands of cannibals, a government of cannibals.

"Democracy" was a pejorative term to the American founders. James Madison in Federalist Paper No. 10 said in a democracy "there is nothing to check the inducement to sacrifice the weaker party..." John Adams added, "Democracy never lasts long. It soon wastes, exhausts, and murders itself. There was never a democracy yet that did not commit suicide." John Marshall said, "Between a balanced republic and a democracy, the difference is like that between order and chaos." Republics are designed to protect liberty by placing restraints on the power of majorities to get what they want.

Majorities oppress when the middle class is too weak to uphold the rule of law (universal laws with nondiscriminatory application). When the rule of law goes, a transfer state arises and all become claimants in shifting coalitions to seize political power in order to steal property from one another.

The central problem addressed by America's Constitutional Convention was how to fashion a republic that would prevent majority rule inimitable to liberty. Madison devised seven checks to thwart a "durable tyrannical majority": (1) limiting powers to those enumerated in a written Constitution; (2) a Bill of Rights protected from majority rule; (3) separated powers between the federal government's three branches; (4) separated powers between federal and state governments; (5) bicameralism; (6) executive veto; and, (7) impeachment power. "Madisonian democracy" places little reliance on the public spirit of citizens to prefer the good of the state above personal interests. Rather, it focuses on the checks and balances to prevent any coalition of interests from being a "durable tyrannical majority."

Liberty is a higher value than democracy. Its foundation is the Rule of Law, that is, the equal, uniform, and predictable application of laws of an abstract and general nature to all men. Some nondemocratic regimes, such as Hong Kong, have fostered liberty. Combining liberty and democracy is best, but many cultures cannot manage it. Adam Smith said it can endure only where a critical mass of people is self-supporting and virtuous. America's founders almost chose the motto "Virtue is Liberty," but decided against restating the obvious. Joseph de Maistre concluded, "Every country has the government it deserves."

Property rights—a prerequisite to liberty—have produced prosperity from Holland's sixteenth century miracle economy to Asia's Tigers. But republics can forfeit liberty after creating economic miracles. The Roman republic fell after it abandoned the rule of law. Paul Johnson noted, "Once the law is humbled, all else that is valuable in a civilized society will vanish, usually with terrifying speed."

Professor R. J. Rummel, who defined wars as conflicts that kill more than a 1,000 people, noted that between 1816 and 1991, of 353 wars, 198 wars were fought between dictatorships and 155 wars were fought between democracies and dictatorships, but no war was fought between democracies. The War of 1812 was the last war between democracies.

EDMUND BURKE
1729–97

Irish, Whig MP, political philosopher, and "father of traditional conservatism," which prizes virtue and social responsibility versus "libertarian conservatism," which prizes maximum freedom. He attacked slavery, sought to remove political disabilities from Catholics, and championed free trade, Parliament, Ireland, India, and the American colonies, saying, "Magnanimity in politics is not seldom the truest wisdom; and a great empire and little minds go ill together." Adam Smith said, "He was the only man who thought on topics as I did."

Seeing that two-thirds of the Anglican clergy supported the French Revolution, Burke wrote the 365-page *Reflections on the Revolution in France* (1790). This most influential conservative work called for evolutionary change in accordance with custom and prescription, per Britain's Glorious Revolution and the American Revolution. Both of these asserted traditional rights, whereas France's Revolution abandoned traditions for abstractions.

The cornerstones of Burke's philosophy were prejudice and prescription. Prejudice was not arbitrary opinions, but the "untaught feelings" and "mass of predispositions" of a people's collective wisdom. This opposed the French Revolution's notion that society could be ordered by abstract speculation. Burke said, "The individual is foolish, but the species is wise."

Prescription provides a rebuttable presumption in favor of long-standing institutions and customs as against rights produced by abstract reasoning. "Historical" rights laid down over generations will best sustain ethical thought and action.

The only thing necessary for the triumph of evil is for good men to do nothing.
> Attributed

It is a general popular error to imagine the loudest complainers for the public to be the most anxious for its welfare.
> In Alison Jones ed., *Chambers Dictionary of Quotations* (1998)

I prefer the collected wisdom of the ages to the abilities of any two men living....

Selected Writings of Edmund Burke,
Modern Library (1961)

The love of lucre, though sometimes carried to a ridiculous excess, a vicious excess, is the grand cause of prosperity to all States.... It is for the satirist to expose the ridiculous; it is for the moralist to censure the vicious...the judge to animadvert on the fraud...but it is for the Statesman to...make use of the general energies of nature, to take them as he finds them.

In Jerry Z. Muller, *The Mind and the
Market* (2002)

When bad men combine, the good must associate; else they will fall, one by one, in unpitied sacrifice, in a contemptible struggle.

*Thoughts on the Cause of the Present
Discontents* (1770)

Your representative owes you, not his industry only, but his judgment; and he betrays instead of serving you if he sacrifices it to your opinion.

Speech to the Electors of Bristol
(November 3, 1774)

The only liberty I mean is a liberty connected with order; that not only exists along with order and virtue, but which cannot exist at all without them.

Ibid.

I do not know the method of drawing up an indictment against a whole people.

Speech, "On Conciliation with the
American Colonies" (March 22, 1775)

In no country perhaps in the world is law so general a study [as in America]....

This study renders men acute, inquisitive, dexterous, prompt in attack, ready in defense, full of resources... They augur misgovernment at a distance, and sniff the approach of tyranny in every tainted breeze.

Ibid.

All government—indeed, every human benefit and enjoyment, every virtue and every prudent act—is founded on compromise and barter.

Ibid.

Among a people generally corrupt, liberty cannot long exist.

Letter to the Sheriffs of Bristol (1777)

Bad laws are the worst sort of tyranny.

Speech at Bristol (1780)

A law against property is a law against industry.

Speech on East India Bill
(December 1, 1783)

The people never give up their liberties but under some delusion.

Speech at Buckinghamshire (1784)

There never was a bad man that had ability for good service.

Impeachment of Warren Hastings
(February 15, 1788)

People will not look forward to posterity who never look backward to their ancestors.

Reflections on the Revolution in France

He that wrestles with us strengthens our nerves and sharpens our skill. Our antagonist is our helper.

Ibid.

A state without the means of some change is without the means of its conservation.

Ibid.

Nothing in progression can rest on its original plan. We might as well think of rocking a grown man in the cradle of an infant.

Ibid.

The power of perpetuating our property in our families is one of the most valuable and interesting circumstances belonging to it, and that which tends the most to the perpetuation of society itself.

Ibid.

Manners are of more importance than laws. Upon them, in a great measure, the laws depend. The law touches us but here and there, and now and then. Manners are what vex or smooth, corrupt or purify, exalt or debase, barbarize or refine us, by a constant, steady, uniform, insensible operation, like that of the air we breathe in.

Ibid.

The most important of all revolutions...a revolution in sentiments, manners, and moral opinions.

Ibid.

But what is liberty without wisdom, and without virtue? It is the greatest of all possible evils; for it is folly, vice, and madness, without restraint.

Ibid.

[Speaking of Marie Antoinette:]...little did I dream that I should have lived to see such disasters fallen upon her in a nation of gallant men, in a nation of men of honor, and of cavaliers. I thought ten thousand swords must have leaped from their scabbards to avenge even a look that threatened her with insult. But the age of chivalry is gone. That of sophisters, economists, and calculators has succeeded, and the glory of Europe is extinguished forever.

Ibid.

In the groves of their academy, at the end of every walk, you see nothing but the gallows.

Ibid.

By hating vices too much, they come to love men too little.

Ibid.

For us to love our country, our country ought to be lovely.

Ibid.

Kings will be tyrants from policy, when subjects are rebels from principle.

Ibid.

Society is indeed a contract...it becomes a partnership not only between those who are living, but between those who are living, those who are dead, and those who are to be born.

Ibid.

We are afraid to put men to live and trade each on his own private stock of reason; because we suspect that this stock in each man is small, and that the individuals would do better to avail themselves of the general bank and capital of nations, and of ages.... Prejudice is of ready application in the emergency;

it previously engages the mind in a steady course of wisdom and virtue, and does not leave the man hesitating in the moment of decision, skeptical, puzzled, and unresolved. Prejudice renders a man's virtue his habit; and not a series of unconnected acts....

> Ibid.

Men are qualified for civil liberty in exact proportion to their disposition to put moral chains upon their own appetites.... Society cannot exist unless a controlling power upon will and appetite be placed somewhere, and the less of it there is within, the more there must be without.

> Ibid.

Tyrants seldom want pretexts.

> Letter to a Member of the National Assembly (1791)

Mere parsimony is not economy.... Expense, and great expense, may be an essential part of true economy.... Economy is a distributive virtue, and consists not in saving but selection.

> Letter to a Lord (1796)

Example is the school of mankind, and they will learn at no other.

> Letters on Regicide (1796)

They argue against a fair discussion of popular prejudices, because...the discovery might be productive of the most dangerous Consequences. Absurd and blasphemous notion! As if all happiness was not connected with the practice of virtue, which necessarily depends upon the knowledge of truth.

> An Indication of Natural Society

There are three estates in Parliament; but, in the Reporters' Gallery yonder, there sits a Fourth Estate more important than they all.

> In Thomas Carlyle, *On Heroes and Hero Worship* (1841)

We know that we have made no discoveries, and we think that no discoveries are to be made in morality; nor many in the great principles of government, nor in the idea of liberty, which were understood long before we were born, altogether as well as they will be after the grave has heaped its mould upon our presumption...

> In William F. Buckley Jr., *Let Us Talk of Many Things* (1999)

The true danger is when liberty is nibbled away, for expedients, and by parts.

To read without reflecting, is like eating without digesting.

No men can act with effect who do not act in concert; no men can act in concert...who are not bound together with common opinions, common affections, and common interests.

The Democratic Party is like a mule without pride of ancestry or hope of posterity.

GOTTHOLD LESSING
1729–81

German, playwright, critic, and a leader of the German Enlightenment who drew German drama away from the classicism of Corneille and Racine and toward the lusty Shakespeare. Lessing was famous for Nathan the Wise, a play about toleration.

For me the greatest beauty always lay in the greatest clarity.

Oliver Goldsmith
1728–74

Irish, poet, playwright, and novelist.

To the last moment of his breath,
On hope the wretch relies;
And even the pain preceding death
Bids expectation rise.
> *The Captivity* (1764), "An Oratorio," act II

How small, of all that human hearts
    endure,
That part which laws or kings can cause
    or cure.
Still to ourselves in every place consign'd,
Our own felicity we make or find.
> *The Traveller* (1764), act 1

A book may be very amusing with
numerous errors, or it may be very dull
without a single absurdity.
> Preface, *The Vicar of Wakefield* (1766)

When lovely woman stoops to folly
And finds too late that men betray,
What charm can soothe her melancholy,
What art can wash her guilt away?
> Ibid., ch. 29

Sweet Auburn! Loveliest village of the
plain.
> [Decrying the depopulation of yeo-
> man farmers due to the Enclosure
> Acts.]
> *The Deserted Village* (1770), l.1

Ill fares the land, to hast'ning ills a prey,
Where wealth accumulates, and men
    decay;
Princes and lords may flourish, or may
    fade;
A breath can make them, as a breath
    has made;

But a bold peasantry, their country's pride,
When once destroyed, can never be
    supplied.
> Ibid., l. 51

It's a damned long, dark, boggy, dirty,
dangerous way.
> *She Stoops to Conquer* (1773), act 1

To make a fine gentleman several trades
are required, but chiefly a barber.

Cheerful at morn, he wakes from short
    repose,
Breasts the keen air, and carols as he goes.

> [Dr. Johnson said of Goldsmith: a
> man who "left scarcely any kind of
> writing untouched and who touched
> nothing he did not adorn."]

Pierre De Beaumarchais
1732–99

French, playwright. In *Barber of Seville*
(1776), the hero was a scheming valet,
Figaro. Both Rossini and Mozart later
wrote operas featuring Figaro. The play
was banned in Europe for attacking an
aristocracy that "closed careers to talent."

Because you are a great lord, you believe
yourself to be a great genius!... You took
the trouble to be born, but no more.
> *The Marriage of Figaro* (1785), act 2, sc. 2

George Washington
1732–99

American, first president (1789–97) and
regarded as the most important world
figure of the eighteenth century. A six-

foot-three son of a gentry man, he was self-taught, and copied a book of *110 Rules of Civility and Decent Behavior*. Not having the connections to rise in the British navy, he became a surveyor. He inherited Mount Vernon (a two-room house) from his brother and married a widow, Martha Curtis, who had 18,000 acres and £40,000 in property. In 1754, at age twenty-three as a Virginia lieutenant colonel, he attacked a French unit in Ohio, l'áffaire Jumonville, which ignited the Seven Years' War, which ended French power in America, which ended colonial dependence on England, which fired America's Revolution. As commander in chief of the Continental Army, he refused the order of John Hancock, president of the Continental Congress, to fight a "general action," but chose instead to wage a "protracted war." His brilliant strategy was to preserve his army in the field as an effective force until the British tired of the war.

In 1783, officers in the "Newburgh conspiracy" wanted Washington to force Congress to pay them. He nixed the cabal by putting on his glasses to read a letter, saying, "Gentlemen, you will permit me to put on my spectacles, for I have not only grown gray, but almost blind, in the service of my country." The ashamed officers relented.

After the war, when he could have been king, he retired. The Confederation began to fray as states imposed tariffs, defaulted on their debts, and veered toward the chaos European royalists had predicted. Washington helped initiate a Constitutional Convention and became its chairman, where he presided over what British prime minister Gladstone called "the greatest work of man ever struck off at a given moment in time, the Constitution of the United States." He set the precedent of giving up the presidency after two terms.

As president, he backed Alexander Hamilton's *Report on the Public Credit* that paid the state and federal war debts in full, thus establishing America's credit. He refused to yield to Jefferson's pleas to join France in fighting Britain.

Benjamin Rush said, "There is not a king in the world who would not look like a *valet de chambre* by his side." When Benjamin West told George III that if America won the war, Washington would return to his estate, the king said, "If he does that he will be the greatest man in the world."

> I can answer for but three things: a firm belief in the justice of our cause, close attention in the prosecution of it, and the strictest integrity.
>
> On accepting command of the Continental
> Army (June 19, 1775)

> I do solemnly swear (or affirm) that I will faithfully execute the Office of President of the United States, and will, to the best of my ability, preserve, protect, and defend the Constitution of the United States.
>
> Oath of the President of the United
> States—New York City (April 30, 1789)

The below farewell letter, which Washington never gave as a speech, stands with the Declaration of Independence and the Gettysburg Address as an American political icon. Since the nineteenth century it has been read annually on Washington's Birthday in Congress. One theme calls for America not to become entangled in European affairs. In fact, after the dissolution of the treaty with France by Adams in 1800, the United States did not ally again until

1917. (Note: "Entangling alliances" was coined in 1801 by Jefferson.) The other theme was that there is no order without law, no law without morality, and no morality without religion.

FAREWELL ADDRESS (EXCERPTS)
SEPTEMBER 17, 1796
POLISHED BY ALEXANDER HAMILTON

Of all the dispositions and habits that lead to political prosperity, Religion and Morality are indispensable supports.... And let us with caution indulge the supposition, that morality can be maintained without religion.

Observe good faith and justice toward all nations. Cultivate peace and harmony with all.... The nation which indulges toward another an habitual hatred or an habitual fondness is in some degree a slave.

[Having one nation, we] will avoid the necessity of those over grown military establishments, which, under any form of government, are inauspicious to liberty, and which are to be regarded as particularly hostile to republican liberty.

Why forgo the advantages of so peculiar a situation? [America's safe distance from Europe.] Why quit our own to stand upon foreign ground? Why, by interweaving our destiny with that of any part of Europe, entangle our peace and prosperity in the coils of European ambition, rivalry, interest, humor or caprice? It is our true policy to steer clear of permanent alliances with any portion of the foreign world.... 'Tis folly for one

nation to look for disinterested favors from another....

> Letter to his brother John in the French and Indian War (July 18, 1755), in L. R. Frank, *Quotationary* (1999)

Discipline is the soul of an army. It makes small numbers formidable; procures success to the weak, and esteem to all.

> Letter to the Virginia Regiments (July 29, 1759)

It is a maxim founded on the universal experiences of mankind that no nation is to be trusted farther than it is bound by its interest.

> Letter to Henry Laurens (November 14, 1778)

Our cause is noble; it is the cause of Mankind!

> Letter to James Warren (March 31, 1779)

I hope I shall always possess firmness and virtue enough to maintain what I consider the most enviable of all titles, the character of an "honest man."

> Letter to Alexander Hamilton (August 28, 1788)

To be prepared for war is one of the most effectual means of preserving peace.

> Address to Congress (January 8, 1790)

[To expect ordinary people to be] influenced by any other principles but those of interest, is to look for what never did and I fear never will happen... The few, therefore, who act upon Principles of Disinterestedness are, comparatively speaking, no more than a drop in the ocean.

> In Paul Johnson, *A History of the American People* (1997)

[To John Adams, successor president] I am fairly out and you are fairly in! See which of us will be happiest!

In L. R. Frank, *Wit and Humor Quotationary*

[Elbridge Gerry's attempt at the Continental Congress in 1787 to limit the size of the Continental Army by law to 10,000 men was sunk by Washington's remark:] "A very good idea. Let us also by law limit the size of any invading force to 5,000 men."

Let us raise a standard to which the wise and honest can repair; the rest is in the hands of God.

[At Valley Forge.]

Leon Gutterman, ed., *Wisdom of the Harvard Classics*, vol. 36 (1961)

RELIGION AND AMERICA'S FOUNDING

Most Founding Fathers were Christians, though a few, like Jefferson, were Deists. The concept of inalienable rights, or natural rights, was central to the Judeo-Christian concept of man made in God's image with dignity accorded to each soul. Islam, Hinduism, and Buddhism, like atheistic creeds, see man as a degraded being of little consequence. Thus, until recently, all the world's democratic republics have been Judeo-Christian.

Secularists, who want to ban public religious expressions, cite Jefferson's letter to the Danbury Baptists, which said that the First Amendment built "a wall of separation between church and state." That amendment stated in part that Congress shall "make no law respecting an estab-lishment of religion..." But the "establishment" clause sought only to bar religious taxes, religious qualifications for public office, and an official state church, which was the specific concern of the Danbury Baptists.

It was also believed that the "free exercise" clause of the First Amendment permitted public prayer and public display of religious symbols. The day after the House approved the First Amendment, it set aside a date for "solemn thanksgiving to God," later entitled Thanksgiving Day. Jefferson attended church in the Capitol. As chairman of the school board, Jefferson assigned the Bible and a hymnal as the principal texts for teaching reading.

John Dickinson said in 1776: "Our liberties do not come from charters....They do not depend on parchments; but come from the King of Kings...." Benjamin Rush said, "The only foundation for a useful education in a republic is to be laid in religion. Without this there can be no virtue, and without virtue there can be no liberty, and liberty is the object and life of all republican governments."

The Declaration gives four Hebrew names to God: Creator, Providence, Judge, and Lawgiver. The first act of the First Continental Congress was to provide for public prayers at their sessions:

> It being the indispensable duty of all nations, not only to offer up their supplications to Almighty God, the giver of all good, for his gracious assistance in a time of distress, but also in a solemn and public manner to give him praise for his goodness in general, and especially for great and signal interpositions of his Providence in their behalf; therefore the United States in Congress assembled,

...do hereby recommend...the observation of ...a day of solemn thanksgiving to God...

Atheism destroys republics because it erases all moral limits on political power. If no higher power endows inalienable rights, there can be no reason to obey the law beyond the fear of punishment.

The U. S. Great Seal reads: *Annuit Coeptis.* [He smiled on our Beginnings.] See Michael Novak, *On Two Wings* (2002).

JOHN ADAMS
1735–1826

American, Washington's vice president, second president (1796–1800), and father of John Quincy Adams, the sixth president. He won the acquittal of Captain Preston, commander of British troops at the Boston Massacre. He drafted Massachusetts' Constitution in 1779, the oldest surviving written constitution. His *Thoughts on Government* became the formula for drafting many state constitutions.

Adams saw unchecked democracy leading to despotism. Unlike Jefferson, he did not trust the people, and unlike Hamilton, he did not trust the aristocrats. Adams did not belong to a party, but he supported a strong central government and tilted toward the British, which aligned him with Hamilton's Federalist Party.

Adams's great success was resisting his largely republican cabinet led by Jefferson that wanted to ally with Napoleon to fight Britain. His great failure was listening to his wife Abigail and passing the Alien and Sedition Acts, outlawing publishing "any false, scandalous, and malicious writing against the Government of the United States."

The rich, therefore, ought to have an effectual barrier in the constitution against being robbed, plundered and murdered, as well as the poor; and this can never be without an independent senate. The poor should have a bulwark against the same dangers and oppressions; and this can never be without a house of representatives of the people. But neither the rich nor the poor can be defended by their respective guardians in the constitution, without an executive power, vested with a negative, equal to either, to hold the balance even between them, and decide when they cannot agree.

"A Defense of the Constitution," in *Works*, vol. VI

Whoever would found a state, and make proper laws for the government of it, must presume that all men are bad by nature.

In Clinton Rossiter, *Conservatism in America*, 2nd rev. ed. (1955)

Man differs by nature from man, almost as much as man from beast.... A physical inequality, an intellectual inequality, of the most serious kind, is established unchangeably by the Author of nature.

Ibid.

Absolute power intoxicates alike despots, monarchs, aristocrats, and democrats.

Ibid.

The moment the idea is admitted into society, that property is not as sacred as the laws of God, and that there is not a force of law and public justice to protect it, anarchy and tyranny commence.

Ibid.

There is danger from all men. The only maxim of a free government ought to be to trust no man living with power to endanger the public liberty.

Diary and Autobiography of John Adams,
vol. 2, (1960)

Liberty cannot be preserved without a general knowledge among the people, who have a right...to that most dreaded and envied kind of knowledge, I mean of the character and conduct of their rulers.

A Dissertation on the Canon and
Feudal Law (1765)

Facts are stubborn things; and whatever may be our wishes, our inclinations, or the dictates of our passions, they cannot alter the state of facts and evidence.

[Adams's successful appeal to the jury in defending Captain Preston in the trial for the "Boston Massacre" in December 1770.]

Public virtue cannot exist in a nation without private virtue, and public virtue is the only foundation of republics.

Letter to Mercy Warren (April 16, 1776)

I must study politics and war that my sons may have liberty to study mathematics...navigation, commerce and agriculture, in order to give their children a right to study painting, poetry, music, architecture, statuary, tapestry, and porcelain.

Letter to Abigail Adams (May 12, 1780)

My country has in its wisdom contrived for me the most insignificant office [the vice presidency] that ever the invention of man contrived....

Letter to Abigail Adams
(December 19, 1793)

Our Constitution was made only for a moral and religious people. It is wholly inadequate to the government of any other.

Letter (1798)

Remember, democracy never lasts long. It soon wastes, exhausts, and murders itself. There never was a democracy yet that did not commit suicide.

Letter to John Taylor (April 15, 1814)

Will you tell me how to prevent riches from becoming the effects of temperance and industry? Will you tell me how to prevent riches from producing luxury? Will you tell me how to prevent luxury from producing effeminacy, intoxication, extravagance, vice and folly?

Letter to Thomas Jefferson

You and I ought not to die before we have explained ourselves to each other.

[Letter to Jefferson, September 10, 1816—one of 152 letters exchanged from 1812 to 1826 between these two conservatives representing anti-Federalist and Federalist views. They knew their letters would summarize for history their views on these timeless political issues. This exchange reanimated their mutual affection, which had been so severely strained during Adams's presidency that they did not speak or correspond for ten years.]

One issue was equality, which Adams thought was a pipe dream. Jefferson responded that there was a "natural aristocracy" among men based on "virtue and talents" and a "pseudo-aristocracy" based on "birth and wealth," which Jefferson attacked by abolishing primogeniture. Another issue was the French Revolution. Jefferson admitted that he had been mistaken to support it.

Adams's last words, on July 4, 1826, the fiftieth anniversary of the Declaration of Independence, were "The country is safe. Jefferson still lives." However, Jefferson had died five hours earlier.

Patrick Henry
1736–99

American, Virginia lawyer, who participated with Jefferson and Richard Henry Lee in the Committee of Correspondence. When he introduced resolutions opposing the Stamp Act, he said, "Caesar had his Brutus; Charles the First his Cromwell; and George the Third—may profit by their example." He was Madison's lieutenant in persuading Congress to adopt the Bill of Rights.

> Mr. President, it is natural to man to indulge in the illusions of hope. We are apt to shut our eyes against a painful truth—and listen to the song of that siren.... For my part, whatever anguish of spirit it might cost, I am willing to know the whole truth, to know the worst, and to provide for it....
>
> Excerpts from speech to the Second Virginia Convention (March 23, 1775), Richmond

> I have but one lamp by which my feet are guided, and that is the lamp of experience. I know no way of judging of the future but by the past.
>
> Ibid.

The battle, sir, is not to the strong alone; it is to the vigilant, the active, the brave.
> Ibid.

> It is in vain, sir, to extenuate the matter. Gentlemen may cry, peace, peace—but there is no peace. The war has actually begun! The next gale that sweeps from the North will bring to our ears the clash of resounding arms! Our brethren are already in the field! Why stand we here idle?...Is life so dear, or peace so sweet, as to be purchased at the price of chains and slavery? Forbid it. Almighty God! I know not what course others may take, but as for me, give me liberty, or give me death.
>
> [Henry was speaking in reaction to the British Governor threatening to seize the privately owned arms of Virginians.]
>
> Ibid.

James Watt
1736–1819

Scottish, in 1769 he invented a 400 percent more fuel-efficient steam engine than the Newcomen engine. It also converted reciprocal motion into a rotary motion that multiplied its applications. He partnered with the ironmaster Matthew Boulton and they fused the theoretical and practical to manufacture engines that made the factory system possible. No longer did factories have to be next to rivers—they could be located near available labor.

A man can produce in a day only a quarter of a horsepower; but an average salary of $16.80 per hour in 2006 can buy each day 1,000 horsepower of electricity, or 4,000 times more physical labor than a man can do. That multiplier made the

Industrial Revolution! As Boulton said, "I sell here, sir, what all the world desires to have, power."

EDWARD GIBBON
1737–94

English, historian and militant atheist who believed Rome fell due to multiple causes of which the principal one was Christianity undermining Rome's martial virtues. Your compiler believes Rome fell due to internecine class warfare.

> The introduction of Christianity had some influence on the decline and fall of the Roman Empire. The clergy successfully preached the doctrines of patience and pusillanimity; the active virtues of society were discouraged; and the last remains of military spirit were buried in the cloister. A large portion of public and private wealth was consecrated to the specious demands of charity and devotion, and the soldiers' pay was lavished on the useless multitudes of both sexes who could only plead the merits of abstinence and chastity.
>
> *The Decline and Fall of the*
> *Roman Empire* (1776)

In the end more than they wanted freedom, they wanted security. When the Athenians finally wanted not to give to society but for society to give to them, when the freedom they wished for was freedom from responsibility, then Athens ceased to be free.

Ibid.

The various modes of worship, which prevailed in the Roman world, were all considered by the people, as equally true;

by the philosopher, as equally false; and by the magistrate, as equally useful.

Ibid., ch. 2

History...is indeed little more than the register of the crimes, follies, and misfortunes of mankind.

Ibid., ch. 3

Corruption, the most infallible symptom of constitutional liberty.

Ibid., ch. 21

I was never less alone than when by myself.

Memoirs of My Life

THOMAS PAINE
1737–1809

American, silver-tongued agitator, who, thirteen months after arriving in America, wrote in 1776 a forty-seven page pamphlet, *Common Sense*, which sold over one hundred thousand copies and which tilted the debate in favor of independence. It argued that (1) England exploited the colonies with its trade policies, (2) attachment to Britain would draw America into Europe's wars, (3) no island should rule a continent, and (4) "a government of our own is our natural right." Its preface read, "I offer nothing more than simple facts, plain arguments and common sense." Paine's war pamphlet series, *The American Crisis*, painted a bumbling George III as a monster.

Paine defended the French Revolution with *The Rights of Man* (1791), which argued for popular sovereignty against constitutional limits on power. He coined "United States of America."

These are the times that try men's souls. The summer soldier and the sunshine patriot will, in this crisis, shrink from the service of his country, but he that stands it now, deserves the love and thanks of man and woman. Tyranny, like hell, is not easily conquered; yet we have this consolation with us, that the harder the conflict, the more glorious the triumph. What we obtain too cheap, we esteem too lightly; 'tis dearness only that gives everything its value.

> *The American Crisis No. 1*
> (December 23, 1776)

War is the Pharo-table of governments, and nations the dupes of the game.

> Ibid.

Moderation in temper is always a virtue, but moderation in principle is always a vice.

> *Rights of Man* (1792)

We have it in our power to begin the world over again.

My country is the world and my religion is to do good.

GEORG C. LICHTENBERG
1742–99

German, physicist who collected aphorisms.

A book is a mirror: when a monkey looks in, no apostle can look out.

> *Aphorisms* (1806), tr. R. J. Hollingdale

When a book and a reviewer's head collide and we hear a hollow sound, is it always the book's fault?

> Ibid.

Perhaps in time the so-called Dark Ages will be thought of as including our own.

> In L. R. Frank, *Quotationary* (1999)

What astonished him was that cats had two holes cut in their furs exactly where their eyes were.

> In L. R. Frank, *Wit and Humor Quotationary* (2000)

THOMAS JEFFERSON
1743–1826

American, third president (1801–9), who, at age thirty-three, wrote the Declaration of Independence. One of the richest men in America, he inherited 5,000 acres and 300 slaves, but died a bankrupt. Always unwigged and often wearing frayed homespun, his manner was that of a country squire. He wrote 90,000 letters and documents but only one book: *Notes on the State of Virginia*. A poor speaker, he rarely talked in large meetings and gave only two presidential speeches, his inaugurals. The signature of his presidency was economy—he cut the national debt 30 percent even as he waged war against the Barbary pirates and acquired the Louisiana Purchase for $15 million (the Mississippi watershed for three cents per acre). Although his authority was dubious, he did not let "metaphysical subtleties" impede expansion.

Jefferson feared aristocrats and the proletariat, preferring yeoman farmers. He wanted America to farm and fish and import all manufactured goods. He feared strong government because it subsidized the powerful. An anti-Federalist, he preferred the Articles of Confederation to the Constitution, and he wanted legislative supremacy over the federal judiciary.

No significant American politician has since advocated the elimination of judicial review.

> It is a very dangerous doctrine to consider the judges as the ultimate arbiters of all constitutional questions. It is one that would place us under the despotism of an oligarchy....
>
> *Writings*, vol. X

His Democratic-Republican Party agrarians favored a limited national government. Alexander Hamilton's Federalists favored organizing a central bank and funding public works. During Woodrow Wilson's administration, the two parties switched their traditional roles. Modern Republicans are the intellectual descendants of Jeffersonian limited government, and modern Democrats favor an activist government that redistributes wealth.

Jefferson, not Washington, warned of "entangling alliances." His phrase was, "Peace, commerce, honest friendship with all nations—entangling alliances with none."

> When in the course of human events, it becomes necessary for one people to dissolve the political bands which have connected them with another, and to assume among the powers of the earth, the separate and equal station to which the laws of nature and of nature's God entitle them, a decent respect to the opinions of mankind requires that they should declare the causes which impel them to the separation.
>
> Declaration of Independence (July 4, 1776), opening paragraph

We hold these truths to be self evident; that all men are created equal; that they are endowed by their creator with certain unalienable rights; that among these are life, liberty, and the pursuit of happiness; that to secure these rights, governments are instituted among men, deriving their just powers from the consent of the governed; that whenever any form of government becomes destructive to these ends, it is the right of the people to alter or to abolish it, and to institute new government, laying its foundation on such principles, and organizing its powers in such form as to them shall seem most likely to effect their safety and happiness. Prudence, indeed, will dictate, that governments long established, should not be changed for light and transient causes; and accordingly all experience hath shewn, that mankind are more disposed to suffer, while evils are sufferable, than to right themselves by abolishing the forms to which they are accustomed. But when a long train of abuses and usurpations, pursuing invariably the same object, evinces a design to reduce them under absolute despotism, it is their right, it is their duty, to throw off such government, and to provide new guards for their future security. Such has been the patient sufferance of these colonies; and such is not the necessity which constrains them to alter their former systems of government. The history of the present King of Great Britain is a history of repeated injuries and usurpations, all having in direct object the establishment of an absolute tyranny over these states. To prove this, let facts be submitted to a candid world.

> [The "truth" that "all men are created equal" had its roots in Judaism, which idea was seeded worldwide by Christianity.]
>
> Ibid.

And for the support of this declaration, with a firm reliance on the protection of divine providence, we mutually pledge to each other our lives, our fortunes, and our sacred honor.

Ibid.

E Pluribus Unum.
Out of many, one.
> [Motto for the national seal selected by Jefferson, Adams, and Franklin. The founders saw diversity as a problem.]

The care of every man's soul belongs to himself. But what if he neglects the care of it? Well what if he neglects the care of his health or estate…? Will the magistrate make a law that he shall not be poor or sick? Laws provide against injury from others, but not from ourselves.

"Scraps Early in the Revolution"
(October 1776), in L. R. Frank,
Quotationary (1999)

[Speaking of slavery:] I tremble for my country when I reflect that God is just.

Notes on the State of Virginia (1785), ch. 18

Were it left to me to decide whether we should have a government without newspapers, or newspapers without a government, I should not hesitate a moment to prefer the latter.

Letter to Col. Edward Carrington
(January 16, 1787)

I hold it, that a little rebellion, now and then, is a good thing, and as necessary in the political world as storms in the physical.

Letter to James Madison
(January 30, 1787)

A strict observance of the written laws is doubtless one of the high duties of a good citizen, but it is not the highest. The laws of necessity, of self-perservation, of saving our country when in danger, are of higher obligation. To lose our country by a scrupulous adherence to written law, would be to lose the law itself, with life, liberty, property and all those who are enjoying them with us; thus absurdly sacrificing the end to the means.

In L. R. Frank, *Freedom* (2003)

And what country can preserve its liberties, if its rulers are not warned from time to time, that this people preserve the spirit of resistance? Let them take arms…. The tree of liberty must be refreshed from time to time with the blood of patriots and tyrants. It is its natural manure.

No man shall ever be debarred the use of arms. The strongest reason for the people to retain the right to keep and bear arms is, as a last resort, to protect themselves against tyranny in government.

Letter to William S. Smith
(November 13, 1787)

I am for free commerce with all nations, political connection with none; and little or no diplomatic establishment.

Letter to Elbridge Gerry
(January 26, 1799)

I have sworn upon the altar of God, eternal hostility against every form of tyranny over the mind of man.
> [On the Jefferson Memorial.]

Letter to Dr. Benjamin Rush
(Sepember 23, 1800)

If there be any among us who would wish to dissolve this Union or to change its republican form, let them stand undisturbed as monuments of the safety with which error of opinion may be tolerated where reason is left free to combat it.

First Inaugural Address (March 4, 1801)

A wise and frugal government, which shall restrain men from injuring one another, which shall leave them otherwise free to regulate their own pursuits of industry and improvement, and shall not take from the mouth of labor the bread it has earned. This is the sum of good government…

Ibid.

The appointment of a woman to office is an innovation for which the public is not prepared, nor am I.

Letter to Albert Gallatin (1807)

When a man assumes a public trust, he should consider himself a public property.

Letter to Baron Humboldt (1807)

Be assured that no person living wishes more sincerely than I do, to see a complete refutation of the doubts I have myself entertained and expressed on the grade of understanding allotted to [Negroes] by nature, and to find that in this respect they are on a par with ourselves. My doubts were the result of personal observation on the limited sphere of my own State, where the opportunities for the development of their genius were not favorable, and those of exercising it still less so. I expressed them therefore with great hesitation; but whatever be their degree of talent it is no measure of their rights. Because Sir Isaac Newton was superior to others in understanding, he was not therefore lord of the person or property of others.

Letter to Henri Gregoire (February 25, 1809), in L. R. Frank, *Quotationary*

There is a natural aristocracy among men. The grounds of this are virtue and talents. There is also an artificial aristocracy founded on wealth and birth, without either virtue or talents…

Letter to John Adams (October 28, 1813)

Merchants have no country.

Letter to Horatio Spafford
(March 17, 1814)

If a nation expects to be ignorant and free, in a state of civilization, it expects what never was and never will be.

Letter to Colonel Charles Yancey
(January 6, 1816)

I know no safe depository of the ultimate powers of the society but the people themselves; and if we think them not enlightened enough to exercise their control with a wholesome discretion, the remedy is not to take it from them, but to inform their discretion.

Letter to William Jarvis
(September 28, 1820)

We are not afraid to follow truth wherever it may lead, nor to tolerate any error so long as reason is left free to combat it.

Letter to William Roscoe
(December 27, 1820)

Were we directed from Washington when to sow and when to reap, we should soon want bread.

Autobiography (1821)

When angry, count ten before you speak; if very angry, an hundred.

A Decalogue of Canons for Observation in Practical Life (February 21, 1825)

Whenever hostile aggressions…require

a resort to war, we must meet our duty and convince the world that we are just friends and brave enemies.

Letter to Andrew Jackson

Advertisements contain the only truth to be relied on in a newspaper.

Letter to Nathaniel Macon

I do not believe... that fourteen out of fifteen men are rogues.... But I have always found that rogues would be uppermost.

Fawn M. Brodie, *Thomas Jefferson: An Intimate History* (1974)

State a problem to a ploughman and a professor. The former will decide it often better than the latter because he had not been led astray by artificial rules.

In Paul Johnson, *History of the American People* (1997)

Let us hear no more of trust in men, but bind them down from mischief by the chains of the Constitution.

In William F. Buckley Jr., *Let Us Talk of Many Things* (1999)

Every man is under the natural duty of contributing to the necessities of the society.

The natural process of things is for government to gain ground and for liberty to yield.

[Jefferson believed education in a democracy should be primarily historical because history:]
by apprising them of the past, will enable them to judge of the future; it will avail them of the experience of other times and other nations; it will qualify them as judges of the actions and designs of men.

Property is the foundation of all civilized society.

To compel a man to furnish contributions of money for the propagation of opinions which he disbelieves is sinful and tyrannical.

Equal rights for all, special privileges for none.

Science is my passion, politics is my duty.

In matters of principle, stand like a rock. In matters of taste, swim with the current.

Government can only do something for the people in proportion to what it can do to the people.

We may consider each generation as a separate nation, with a right, by the will of the majority, to bind themselves, but none to bind the succeeding generation, more than the inhabitants of another country.

I place economy among the first and most important virtues... We must make our choice between economy and liberty, or profusion and servitude.... If we can prevent the government from wasting the labors of the people under pretense of caring for them, we will be wise.

The policy of the American government is to leave their citizens free, neither restraining nor aiding them in their pursuits.

Great innovations should not be forced on slender majorities.

We must dream of an aristocracy of achievement arising out of a democracy of opportunity.

My reading of history convinces me that most bad government results from too much government.

Rebellion to tyrants is obedience to God.
[An Oliver Cromwell quotation Jefferson selected for his personal seal.]

Jefferson's Kentucky Resolutions of 1798 argued that the Sedition Act was unconstitutional because it violated natural rights that gave each state the right to nullify the act within its boundary, and it gave the state the right to secede. These arguments were later used by John C. Calhoun.

Eternal vigilance is the price of liberty.
A phrase ascribed to Jefferson, but coined by John Philpot Curran (1750–1817)

Jefferson, as chairman of William and Mary, abolished the departments of theology and Greek and Hebrew languages, and started departments in medicine, chemistry, and modern languages. He wanted to be remembered for the Declaration of Independence, the Virginia Statute of Religious Liberty, and founding the University of Virginia.

Is it the Fourth?
Last words

Near death, Jefferson said, "John Adams will see that things go forward." The last words of John Adams, who survived Jefferson by five hours, were, "The country is safe. Jefferson still lives."

ANTOINE L. LAVOISIER
1743–94

French, "father of modern chemistry," who was to chemistry what Newton was to physics. He introduced quantitative methods and discovered (1) the nature of combustion, (2) the elements (indecomposable materials), and (3) the conservation of mass: "Nothing is created in the operations either of art or of Nature, and it can be taken as an axiom that in every operation an equal quantity of matter exists both before and after the operation." Previously, it had been thought that air and water were elementary substances and that fire released "phlogiston."

Lavoisier, a liberal who supported the French Revolution, was denounced by Marat. The judge sentencing Lavoisier to be guillotined said, "The republic has no need of savants." Later, the mathematician Lagrange reposted, "It took them only an instant to cut off that head, and a hundred years may not produce another like it." Note: Lavoisier had earlier exploded a phlogiston theory of the hopeful young chemist Jean-Paul Marat.

JOHN JAY
1745–1829

American, author of five Federalist Papers, delegate to the Continental Congress, secretary of foreign affairs, signer of Jay's Treaty, and the first chief justice.

Providence has been pleased to give this one connected country, to one united people, a people descended from the same ancestors, speaking the same language, professing the same religion,

attached to the same principles of government, very similar in their manners
and customs....
    [America's founding culture was
Anglo-Saxon, not Eurocentric.]
                                Federalist No. 2

HANNAH MORE
1745–1833

English, pamphlet writer, and feminist.

He liked those literary cooks
Who skim the cream of others' books;
And ruin half an author's graces
By plucking bon-mots from their
    places.
                        Florio (1786), pt. 1, 1.123

How much it is to be regretted, that the
British ladies should ever sit down con-
tented to polish, when they are able to
reform; to entertain, when they might
instruct; and to dazzle for an hour, when
they are candidates for eternity!
Essays on Various Subjects...for Young Ladies
                (1777), "On Dissipation"

JOHN PAUL JONES
1747–92

American, naval captain.

I wish to have no connection with any
ship that does not sail fast; for I intend
to go in harm's way.
                Letter to le Ray de Chaumont
                        (November 16, 1778)

I have not yet begun to fight.
    [After being asked in 1779 to surren-
    der his ship, the *Bon Homme Richard*,

which soon sank, Jones, sailed away
in the British ship he had captured,
the *Serapis*—a unique event in naval
warfare. Jones won because a Marine
on his own initiative climbed out
on the Richard's yardarm and threw
grenades into the hatch of the Serapis, which started a fire that would
have blown the ship apart had it not
been surrendered.]

JEREMY BENTHAM
1748–1832

English, founder of utilitarianism, a doctrine that holds: "That action is right
which promotes the greatest happiness for
the greatest number of people." Bentham
believed laissez-faire economics would
maximize wealth creation, which would
bring the greatest happiness to the greatest
number. But utilitarianism has no moral
norms. Lenin, Stalin, Mao, and Hitler were
all professed utilitarians. Utilitarians today
are usually socialists.
    Opposite of the Kantians, utilitarians
believe motivation is unimportant, consequences are all. Any act is morally right if it
results in the greatest good for the greatest
number.

The greatest happiness of the greatest
number is the foundation of morals and
legislation.
*An Introduction to the Principles of Morals
        and Legislation* (1789), ch. 1

[The legal regime that secures private
property is] the noblest triumph of
humanity over itself....
            Principles of the Civil Code

...it is that right [to private property] which has vanquished the natural aversion to labor, which has given to man the empire of the earth; which has brought to an end the migratory life of nations, which has produced the love of country and a regard for posterity.

Ibid.

To be the most effectively benevolent man who ever lived.
[His goal.]
In Mary P. Mack *International Encyclopedia of the Social Sciences* (1968), vol. 2

EMMANUEL JOSEPH SIEYES
1748–1836

French, abbot, and member of the National Assembly. He engineered the coup d'etat of 18 *Brumaire* 1799, which brought Napoleon to power as first consul.

La mort sans phrases.
Death without useless talk.
[His vote to execute Louis XVI.]

What is the Third Estate? Everything. And what has it been until the present time? Nothing. And what does it demand? To be something.

J'ai vécu.
I survived.
[When asked what he had done during the Reign of Terror.]

JOHANN WOLFGANG VON GOETHE
1749–1832

German, regarded as the greatest figure in German literature. Goethe, Schiller, Herder,

among others, formed the *Sturm-und-Drang* romantic rebellion against Napoleon's holocaust and the classical order of Corneille and Racine. They preferred the imaginative robustness of Homer and Shakespeare to artificial classical allusions. Goethe admired America: *"Amerika, du hastes besser,"* or, *"America you have it better."*

Goethe, mesmerized by feminine beauty, wrote fifteen hundred love letters to Charlotte Buff, one of his many amours. He struggled against the "brevity of beauty and the elusiveness of truth." At twenty-five he became a celebrity for *The Sorrows of Young Werther* (1774). Werther kills himself for love of Charlotte, who is engaged to Albert, his friend whom he will not betray. So many committed suicide after reading it that it was banned in much of Europe. Many young men took to wearing Werther's trademark blue coat and yellow pants. It exudes *Weltschmerz*, sorrow about the world, and *Ischmerz*, sorrow over one's condition. Werther's suicide note to Charlotte read:

Albert is your husband—well, what of it? Husband! In the eyes of the world—and in the eyes of the world is it sinful for me to love you, to want to tear you from his embrace into my own? Sin? Very well, I am punishing myself.... From this moment you are mine! Mine, oh Lotte-! I am going on ahead! Going unto my Father, your Father. I shall tell Him my sorrows and He will comfort me until that time when you come and I fly to meet you, hold you and remain with you in a perpetual embrace in the sight of the eternal.

There is strong shadow where there is much light.

Gotz von Berlichingen (1773), act 1

…any single fool can live arbitrarily.
> In L. Lewisohn, *Goethe*, letters of
> (January 3, 1781)

One ought, every day at least, to hear a little song, read a good poem, see a fine picture, and, if it were possible, to speak a few reasonable words.
> *Wilhelm Meisters Apprenticeship*, bk. 5, ch. 1

An unused life is but an early death.
> *Iphigenie auf Tauris* (1787), act 1. sc. 1

You must be master and win, or lose and serve, triumph or suffer, be the hammer or the anvil.
> *Der Gross Cophta* (1791), act 2

THE MAXIMS AND REFLECTIONS OF GOETHE (1892)
TR. T. BAILEY SAUNDERS

Everything that frees our spirit without giving us control of ourselves is ruinous.

The greatest difficulties lie where we are not looking for them.

Nothing is more terrible than ignorance in action.

Genius is knowing when to stop.

Whatever you do, or dream you can do, begin it. Boldness has genius, power and magic in it.

When ideas fail, words come in very handy.

Girls we love for what they are; young men for what they promise to be.

To act is easy; to think is so hard.

Terrible is he who has nothing to lose.

No one who has not seen the Sistine Chapel can have a clear idea of what a human being may achieve.

Without haste, but without rest.
> [Goethe's Motto]
> *Zahme Xemien* (1796)

A teacher who can arouse a feeling for one single good action, for one single good poem, accomplishes more than he who fills our memory with rows on rows of natural objects, classified with name and form.
> *Elective Affinities* (1808), bk. II, ch. 7

FAUST
1808–32

Man errs as long as he strives.
> Pt. I, "Prologue in Heaven"

Philosophy have I digested,
The whole of Law and Medicine,
From each its secrets I have wrested,
Theology, alas, thrown in.
Poor fool, with all this sweated lore,
I stand no wiser than I was before.
> Ibid., pt. 1, "Night, Faust's Study"

The glory's naught, the deed is all.
> Ibid., pt. IV, "Mountain Heights"

Who strives always to the utmost,
For him there is salvation.
> [Said by the angels as they rescue Faust from Mephistopheles.]
> Ibid., pt. V, "Mountain Gorges"

In Marlowe's *The Tragical History of Doctor Faustus* (1604), Dr. Faustus sold his soul to the Devil to gain forbidden knowledge and become the "great Emperor of the world." But Goethe's Faust is a hero beloved of God, seeking experiences after becoming disillusioned with knowledge. Faust agrees to give his soul to a demon, the attractive Mephistopheles, in exchange for a greater capacity for experience, if he ceases to strive to make the world better or if life ever becomes so enthralling that he wants to live in it forever and will say

> When to the moment I shall say
> "Linger awhile! So fair thou art!"
> Then mayst thou fetter me straightway
> Then to the abyss will I depart!

Mephistopheles tempts Faust with power, knowledge, the lovely Gretchen, and even Helen of Troy, but to no avail. But Faust says, "Stay! Thou art so fair" after reclaiming land from the sea. Because the experience Faust deemed to be fair was helping other people, the Devil lost his wager with God that he could tempt Faust from God's service. So God rescued Faust. Faust's moral is that damnation comes from ceasing to strive to turn chaos into order. God knows man must err as he strives. Goethe wrote *Faust* over 59 of his 83 years.

> Doubt grows with knowledge...[so] quietly revere the unfathomable.
> > Proverbs in Prose

> Everywhere, we learn only from those whom we love.
> > In Peter Eckermann, *Conversations with Goethe, 1836–1848*, tr. John Oxenford
> > (1850)

Give me the benefit of your convictions, if you have any, but keep your doubts to yourself, for I have enough of my own.
> > Ibid.

Vernunft wird Unsinn/Wohltat, Plage.
Reason becomes nonsense/Boons afflictions.
> [Goethe's disenchantment with the Enlightenment and the French Revolution.]

Live dangerously and you live right.

In the realm of ideas, everything depends on enthusiasm; in the real world, all rests on perseverance.

Legislators and revolutionaries who promise equality and liberty at the same time are either psychopaths or mountebanks.

Correction does much, but encouragement does more.

Daring ideas are like chessmen moved forward; they may be beaten, but they may start a winning game.

If everyone sweeps before his own front door, then the street is clean.

Few men have imagination enough for reality.

It never occurs to fools that merit and good fortune are closely united.

There are but two roads that lead to an important goal and to the doing of great things: strength and perseverance. Strength is the lot of but a few privileged men; but austere perseverance, harsh and continuous, may be employed by the smallest of us, and rarely fails of its purpose, for its silent power grows irresistibly greater with time.

Treat people as if they were what they ought to be and you help them become what they are capable of becoming.

More light.

Last words

HONORE GABRIEL, COMTE DE MIRABEAU
1749–91

French, delegate to the 1789 Estates General where he championed a constitutional monarchy. His untimely death enabled the Jacobins to overthrow his republican policies and take France down the path to chaos and dictatorship. His father, Victor, Marquis de Mirabeau, the leading physiocrat, had jailed him in his youth for wildness.

Begin with the infant in the cradle; let the first word he lisps be Washington.

War is the national industry of Prussia.

PIERRE SIMON DE LAPLACE
1749–1827

French, scientist. He argued that if an intelligence knew the position and motion of all atoms, it could calculate the past and future. Per Newton, he saw the world as a machine: complex, but governed by cause and effect and thus predictable. Quantum mechanics and Werner Heisenberg's "uncertainty principle" reintroduced chance and free will.

All the effects of nature are only the mathematical consequences of a small number of immutable laws.

E. T. Bell, Men of Mathematics

JAMES MADISON
1751–1836

American, fourth president (1809–17), five feet, six-inches tall and taciturn "father of the Constitution and the Bill of Rights." He and Alexander Hamilton asked the Congress under the Articles of Confederation to issue a call for a convention of the states to meet in Philadelphia in 1787 to make rules for governing commerce between the states. That convention produced the Constitution, under which the new national government derived its powers from the people, not from the states or from the nation, thus Madison's, "We the People." Madison also provided the Virginia Plan, which gave each state two senators, and the Three-fifths Rule, which solved the knotty problem of slavery. Those two compromises made the Constitution possible. He wrote the notes of the Constitutional Convention. He said insightfully, "The diffusion of knowledge is the only true guardian of liberty." A man of affairs, he became one of the world's greatest political theorists.

Madison, Hamilton, and Jay in 1787–88 wrote *The Federalist Papers*, eighty-five newspaper articles that explained the intent of the Constitution's framers. Federalists 10 and 51 outlined "Madisonian democracy": "the causes of faction cannot be removed and that relief is only to be sought in the means of controlling its effects." That is, democracy's best chance for survival lies in the power to check the most powerful factions, given the constant struggle between factions as they form new combinations. Madison's genius was to structure the Constitution to prevent the coalescing of a "durable tyrannical majority." He believed only the separation of powers and checks and balances could maintain liberty, not man's virtue, although the absence of virtue dooms any republic, no matter what checks and balances are employed.

The principal anti-Federalist argument was that a central government would be less democratic than state governments. Madison countered by saying that the larger the republic, the more competing interests contending against each other, so it would be more democratic than the state governments.

Madison and Jefferson in "the great collaboration" founded the Democratic Party. Madison yielded the public spotlight to Jefferson, who yielded to Madison on substance. Madison was a disciple of Hume and Adam Smith, that is, keep government from interfering in the economy.

> The protection of these faculties [for acquiring property] is the first object of government.
>
> *The Federalist* (1787), no. 10

> …democracies have ever been spectacles of turbulence and contention; have ever been found incompatible with personal security or the rights of property; and have in general been as short in their lives as they have been violent in their deaths.
>
> Ibid.

> The most common and durable source of factions has been the various and unequal distribution of property. Those who hold and those who are without property have ever formed distinct interests in society.
>
> Ibid.

> The Constitution preserves the advantage of being armed which Americans possess over the people of almost every other nation…[where] governments are afraid to trust the people with arms.
>
> Ibid., no. 46

> The accumulation of all powers legislative, executive and judiciary in the same hands…may justly be pronounced the very definition of tyranny.
>
> Ibid., no. 47

> Ambition must be made to counteract ambition.... If men were angels, no government would be necessary.... In framing a government which is to be administered by men over men, the great difficulty lies in this: you must first enable the government to control the governed and in the next place oblige it to control itself.
>
> Ibid., no. 51

> In all very numerous assemblies, of whatever characters composed, passion never fails to wrest the scepter from reason. Had every Athenian citizen been a Socrates, every Athenian assembly would still have been a mob.
>
> Ibid., no. 55

> It will be of little avail to the people that laws are made by men of their choice, if the laws be so voluminous that they cannot be read, or so incoherent that they cannot be understood…that no man who knows what the law is today can guess what it will be tomorrow.
>
> *Federalist Papers*

To secure the public good and private rights against the danger of the property-less or proletarians and at the same time preserve the spirit and form of popular government was then the great object to which the Convention inquires were directed.

> Letter to Jefferson (October 24, 1887)

I believe there are more instances of the abridgment of freedom by gradual and silent encroachments of those in power than by violent and sudden usurpations.

> Speech at Virginia Ratifying Convention
> (June 16, 1788)

Is there no virtue among us? If there be not, we are in a wretched situation. No theoretical checks—no form of government, can render us secure. To suppose that any form of government will secure liberty or happiness without any virtue in the people is a chimerical idea.

> Ibid.

Wherever the real power in a Government lies, there is the danger of oppression. In our Governments the real power lies in the majority of the Community, and the invasion of private rights is chiefly to be apprehended, not from acts of Government contrary to the sense of its constituents, but from acts in which the Government is the mere instrument of the major number of the constituents.

> Letter to Thomas Jefferson
> (October 17, 1788)

Government is instituted to protect property of every sort; as well that which lies in the various rights of individuals, as that which the term particularly expresses. This being the end of government, that alone is a just government, which impartially secures to every man, whatever is his own.

> *National Gazette* essay (March 27, 1792)

Of all the evils to public liberty, war is perhaps the most to be dreaded, because it comprises and develops every other. War is the parent of armies; from these proceed debts and taxes. And armies, and debts, and taxes, are the known instruments for bringing the many under the dominion of the few....No nation could preserve its freedom in the midst of continual warfare.

Having outlived so many of my contemporaries...I may be thought to have outlived myself.

The truth is that all men having power should be distrusted.

JOSEPH DE MAISTRE
1753–1821

French, diplomat, and Catholic royalist.

Every country has the government it deserves.

> *Lettrès* (1851), vol. 1, letter 53
> (August 15, 1811)

THOMAS BOWDLER
1754–1825

English, editor.

I acknowledge Shakespeare to be the world's greatest dramatic poet, but regret that no parent could place the uncorrected book in the hands of his daughter.

> *Family Shakespeare* (1818), Preface

JOSEPH JOUBERT
1754–1824

French, essayist, epigramist, and moralist.

> Children have more need of models than critics.
>> *Pensées* (1842), tr. Paul Auster (1983)

> Words, like eyeglasses, blur everything that they do no make clearer.
>> Ibid.

> Genius begins great works; labor alone finishes them.

MARIE-JEANNE ROLAND
1754–93

French, poet, "muse of the Girondists," liberal aristocrats lead by Mirabeau, who favored a constitutional monarchy. But as Georg Büchner said, "The revolution is like Saturn—it eats its own children." The Girondists lost favor when their war on Austria and Prussia (initiated to rally the nation) went badly. Danton and Marat of the Jacobin Club in August 1792 captured the Hotel de Ville, slaughtered the Swiss Guard at the Tuileries, took Louis XVI captive, and liquidated most Girondists.

> O Liberty! O Liberty! What crimes are committed in thy name!
>> [Said when passing a statue to liberty while riding in a tumbrel to be guillotined.]
>> Lamartine, *Histoire des Girondins* (1847)

LOUIS XVI
1754–93

French, king, who was bewildered, phlegmatic, and, married to Marie Antoinette, who never said of the hungry in Paris, "If they have no bread, let them eat cake." But she was extravagant and was called "Mrs. Deficit." To avoid personal economies, she forced the resignation of Turgot, controller general of finance, who had balanced the budget by cutting costs, taxing the clergy and nobility, and abolishing state-supported monopolies. A leap in confidence enabled Turgot to refinance part of France's debt at 4 percent rather than at 12 percent. After Turgot's reforms were overturned, inflation exploded. Also, Louis spent 1 billion *livres* to support the American revolutionists. The day the Bastille was stormed, Louis went hunting and wrote in his diary, "Nothing happened." The next day, Louis asked, "Is it a revolt?" The Duke de la Rochefoucauld retorted, "No, sire, it is a revolution." Louis had no sense of the great discontinuity that was about to sweep away his monarchy and transform the world.

CHARLES MAURICE TALLEYRAND
1754–1838

French, nobleman, and defrocked bishop. He defended the church in the National Assembly until he introduced a bill to expropriate church properties. He was Napoleon's foreign minister, but he persuaded the Senate to depose Napoleon in 1814, after which he represented France at the Congress of Vienna. He persuaded the tsar to reinstate the Bourbons on the French throne and served as Louis XVIII's foreign minister and Louis Philippe's chief adviser. His opportunism was exceeded only by that of Joseph Fouché.

> They have learned nothing, and forgotten nothing.
> [Of the Bourbons.]
>> Letter to M. Mallet du Pan (1796)

> [When Napoleon asked him what he had meant by saying "nonintervention," Talleyrand replied:]
> Sire, it means about the same as intervention.
>> In L. R. Frank, *Quotationary* (1999)

> Treason, your majesty, is a question of dates.
>> In Paul Johnson, *The Birth of the Modern* (1991)

> You can do everything with bayonets, Sire, except sit on them.

> [Hearing of Napoleon's death, Talleyrand commented:]
> Not an event, more a news-item.
>> In Harold Nicholson, *The Congress of Vienna*

> I consider Napoleon, Pitt, and Hamilton as the three greatest men of our age, and if I had to choose, I would unhesitatingly give the first place to Hamilton.
>> In Jean E. Smith, *John Marshall* (1996)

> [Talleyrand during the July Revolution of 1830 heard rioting and said:] "Ah, the tocsin! We're winning." [Asked "Who is we?" Talleyrand replied:] "I'll tell you who we are tomorrow."

> She is intolerable, but that is her only fault.

> To avoid being called a flirt, she always yielded easily.

> Women sometimes forgive a man who forces the opportunity, but never a man who misses one.

> *Surtout, Messieurs, point de zele.*
> Above all, gentlemen, no zeal.

> Wellington said of Talleyrand, "He is not lively or pleasant in conversation, but now and then he comes out with a thing you remember all the rest of your life."

> Died has he. I wonder what he meant by that?
> [Metternich on hearing of his death.]

NATHAN HALE
1755–76

American, patriot.

> I regret that I have but one life to lose for my country.
> [He was hanged by the British as a spy.]

ALEXANDER HAMILTON
1755–1804

American, the "little lion of Federalism" (at five-feet, six-inches) who, under the pen name Publius, wrote 51 of the 85 newspaper articles (*Federalist Papers*) urging ratification of the Constitution. He championed an activist government of "implied powers" to fund public improvements and establish a national bank. He is often called the "father of American capitalism" and the "patron saint of Wall Street." Thomas Jefferson lamented, "We can pay off his debts in fifteen years, but we can never get rid of his financial system." Jefferson's vision for America was a loose confederation of agricultural states, while Hamilton favored a strong federal government for an new economy including banks, manufacturing, corporations, and stock exchanges.

Hamilton is considered one of the five greatest Founding Fathers for securing the ratification of the Constitution and establishing U.S. credit, which required getting Southern support for the federal assumption of state war debts. To broker that deal, Hamilton made Washington, D.C., the capital, not Philadelphia. In 1789, U.S. public securities traded at 25 percent of face value on European markets, but rose to 110 percent before Hamilton stepped down. With established credit, the United States financed its growth at low interest rates in the nineteenth century by selling bonds in Europe. Latin America stagnated because it never established its credit.

Hamilton, George Washington's de facto prime minister, led the pro-British Federalist Party in opposition to Jefferson/Madison's pro-French Democratic-Republican Party. He expressed the core of conservatism when he said, "I have thought it my duty to exhibit things as they are, not as they ought to be." Aaron Burr killed Hamilton in a duel.

> Every man ought to be supposed a knave; and to have no other end, in all his actions, but private interest. By this interest we must govern him; and, by means of it, make him co-operate to public good, notwithstanding his insatiable avarice and ambition. Without this, we shall in vain boast of the advantages of any constitution.
>
> *Works*, vol. II

A national debt, if it is not excessive, will be to us a national blessing.
> *Works*, vol. I, in a letter to Robert Morris
> (April 30, 1781)

A power over a man's subsistence amounts to a power over his will.
> *Federalist Papers*

A nation, despicable by its weakness, forfeits even the privilege of being neutral.
> *Federalist*, no. 11

If the representatives of the people betray their constituents, there is no recourse left but in the exertion of that original right of self-defense which is paramount to all forms of positive government.
> Ibid., no. 28

The complete independence of the courts of justice is peculiarly essential in a limited Constitution. By a limited Constitution, I understand one which contains certain specified exceptions to the legislative authority; such, for instance, as that it shall pass no bills of attainder, no ex post facto laws, and the like. Limitations of this kind can be preserved in practice no other way than through the medium of courts of justice, whose duty it must be to declare all acts contrary to the manifest tenor of the Constitution void. Without this, all the reservations of particular rights or privileges would amount to nothing.
> Ibid., no. 78

History teaches that among the men who have overturned the liberties of republics, the greatest number have begun their career by paying obsequious court to the people; commencing demagogues and ending tyrants.
> Ibid., no. 78

Foreign influence is truly the Grecian horse to a republic. We cannot be too careful to exclude its entrance. Nor ought we to imagine that it can only make its approaches in the gross form of direct bribery. It is then most dangerous when it comes under the patronage of our passions, under the auspices of national prejudice and partiality.

Walter A. McDougall, *Promised Land, Crusader State: The American Encounter with the World Since 1776,* (1997)

Sparta, Athens, Rome, and Carthage were all republics…Yet were they as often engaged in wars, offensive and defensive, as the neighboring monarchies of the same times….Few nations have been more frequently engaged in war [than Great Britain]…

In Henry Kissinger, *Diplomacy* (1994)

[Hamilton wrote at age twelve:] I condemn the groveling conditions of a clerk…and would willingly risk my life, though not my character, to exalt my station….I mean to prepare the way for futurity.

The people!—the people is a great beast.

JOHN MARSHALL
1755–1835

American, fourth chief justice of the Supreme Court (1801–35). Marshall transformed the Constitution from a state compact into a national charter, with the Supreme Court as the arbiter of the rules for American governance. As the great biographer Jean Edward Smith wrote in his *John Marshall* (1996), "If George Washington founded the country, John Marshall

defined it." John Adams, said, "My gift of John Marshall to the people of the United States was the proudest act of my life."

In *Marbury v. Madison* (1803), Marshall established judicial review, to wit, the Supreme Court's authority to declare unconstitutional acts of the Congress and the executive. That was contrary to English tradition and to the views of Jefferson, who argued the Constitution was merely equal to laws passed by Congress. But no prominent politician since Jefferson has questioned the constitutionality of judicial review. The framers understood the need for an independent judiciary. James Madison said in the first session of Congress that the judiciary was "an impenetrable bulwark against every assumption of power in the Legislative or Executive."

It is emphatically the province and duty of the judicial department to say what the law is…. This is the very essence of judicial duty…. The powers of the legislature are defined and limited; and that those limits may not be mistaken, or forgotten, the Constitution is written.

Marbury v. Madison (1803)

The very essence of civil liberty is the right of every individual to claim the protection of the laws whenever he receives an injury.

Ibid.

Marshall in *Marbury v. Madison* gave Jefferson a minor tactical victory, but gave the Federalists an overwhelming strategic victory by holding that the Supreme Court had the power to declare laws unconstitutional. As the new president, Jefferson had refused to deliver a duly signed midnight appointment by President Adams of

Marbury as a justice of the peace. Marshall held that the law requiring such delivery was unconstitutional.

Marbury v. Madison does not mean that the Supreme Court sits as a board of review over acts of the Congress and the executive branch. The court only has jurisdiction in cases of law or equity properly before it, and Congress might have the power to eliminate the Supreme Court's appellate jurisdiction, leaving it only its narrow original jurisdiction over cases involving ambassadors and ministers and cases in which states are parties.

In *Cohens v. Virginia* (1821), Marshall established the supremacy of the Supreme Court over state laws and courts.

Marshall emphasized that the Constitution had been approved by the people in special conventions, not by state governments. That the conventions had been held in the states was an expedient. Unlike the sovereign British Parliament, in America the people had granted power to the government, so the people were sovereign. The U.S. government is thus bound by the same laws as a private citizen. Marshall saw the judiciary's role as the defender of constitutional liberty. In thirty-four years he led the majority in 1,100 cases and dissented only eight times.

In *McCulloch v. Maryland* (1819), he upheld the federal government's power to create a national bank. That favored Hamilton's argument for the implied powers of the national government over the concept that the government's powers were limited to those specifically enumerated. Marshall wrote:

> We must never forget that it is a constitution we are expounding...something

organic, capable of growth, susceptible to change.... This provision is made in a constitution, intended to endure for ages to come, and consequently, to be adapted to the various crises of human affairs.
>
> *McCulloch v. Maryland*, 4 Wheaton 316, 407, 415

He secured capitalism by protecting property rights from government intervention. In *Fletcher v. Peck* (1810), Marshall held a contract valid even if its terms were onerous; in 1819 in the Dartmouth College case, he held corporations have similar property rights as individuals; in *Gibbons v. Ogden* (1824), he ruled a state-granted monopoly unconstitutional because it interfered with Congress' power to regulate interstate commerce; and in *Sturges v. Crowninshield* (1819), he ruled unconstitutional a debtor-friendly state bankruptcy law that violated the constitutional right to contract. His protection of the sanctity of contracts made it possible to invest capital with confidence.

Marshall and Hamilton were the two great capitalists of the early republic who revered Adam Smith's *Wealth of Nations*. Paul Johnson in *The Birth of the Modern* (1991) said Marshall:

> was able to turn the Supreme Court into an elitist fortress, using all the resources of the U.S. Constitution and the English Common law to assert the gravitational value of property and commercial law and so to prevent the United States from falling victim to the anti-capitalist demagoguery which repeatedly swept across the states of Latin America and hindered its wealth-producing process. In doing so, he became one of the principal architects of the modern world.

John Marshall was a man's man raised in a frontier log cabin. Taught to read by his father, he loved the poetry of Horace and Pope and the histories of Livy, who celebrated republican virtues. During the Revolutionary War he was a heroic officer. He began as a surveyor and then read law. His temperament was even and his manners unassuming, and he was a devoted husband. He said, "I would have had my wife if I had had to climb Alleghenys of skulls and swim Atlantics of blood." All teenagers should read Jean Smith's biography of Marshall.

> We ought to have commercial intercourse with all, but political ties with none. Let us buy as cheap and sell as dear as possible. Let commerce go where individual…interest will carry it; but let us never connect ourselves with any people whatever.
>
>   In Jean E. Smith, *Marshall* (1996)

Philadelphia's Liberty Bell was first rung in Independence Hall in 1776 to celebrate American Independence. It cracked in 1835 while tolling the death of John Marshall, and was thereafter silent.

HENRY LEE
"LIGHT HORSE HARRY"
1756–1818

American, general, and father of Robert E. Lee.

> To the memory of the Man, first in war, first in peace, and first in the hearts of his countrymen.
>
>   Eulogy for George Washington
>   in the House of Representatives,
>   (December 26, 1799)

To preserve liberty it is essential that the whole body of the people always possess arms and be taught alike, especially when young, how to use them.

WILLIAM BLAKE
1757–1827

English, mystic, poet, engraver, painter, and first English "Romantic." He revolted against the Enlightenment that reduced man to a thinking machine and ignored spirit. He said, "Everything that lives is holy. We are all part of the Divine, and our great gift is imagination, not reason."

He painted portraits of "visionary heads" of ancient kings and saints, who came as spirits to sit in his studio. His wife said, "I have very little of Mr. Blake's company; he is always in Paradise."

Blake's "The Chimney Sweeper" is the most powerful indictment of the Industrial Revolution, and even God is condemned as a false father.

> When my mother died I was very young,
> And my father sold me while yet my
>   tongue
> Could scarcely cry weep weep weep weep,
> So your chimneys I sweep & in soot I
>   sleep.
>   "The Chimney Sweeper," st. 1

> And all must love the human form,
> In heathen, Turk or Jew;
> Where mercy, Love and Pity dwell
> There God is dwelling too.
>   *Songs of Innocence* (1789), "The Divine
>   Image"

> Then cherish pity, lest you drive an
>   angel from your door.
>   Ibid., "Holy Thursday"

Tiger Tiger, burning bright,
In the forests of the night;
What immortal hand or eye,
Could frame thy fearful symmetry?
> *Songs of Experience* (1794), "The Tiger"

To see a world in a grain of sand,
And a heaven in a wild flower;
Hold infinity in the palm of your hand,
And eternity in an hour.
> *Auguries of Innocence* (1803)

A truth that's told with bad intent
Beats all the lies you can invent.
> Ibid.

A Robin Redbreast in a Cage
Puts all Heaven in a Rage.
> Ibid.

A Fool sees not the same tree that a Wise
Man sees.
> *The Marriage of Heaven and Hell* (1790-
> 93), "Proverbs of Hell"

Prudence is an ugly old maid courted by
incapacity.
> Ibid.

One law for the Lion and Ox is
oppression.
> Ibid.

He who would do good to another man
must do it in Minute Particulars.
General Good is the plea of the scoundrel,
hypocrite, and flatterer...
> *Jerusalem* (1804-07), Plate 77

And was Jerusalem builded here
Among these dark Satanic mills?
> Ibid., "Milton"

I can look at the knot in a piece of
wood until it frightens me.
> In Paul Johnson, *The Birth of the Modern*
> (1991)

The hand of Vengeance sought the bed
To which the purple tyrant fled;
The iron hand crush'd the tyrant's head,
And became a tyrant in his stead.
> [Comment on the French Revolution.]

JAMES MONROE
1758–1831

American, fifth president (1817–25). The
Monroe Doctrine was proclaimed in 1817
when Britain asked America to join her in
preventing the French from replacing the
Spanish in Latin America. Monroe acted
alone, due to John Quincy Adams, who did
not want the U.S. to "come in as a cockboat
in the wake of a British man-of-war."

National honor is national property of
the highest value.
> First Inaugural (March 4, 1817)

In the wars of the European powers in
matters relating to themselves we have
never taken any part, nor does it com-
port with our policy so to do....[But]
the American continents, by the free
and independent condition which they
have assumed and maintain, are henceforth not to be considered as subjects
for future colonization by any European
powers.
> [Monroe Doctrine]
> [The "Roosevelt Corollary" held
> that the U.S. may intervene to pro-
> tect U.S. interests.]
> Ibid.

HORATIO NELSON
1758–1805

English, admiral, who died on his flagship, HMS *Victory*, at the Battle of Trafalgar, which eliminated any possibility of Napoleon invading England. At Trafalgar, Nelson's 27 ships captured or destroyed 19 of France's 33 ships. Nelson had also beaten French fleets at Calvi (1794), Tenerife (1797), the Battle of the Nile (1798), and Copenhagen (1801). Nelson wore his admiral stars on the quarterdeck of HMS *Victory*, where he was shot by a sniper, but the Duke of Wellington and staff dressed as civilians in battles to confuse snipers. In combat, U.S. Marine officers and NCOs cover their insignia of rank.

> I have only one eye...I really do not see the signal.
>> [At the Battle of Copenhagen, Nelson raised his spyglass to his blind eye to not see the signal to disengage; and, Nelson won the battle. MacArthur said, "Generals become famous for the orders they refuse to obey." The navy never "retreats", it "disengages."]
>>> R. Southey, *Life of Nelson* (1813)

> But, in case signals can neither be seen nor perfectly understood, no captain can do very wrong if he places his ship alongside that of the enemy.
>> Memorandum to the fleet
>> (October 9, 1805)

> I have always been a quarter of an hour before my time, and it has made a man of me.

> [Talking with his officers, Nelson picked up a poker and said:]
> It matters not at all in what way I lay this poker on the floor. But if Bonaparte should say it must be placed in this direction, we must instantly insist on its being laid in some other way.

> England expects every man will do his duty.
>> Signal at Battle of Trafalgar,
>> (October 21, 1805)

> Thank God, I have done my duty.
>> Nelson dying after the battle of Trafalgar

ROBERT BURNS
1759–96

Scottish, the "Plowman Poet" and the "Scottish National Poet."

> What signifies the life o' man,
> An 'twere na for the lasses, O.
>> "Green Grow the Rashes" (1784)

> The best laid schemes o' Mice an' Men
> Gang aft a-gley.
>> "To a Mouse" (1785)

> O wad some power the giftie gie us
> To see oursel's as ithers see us!
> It wad frae monie a blunder free us
> An' foolish notion.
>> "To a Louse" (1786)

> Should auld acquaintance be forgot, and
>> never brought to min'?
> Should auld acquaintance be forgot,
> And days o' lang syne?
>> "Auld Lang Syne" (1788), st. 1

> For auld lang syne, my dear,
> For auld lang syne,
> We'll tak a cup o' kindness yet,
> For auld lang syne.
>> Ibid., Chorus

Everyone, more or less, in the words of
the old Scots Proverb, 'Has his cods in
a cloven stock, and maun wyse them out
the best way he can.'

> Letter (June 30, 1788)

My heart's in the Highlands, my heart
   is not here;
My heart's in the Highlands a chasing
   the deer.

> "My Heart's In the Highlands" (1790)

John Anderson, my jo, John
When we were first acquent,
Your locks were like the raven,
Your bonnie brow was brent;
But now your brow is beld, John,
Your locks are like the snow;
But blessings on your frosty pow,
John Anderson, my jo!

> "John Anderson, My Jo" (1790), st. 1

John Anderson, my jo, John,
We clamb the hill thegither;
And monie a canty day, John
We've had wi'ane anither;
Now we maun totter down, John
But hand in hand we'll go,
And Sleep thegither at the foot,
John Anderson, my jo.

> Ibid., st. 2

Whare sits our sulky, sullen dame,
Gathering her brows like gathering storm,
Nursing her wrath to keep it warm.

> "Tam o' Shante, A Tale" (1790)

Inspiring, bold John Barleycorn!
What dangers thou canst make us scorn!
Wi' tippenny, we fear nae evil;
Wi usquabae [whisky], we'll face the
   devil!

> Ibid.

Nae man can tether time or tide.

> Ibid.

To see her is to love her,
And love but her forever;
For nature made her what she is,
And never made anither.

> "Bonnie Lesley" st. 2

What though on hamely fare we dine,
Wear hodden-gray, and a' that;
Gie fools their silks, and knaves their
   wine,
 A man's a man for a' that;
For a' that, and a' that;
Their tinsel show, and a' that;
The honest man, though e'er sae poor,
Is king o' men for a' that.

> "For A' That and A' That" (1795), st. 2

Then let us pray that come it may,
 As come it will for a' that.
That sense and worth, o'er a' the earth,
 May bear the gree, and a' that.
For a' that and a' that
It' coming yet, for a' that,
That man to man the world o'er
Shall brothers be for a' that.

> Ibid., st. 5

My Luve's like a red, red rose
That's newly sprung in June;
O my luve's like the melodie
That's sweetly play'd in tune.
As fair art thou, my bonie lass,
So deep in luve am I;
And I will luve thee still, my Dear,
Till a' the seas gang dry.
Till a' the seas gang dry, my Dear,
And the rocks melt wi' the sun:
O I will luve thee still, my Dear,
While the sands o' life shall run.

> "A Red, Red Rose" (1794)

Gin a body meet a body
Coming thro' the rye,
Gin a body kiss a body
Need a body cry?
"Coming thro' the Rye" (1796), st. 2

We cam na here to view your warks,
In hopes to be mair wise,
But only, lest we gang to Hell,
It may be nae surprise.
"Carron Iron Works"

God knows, I'm no the thing I should be,
Nor am I even the thing I could be.
"Posthumous Pieces To Reverend
John M. Math," st. 8

A man may drink and no be drunk;
A man may fight and no be slain;
A man may kiss a bonnie lass,
And aye be welcome back again.

JOSEPH FOUCHÉ
1759–1820

French, statesman and one of history's biggest opportunists. He organized the first secret police, a model followed by Himmler and Beria. He led the French secret police from 1792 to 1820, switching to each new government just in time.

He began a Girondin; he became a Jacobin; yet he arrested Robespierre after the French turned against the Terror. Fouché betrayed the Revolution to support Napoleon's 18 *Brumaire* coup (November 9, 1799). He deserted Napoleon after the Battle of Waterloo in 1815, and was elected president of the provisional government. Made a titled aristocrat by Louis XVIII, Fouché executed the monarchy's republican enemies, his former comrades.

After Napoleon's return from Elba, Fouché drew a list of people to be shot. Talleyrand saw his name on it and said: "One must at least do him the justice of acknowledging that he has omitted none of his friends."

It is worse than a crime; it is a blunder.
[Of Napoleon's execution of the Duc d'Enghien.]
In Albert Carr, *Napoleon Speaks*
(1941) ch.8

WILLIAM PITT (THE YOUNGER)
1759–1806

English, Tory PM, 1783–1801 and 1804–06. A votary of Adam Smith, he lowered tariffs and substituted sales taxes for taxes on capital. The economy grew rapidly. During George III's illness, Pitt substituted "cabinet government" for the Privy Council, which stripped the monarchy of its last power. His coalition defeated Napoleon in 1815.

Necessity is the plea of every infringement of human freedom. It is the argument of tyrants; it is the creed of slaves.
Speech on the India Bill
(November 18, 1783)

GEORGES JACQUES DANTON
1759–94

French, Jacobin who led the mob to storm the Tuileries and imprison Louis XVI, after which Danton became the chief executive. The Girondists, the National Assembly's republicans and radicals, became conservatives in the National Convention and the Jacobins were the new radicals. The Reign of Terror began in June 1793 when the Jacobins executed the Girondists, and it ended in July 1794 with Robespierre's execution. In between, Danton was executed for opposing rule by the Directory, which Robespierre controlled. On route to the guillotine Danton said, "Vile Robespierre! The scaffold claims you, too. You will follow me." The competition between Danton and Robespierre was like that between Trotsky and Stalin. All four were bloodthirsty opportunists vying for total power.

> De l'audace, encore de l'audace, et toujours de l'audace, et la France est sauvée.
> Audacity, and more audacity, and ever more audacity, and France is saved.
> Speech (September 2, 1792), on the eve of the September Massacre

> What care I that I am called a 'drinker of blood?' Well, let us drink the blood of the enemies of humanity.
> Address, National Assembly (1793)

FRIEDRICH VON SCHILLER
1759–1805

German, philosopher, poet, playwright, and a leader of German Romanticism and the *Sturm-und-Drang* reaction against the Enlightenment's formalism. They stressed natural feelings and German folk stories. Both Napoleon and Hitler banned Schiller's works. F. A. Hayek said, "Schiller did probably as much as any man to spread liberal ideas in Germany." This pan-European poet's three greatest plays celebrated three freedom fighters: William Tell, Joan of Arc, and Don Carlos.

> The universe is one of God's thoughts.
> "Theosophie des Julius,"
> *Philosophische, Briefe* (1786)

> Folly, thou conquerest, and I must yield!
> Against stupidity the very gods
> Themselves contend in vain...
> *The Maid of Orleans* (1800), act 3, sc. 5

> To brave the lake in all its wrath! 'Twas not
> To put your trust in God! 'Twas tempting Him.
> *William Tell* (1804), act 3, sc. 1

William Tell is Switzerland's legendary hero who refused to doff his hat to the Austrian governor and so was compelled to shoot an apple off his son's head with a crossbow. The governor locked up Tell anyway, but he was rescued, after which he led a successful national revolt.

> He who reflects too much will accomplish little.
> Ibid.

MARY WOLLSTONECRAFT
1759–97

Irish, whose *A Vindication of the Rights of Man* (1790) attacked Burke's *Reflections*. A leftist, she wanted to abolish inheritance, capital punishment, and marriage. Her daughter, Mary, married Shelley.

She wrote the first great feminist document, *A Vindication of the Rights of Women* (1792), which urged woman suffrage, the same education for both sexes, equal property rights, and so forth. However, she believed the purpose of educating women was to make them better wives and mothers.

> Weakness may excite tenderness and gratify the arrogant pride of man; but

the lordly caresses of a protector will not gratify a noble mind that pants for and deserves to be respected.

> *A Vindication of the Rights of Women*
> (1792), pt. 1., ch. 2

Women are systematically degraded by receiving the trivial attentions which men think it manly to pay to the sex, when, in fact, men are insultingly supporting their own superiority.

> Ibid., ch. 4

JOSEPH ROUGET
1760–1836

French, army officer, who composed the "War Song for the Army on the Rhine" before the French Revolution. Revolutionists from Marseilles sang the song on entering Paris on July 30, 1792, so it became "La Marseillaise." The revolutionists changed "To arms the brave" into "To arms citizens." Condemned to the guillotine, Rouget was spared when the mob learned he had authored it.

> *Allons, enfants de la Patrie!*
> *Le jour de gloire est arrive!*
> *Contre nous de la tyrannic*
> *L'etendard sanglant est leve.*
>
> *Aux armes, citoyens!*
> *Formex les bataillions!*
> *Marchons! marchons! Qu'un sang impur*
> *Abreuve nos sillons.*

Onward, children of the nation
The day of glory has come!
We stand against tyranny
Our bloody standard is raised.

To arms citizens!
Form your battalions!

Let us march on where the impure
  blood [of our enemies]
Will drench our fields.

> *"La Marseillaise"* (1792)

COMTE HENRI DE SAINT-SIMON
1760–1825

French, social philosopher. Friedrich Hayek said Saint-Simon at France's L'École Polytechnique gave birth to socialism. As the most important precursor to Marx, he believed state capitalism run by technocrats could reorganize society along scientific lines to eliminate the inefficiencies of competition and provide justice for all. *Saint-Simonisme* called for a scientific utopia with government ownership of the means of production. Bureaucrats would replace priests and kings. He invented plebiscites and the "self-determination" doctrine of Woodrow Wilson. He advocated a new religion of Faith in Progress and a United Nations.

Saint-Simon argued that women were incapable of abstract thought because they rarely succeeded in poetry, music composition, painting, and other arts. Thus, women should not be eligible to vote.

JOHANN GOTTLIEB FICHTE
1762–1814

German, philosopher loved by the Kaiser and Hitler. He held Germans to be the urvolk, "nature's chosen people," who were to create a great state and teach its culture to the world. The German prince should rule his people according to the law, but there is no limitation on his power over other peoples. Between states "there is neither law nor justice, only the law of strength." Fichte's notion of unlimited Reich power outside of Germany became Lenin's "Revolutionary Conscience" and Hitler's "Higher Law of the Party." Fichte evinces the intellectuals' eagerness to use the military to impose their schemes on others, that is, the "natural alliance between the penmen and the swordsmen," per Paul Johnson in *The Birth of the Modern* (1991).

ROBERT G. HARPER
1765–1825

American, diplomat.

> Millions for defense, but not one cent for tribute.
> [The above was a toast to Charles C. Pinckney after he told Talleyrand's emissary he would not give him six cents. The emissary had sought a $50,000 bribe and a public apology for John Adams's anti-French address to Congress to get an appointment to discuss France's seizure of three hundred U.S. ships. Note: later Adams waived $20 million of losses in U.S. shipping seized by the French to terminate the alliance with France. This cost Adams his reelection by infuriating the Federalists, but it saved the U.S. from war with France.]

JOHN DALTON
1766–1844

English, chemist, "father of modern atomic theory" who proved that matter is composed of tiny, indestructible objects, which make molecules and elements. He characterized elements by their atomic weights. Jacob Bronowski calls Dalton's discovery of the nature of atoms the "most powerful idea in modern science."

> John Dalton for fifty seven years measured the rainfall and the temperature— a singularly monotonous enterprise. Of all that mass of data, nothing whatever came. But of his one searching, almost childlike question about the weights that enter the construction of these simple molecules—out of that, came modern atomic theory.
> Jacob Bronowski, *The Ascent of Man* (1973)

THOMAS R. MALTHUS
1766–1834

English, political economist, and demographic pioneer, who thought wars, epidemics, famines, and late marriages were necessary to keep population in check because an unchecked population increases at a geometric rate while subsistence increases at only an arithmetical rate. He cited British North America, whose population doubled every twenty-five years.

Malthus's model had been right up until his time. Like Marx, he failed to perceive that an Industrial Revolution was increasing wealth faster than population growth. In the nineteenth century, England's population increased sixfold even as her per capita income also increased sixfold. Dickens satirized Malthus in *A Christmas Carol*, where Ebenezer Scrooge said the poor might as well die to "decrease the surplus population."

Malthus's other mistakes were supporting the Corn Laws (protection for landed aristocrats) and opposing Say's Law (supply creates demand). Malthus argued that an "effective demand" needed to be imposed from outside the capitalist system or surplus goods would pile up. John Maynard Keynes revived Malthus's flawed economics in the 1930s.

> Population, when unchecked, increases in a geometrical ratio. Subsistence only increases in an arithmetical ratio.
> *Essay on the Principle of Population* (1798)

> ...the causes of the wealth and poverty of nations—the grand object of all inquiries in Political Economy.
> Letter to Ricardo (January 26, 1817), in David S. Landes, *The Wealth and Poverty of Nations* (1998)

ANNE LOUISE GERMAINE DE STAËL
1766–1817

French (Swiss born), novelist called the "den mother of the romantics" by historian Paul Johnson for raising an anti-Napoleon, pro-liberty banner. Exiled by Napoleon, she led in Weimar a salon of artists who made German Romanticism the rage in Europe, especially through her *De L'Allemagne* (1811). In her *Delphine* (1802), the heroine embodied the "new woman"—a superior being of mind and willpower who was isolated by the conventions of her society.

> To be totally understanding makes one very indulgent.
> *Corinne* (1807), bk. 18, ch. 5

> The primary requirement for a writer is to feel keenly and strongly.
> *De L'Allemagne* (1811)

I'm glad I am not a man, for if I were, I would be obligated to marry a woman.

JOHN QUINCY ADAMS
1767–1848

American, sixth president (1825–1829) and son of the second president. As Monroe's secretary of state, Adams negotiated the Monroe Doctrine and the release of Spain's claims to Florida.

> The American Republic invites nobody to come. We will keep out nobody. Arrivals will suffer no disadvantages as aliens. But they can expect no advantages either, Native-born and foreign-born face equal opportunities. What happens to them depends entirely on their individual ability and exertions, and on good fortune.
> *Niles Weekly Register*, 18 (1820)

> Whatever the standard of freedom and independence has been or shall be unfurled, there will [America's] heart, her benedictions, and her prayers be. But she goes not abroad in search of monsters to destroy. She is the well wisher to the freedom and independence of all. She is the champion and vindicator only of her own....
> Speech (July, 4 1821), as secretary of state in response to the Greek appeal for America's help to liberate Greece from the Ottomans

> Individual liberty is individual power, and as the power of a community is a mass compounded of individual powers, the nation which enjoys the most freedom must necessarily be in proportion to its numbers the most powerful nation.
> Letter to James Lloyd (October 1, 1822)

Posterity! You will never know how much it cost the present generation to preserve your freedom. I hope you will make good use of it.

In 1814, negotiations over ending the War of 1812 were deadlocked over British insistence on a homeland for Indians in northeastern America. They were offered citizenship and a square mile of land per family, but they wanted to live as hunters on twenty-five square miles of land per person, enough for five hundred settlers. Adams asked if it were "in human power to check progress by a bond of paper?"

To condemn vast regions of territory to perpetual barrenness [so] a few hundred savages might find wild beasts to hunt upon it, was a species of game law that a nation descended from Britons would never endure. It was incompatible with the moral as well as the physical nature of things. [Any treaty limiting settlements for Indians] …was opposing a feather to a torrent.

In Paul Johnson, *The Birth of the Modern* (1991)

ANDREW JACKSON
1767–1845

American, seventh president (1829–37), who solved the "Indian problem" by offering them U.S. citizenship and 640 acres (a square mile) per family or requiring them to move west of the Mississippi to live on reservations. He disobeyed a Supreme Court decision on tribal land in Georgia, saying, "John Marshall has made his decision, let him enforce it." After his victories in the Indian Wars, he defended New

Orleans in the War of 1812. Jackson's militia, plus free blacks and pirates, defeated the British regulars, with only 71 American casualties versus 2,037 British casualties.

Jackson named Jefferson's Democratic-Republican Party the Democratic Party. He sought to benefit the common man by operating a frugal, minimalist government. His "spoils system" replaced government employees with political loyalists, and his cabinet reflected a point of view rather than a cross section of the American elite.

He vetoed the recharter of the Second Bank of the United States (precursor to the Federal Reserve) and withdrew all government deposits from it to hand out to favored private banks. This disastrous decision enabled private banks to give easy credit, leading to their collapse and the Panic of 1837–44, a depression second only to the Great Depression. This is one example of the pattern of liberals who demonize economic success to advance their political fortunes to the great misery of the people.

Jackson fought in the Revolutionary War at age twelve. Captured, he refused to clean a British officer's boots and was sabered across the face.

Mother: Stop that Andrew. Do not let me see you cry again. Girls were made to cry, not boys.
Jackson: What are boys made for, mother?
Mother: To fight.

Mother: Never sue anybody for slander or assault. Always settle them cases yourself.

The individual who refuses to defend his rights when called by his Government, deserves to be a slave, and must be punished as an enemy of his country and friend to her foe.

> Proclamation to the people of Louisiana
> from Mobile (September 21, 1814)

Each public officer who takes an oath to support the constitution swears that he will support it as he understands it, and not as it is understood by others.

> [On vetoing the recharter of the Bank of the United States, July 10, 1832.]
> In H. S. Commager, *Documents of American History,* vol. 1 (1963)

I don't give a damn for any man who can't spell a word more than one way.

> Attributed

One man with courage makes a majority.

> Attributed

JEAN BAPTISTE SAY
1767–1832

French, industrialist/economist, the first to see entrepreneurs as risk-takers. He corrected Adam Smith's big mistake, the Labor Theory of Value, which held that labor costs determine prices. Say argued that value reflected consumer preferences, so prices reflect what customers are willing to pay.

Say is known for "supply creates demand," or "products are paid for with products." This does not mean that if one makes a widget another will buy it. It means there can be no consumption without first having production. More profoundly, there cannot be sustained overproduction in a free economy. Say was not referring to individual products, but to the economy. If productivity doubles next year, we would not consume twice as much salt. Rather part of the capital invested in salt would be shifted to other industries to produce what consumers wanted. Recessions result from misallocating resources, as when too much salt is produced. This usually results from government interventions that hamper adjustment to the changing supply/demand curves.

Say's Law means it is unwise to try to remedy economic downturns with Keynesian policies to increase demand—it is better to remove the political obstacles to increasing production in desired goods.

> [Political economy] recognizes the right of private property solely as the most powerful of all encouragement's to the multiplication of wealth....
> *A Treatise on Political Economy* (1803)

CHARLOTTE CORDAY
1768–93

French. She killed Jean-Paul Marat to avenge his guillotining twenty-one Girondists. She entered Marat's room on the pretense of bringing him a list of more Girondists to guillotine. Marat was founder of the newspaper, *L'Ami du Peuple* and one of the bloody troika, along with Robespierre and Danton. When Marat, sitting in his bathtub, demanded to see the list of traitors, Corday plunged a knife into his chest.

> The crime, not the scaffold, is the real disgrace.
> [On the eve of her execution.]

WRITINGS OF JUNIUS
1769–72

English, anonymous writer to the *Public Advertiser,* who attacked King George III.

> Let it be impressed upon your minds, let it be instilled into your children, that the liberty of the press is the palladium of all the civil, political, and religious rights.

NAPOLEON BONAPARTE
1769–1821

French (Corsican born), five-foot, two-inch dictator, who co-opted France's intellectuals into supporting perpetual war. Aldous Huxley called him the world's "ablest bandit." Madame de Stael said, "He regards a human being like a thing.... Neither pity nor attraction, nor religion nor attachment would ever divert him from his ends.... I felt in his soul cold steel." Rather than criticize Napoleon as their Hitler, the French revere him. Lamartine said, "Frenchmen will forget liberty, if you give them glory."

Napoleon was revered by his soldiers because he dressed austerely like them, ate plain dinners in fifteen minutes, knew how to speak to simple people, and was tireless. He slept only a few hours nightly and could dictate 125 letters a day.

After his military victories for the Directory, he seized power as first consul in 1799, consul for life in 1802, and emperor in 1804. His Code Napoleon rationalized commercial law in Western Europe, and his Vatican Concordat of 1801 reestablished Catholicism as France's state church. His *Grande Armée* was annihilated in 1812 when he attacked Russia, the last obstacle to his controlling Continental Europe (615,000 French and allies entered; 150,000 exited). Russian General Kutuzov bled the French to death with scorched earth in one of the coldest winters on record. Exiled to Elba Island, Napoleon returned in 1814 to France, but was defeated at Waterloo in 1815 and exiled to St. Helena Island where he died. Waterloo was the only battle in which he could not closely direct the action from horseback due to his inflamed hemorrhoids.

Napoleon used many new military technologies: divisional organization, dispersion until the battle, and reduced weight of artillery for mobility. Strategically, he passed the enemy's flank to cut its communications, forcing the enemy's withdrawal from prepared positions. Tactically, he enveloped the enemy's rear to spread confusion and delivered a decisive blow at a weak point with massed artillery. Yet, he said he followed no principles of war—he was the supreme opportunist who responded to each factual situation differently. His quotations were collected as *Napoleon's Maxims of War.*

Napoleon's weakness was grand strategy. He got bogged down in Spain, failed to concentrate on England's navy, and invaded Russia. Napoleon lost at Waterloo because heavy rain delayed his attack. That allowed the Prussian army to get to Waterloo before he had finished off the British.

Napoleon, like Louis XIV and Hitler, sought to rule Europe and left his country shattered. Because Napoleon opposed the *ancien régimes,* most intellectuals supported him, except Edmund Burke and the German Romanticists. Yet, Napoleon had no interest in liberty, and his constitutions curtailed more liberties than the constitutions he replaced.

Two million soldiers perished in his battles and 8 million civilians died from starvation and other related causes. He generated support in France by reducing income taxes from 50 percent to 30 percent. He lost popular support when he later raised taxes because he could no longer loot enough from the conquered nations.

Benjamin Constant encapsulated Napoleon in his *De L'Esprit de la Conquête* (1813): "Human beings are sacrificed to abstractions—a holocaust of individuals is offered up to 'the People.' " As Goya said, "The dream of reason produces monsters."

In 1813, after the Russian debacle, Napoleon rejected Metternich's peace terms, saying, "My reign will not outlast the day when I have ceased to be strong and therefore to be feared." Further:

> *Napoleon:*   A man like me cares little
> for the lives of a million
> men.
> *Metternich:* If only the words you have
> just spoken could be heard
> from one end of Europe to
> the other.
> *Napoleon:*   I may lose my throne. But
> I shall bury the whole
> world in its ruins.
> *Metternich:* Sire, you are a lost man.
>
> In Paul Johnson, *The Birth of the
> Modern* (1991)

They should have swept down five hundred with grapeshot, and the rest would have fled.
[As witness to Louis XVI capitulating to a mob invading the Tuileries Palace.]
In L. R. Frank, *Quotationary* (1999)

Whilst an individual owner, with a personal interest in his property, is always wide awake, and brings his plans to fruition, communal interest is inherently sleepy and unproductive, because individual enterprise is a matter of instinct, and communal enterprise is a matter of public spirit, which is rare.
Letter to brother Lucien,
December 31, 1799, in Will Durant,
The Story of Civilization (1975), vol. 11

Go, sir, gallop, and don't forget that the world was made in six days. You can ask me for anything you like, except time.
[To an aide, 1803.]
From R. M. Johnston, *The Corsican*

War is not at all such a difficult art as people think....In reality it would seem that he is vanquished who is afraid of his adversary and that the whole secret of war is this.
To Tsar Alexander, Tilsit, 1807.

Act swiftly and vigorously....I shall sanction everything that is vigorous, spirited, and politic.
Letter to Marshal Bessiéres
(November 20, 1809)

Confront boldness by being still bolder.
In L. R. Frank, *Quotationary* (1999)

My son should read much history and meditate upon it; it is the only true philosophy.
"Political Testament" (April 1821)

...in audacity and obstinacy will be found the safety and conservation of the men.
Maximes de Guerre (November 15, 1831)

In war never do what the enemy wishes you to do, for this reason alone, because he wishes it. A field of battle, therefore, which he has previously sited and reconnoitered, should be avoided.

> Ibid., no. 16

Better one bad general than two good ones.

Nothing is more important in war than unity of command.

> Ibid., no. 64

Read over and over again the campaigns of Alexander, Hannibal, Caesar, Gustavo's, Turenne, and Frederic. Make them your models. This is the only way to become a great general and to master the secrets of the art of war.

> Ibid., no. 78

What is most desirable and distinguishes the exceptional man is the balance of intelligence and ability with character or courage. If courage is predominant, the general will hazard far beyond his conceptions; and on the contrary, he will not dare to accomplish his conceptions, if his character or his courage are below his intelligence.

> Ibid., no. 81

War is composed of nothing but accidents, and, although holding to general principles, a general should never lose sight of everything to enable him to profit from these accidents; that is the mark of genius. In war there is but one favorable moment; the great art is to seize it.

> Ibid., no. 95

If I were to give liberty to the press, my power could not last three days.

> In L. R. Frank, *Quotationary* (1999)

A leader is a dealer in hope.

> Jules Bertaut Napoleon in *His Own Words*
> (1916), ch. 4

One should never forbid what one lacks the power to prevent.

> In L. R. Frank, *Quotationary* (1999)

Never attack in front a position that can be taken by turning!

> Ibid.

Success is the greatest orator in the world.

> In Norman Davies, *Europe: A History*
> (1996)

All empires die of indigestion.

> Ibid.

One always has a chance of recovering lost ground, but lost time—never.

> Ibid.

A soldier will fight long and hard for a bit of colored ribbon.

> To captain of HMS *Bellerophon*
> (July 1815)

I defy anyone to trick me. Men would have to be exceptional rascals to be as bad as I assume them to be.

> In L. R. Frank, *Wit and Humor*
> *Quotationary*

Aptitude for maneuver is the supreme skill in a general; it is the most useful and rarest of gifts by which genius is estimated.

From the sublime to the ridiculous is but a step.

> [In 1813 about the retreat from Russia.]

On s'éngage et puis on voit.
Engage and then see what happens.

Separate to live, unite to fight.

If you start to take Vienna—take Vienna.

The outcome of the greatest events is always determined by a trifle.

Liberty is a need felt by a small class of people whom nature has endowed with nobler minds… Consequently, it may be repressed with impunity. Equality on the other hand, pleases the masses.

What is history but a fable agreed upon?

Merde en bas de soie.
You are shit in a silk stocking.
    [To Talleyrand's objection to invading Spain.]

Nothing is more difficult, and therefore more precious, than to be able to decide.

The desire for perfection is the worst disease that ever afflicted the human mind.

The best way to keep one's word is not to give it.

Circumstances? I make circumstances!

The people to fear are not those who disagree with you, but those who disagree with you and are too cowardly to let you know.

I fear three newspapers more than a hundred thousand bayonets.

Good intelligence is nine-tenths of any battle.

An army of rabbits commanded by a lion is better than an army of lions commanded by a rabbit.

Even in offensive war, the merit lies in having only defensive conflicts and obliging your enemy to become the assailant.

The whole art of war consists in a well-reasoned and extremely circumspect defensive, followed by a rapid and audacious attack.

The first quality of a soldier is constancy in enduring fatigue and hardship. Courage is only the second.

It is very difficult for a nation to create an army when it has not already a body of officers and noncommissioned officers to serve as a nucleus, and a system of military organization.

Every French soldier carries a marshal's baton in his knapsack.

There are no bad regiments; there are only bad colonels.

Any commander in chief who undertakes to carry out a plan which he considers defective is at fault; he must put forward his reasons, insist on the plan being changed and finally tender his resignation rather than be the instrument of his army's downfall…. A military order requires passive obedience only when it is issued by a superior who is present at the seat of war.

A cavalry general should…know the value of seconds, despise life and not trust to chance.

Let China sleep for when she wakes the world will tremble.

A man becomes the creature of his uniform.

Italy is a boot and should only be invaded from the top.

An army marches on its stomach.

In war, the moral element is to all others as three is to one.

Napoleon's campaign in Egypt discovered the Rosetta Stone, a block of black granite with the same text in hieroglyphics, Greek, and common Egyptian, enabling the translation of hieroglyphics.

DAVID EVERETT
1769–1813

American, lawyer, and writer.

Large streams from little fountains flow,
Tall oaks from little acorns grow;
And though now I am small and young,
Of judgment weak and feeble tongue,
Yet all great, learned men, like me
Once learned to read their ABC.
"Tall Oaks from Little Acorns Grow"
(1790)

ARTHUR WELLESLEY, DUKE OF WELLINGTON
1769–1852

Anglo-Irish, general, and PM (1828–30). The "Iron Duke" won the Peninsular War in Spain (1808–14) and defeated Napoleon in 1815 at O'Hain, Belgium, which battle he named after the village of Waterloo. He was as small as Napoleon.

The only thing I am afraid of is fear.
From Philip Henry, *Notes of Conversations with the Duke of Wellington* (1888)

Nothing except a battle lost can be half so melancholy as a battle won.
Letter to Lady Frances Shelley after the Battle of Waterloo (June 19, 1815)

Hard pounding this, gentlemen, let's see who will pound longest.
[At the Battle of Waterloo.]
In Sir Walter Scott, *Paul's Letters* (1816)

…a damned nice thing, the nearest run thing you ever saw in your life.
[After the Battle of Waterloo.]
In Thomas Creevey, *The Creevey Papers*, H. Maxwell, ed. (1904)

The battle of Waterloo was won on the playing fields of Eton.
In Sir William Fraser, *Words on Wellington* (1889)

I used to say of [Napoleon] that his presence on the field made the difference of 40,000 men.
In Philip Henry Stanhope, *Notes of Conversations with the Duke of Wellington* (1888)

There is no mistake; there has been no mistake; and there shall be no mistake.
Wellingtoniana (1832)

All the business of war, and indeed all the business of life, is to endeavor to find out what you don't know by what you do;

that's what I called "guessing what was at the other side of the hill."

John Wilson Croker, *The Croker Papers* ed. Bernard Pool (1885), vol. 3, ch. 28

If you will believe that, you will believe anything.

In Elizabeth Longford's, *Pillar of State* (1972) ch. 10

I don't know what effect these men will have upon the enemy, but, by God, they frighten me.

[Speaking of his English reinforcements.]

Publish and be damned.

[Replying to an extortionist threat by the courtesan to publish her memoirs.]

[After one of his maids drowned herself for unrequited love of a gardener, the duke assembled his maids and told them he hoped they would] put up with the misfortunes of this world and not destroy themselves.

In Vienna after the Battle of Waterloo when French officers snubbed Wellington by turning their backs toward him, Wellington remarked, "I have seen their backs before, Madame."

Little, Brown Book of Anecdotes (1985), Clifton Fadiman, ed.

LUDWIG VAN BEETHOVEN
1770–1827

German, Romantic composer. When deafness caused him to stop playing and concentrate on composing, his compositions soared; for example, the Third "Eroica" Symphony, the Fifth Symphony, the Sixth "Pastoral" Symphony, and the Fifth Piano Concerto. He liked best his Quartet in C-sharp Minor, Opus 131. When totally deaf, he composed his most popular work, the Ninth Symphony, with its choral finale, the "Ode to Joy." He said to one critic, "They are not for you, but for a later age."

Music is a higher revelation than philosophy.

Letter to Bettina von Arnim (1810)

I shall hear in heaven.

Last words. In Ian Crofton, *A Dictionary of Musical Quotations* (1985)

[Bakunin:] All, all will perish…only one thing will not perish but last forever: the Ninth Symphony.

CLASSICAL MUSIC

For the cognoscenti, music is divided between "popular music" and "concert music," which is music intended to be played in concert halls or opera houses and which is longer and has more information content than popular music. "Classical music" is concert music composed between 1750 and 1857. Among the favorite classical composers are Bach, Beethoven, and Brahms (the "Three Bs"). Beethoven called Bach "the immortal god of harmony." Arguably, music is the most abstract and sublime of all arts, and it relieves one of thinking.

The immortals of early classical music are Pachelbel (1653–1706), Telemann (1681–1767), Bach (1685–1750), Handel (1685–1759), Haydn (1732–1809), and Mozart (1756–91). The romantic music immortals are Beethoven (1770–1827) Schubert (1797–1828), Mendelssohn (1809–47), Chopin (1810–49), Liszt (1811–86), Brahms (1833–97), Tchaikovsky (1840–93), Dubussy (1862–1918), and Rachmaninov (1873–1943). Great composers of grand opera include: Rossini (1792–1868), Wagner (1813–83), Verdi (1813–1901), and Puccini (1858–1924).

GEORG WILHELM FRIEDRICH HEGEL
1770–1831

German, preeminent nineteenth century philosopher, whose central idea was that man is a social being who is nothing until he is identified with society. The state is the all-important agency because it is the platform for creating all social institutions. Life's purpose is achievement, and dying for the state is the essence of humanity.

Hegel's idealism was different from Bishop Berkeley's, who held that a thing existed only if perceived by a human or divine mind. To Hegel, things existed independent of anyone experiencing them. But, most real is the logic, the reasoning, which is not subjective, but universal: "What is rational is actual and what is actual is rational."

To Hegel a "world-spirit" (Zeitgeist) pushes history from lower to higher forms in a march of progress toward freedom. Each age has its peculiar Zeitgeist, or moral tone, that effects the lives of all. History advances through a "dialectic" where the truth of a "thesis" creates an "antithesis," carrying a new truth which leads to a "synthesis" into a higher truth. The synthesis becomes the next thesis, and the cycle repeats until "the end of history," where perfect government will have been created.

Note: The American Leo Strauss (1899–1973) reacted against a Hegelian dialectic that inevitably draws man ever closer to the truth by progressive steps. Rather, it is possible the ancient philosophers came closest to the truth. Evidence for this is that the totalitarianisms of the twentieth century were retrograde, barbarian tribal movements. For Strauss, America's founding politics were not progressive, but rooted in the universal "natural right" theories of ancient Rome, Greece, and the Bible. Strauss argues that, since Machiavelli, political philosophers have been engaged in trying to change the world rather than understand it. But in recent years, some have been revisiting natural law as the surest defense against relativist ethics.

To Hegel, "truth is the whole." Reality is a metaphysical system.

Hegel said all human relations are of master to slave. Marx used Hegel's master-slave concept for his theory of classes struggling for mastery.

To Hegel the most distinctive feature of the modern world is the market, which frees man from serfdom and allows him to express his individuality.

Hegel did not see the relationship of the state and the market as antagonistic. The market created the wealth that made the state powerful; the state created institutions that made the market viable.

The modern economy created pauperism, which is different from poverty or a lack of resources. Pauperism is a state of mind where men lose the habits of industriousness by relying on the modern state's charity. Paupers are a danger to civil society:

Thus to be independent of public opinion is the first formal condition of achieving anything great or rational whether in life or in science.

Lectures on the Philosophy of World History (1830)

The history of the world is none other than the progress of the consciousness of freedom.

Ibid.

Whatever worth and spiritual reality man possesses are his solely by virtue of the state.

Philosophy of History, introduction (1832), tr. H. B. Nisbet (1975)

We may affirm absolutely that nothing great in the world has been accomplished without passion.

Ibid.

It is a matter of perfect indifference where a thing originated; the only question is: "Is it true in and for itself?"

Ibid., pt. II, sec. 3, ch. 2

No man is a hero to his valet; not, however, because the man is not a hero, but because the valet is a valet.

7
THE ROMANTIC AGE

Rousseau, the "father of Romanticism," sketched its main lines: reliance on feeling over reason, revolt against convention, enlightened dictatorship over democracy, and rejection of neoclassicism, Cartesian rationalism, and Newtonian physics for an irrational, volcanic, and pagan nature. But above all, Rousseau worshiped equality and man's innate goodness that can be trained to serve equality. Stated positively, Romanticism reacted against the narrowing aspects of the Enlightenment, that is, against its inadequate responses to the entire range of human experience. Romantics included: (Germany) Goethe, Schiller, Heine, Fichte, Kant, Hegel, and Beethoven; (France) Mme. de Staël, Balzac, Hugo, Vigny, Dumas Père, Chateaubriand, Baudelaire, Sand, and Stendhal; (America) Cooper, Irving, Poe, Emerson, Thoreau, Hawthorne, Melville, Longfellow, and Whitman.

The English Romantic age (1798 to 1832) begins with the publication of the *Lyrical Ballads* of Wordsworth and Coleridge and ends with Sir Walter Scott's death in 1832. Wordsworth rebelled against the classical age dominated by Dryden and Pope, who deemed poetry to be "a mirror held up to nature" to instruct and give pleasure. Wordsworth said in the preface to *Lyrical Ballads*, "Poetry is the spontaneous overflow of powerful feelings; it takes its origin from emotion recollected in tranquility." Lyrical poetry is written in the first person and is about the poet's state of mind. It emphasizes nature's effect on the human psyche by exploring the lives of ordinary people, and it omits classical allusions. Thomas Gray, Robert Burns, and William Blake were forerunners of English Romanticism.

Except for Edmund Burke, most British Romantics supported the French Revolution, but some, such as the Lake Poets (Wordsworth, Coleridge, and Southey), were so repulsed by the Reign of Terror that they changed into Tories. Shelley, Keats, Hazlitt, and Byron never lost their revolutionary zeal, believing equality could be realized without terror, if only better men were put in charge. French Romantics who lived through the Revolutionary terror and wars, like Balzac, Dumas (Père), Hugo, and Chateaubriand, repudiated dictatorships in favor of constitutional monarchy.

Equality—a notion contrary to all experience and all rationality, a notion springing solely from primitive tribal solidarity— was Romanticism's supreme value. Rousseau said that as soon as property was introduced, equality disappeared and strife began. To Rousseau, laws and institutions had arisen to protect property and thus to promote inequality. Men should enter a new social contract to construct a government to redress inequality.

The Romantic era experienced a heightened awareness of inequality because for first time wealth was being created at such a prodigious rate that poverty was no longer inevitable for almost all people. Concern over inequality led many Romantics to socialism, which is the bridge over Victorianism that connects Romanticism to modernism.

The Victorian age that succeeded Romanticism developed more formidable social constraints than the Enlightenment's, against which Romanticism had rebelled. The Victorian constraints arose during the greatest expansion of liberty and democracy in history. Victorians found equality to be absurd. If any trait epitomizes Victorianism and opposes Romanticism, it is the meritocracy that springs from competition, the antipode of equality.

WILLIAM WORDSWORTH
1770-1850

English, poet laureate, often accounted the third greatest man of English letters after Shakespeare and Milton. A "Lakeland poet" with Coleridge and Southey, Wordsworth and Coleridge launched English Romanticism in their jointly published *Lyrical Ballads* in 1798. In Paris he supported the French Revolution, but was shocked by its terror. Like Rousseau, he exulted in nature, but unlike Rousseau, was bound by traditional morality.

Wordsworth believed the only good life is bound in duty to others. Wordsworth displayed the suffering of common people as in "The Ruined Cottage," in which the loving Margaret and her children perish from what is best in her, her hope for the return of her runaway husband.

Oh Sir, the good die first,
And they whose hearts are dry as

summer dust,
Burn to the socket. Many a passenger
Has blessed poor Margaret for her
gentle looks
When she upheld the cool refreshment
drawn
From that forsaken spring, and no one
came
But he was welcome, no one went away
But that it seemed she loved him. She
is dead.
"The Ruined Cottage," 1797

That best portion of a good man's life
His little, nameless, unremembered, acts
Of kindness and of love.
"Lines Composed a Few Miles above Tintern Abbey," 1798

She dwelt among the untrodden ways
Besides the springs of Dove,
A Maid whom there were none to praise
And very few to love;
"She Dwelt among the Untrodden Ways"
(1799), st. 1

She lived unknown, and few could know
When Lucy ceased to be;
But she is in her grave, and, oh,
The difference to me!
Ibid., st. 3

I travelled among unknown men
In lands beyond the sea;
Nor England! Did I know till then
What love I bore to thee.
"I Travelled among Unknown Men"
(1799), st. 1

Bliss was it in that dawn to be alive,
But to be young was very heaven!
[Of the French Revolution.]
The Prelude (1805), bk. XI, ll.108-9

My heart leaps up when I behold
A rainbow in the sky;
So was it when my life began;
So is it now I am a man;
So be it when I shall grow old,
Or let me die!
The Child is father of the Man…
                    "My Heart Leaps Up," 1807

…every great and original writer, in proportion as he is great or original, must
himself create the taste by which he is to
be relished.
    Letter to Lady Beaumont (May 21, 1807)

I wandered lonely as a cloud
That floats on high o'er vales and hills,
When all at once I saw a crowd,
A host of golden daffodils,
Beside the lake, beneath the trees
Fluttering and dancing in the breeze.
    "*I Wandered Lonely as a Cloud*," (1815), st. 1

Continuous as the stars that shine
And twinkle on the Milky Way,
They stretched in never-ending line
Along the margin of a bay:
Ten thousand saw I at a glance,
Tossing their heads in sprightly dance.
                              Ibid., st. 2

The waves beside them danced; but they
Outdid the sparkling waves in glee;
A poet could not but be gay,
In such a jocund company;
I gazed—and gazed—but little thought
What wealth the show to me had
    brought:
                              Ibid., st. 3

For oft, when on my couch I lie
In vacant or in pensive mood,
They flash upon that inward eye

Which is the bliss of solitude;
And then my heart with pleasure fills,
And dances with the daffodils.
                              Ibid., st. 4

Still glides the stream, and shall for ever
    glide;
The Form remains, the function never
    dies;
While we, the brave, the mighty, and
    the wise,
We Men, who in our morn of youth
    defied
The elements, must vanish;—be it so!
    The River Duddon, "After-Thought" (1820),
                                  st. 2

Enough, if something from our hands
    have power
To live, and act, and serve the future hour;
And if, as toward the silent tomb we go,
Through love, through hope, and Faith's
    transcendent dower,
We feel that we are greater than we know.
                              Ibid., st. 3

SIR WALTER SCOTT
1771–1832

Scottish, novelist, lawyer, Tory, and poet,
who made a fortune embodying the heroic
spirit of Scotland with its kilts, sporrans,
bonnets, tartans, bagpipes, and Gaelic
battle songs. He invented the historical
novel, as in *Rob Roy* (1818) and *Ivanhoe*
(1819). The first novelist to be historically
accurate, he created a historical consciousness unique to his age. In the nineteenth
century, people read histories for pleasure
like they read mysteries today. Hugo, Balzac, Tolstoy, Alfred de Vigny, and James
Fenimore Cooper followed Scott in using

history to add realism to their work. He created a mass market for novels, which benefited Dickens and others like him.

He published anonymously his first work, the *Waverly Novels*, which magnified public interest for eleven years in the "Great Unknown." He started a new industry, Highland tourism. As honorable as his heroes, Scott spent his later years paying the debts of his publishing partners.

> Breathes there the man, with soul so dead,
> Who never to himself hath said,
> This is my own, my native land!
> Whose heart hath ne'er within him
>   burn'd
> As home his footsteps he hath turn'd,
> From wandering on a foreign strand?
> > *The Lay of the Last Minstrel* (1805),
> > canto VI, st. 1 (partial)

> O what a tangled web we weave,
> When first we practice to deceive!
> > *Marmion* (1808), canto IV, st. 17

> A lawyer without history or literature is a mechanic, a mere working mason; if he possesses some knowledge of these, he may venture to call himself an architect.
> > *Guy Mannering* (1815), ch. 37

> The hour's come, but not the man.
> > *The Heart of Midlothian* (1818), ch. 4

> I am a Scot and therefore I had to fight my way into the world.
> > Arthur Herman, *How the Scots Invented the Modern World* (2001)

> One hour of life crowded to the full with glorious action and filled with noble risks is worth whole years of those mean observances of paltry decorum.

From the time that the mother binds the child's head till the moment that some kind assistant wipes the brow of the dying, we cannot exist without mutual help.

SYDNEY SMITH
1771–1845

English, clergyman, essayist, and a founder of the *Edinburgh Review*, a Whig periodical that was the most influential periodical in the English-speaking world for a century. It was not written for the literati, but for educated laymen, and it addressed progress in every human endeavor. It savaged the Romantic writers and praised the Victorian ones.

> What is real piety? How to evince true attachment to the Church? The answer is plain: by sending strawberries to a clergyman.

> In the four corners of the globe, who reads an American book? or goes to an American play? or looks at an American picture or statue? What does the world yet owe to American physicians or surgeons?... Finally, under which of the old tyrannical governments of Europe is every sixth man a slave, whom his fellow creatures may buy and sell and torture?
> > *Edinburgh Review* (January-May 1820)

> He was a one-book man. Some men have only one book in them, others, a library.
> > Lady Holland (his daughter),
> > *Memoir of the Reverend Sydney Smith* (1855), vol. 1, ch. 1

> Marriage resembles a pair of shears, so joined that they cannot be separated;

often moving in opposite directions, yet always punishing anyone who comes between them.

> Ibid.

In composing, as a general rule, run your pen through every other word you have written; you have no idea what vigor it will give your style.

> Ibid.

Avoid shame, but do not seek glory— nothing's so expensive as glory.

> Ibid., ch. 4

Great men hallow a whole people and lift up all who live in their time.

> Ibid., ch. 7

He has spent all his life in letting down empty buckets into empty wells; and he is frittering away his age in trying to draw them up again.

> Ibid., ch. 9

Never give way to melancholy; resist it steadily, for the habit will encroach.

> Ibid., ch. 10

I never read a book before reviewing it; it prejudices a man so.

> H. Pearson, *The Smith of Smiths* (1934)

I am just going to pray for you at St. Paul's, but with no very lively hope of success.

> Ibid., ch. 10

We need to be reminded more than we need to be instructed.

Whatever you are by nature, keep to it; never desert your own line of talent. Be what nature intended you for, and you will succeed.

A comfortable house is a great source of happiness. It ranks immediately after health and a good conscience.

It is the calling of great men, not so much to preach new truths as to rescue from oblivion those old truths, which it is our wisdom to remember and our weakness to forget.

Among the smaller duties of life I hardly know any one more important that that of not praising where praise is not due.

In the country I always fear that creation will expire before teatime.

It is the greatest of all mistakes to do nothing because you can do only a little. Do what you can.

The real object of education is to give children resources that will endure as long as life endures; habits that time will ameliorate, not destroy; occupations that will render sickness tolerable, solitude pleasant, age venerable, life more digni-fied and useful, and death less terrible.

SAMUEL COLERIDGE
1772–1834

English, romantic poet, philosopher, and devout Christian. Rheumatic fever led to his taking laudanum, an opiate deriva-tive that destroyed his family and his poetic creativity. After his wife left him, he beat his addiction and became a political philosopher.

A conservative, he knew that evil came from man's nature. He saw that Shelley and other utopians loved man in the abstract, but were heartless to people around them. Their "love" for mankind masked a desire to control mankind. Coleridge's philosophy helped keep Britain on a reformist, nonrevolutionary track. He described his character as "indolence capable of energies."

> "God save thee, ancient Mariner!
> From the fiends, that plague thee thus!
> Why look'st thou so?"—With my crossbow
> I shot the ALBATROSS
> > "The Rime of the Ancient Mariner"
> > (1798), pt. 1, l. 80

> Day after day, day after day,
> We stuck, nor breath nor motion;
> As idle as a painted ship
> Upon a painted ocean.
> > Ibid., pt. II, l. 115

> Water, water, everywhere,
> And all the boards did shrink;
> Water, water, every where,
> Nor any drop to drink.
> > Ibid., l. 120

> Ah! Well a day! What evil looks
> Had I from old and young!
> Instead of the cross, the albatross
> Around my neck was hung.
> > Ibid., l. 140

> The many men, so beautiful!
> And they all dead did lie;
> And a thousand slimy things
> lived on; and so did I.
> > Ibid., pt. IV, l. 235

> A spring of love gushed from my heart,
> And I blessed them unaware;

> Sure my kind saint took pity on me,
> And I blessed them unaware.
> > [on seeing water snakes]
> > Ibid., l. 285

> The selfsame moment I could pray;
> And from my neck so free
> The Albatross fell off, and sank
> Like lead into the sea.
> > Ibid., l. 290

> He prayeth well, who loveth well
> Both man and bird and beast.
> He prayeth best, who loveth best
> All things both great and small;
> For the dear God who loveth us,
> He made and loveth all.
> > Ibid., pt. 7, l. 615

> And the Devil did grin, for his
> > darling sin
> Is pride that apes humility.
> > "The Devil's Thoughts" (1799), st. 6

> In Xanadu did Kubla Khan
> A stately pleasure-dome decree;
> Where Alph, the sacred river, ran
> Through caverns measureless to man
> Down to a sunless sea...
> > "Kubla Khan" (1816)

> A savage place! As holy and enchanted
> As e'er beneath a waning moon was
> > haunted
> By woman wailing for her demon-lover...
> > Ibid.

> Ancestral voices prophesying war!
> > Ibid.

Camille Paglia in her *Break, Blow, Burn* (2005) says "Kubla Khan" is a "half-mad artist in creative rapture." Coleridge is reciting the difficulty of the artist having a creative imagination in a hostile and indifferent world. Paglia holds, "Great artists radically transform us, permanently repopulating our consciousness with their own obsessions."

> No man was ever yet a great poet, without being at the same time a profound philosopher.
> *Biographia Literaria* (1817), ch. 15

> The river Rhine, it is well known,
> Doth wash your city of Cologne;
> But tell me, Nymphs, what power divine
> Shall henceforth wash the river Rhine?
> "Cologne" (1834)

> Praises to the unworthy are felt by ardent minds as robberies of the deserving.

DAVID RICARDO
1772–1823

English, speculator, and MP, who advocated laissez-faire economics, not from a theory of natural rights, but from a utilitarian philosophy of social benefit. His *Principles of Political Economy and Taxation* (1817) developed the free trade theory of comparative advantage, that is, that each country should produce what it produces best and then trade for what other countries produce best, for example, trade English wool for Portuguese wine. He also saw that a division of labor between talented and untalented individuals benefits both, for example, a doctor hires a laborer to cut his grass, even if the doctor can cut the grass as well or better than the laborer. Ricardo proved that open trade among nations produces the greatest wealth for all. Trade is not a zero-sum game because it encourages each nation to specialize in its comparative advantage. No notable economist has ever challenged that thesis.

Unfortunately, he also endorsed Adam Smith's Labor Theory of Value (value is determined by the amount of labor to produce a good). That ignored the contributions of entrepreneurial risk-taking, capital, and innovation, and led to Karl Marx's erroneous theory of labor exploitation.

> Nothing contributes so much to the prosperity and happiness of a country as high profits.
> *On Protection to Agriculture* (1822), ch. 5

PRINCE METTERNICH
1773–1859

Austrian, statesman who was the principal organizer at the Congress of Vienna in 1815 of the Holy Alliance that repressed democracy and later prompted the European revolutions of 1848. Czar Alexander I of Russia wanted to depose autocratic kings and impose new ones subject to liberal constitutions. Metternich used his gifts to side-track Alexander and preserve the autocratic rulers.

> The greatest gift of any statesman rests not in knowing what concessions to make, but recognizing when to make them.

JOHN RANDOLPH
1773–1833

American, congressman from Virginia, renowned for his venomous wit.

> I am an aristocrat. I love liberty; I hate equality.

He is a man of splendid abilities, but utterly corrupt. He shines and stinks like rotten mackerel by moonlight.
[Of Edward Livingston.]

[When Randolph and Henry Clay of Kentucky, two bitter political rivals, walked toward each other on a narrow footpath, Randolph snapped, "I never give way to scoundrels." Clay responded as he stepped off the path, "I always do."]
Little Brown's Book of Anecdotes (1985),
Clifton Fadiman ed.

...I can never assent to it [that all men are born equal] for the best of all reasons, because it is not true.... Who should say that all the soil in the world is equally rich..?
Register of Debates, Nineteenth Congress,
Second Session, II, 129

ROBERT SOUTHEY
1774–1843

English, historian, poet laureate, and Jacobin who ended a conservative. He and Coleridge married sisters. His most quoted work is the antiwar poem about the War of the Spanish Succession.

And everybody praised the Duke
Who this great fight did win.
"But what good came of it at last?"
Quoth little Peterkin.
"Why that I cannot tell," said he,
"But 'twas a famous victory."
"The Battle of Blenheim," st. 11

JANE AUSTEN
1775–1817

English, one of the greatest woman novelists. She lived with her unmarried sisters in a country parsonage and wrote about poor gentrified families struggling to find husbands for their daughters. She was published anonymously or posthumously. Now she is more widely read than Dickens, although she wrote only six novels, of whom *Emma* and *Persuasion* may be the most powerful.

Her *Sense and Sensibility* (1811) features two sisters, Elinor and Marianne Dashwood, who are both jilted when they expect proposals. Elinor bears up with dignity and gets her intended, Edward Ferrars, while Marianne throws herself at her intended and has to settle for an old admirer.

In *Pride and Prejudice* (1813), Mrs. Bennet of the gentry schemes to marry her five daughters to aristocrats. A rich aristocrat, Darcy, represents "pride" given his high-handed marriage proposal to Elizabeth Bennet, who represents "prejudice" in her reaction to Darcy's pride. Yet she decides that "to be mistress of Pemberley might be something!"

It is a truth universally acknowledged, that a single man in possession of a good fortune, must be in want of a wife.... However little known the feelings or views of such a man may be on his first entering a neighbourhood, this truth is so well fixed in the minds of the surrounding families, that he is considered as the rightful property of some one or other of their daughters.
Opening lines, *Pride and Prejudice* (1813)

Loss of virtue in a female is irretrievable...
one false step involves her in endless ruin.

Ibid., ch. 47

There is not one in a hundred of either
sex who is not taken in when they marry.
Look where I will, I see that it is so; and
I feel that it must be so, when I consider
that it is, of all transactions, the one in
which people expect most from others,
and are least honest themselves.

Mansfield Park (1814), ch. 5

One half of the world cannot understand
the pleasures of the other.

Emma (1815), ch. 9

A woman, if she have the misfortune of
knowing anything, should conceal it as
well as she can... imbecility in females is a
great enhancement of their personal charms.

Northanger Abbey (1818), ch. 14

...a world of rural gentility and idleness,
of heirs, nonheirs, and poor intriguers—
pretenders to unearned wealth. It was a
world that possessed considerable appeal,
quietly lying in wait to draw the tired
and incapable and handsome seekers of
social rent into the nirvana of triviality.

David Landes said of Austen's work in *The*
Wealth and Poverty of Nations (1998)

THE NOVEL

Cervantes' *Don Quixote* was the first
novel—a long, realistic book about the life
of an individual, which book is not based
on a myth nor is a "romance"—escapist
stories of exalted persons in impossible
situations. Dr. Johnson said novelists try
to "exhibit life in its true state." Defoe and
Fielding wrote the first British novels. In
the nineteenth century, the novel became
intensely realistic, as per Flaubert's minute descriptions of daily life and Dostoyevsky's psychological realism. Many
modernist novelists in the twentieth century wrote novels for the elite that emphasized neither plot nor character, but which
described the chaos of an individual's
stream of consciousness.

AMERICAN ECONOMY
1776

America's plentiful resources and scarcity of people shaped her culture. New
England's great cash crops were lumber
and codfish, and she built ships at half the
cost of Europe because abundant timber
was located near running water that could
float logs to the ports and also power the
sawmills. The middle colonies exported
tobacco and the southernmost exported
rice and indigo. Most American farms
exceeded 100 acres, compared to France,
where 97 percent of farms were less than 25
acres. Only 5 percent of white males were
poor because cheap land was abundant
and few worked for anyone else after age
twenty-five. One could buy arable land for
$1.25 per acre with only 25 percent down!

500,000 Europeans flocked to America as indentured laborers—self-selected
risk-takers. With its natural abundance
and liberties, America's economy surged
from being only 5 percent of the British
economy in 1700 to 40 percent by 1776. To
avoid heavy taxation, Europeans flocked
to America, where the average colonist in
1770 paid one shilling in taxes compared
to twenty-six shillings in England. An
American farm in 1800 with eight horses
paid about twelve dollars a year in taxes.

HENRY CLAY
1777–1852

American, statesman, "the Great Pacifier" for the Compromises of 1820 and 1850. The North benefited because its strength increased relative to the South's. Clay attacked abolitionism and slavery, believing it would expire naturally. That ended his chances for the presidency. His "American System" advocated that the federal government build projects, act as a central banker, and pass protective tariffs.

> Sir, I would rather be right than be President.
> [Clay's Compromise of 1850 alienated the antislavery states.]
> Carl Schurz, *Life of Henry Clay*, ch. 21 on speech, 1839

> Of all human powers operating on the affairs of mankind, none is greater than that of competition.

NATHAN M. ROTHSCHILD
1777–1836

English, banker, one of five sons of Meyer Rothschild, who founded a bank with branches in London, Paris, Vienna, Frankfurt, and Naples. The Rothschilds midwifed the modern world by being the first to assist governments to finance major peacetime projects, as Michael Milken restructured U.S. industry by securitizing loans to firms lacking established credit, leading to the 1980–2007 boom.

The world's richest man died from an infected cut now easily curable with inexpensive antibiotics.

> The time to buy is when blood is running in the streets. [And] Always sell too soon.
> [Rothschild's two rules for investing]

Legend says that after Rothschild received early word by carrier pigeon and a fast yacht of Wellington's victory at Waterloo, he had his agents ostentatiously start to sell bonds. Traders assumed Nathan's selling meant Wellington had lost, so the market crashed. Then, Nathan made a fortune buying bonds at distressed prices.

> It requires a great deal of boldness and a great deal of caution to make a great fortune; and when you have got it, it requires ten times as much wit to keep it.

WILLIAM HAZLITT
1778–1830

English, essayist; first full time literary critic.

> There is not a more mean, stupid, dastardly, pitiful, selfish, spiteful, envious, ungrateful animal than the Public. It is the greatest of cowards, for it is afraid of itself.
> *Table Talk* (1821), "On Living to One's Self"

> We never do anything well till we cease to think about the manner of doing it.
> *Sketches and Essays* (1938) "On Prejudice"

> Without the aid of prejudice and custom, I should not be able to find my way across the room.
> Ibid.

Stephen Decatur
1779–1820

American, crusading admiral against Islamic pirates in the Tripolitan War of 1805 and Algerine War of 1815, which ended the U.S. paying tribute to the Barbary states of Algeria, Tunisia, and Tripolitania. The beys broke treaties as soon as the U.S. and European fleets sailed away, so piracy was not actually ended until France occupied Algeria in 1830. Similarly, Britain had to occupy the Arabian Gulf states to stop their piracy in the Indian Ocean.

> Our country! In her intercourse with foreign nations, may she always be in the right; but our country, right or wrong.
>> Toast in 1816, in *Life of Decatur* (1846), ch. 14, by A. S. Mackenzie

> [Carl Schurz, speaking at an anti-imperialist conference, amended Decatur's toast on October 17, 1899:] Our country right or wrong. When right, to be kept right; when wrong, to be put right.

Francis Scott Key
1779–1843

American, captive on a British warship in 1814 when it shelled Fort McHenry, which guarded Baltimore. His poem was adopted as the National Anthem in 1931.

> Oh, say, can you see by the dawn's early light,
> What so proudly we hailed at the twilight's last gleaming?
> Whose broad stripes and bright stars, through the perilous fight,

O'er the ramparts we watched were so gallantly streaming?
And the rockets' red glare, the bombs bursting in air,
Gave proof through the night that our flag was still there.
Oh, say, does that star-spangled banner yet wave
O'er the land of the free and the home of the brave?
>> "The Star-Spangled Banner"
>> (September 14, 1814)

Clement C. Moore
1779–1863

American, classical scholar. He wrote his poem as a Christmas present to his sick little daughter.

> 'Twas the night before Christmas, when all through the house
> Not a creature was stirring—not even a mouse;
> The stockings were hung by the chimney with care,
> In hopes that St. Nicholas soon would be there.
> The children were nestled all snug in their beds,
> While visions of sugar plums danced in their heads.
>> "The Night Before Christmas" (1823), st. 1

Karl Von Clausewitz
1780–1831

Prussian, general, writer on grand strategy who advocated "total war," that is, "destroy the enemy's potential for waging war by attacking the enemy's economy and citizens." The previous objective had been "to destroy the enemy's fighting forces." The first total war was the Boer War, during which the British herded Boer children into death camps to discourage the Boers fighters. Peter Drucker wrote, "In modern war, there are no civilians."

John Keegan in *A History of Warfare* (1993) argues Clausewitz wrote about "ideal war," i.e., what war should be, not what it was. For example, in World War I the bloodlust of the warring parties overrode all political logic. Thus, "true war" is different from Clausewitz's "ideal war."

ON WAR
1832–34

War is therefore a continuation of politics by other means. It is not merely a political act but a real political instrument, a continuation of political intercourse, a conduct of political intercourse by other means. What still remains peculiar to war relates merely to the peculiar character of the means it employs.

War is the province of chance. In no other sphere of human activity must such a margin be left for this intruder.

Everything is very simple in war, but the simplest thing is difficult.

If the enemy is to be coerced, you must put him in a situation that is even more unpleasant than the sacrifice you call on him to make.

Let us not hear of generals who conquer without bloodshed.

The theory of warfare tries to discover how we may gain a preponderance of physical forces and material advantages at the decisive point.

Never forget that no military leader has ever become great without audacity.

There is only one decisive victory, the last.

Arming the Nations

OTHER FACTS

English military analyst J. F. C. Fuller enumerated nine "principles of war," known by the acronym MOOSEMUSS: Mass, Objective, Offensive, Surprise, Economy of force, Maneuver, Unity of effort, Security, and Simplicity.

CHARLES CALEB COLTON
1780–1832

English, clergyman.

Imitation is the sincerest form of flattery.
Lacon or Many Things in Few Words (1823),
vol. 1, no. 217

Examinations are formidable even to the best prepared, for the greatest fool may ask more than the wisest man can answer.

Ibid., no. 322

That writer does the most who gives his reader the most knowledge, and takes from him the least time.

JOHN C. CALHOUN
1782–1850

American, vice president under John Quincy Adams and Andrew Jackson.

His doctrine of the "concurrent majority" argued that state governments could "nullify" decisions of the federal government. The Senate filibuster is the surviving remnant.

> If we remain quiet...and let our destinies work out their own results, we shall do more for liberty, not only for ourselves but also for the example of mankind, than can be done by a thousand victories.
> [Calhoun opposing intervention in Hungary.]
> Robert H. Ferrell, *American Diplomacy: A History* (1959)

Now, as individuals differ greatly from each other, in intelligence, sagacity, energy, perseverance, skill, habits of industry and economy, physical power, position and opportunity, the necessary effect of leaving all free to exert themselves to better their condition, must be a corresponding inequality between those who may possess these qualities and advantages in a high degree, and those deficient in them... It is, indeed, this inequality of condition between the front and rear ranks, in the march of progress, which gives so strong an impulse to the former to maintain their position, and to the latter to press forward into their files. This gives to progress its greatest impulse.

Disquisition on Government Works 1. 35

DANIEL WEBSTER
1782–1852

American, Massachusetts senator, whose support for the 1850 Compromise infuriated the abolitionist Whigs, who formed the Republican Party. Webster and Clay felt that slavery was a doomed institution. They hoped to avoid a civil war until slavery died a natural death.

> Every man's life, liberty and property are in danger when the Legislature is in session.

> There is always room at the top.
> [When advised not to enter the crowded legal field.]

> Nothing will ruin the country if the people themselves will undertake its safety; and nothing can save it if they leave that safety in any hands but their own.

> Justice is the great interest of man on earth. It is a ligament which holds...civilized nations together.

WASHINGTON IRVING
1783–1859

American, the first celebrated U.S. author. His "Rip Van Winkle" in *The Sketch Book* (1820) was lifted from Christopher Wieland's *Travels through Germany*. While hunting, Rip ran into little men led by Hendrick Hudson playing ninepins. After drinking from their keg, he fell asleep for twenty years and awoke to find his ill-humored wife had died and his favorite tavern's portrait of King George III had been replaced with Washington's.

In "The Legend of Sleepy Hollow," Ichabod Crane, a young Yankee schoolmaster in a Dutch settlement, is attracted to Katrina Van Tassel, whose hand is also sought by Van Brunt (Brom Bones). Brom Bones tells of a headless horseman at a party given by the Van Tassels. Ichabod then rides his horse, Gunpowder, home. The next day a smashed pumpkin and a grazing Gunpowder are found nearby, but Ichabod is never seen again.

> A father may turn his back on his child; brothers and sisters may become inveterate enemies; husbands may desert their wives and wives their husbands. But a mother's love endures through all; in good repute, in bad repute, in the face of the world's condemnation, a mother will love on, and still hopes that her child may turn from his evil ways, and repent; still she remembers the infant smiles that once filled her bosom with rapture, the merry laugh, the joyful shout of his childhood, the opening promise of his youth; and she can never be brought to think him all unworthy.

> Who ever hears of fat men heading a riot?

STENDHAL
1783–1842

French, novelist, and officer in Napoleon's invasion of Russia. In *The Red and the Black* (1830), the hero and villain is Julien Sorel, a brilliant but poor provincial determined to advance through a military career (the red) or the church (the black). He has an affair with Madame de Rênal and flees when discovered. As secretary to Marquise de La Mole, Julien falls in love with and impregnates his daughter, Mathilde. Once engaged, the Marquise gives Julien land and a title, but takes them back after he receives a letter from Madame de Rênal telling all. Julien shoots at Madame de Rênal

and is sentenced to death for attempted murder. Julien refuses to defend himself or allow Madame de Rênal or Mathilde to rescue him. Madame de Rênal commits suicide after the execution of Julien.

> Almost all our misfortunes in life come from the wrong attitudes we have... To know men thoroughly, to judge events sanely is, therefore, a great step towards happiness.
>
> *Journal* (December 10, 1801)

> A wise woman never yields by appointment. It should always be an unforeseen happiness.
>
> *De L'Amour* (1822), ch. 1

> [T]he most shocking fault of women is that they make the public the judge of their lives.
>
> Ibid., ch. 60

> I see but one rule: to be clear. If I am not clear, all my world crumbles to nothing.
>
> Letter to Balzac (1840)

> Wit lasts no more than two generations.
>
> Ibid.

> I have had proof this evening that when music is perfect, it sets the heart in exactly the same condition as that produced by the presence of the beloved; which is to say music gives the most intense happiness available on this earth.
>
> *On Love* (1822)

> One can acquire everything in solitude, but character.

LEIGH HUNT
1784–1859

English, poet, essayist, and critic.

> Jenny kiss'd me when we met,
> Jumping from the chair she sat in;
> Time, you thief, who love to get
> Sweets into your list, put that in!
>
> Say I'm weary, say I'm sad,
> Say that health and wealth have miss'd me,
> Say I'm growing old, but add,
> Jenny kiss'd me.
>
> "Jenny Kiss'd Me" Rondeau (1838)

LORD PALMERSTON
1784–1865

British, prime minister (1855–58, 1859–65) who checked the Russians in the Crimea and made Great Britain the nineteenth century's world power.

> [Lord Palmerston said only three people understood Schleswig-Holstein: The Prince Consort, who was dead; a German professor, who had gone mad; and himself, who had forgotten all about it.]
>
> In Norman Davies, *Europe: A History* (1996)

> We have no eternal allies and we have no perpetual enemies. Our interests are eternal and perpetual, and those interests it is our duty to follow.
>
> House of Commons (March 1, 1848)

> Die, my dear Doctor, that's the last thing I shall do.
>
> Last words. In Peter Andrews, "Famous Last Apothegms," *Horizon* (January 1977)

CONSTITUTION OF THE UNITED STATES
WRITTEN 1787, RATIFIED 1789

That the United States is the longest surviving republic testifies to the genius of the Founding Fathers, who were all men of affairs; not one was an academic. The Constitution limited government power more than any other government in history. It grants government only limited powers, and it can be amended only by cumbersome procedures of supra-majority votes. Because the Declaration of Independence holds that men are endowed by their Creator with inalienable rights, the Constitution cannot be amended to abridge those rights even with supra-majority votes. It separates federal executive, legislative, and judicial powers, and federal and state powers. It was designed to govern selfish citizens, and has survived by preventing the coalescing of a "durable tyrannical majority."

The Constitution was drafted after Adam Smith published *The Wealth of Nations*. It demolished mercantilism, which had plagued Europe with inefficient state and private monopolies, systems of privilege, and government guidance of the economy. Smith argued competition would create prosperity, and government's primary economic role was to prevent the use of force and fraud.

Joseph Ellis in his *Founding Brothers* (2000) concludes that the Constitution survived because neither the Federalists (Washington, Hamilton, Adams) nor the Republicans (Jefferson, Madison) triumphed in their battle to define the Revolution. Popular sovereignty, which had caused the lives of republics to be short, was constrained by a limited, written constitution. The whole point of a written constitution was to protect permanent values against the transient whims of shifting majorities. An interesting fact is that the U.S. Constitution is written on twelve pages while the unsigned Constitution of the European Union is over 800 pages.

We the People of the United States in Order to form a more perfect Union, establish Justice, insure domestic Tranquility, provide for the common Defense, promote the general Welfare, and secure the Blessings of Liberty to ourselves and our Posterity, do ordain and establish this Constitution for the United States of America.

Preamble

GEORGE NOEL GORDON, LORD BYRON
1788–1824

English, Romantic poet, who became an overnight success with the 1812 publication of his semiautobiographic *Childe Harold's Pilgrimage*. Byron exclaimed, "I awoke one morning and found myself famous." After his brief marriage fell apart amid accusations of incest, he fled to Italy in 1816 and wrote his greatest verse, *Don Juan*. He crusaded against Islam, and gave his fortune and his life to free Greece from Turkey in 1823.

One mistress, Lady Caroline Lamb, called him, "Mad, bad, and dangerous to know." He slept with over two hundred women in two and a half years in Italy where married women, like the men, believed they had a right to a lover, a *cavaliere servente*.

[When his classmate at Harrow, Robert Peel, was being beaten by a bully, Byron asked how many stripes he intended to give Peel. When the bully demanded why he asked, the clubfooted Byron responded, "I would take half."]

Little Brown Book of Anecdotes (1985),
Clifton Fadiman, ed.

With just enough of learning to misquote.

English Bards and Scotch Reviewers (1809)

Maid of Athens, ere we part,
Give, oh give me back my heart.
Or, since that has left my breast,
Keep it now and take the rest!

"Maid of Athens" (1810), .1

War, war is still the cry,—"war even to the knife!"

Childe Harold's Pilgrimage (1812-18),
canto 1, st. 16

Hereditary bondsmen! know ye not
Who would be free themselves must
    strike the blow?

Ibid., canto 2, st. 76

There is pleasure in the pathless woods,
There is a rapture on the lonely shore,
There is society, where none intrudes,
By the deep sea, and music in its roar;
I love not man the less, but nature more,
From these our interviews, in which I steal
From all I may be, or have been before,
To mingle with the universe, and feel
What I can ne'er express, yet cannot all
    conceal.

Ibid., canto 4, st. 178

She walks in beauty, like the night
Of cloudless climes and starry skies,
And all that's best of dark and bright
Meet in her aspect and her eyes;

Thus mellowed to that tender light
Which heaven to gaudy day denies.
　[Byron's most loved poem.]
　　"She Walks in Beauty" (1815), st. 1.

One shade the more, one ray the less,
Had half impaired the nameless grace
Which waves in every raven tress
Or softly lightens o'er her face,
Where thoughts serenely sweet express
How pure, how dear their
　dwelling-place.
　　　　　　　　　Ibid., st. 2

And on that cheek, and o'er that brow,
So soft, so calm, yet eloquent,
The smiles that win, the tints that glow,
But tell of days in goodness spent,
A mind at peace with all below,
A heart whose love is innocent!
　　　　　　　　　Ibid., st. 3

What is hope? nothing but the paint on
the face of Existence; the least touch of
truth rubs it off, and then we see what a
hollow-cheeked harlot we have got hold
of.
　　　　　Letter to Thomas Moore
　　　　　　(October 28, 1815)

Our cloudy climate, and our chilly
　women.
　　　　　　"Beppo" (1818), st. 49

What men call gallantry, and gods
　adultery,
Is much more common where the
　climate's sultry.
　　"Don Juan" (1818–24), canto 1, st. 63

A little still she strove, and much repented,
And whispering, "I will ne'er
　consent,—consented."
　　　　　　　　　Ibid., st. 117

Man's love is of man's life a thing apart;
'Tis woman's whole existence.
　　　　　　　　　Ibid., st. 194

Let us have wine and women, mirth
　and laughter,
Sermons and soda water the day after.
　　　　　　Ibid., canto 2, st. 178

All tragedies are finished by a death,
All comedies are ended by a marriage;
The future states of both are left to faith.
　　　　　　　　　Ibid., st. 9

He was the mildest manner'd man
That ever scuttled ship or cut a throat.
With such true breeding of a gentleman,
You never could divine his real thought.
　　　　　　　　　Ibid., st. 41

And if I laugh at any mortal thing
'Tis that I may not weep.
　　　　　　Ibid., canto 4, st. 4

Our hair grows grizzled, and we are not
　what we were.
　　　　　　Ibid., canto 12, st. 1

Ready money is Aladdin's lamp.
　　　　　　　　　Ibid., st. 12

'Tis strange—but true; for truth is
　always stranger;
Stranger than fiction.
　　　　　　Ibid., canto 14, st. 101

The Devil hath not, in all his quiver's
　choice,
An arrow for the heart like a sweet voice.
　　　　　　Ibid., canto 15, st. 13

A lovely being, scarcely formed or
　molded,

A rose with all its sweetest leaves yet
folded.

Ibid., st. 43

How little do we know that which we are!
How less what we may be!

Ibid., st. 99

I am ashes where once I was fire.
And the bard in my bosom is dead;
What I loved I now merely admire,
And my heart is as gray as my head.

"The Countess of Blessington," 1823

Ah, surely nothing dies but something
mourns.

In commitment, we dash the hopes of a
thousand potential selves.

Sir Robert Peel
1788–1850

English, Tory prime minister (1834–35 and
1841–46), after whom the English police-
men are nicknamed "bobbies." In 1846,
knowing it would split the Tory Party
and require his resignation, he repealed
the Corn Laws (tariffs on foreign grain)
and the two-hundred-year-old Navigation
Acts. Cheap grain permitted people to flee
tenant farming to become factory workers.
Free trade made Britain the world's leader
in shipping, commerce, insurance, and
finance. Note: the English textile entrepreneurs, Richard Cobden and John Bright,
had led the Anti-Corn-Law League and
had argued for the unilateral reduction of
tariffs without requiring "concessions."
Abolishing tariffs helped poor people and
promoted peace by taking politics out of
international trade. When Peel died, the
poor wept openly for their protector and
gave their pennies to build his statute.

Deprive me of power tomorrow, but you
can never deprive me of the consciousness that I have exercised the powers
committed to me from no corrupt or
interested motives, from no desire to
gratify ambition, or to attain any personal object.

On repeal of the Corn Laws
(May 15, 1846)

Arthur Schopenhauer
1788–1860

German, the "dismal philosopher," who
held that the ultimate reality was the
struggle of all organic matter against all
other organic matter. Moreover, the world
is basically evil. Happiness is only momentary respites from pain, so "Life must be
some kind of mistake," and "It is a sin to
be born." Our will to survive can never be
satisfied, so life is suffering, which is "the
thing in itself." The only escape is by intellect to vanquish all desire.

To be alone is the fate of all great
minds—a fate deplored at times, but still
always chosen as the less grievous of two
evils.

Essays, Sec. 24

Necessity is the constant scourge of the
lower orders; ennui that of the higher
classes.

The World as Will and Idea (1819)

Every lover, after the ultimate consummation of the great work, finds himself
cheated; for the illusion has vanished by

means of which the individual was here the dupe of the species.

Supplements to The World as Will and Idea,
ed. Richard Taylor

Happy marriages are well known to be rare; just because it lies in the nature of marriage that its chief end is not the present but the coming generation.

Ibid.

The fundamental fault of the female character is that it has no sense of justice.... They are dependent not upon strength, but upon craft, and hence their instinctive capacity for cunning, and their incredible tendency to say what is not true.

Ibid.

It is only the man whose intellect is clouded by his sexual impulses that could give the name of fair *sex* to that under-sized, narrow-shouldered, broad-hipped, and short-legged racc.... Neither for music, nor for poetry, nor for fine art have they really and truly any sense, it is mere mockery if they make a pretense of it in order to assist their endeavor to please.

Ibid.

After your death you will be what you were before your birth.

The closing years of life are like the end of a masquerade party, when the masks are dropped.

Much of the wisdom of one age is the folly of the next.

JAMES F. COOPER
1789–1851

American, novelist, whose *The Pioneers* (1823) introduced the frontier hero, Natty Bumppo (Hawkeye), an incorruptible woodsman. Natty also starred in the other *Leatherstocking Tales*: *The Last of the Mohicans* (1826), *The Prairie* (1827), *The Pathfinder* (1840), and *The Deerslayer* (1841). Wildly popular Europe-wide, in France, Cooper was known as *"le* Walter Scott *des sauvages."* European children learned to walk "Indian file." The last of the Mohicans was Chingachgook, father of Uncas.

> Equality of condition is incompatible with civilization, and is found only to exist in those communities that are but slightly removed from the savage state. In practice, it can only mean a common misery.
>
> *The American Democrat* (1838)

THE FRENCH REVOLUTION
1789–99

The French Revolution began when Louis XVI for the first time in 174 years convened the Estates-General in 1789 and entreated it to raise taxes to quell a ruinous inflation. By tradition, the Estates-General sat as three bodies, Nobility, Clergy, and Commons, but the Commons demanded that all sit as one body. Louis refused and shut out the Commons. The delegates reassembled on an indoor tennis court to proclaim themselves a National Assembly and took the "tennis court oath" to remain united. After Louis fired Necker, a reformist minister, it was rumored that the king would disband the assembly, so a journalist, Camille Desmoulins, organized a mob to take thirty thousand muskets from the Hôtel des Invalides and storm the Bastille, a royal prison symbolizing repression. In 1791 the Constituent Assembly proclaimed the Declaration of the Rights of Man, which abolished hereditary privileges and called for new elections that swept away all the moderate leaders in a new Legislative Assembly.

Louis tried to flee to join expatriate nobles but was caught. When the war against Austria went badly, Louis was arrested and the Reign of Terror began as power shifted to the radical Jacobin Party (Society of Friends of Liberty and Equality)—three thousand socialist journalists and lawyers who liquidated the republicans, the Girondists. Pierre Vergniaud, a Girondist leader who had voted to execute Louis, exclaimed when he faced the scaffold, "The Revolution, like Saturn, is devouring its children."

The Jacobins were known as the "men of the mountain" or "montagnards," because they sat on the highest benches in the hall. They were also called "leftists," because they sat to the left of the speaker. Robespierre, leader of the Jacobins, ruled as head of the Committee of Public Safety and murdered about twenty-five thousand people, including Danton and Desmoulins. In an address to the Constituent Assembly, Robespierre said, "Does any man tremble as I speak? Then I say he is guilty."

The Revolution, which proclaimed, "Liberté, Fraternité, and Égalité," sacrificed liberty to equality, and fraternity never mattered. It promoted three fatal ideas: utopia can be founded on abstract principles; equality can be enforced by the state; and the idealization of violence. Frederic

Bastiat's *The Law* (1998) quotes the leading revolutionists:

Saint-Just: "The legislator commands the future. It is for him to will the good of mankind. It is for him to make men what he wills them to be."

Robespierre: "Terror is nothing but prompt, severe, inflexible justice; it is therefore an emanation of virtue.... The principle of the republican government is virtue, and the means required to establish virtue is terror."

Le Pelletier: "Considering the extent of human degradation, I am convinced that it is necessary to effect a total regeneration and, if I may so express myself, of creating a new people."

Frederic Bastiat's response: "Ah, you miserable creatures! You who think that you are so great! You who judge humanity to be so small! You who wish to reform everything! Why don't you reform yourselves?"

Alarmed by Robespierre's blood lust, the convention arrested him on 9 *Thermidor* (July 27, 1794), the "Thermidorian Reaction," and established the Directory. Napoleon's 18 *Brumaire* (November 9, 1799) coup d'ètat established him as First Consul of the Directory. He became "consul for life" in 1802 and emperor in 1804.

Only 8 percent of those murdered in quasi-judicial executions were aristocrats or clergymen; most were disloyal liberals and peasants. Citizens in "counterrevolutionary" cities were herded into river barges, *noyades*, which were sunk in the evening and refloated in the morning for the next group. Saint-Just ("Archangel of the Terror") executed the "indifferents" as well as traitors. In the tumbrel to the square, Danton warned Robespierre, "the Incorruptible," that he would follow him to the guillotine—affectionately called *nôtre chère mere,* or "our dear mother." In Erik Von Kuehnelt-Leddihn's phrase, the guillotine was the first of the "Left Wing's G's: guillotine, gallows, Gestapo, gas-chamber, and gulag." See Paul Johnson, *Birth of the Modern*:

> The French Revolution had opened an era of intense politicization.... In Latin America, every would-be plunderer or ambitious bandit now called himself a "liberator"; murderers killed for freedom; thieves stole for the people.

General Westermann, who murdered one hundred thousand Catholic counter-revolutionaries, reported to Danton:

> The Vendée is no more. I have trampled their children beneath our horses' feet; I have massacred their women so they will no longer give birth to brigands. I do not have a single prisoner to reproach me. I have exterminated them all. The roads are sown with corpses... Mercy is not a revolutionary sentiment.
>
> In Norman Davies, *Europe: A History*
> (1996)

France, which had been Europe's leading nation for centuries, has never recovered from the Jacobin's mass murders and their attempts to create a new Adam. A calendar of twelve months of thirty days, plus five days at the end of the year was hatched. Each month had three deciles with one day of rest per decile. Deeming atheism to be a "luxury of aristocrats," Robespierre installed the Cult of the Supreme Being with a Festival of Reason. Divorce was the "revolutionary sacrament." But de Tocqueville noted that the Revolution did not demolish the *ancien regime's* prisons; it enlarged them.

But the Revolution did democratize dress. Wigs and silver buckles on shoes were abandoned. Male aristocrats had worn knee britches *(culottes)* with garters and silk stockings. Equality demanded that everyone dress like workmen, that is, wear trousers *(sans-culottes)*. The red "phrygian" cap given by the Romans to manumitted slaves became the emblem of freedom, as did the red, white, and blue cockade. Also, everyone was called "citizen" or "citizeness" to blur any indicia of rank. The Communists later changed "citizen" to "comrade."

BILL OF RIGHTS
CERTIFIED DECEMBER 15, 1791

Madison drafted the first ten amendments to the U.S. Constitution to protect individual rights against majority rule of the federal government. Most were applied to the states via later judicial interpretations of the Fourteenth Amendment, which did not allow the federal government "to abridge the privileges and immunities" of U.S. citizens, "to deprive any person of life, liberty, or property without due process of law," or "to deny any person within its jurisdiction the equal protection of the laws."

> *First Amendment*: Congress shall make no law respecting an establishment of religion or prohibiting the free exercise thereof; or abridging the freedom of speech, or of the press; or the right of

the people peaceably to assemble and to petition the Government for a redress of grievances.

Second Amendment: A well regulated militia, being necessary to the security of a free state, the right of the people to keep and bear Arms, shall not be infringed.

Third Amendment: No Soldier shall, in time of peace be quartered in any house, without the consent of the Owner, nor in time of war, but in a manner to be prescribed by law.

Fourth Amendment: The right of the people to be secure in their persons, houses, papers, and effects, against unreasonable searches and seizures, shall not be violated, and no Warrants shall issue, but upon probable cause, supported by Oath or affirmation, and particularly describing the place to be searched, and the persons or things to be seized.

Fifth Amendment: No person shall be held to answer for a capital, or otherwise infamous crime unless on a presentment or indictment of a Grand Jury, except in cases arising in the land or naval forces, or in the Militia, when in actual service in time of War or public danger; nor shall any person be subject for the same offense to be twice put in jeopardy of life or limb; nor shall be compelled in any criminal case to be a witness against himself, nor be deprived of life, liberty or property, without due process of law; nor shall private property be taken for public use, without just compensation.

Sixth Amendment: In all criminal prosecutions, the accused shall enjoy the right to a speedy and public trial, by an impartial jury of the State and district wherein the crime shall have been committed, which district shall have been previously ascertained by law, and to be informed of the nature and cause of the accusation; to be confronted with the witnesses against him, to have compulsory process for obtaining witnesses in his favor, and to have the Assistance of Counsel for his defense.

Seventh Amendment: In Suits at common law, where the value in controversy shall exceed twenty dollars, the right of trial by jury shall be preserved, and no fact tried by a jury shall be otherwise reexamined in any Court of the United States, than according to the rules of the common law.

Eighth Amendment: Excessive bail shall not be required, nor excessive fines imposed, nor cruel and unusual punishments inflicted.

Ninth Amendment: The enumeration in the Constitution of certain rights shall not be construed to deny or disparage others retained by the people.

Tenth Amendment: The powers not delegated to the United States by the Constitution, nor prohibited by it to the States, are reserved to the States respectively, or to the people.

MICHAEL FARADAY
1791–1867

English, inventor of the electric motor and the dynamo, who taught himself to read. He discovered the laws of electrolysis, which tied together electricity and chemical change.

> Time, Sir is all I require…. Oh! That I could purchase at a cheap rate some of our modern gent's spare hours!
> In Paul Johnson, *The Birth of the Modern* (1991)

The man who is certain he is right is almost sure to be wrong; and he has the additional misfortune of inevitably remaining so. All theories are fixed upon uncertain data, and all of them want alternation and support.

> Ibid.

SAMUEL MORSE
1791–1872

American (born Scot), invented the telegraph and Morse code. That led to Bell's telephone and Marconi' radio, which was based on inventing the vacuum tube, leading to transistors and computers.

> What hath God wrought!!
> [First telegraphic message—from the Supreme Court Building to Baltimore.]

PERCY BYSSHE SHELLEY
1792–1822

English, poet, who condemned private property, but kept his inherited fortune. He was unable to live on a 1,000-pound annual annuity (a workman's annual wage was 50 pounds). Shelley, an atheist, felt that poets, not the church, should give moral guidance. But Shelley let his four bastard children die in orphanages, and

his second wife, Mary Shelley, hoped their son Percy would be "ordinary" and not a "self-centered bohemian genius." Shelley, like Byron, is absent from the Poets' Corner in Westminster Abbey due to his "immoral conduct." He also tried, from a safe distance, to incite Britain's masses to rebel by his *Masque of Anarchy*:

> Rise like lions after slumber
> In unvanquishable number
> Shake your chains to earth like dew
> Which in sleep had fall'n on you
> You are many—they are few.

Shelley held love to be the key to morality, yet he changed mistresses with the seasons. T. S. Eliot called Shelley's poetry "an affair of adolescence." Southey thought Shelley had led a tragic and miserable life because "he adopted the Devil's own philosophy that nothing ought to stand in the way of his own gratification." Today the novel *Frankenstein* by Shelley's wife is better known than his best lyrics, "Ode to the West Wind" and "To a Skylark."

> If God has spoken, why is the universe not convinced?
> *Notes to Queen Mab* (1813)

> Love is free; to promise forever to love the same woman is not less absurd than to promise to believe that same creed.
> Ibid.

> I met a traveler from an antique land
> Who said: Two vast and trunkless legs of stone
> Stand in the desert…Near them, on the sand,
> Half sunk, a shattered visage lies, whose frown,

And wrinkled lip, and sneer of cold
　　command...
And on the pedestal these words appear:
"My name is Ozymandias, king of kings;
Look on my works, ye Mighty and
　　despair!"
Nothing beside remains. Round the decay
Of that colossal wreck, boundless and
　　bare
The lone and level sands stretch far away.
　　　[Ozymandias is Rameses the Sec-
　　　ond, the Egyptian king who ruled
　　　from 1290 B.C.]
　　　　　"Ozymandias of Egypt" (1817)

The trumpet of a prophecy! O Wind,
If winter comes, can spring be far behind?
　　　"Ode to the West Wind" (1819), l. 68

I have a passion for reforming the world.
　　　　　Prometheus (1820), Preface

Poets are the unacknowledged legislators
of the world.
　　　Closing words, *A Defense of Poetry* (1821),
　　　　　ed. Albert S. Cook (1890)

A modern equivalent to Shelley was the
Beatle John Lennon—an atheist and self-
styled socialist who wrote many songs
about sharing, but who died grasping $275
million!

WILLIAM CULLEN BRYANT
1794–1878

American, romantic poet, and publisher.

So live, that when thy summons comes
　　to join
The innumerable caravan which moves
To that mysterious realm, where each
　　shall take

His chamber in the silent halls of death,
Thou go not, like the quarry-slave at
　　night,
Scourged to his dungeon, but, sustained
　　and soothed
By an unfaltering trust, approach thy
　　grave,
Like one that wraps the drapery of his
　　couch
About him, and lies down to pleasant
　　dreams.
　　　　"Thanatopsis" (1817-21), (partial)

CORNELIUS VANDERBILT
1794–1877

American, "the Commodore," an industrialist. He created the first modern American industry, steamships. Robert Fulton
operated a steamboat on the Hudson River
under a New York monopoly. Vanderbilt
sued and won in *Gibbons v. Ogden* (1824),
which struck down Fulton's monopoly.
Steamship ticket prices from Albany to
New York City fell from seven dollars to
three dollars. The Commodore later combined several old railroads to make the
New York Central (New York to Chicago)
into the most profitable railroad. When a
competitor lowered rates below variable
costs, the Commodore bought herds of
cattle to ship on his competitor's line.

Danile Drew, "the Great Bear," was a
director of the Erie Railroad, the "scarlet
woman of Wall Street." When Vanderbilt
tried to buy a controlling interest, Drew,
Jay Gould, and Jim Fisk had Erie illegally
issue new stock until enjoined by a New
York judge. They fled to Jersey City and
later paid a half a million dollars to New
York legislators to legalize the "watering"
of Erie's stock. Vanderbilt said that "has

learned me it never pays to kick a skunk."
Drew died penniless after the Panic of
1873, and Fisk was murdered by the lover
of his mistress. Gould, the "Mephistopheles of Wall Street," almost cornered the
gold market in 1869.

> Building railroads from nowhere to
> nowhere at public expense is not a legiti-
> mate business.

> [When two associates stole from
>   him, he wrote to them:]
> Gentlemen: You have undertaken to
> cheat me. I won't sue you, for the law is
> too slow. I'll ruin you.
>   [He did.]

RAILROADS

George Stephenson (Scottish) built the first
railroad for steam locomotives in 1825 to
haul coal between mines at Darlington,
England, and the port at Stockton. Stephenson's *Rocket* engine averaged fourteen
miles per hour over sixty miles.

In the nineteenth century, Britain developed the highest density of railroads in the
world (seven times that of France or Germany). That gave Britain an advantage in
leading the Industrial Revolution.

In America, railroads created a continental economy. The first transcontinental railway was the moon project of the
nineteenth century: It took six years and
$100 million to build, and reduced coast-
to-coast travel time from three months to
one week. Between 1869 and 1893, five
transcontinental railroads were built. The
last, Jim Hill's Great Northern, was built
without public subsidy and was the most
efficient. Railroads cut shipping costs 95
percent and created economies of scale
that allowed national companies to kill off
local monopolies.

The railroad and horse-and-coach lob-
bies persuaded Parliament to prohibit
steam carriages on Britain's toll roads. That
political regulation prevented the development of the auto in Britain.

THOMAS CARLYLE
1795–1881

Scottish, essayist, and historian, who
believed history was driven by great men,
not by impersonal forces, like Marx's notion
of class struggle. A pro-slavery traditionalist who called economics the "dismal science," he attacked laissez-faire capitalism
as "anarchy plus the constable."

> Were we required to characterize this
> age of ours by any single epithet, we
> should be tempted to call it…the Age of
> Machinery….
>
>> *Sign of the Times* (1829)

> The fearful Unbelief is unbelief in yourself.
>
>> *Sator Resartus* (1834)

> Shall I tell you what is the most intolera-
> ble sort of slavery, the slavery over which
> the very gods weep? It is the slavery of
> the strong to the weak; of the great and
> noble minded to the small and mean.
>
>> Ibid.

> He who first shortened the labor of
> Copyists by device of Movable Types was
> disbanding hired Armies and cashiering
> most Kings and Senates, and creating a
> whole new Democratic world….
>
>> Ibid., bk. 1, ch. 5

Man is a tool using animal…. Without tools he is nothing, with tools he is all.

> Ibid.

The end of man is an action, and not a thought, though it were the noblest.

> Ibid., bk. 2, ch. 6

France was long a despotism tempered by epigrams.

> *History of the French Revolution* (1837),
> pt.1, bk. 1, ch. 1

Experience is the best of schoolmasters, only the school-fees are heavy.

> *Critical & Miscellaneous Essays* (1838–57)

Our grand business undoubtedly is, not to see what lies dimly at a distance, but to do what lies clearly at hand.

> Ibid.

The three great elements of modern civilization: Gunpowder, Printing, and Protestant Religion.

> Ibid., "The State of German Literature"

The true University of these days is a Collection of Books.

> *On Heroes, Hero-Worship and the Heroic*
> (1841), "The Hero as Man of Letters"

Adversity is sometimes hard upon a man; but for one man who can stand prosperity, there are a hundred that will stand adversity.

> Ibid.

History is the essence of innumerable biographies.

> Ibid., "On History"

Understand well it is the deep commandment, dimmer or clearer, of our

whole being, to be free. Freedom is the one purport wisely aimed at, or unwisely, of all man's struggles, toiling, and sufferings on this earth.

> "Heroes and Hero-Worship" Lectures,
> London (May 5, 1841)

The first duty of man is that of subduing fear. We must get rid of fear; we cannot act till then.

> Ibid.

In the long run every Government is the exact symbol of its People, with their wisdom and unwisdom; we have to say, like People like Government.

> *Past and Present* (1843), bk. III, ch. 4

Blessed is he who has found his work; let him ask no other blessing. He has a life-purpose.

> Ibid., ch. 11

"Gad! she'd better!"
> [On hearing that Margaret Fuller "accepted the universe."]
> William James, *Varieties of Religious*
> *Experience* (1902), lecture 2

[Carlyle consigned publishers of indexless books:]
"to be damned beyond Hell…"

Give me a man who sings at his work.

The block of granite which was an obstacle in the path of the weak, becomes a steppingstone in the path of the strong.

Show me the man you honor, and I will know what kind of a man you are, for it shows me what your ideal of manhood is, and what kind of man you long to be.

The true epic of our times is not arms and the man, but tools and the man, an infinitely wider kind of epic.

JOHN KEATS
1795–1821

English, lyric poet, whose life was cut short by tuberculosis. His "La Belle Dame Sans Merci" is the best of Romantic medievalism.

If poetry comes not as naturally as the leaves to a tree, it had better not come at all.
  Letter to John Taylor (February 27, 1818)

A thing of beauty is a joy forever.
  Endymion (1818), bk. 1, l. 1

When old age shall this generation waste,
Thou shalt remain, in midst of other woe
Than ours, a friend to man, to whom
    thou say'st,
"Beauty is truth, truth beauty,"—that is all
Ye know on earth, and all ye need to
    know.
    [Keats says the purpose of art is beauty that lives on to bring joy to the future.]
    "Ode on a Grecian Urn" (1820), st. 5

Oh, what can ail thee knight at arms
Alone and palely loitering?
The sedge has withered from the lake
And no birds sing.
  "La Belle Dame Sans Merci" (1820), st. 1

I met a Lady in the Meads,
Full beautiful, a faery's child,
Her hair was long, her foot was light
And her eyes were wild.
    Ibid., st. 4

And there she lulled me asleep,
And there I dreamed, Ah Woe betide!
The last dream I ever dreamt
On the cold hill side.
    Ibid., st. 9

I saw pale kings, and princes too,
Pale warriors, death-pale were they all:
They cried – "La Belle Dame sans Merci
Hath thee in thrall!"
    Ibid., st. 10

NICHOLAS I
1796–1855

Russian emperor, whose motto was "orthodoxy, autocracy, and national union."

Russia has two generals in whom she can confide—Generals January and February.

HEINRICH HEINE
1797–1856

Germany's great Romantic poet, whose lyrics defy translation. He was a revolutionary self-exiled to Paris where he wrote tragic poetry and prose.

Gross ist die Ahulichke it der be iden schonen.
For Sleep is good, but Death is better still—The best is never to be born at all.

Whenever they burn books they will also, in the end, burn human beings.
    Almansor: A Tragedy (1823)

Mark this well, you proud men of action: You are nothing but the unwitting agents of the men of thought who often, in quiet self-effacement, mark out most exactly all your doings in advance. Maximilian Robespierre was nothing but the hand of Jean Jacques Rousseau, the bloody hand that drew from the womb of time the body whose soul Rousseau had created.

History of Religion and Philosophy in Germany (1834), vol. 3

People in those old times had convictions; we moderns only have opinions. And it needs more than a mere opinion to erect a Gothic cathedral.

The French Stage (1837), ch. 9

You talk of our having an idea; we do not have an idea. The idea has us, and martyrs us, and scourges us, and drives us into the arena to fight and die for it, whether we want to or not.

In L. R. Frank, *Quotationary* (1999)

Christianity has occasionally calmed the brutal German lust for battle.... When once that restraining talisman, the Cross, is broken...the old stone gods will leap to life among forgotten ruins and Thor will crash down his mighty hammer on the Gothic cathedrals.

Quoted in Carr, *The Paths of Dictatorship* (1959)

If the Romans had been obliged to learn Latin, they would never have found time to conquer the world.

Ordinarily he is insane, but he has lucid moments when he is only stupid.

The only thing we learn from history is that we learn nothing from history.

A blaspheming Frenchman is a spectacle more pleasing to the Lord than a praying Englishman.

Of course [God] will pardon me. It's his trade.

Last words

CHARLES LYELL
1797–1875

Scottish, scientist whose *Principles of Geology* (1830) said earth had existed for an immense time. That wrecked the Bible's seven-day chronology.

Nature is not repose, but war. It is not rest, but change. It is not preservation but successive production and annihilation.

MARY WOLLSTONECRAFT SHELLEY
1797–1851

English, novelist. Mary and Percy Bysshe Shelley invited John Polidori and Lord Byron to dinner, after which they told ghost stories. Byron challenged each to write a ghost story, whence came Polidori's *Vampyre* and Mary's Gothic science fiction *Frankenstein* (1818). Mary Shelley's novel, written at age eighteen, featured the magical power of electricity, which was then little understood.

SOJOURNER TRUTH
1797–1854

American, abolitionist, and suffragist, who was born a slave but became an evangelist in the North.

Well, chilern, whar dar is so much racket dar must be something out o'kilter. I tink dat twixt de niggers of de Souf and de women at de Norf all a talkin' bout rights, de white men will be in a fix pretty soon.

Women's Rights Convention, Akron, Ohio
(1851)

AUGUSTE COMTE
1798–1857

French, founder of positivism (positive science) and sociology (study of human society). The "positive" is science, a new understanding after the failures of religion and metaphysics. Truth is only what can be proved scientifically.

Comte's *Système de Politique Positive* (1854) explained positivism: "Love our principle, order our foundation, progress our goal." He sought a rational society with everyone helping others. But he left no room for freedom. Only scientists, like him, could provide the direction. His "religion of mankind" worshiped humanity as the "Great Being," and recognized great men as saints. T. H. Huxley panned positivism as "Catholicism minus Christianity." Marvin Minsky said the positivists turned man into a cog, a "machine made of meat." Marx combined Comte's positivism with Saint-Simon's socialism to make "scientific socialism."

HONORÉ DE BALZAC
1799–1850

French, unabashed monarchist who was a realist novelist known for *La Comèdie Humaine,* a slightly connected series of novels and short stories that described French society of his time.

In *Le Père Goriot (Goriot, the Father)* (1835), Goriot gives everything he has as dowries to his two daughters so they can marry wealthy, titled men. Ashamed of their impoverished father, they send two empty carriages to his funeral. But Goriot, like King Lear, is also guilty because he raised his daughters to be idle and grasping.

In *Cousin Betty* (1846), an evil aunt, Lisbeth Fischer, masks her bitterness behind a facade of kindness to thwart her niece's romance. *Eugénie Grandet* (1833) depicts a Scrooge-like miser, M. Grandet. The lawyer, Rastignac, begins his career as a young idealist and ends as a corrupt bloodsucker. Balzac's archvillain, Vautrin, the chief criminal in Paris, becomes head of the Sûreté.

I am a galley slave to pen and ink.
Letters (1832)

Nothing in the world exists in a single block. Everything is a mosaic.

The young man is consumed with passion for a beautiful woman he has not met. She is called fame.
[A dying Balzac said the only doctor who could help was Bianchon, a character in his *Le Père Goriot.*]

ALEXANDER PUSHKIN
1799–1837

Russian, poet, novelist, and playwright. He proved that great literature could be written in Russian. In his great novel, *Eugene Onegin,* Onegin kills his only friend in a duel and spurns Tatyana, a woman desperately in love with him. He falls in love with Tatyana later after she is married, only to be rejected in turn. Pushkin was killed in a duel with an officer who had an affair with his wife.

A woman's love for us increases
The less we love her, sooth to say-
She stoops, she falls, her struggling ceases;
Caught fast, she cannot get away.
>   *Eugene Onegin* (1823), ch. 4., st. 1, tr.
>   Babette Deutsch

Calmly he contemplates alike the just
And unjust, with indifference he notes
Evil and good, and knows not wrath
    nor pity.
>   *Boris Godunov* (1825)

THOMAS BABINGTON MACAULAY
1800–1859

English, historian, poet, Whig MP, who saw the expansion of democracy and capitalism as a march toward progress and who lauded peace, private property, and scientific progress. He supported the "Whig interpretation of history": abolish slavery, repeal anti-Semitic laws, limits on government, and expansion of individual rights. His "Southey's Colloquies" (1830), argued that Britain's Industrial Revolution had resulted from lower taxes and more secure private property. Perhaps the most eloquent historian, he confounded learned readers by beginning the discussion of obscure events with the phrase, "As every schoolboy knows…" Lord Grenville said, "I wish I were as sure about anything as Macaulay is about everything."

Free trade, one of the greatest blessings that a government can confer on a people, is in almost every country unpopular.
>   *Essay on Mitford's History of Greece* (1824)

His imagination resembled the wings of an ostrich. It enabled him to run, though

not to soar. When he attempted the highest flights, he became ridiculous; but while he remained in a lower region, he outstripped all competitors.
>   "John Dryden," *Edinburgh Review*
>   (January 1828)

The gallery in which the reporters sit has become a fourth estate of the realm.
>   *On Hallam's Constitutional History* (1828)

An acre in Middlesex is better than a principality in Utopia.
>   "Lord Bacon," *Edinburgh Review*
>   (July 1837)

From the poetry of Lord Byron they drew… a system in which the two great commandments were to hate your neighbor and to love your neighbor's wife.
>   Essay to *Edinburgh Review* (1843), vol. 1.,
>   "Moore's Life of Lord Byron"

Then out spake brave Horatius,
The Captain of the Gate:
To every man upon this earth
Death cometh soon or late.
And how can man die better
Than facing fearful odds,
For the ashes of his fathers,
And the temples of his Gods?
>   "Lays of Ancient Rome" (1842), st. 27

The Puritan hated bear-baiting, not because it gave pain to the bear, but because it gave pleasure to the spectators.
>   *History of England* (1849), vol. 1, ch. 2

The ambassador of Russia and the grandees who accompanied him were so gorgeous …and so filthy that nobody dared to touch them. They came to the court balls dropping pearls and vermin.
>   Ibid., vol. 5 ch. 23

...the most frightful of all spectacles, the strength of civilization without its mercy.
> Quoted in *Winston Churchill*, Martin Gilbert, vol. IV ch. 23

Your Constitution is all sail and no anchor.
> [Referring to the U. S. Constitution.]
> Letter to H. S. Randall (May 23, 1857)

The rules of evidence in law save scores of culprits whom judges, jury and spectators firmly believe to be guilty....But it is clear that an acquittal so obtained cannot be pleaded in bar of the judgment of history.
> *Essay on Warren Hastings*

Many politicians of our time are in the habit of laying it down as a self-evident proposition that no people ought to be free till they are fit to use their freedom. The maxim is worthy of the fool in the old story, who resolved not to go into the water till he had learned to swim.
> In L. R. Frank, *Freedom*, 2003

Nothing but the mint can make money without advertising.

8

INDUSTRIALIZATION AND THE VICTORIAN AGE

Britain's Industrial Revolution stretched from the invention of the steam engine in 1769 to the end of Queen Victoria's rule in 1901, during which Britain switched from water, wind, and wood power to coal and oil power. In 1785, Britain's population totaled 9 million, of whom 80 percent worked in agriculture; by 1865 it totaled 29 million, of whom 60 percent worked in industry. It was an age of freedom in which private corporations ushered in historically unparalleled progress. As Paul Johnson wrote in *The Recovery of Freedom* (1980):

> The Industrial Revolution [began] in late eighteenth century England. It was a period of minimum government.... As a matter of fact, the Industrial Revolution, perhaps the most important single event in human history, seems to have occurred without the English government even noticing.

From the Romans to the Industrial Revolution, life was a losing race against famine and pestilence. Real per capita income rose only 50 percent in two thousand years. In 1800 the world's typical person had income equal to only 2 percent of U.S. income in 2005. Life was centered on growing food and gathering wood to burn, until entrepreneurs built steam engines that scrambled the old order and sped up everything. Machinery too big for homes was sited in factories, so villages emptied as mill towns arose. After steam engines and railroads, new services arose: prepaid postal service, daily newspapers, universal limited liability corporations, civil service, banks, telegraph (1835), telephone (1877), and radio (1895).

Cotton cloth, once the cloth of the super rich, became widely available, which was critical to health because cotton could be easily cleaned and wool could not. Cotton cloth by 1860 had fallen by 99 percent in price from 1785. Former luxuries for kings became common goods for the people.

The Victorian meritocratic order empowered all exceptional individuals. George Stephenson, who invented the steam locomotive, taught himself to read. Humphrey Davy, a carpenter's son, ran the Royal Society's laboratory. Michael Faraday, son of a blacksmith, invented the electric motor and the electric dynamo. John Dalton, "father of modern atomic theory," financed his studies by gambling.

European entrepreneurs flocked to Great Britain because it had the world's only effective patent laws. Mark Brunel, a Frenchman, became the most famous British inventor of machinery. His circular saw reduced the cost of lumber by 90 percent.

Industrialization vastly improved the lives of poor people. As bad as Dickens depicted factory conditions in England, people willingly, desperately, fled the grinding poverty and insecurity of tenant farming for the improved living conditions of factory workers. Industrial work was the first nonmartial opportunity in history for tenant farmers and servants to better themselves without emigrating.

The broadest measure of well-being is life expectancy. In preindustrial England, the average life span was about thirty-five years, the same as in imperial Rome. England's average life span and its population rose as living standards rose. Greenies who long for the precapitalist life, for "Merrie England,"would find there appalling destitution, and they would bury most of their own children.

Some nineteenth century writers,like Flaubert, Zola, and Baudelaire, failed to see how the meritocratic Victorian culture empowered entrepreneurs to enrich society so that most people would no longer be condemned to destitution. By mocking Victorian virtues and the bourgeoisie, they prepared the way for the Bolsheviks and National Socialists.

Peter Drucker said the West's bourgeoisie in the nineteenth century increased the rate of productivity growth from less than one-tenth of 1 percent per annum to 4 percent per annum. That led in the nineteenth century to a 40 percent reduction in working hours for workers and a twenty-fold increase in real wages. Yet most intellectuals hate entrepreneurs, whom they charge are "robber barons." Worse, they glamorize dictators who promise "social justice," that is, robbery of the creative minority whose work enriches all. Per Paul Johnson, intellectuals in the nineteenth century set the "world adrift in a relativistic universe" which "was a summons to…gangster statesmen to emerge. They were not slow to make their appearance."

Victorians are criticized for being hypocrites, but their values managed industrialization and made the nineteenth century the most peaceful one. Victorians did not see themselves as being virtuous—indeed, no group has ever been so conscious of their vices as they struggled to emulate the highest standards. Compared to the horrors of Soviet industrialization, during which life spans plummeted, the privations of British industrialization were beatific.

Why was it that Great Britain started the Industrial Revolution and became the "workshop of the world"? Tom Bethell's *The Noblest Triumph* (1998) argues that the answer is Britain's common law that removed medieval restrictions on property rights, like "just prices," monopolistic guilds, union strikes, and usury laws. The willingness of government to foreclose mortgages enabled Britain to develop the first general credit system, and its Parliamentary Enclosure Acts privatized common land, which spurred a dramatic increase in farm productivity. More generally, the British culture supported obeying the law. One could invest without fear of confiscation or having to bribe officials. Thus, from all over Europe physical capital and human capital migrated to Britain.

Most Victorians, like Macaulay, rejoiced in the blessings of progress. In 1900, when Henry Adams visited the Gallery of Machines in the Great Exposition in Paris, he concluded, "Man had translated himself into a new universe which had no common scale of measurement with the old." But some despaired at how "progress" undermined traditional life. Karl Marx put it this way in *The Communist Manifesto*:

> Constant revolutionizing of production, uninterrupted disturbance of all

social conditions, everlasting uncertainty and agitation distinguish the bourgeois epoch from all earlier ones. All fixed, fast-frozen relationships, with their train of ancient and venerable prejudices and opinions, are swept away, all new-formed ones become antiquated before they can ossify. All that is solid, melts into air, all that is holy is profaned….

Similarly, Matthew Arnold wrote:

For what wears out the life of mortal
    men?
'Tis that from change to change their
    being rolls;
It's that repeated shocks, again, again,
Exhaust the energy of strongest souls.

Peter Drucker prefers "Four Entrepreneurial Surges": (1) commercial revolution (1650) with large oceangoing ships; (2) Industrial Revolution (1769), with the steam engine, as augmented by the railroad; (3) second Industrial Revolution of the late nineteenth century: electricity, telephone, steel, chemicals, pharmaceuticals, automobiles, and airplanes; 4) today's information and biology revolutions.

HELMUTH VON MOLTKE
1800–1891

Prussian, field marshal, whose army defeated Austria in 1866 and France in 1871. He told about a major who explained a blunder by saying he was following orders. Prince Frederick replied, "His Majesty made you a major because he believed you would know when not to obey his orders." The German concept of "mission tactics" requires that the highest commander to the youngest soldier must do what the situation requires as he sees it without waiting for orders and even in contravention of orders.

You need the lazy and stupid—they will fill the ranks. You need the lazy and intelligent—they will be your staff officers. The energetic and intelligent will be your top commanders. But, at all cost, weed out the energetic and stupid.

First ponder, then dare.

FREDERIC BASTIAT
1801–50

French, political economist, and natural rights philosopher, who explained how free economies exhibit an unplanned regularity. Complaints about free markets are complaints about choices made by free people. His "A Petition" (1845) told how French candle makers sought protection from a ruinous foreign competitor, to wit, the sun. The candle makers requested regulations requiring that curtains be hung over all windows during daylight.

Bastiat exposed the "broken window" fallacy. If a window is broken, this does not stimulate the economy by creating a demand for labor and capital to repair it. Money used to fix the window would have been used for some other thing and society would have been richer for having the window and the new thing. Ludwig von Mises said, "War prosperity is like the prosperity that an earthquake or a plague brings."

Bastiat asked a key question: If people delegate power to the government, how can the government acquire powers that the individuals never had? For example, if a person does not have the right to seize rich Peter's property to give to poor Paul, how does government ever acquire that right?

> The state is that great fiction by which everyone tries to live at the expense of everyone else.
> "The State," *The Law* (1850), tr. Dean Russell

> When plunder is organized by the law for the profit of those who make the law, all the plundered classses try somehow to enter—by peaceful or revolutionary means—into the making of laws.
> Ibid.

> Thus we have an infinite number of plans for organizing legal plunder: tariffs, protection, benefits, subsidies, progressive taxation, guaranteed jobs, guaranteed profits, minimum wages, a right to relief, a right to the tools of labor, free credit, and so on and so on. All these plans as a whole—with their common aim of legal plunder—constitute socialism.
> Ibid.

> If goods don't cross borders, soldiers will.

DAVID G. FARRAGUT
1801–70

American, admiral. At the Battle of Mobile Bay on August 5, 1864, Farragut either had to pass under Fort Morgan's guns or sail on the other side of the bay mined by "torpedoes" (submerged mines). His recorded words were, "Damn the torpedoes! Captain Drayton, go ahead! Jouett, full speed!" He hit a mine, but it did not explode.

> Damn the torpedoes—full speed ahead.
> Attributed

> Remember also that one of the requisite studies for an officer is *man*. Where your analytical geometry will serve you once, a knowledge of men will serve you daily. As a commander, to get the right man in the right place is one of the questions of success or defeat.
> Letter to his son (October 13, 1864).

ALEXANDRE DUMAS, PÈRE
1802–70

French, novelist, and playwright, who wrote *The Three Musketeers* (1844) and *The Count of Monte Cristo* (1844), a story of the revenge taken by Edmond Dantès for false imprisonment.

> All for one, one for all, that is our motto.
> [Spoken by D'Artagnan, who on his arrival in Paris challenges the three musketeers, Porthos, Athos, and Aramis, to duels, which are interrupted by the arrival of Cardinal Richelieu's soldiers. The four unite against Richelieu to save the crown. This was the best-selling novel of the nineteenth century.]
> *Les Trois Mousquetaires* (1844), ch. 9

VICTOR HUGO
1802–85

France's Shakespeare: Romantic novelist, lyric poet, playwright, and republican who fled France in 1851 but returned in triumph in 1870 after the fall of Napoleon III. He believed poets should inspire and uplift, not write narcissistically about their personal feelings. *The Hunchback of Notre Dame* (1831) and *Les Misérables* (1862) illustrate his indictment of France's criminal justice system. Quasimodo, the hunchback and deaf-mute bell-ringer of Notre Dame, tries to protect the virgin beauty Esmeralda from Archdeacon Frollo, who denounces her as a witch because she refuses his advances. After her execution, Quasimodo throws Frollo from the bell tower. Hugo shows that man is both animal and spirit, monstrous and sublime.

I miss you, I am estranged from myself.
Hermani (1830), act 1, sc. 2

An invasion of armies can be resisted, but not an idea whose time has come. [or] Nothing is so powerful as an idea whose time has come.
Conclusion to *Histoire d'un Crime* (1852)

A woman's particular talent is to understand a man better than he understands himself.
Les Misérables (1862), vol. 1., bk. 1, ch. 9

The supreme happiness of life is the conviction that we are loved.
Ibid., bk. 5, ch. 4

In *Les Misérables* (1862) hero-entrepreneur Jean Valjean brings prosperity to a poor town, but he is persecuted by a minion of an oppressor state, Detective Javert. Valjean had been imprisoned five years for stealing bread to feed a starving family, and nineteen years more for his escape attempts. He escapes and becomes an industrialist and mayor. He discovers Javert is trying another person as Jean Valjean, so he gives himself up to save the innocent man. To protect his daughter, Cosette, he escapes

again. In the 1848 Revolution, Javert is captured, but Valjean saves him. Javert cannot understand this mercy, so he drowns himself. Javert is an inhumane martinet, but not without honor.

A fixed idea ends in madness or heroism.
Ninety-Three (1879), vol. 3, ch.1

Earnestness is the salt of eloquence.

People do not lack strength; they lack will.

Everything bows to success, even grammar.

RALPH WALDO EMERSON
1803–82

American, Unitarian minister who lost his faith, philosopher, poet, and wisdom writer who said, "The world belongs to the energetic." "America's Seneca" believed the Supreme Mind or God is mixed in the world. Each man's soul is part of God: "Every man hath in him the divine Reason." To live by divine Reason is man's purpose.

Emerson was a Panentheist, one who sees God immanently interpenetrating all nature, yet distinct (transcendent) from nature, the religion of Albert Schweitzer and Alfred North Whitehead. This differs from a Pantheist who sees God and nature as the same thing. Deists, like Thomas Jefferson, see God as transcendent from the world (God creates a world machine and lets it runs as it will). Theists see God as transcendent, but also immanent (present and active in the world with miracles).

Emerson was a Romantic: Man is divine. Today transcendentalists are called mystics. Their downside is the denial of

Original Sin, and thus the views that man can be perfected by education and Utopia can be organized.

By the rude bridge that arched the flood,
Their flag to April's breeze unfurl'd;
Here once the embattl'd farmers stood,
And fired the shot heard round the world.
"Concord Hymn" (July 4, 1837), st. 1

On this green bank, by this soft stream,
We set today a votive stone;
That memory may their deed redeem,
When, like our sires, our sons are gone.
[On April 19, 1775, John Parker ordered the Minutemen: "Stand your ground. Don't fire unless fired upon, but if they mean to have a war, let it begin here."]
Ibid., st. 3

Meek young men grow up in libraries, believing it their duty to accept the views which Cicero, which Locke, which Bacon have given, forgetful that Cicero, Locke and Bacon were only young men in libraries when they wrote those books.
The American Scholar Address, Harvard University (August 31, 1837)

The great man makes the great thing. Wherever Macdonald sits, there is the head of the table.
Ibid.

This time, like all times, is a very good one, if we but know what to do with it.
Ibid.

If the single man plant himself indomitably on his instincts, and there abide, the huge world will come round to him.
Ibid.

Tobacco, coffee, alcohol, hashish, prussic acid, strychnine, are weak dilutions; the surest poison is time.
Essays, First Series (1841)

Great geniuses have the shortest biographies.
Ibid.

Beware when the great God lets loose a thinker on this planet. Then all things are at risk.
Ibid.,"Circles"

People wish to be settled; only as far as they are unsettled is there any hope for them.
Ibid.

God offers to every mind its choice between truth and repose. Take which you please,—you can never have both.
Ibid., "Intellect"

In skating over thin ice our safety is in our speed.
Ibid., "Prudence"

A foolish consistency is the hobgoblin
of little minds,
Adored by little statesmen and philosophers and divines.
Ibid., "Self-Reliance"

An institution is the lengthened shadow of one man.
Ibid.

Trust thyself. Great men have always done so. And we are now men, not minors and invalids in a protected corner, but guides, redeemers, and benefactors advancing on Chaos and the Dark.
Ibid.

Whoso would be a man, must be a nonconformist. He who would gather immortal palms must not be hindered by the name of goodness, but must explore if it be goodness.

Ibid.

To be great is to be misunderstood.

Ibid.

Character is that which can do without success.

Essays: Second Series (1844), "Character"

Character is higher than intellect.

Ibid.

No change of circumstances can repair a defect of character.

Ibid.

The only gift is a portion of thyself.

Ibid., "Gifts"

Every actual State is corrupt. Good men must not obey the laws too well.

Ibid., "The Poet"

EMERSON'S JOURNALS (EXCERPTS)

To different minds, the same world is a hell, and a heaven.

(December 20, 1822)

At home I dream that at Naples, at Rome, I can be intoxicated with beauty and lose my sadness. I pack my trunk, embrace my friends, embark on the sea, and at last wake up in Naples and there beside me is the Stern Fact, the Sad Self unrelenting, identical, that I fled from.... My Giant goes with me wherever I go.

(May 28, 1839)

There is always a certain meanness in the argument of conservatism, joined with a certain superiority in its facts.

(December 9, 1841)

All life is an experiment. The more experiments you make the better.

(November 11, 1842)

Never strike a king unless you are sure you shall kill him.

(August 1843)

Books are worth reading that sketch a principle, as lectures do. All others are tickings of a clock. And we have so much less time to live—the robbers.

(October 1848)

I hate quotations. Tell me what you know.

(May 1849)

The word "liberty" in the mouth of Mr. Webster sounds like the word "love" in the mouth of a courtesan.

(February 12, 1851)

Our very defects are...shadows of our virtues.

I trust a good deal to common fame, as we all must. If a man has good corn, or wood, or boards, or pigs, to sell, or can make better chairs or knives, crucibles, or church organs, than anybody else, you will find a broad hard-beaten road to his house, though it be in the woods.

In all my lectures, I have taught one doctrine, namely, the infinitude of the private man.

There is properly no history; only biography.

Essays, First Series (1841)

So nigh is grandeur to our dust,
So near is God to man.
When Duty whispers low, "Thou must,"
The youth replies, "I can."
Poems (1847), "Voluntaries III"

It is time to be old,
To take in sail.
Ibid., "Terminus," opening line

Rhodora! if the sages ask thee why
This charm is wasted on the earth and
 sky,
Tell them dear, that if eyes were made
 for seeing,
Then Beauty is its own excuse for being.
Ibid., "The Rhodora"

Things are in the saddle
And ride mankind.
Ibid., "Ode to W. H. Channing"

Concentration is the secret of strength in politics, in war, in trade, in short in all management of human affairs.... so should you stop off your miscellaneous activity and concentrate your force on one or a few points.
Representative Men (1850)

He is great who is what he is from Nature, and who never reminds us of others.
Ibid.

Keep cool, it will be all one a hundred years hence.
The Conduct of Life (1860), "The Skeptic"

Great men, great nations [perceive] the terror of life, and have manned themselves to face it.
Ibid., "Fate"

Fine manners need the support of fine manners in others.
Ibid.

Our chief want in life is somebody who shall make us do what we can.
Ibid., "Considerations"

New York is a sucked orange.
Ibid., "Culture"

Beauty without grace is the hook without the bait.
Ibid., "Beauty"

Life is a search after power.
Ibid., "Power"

The basis of political economy is noninterference
Ibid., "Wealth"

Every man is a consumer and ought to be a producer....
Ibid.

Art is a jealous mistress, and if a man have a genius for painting, poetry, music, architecture, or philosophy, he makes a bad husband and an ill provider.
Ibid.

The louder he talked of his honour, the faster we counted our spoons.
Ibid., "Worship"

Raphael paints wisdom; Handel sings it, Phidias carves it, Shakespeare writes it, Wren builds it, Columbus sails it, Luther preaches it, Washington arms it, Watt mechanizes it.
Society and Solitude (1870), "Art"

Hitch your wagon to a star.
Ibid., "Civilization"

The greatest meliorator of the world is selfish, huckstering trade.
Ibid., "Works and Days"

The true test of civilization is, not the census, nor the size of cities, nor the crops—no, but the kind of man the country turns out.
Ibid.

Conversation is the laboratory and workshop of the student.
Ibid., "Clubs"

The ornament of a house is the friends who frequent it.
Ibid., "Domestic Life

Can anybody remember when the times were not hard and money not scarce?
Ibid., "Works and Days"

Next to the originator of a good sentence is the first quoter of it.
Letters and Social Aims (1876), "Quotation & Originality"

Great men are they who see that spiritual is stronger than any material force, that thoughts rule the world.
Ibid., "Progress and Culture"

By necessity, by proclivity, and by delight, we all quote.
Ibid.

We are as much informed of a writer's genius by what he selects as by what he originates.
Ibid.

What you are stands over you and thunders so that I cannot hear what you say to the contrary.
Ibid.

What is a weed? A plant whose virtues have not yet been discovered.
Fortune of the Republic (1878)

Speak the affirmative; emphasize your choice by utter ignoring of all that you reject.
Lectures on Biographical Sketches (1883)

Talents differ. If I cannot carry forests on my back, neither can you crack a nut.
"The Mountain and the Squirrel"

By God, I will not obey this filthy enactment!
[Of the Fugitive Slave Act.]

America is another name for opportunity.

In a free and just commonwealth, property rushes from the idle and imbecile to the industrious, brave and persevering.
E. Wagenknecht, Ralph Waldo Emerson: Portrait of a Balanced Soul (1974)

To laugh often and much; to win the respect of intelligent people and the affection of children; to earn the appreciation of honest critics and endure the betrayal of false friends; to appreciate beauty, to find the best in others; to leave the world a bit better, whether by a healthy child, a garden patch or a redeemed social condition; to know even one life has breathed easier because you have lived. This is to have succeeded.

The characteristic of heroism is its persistency. All men have wandering impulses, fits and starts of generosity. But when you have chosen your part, abide by it, and do not weakly try to reconcile yourself with the world. The heroic cannot be the common, nor the common heroic.

Trust the instinct to the end, though you can render no reason.

Steam is no stronger now than it was a hundred years ago, but it is put to better use.

Many times the reading of a book has made the future of a man.

Every idea is a prison.

Every man is a borrower and a mimic; life is theatrical and literature a quotation.

No member of a crew is praised for the rugged individuality of his rowing.

Each [Liberalism and Conservatism] is a good half, but an impossible whole.

I pay the schoolmaster but tis the school boys that educate my son.

Take notes on the spot, a note is worth a cart-load of recollections.

Ah! Sometimes gunpowder smells good. [Reaction to the outbreak of the Civil War.]

It's like another candle has been lit when a happy person comes in the room.

EDWARD BULWER-LYTTON (OWEN MEREDITH) *1803–73*

English, playwright.

The pen is mightier than the sword.
Richelieu (1839), act II, sc. 2

In science, read by preference the newest works; in literature, the oldest. The classics are always modern.

BENJAMIN DISRAELI *1804–81*

English, Tory prime minister 1868 and 1874–80, and the favorite of Queen Victoria due to his imperialist and protectionist policies. He saw England as being "two nations": the rich and the poor, and like Caesar, his "Tory democracy" intended to ally the aristocracy with the working class. His Factory Acts of 1874 and 1878 and protectionism abandoned the Whig's laissez-faire politics that had enabled England to lead the world into industrialization and out of destitution. His Trade Union Act voided Common Law prohibitions against union monopolies and restraints on trade.

While Disraeli realized the empire, and India especially, was a net financial drain, its glory united the working class behind the Tories. Even though he called Britain's colonies "a millstone around our neck," Disraeli invaded the Transvaal, Afghanistan, the Malay Peninsula, Egypt, and so on.

Niall Ferguson's *Empire* (2003) notes that Britain invested more in India than it took out. Lance Davis's *Mammon and the Pursuit of Empire* (1987) concluded that Britain lost money on all of its colonies. William Graham Sumner argued that colonies were much desired by politicians and missionaries, but by few capitalists. Cecil Rhodes got rich in Africa by passing the higher "external" costs of colonization onto Britain. One external cost of colonization was World War I. The developed nations actually exported trivial amounts to their colonies and received trivial imports from them.

Read no history—only biography, that is life without theory.
Contarini Fleming (1832), pt. 1., ch. 14

No government can be long secure without a formidable Opposition.
Coningsby (1844), bk. 2, ch. 1

Youth is a blunder; Manhood a struggle; Old Age a regret.
Ibid., bk. 3, ch. 1

The question is this: Is man an ape or an angel? I, my lord, I am on the side of the angels.
Speech to the Oxford Diocese
(November 25, 1864)

Many thanks for your book; I shall lose no time in reading it.
In Wilfred Meynell, *The Man Disraeli*
(1927)

[When asked the difference between a calamity and a misfortune, he replied:] If Gladstone fell into the Thames, that would be a misfortune, and if anybody pulled him out that, I suppose, would be a calamity.
In Leon A. Harris, *The Fine Art of
Political Wit* (1966), ch. 4

There are three kinds of lies: lies, damned lies and statistics.
Attributed, in Mark Twain, *Autobiography*
(1924), vol. 1

I have never been in [a distant land] without finding a Scotchman, and I never found a Scotchman who was not at the head of the poll.
In Arthur Herman, *How the Scots Invented
the Modern World* (2001)

I never deny; I never contradict; I sometimes forget.
[His relationship with Queen Victoria.]
In L. R. Frank, *Wit and Humor
Quotationary* (2000)

[Gladstone said, "Mr. Disraeli, you will probably die by the hangman's noose or a vile disease."] Sir, that depends upon whether I embrace your principles or your mistress.
Ibid.

Gladstone made his conscience not his guide but his accomplice.
Ibid.

She is an excellent creature, but she can never remember who came first, the Greeks or the Romans.

Next to knowing when to seize an opportunity, the next important thing in life is to know when to forgo an advantage.

Plagiarists, at least, have the merit of preservation.

The only thing that has driven more men mad than love is the currency question.

[Of Daniel O'Connell:] He has committed every crime that does not require courage.

As a general rule the most successful man in life is the man who has the best information.

If the English hear that Palmerston still has a mistress at eighty, they will make him a dictator!

A man who is not a Liberal at sixteen has no heart; a man who is not a Conservative at sixty has no head.

Mr. Gladstone has not a single redeeming defect. He is honest in the most odious sense of the word.

Mr. Gladstone is a sophistical rhetorician inebriated with the exuberance of his own verbosity.

NATHANIEL HAWTHORNE
1804–64

American, novelist, and short story writer: *Twice-Told Tales* (1842). In *The Scarlet Letter* (1850), Hester Prynne must wear a scarlet *A* for her adultery, but she refuses to name her lover, Arthur Dimmesdale, the minister who denounces her sin. The real villain is Hester's elderly husband, Roger Chillingworth, who torments Arthur until he dies on the pillory confessing his sin—his open shirt reveals a scarlet *A* imprinted on the flesh of his chest.

In *The House of Seven Gables* (1851), a Gothic romance, Judge Pyncheon convicts Matthew Maule of witchcraft in order to steal his land, and Maule curses him. The judge dies horribly after building a house

with seven gables. The curse continues for generations, which is Hawthorne's theme that the sins of the fathers are visited on future generations.

> Preach! Write! Act! Do anything save to lie down and die.
>
> *The Scarlet Letter* (1850)

> Let men tremble to win the hand of a woman, less they win along with it the utmost passion of her heart.
>
> Ibid., ch. 15

> Life is made up of marble and mud.
>
> *The House of Seven Gables* (1851), ch. 2

AMANDINE LUCILE DUPIN (GEORGE SAND)
1804–1876

French, novelist and Chopin's lover.

> I would rather believe that God did not exist than believe that He was indifferent.
>
> *Impressions et Souvenirs* (1896)

> As things are, they [women] are ill-used. They are forced to live a life of imbecility, and are blamed for doing so. If they are ignorant, they are despised, if learned, mocked. In love they are reduced to the status of courtesans. As wives they are treated more as servants than as companions.
>
> "La Fauvette du Docteur," *Almanach du Mois* (November 1844)

HANS CHRISTIAN ANDERSEN
1805–75

Dane, author of 160 fairy tales, such as "The Ugly Duckling." This unhappy, ugly man, like Aesop with his animal fables, has delighted generations of young and old by illuminating the universal morals of humanity in captivating stories.

"But the Emperor has nothing on at all," cried a little child.
> "The Emperor's New Clothes," *Danish Fairy Legends and Tales* (1846)

She was delicate and fair as moonlight.

WILLIAM LLOYD GARRISON
1805–79

American, antislavery publicist, whose weekly *The Liberator* operated on a shoe-string promoting abolition for thirty-five years. He joined the Colonization Society, which sought to return blacks to Africa.

I will be as harsh as truth and as uncom-promising as justice. On this subject I do not wish to think or speak, or write, with moderation. I am in earnest. I will not equivocate; I will not excuse; I will not retreat a single inch; and I will be heard.
> *The Liberator*, motto (1831), vol. I, no. 1

No! No! Tell a man whose house is on fire to give a moderate alarm; tell him to moderately rescue his wife from the hands of the ravisher...but urge me not to use moderation.
> Ibid.

The compact which exists between the North and the South is a covenant with death and an agreement with hell.
> *Resolution adopted by the Anti-Slavery Society* (January 27, 1843)

ALEXIS DE TOCQUEVILLE
1805–59

French, political scientist. He wrote *Democracy in America, Volume I* (1835) when twenty-eight years old after traveling nine months in the U.S., and *Volume II* in 1840. Many believe this is the best book on America and on democracy. He explored why America's Revolution had succeeded while France's had failed. He concluded in *Volume I*:

Among the new objects that attracted my attention during my stay in the United States, none struck my eye more vividly than the equality of conditions [equality of opportunity]. I discovered without difficulty the enormous influence that this primary fact exerts on the course of society; it gives a certain direction to public spirit, a certain turn to the laws...and modifies everything its does not produce.... We do not find [in the United States], as among an aristocratic people, one class that keeps quiet because it is well off; and another that does not venture to stir because it despairs of improving its condition.

Tocqueville argued "American Exceptionalism" had been created by: 1) "equality of conditions" and 2) Christianity. Equality of opportunity enables all citizens to contribute their talents, which is absent in states with privileged citizens. Christianity is a double bulwark against an oppressive state by imposing a duty to obey just laws and by endowing man with natural rights that supersede state power.

In *A History of the American People* (1997), Paul Johnson supports Tocqueville by opining that the Christian revival, the

Great Awakening in the eighteenth century, sounded the death knell of British colonialism and the Second Great Awakening in the nineteenth century sounded the death knell of slavery.

Not until I went into the churches of America and heard her pulpits flame with righteousness, did I understand the secret of her genius and power. America is great because America is good…and if America ever ceases to be good …America will cease to be great.

Democracy in America (1835)

Society can exist only when a great number of men…hold the same opinions upon many subjects, and when the same occurrences suggest the same thoughts in their minds.

Ibid.

…I have nowhere seen a woman occupying a loftier position [than in America]; and if I were asked…to what the singular prosperity and growing strength of that people ought mainly to be attributed, I should reply: to the superiority of their women.

Ibid.

America is a land of wonders, in which everything is in constant motion and every change seems an improvement. The idea of novelty is there indissolubly connected with the idea of amelioration.

Ibid., ch. 18

In the United States religion…directs the manners of the community, and by regulating domestic life, it regulates the state.

Ibid., pt. 2, ch. 7

I know of nothing more opposite to revolutionary attitudes than commercial ones.

Ibid., pt. 3, ch. 21

There are at the present time two great nations in the world—the Russians and the Americans. The American relies upon his personal interest to accomplish his ends…. The Russian centers all his authority of society in a single arm.

Ibid., vol. 2. (1840), pt. 1, ch. 1

One of the happiest consequences of the absence of government…is the development of individual strength that inevitably follows.

De Tocqueville, *Oeuvres Complètes* (1981), vol.18, V, I, 89

Everyone takes it for granted that education will be moral and religious. There would be a general outcry, a kind of popular uprising, against anyone who tried to introduce a contrary system, and everyone would say it would be better to have no education at all than an education of that sort. It is from the *Bible* that all the children learn to read.

Ibid., p. 85

The man who asks of freedom anything other than itself is born to be a slave.

L'Ancien Régime et La Révolution, J. P. Mayer, ed. (1856)

The president, who exercises a limited power, may err without causing great mischief…. Congress may decide amiss without destroying the union…. But if the Supreme Court is ever composed of imprudent or bad men, the union may be plunged into anarchy or civil war.

ELIZABETH B. BROWNING
1806–61

English, poet, and wife of Robert Browning. Her forty-four sonnets tell of her withdrawal from society and how her love for Robert brought her back. They made her more famous than Robert.

> How do I love thee? Let me count the
> ways.
> I love thee to the depth and breadth and
> height
> My soul can reach, when feeling out of
> sight
> For the ends of being and ideal grace.
> I love thee to the level of everyday's
> Most quiet need, by sun and
> candle-light.
> I love thee freely, as men strive for Right;
> I love thee purely, as they turn from
> Praise.
> I love thee with the passion put to use
> In my old griefs, and with my child-
> hood's faith
> I love thee with the love I seemed to lose
> With my lost Saints,—I love thee with
> the breath
> Smiles, tears, of all my life!—and, if
> God choose,
> I shall but love thee better after death.
>> *Sonnets from the Portuguese* (1850), no. 21

JEFFERSON DAVIS
1806–1889

American, president of the Confederate States of America. He doomed the Confederacy by violating "unity of command" (geographic army departments) and by appointing an incompetent commander in the west, Braxton Bragg.

All we ask is to be let alone.
>> Inaugural Address to the First
>> Confederate Congress (February 18, 1861)

[Jefferson Davis's fiancée wrote:]
"Would you believe it, he is refined and cultivated, and yet he is a Democrat!"
[Gentlemen were Whigs.]
>> *Jefferson Davis: A Memoir by his Wife*, vol. 1

JOHN STUART MILL
1806–73

Scottish, utilitarian political-economist, who rejected natural rights defenses of liberty. He defended liberty on the grounds that it led to the greatest good for the greatest number. In *On Liberty* (1859), Mill pleaded for freedom of speech on three practical grounds: suppression of "false opinion" involves an assumption of infallibility; even if the opinion is false, it might bring new understanding; and even if the opinion is wholly true, people will doubt it unless it is challenged.

Mill understood that a utilitarian doctrine would foster tyranny unless there were guarantees for liberty. He allowed the individual to do as he wished, unless it "would bring harm to another." Mill called the Conservative Party "the stupider party" because he never understood that the wisdom of the species gained through trial and error is more likely to be true than rational speculation.

In the first edition of his *Principles of Political Economy*, Mill criticizes socialism/communism for being economically infeasible; a year later in the revised second edition, he is neutral to those ideologies; and in the third edition, he elaborates a socialist vision of society of high taxes, extensive welfare programs, and confiscation of all property on death. Under Mill, where one would have only a life estate interest in property earned and saved, the state would supplant the family.

> If all mankind minus one, were of one opinion, and only one person were of the contrary opinion, mankind would be no more justified in silencing that one person, than he, if he had the power, would be justified in silencing mankind.
>
> *On Liberty* (1859)

> He who knows only his own side of the case, knows little of that.
>
> Ibid.

> A people may prefer a free government, but if from indolence, or carelessness, or cowardice, or want of public spirit, they are unequal to the exertions necessary for preserving it…they are more or less unfit for liberty; and…they are unlikely long to enjoy it.

GIUSEPPE GARIBALDI
1807–82

Italian, revolutionary hero of the Risorgimento. A republican, his forces supported King Victor Emmanuel of Italy against the Austrians and French. His one thousand "red shirts" conquered Sicily and Naples, which he turned over to King Emmanuel.

> I offer neither pay, nor quarters, nor provisions; I offer hunger, thirst, forced marches, battles and death.
>
> George M. Trevelyan, *Garibaldi's Defense of the Roman Republic*

ROBERT E. LEE
1807–70

American, general (Confederate Army of Northern Virginia), "the gray fox." Lee, known at West Point as the "marble model," was his class's first captain, and he stood second academically. He is the only cadet ever to be graduated from an American military service academy without receiving a demerit. Churchill viewed Lee as "one of the noblest Americans who ever lived and one of the greatest captains known to the annals of war." Theodore Roosevelt honored him as "the very greatest of all the great captains the English-speaking peoples have brought forth."

One pillar of Lee's Christian philosophy was self-discipline, believing no one could lead who was not master of himself. As Lee said, "I cannot consent to place in the control of others one who cannot control himself." Advising a mother on how to instruct her infant son, Lee said, "Teach him he must deny himself." The second pillar was humility, because a leader must subordinate himself to his cause to inspire others to do so. This was Jim Collins's big discovery in *Good to Great* (2001) about what makes a great executive. The third pillar was total realism—the courage to face the bleakest truth and deal with it. The fourth pillar was to lead by example, not by force. Lee said, "As a general principle you should not force young men to do their duty, but let them do it voluntarily and thereby develop their characters." Further, Lee said, "Young men must not expect to escape contact with evil, but must learn not to be contaminated by it. That virtue is worth but little that requires constant watching and removal from temptation."

You must study to be frank with the world: frankness is the child of honesty and courage. Say just what you mean to do on every occasion, and take it for granted that you mean to do right. If a friend ask a favour, you should grant it, if reasonable; if not, tell him plainly why you cannot: you will wrong him and yourself by equivocation of any kind. Never do a wrong thing to make a friend or keep one.... Above all, do not appear to others what you are not. If you have any fault to find with any one, tell him, not others, of what you complain; there is no more dangerous experiment than that of undertaking to be one thing before a man's face and another behind his back. We should live so as to say and do nothing to the injury of any one. It is not only best as a matter of principle, but it is the path to peace and honour.... Duty, then, is the sublimest word in our language. Do your duty in all things.... You cannot do more, you should never wish to do less.

Letter to his son at West Point. In H. W. Crocker III, *Robert E. Lee on Leadership* (1999)

I am opposed to the theory of doing wrong that good may come of it. I hold to the belief that you must act right whatever the consequences.

Ibid., letter to his son Custis

In this enlightened age there are few, I believe, but that will acknowledge that slavery as an institution is a moral and political evil in any country.... I think it, however, a greater evil to the white than to the black race....

[Lee freed the slaves he inherited from his father-in-law as soon as possible and, like Benjamin Franklin,

he freed the only slave he had while a young officer.]

Letter to Mrs. Lee (December 6, 1856), in L. R. Frank, *Quotationary* (1998)

It is well that war is so terrible or we would grow too fond of it.

[After 9,000 Yankees had perished in assaults on Marye's Heights at Fredericksburg]

Letter to James Longstreet (December 13, 1862)

After four years of arduous service marked by unsurpassed courage and fortitude, the Army of Northern Virginia has been compelled to yield to overwhelming numbers and resources....You may take with you the satisfaction that proceeds from the consciousness of duty faithfully performed....

Robert E. Lee's Farewell to His Army (April 10, 1865), his General Orders No. 9

After the fall of Richmond, Jefferson Davis urged Lee to fight a guerrilla war. Lee chose instead to go to Appomattox, saying, "There is nothing left for me to do but to go and see General Grant, and I would rather die a thousand deaths....[but] it is our duty to live." He later said, "I surrendered as much to Lincoln's goodness as I did to Grant's armies." After Appomattox he urged his men to "be as good citizens in peace as you have been good soldiers in war." To bind up the wounds, he later told the South, "Abandon your animosities and make your sons Americans."

After the Civil War, Lee refused a huge advance for his memoirs, saying, "I should be trading on the blood of my men." He also turned down a $50,000 job in order to become president of Washington College, which paid $1,500, saying, "I have led the young men of the South in battle, I must teach their sons to discharge their duty in life."

> [Lee refused $10,000 to lend his name as titular head of an insurance company, saying:]
> Excuse me, sir; I cannot consent to receive pay for services I do not render.
> In L. R. Frank, *Quotationary* (1999)

We have but one rule here and it is that every student must be a gentleman.
> [As President of Washington College responding to a request for the rules.]
> Ibid.

Children should be governed by love, not fear.

A gentleman is a man who never makes anyone feel inferior.
> [After the war, when a black man went up to kneel at the communion rail of St. Paul's Episcopal Church in Richmond, the congregation froze until Lee walked up from a back pew to kneel beside him.]

Lee knew that the North had overwhelming numbers and no foreign power would aid the South, so the only hope was that the North would tire of war, as the British had tired of the American Revolution. Thus he adopted a strategy of inflicting more casualties than he suffered, but this attrited his small army. His strategy might have won if Nathan B. Forrest had commanded the West, not the incompetent Braxton Bragg.

> One thing they had in common—a belief in Southern rights. That one of those

rights involved the dark institutions of chattel slavery is not pertinent because few of them owned slaves or hoped to own them. That tariff and free trade entered into it is not pertinent, either. These were pastorals, and their economics were bounded by their fields and wood lots.... They were terrible in battle. They were generous in victory. They rose up from defeat to fight again, and while they lived they were formidable. There were not enough of them. That is all.
> Marine officer John W. Thomason Jr. on the devotion of Lee's "hard-dying" troops

Strike the tent.
> Last words

Sewanee Military Academy required all juniors to write a twenty-page paper on Robert E. Lee. America's high schools should follow that example, that is, build the character of students while improving their writing skills.

Henry Wadsworth Longfellow
1807–82

American, the world's most popular poet of his era, and the first American in Westminster Abbey's Poets' Corner. The academy rejected him for being a "fireside poet," one who writes beautifully and is enjoyable to read. Today's split between academic and popular audiences is gargantuan.

The lowest ebb is the turn of the tide.

Music is the universal language of mankind.
> *Outre Mer* (1835)

Life is real! Life is earnest!
And the grave is not its goal;
Dust thou art, to dust returnest,
Was not spoken of the soul.
"A Psalm of Life," *Voices of the Night*
(1839), st. 2

Lives of great men all remind us
We can make our lives sublime,
And, departing, leave behind us
Footprints on the sands of time.
Ibid., st. 7

Under a spreading chestnut tree
The village smithy stands;
The smith, a mighty man is he,
With large and sinewy hands;
And the muscles of his brawny arms
Are strong as iron bands.
"The Village Blacksmith" (1842), st. 1

Each morning sees some task begin,
Each evening sees it close;
Something attempted, something done,
Has earned a night's repose.
Ibid., st. 7

And the night shall be filled with music
And the cares that infest the day
Should fold their tents, like the Arabs,
And silently, steal away.
"The Day Is Done" (1844)

I shot an arrow into the air,
It fell to earth, I knew not where;
For, so swiftly it flew, the sight
Could not follow it in its flight.
"The Arrow and the Song" (1845), st. 1

I breathed a song into the air,
It fell to earth, I knew not where;
For who has sight so keen and strong,
That it can follow the flight of song?
Ibid., st. 2

Long, long afterward, in an oak
I found the arrow, still unbroke;
And the song, from beginning to end,
I found again in the heart of a friend.
Ibid., st. 3

Thou, too, sail on O Ship of State!
Sail on, O Union, strong and great!
Humanity with all its fears,
With all the hopes of future years,
Is hanging breathless on thy fate!
"The Building of the Ship" (1849), l. 378

There was a little girl
Who had a little curl
Right in the middle of her forehead,
When she was good
She was very, very good,
But when she was bad she was horrid.

By the shores of Gitche Gumee,
By the shining Big-Sea-Water,
Stood the wigwam of Nokomis,
Daughter of the Moon, Nokomis.
"The Song of Hiawatha' (1855), pt. III

As unto the bow the cord is,
So unto the man is woman,
Though she bends him, she obeys him,
Though she draws him, yet she follows,
Useless each without the other.
Ibid., pt. X

If I am not worth the wooing,
I surely am not worth the winning.
"The Courtship of Miles Standish" (1858),
pt. 3

Listen, my children, and you shall hear,
Of the midnight ride of Paul Revere,
On the eighteenth of April, in Seventy-five
Hardly a man is now alive
Who remembers that famous day and
year.

[This celebrates the ride from Boston to Lexington to alert the militia of the approach of the British, after the signal from the Old North Church bell tower.]
"Paul Revere's Ride," *Tales of the Wayside Inn*, (1863–1874), st. 1

One if by land, and two if by sea;
                    Ibid., st. 2 (partial)

Ships that pass in the night, and speak
    to each other in passing;
Only a signal shown and a distant voice
    in the darkness;
So on the ocean of life we pass and
    speak to one another,
Only a look and a voice; then darkness
    again and a silence.
            Ibid., "The Theologian's Tale"

Let him not boast who puts his armor on
As he who puts it off, the battle done.
        "Morituri Salutamus" (1875), st. 9

Not in the clamor of the crowded street,
Not in the shouts and plaudits of the
    throng,
But in ourselves, are triumph and defeat.
        "The Poets," *A Book of Sonnets* (1876)

"It is too late!" Ah, nothing is too late--
Cato learned Greek at eighty; Sophocles
Wrote his grand "Oedipus," and
    Simonides
Bore off the prize of verse from his
    compeers
When each had numbered more than
    fourscore years….
Chaucer, at Woodstock, with his
    nightingales,
At sixty wrote the "Canterbury Tales."
Goethe, at Weimar, toiling to the last,

Completed "Faust" when eighty years
    were past.
What then? Shall we sit idly down and
    say,
"The night has come; it is no longer
    day"?
For age is opportunity no less
Than youth itself, though in another
    dress.
And as the evening twilight fades away,
The sky is filled with stars, invisible by
    day.
It is never too late to start doing what
    is right.
Never.
                    "Never Too Late"

All things must change
To something new, to something strange.

Most people would succeed in small
things if they were not troubled by great
ambitions.

JOHN GREENLEAF WHITTIER
1807–92

American, poet, Quaker, and abolitionist
editor.

For of all sad words of tongue or pen,
The saddest are these: "It might have
    been!"
God pity them both! And pity us all,
Who vainly the dream of youth recall.
    [Poem of the incipient love of young
    people who never come together
    because of their social stations. Both
    regret throughout their lives that
    they went separate ways.]
            "Maud Muller" (1856), st. 53

Up rose old Barbara Frietchie then,
Bowed with her fourscore years and ten;
    "Barbara Frietchie" (1864), st. 9

She leaned far out on the window-sill,
And shook it forth with a royal will.
                Ibid., st. 17

"Shoot, if you must, this old gray head,
But spare your country's flag," she said.
    [Stonewall Jackson ordered his men
    not to harm Barbara Frietchie, a
    ninety-five-year-old lady who waived
    a Union flag out of her window while
    Confederate troops marched through
    Frederick, Maryland.]
                Ibid., st. 18

CHARLES R. DARWIN
1809–82

English, naturalist, whose *Origin of Species* (1859) ranks with the works of Galileo, Newton, Adam Smith, and Marx as the most consequential books since the Bible and Koran.

The notion that all species evolved through a struggle for existence dates back to Anaxagoras in 500 B.C. and Empedocles in 495 B.C. Darwin set out to prove that old notion by gathering data on a voyage on the HMS *Beagle* (1831–36) to the Galápagos Islands. He concluded that plants and animals change for unknown reasons, and the new forms survive if they adapt to their environments better than the older ones. Science later discovered random DNA mutations cause genetic variations.

Charles Lyell and Thomas Malthus inspired Darwin's theory of evolution by natural selection. Lyell's *Principles of Geology* (1830) argued that the earth was formed billions of years earlier, which gave time for evolution; not on October 26, 4004 B.C., per Archbishop Usher's extrapolation in 1650 of the Bible's Begats. Malthus's "Essay on the Principle of Population" (1798) argued that competition among men for food resulted in the survival of only the strong, leading to Darwin's formulation of "natural selection."

Darwin, a militant atheist self-styled the "devil's chaplain," asserted the world was run by the laws of physics, chemistry, and biology, not by God. His theory of evolution explained design in the universe without a Creator. Note, many theologians argue that evolution is consistent with the Bible, albeit not with its literal interpretation.

There is a downside to Darwin's theory. In the *Descent of Man* (1871) he wrote, "the various races...differ much from each other....At some future period, the civilized races of man will almost certainly exterminate and replace the savage races throughout the world." He also argued that it was injurious to civilization to care for and keep alive "the imbecile, the maimed, and the sick." It is arguable that Darwin's theory caused the twentieth century's world wars, the murder of hundreds of millions by Communists and Nazis, and the abortion of hundreds of millions of babies. Karl Marx said of *Origin of Species*, "This is the book which contains the basis in natural history for our views." Hitler's racial philosophy was 100 percent grounded in natural selection, as was the Kaiser's and that of the eugenics movement. For details, see Ann Coulter's *Godless* (2006).

The theory of evolution by natural selection has been attacked on scientific grounds. For example, Darwin's *Origin of Species* fingered one of its weaknesses:

If it could be demonstrated that any complex organ existed which could not possibly have been formed by numerous, successive, slight modifications, my theory would absolutely break down.

Professor of biochemistry Michael J. Behe in *Darwin's Black Box* (1996) argues that there are "irreducibly complex" biological systems in which every part would have to appear simultaneously for the system to function; they could not arise by "successive, slight modifications." Indeed, the atheist astrophysicist Sir Fred Hoyle said the chance of the enzymes basic to life arising randomly were 1 to 1 followed by 40,000 zeros! Hoyle concluded that a "common sense interpretation of the facts" is that "a superintellect has monkeyed with physics, as well as with chemistry and biology…"

Gregor Mendel (1822–84) discovered the principles of genetics by crossbreeding sweet peas. Crossing tall and short plants does not produce an average size. Genes from one plant will dominate in the first generation and will not be blended with genes from the other plant. In later generations, dominant and recessive genes will appear in the ratio of 3:1. His "segregation law" holds that traits inherited of parents are mixed but remain separate, one dominant and one recessive in each offspring.

Darwin and Mendel jointly built the foundation for the life sciences without being aware of each other. Darwin saw that all living things "trace their ancestry to a single, common source," and Mendel explained the mechanism for this. However, Darwin's theory did not gain wide acceptance until the 1920s after scientists actually accepted the theory that the earth was billions of years old.

Jean B. Lamarck (d. 1829) expounded a theory of evolution whereby organisms pass to offspring characteristics developed during their lives: the "inheritance of acquired characteristics." Soviet agronomist Trofim D. Lysenko (d. 1976), adopted Lamarck's genetic theory, which was congenial with Communism that education could create a "new Soviet man." When Lysenko's seeds failed to produce, Lysenko's theory was not questioned—the farmers were shot for sabotage.

I have called this principle, by which each slight variation, if useful, is preserved, by the term of Natural Selection.
On the Origin of Species (1859), ch. 3

From the war of nature, from famine and death, the most exalted object which we are capable of conceiving, namely the production of the higher animals, directly follows….from so simple a beginning endless forms most beautiful and most wonderful have been and are being evolved.
Ibid., ch. 15

Man is descended from a hairy-tailed quadruped, probably arboreal in his habits.
The Decent of Man and Selection in Relation to Sex, 2nd ed. (1874)

At some future period, the civilized races of man will almost certainly exterminate and replace the savage races throughout the world.
Ibid.

The *Old Testament*, from its manifestly false history of the earth, and from its attributing to God the feelings of a revengeful tyrant, was no more to be trusted than the sacred books of the Hindoos, or the beliefs of any barbarian.

Man is more courageous, pugnacious and energetic than woman, and has a more inventive genius.

[When the wife of the Bishop of Worcester heard that Darwin claimed that man descended from monkeys, she said,] "My dear, let us hope it isn't true! But if it is, let us pray it doesn't become widely known!"

EDWARD FITZGERALD
1809–83

English, poet, who creatively translated 101 of the 1,200 quatrains of the *Rubáiyát of Omar Khayyám* (d. A.D. 1123), a Persian mathematician, astronomer, poet, and hedonist. Rubáiyát means a quatrain rhyming: aaba.

And, as the cock crew, those who stood
    before
The Tavern shouted—"Open then the
    Door!
You know how little while we have to
    stay,
And, once departed, may return no more."
                 Ibid., st. 3

Come fill the Cup, and in the fire of
    Spring
Your winter-garment of Repentance
    fling;
The Bird of Time has but a little way
To flutter, and lo the Bird is on the
    Wing.
                 Ibid., st. 7

A book of Verses—underneath the
    Bough
A Jug of Wine, A Load of Bread—and
    Thou
Beside me singing in the Wilderness-
Oh, Wilderness were Paradise enow!
    [enough]
                Ibid., st. 12

For some we loved, the loveliest and the
    best
That from his Vintage rolling Time
    hath press.
Have drunk their Cup a Round or two
    before
And one by one crept silently to rest.
                Ibid., st. 22

Myself when young did eagerly
    frequent
Doctor and Saint, and heard great
    argument
About it and about: but evermore
Came out by the same door where in I
    went.
                Ibid., st. 27

O threats of Hell and Hopes of
    Paradise!
One thing at least is certain—This Life
    flies;
One thing is certain and the rest is Lies;
The Flower that once has blown for
    ever dies.
                Ibid., st. 63

The Moving Finger writes; and, having
    writ,
Moves on: nor all your Piety nor Wit
Shall lure it back to cancel half a Line,
Nor all your Tears wash out a Word
    of it.
                Ibid., st. 71

In the *Book of Daniel*, the king of Babylon, Belshazzar, son of Nebuchadnezzar who raided the Temple and took the Israelites into captivity, had a banquet. A human finger began to write on the wall letters of an unknown language. Daniel was brought in to interpret it. He said, "God has numbered the days of your reign and brought it to an end. You have been weighed on the scales and been found wanting." That night Persia invaded Babylon.

> I wonder often what the vintners buy
> One half so precious as the stuff they
> sell.
> > *Ibid.*, st. 95

> And when like her, O Saki, you shall pass
> Among the Guests Star-scatter'd on the
> Grass,
> And in your joyous errand reach the spot
> Where I made One, turn down an
> empty Glass.
> > *Ibid.*, st. 101

WILLIAM GLADSTONE
1809–98

Scottish, free trader, Liberal Party prime minister, 1868–1874, 1880–1885, 1886, and 1892–1894. He cut tariffs 95 percent, cut the income tax from 10 percent to 1.25 percent, opposed imperialism, sought home rule for Ireland, and favored free trade. His rival, the imperialist and protectionist Tory, Disraeli, degraded property rights to placate labor unions. Gladstone's foreign policy principles were: promote peace, avoid alliances, treat nations equally, and that "the foreign policy of England should always be inspired by the love of freedom…."

Gladstone knew Britain's power was based not on colonies, but on liberty, which had caused her to lead the world in industrial development. Colonies were financial rat holes. In the 1950s, Britain had to cut off the millstones of her colonies to survive.

> All the world over, I will back the masses against the classes.
> > Speech, Liverpool (June 28, 1886)

> He is a wise man who wastes no energy on pursuits for which he is not fitted; and he is still wiser who, from among the things that he can do well, chooses and resolutely follows the best.

> [Henry Labourchere said of Gladstone:] I don't object to the old man keeping a card up his sleeve, but I do object to his asserting that God put it there.

Gladstone declined to buy a painting of a seventeenth century aristocrat because it was too expensive. Later, he saw the painting in the house of a host, who claimed it to be his ancestor. Gladstone murmured, "Three pounds less and he would have been my ancestor."

> A radical is a liberal in earnest.

NIKOLAI GOGOL
1809–52

Russian, novelist of Russian realism. Gogol's melancholy focus on the lives of ordinary people changed Russian literature. After reading Gogol, Pushkin said, "Goodness, how sad is our Russia."

Gogol's *Dead Souls* (1842) has the swindler Chichikov buying serfs who have died since the last census, which lets landown-ers avoid paying taxes on them until the next census and lets Chichikov mortgage the serfs to speculate in land.

In *The Overcoat* (1842), a poor clerk, Akaky, is told by a tailor that his overcoat is too threadbare to be patched. Akaky scrimps to buy a new overcoat. It is stolen and his desperate appeals to the authori-ties to help him are ignored. Akaky dies. Soon, a phantom steals the overcoats of bureaucrats. This was the first Russian work to deal with downtrodden folk, lead-ing Dostoevsky to write, "We all came from beneath Gogol's *Overcoat*."

OLIVER WENDELL HOLMES
1809–94

American, physician, whose *Atlantic Monthly* essays were collected in *The Auto-crat of the Breakfast Table* (1858) and *The Professor at the Breakfast Table* (1859). A Victorian Brahmin, he excoriated egali-tarianism and materialism. A tolerant con-servative, he allowed time for progress to uplift the workingman. His "Old Iron-sides" (1830) saved from dismantling the forty-four-gun frigate *Constitution*, which had won thirty-two engagements.

Thou say'st an undisputed thing
In such a solemn way.
"To an Insect" st. 7

Old Time is a liar! We're twenty tonight!
"The Boys" st. 1

We are all tattooed in our cradles with the beliefs of our tribe...
The Poet at the Breakfast Table (1852)

Give us the luxuries of life, and we will dispense with its necessaries.
The Autocrat of the Breakfast Table (1858)

The world's great men have not com-monly been great scholars, nor its great scholars great men.
Ibid.

The axis of the earth sticks out visibly through the center of each and every town or city.
Ibid.

To reach the port of heaven, we must sail sometimes with the wind and some-times against it—but we must sail and not drift, nor lie at anchor.
Ibid.

Build thee more stately mansions, O my
soul,
As the swift seasons roll! Leave thy
low-vaulted past!
Let each new temple, nobler than the last
Shut thee from heaven with a dome
more vast,
Till thou at length art free,
Leaving thine outgrown shell by life's
unresting sea.
Ibid., "The Chambered Nautilus"

Have you heard of the wonderful one-hoss shay
That was built in such a logical way
It ran a hundred years to a day?
[Every part disintegrated on the same day.]
Ibid., "The Deacon's Masterpiece"

Rough work iconoclasm, but the only way to get at truth.
The Professor at the Breakfast Table (1859)

Alas for those that never sing,
But die with all their music in them!
"The Voiceless"

I firmly believe that if the whole *materia medica* could be sunk to the bottom of the sea, it would be all the better for mankind and all the worse for the fishes.
> In George Will, *With a Happy Eye* (2002) [Will said that it was not until about 1910 that doctors did more good than harm.]

The young man knows the rules, but the old man knows the exceptions.

Many ideas grow better when transplanted into another mind than in the one where they sprung up. That which was a weed in one becomes a flower in the other....

ABRAHAM LINCOLN
1809–65

American, sixteenth president (1861–65). Like George Washington and John Marshall, Lincoln was born poor, tall, had only one year of formal education, and first worked as a surveyor. He was elected president with the smallest percentage of the popular vote: 39.9 percent. His greatest decisions were hiring Jay Cooke to sell war bonds to the public and Ulysses S. Grant to command the army.

Business failed	'31
Defeated for legislature	'32
Business failed	'34
Nervous breakdown	'36
Defeated for legislature	'38
Defeated for Congress	'44
Defeated for Congress	'46
Defeated for Congress	'48
Defeated for Senate nomination	'55
Defeated for vice president	'56
Defeated for Senate	'58
Elected president	'60

Good boys who to their books apply
Will all be great men by and by.
> In L. R. Frank, *Quotationary* (1999)

You must remember that some things that are legally right are not morally right.
> [In refusing to take a $500 case against a widow with six children.]
Ibid.

If you would win a man to your cause, first convince him that you are his sincere friend.
> Speech to Washington Temperance Society (February 22, 1842)

I hate [slavery] because it deprives the republican example of its just influence in the world—enables the enemies of free institutions, with plausibility, to taunt us as hypocrites—causes the real friends of freedom to doubt our sincerity.
> Speech, Peoria, Ill. (October 16, 1854)

Always bear in mind that your own resolution to succeed is more important than any other one thing.
> Letter to Isham Reavis (November 5, 1855), in L. R. Frank, *Quotationary* (1999)

"A house divided against itself cannot stand," I believe this government cannot endure permanently half slave and half free.
> Republican State Convention (June 16, 1858)

All I ask for the Negro is that if you do not like him, let him alone. If God gave him but little, that little let him enjoy.

Speech (July 17, 1858)

I am not, nor ever have been, in favor of bringing about in any way the social and political equality of the white and black races—I am not, nor ever have been, in favor of making voters or jurors of Negroes,—nor of qualifying them to hold office, nor to intermarry with white people.

[Lincoln advocated the colonization of former slaves in Africa to spare the United States what he called "the troublesome presence of the free Negroes."]

First Debate (August 21, 1858)

Public sentiment is everything. With public sentiment, nothing can fail. Without it, nothing can succeed. Consequently, he who molds public sentiment goes deeper than he who enacts statutes or pronounces decisions.

Speech, Columbus, Ohio (September 16, 1859)

It is said an Eastern monarch once charged his wise men to invent him a sentence which should be true and appropriate in all times and situations. They presented him the words: "And this, too, shall pass away."

Address, Wisconsin State Agricultural Society (September 30, 1859)

We are not enemies, but friends. We must not be enemies. Though passion may have strained, it must not break our bonds of affection. The mystic chords of memory, stretching from every battlefield and patriot grave to every living heart and hearth-stone all over this broad land, will yet swell the chorus of the Union when again touched, as surely they will be, by the better angels of our nature.

First Inaugural Address (March 4, 1861)

It is difficult to make a man miserable while he feels he is worthy of himself and claims kindred to the great God who made him.

Speech on "Colonization to a Committee of Colored Men" (August 14, 1862)

My paramount object in this struggle is to save the Union, and is not either to save or to destroy slavery. If I could save the Union without freeing any slave, I would do it; and if I could save it by freeing some and leaving others alone, I would also do that. What I do about slavery and the colored race, I do because I believe it helps to save the Union...

Letter to Horace Greeley (August 30, 1862)

The dogmas of the quiet past are inadequate to the stormy present. The occasion is piled high with difficulty, and we must rise with the occasion. As our case is new, so we must think anew, and act anew.

Message to Congress (December 1, 1862)

Fourscore and seven years ago our fathers brought forth upon this continent a new nation, conceived in liberty and dedicated to the proposition that all men are created equal.

Now we are engaged in a great civil war, testing whether that nation or any nation so conceived and so dedicated can long endure. We are met on a great battlefield of that war. We have come to dedicate a portion of that field, as a final resting place for those who here gave their lives that this nation might live. It is altogether fitting and proper that we should do this.

But, in a larger sense, we cannot dedicate—we cannot consecrate—we cannot hallow—this ground. The brave men, living and dead, who struggled here, have consecrated it far above our poor power to add or detract. The world will little note nor long remember what we say here, but it can never forget what they did here. It is for us, the living, rather to be dedicated here to the unfinished work which they who fought here have thus far so nobly advanced. It is rather for us to be here dedicated to the great task remaining before us—that from these honored dead we take increased devotion to that cause for which they gave the last full measure of devotion; that we here highly resolve that the dead shall not have died in vain, that this nation, under God, shall have a new birth of freedom; and that government of the people, by the people, and for the people, shall not perish from the earth.

> [Lincoln's ten sentences are memorialized while the two-hour speech of Edward Everett has long been forgotten.]

Gettysburg Address (November 19, 1863)

The Lord prefers common-looking people, that is why he makes so many of them.

Letter to John Hay (December 23, 1863)

Property is the fruit of labor; property is a positive good in the world. That some should be rich shows that others may become rich, and hence is just encouragement to industry and enterprise. Let not him who is houseless pull down the house of another, but let him labor diligently and build one for himself; thus, by example, assuring that his own shall be safe from violence when built.

To New York Workingmen's Association, in Washington D.C. (March 21, 1864)

I don't believe in a law to prevent a man from getting rich; it would do more harm than good. When one starts poor, as most do in the race of life, free society is such that he knows he can better his condition; he knows there is no fixed condition of labor for his whole life.

> [He called this the True American System.]

It is best not to swap horses when crossing streams.

Speech (June 9, 1864)

With malice toward none; with charity for all; with firmness in the right, as God gives us to see the right, let us strive on to finish the work we are in, to bind up the nation's wounds, to care for him who shall have borne the battle, and for his widow and orphan, to do all which may achieve and cherish a just and lasting peace among ourselves and with all nations.

Second Inaugural Address (March 4, 1865)

Important principles may and must be inflexible.

Speech, Washington, D.C., (April 11, 1865)

A governor of a certain state was visiting the state prison, and stopped to talk with a number of prisoners. They told him their story, and in every instance it was one of wrong suffered by an innocent person. There was one man, however, who admitted his crime and the justice of his sentence. "I must pardon you," said the governor: "I can't have you in here corrupting all these good men." [Story told by Lincoln.]

In L. R. Frank, *Quotationary* (1999)

So you're the little woman who wrote the book that made this great war!

[On meeting Harriet Beecher Stowe.]

He reminds me of the man who murdered both his parents, and then when sentence was about to be pronounced, pleaded for mercy on the grounds that he was an orphan.

My dear McClelland: If you don't want to use the Army, I should like to borrow it for a while.

If by the mere force of numbers a majority should deprive a minority of any clearly written constitutional right, it might, in a moral point of view, justify revolution—it certainly would if such a right were a vital one.

A lawyer's time and advice is his stock-in-trade.

[Sign in Lincoln's law office.]

All that I am or ever hope to be, I owe to my sainted mother.

I regard no man as poor who has a godly mother.

Let the people know the truth and the country is safe.

You can fool all the people some of the time; you can even fool some of the peo-

ple all the time; but you can't fool all of the people all the time. [Also attributed to Phineas Barnum.]

[Mary Todd Lincoln said of Abraham Lincoln]
He is of no account when he is at home. He never does anything except to warm himself and read. He is the most useless, good-for-nothing man on earth.

Sayings and Anecdotes of Lincoln (1940)

I cannot meddle in your case. I could as easily bail out the Potomac River with a teaspoon as attend to all the details of the army.

[Remark to soldier with a petty grievance.]

In L. R. Frank, *Wit and Humor Quotationary*

You cannot help men permanently by doing for them what they could and should do for themselves.

You conquer your enemies by making them your friends.

EDGAR ALLAN POE
1809–49

American, poet, who invented the detective story, *The Murders in the Rue Morgue* (1841), the horror story, *The Pit and the Pendulum* (1842), the supernatural story, *The Fall of the House of Usher* (1839), and science fiction, *Heureka* (1848). In *The Purloined Letter* (1845), Poe taught us to hide something in the most obvious place because no one will look there. Poe's work brought him fame, but no money. He died an impoverished young alcoholic, but he may have had a greater impact on European literature than any other American.

From childhood's hour I have not been
As others were—I have not seen
As others saw.
> "Alone" (1829)

Helen, thy beauty is to me
Like those Nicean barks of yore,
That gently, o'er a perfumed sea,
The weary, way-worn wanderer bore
To his own native shore.
> "To Helen" (1831), st. 1

Those who dream by day are cognizant
of many things which escape those who
dream only by night.
> "Eleonora" (1841)

That the play is the tragedy, "Man."
And its hero, the Conqueror Worm.
> "The Conqueror Worm" (1843), st. 5

Thy Naiad airs have brought me home
To the glory that was Greece
And the grandeur that was Rome.
> Ibid., st. 2. (partial)

Once upon a midnight dreary, while I
    pondered, weak and weary,
Over many a quaint and curious volume
    of forgotten lore-
While I nodded, nearly napping, sud-
    denly there came a tapping,
As of some one gently rapping, rapping
    at my chamber door.
"'Tis some visitor," I muttered, "tapping
    at my chamber door-
Only this and nothing more."
> "The Raven" (1845), st. 1

And the Raven, never flitting, still is
    sitting, still is sitting
On the pallid bust of Pallas just above
    my chamber door;
And his eyes have all the seeming of a

demon's that is dreaming
And the lamp-light o'er him streaming
    throws his shadow on the floor;
And my soul from out that shadow that
    lies floating on the floor
Shall be lifted—nevermore!
> Ibid., st. 16

The skies they were ashen and sober;
The leaves they were crisped and sere-
The leaves they were withering and sere:
It was night in the lonesome October
Of my most immemorial year....
It was down by the dank tarn of Auber,
In the ghoul-haunted woodland of Weir.
> "Ulalume" (1847), st. 1

It was many and many a year ago,
In a kingdom by the sea,
That a maiden there lived who you may
    know
By the name of Annabel Lee;-
And this maiden she lived with no other
    thought
Than to love and be loved by me.
> [Poe wrote "Annabel Lee" in mem-
> ory of his wife, Virginia Clemm,
> whom he married when she was
> thirteen. Poe drank himself to death
> two years after Virginia died.]
> "Annabel Lee" (1849), st. 1

I was a child and she was a child,
In this kingdom by the sea;
But we loved with a love that was more
    than love-
I and my Annabel Lee-
With a love that the winged seraphs of
    heaven
Coveted her and me.
> Ibid., st. 2

So that her highborn kinsmen came
And bore her away from me,

To shut her up in a sepulchre
In this kingdom by the sea.
                    Ibid., st. 3. (partial)

Gaily bedight,
A gallant knight,
In sunshine and in shadow,
Had journeyed long,
Singing a song,
In search of Eldorado.
But he grew old-
This knight so bold-
And o'er his heart a shadow
Fell as he found
No spot of ground
That looked like Eldorado.
                    "Eldorado" (1849), st. 1

And, as his strength
Failed him at length,
He met a pilgrim shadow-
"Shadow," said he,
"Where can it be-
This land of Eldorado?"
                    Ibid., st. 2

"Over the Mountains
Of the Moon,
Down the Valley of the Shadow,
Ride, boldly ride,"
The shade replied,-
"If you seek for Eldorado."
                    Ibid., st. 3

I hold that a long poem does not exist.
    [To Poe, long poems were "con-
    nective versifications" surrounding
    small bits of real poetry.]
                    The Poetic Principle (1850)

I would define, in brief, the poetry of
words as the rhythmical creation of
Beauty. Its sole arbiter is taste.
                    Ibid.

My enemies referred my insanity to
the drink rather than the drink to the
insanity.

PIERRE-JOSEPH PROUDHON
1809–65

French, anarchist who believed the state
was as evil as capitalism. Unlike his revolutionary disciple Bakunin, Proudhon
believed government would disappear
peacefully and the abuses of private property would fade away. He inspired trade
unions, which were often opponents of
socialism. Like Mahatma Gandhi, he
favored an economy consisting of craftsmen owning their own tools.

Property is theft.
                    What is Property? (1840), ch. 1

Communism is the exploitation of the
strong by the weak.
                    Ibid.

LORD ALFRED TENNYSON
1809–92

English, poet laureate, Victorian England's
most popular poet, and the favorite Victorian target of modernist intellectuals for
his patriotism.

"Forward, the Light Brigade!"
Was there a man dismayed?
Not though the soldier knew
Some one had blundered:
Theirs not to make reply,
Theirs not to reason why,
Theirs but to do and die:
Into the valley of Death

Rode the six hundred.
　"Charge of the Light Brigade" (1854), st. 2

Cannon to right of them,
Cannon to left of them
Volley'd and thunder'd
Stormed at with shot and shell,
Boldly they rode and well,
Into the jaws of Death,
Into the mouth of Hell
Rode the six hundred.

Ibid., st. 3

In the Battle of Balaklava in 1854, the British Light Brigade charged two miles down a narrow valley with Russian cannon on both sides. Only 198 of the 607 cavalrymen returned. Marshal Bosquet (French), who witnessed the charge, said, "It is magnificent, but it is not war." Lord Raglan's order:

> Lord Raglan wishes the cavalry to advance rapidly to the front and try to prevent the enemy carrying away the guns. Troop of horse artillery may accompany. French cavalry is on your left. Immediate.

This order was ambiguous: There were three different sets of Russian batteries, but Raglan was referring to a battery of British naval guns, which Raglan could see, but which Lord Lucan could not see. Captain Nolan, who delivered the order, was not privy to Lord Raglan's thoughts. But when Lord Lucan asked, "Attack, sir, attack what guns," Nolan pointed into the valley saying, "There, my lord, is your enemy. There are your guns!" When Lord Cardigan, Light Brigade commander, received the order to attack, he thought it madness and protested. When Lucan confirmed the order, Cardigan said, "Here goes the last of the Brudenells." The Light Brigade carried the Russian guns but lacked spikes to spike them. When immediately counterattacked, the brigade rode back under the same cannon fire.

OTHER FACTS

The U.S. Army uses the "five paragraph order" to avoid such disasters. It is the commander's responsibility to communicate so clearly that the order cannot be misinterpreted.

In the spring a young man's fancy
Lightly turns to thoughts of love.
　"Locksley Hall" (1842), l. 20

Knowledge comes, but wisdom lingers.
　Ibid., l. 141

Though much is taken, much abides;
　and though
We are not now that strength which in
　old days
Moved earth and heaven; that which we
　are, we are,
One equal temper of heroic hearts,
Made weak by time and fate, but strong
　in will
To strive, to seek, to find, and not to yield.
　"Ulysses" (1842), ll. 65-70

My strength is the strength of ten,
Because my heart is pure.
　"Sir Galahad" (1842), st. 1

'Tis better to have loved and lost,
Than never to have loved at all.
　"In Memoriam A. H. H." (1850), canto
27, st. 4

But what am I?
An infant crying in the night:
An infant crying for the light:
And with no language but a cry.
                          Ibid., canto 54, st. 5

Are God and Nature then at strife,
That Nature lends such evil dreams?
So careful of the type she seems,
So careless of the single life,
                          Ibid., canto 55, st. 2

Who trusted God was love indeed
And love Creation's final law
Tho' Nature, red in tooth and claw,
With ravine, shriek'd against His creed.
                          Ibid., canto 56, st. 4

God's finger touch'd him, and he slept.
                          Ibid., canto 85, st. 5

Ring out, wild bells, to the wild sky,
The flying cloud, the frosty light:
The year is dying in the night;
Ring out, wild bells, and let him die.
                          Ibid., canto 106, st. 1

Ring out the old, ring in the new.
Ring, happy bells, across the snow:
The year is going, let him go
Ring out the false, ring in the true.
                          Ibid., st. 2

Ring in the valiant man and free,
The larger heart, the kindlier hand;
Ring out the darkness of the land,
Ring in the Christ that is to be.
                          Ibid., st. 8

At the University of the South, at midnight on New Year's Eve, the youngest and the oldest persons in attendance alternate reading the verses of "Ring Out," then all hold hands to sing "Auld Lang Syne."

In "In Memoriam A. H. H.," one of the greatest elegies, Tennyson agonizes over the death of his friend. In a battle between science and faith, Tennyson's moods swing from anger at a cold, mechanistic universe of "nature, red in tooth and claw" to a faith that "Love is and was my king and lord…"

Man dreams of fame while woman wakes to love.
                 Idylls of the King (1859), "Merlin and
                          Vivien," l. 478

PHINEAS T. BARNUM
1810–91

American, circus showman, who created "The Greatest Show on Earth."

There's a sucker born every minute.

[So many people came to Barnum's American Museum in New York City that long lines developed. To hurry up the people inside, he posted a large sign over the exit door:]
To the egress.

CONTE CAMILLO BENSO DI CAVOUR
1810–61

Italian, architect of Italian unification who mobilized French support for the House of Savoy to rule a unified Italy. He founded *Il Risorgimento*, a newspaper advocating a liberal, monarchical Italy.

In 1815 the Congress of Vienna divided Italy into principalities under Austrian control, except for Sardinia. A series of revolutions and wars from 1815 to 1870 called *il Risorgimento* or "the Resurgence," unified Italy under Cavour's program. Victor

Emmanuel II of Sardinia was crowned king of Italy after the Austro-Prussian War of 1866. Mazzini represented the republican parties, and Garabaldi's one thousand "redshirts" annexed Sicily and Naples to Italy. Cavour was asked how he would discharge his debt to the European liberals who had helped him unify Italy. He replied that he would astonish everyone with his ingratitude.

> What scoundrels we would be if we did for ourselves what we are ready to do for Italy.
>> In Edward J. Conry, "The Indivisibility of Ethics," *New York Times* (March 3, 1991)

> I have discovered the art of fooling diplomats; I speak the truth and they never believe me.

HORACE GREELEY
1811–72

American, publisher of the *New York Tribune.*

> Go West young man, and grow up with the country.
>> "Hints Toward Reform" (1850)

> I never said all Democrats were saloon keepers. What I said was that all saloon keepers were Democrats.
>>> Attributed

HARRIET BEECHER STOWE
1811–96

American, abolitionist, and feminist, from Connecticut. Her *Uncle Tom's Cabin* (1851) sold 300,000 copies its first year. It stripped away the veneer of acceptability of the South's "peculiar institution" of slavery and laid bare its fundamental injustice. It tells about a religious slave who rescues a white child but is sold by the child's father to Simon Legree, a sadist who flogs Tom to death for his goodness. A poignant scene describes Eliza's escape across ice floes on the Ohio River carrying her child with the slave trader, Haley, in hot pursuit.

An unsympathetic Southern reviewer said of the author, "The Petticoat lifts of itself and we see the hoof of the beast under the table." Others observed that slaves lived twice as long in the South as in Africa and that slaves rarely accepted manumission, if it meant returning to Africa.

> If ever Africa shall show an elevated and cultivated race—and come it must, some time, her turn to figure in the great drama of human improvement—life will awake there with a gorgeousness and splendor of which our cold western tribes faintly have conceived.
>> *Uncle Tom's Cabin* (1851), ch. 16

> Whipping and abuse are like laudanum; you have to double the dose as the sensibilities decline.
>> Ibid., ch. 20

WILLIAM MAKEPEACE THACKERAY
1811–63

English novelist. His *Vanity Fair: A Novel without a Hero* (1848) pits Becky Sharp, an ambitious and amoral poor girl, against Amelia Sedley, a well-born and passive rich girl.

> I think I could be a good woman, if I had five thousand a year.
> [Becky Sharp]
>> *Vanity Fair* (1848), ch. 1

The world is a looking glass, and gives back to every man the reflection of his own face. Frown at it, and it will in turn look sourly upon you; laugh at it and with it, and it is a jolly kind companion.
Ibid., ch. 2

Charlotte, having seen his body
Borne before her on a shutter,
Like a well-conducted person,
Went on cutting bread and butter.
[A satire of Goethe's *Young Werther*.]
"Sorrows of Werther," st. 4

ROBERT BROWNING
1812–89

English, poet, aka "Mrs. Browning's husband" because she was more famous. Posthumously, she declined into a minor figure, and he was recognized as the trailblazer of "dramatic monologue," the most prevalent form of twentieth-century poetry.

The year's at the spring
And the day's at the morn;
Morning's at seven;
The hillside's dew-pearled;
The lark's on the wing;
The snail's on the thorn:
God's in his heaven–
All's right with the world.
"Pippa Passes" (1841), pt. 1

Less is more.
"Andrea del Sarto" (1855), l. 78

Ah, but a man's reach should exceed his grasp,
Or what's a heaven for?
Ibid., l. 97

Why stay on the earth except to grow.
"Cleon" (1855), l. 114

Grow old along with me!
The best is yet to be,
The last of life, for which the first was made...
[The rabbi compares life to a potter's cup whose base is youth and whose wall (later life) gives value to the whole.]
"Rabbi Ben Ezra" (1864), st. 1

A minute's success pays the failure of years.
"Apollo and the Fates" (1886), st. 42

Browning's Pied Piper contracted with the town of Hamelin to rid it of rats. He walked through town playing his pipe and the rats followed him to drown in the river. The town refused to pay seeing how easily he had killed the rats. The Pied Piper came back and enchanted the town's children, who followed him in the woods and disappeared forever.

CHARLES DICKENS
1812–70

English, social critic, and perhaps the greatest novelist. Raised with his father in debtor's prison, he portrayed urban poverty and crusaded against the mistreatment of children. He felt *David Copperfield* was his best novel—it depicted his childhood as fiction. He was read by royals, aristocrats, the middle class, and laborers. Chesterton called Dickens "the spokesman of the poor."

He drew the most memorable characters in literature, from Samuel Pickwick, the adventurer; to the grasping Scrooge; to the loving Tiny Tim; to the ever-optimistic, but impecunious Mr. Micawber, who waits for "something to turn up"; to the "umble" Uriah Heep (malice cloaked in humility); to the sadistic Murdstones; to the villainous Fagin; to the vindictive Miss Havisham; to the fierce Madame DuFarge; to the gallant Sidney Carton. Chesterton and Harold Bloom hold *The Pickwick Papers* to be Dickens's greatest work.

Hard Times condemns industrialization and its factory system for destroying both individual pride and a sense of community. More generally, it impoverishes man's spirit, as shown in the words of the utilitarian schoolmaster Gradgrind: "Now, what I want is Facts. Teach these boys and girls nothing but Facts. Facts alone are wanted in life. Plant nothing else, and root out everything else."

> He had used the word in its Pickwickian sense...he had merely considered him a humbug in a Pickwickian point of view.
> Ibid., ch. 1

Despair seldom comes with the first severe shock of misfortune. A man has confidence in untried friends...he has hope—the hope of happy inexperience.
Ibid., ch. 20

Be very careful o' widders all your life.
Oliver Twist (1837-38), ch. 2

Please, sir, I want some more.
Ibid.

Known by the sobriquet of 'The artful dodger.'
Ibid.

"If the law supposes that," said Mr. Bumble,... "the law is an ass...an idiot."
Ibid., ch. 51

There are strings in the human heart that had better not be vibrated.
Barnaby Rudge (1841), ch. 22

Secret, and self-contained, and solitary as an oyster.
[Of Ebenezer Scrooge.]
A Christmas Carol (1843)

Bah, Humbug!
[Scrooge.]
Ibid.

I wear the chain I forged in life.
[Marley's ghost.]
Ibid.

"God bless us every one!" said Tiny Tim, the last of all.
Ibid.

"Barkis is willin."
[Proposal of Barkis, a cart driver, to Clara Peggoty.]
David Copperfield (1850), ch. 5

I have known him come home to supper with a flood of tears, and a declaration that nothing was now left but a jail; and go to bed making a calculation of the expense of putting bow windows to the house, 'in case anything turned up,' which was his favorite expression.
[Of Mr. Micawber.]
Ibid., ch. 11

Annual income twenty pounds, annual expenditure nineteen six, result happiness. Annual income twenty pounds, annual expenditure twenty pounds ought and six, result misery.

Ibid., ch. 12

It's a mad world. Mad as Bedlam.
    [Mr. Micawber.]

Ibid., ch. 14

Fog everywhere. Fog up the river, where it flows among green aits and meadows; fog down the river, where it rolls defiled among the tiers of shipping and the waterside pollution's of a great (and dirty) city. Fog on the Essex marshes, fog on the Kentish heights. Fog creeping into the cabooses of collier-brigs; fog lying out on the yards and hovering in the rigging of great ships…And hard by Temple Bar, in Lincoln's Hall, at the very heart of the fog, sits the Lord High Chancellor in his High Court of Chancery.

Bleak House (1853), ch. 1

This is the Court of Chancery…there is not an honourable man among its practitioners who would not give—who does not often give—the warning, "Suffer any wrong that can be done you, rather than come here!"

Ibid.

Jarndyce and Jarndyce drones on. This scarecrow of a suit has, in course of time, become so complicated, that no man alive knows what it means. The parties to it understand it least but it has been observed that no two Chancery lawyers can talk about it for five minutes without coming to a total disagreement as to all the premises. Innumerable children have been born into the case; innumerable young people have married into it; innu-

merable old people have died out of it. Scores of persons have deliriously found themselves made parties in Jarndyce and Jarndyce, without knowing how or why; whole families have inherited legendary hatreds with the suit. The little plaintiff or defendant, who was promised a new rocking horse when Jarndyce and Jarndyce should be settled, has grown up, possessed himself of a real horse, and trotted away into the other world. Fair wards of court have faded into mothers and grandmothers, a long procession of Chancellors has come in and gone out; the legion of bills in the suit have been transformed into mere bills of mortality; there are not three Jarndyceses left upon the earth…but Jarndyce and Jarndyce still drags its dreary length before the Court, perennially hopeless.

Ibid.

This case is finally settled in the protagonist's favor, but all the funds had been dissipated in the litigation. The novel tracks the delays and archaic absurdities of a court that had refused a remedy to Dickens for the pirating of his *A Christmas Carol*.

Bleak House also caricatures Mrs. Jellyby, who "devotes herself entirely to the public." She abandons her children and husband in her absorption in educating the distant African natives of Borrioboola-Gha.

A person who can't pay, gets another person who can't pay, to guarantee that he can pay.

Little Dorrit (1857 - 58), bk. I, ch. 23

It was the best of times, it was the worst of times, it was the age of wisdom, it was the age of foolishness, it was the epoch of belief, it was the epoch of incredulity, it was the season of Light, it was the season of Darkness, it was the spring of hope, it was the winter of despair.

A Tale of Two Cities (1859), bk. I, ch. 1

It is a far, far better thing that I do, than I have ever done; it is a far, far better rest that I go to, than I have ever known.

[Sidney Carton, who loves Lucie Manette, takes her husband's place on the guillotine.]

Ibid., bk. III, ch. 15

Great books are wine and mine are water. But, everyone drinks water.

EDWARD LEAR
1812–88

English, writer, known for his fantasy humor published in five books of non-sense verse.

There was an Old Man with a beard,
Who said, "It is just as I feared!—
Two Owls and a Hen,
Four Larks and a Wren,
Have built their nest in my beard!"

A Book of Nonsense (1846)

The Owl and the Pussy-Cat went to sea
In a beautiful pea-green boat.
They took some honey, and plenty of
   money,
Wrapped up in a five-pound note.
The Owl looked up to the Stars above
And sang to a small guitar,
"Oh lovely Pussy!, my love,
What a beautiful Pussy, you are."

"The Owl and the Pussy-Cat," st. 1.,
Nonsense Songs (1871)

Pussy said to the Owl, "You elegant Fowl!
How charmingly sweet you sing!
O let us be married! Too long we have
   tarried:
But what shall we do for a ring?"
They sailed away for a year and a day,
To the land where the Bong-tree grows,
And there in a wood a Piggy-wig stood
With a ring at the end of his nose.

Ibid., st. 2

They dined on mince, and slices of quince,
Which they ate with a runcible spoon;
And hand in hand on the edge of the
   sand,
They danced by the light of the moon.

Ibid., st. 4

SAMUEL SMILES
1812–1904

Scottish, physician, and writer. He championed Victorian values and free enterprise and invented the motivational book with his *Self-Help* (1859). His short biographies popularized the heroes of the Industrial Revolution, especially great men who had risen from humble origins.

A man is already of consequence in the world when it is known that he can be relied on—that when he says he knows a thing, he does know it—that when he says he will do a thing, he can do it, and does.

Character (1871)

We each day dig our graves with our teeth.

Duty (1880) ch. 16

The shortest way to do many things is to do only one thing at once.

Self-Help (1859), ch. 9

Sow a thought, and you reap an act;
Sow an act, and you reap a habit;
Sow a habit, and you reap a character;
Sow a character, and you reap a destiny.
Quoted by Smiles in *Life and Labor* (1887)

SØREN KIERKEGAARD
1813–55

Danish, Christian philosopher, and "father of existentialism": Each person must make moral choices. The self is not born but is made by decisions. Because man cannot know for sure what God's purpose is, man must take a suprarational "leap of faith" to follow God's will, failing which leads to despair. Like Tertullian, who had said, "I believe because it is absurd," Kierkegaard held that there are no rational proofs of God.

Dostoyevsky, Nietzsche, and Husserl in the nineteenth-century developed ideas that influenced twentieth-century secular existentialists, such as Heidegger, Jaspers, Sartre, Beckett, and Camus, who focused on the "absurd" of life. Existentialists hold that there is no essential self. Man is nothing but what he makes of himself, so he is responsible.

Life can only be understood backwards; but it must be lived forwards.
Journals and Papers (1843), vol. 1

Prayer does not change God, but it changes him who prays.

GIUSEPPE VERDI
1813–1901

Italian. Either Verdi is the greatest operatic composer (*Rigoletto, Il Trovatore, La Traviata, Aida*), or it is Giacomo Puccini (1858–1924) (*Tosca, La Boheme,* and *Madame Butterfly*). Verdi composed 28 operas, and it is claimed that his *La Traviata* (1853) has been staged somewhere around the world every evening for over 100 years. The greatest opera houses are Teatro Alla Scala in Milan, Festspielhaus in Bayreuth, Staatsoper in Vienna, L'Opera in Paris, Royal Opera House in London, and the Metropolitan Opera House in New York. "Opera" is the plural of *opus* (work). It originated in Italy in the seventeenth-century as a "fable set to music." In the nineteenth-century, opera became serious, rather than spectacles of sexual intrigues.

You may have the universe if I may have Italy.
"Attila"

RICHARD WAGNER
1813–83

German, anti-Semitic composer, who aspired to replace the opera with a grand "musical drama" woven together with "leitmotivs." His *Ring of the Nibelung* consisted of the separate musical dramas *Das Rehingold, Die Valkyrie, Der Junge Siegfried,* and *Gotterdammerung (The Twilight of the Gods).* Other works include *Lohengrin, Tannhauser, Die Meistersinger,* and *Tristan und Isolde,* which is often acclaimed the beginning of modern music.

Wagner's works are interspersed with spellbinding music. A wag described Wagner's music as "fog shot through with lightning." Wagner designed the Festspielhaus in Bayreuth.

A master needs quiet. Calm and quiet are his most imperative needs. Isolation and complete loneliness are my consolation and my salvation.

In Alfred Hock, *Reason and Genius* (1960)

One cannot judge *Lohengrin* from a first hearing, and I certainly do not intend to hear it a second time.

[Rossini]

Wagner's music is better than it sounds.

[Mark Twain]

The Nibelungs are dwarfs who guard a ring of great power that carries a curse. To take the ring, Siegfried slays Fafnir, a dragon guardian, whose blood makes Siegfried invulnerable, except for a spot on his back that had been covered by a leaf. He finds Brunhilde, a Valkyrie whom Wotan had punished by placing her asleep on a mountain in the center of a magic ring of fire that can only be crossed by a hero. Siegfried rescues and marries Brunhilde and leaves her the ring as he goes off on an adventure. Hagen, son of a dwarf Siegfried had killed, gives Siegfried a drug that makes him forget Brunhilde and pursue Gudrun. Brunhilde, enraged at Siegfried's unfaithfulness, prompts Hagen to thrust his spear in his one vulnerable spot, just as the drug wears off and Siegfried remembers Brunhilde. Brunhilde mounts Siegfried's funeral pyre and slays herself with Siegfried's sword.

Wagner's *Ring* is mostly sourced from the Scandinavian *Völsunga Saga*, not the Austrian epic poem *The Nibelungenlied*, in which Siegfried marries Kriemhild, sister of the king of Burgundy, whom Brunhilde marries. Hagen slays Siegfried to get Kriemhild, and a treasure is lost because Hagen hides it in the Rhine before Kriemhild slays him.

MIKHAIL ALEKSEYEVICH BAKUNIN
1814–76

Russian, rich aristocrat, who became a violent anarchist. He spoke against Marx and was expelled from the Communist International. He accused Marxists of establishing a "pedantocracy," a regime of unemployable socialist intellectuals.

From each according to his faculties, to each according to his needs.

Anarchist Declaration (1870)

CHARLES MACKAY
1814–89

Scottish, poet, and historian, whose *Extraordinary Popular Delusions and the Madness of Crowds* (1841) described how in Holland in the 1630s during the Tulipmania, a Semper Augustus bulb fetched 6,000 guilders, enough to build a fine house. That was followed by John Law's Mississippi Bubble in France and the South Sea Bubble in England in the 1720s, the British Canal Bubble of the 1790s, Britain's South American Mining Bubble of the 1820s, the American Railroad Bubble of the 1870s, the American Auto-Radio-Electricity Bubble of the 1920s, the Japanese Real Estate Bubble of the 1980s, and America's 1990s Dot-Com Bubble. According to Peter Drucker, a decade after its bubble, the new technology makes huge contributions to economic productivity.

You have no enemies you say?
Alas, my friend, the boast is poor.
He who has mingled in the fray
Of duty, that the brave endure,
Must have made foes. If you have none,

Small is the work that you have done.
You've hit no traitor on the hip,
You've dashed no cup from perjured lip,
You've never turned the wrong to right,
You've been a coward in the fight.

"Enemies"

CONGRESS OF VIENNA
1815

The Congress of Vienna, after Napoleon's defeat at Waterloo, redrew the map of Europe. Unlike at the Treaty of Versailles in 1914, in which Germany was excluded, France was represented at the Congress. The Congress wanted to ensure a stable France, and Europe enjoyed one hundred years of peace thereafter. Castlereagh, England's foreign secretary, achieved a "balance of power" by strengthening Prussia and Austria as bulwarks against Russia. When attacked in Parliament on moral grounds, Castlereagh replied: "The Congress of Vienna was not assembled for the discussion of moral principles, but for great practical purposes, to establish effectual provision for the general security."

OTTO VON BISMARCK
1815–98

German, "Iron Chancellor," who unified Germany by starting and winning wars against Denmark (1864), Austria (1866), and France (1870). He robbed the socialists of their energy by adopting their sensible policies, such as workmens compensation and old-age benefits. He resigned to protest Kaiser Wilhelm II, who sought colonies and alienated Britain by building a fleet. Bismarck understood the lunacy of subordinating Germany's economy to the vainglory of acquiring colonies.

Prussia must keep her power together for the auspicious moment. The great questions of the age are not settled by speeches and majority votes, but by iron and blood.

Speech to Prussian Delegates
(September 30, 1862)

Politics is not an exact science.

Speech, Prussian Delegates
(December 18, 1863)

Politics is the art of the possible.

Letter to Prince Meyer von Waldeck
(August 11, 1867)

Universal suffrage is the government of a house by its nursery.

In L. R. Frank, *Quotationary* (1999)

[Nation-states travel on a] stream of time [which they can] neither create nor direct, [but upon which they can] steer with more or less skill and experience.

In Planze, *Bismarck and the Development of
Germany*

In Prussia it is only kings who make revolutions.

I am accustomed to paying men back in their own coin.

The Balkans are not worth the bones of a single Pomeranian grenadier.

He who has his thumb on the purse has the power.

If there is ever another war in Europe, it will come out of some damned silly thing in the Balkans.

Law is like sausage. If you like it, you shouldn't watch it being made.

[When asked the most important fact, Bismarck said:] The fact that North America speaks English.

All treaties between great states cease to be binding when they come in conflict with the struggle for existence.

SAMUEL COLT
1814–62

American, arms manufacturer, whose 1836 six-shot "Peacemaker" won the West. His Colt 45 pistol was nicknamed "the equalizer." The saying was, "God made man and Colt made him equal."

DANIEL DECATUR EMMETT
1815–1904

American, Ohio songwriter, who played "Dixie Land" in 1859 in New York City in a minstrel.

I wish I was in de land ob cotton,
Old times thar are not forgotten.
Look away! look away! look away! Dixie
    Land
In Dixie whar I was born in,
Early on one frosty mornin',
Look away! look away! look away! Dixie
    land!
               "Dixie Land" (1859), st. 1

Den I wish I was in Dixie! Hooray!
    Hooray!
In Dixie land we'll take our stand, to lib
    an' die in Dixie,
Away, away, away down south in Dixie!

Away, away, away down south in Dixie!
               Ibid., Chorus

After Lee's surrender, Lincoln had his band play "Dixie" at the White House because, "That wonderful song now belongs to all Americans."

SPANISH AMERICAN LIBERATION
1815–1825

The liberation of Spanish America created the largest number of new independent states until the 1960s decolonialization. This was a civil war of Spanish landowners backed by Spain against the lower classes, who were largely Indian and African. There were no volunteer armies, only mercenaries who looted. The principal liberator was Simón Bolívar, a wealthy Creole planter and slave owner in Venezuela who hated Spain. His army's crossing of the high Andes was far more extraordinary than Hannibal's and Napoleon's crossings of the Alps. Bolívar in 1819 liberated Venezuela and Colombia, and he helped liberate Chile, Bolivia, and Peru. Bolívar denounced "popular elections"; he wanted to be king of a united Spanish empire. He said, "Democracy on my lips, aristocracy here [placing his hand over his heart]." See Paul Johnson, *The Birth of the Modern* (1991).

ELIZABETH CADY STANTON
1815–1902

American, intellectual of the woman's suffrage movement, and coauthor of *The History of Woman Suffrage* (1881) with Susan Anthony and Mathilda Gage. Stanton organized the first Woman's Rights Convention in Seneca Falls in 1848. She based the right to woman's suffrage on natural rights. Stanton was the woman's suffrage strategist, while Anthony was its leader. Anthony said, "Always I have felt that I must have Mrs. Stanton's opinion of things before I knew where I stood myself."

> All men and women are created equal.
> First Woman's Rights Convention, Seneca
> Falls, New York (July 19–20, 1848),
> "Declaration of Sentiments"

> We are, as a sex, infinitely superior to men.
> Diary Entry (1890)

> The Bible and Church have been the greatest stumbling blocks in the way of women's emancipation.
> In *Free Thought Magazine*, vol. XIV
> (September 1896)

> The queens of history compare favorably with the kings.

> ...the woman is uniformly sacrificed to the wife and mother.

CHARLOTTE BRONTË
1816–55

English, poet, novelist, and elder sister to Emily and Anne. They were raised in a parsonage, where they lived in a secluded world and wrote imaginary novels and poetry. Their first poetry was published using three male pseudonyms. Charlotte's *Jane Eyre* (1847) introduced a new kind of heroine who was intelligent and independent. An orphan raised in a charity house, Jane becomes the tutor of the ward of Edward Rochester, whose wife is insane. After they fall in love, Jane declines his proposal to be his mistress, knowing her refusal means she will be left destitute. She is a heroine who eschews female subservience; she will marry Rochester only after he is blinded — when she is dominant.

> ...women feel just as men feel; they need exercise for their faculties, and a field for their efforts as much as their bothers do; they suffer from too rigid a restraint, too absolute a stagnation, precisely as men would suffer...it is thoughtless to condemn them, or laugh at them, if they seek to do more than custom has pronounced necessary for their sex.
> *Jane Eyre* (1847), ch. 12

JOHN GODFREY SAXE
1816–87

American, attorney and poet.

> It was six men of Indostan
>   To learning much inclined
> Who went to see the Elephant
> (Though all of them were blind)
>   That each by observation
> Might satisfy his mind.
>
> The First approached the Elephant,
>   And happening to fall
> Against his broad and sturdy side,
>   At once began to bawl:
> "God bless me! But the Elephant
> Is very like a wall."
>
> The Second, feeling at the tusk,
>   Cried "Ho what have we here
> So very round and smooth and sharp?
>   To me 'tis mighty clear

This wonder of an Elephant
    Is very like a spear!"

The Third approached the animal,
    And happening to take
The squirming trunk within his hands,
    Thus boldly up and spake:
"I see," quoth he, "the Elephant
    Is very like a snake!"

The Fourth reached out an eager hand,
    And felt about the knee.
"What most this wondrous beast is like
    Is might plain," quoth he;
"'Tis clear enough the Elephant
    Is very like a tree!"

The Fifth, who chanced to touch the ear,
    Said: "E'en the blindest man
Can tell what this resembles most;
    Deny the fact who can,
This marvel of an Elephant
    Is very like a fan!"

The Sixth no sooner had begun
    About the beast to grope,
Than, seizing on the swinging tail
    That fell within his scope,
"I see" quoth he, "the Elephant
    Is very like a rope!"

And so these men of Indostan
    Disputed loud and long.
Each in his own opinion
    Exceedingly stiff and strong.
Though each was partly in the right,
    And all were in the wrong!
        "The Blind Men and the Elephant"

FREDERICK DOUGLASS
1817–95

American, journalist and abolitionist. The son of an unknown white man and a black woman, Douglass was raised as a slave, escaped in 1838, and his freedom was later bought by British abolitionists.

Property will produce for us the only condition upon which any people can rise to the dignity of genuine manhood.... Knowledge, wisdom, culture, refinement, manners are all founded on work and the wealth which work brings.... Without money, there's no leisure, without leisure no thought, without thought no progress.
    In Jim Powell, *The Triumph of Liberty*
        (2000)

What, to the American slave, is your Fourth of July? I answer: a day that reveals to him, more than all other days in the year, the gross injustice and cruelty to which he is the constant victim. To him, your celebration is a sham; your boasted liberty, an unholy license; your national greatness, swelling vanity; your sounds of rejoicing are empty and heartless; your denunciation of tyrants, brass-fronted impudence; your shouts of liberty and equality, hollow mockery; your prayers and hymns, your sermons and Thanksgivings, with all your religious parade and solemnity, are, to Him, mere bombast, fraud, deception, impiety, and hypocrisy—a thin veil to cover up crimes which would disgrace a nation of savages.
    Speech (July 4, 1852),
        Rochester, New York

The existence of slavery in this country brands your republicanism as a sham, your humanity as a base pretense, and your Christianity as a lie.

Ibid.

HENRY DAVID THOREAU
1817–62

American, individualist, transcendentalist, and poet. Opposing the Mexican War because it would add a slave state to the Union, he wrote the essay "Civil Disobedience," which inspired Tolstoy, Gandhi, and King with the political strategy of passive disobedience. He approved violence to oppose slavery. Note: It was a felony in the Soviet Union to own a copy of "Civil Disobedience."

I heartily accept the motto, "That government is best which governs least"… We should be men first and subjects afterwards. It is not desirable to cultivate a respect for the law, so much as for the right…. If the law is of such a nature that it requires you to be an agent of injustice to another, then, I say, break the law. Let your life be a counter friction to stop the machine….

"Civil Disobedience" (1849)

Moreover, any man more right than his neighbors constitutes a majority of one already.

Ibid.

[Thoreau was jailed overnight for refusing to pay Massachusetts' poll tax because he objected to war with Mexico. Emerson visited him and asked why he was there. Thoreau responded:]
"Waldo, why are you not here?"

Everyone has a devil in him that is capable of any crime in the long run.

A Week on the Concord and Merrimack Rivers (1849), "Wednesday"

The poet is a man who lives at last by watching his moods. An old poet comes at last to watch his moods as narrowly as a cat does a mouse.

Journal (August 28, 1851)

Thoreau's *Walden* recounted his two years in a cabin on Emerson's Walden Pond, a mile and a half from town. His purpose was to "front only the essential facts of life, and see if I could not learn what it had to teach, and not, when I came to die, discover that I had not lived." Note: After Thoreau sold his family's manufacturing company, he pocketed the proceeds, which made him well-to-do.

If a plant cannot live according to its nature, it dies; and so does a man.

I have traveled a good deal in Concord.

Walden; or Life in the Woods (1854), "Economy"

Public opinion is a weak tyrant compared with our own private opinion. What a man thinks of himself, that it is which determines, or rather indicates, his fate.

Ibid.

As if you could kill time without injuring eternity.

Ibid.

If I knew for a certainty that a man was coming to my house with the conscious design of doing me good, I should run for my life.

Ibid.

The mass of men lead lives of quiet desperation.

> Ibid.

Beware of all enterprises that require new clothes.

> Ibid.

Our life is frittered away by detail.... Simplify, simplify!

> Ibid., "Where I lived and What I Lived For"

Love your life, poor as it is. You may perhaps have some pleasant, thrilling, glorious hours, even in a poorhouse. The setting sun is reflected as brightly from the windows of the almshouse as from the rich man's abode.

> Ibid., "Conclusion"

Why should we be in such desperate haste to succeed…? If a man does not keep pace with his companions, perhaps it is because he hears a different drummer. Let him step to the music which he hears, however measured or far away.

> Ibid.

What is the use of a house if you haven't got a tolerable planet to put it on?

None are so old as those who have outlived enthusiasm.

Any fool can make a rule and every fool will mind it.

Do what you love. Know your own bone; gnaw at it, bury it, unearth it, and gnaw it still.

What recommends commerce to me is its enterprise and bravery.

I have received no more than one or two letters in my life that were worth the postage.

JOSH BILLINGS
1818–85

American, humorist and auctioneer.

It is better to know nothing than to know what ain't so.

> "Solemn Thoughts," *Everybody's Friend* (1874)

Newfoundland dogs are good to save children from drowning, but you must have a pond of water handy and a child, or else there will be no profit in boarding a Newfoundland.

Thrice is he armed that hath his quarrel just;
And four times he who gets his fist in fust.

EMILY BRONTË
1818–48

English, novelist and poet. Her gloomy novel *Wuthering Heights* (1847) tells of ill-fated lovers, the orphan Heathcliff and Catherine Earnshaw, whose house, Wuthering Heights, sits on the desolate Yorkshire moors. Catherine grows up with and loves Heathcliff but rejects his proposal because he is poor. She marries Edgar Linton. Heathcliff returns later wealthy and determined to avenge his persecution as a child by Catherine's brother, Hindley, and Catherine's rejection. She dies in childbirth, after which Heathcliff starves himself. Today, *Wuthering Heights* is accounted to be better than her sister

Charlotte's novel *Jane Eyre* (1847), which was more celebrated then.

> My love for Linton is like the foliage in the woods; time will change it, I'm well aware, as winter changes the trees—My love for Heathcliff resembles the eternal rocks beneath....
>
> *Wuthering Heights* (1847), ch. 9

> Kiss me again; and don't let me see your eyes! I forgive what you have done to me, I love my murderer—but yours! How can I?
>
> [Heathcliff's love for Catherine.]

KARL HEINRICH MARX
1818–83

German, whose socialist ideas ignited wars and civil wars.

Marxism is a victim's ideology; it channels the resentments of the weak and risk-averse against the successful creative minority. Marxism also aped Catholicism's hatred of competition and usury. Marx's modern side was a machinery fetish. He theorized that machines were becoming so efficient that companies would lay off most workers, so there would be too few people with jobs to buy the products. Industry would become increasingly concentrated as big firms gobbled little ones, so at the end there would be only "millionaires and paupers." Underconsumption would collapse the economy, so the masses would seize the machines.

Marxism is founded on two gross errors. The "labor theory of value" holds that value is determined by the labor content in goods, so profits are the theft of "surplus value" created by labor. Because employers steal profits from their workers, there will be "class war." Note: Just as the Ptolemaists had had to introduce complexities to justify their erroneous geocentric theory, so Marx had to write a tortured *Das Kapital* to salvage his fatally flawed labor theory of value. Note: Carl Menger later proved "value" is solely "consumer preference."

Second, Marx's "dialectical materialism," or economic determinism, held that the mode of production determines the social superstructure of law, politics, and so forth. Marx wrote:

> The mode of production in material life conditions the social, political and intellectual life processes in general.
>
> *A Contribution to the Critique of Political Economy* (1859), *The Marx-Engels Reader*, 2nd ed., ed. Robert C. Tucker (1978), Preface

But laws and customs shape the economy more than vice-versa. For example, Muslim laws prohibiting charging interest and speculating in goods have inhibited the industrialization of Muslim nations.

> A specter is haunting Europe—the specter of Communism.
>
> [Opening line.]
>
> *Communist Manifesto* (1848)

> The theory of the Communists may be summed up on one sentence: Abolition of private property.
>
> Ibid.

> Abolition of the family and abolition of all right of inheritance.
>
> Ibid.

> The Communists disdain to conceal their views and aims. They openly declare that their ends can be obtained

only by forcible overthrow of all existing social conditions. Let the ruling classes tremble at a Communist revolution. The proletarians have nothing to lose but their chains. They have a world to win. Working men of all countries, unite!

Ibid.

Religion is the opiate of the masses.
["Marxism is the opiate of the intellectuals."]
The Critique of Hegel's Philosophy of Right (1844)

I hope the bourgeoisie as long as they exist will have cause to remember my carbuncles.
[Referring to the boils he endured writing *Das Kapital* in the British Museum.]

Letter to Engels

Hegel says somewhere that all great events and personalities in world history reappear in one fashion or another. He forgot to add: the first time as tragedy, the second as farce.

Eighteenth Brumaire of Louis Bonaparte
(1852), pt. 1

The bourgeoisie, during its rule of scarce one hundred years, has created more massive and more colossal productive forces than have all preceding generations together.

Marx was antiscientific: He was a dishonest researcher who fabricated statistics to counter the overwhelming evidence that in Great Britain the condition of working-men had been improving in proportion to the rise of GDP. See Paul Johnson, *The Pick of Paul Johnson* (1985).

Marx, who never visited a factory, was inept. All of his predictions were wrong:

1) that under capitalism profits and wages would decline and technical progress would end; 2) a surplus of industrial workers would create an "industrial reserve army" that would prevent wages from rising above subsistence; 3) capitalism would die in a crisis of overproduction because the impoverished masses could not buy the output; 4) the middle class would disappear, provoking a revolutionary crisis; and, 5) under Communism the state would fade away. A wag said, "Proof of his far-sightedness is that none of his predictions have come true yet."

Marx was a racist; he approved of colonialism for Asia, Africa, and Latin America because "the primitive races need a European push to begin their historical development."

Worst, Marx stole epigrams without attribution: Schapper coined "Workers of all countries, unite"; Marat coined "the proletarians have nothing to lose but their chains"; Heine coined "Religion is the opium of the people"; Blanqui coined "the dictatorship of the proletariat"; Blanc coined "From each according to his faculties, to each according to his needs"; and Birrell coined "dust bin of history."

HISTORY OF SOCIALISM

According to Friedrich Hayek, humans began as socialists, that is, hunter-gatherers who lived by two rules: tribal solidarity and predation of others. Socialists still cling to these rules. For Communists the tribe is the worker, who deserves solidarity, and the outsider is the "bourgeoisie," who deserves predation. For National Socialists, the tribe is the "Aryan race," which deserves solidarity, and the outsider is the "Jew," who deserves predation.

To Hayek, progress requires an "extended order of human cooperation," that is, voluntary exchange with all by contract. Contracting with total strangers vastly multiplies the possible number of exchanges. That increases opportunities for specialization of labor and competition, drivers of wealth creation.

As capitalism evolved out of feudalism, tracts favoring communal ownership emerged, like Sir T. More's *Utopia* (1516), James Harrington's *The Commonwealth of Oceana* (1656), Morelly's *Le Code de la Nature* (1755), and William Godwin's *Inquiry Concerning Political Justice* (1793). The latter forecast that industrialization would prompt revolt, leading to a classless society. Godwin, like Rousseau, believed men were perfectible and reason would enable them to live peacefully without the compulsion of laws. Yet all these utopias enforce intrusive codes of behavior, the antithesis of liberty.

After the Napoleonic wars, Saint-Simon advocated state capitalism, August Comte promoted rule by technocrats, and Simone de Sismondi argued that competition causes overproduction, depression, imperialism, and war. Charles Fourier believed people should join groups of one hundred families, a "phalanx," to share goods and women. Robert Owen endorsed free love and coined "socialism." He implemented Fourier's ideas in his New Lanark spinning mill in England and in his New Harmony village in Indiana, both of which failed. Louis Blanc and Étienne Cabet demanded that states redistribute wealth. Louis Blanqui's motto was *"Ni Dieu, ni maître"* "Neither God, nor boss."

The next generation of European leftists fashioned modern socialism. Ferdinand Lassalle formed the German Workers' Union to nationalize industry through democracy. Karl Marx and Frederick Engels advocated violent revolution to nationalize industry. The anarchists Proudhon and Bakunin thought Communism was worse than capitalism. In England, Sidney Webb formed the Fabian Society to socialize industry via democracy. The Russian Social Democratic Party split into Lenin's Bolsheviks, who favored a centralized party hierarchy, versus Martov's Mensheviks, who favored a democratic structure. [See Norman Davies *Europe: A History* (1996).]

After World War I, socialists took charge in Russia, Italy, Germany, and other countries, and socialism became the prevailing doctrine of Western intellectuals. Many governments that were not strictly socialist put many socialist principles into practice by redistributing wealth and creating regulatory bureaucracies.

The socialist common denominator is the belief that politics allocates wealth better than markets. But socialism never works: (1) socialism provides no rational price signals, so their economies are blind; and (2) socialism eliminates risk-takers or entrepreneurs who create the industries of the future in capitalist economies. Entrepreneurs are rarely found in bureaucratic economies organized to protect the status quo. Thus, Harold Bloom called Marxism a "cry of pain rather than a science."

IVAN S. TURGENEV
1818–83

Russian, novelist and Westernizer. His *Fathers and Sons* (1862) featured the young nihilist Bazarov, who believed a good chemist "is twenty times as useful as any poet." Nihilism is the notion that only science has validity. Bazarov became a paragon for Russian radicals, but a devil for the Slavophiles. Turgenev portrayed the revolutionary impulse in Russia in the mid-nineteenth century:

> "Do you who desire to cross this threshold, do you know what awaits you?
> I know, replied the girl.
> Cold, hunger, abhorrence, derision, contempt, abuse, prison, disease, and death!
> I know, I am ready, I shall endure all blows.
> Not from enemies alone, but also from relatives, from friends.
> Yes, even from them…
> Are you ready even to commit a crime?
> I am ready for crime, too.
> Do you know that you may be disillusioned in that which you believe, that you may discover that you were mistaken, that you ruined your young life in vain?
> I know that, too.
> Enter!
> The girl crossed the threshold, and a heavy curtain fell behind her.
> Fool! Said someone, gnashing his teeth.
> Saint! Someone uttered in reply."

GEORGE ELIOT
1819–80

English, freethinking novelist, whose real name was Mary Ann Evans. She was known for her probing character analysis in *Middlemarch* (1871).

It is good to be unselfish and generous; but don't carry that too far. It will not do to give yourself to be melted down for the benefit of the tallow trade....

Sesame and Lilies (1865)

I should like to know what is the proper function of women, if it is not to make reasons for husbands to stay at home, and still stronger reasons for bachelors to go out.

The Mill on the Floss (1860), bk. VI, ch. 6

Character is not cut in marble; it is not something solid and unalterable. It is something living and changing, and may become diseased as our bodies do.

Ibid.

JULIA WARD HOWE
1819–1910

American, Unitarian, abolitionist, and feminist.

> Mine eyes have seen the glory of the coming of the Lord;
> He is trampling out the vintage where the grapes of wrath are stored;
> He hath loosed the fateful lightning of His terrible, swift sword;
> His truth is marching on.

"Battle Hymn of the Republic"
(1862), st. 1

JAMES RUSSELL LOWELL
1819–91

American, poet, critic, and Boston Brahmin who yearned for order in a time of change. He began as a socialist. Older, he declared the Chicago Haymarket Riot ruffians "were well hanged."

> Truth forever on the scaffold, Wrong forever on the throne.
> > "The Present Crisis" (1844), st. 5

> No, never say nothin' without you're compelled tu,
> An' then don't say nothin' thet you can be held tu.
> > *The Biglow Papers' Series II* (1866), "The Courting," no. 5

> Not failure, but low aim, is a crime.
> > "For an Autograph" st. 5, *Under the Willows* (1868)

> There is no good in arguing with the inevitable. The only argument available with an east wind is to put on your overcoat.
> > "Democracy" Speech in Birmingham, England (October 6, 1884)

> Every man feels instinctively that all the beautiful sentiments in the world weigh less than a single lovely action.
> > *Literary Essays, vol. II* (1870–90), "New England Two Centuries Ago"

> True scholarship consists in knowing not what things exist, but what they mean; it is not memory but judgment.

HERMAN MELVILLE
1819–91

American, novelist, who wrote about living among cannibals (*Typee*, 1846), his life in Tahiti (*Omoo*, 1847), and his whaling (*Moby Dick*, 1851). His *White Jacket* (1850) protested flogging and led to a congressio-

nal ban of it. He finished *Billy Budd* (1891) just months before he died. Only Hawthorne praised his work, so for the last thirty years of his life he sought obscurity as a minor customs officer.

> Sailor or landsman, there is some sort of Cape Horn for all.
> > *White Jacket* (1850), ch. 26

> Call me Ishmael.
> > [Opening line meaning "outcast," son of Abraham and his Arab mistress, Hagar.]
> > *Moby Dick* (1851), ch. 1

> "A whale-ship was my Yale College and my Harvard."
> > Ibid., ch. 24

> All my means are sane, my motive and object mad.
> > Ibid., ch. 41

> To produce a mighty book, you must choose a mighty theme.
> > Ibid., ch. 104

> 'I will have no man in my boat,' said Starbuck, 'who is not afraid of a whale.' By this, he seemed to mean, not only that the most reliable and useful courage was that which arises from the fair estimation of the encountered peril, but also that an utterly fearless man is a far more dangerous comrade than a coward.

Captain Ahab sails the whaler the *Pequod* in search of the albino whale, Moby Dick, seeking revenge for losing a leg in an earlier encounter. Obsessed with keeping on Moby Dick's trail, Ahab refuses to help search for survivors from the longboats of the *Rachel*. Ahab is killed by his obsession as he is ensnared in the line of the harpoon he has thrust into the side of Moby Dick, which rams and sinks the *Pequod*. Only Ishmael survives, floating on Queequeg's coffin until picked up by the *Rachel*, still looking for her lost children.

One interpretation is man's struggle with evil. The white whale personifies all that is wicked and beautiful, dangerous and compelling. Ahab reflects in chapter 36 on our unequal struggle against fate:

> How can the prisoner reach outside except by thrusting through the wall? To me, the white whale is that wall, shoved near me. Sometimes I think there's naught beyond. But 'tis enough. He tasks me; he heaps me; I see in him outrageous strength, with an inscrutable malice sinewing it. ...and be the white whale agent, or be the white whale principal, I will wreak that hate upon him.

Ishmael is a philosopher trying to understand. Starbuck, the first mate, knows he serves a madman who endangers them all, but moderation stays him from assassinating Ahab. In the Bible, Ahab, a king of Israel, was led into idolatry by his wife, Jezebel.

JOHN RUSKIN
1819–1900

English, art critic, who loved the pre-Raphaelite painters and hated the effects of industrialism.

> The essence of Lying is in deception, not in words; a lie may be told in silence....
> *Modern Painters, vol. 1.* (1843), pt. IX, ch. 7

Remember that the most beautiful things in the world are the most useless; peacocks and lilies for instance.
The Stones of Venice (1851–53), vol. 1, ch. 2

No great intellectual thing was ever done by great effort; a great thing can only get done by a great man, and he does it without effort.
Pre-Raphaelitism (1851)

There is no law of history any more than of a kaleidoscope.
Letter to James Froude (February 1864)

All books are divisible into two classes: the books of the hour, and the books of all time.
Sesame and Lilies (1865), "Of King's Treasuries," sec. 8

A state without virtue, without law, without honor, [a soldier] is not bound to defend.
The Crown of Wild Olive (1866)

Life without industry is guilt, and industry without art is brutality.
Lectures on Art (1870), III, "The Relation of Art to Morals"

Great nations write their autobiographies in three manuscripts, the book of their deeds, the book of their words and the book or their art. Not one of these books can be understood unless we read the two others, but of the three the only trustworthy one is the last.
St. Mark's Rest (1877), preface

Though you may have known clever men who were indolent, you never knew a great man who was so; and when I hear a young man spoken of as giving promise of great genius, the first question I ask about him always is, "Does he work?"

On the whole, it is patience which makes the final difference between those who succeed or fail in all things. All the greatest people have it in an infinite degree… the patient weak ones always conquer the impatient strong.

A life being very short, and the quiet hours of it few, we ought to waste none of them in reading valueless books.

MAX SCHNECKENBURGER
1819–49

German, poet.

A voice resounds like thunder-peal,
'Mid clashing waves and clang of steel:-
"The Rhine, the Rhine, the German
    Rhine!
Who guards today my stream divine?"
Dear Fatherland, no danger thine:
Firm stand thy sons to watch the Rhine!
"The Rhine" st. 1

QUEEN VICTORIA
1819–1901

English, queen of Great Britain and Ireland (1837–1901), empress of India (1876–1901). She reigned longer than any English monarch and she so personified her age that it was named after her. She married her cousin, Prince Albert of Saxe-Coburg, whose death she grieved for years.

I will be good.
    [On viewing the chart of succession.]

Great events make me quiet and calm; it is only trifles that irritate my nerves.
(April 4, 1848)

He speaks to me as if I were a public meeting.
    [Of Gladstone.]
In G. W. E. Russell, Collections and
Recollections (1898), ch. 14

We are not amused.
    [Viewing an act imitating her.]
January 2, 1900. In Caroline Holland,
Notebooks of a Spinster Lady (1919), ch. 21

Lie still and think of the Empire.
    [Her marriage advice to her daughter.]
In Agnes Hooper Gottlieb, et al., 1,000
Years, 1,000 People (1998)

WALT WHITMAN
1819–92

American, Romantic poet, who wrote about man's dignity. He could not find a publisher for *Leaves of Grass,* so he self-published it in 1855 and spent his life writing eight revised editions. Its centerpiece was "Song of Myself." He exposed himself as a tormented, divided being. He planted news stories about himself, saying, "The public is a thick-skinned beast and you have to keep whacking away on its hide to let it know you're there." Emerson spoke of Whitman as "half song-thrush, half alligator." Harold Bloom thinks Whitman's "When Lilacs Last in the Dooryard Bloom'd" is the greatest American poem.

The United States themselves are essentially the greatest poem.
Leaves of Grass (1855), preface

I hear America singing, the varied carols
I hear.
Ibid.

As soon as histories are properly told
there is no more need of romances.
Ibid.

Do I contradict myself?
Very well then I contradict myself,
(I am large, I contain multitudes.)
Ibid., "Song of Myself"

Captain! my Captain! our fearful trip is
   done!
The ship has weather'd every rack, the
   prize we sought is won,
The port is near, the bells I hear, the
   people all exulting.
While follow eyes the steady keel, the
   vessel grim and daring.
   [Memorial for Abraham Lincoln.]
Ibid., "O Captain! My Captain," st. 1
(partial)

A noiseless patient spider,
I mark'd where on a little promontory it
   stood isolated,
Mark'd how to explore the vacant vast
   surrounding,
It launch'd forth filament, filament, fila-
   ment out of itself,
Ever unreeling them, ever tirelessly
   speeding them.
Ibid., "A Noiseless Patient Spider," st. 1

And you O my soul where you stand,
Surrounded, detached, in measureless
   oceans of space,
Ceaselessly musing, venturing, throwing, seeking the spheres to connect
   them,
Till the bridge you will need be form'd,
   till the ductile anchor hold,

Till the gossamer thread you fling catch
   somewhere, O my soul.
Ibid., st. 2

To have great poets, there must be great
   audiences too.
Notes Left Over (1882), "Ventures, on an
Old Theme"

The secret of it all, is to write in the rush,
the throb, the flood, of the moment—to
put things down without deliberation—
without worrying about their style—
without waiting for a fit time or place.
I always worked that way…. By writing
at the instant the very heartbeat of life
is caught.
In L. R. Frank, *Quotationary* (1999)

There is no week nor day nor hour, when
tyranny may not enter upon this country, if the people lose their roughness and
spirit of defiance….
Notes for Lecturers on Democracy

SUSAN BROWNELL ANTHONY
1820–1906

American, cofounder with Elizabeth Cady
of the National Women's Suffrage Association (1869), and a leader in the temperance and antislavery movements. She was
most responsible for the passage in 1920
of the Nineteenth Amendment, which
accorded woman suffrage. Prior to 1918,
only Norway and Finland allowed woman
suffrage.

The true republic: men, their rights and
nothing more; women, their rights and
nothing less.
Motto. In L. R. Frank, *Quotationary*
(1999)

Equal pay for equal work.

The Revolution (March 18, 1869)

[How do you plead?] Guilty! Guilty of trying to uproot the slavery in which you men have placed us women. Guilty of trying to make you see that we mothers are as important to this country as are the men. Guilty of trying to lift the standard of womanhood, so that men may look with pride upon their wives' awareness of public affairs. But, Your Honor, not guilty of acting against the Constitution of the United States, which says that no person is to be deprived of equal rights under the law.... You, you blind men, have become slaveholders of your own mothers and wives.

> [Her response in 1872 to the charge of illegal voting. Found guilty and fined one hundred dollars, she did not pay.]

Marriage, to women as to men, must be a luxury, not a necessity; an incident of life, not all of it.

Speech on Social Purity (1875)

When I was young, if a girl married poverty, she became a drudge; if she married wealth, she became a doll.

In L. R. Frank, *Quotationary* (1999)

Suffrage is the pivotal right....

"The Status of Women, Past, Present and Future" *The Arena* (May 1897)

FEMINISM, OR WOMEN'S LIBERATION

During the Enlightenment, feminists first began to dispute the legal subjugation of women and seek to secure equal rights so that they would no longer be the property of their fathers and husbands. The movement also sought to change social mores so as to make women's choices acceptable. Prior to the last century, only a few male thinkers, such as Plato, Francis Hutcheson, and J. S. Mill, had defined rights without regard to gender. Mary Wollstonecraft was one of the first women to demand equal rights in her *A Vindication of the Rights of Women* (1792). But little happened until new technologies made mental skills more economically productive than upper-body strength.

Most women and men worked in their homes until the Industrial Revolution drew men into factories and offices. After a century's lag, women followed due to the Remington typewriter (1873), telephones, public education, and World Wars I and II. America's Nineteenth Amendment (woman suffrage) was passed in 1920, contemporaneously with European woman suffrage. The Western ethos of liberty continued an expansion of women's rights and reduction of discrimination against women.

FRIEDRICH ENGELS
1820–95

German, Communist who collaborated with Marx to write *The Communist Manifesto* and who edited *Das Kapital*. Out of his inheritance, Engels gave Marx a 350-pound annual stipend, which was seven times a workingman's income. Socialism has typically been financed by the heirs of fortunes.

> The proletariat uses the State not in the interests of freedom but in order to hold down its adversaries.

Letter to Bebel (August 18, 1875)

These two great discoveries, the materialistic conception of history and the revelation of the secret of capitalistic production through surplus value, we owe to Marx. With these discoveries socialism becomes a science.

Socialism, Utopian and Scientific (1892)

The first condition for the liberation of the wife is to bring the whole female sex into public industry and…this in turn demands the abolition of the monogamous family as the economic unit of society.

The Origin of the Family, Private Property and the State

WILLIAM TECUMSEH SHERMAN
1820–91

American, general who believed the Civil War unnecessary, but who became the Union's best field general. He burned Atlanta and marched to the sea to Savannah and Charleston, burning every building and killing every animal in a sixty-mile-wide swath.

I can make the march and I can make Georgia howl. I propose to kill even the puppies.

If nominated I will not accept; if elected I will not serve.
[Message to Republican Convention in 1884.]

We must act with vindictive earnestness against the Sioux, even to their extermination, men, women and children.

Letter to General Ulysses S. Grant, (December 28, 1866). In L. R. Frank, *Quotationary* (1999)

War is at best barbarism….Its glory is all moonshine….War is hell.

Speech, Michigan Military Academy (June 19, 1879)

If we must be enemies, let us be men, and fight it out as we proposed to do, and not deal in hypocritical appeals to God and Humanity.

HERBERT SPENCER
1820–1903

English, radical libertarian whose *Social Statics* (1850) preceded Darwin's *Origin of Species* by nine years. He coined "survival of the fittest" and "evolution." Nature moves from the simple to the complex, "not as an accident, but as a necessity." This includes civilizations. Initially they are military societies, but commerce requires an evolving freedom.

His "social Darwinism" used Darwin's theory of evolution as a unifying principle for understanding society. It placed human races in a hierarchy from the most primitive to the most advanced, the Europeans. Spencer's ideas about the natural evolution of society through individuals cooperating rather than central planning influenced Hayek and other twentieth-century conservatives.

Progress, therefore, is not an accident, but a necessity…. It is a part of nature.

Social Statics (1881)

We have unmistakable proof that throughout all past time, there has been a ceaseless devouring of the weak by the strong.

First Principles (1861)

This survival of the fittest which I have here sought to express in mechanical terms, is that which Mr. Darwin has called "natural selection or the preservation of favored races in the struggle for life."

Principles of Biology (1864-67), pt. III, ch. 12

All socialism involves slavery....That which distinguishes the slave is that he labours under coercion to satisfy another's desires.

The Coming Slavery (1884)

The ultimate result of shielding men from the effects of folly is to fill the world with fools.

Essays (1891), "State Tampering with Money Banks"

When a man's knowledge is not in order, the more of it he has the greater will be his confusion.

HARRIET TUBMAN
c.1820–1913

American, "conductor of the Underground Railway." In 1849 she escaped from Maryland, where she had been enslaved. She returned twenty times to rescue more than three hundred slaves.

I had crossed the line. I was free; but there was no one to welcome me to the land of freedom. I was a stranger in a strange land; and my home, after all, was down in Maryland.

HENRI FREDERIC AMIEL
1821–81

Swiss, critic and diarist.

The great artist is the simplifier.

Amiel's Journal Intime (1849–72)

An error is the more dangerous the more truth it contains.

Ibid.

Charm: the quality in others that makes us more satisfied with ourselves.

Ibid.

For purposes of action nothing is more useful than narrowness of thought combined with energy of will.

FYODOR DOSTOYEVSKY
1821–88

Russian, novelist, imprisoned in Siberia for spreading Fourierist doctrines. He was standing in front of a firing squad when his sentence was commuted. Devoted to Eastern Orthodoxy, he was a Slavophile who believed Russia's divine mission was to reinvigorate Christianity. He criticized Western science and materialism, which brought in its train secularism and socialism; so he opposed the modernizing Westernizers, such as Turgenev.

In *Crime and Punishment* (1866), Raskolnikov is an impoverished young intellectual who believes he is exempt from the moral law because he, like Napoleon, is an "extraordinary world spirit" who has the right to be amoral in order to create a New Jerusalem. He kills an old pawnbroker and her sister, needing their money to set him on the path of becoming a creative world spirit. In time, the meaninglessness of his scientific utopianism is revealed to him as he sees that his addiction to ideas has turned his sister into a prostitute. His self-loathing grows and he confesses his crime to Sonya, who leads him to confess to the police. In prison he recovers his soul by rejecting the Enlightenment.

Dostoyevsky's prophetic novel is *The Possessed (The Devils)* (1870-72) which shows how Western ideas in Russia degenerated into nihilism, which unleashed demons. He skewers Russia's liberal intellectuals whose children become nihilists and terrorists. He wrote, "Starting from unlimited freedom, I arrive at unlimited despotism." He saw terrorism as a by-product of the loss of religious faith, so a liberal apocalypse could be avoided only by returning to Russian Orthodox Christianity.

Dostoyevsky stands at the pinnacle with Homer, Virgil, Dante, Cervantes, Shakespeare, Goethe, Hugo, Dickens, and Eliot. *The Brothers Karamazov* (1881), may be the greatest novel of all time.

> It would be interesting to know what it is men are most afraid of. Taking a new step, uttering a new word.
> *Crime and Punishment* (1866), tr. David
> Magarshack (1951), pt. 1, ch. 1

> Man grows use to everything, the scoundrel!
> [Raskolnikov.]
> Ibid., pt. 1, ch.2

> If you were to destroy in mankind the belief in immortality...nothing then would be immoral, everything would be permissible, even cannibalism, and no law would have any force.
> *The Brothers Karamazov* (1881), tr.
> Constance Garnett (1912), bk. 2, ch. 6

> They think to order all things wisely; but having rejected Christ they will end by

> drenching the world with blood.
> Ibid., bk. 5, ch. 5

> [Father Zossima:] How many ideas have there been in the history of man which were unthinkable ten years before they appeared?
> Ibid., bk. 6, ch. 2.

> Who doesn't desire his father's death?
> Ibid., bk. 12, ch. 5

> ...there is nothing higher and stronger and more wholesome and good for life in the future than some good memory, especially a memory of childhood, of home....

> [After the brother Dimitri is wrongly convicted of murdering his father, he plans an escape to America, saying:] "I hate that America already! And though they may be wonderful at machinery, everyone of them, damn them, they are not of my soul. I love Russia, Alyosha, I love the Russian God, though I am a scoundrel...."

Ivan, a rationalist and atheist, tells his brother, Alyosha, a priest, about "the Grand Inquisitor" of Spain, who recognizes Christ on a day when one hundred heretics are burned. The Grand Inquisitor arrests Christ and berates him for His cruelty to man by rejecting Satan's three temptations, thereby confirming man's free will. But man is weak and sinful, so he cannot bear freedom. Thus, the church was formed to bear the burdens of freedom and sin from the people. This the church does, not out of pursuit of power, but from pity for mankind.

Dostoevsky was originally Ivan but he became Alyosha; he was addicted to gambling, like Dimitri; he was an epileptic, like Smerdyakov; and he gave his first name to the father Karamazov.

> Beauty will save the world.
> Quoted by Solzhenitsyn in Nobel Prize speech (1970)

> In the abstract love of humanity, one always loves only oneself.

> Neither man nor nation can exist without a sublime idea.

CROWFOOT
1821–90

Blackfoot warrior.

> What is life? It is the flash of a firefly in the night. It is the breath of a buffalo in the wintertime. It is the little shadow that runs across the grass and loses itself in the sunset.
> Last words.

GUSTAVE FLAUBERT
1821–80

French, novelist, known for *Madame Bovary* (1857), a novel about the adulteries and suicide of Emma, who was suffocated by the dullness of her village husband and Victorian morals. Emma reads romances and longs for exotic sex. Flaubert and Baudelaire were *épatistes,* who crusaded to smear the middle class, that is, *"Pour épater le bourgeoisie"* (To startle the middle class). Marx and Lenin transformed this literary hatred of the bourgeoisie into genocidal political hatred.

> My wants have no limits. I go forward always, freeing spirits… without fear, without compassion, without love, without God. I am called science.
> *The Temptation of St. Antony* (1874)

> The author in his work must be like God in the universe, present everywhere and visible nowhere.
> In Agnes Hooper Gottleib, et al., *1,000 Years, 1,000 People* (1998)

> Hatred of the bourgeoisie is the beginning of wisdom.
> Letter to George Sand (May 10, 1867)

NATHAN BEDFORD FORREST
1821–77

American, Confederate general.

> Whenever you see a Yankee, show fight. If there ain't but one of you and a hundred of them, show fight. They'll think a heap more of you for it.
> [Forrest's only general order.]

At Appomattox when Grant asked who was the best Confederate general, Lee said, "A man I have never seen sir. His name is Forrest." Forrest often tricked enemy forces larger than his to surrender. He would circle his troops several times around a hill to indicate his forces were superior. Seeing he had been tricked, a Colonel Streit demanded the return of his 1,700 men and ten cannon so he could fight Forrest's 400 men and three cannon. Forrest never put prisoners to the sword, but the Yankees lied that he had massacred blacks at Fort Pillow.

"I git thar fustest with the mostest" and "I hit 'em whar they ain't" his explanations of how he won all his battles. He surrendered only after Lee had surrendered to Grant and Johnson to Sherman. Always outnumbered in the campaign theater, he usually outnumbered the enemy at the point of attack by concentration, deception, and rapid movement. He often crossed enemy lines with one aide to make a personal reconnaissance of the enemy's positions. His forces grew larger and became better equipped during each campaign. At the end of each campaign, Braxton Bragg ordered him to turn over his forces, so Forrest had to raise a new regiment of raw recruits for each campaign.

Unlike the federal cavalry, Forrest (and John Mosby) threw away the sword as useless and armed each man with a rifle and two pistols. Yankees called him the "Wizard of the Saddle." Forrest said of the many freemen blacks who fought under his command

> "Better Confederates did not live."
>
> Andrew Lytle, *Bedford Forrest and His Critter Company*, Green Key Press (1984).

ARDANT DU PICQ
1821–70

French, colonel, who wrote *Battle Studies* (1880):

> In battle, two moral forces, even more than two material forces, are in conflict.

> The surprised adversary does not defend himself, he tries to flee.

> Man's bravery is born of his strength and it is not absolute. Before a stronger he flees without shame…. Man must test himself before acknowledging a stronger. But once the stronger is recognized, no one will face him.

> In studying ancient combats, it can be seen that it was almost always an attack from the flank or rear, a surprise action, that won battles….

> In ancient conflicts, demoralization and flight began in the rear ranks.

> Discipline itself depends on moral pressure which actuates men to advance from sentiments of fear or pride. But it depends also on surveillance, the mutual supervision of groups of men who know each other well. A wise organization insures that the personnel of combat groups changes as little as possible, so that comrades in peace time maneuvers shall be comrades in war.

> Discipline cannot be secured or created in a day. It is an institution, a tradition.

> Four brave men who do not know each other will dare not attack a lion. Four less brave, but knowing each other well, sure of their mutual aid, will attack resolutely. There is the science of the organization of armies in a nutshell.

MATTHEW ARNOLD
1822–88

English, poet, literary critic, and "anti-Victorian" who opposed industrialization. He did not so much object to the Victorians' materialism and indifference to the poor as their being "Philistines" too ignorant to enjoy civilized living. He feared a world becoming "more comfortable for the masses, and more uncomfortable for those of any natural gift or distinction..."

Beautiful city [Oxford]!...whispering from her towers the enchantments of the Middle Ages....Home of lost causes, and forsaken beliefs, and unpopular names and impossible loyalties!

Essays in Criticism First Series
(1865), preface

Ah, love, let us be true
To one another! for the world, which
    seems
To lie before us like a land of dreams,
So various, so beautiful, so new
Hath really neither joy, nor love, nor
    light,
Nor certitude, nor peace, nor help for
    pain;
And we are here as on a darkling plain
Swept with confused alarms of struggle
    and flight,
Where ignorant armies clash by night.

"Dover Beech" (1867), st. 4

Culture, the acquainting ourselves with the best that has been known and said in the world, and thus with the history of the human spirit.

Literature and Dogma, preface to 1873
edition

Culture is the eternal opponent of the two things which are the signal marks of Jacobinism—its fierceness and its addiction to an abstract system.

In Robert Conquest, *Reflections on a Ravaged Century* (2000)

RUDOLF JULIUS CLAUSIUS
1822–88

German, physicist.

The energy of the universe is constant—the entropy of the universe tends toward a maximum.

Mayer and Helmholtz discovered in 1847 the law of conservation of energy or first law of thermodynamics: energy can neither be created nor destroyed; it can only change form. Clausius discovered the second law: "The entropy of the universe tends to a maximum" because heat can never spontaneously pass from a colder body to a warmer one. Heat continuously disperses, and eventually will be "dissipated" into low, lifeless warmth throughout the universe, or "heat death."

ULYSSES S. GRANT
1822–85

American, union commander 1864–65, eighteenth president (1869–77). He defeated Robert E. Lee by relentless attrition. He threatened to resign his command if President Johnson did not quash the indictment of Robert E. Lee for treason. As president, Grant returned to hard currency by withdrawing all greenbacks from circulation, which allowed the economy to flourish for decades.

No terms except an unconditional and immediate surrender can be accepted. I propose to move immediately upon your works.

[Ultimatum for surrender of Fort Donelson, Tennessee, on February 16, 1862.]

I purpose [*sic*] to fight it out on this line, if it takes all summer. [Dispatch to Washington.]

Spotsylvania, Virginia, (May 11, 1864)

I know no method to secure the repeal of bad or obnoxious laws so effective as their stringent execution.

Inaugural Address (March 4, 1869)

When in doubt, fight.

[Motto of Ulysses S. Grant]

LOUIS PASTEUR
1822–95

French, chemist, father of bacteriology, and possibly the most important person in medicine. He debunked the theories that diseases came from poisonous vapors, imbalances in bodily humors, or internally generated germs. He proved that disease comes from bacteria in the environment. He invented immunization for rabies and anthrax and pasteurization to kill food bacteria: Heat milk to 145 degrees F. for thirty minutes and then cool quickly.

Where observation is concerned, chance favors only the prepared mind.

Lecture, University of Lille
(December 7, 1854)

Let me tell you the secret that has led me to my goal. My strength lies solely in my tenacity.

DISEASE

Paracelsus (1493–1541), Swiss physician, who refuted the doctrine that ill health resulted from an imbalance of the "humors." Disease came from outside the body, so medicine had to find specific chemicals to help the body repel specific invaders. Edward Jenner (1749–1823) invented inoculation after noticing that milkmaids frequently had a mild cowpox but rarely smallpox. Catherine the Great of Russia vaccinated herself to show confidence in Jenner's procedure. Pasteur's discovery of bacteria made possible the discovery of antiseptics by the Scottish surgeon, Joseph Lister, who in 1866 cleaned open wounds with carbolic acid and boiled surgical instruments and dressings.

Ignaz Semmelweis (1818–65), a Hungarian obstetrician, discovered in 1848 that washing hands and instruments in chlorinated lime reduced the obstetrics mortality rate by 90 percent and postsurgical fatalities by half. Unsanitary doctors were spreading puerperal ("child-bed") fever. For his theory, he was judged insane and put in a madhouse. His discovery—backed by clinical trials—was ignored because he could not explain the unknown science of pathogens.

Alexander Fleming in 1928 left out a dish of staphylococcus bacteria. Later he saw that a bread mold he called Penicilium-Notatum had killed the bacteria around it. But he abandoned the mold because he could only produce minute quantities. In 1937, two other British researchers, Ernst Chain and Harold Florey, received funds from the Rockefellers to mass-produce and purify penicillin, after the U.S. and British governments refused to fund them.

MARY BOYKIN CHESNUT
1823–86

American, diarist of the Civil War. She chronicled Southern society and the lives of Confederate civilian and military leaders.

> They live in nice New England homes, clean, sweet-smelling, shut up in libraries, writing books which ease their hearts of their bitterness against us. What self-denial they do practice is to tell John Brown to come down here and cut our throats in Christ's name.
>
> *Diary from Dixie* (November 28, 1861)

ERNEST RENAN
1823–1892

French, historian. His *Life of Jesus* (1863) criticized the historical accuracy of the Bible, arguing it should be treated as other histories.

> God, if there is a god, save my soul, if I have a soul.
>
> "Agnostic's Prayer"

> The simplest schoolboy is now familiar with facts for which Archimedes would have sacrificed his life.
>
> *Souvenirs d'Énfance et de Jeunesse* (1863)

THOMAS JONATHAN "STONEWALL" JACKSON
1824–63

American, Confederate general. He acquired the sobriquet "Stonewall" at the first Battle of Bull Run when General Bee said, "Look at Jackson's brigade! It stands there like a stone wall. Rally around the Virginians!" Usually Jackson had his men lie down while he stood in front facing the enemy's fire. This eccentric, unclubable man hated slavery and was a dour disciplinarian who said, "I like strong drink—so I never touch it." Lee used Jackson's "foot cavalry" of 16,000 men to occupy four times as many federals and screen his western flank in the Shenandoah Valley. After Lee and Jackson's great victory at Chancellorsville (60,000 Confederates routed 135,000 Federals), a Confederate picket accidentally killed Jackson. Thereafter, the South only won at Chickamauga and Nathan B. Forrest's battles.

> Always mystify, mislead, and surprise the enemy, if possible; and when you strike and overcome him, never let up in the pursuit.... Never fight against heavy odds...hurl your own force on only a part, and that the weakest part of the enemy and crush it. Such tactics will win every time, and a small army may thus destroy a large one in detail, and repeated victory will make it invincible.
>
> In G. F. R. Henderson, *The Science of War* (1905), ch. 2, ed. Neil Malcolm

> [The weaker side] must make up in activity what it lacks in strength.
>
> Letter (April 1963). In L. R. Frank, *Quotationary* (1999)

> To move swiftly, strike aggressively is the secret of a successful war.
>
> In Robert Fitton, *Quotations From the World's Greatest Motivators* (1997)

> Let us cross over the river, and rest under the shade of the trees.
>
> Last words

THOMAS HENRY (T.H.) HUXLEY
1825–95

English, biologist, paleontologist, "Darwin's bulldog," and coiner of the term, "agnosticism."

The great tragedy of Science—the slaying of a beautiful hypothesis by an ugly fact.
Collected Essays (1893-94), "Biogenesis and Abiogenesis" (1870)

If a little knowledge is dangerous, where is the man who has so much as to be out of danger?
Collected Essays, vol. 3, (1895), "On Elementary Instruction in Physiology" (1877)

It is the customary fate of new truths to begin as heresies and to end as superstition.
Science and Culture and Other Essays (1880), "The Coming of Age of the Origin of Species"

Irrationally held truths may be more harmful than reasoned errors.
Ibid.

[In a public debate with Bishop Wilberforce, Huxley replied:]
I would not be ashamed to have a monkey as an ancestor, but I would be ashamed to be connected with a man who used great gifts to obscure the truth.
In Norman Davies, *Europe: A History* (1996)

There is no alleviation for the sufferings of mankind except veracity of thought and the resolute facing of the world as it is.

Every great advance in natural knowledge has involved the absolute rejection of authority.

There is a well-worn adage that those who set out upon a great enterprise would do well to count the cost. I am not sure that this is always true. I think that some of the very greatest enterprises in this world have been carried out successfully simply because the people who undertook them did not count the cost....

WALTER BAGEHOT
1826–77

English, editor of *The Economist*, the leading laissez-faire and free-trade magazine. Bagehot [pronounced *Bajet*] was an admired Victorian.

The great qualities, the imperious will, the rapid energy, the eager nature fit for a great crisis are not required—are impediments—in common times.
The English Constitution (1867)

One of the greatest pains to human nature is the pain of a new idea.
Physics and Politics (1869), ch. 5

The most melancholy of human reflections, perhaps, is that on the whole it is a question whether the benevolence of mankind does more good or harm.
Ibid.

STEPHEN COLLINS FOSTER
1826–64

American, first great American composer. He hailed from New York and made only one trip to the South. His songs include "My Old Kentucky Home," "Old Dog Tray," "Camptown Races," "Nelly Bly," "Old Black Joe," "Jeannie with the Light Brown Hair," and "Beautiful Dreamer."

> Way down upon de Swanee ribber,
> Far, far way,
> Dere's wha' my heart is turning ebber,
> Dere's wh' de old folks stay.
> All up and down de whole creation,
> Sadly I roam,
> Still longing for de old plantation,
> And for de old folks at home
> > "Old Folks at Home," st. 1

GEORGE FRISBIE HOAR
1826–1904

American, a founder of the Republican Party.

> The men who do the work of piety and charity in our churches...the men who own and till their own farms...and the men who went to war and saved the nation's honor, by the natural law of their being find their place in the Republican Party. While the old slave owner and slave driver, the saloon keeper, the ballot box stuffer...the criminal class of the great cities and the men who cannot read or write, by the natural law of their being find their congenial place in the Democratic Party!

HENRIK IBSEN
1828–1906

Norwegian, playwright, "father of the modern theater," who emphasized character development rather than intricate plots and addressed modern problems, such as venereal disease. He eschewed artificial conventions, such as asides, and required outcomes to be realistic. Eric Bentley said of Ibsen, "Everything that isn't a copy of him is a reaction to him." Using natural dialogue, he wrote about man against society.

Ibsen wrote of sinister, destructive men and women, such as Hedda Gabler, who resembled the pet scorpion he kept bottled on his writing desk in his gloomy house. George Bernard Shaw praised Ibsen for destroying heroic icons, as in *Peer Gynt*:

> What is a man's first duty? The answer is brief: to be himself.
> > *Peer Gynt* (1867), act 4

In this fantasy-comedy, there is no more inner self to Peer Gynt than there is to an onion. Yet this hero-villain is admired for his courage in hunting the troll king, the Great Boyg, and the Button-Moulder, who threatens Gynt with, "Friend, it's time to be melted." Gynt, a merchant who ships to China both missionaries and idols, expresses his philosophy:

> The Gyntian self—it's an army corps
> Of wishes, appetites, desires,
> The Gyntian self is a mighty sea
> Of whim, demand, proclivity—

In *A Doll's House* (1879), Ibsen attacks the Victorian ideals of duty and honor. Nora Helmer leaves her husband and child. She complains that her husband, Torvald, a banker who calls her his "little lark" and "little featherbrain," treats her like a doll. Many credit/blame Ibsen as a feminist, though some interpret *A Doll's House* as exhorting radical individualism in general. Nora is the opposite of Virgil's Aeneas, who sacrificed all to do his duty.

> Torvald: First and foremost, you are a
> wife and mother.
> Nora: That I don't believe any more.
> I believe that first and fore
> most I am an individual, just
> as much as you are.
> *A Doll's House* (1879), act III

In *Ghosts* (1881), the father dies of syphilis, which is inherited by his son who also dies of it while the sister is driven into prostitution due to the family's impoverishment. This shows the sins of the father are visited down through the generations; that we are all connected to ghosts from the past.

> But I'm coming to believe that all of us are ghosts.... It's not just what we inherit from our mothers and fathers. It's also the shadows of dead ideas and opinions and convictions. They're no longer alive, but they grip us all the same, and hold on to us against our will.
> *Ghosts* (1881), act 2

In *The Wild Duck* (1884), an officious idealist tries to relieve his friend of his illusions and ends up prompting his friend to reject his daughter. The meddler then tries to patch things up and inadvertently prompts her to commit suicide.

In *Hedda Gabler* (1890), a professor's wife, Hedda, a ruthless neurotic who hates her dull husband, seduces professor Lovborg, who is her husband's competitor for a promotion. Wanting the emoluments of the promotion, she lures Lovborg into dissipation, burns his manuscript, and, when he is in despair, hands him a pistol and urges him "to die beautifully." He dies horribly.

He has the luck to be unhampered by either character, or conviction, or social position, so that Liberalism is the easiest thing in the world for him.

> *The League of Youth*, act 5

Rob the average man of his life-illusion, and you rob him of his happiness as well.

> *The Wild Duck* (1884), act 5, in L. R. Frank,
> *Quotationary* (1999)

GEORGE MEREDITH
1828–1909

English, novelist, and poet.

> Kissing don't last: cookery do!
> *The Ordeal of Richard Feverel* (1859), ch. 28

A witty woman is a treasure; a witty beauty is a power.

> *Diana of the Crossways* (1885), ch. 1

LEO N. TOLSTOY
1828–1910

Russian, novelist, who developed the realistic novel with his masterpieces *War and Peace* (1869) and *Anna Karenina* (1873). Tolstoy, a soldier, became a pacifist; a philanderer, he became a Puritan; an aristocrat, he became a peasant's advocate; a Christian, he came to deny Christ. His moral philosophy emphasized love and asceticism (people should work with their hands and be content to be poor). His nonviolent philosophy preceded Gandhi and Martin Luther King Jr.

War and Peace's 1,600 pages has 500 characters. Natasha Rostova and Pierre Bezukhov shared his philosophy. Harold Bloom says the hidden truths of Tolstoy were his "nihilism and his inability to abide nihilism." Bloom charges Tolstoy was the greatest solipsist, unable to love anyone, including his thirteen children. Rejecting a loving God, he revered love and was anguished never to find it.

The strongest of all warriors are these two—Time and Patience.
War and Peace (1869), bk. 10, ch. 16

You are like this house. You suffer, you show your wounds. But you stand.
[Conclusion of the film *War and Peace*: Natasha (Audrey Hepburn) to Pierre (Henry Fonda).]

Happy families are all alike; every unhappy family is unhappy in its own way.
[Opening words.]
Anna Karenina (1875)

I sit on a man's back, choking him and making him carry me, and yet assure myself and others that I am very sorry for him and wish to ease his lot by all possible means—except by getting off his back.
What Then Must We Do? (1886), ch. 16, tr. A. Maude

Art is a microscope which the artist fixes on the secrets of his soul, and shows to people these secrets which are common to all.
Diaries (May 17, 1896)

Art is a human activity having for its purpose the transmission to others of the highest and best feelings to which men have risen.
What Is Art? (1898), ch. 8

The difference between reactionary repression and revolutionary repression is the difference between cat shit and dog shit.
In L. R. Frank, *Quotationary* (1999)

There is no happiness in life, only occasional flares of it. You must learn to live on them.
In Agnes Hooper Gottlieb, et. al., *1,000 Years, 1,000 People* (1998)

Life is God, and to love life is to love God.

Six feet of land was all that he needed.
"How Much Land Does A Man Need?" (1886)

The above is from a poignant short story of a poor peasant, Pahom, who dedicated his life to acquiring ever more land. He heard the Bashkirs sold all the land one could walk around in a day for a thousand rubles. If the purchaser failed to complete the circuit, he got nothing. Pahom walked out ever farther to include various fields. He died racing back to beat the sunset, so all the land he needed was six feet for a grave. James Joyce thought this was the best story ever written, but Harold Bloom thinks the best story ever written is Tolstoy's novella, *Hadji Murad*.

JULES VERNE
1828–1905

French, science fiction writer, best known for his *A Voyage to the Center of the Earth* (1864), *Twenty Thousand Leagues Under the Sea* (1870), and *Around the World in Eighty Days* (1873). In sixty novels he invented automobiles, subways, submarines, airplanes, movies, guided missiles, air conditioning, the fax machine, and so on.

EMILY DICKINSON
1830–86

American, modernist poet and spinster who focused on unconsummated love, decay, loneliness, death, and God—perhaps to understand them. She published only 11 of 2000 poems because a critic said her poetry would not be appreciated. But the 1890 first edition required six printings in six months! Only 24 poems had titles, so an editor numbered the rest. No other poet has written with her combination of simplicity and profundity.

Harold Bloom says Dickinson and Whitman are the two geniuses in American literature. Her "best" poems, according to Bloom, are omitted in *Great Quotations*, except number 761, because your compiler does not understand them.

> From Blank to Blank—[Ruin to Ruin?]
> A Threadless Way [Threadless for a
>   labyrinth?]
> I pushed Mechanic feet—
> To stop—or perish—or advance—
> Alike indifferent—
>   "No. 761" (c. 1863), st. 1

> If end I gained
> It ends beyond
> Indefinite disclosed—
> I shut my eyes—and groped as well
> 'Twas light—to be Blind—[Better not
>   to try to understand?]
>   Ibid., st. 2

> Success is counted sweetest
> By those who ne'er succeed.
>   "No. 67" (c. 1859)

I'm Nobody!
Who are you?
Are you—Nobody—too?
Then there's a pair of us!
Don't tell! they'd advertise—you know.
How dreary—to be—Somebody!
How public—like a Frog-
To tell one's name—the lifelong June-
To an admiring bog!
                    "No. 288" (c. 1861)

Because I could not stop for Death,
He kindly stopped for me-
The Carriage held but just Ourselves
And Immortality.
                    "No. 712" (c. 1863), st. 1

I never saw a Moor-
I never saw the Sea-
Yet know I how the Heather looks
And what a Billow be.
                    "No. 1052" (c. 1865), st. 1

I never spoke with God
Nor visited in Heaven-
Yet certain am I of the spot
As if the Checks were given-
                    Ibid., st. 2

A word is dead
When it is said,
Some say.
I say it just
Begins to live
That day.
                    "No. 1212" (c. 1872)

There is no frigate like a book
To take us lands away,
Nor any coursers like a page
Of prancing poetry.
This traverse may the poorest take
Without oppress of toll;
How frugal is the chariot

That bears a human soul!
"No. 1263" (c. 1873)

She dealt her pretty words, like blades,
As glittering they shone,
And everyone unbarred a nerve
Or wantoned with a bone.
In Further Poems (1924)

Assent—and you are sane—
Demur—you're straightway dangerous
And handled with a Chain.

MARIE VON EBNER-ESCHENBACH
1830–1916

Austrian, novelist, and poet, famous for realism.

Imaginary ills are incurable.
Aphorisms (1905), tr. David Scrase (1994)

Happy slaves are the bitterest enemies of freedom.
Ibid.

We are so vain that we even care for the opinion of those we don't care for.
Ibid.

Privilege is the greatest enemy of right.
Ibid.

Much less evil would be done on earth if evil could not be done in the name of good.
In L. R. Frank, *Quotationary* (1999)

CHRISTINA ROSSETTI
1830–94

English, poet, known for religious symbolism and intensity of feeling. She was the sister of the poet and painter Dante Gabriel Rossetti, who was part of the pre-Raphaelite brotherhood that accused Romantics of being so absorbed in seeking beauty that they forgot to search for the truth.

Does the road wind up-hill all the way?
Yes, to the very end.
Will the day's journey take the whole
long day?
From morn to night, my friend.
"Up-Hill" (1862), st. 1

But is there for the night a
resting-place?
A roof for when the slow dark hours
begin.
May not the darkness hide it from my
face?
You cannot miss that inn.
Ibid., st. 2

Shall I meet other wayfarers at night?
Those who have gone before.
Then must I knock, or call when just in
sight?
They will not keep you standing at that
door.
Ibid., st. 3

Shall I find comfort, travel-sore and
weak?
Of labour you shall find the sum.
Will there be beds for me and all who
seek?
Yea, beds for all who come.
Ibid., st. 4

An emerald is as green as grass;
A ruby red as blood;
A sapphire shines as blue as heaven;
A flint lies in the mud.

> "Precious Stones," st. 1

A diamond is a brilliant stone,
To catch the world's desire;
An opal holds a fiery spark;
But a flint holds fire.

> Ibid, st. 2.

Who has seen the wind?
Neither you nor I:
But when the trees bow down their
   heads,
The wind is passing by.

> "Who Has Seen the Wind?" (1872), st. 1

LOUISA MAY ALCOTT
1832–88

American, whose novel *Little Women* (1868) is an autobiography of four poor, gentrified sisters. Preteen girls love it. Her novel about adultery, *A Long Fatal Love Chase*, was published in 1995.

...men have to work, and women to marry for money. It's a dreadfully unjust world....

> *Little Women* (1868), pt. I

"...girls are so queer you never know what they mean. They say No when they mean Yes, and drive a man out of his wits for the fun of it...."

> Ibid., pt. II, ch. 35

Energy is more attractive than beauty in a man.

> *Behind a Mask* (1886), ch. 21

Philosopher: A man up in a balloon, with his family and friends holding the ropes which confine him to earth and trying to haul him down.

LEWIS CARROLL
1832–98

English, Oxford math professor, who told stories to Dean Liddell's children, including Alice, who implored him to write his story of her falling down a rabbit hole when she was seven years old. Next to the Bible and the Koran, *Alice in Wonderland* and *Through the Looking Glass* are the world's most quoted books. The illustrations by Sir John Tenniel add to its majesty. *Wonderland* is more enticing; *Through the Looking Glass* has better poems.

Curiouser and curiouser!
   [Alice]

> *Alice's Adventures in Wonderland*
> (1865), ch. 1

How cheerfully he seems to grin,
How neatly spreads his claws,
And welcomes little fishes in
With gently smiling jaws!

> Ibid., "The Crocodile," st. 2

[A "caucus race"]
There was no "One, two, three and away!" but they began running when they liked and left off when they liked.... the Dodo suddenly called out "The race is over!" and they all crowded round it, panting, and asking "But who has won?"...At last the Dodo said "Everybody has won, and all must have prizes."

> Ibid., ch. 2

"If everybody minded their own business," said the Duchess in a hoarse growl, "the world would go round a deal faster than it does."

Ibid., ch. 6

"Would you tell me, please, which way I ought to go from here?" [Alice]
"That depends a good deal on where you want to get to," said the Cheshire Cat.
"I don't much care where," said Alice.
"Then it doesn't matter which way you go," said the Cheshire Cat.

Ibid.

"All right," said the Cheshire Cat; and this time it vanished quite slowly, beginning with the end of the tail, and ending with the grin, which remained some time after the rest of it had gone.

Ibid.

"Then you should say what you mean."
    the March Hare went on.
"I do," Alice hastily replied: "at least —at least I mean what I say—and that's the same thing, you know."
"Not the same thing a bit!" said the Hatter. "Why, you might just as well say that 'I see what I eat' is the same thing as 'I eat what I see'!"

Ibid., ch. 7

[When the Hatter glared at the March Hare for failing to fix his watch by applying butter to it, the March Hare exclaimed in his defense,] "It was the best butter, you know."

Ibid.

"Take some more tea," the March Hare said to Alice, very earnestly.
"I've had nothing yet," Alice replied in

an offended tone; "so I can't take more."
"You mean you can't take less," said the Hatter: "It's very easy to take more than nothing."

Ibid.

[The March Hare and the Dormouse were drawing things that began with an "M."]
"Why with an M?" said Alice.
"Why not?" said the March Hare.

Ibid.

Duchess: Everything's got a moral, if only you can find it.

Ibid., ch. 9

Alice: Where should I begin, please your majesty?
King: Begin at the beginning and go on till you come to the end: then stop.

Ibid., ch. 12

Queen: Sentence first, verdict afterwards.

Ibid.

"Off with her head!" the Queen shouted at the top of her voice. Nobody moved.
"Who cares for you?" said Alice (she had grown to her full size by this time). "You're nothing but a pack of cards!"

The sequel, *Through the Looking Glass* (1865), like *Wonderland*, has twelve major characters and it revolves around a game of chess as *Wonderland* revolved around cards. In it, to get to where you want to go, you must go in the opposite direction, just as the White Queen lived backward and remembered things before they happened. When Tweedledum tells Alice she will vanish if the Red King wakes up, it is reminiscent of Bishop Berkeley saying that nothing exists unless it is perceived in the mind of God. The last lines of the final poem include: "Life, what is it but a dream?"

Twas brillig, and the slithy toves
Did gyre and gimble in the wabe;
All mimsy were the borogroves,
And the mome raths outgrabe.
Through the Looking Glass (1865), ch. 1.,
"Jabberwocky" st. 1

"Beware the Jabberwock, my son!
The jaws that bite, the claws that catch!
Beware the Jubjub bird, and shun
The Fruminous Bandersnatch!"
Ibid., st. 2

He took his vorpal sword in hand:
Long time the maxome foe he sought,-
So rested he by the Tumtum tree,
And stood awhile in thought.
Ibid., st. 3

And, as in uffish thought he stood,
The Jabberwock, with eyes of flame,
Came whiffling through the tulgey
   wood,
And burbled as it came!
Ibid., st. 4

One, two! One, two! And through and
   through
The vorpal blade went snicker-snack!
He left it dead, and with his head
He went galumphing back.
Ibid., st. 5

"And hast thou slain the Jabberwock?
Come to my arms, my beamish boy!"
"O frabjous day! Callooh, Callay!"
He chortled in his joy.
Ibid., st. 6

"Now, here, you see it takes all the running you can do to keep in the same place. If you want to get somewhere else, you must run at least twice as fast as that!" [Queen.]
Ibid., ch. 2

The Walrus and the Carpenter
Were walking close at hand:
They wept like anything to see
Such quantities of sand.
"If this were only cleared away,"
They said, "It would be grand!"
Ibid., ch. 4., "The Walrus and the
Carpenter" st. 4

"If seven maids with seven mops
Swept it for half a year,
Do you suppose," the Walrus said,
"That they could get it clear?"
"I doubt it," said the Carpenter,
And shed a bitter tear.
Ibid., st. 5

"O Oysters, come and walk with us!"
The Walrus did beseech.
"A pleasant talk, a pleasant walk,
Along the briny beach:
We cannot do with more than four,
To give a hand to each."
Ibid., st. 6

"The time has come," the Walrus said,
"To talk of many things:
Of shoes—and ships—and sealing wax
Of cabbages—and kings-
And why the sea is boiling hot-
And whether pigs have wings."
Ibid., st. 11

"It seems a shame," the Walrus said,
"To play them such a trick.
After we've brought them out so far,
And made them trot so quick!"

The Carpenter said nothing but
"The butter's spread too thick!"

> Ibid., st. 16

"I weep for you," the Walrus said:
"I deeply sympathize."
With sobs and tears he sorted out
Those of the largest size,
Holding his pocket-handkerchief
Before his steaming eyes.

> Ibid., st. 17

"I like the Walrus best," said Alice:
  "because he was a little worried for
  the poor oysters."
"He ate more than the Carpenter,
  though," said Tweedledee...
"That was mean!" Alice said indignantly.
  "Then I like the Carpenter best—if
  he didn't eat as many as the Walrus."
"But he ate as many as he could get,"
  said Tweedledum.

> Ibid., ch. 4

I'm very brave generally, only today I
happen to have a headache.
  [Tweedledum and Tweedledee were
  twins.]

> Ibid.

Queen: The rule is jam to-morrow, and
jam yesterday—but never jam today.

> Ibid., ch. 5

"It's a poor sort of memory that
only works backwards," the Queen
remarked.... "There's the King's Messenger. He's in prison now, being punished;
and the trial doesn't even begin till next
Wednesday; and of course the crime
comes last of all."

"Suppose he never commits the crime?"
said Alice.

"That would be all the better, wouldn't
it?" the Queen said.

> Ibid.

"There's no use trying," she said: "one
  can't believe impossible things."
"I daresay you haven't had much practice," said the Queen. "When I
  was your age, I always did it for
  half-an-hour a day. Why sometimes
  I've believed as many as six impossible things before breakfast."

> Ibid.

"When I use a word," Humpty Dumpty
  said, in rather a scornful tone, "it
  means just what
I choose it to mean—neither more nor
  less."
"The question is, " said Alice, "whether
  you can make words mean so many
  different things."
"The question is," said Humpty Dumpty,
  "which is to be master—that's all."

> Ibid., ch. 7

"Just the place for a Snark!" I have said
  it twice:
That alone should encourage the crew.
"Just the place for a Snark!" I have said
  it thrice:
"What I tell you three times is true."

> "The Hunting of the Snark" sec. 1, st. 2

But the judge said he never had
  summed up before;
So the Snark undertook it instead,
  And summed it so well that it came to
  far more
Than the Witnesses ever had said!

> Ibid., sec. 6, st. 11

The hunting of the Snark is undertaken
by a barrister, a bellman, a butcher, a

banker, a broker, a baker, a boots, and a bonnet maker who use a map of a shoreless ocean without an equator or meridians. We are never told what a Snark is, although there are some clues, such as: "It frequently breakfasts at five o'clock tea And dines on the following day."

JOHN MARSHALL HARLAN
1833–1911

American, Associate Justice (1877–1911).

In the view of the Constitution, in the eyes of the law, there is in this country no superior dominant ruling class of citizens. There is no caste system here. Our Constitution is colorblind, and neither knows nor tolerates classes among citizens. In respect of civil rights, all citizens are equal before the law.
[This was the sole dissenting opinion in *Plessy v. Ferguson*, 163 U. S. 537, 559 (1896), which ruled that railway cars segregated by race were constitutional, if they were equal.]

ROBERT G. INGERSOLL
1833–99

American, lawyer, and the "great agnostic."

In nature there are neither rewards nor punishments—there are consequences.
Some Reasons Why (1881) pt. 8, "The New Testament"

Every cradle asks us, "Whence?" and every coffin, "Whither?" The poor barbarian, weeping above his dead, can answer these questions as intelligently as the robed priest of the most authentic creed.
Eulogy at a child's grave

LORD ACTON
1834–1902

English, Liberal MP, and professor of history at Cambridge, who never wrote a book but is widely quoted on liberty, which, like Hegel, he believed to be the grand theme of history. He found liberty's origins in the biblical Hebrew belief in a higher law that applies to everyone, even kings.

[Liberty] is the delicate fruit of a mature civilization.... At all times sincere friends of freedom have been rare, and its triumphs have been due to minorities, that have prevailed by associating themselves with auxiliaries whose objects often differed from their own; and this association, which is always dangerous, has been sometimes disastrous.... The most certain test by which we judge whether a country is really free is the amount of security enjoyed by minorities.
"The History of Freedom in Antiquity" (1877), *The History of Freedom and Other Essays*, ed. J. N. Figgis and R. V. Laurence, (1907)

Liberty is not a means to a higher political end. It is itself the highest political end.
Ibid.

There is no error so monstrous that it fails to find defenders among the ablest men.
Letter to Mary Gladstone (April 24, 1881)

All power tends to corrupt; absolute power corrupts absolutely.

> Letter to Bishop Creighton
> (April 5, 1887)

There is no worse heresy than that the office sanctifies the holder of it.

> Ibid.

ARTEMUS WARD
1834–67

American humorist.

I have abstained from having any sentiments or principles. My pollertics, like my religion, bein of a exceedin accomodatin character.

> "The Crisis," *The Complete Works of Artemus Ward* (1898)

I have already given two cousins to the war, & I stand ready to sacrifiss my wife's brother ruther'n not see the rebelyin krusht.

> Ibid.

It's not so much what folks don't know that causes problems, it's what they do know that ain't so.

> Ibid.

JAMES MCNEILL WHISTLER
1834–1903

American, painter who moved to London.

[Asked why he charged two hundred guineas for two days, work, he replied:] "No, I ask it for the knowledge of a lifetime."

> *The Gentle Art of Making Enemies* (1890)

Oscar Wilde: How I wish I had said that.
Whistler: You will, Oscar, you will.

> In L. C. Ingleby, *Oscar Wilde* (1907)

Had silicon been a gas, I would have been a major general.
[Of failing chemistry at West Point.]

> Joseph Pennell, *The Life of James McNeill Whistler* (1908)

SAMUEL BUTLER
1835–1902

English satirist, whose utopia was named *Erehwon*, "nowhere" spelled backward. Dwellers in Erehwon stopped making machines for fear they would become smarter than themselves.

A hen is only an egg's way of making another egg.

> *Life and Habit* (1877), ch. 8

It was very good of God to let Mr. Carlyle and Mrs. Carlyle marry one another and so make only two people miserable instead of four.

> Letter to Miss E. M. A. Savage
> (November 21, 1884)

It has been said that though God cannot alter the past, historians can....

> *Erewhon Revisited* (1901), ch. 14

Life is the art of drawing sufficient conclusions from insufficient premises.

> Ed. Henry Festing Jones, *Note-Books of Samuel Butler* (1912), ch. 1

Every man's work, whether it be literature or music or pictures or architecture or anything else, is always a portrait of himself....

The Way of All Flesh (1903), ch. 14

I do not mind lying, but I hate inaccuracy.
  Ibid., "Truth and Convenience: Falsehood"

The *Ancient Mariner* would not have taken so well if it had been called *The Old Sailor.*

Ibid., "Titles and Subjects"

I never write on any subject unless I believe the opinion of those who have the ear of the public to be mistaken.

ANDREW CARNEGIE
1835–1919

American (Scottish-born), industrialist, who sold Carnegie Steel Company for $480 million to J. P. Morgan, who organized the U.S. Steel Corporation. This five-foot, three-inch immigrant worked at age thirteen for $1.25 a week. His family immigrated to America after a power loom replaced his father.

At age fourteen he found $500, which he advertised to find the owner and return it. He was hired by a railroad executive who admired his talent in Morse code. Many industrialists rose out of poverty, such as Cyrus McCormick, Cornelius Vanderbilt, John D. Rockefeller, Richard Sears, Montgomery Ward, and James Cash Penney, Henry Ford, David Sarnoff, and Frederick Weyerhauser.

Carnegie made his poke by financing men doing business with his railroad, such as George Pullman. He switched from railroads to steel in 1873 after the Bessemer blast furnace reduced cost. By 1900, Carnegie out-produced all of England's

mills. He vastly improved steel quality and cut the price of steel rails from $160 to $17 a ton. He was the first to expound on "economies of scale."

When a socialist implored him to distribute his wealth, Carnegie divided his worth by the people in the world and offered the socialist his share, sixteen cents. Carnegie distributed his wealth by building twenty-eight hundred public libraries, along with parks, swimming pools, auditoriums, churches, and medical laboratories. A cub reporter cabled back to Europe a story on Andrew Carnegie, "You'll never believe the sort of money there is in running libraries."

Three generations from shirt sleeves to shirt sleeves.

Triumphant Democracy (1886)

Those who would administer [charity] wisely must, indeed, be wise, for one of the serious obstacles to the improvement of our race is indiscriminate charity. It were better for mankind that the millions of the rich were thrown into the sea than spent to encourage the slothful, the drunken, the unworthy. Of every thousand dollars spent in so-called charity today, it is probable that nine hundred and fifty dollars is unwisely spent—so spent, indeed, as to produce the very evils which it hopes to mitigate or cure.

  "Wealth," *North American Review* (June 1889), in L. R. Frank, *Quotationary* (1999)

The man who dies rich dies disgraced.

Ibid.

There is scarcely an instance of a man who has made a fortune by speculation and kept it.

The Empire of Business

The Republic may not give wealth or happiness; she has not promised these. It is the freedom to pursue these, not their realization, we can claim. But if she does not make the emigrant happy or prosperous, this she can do and does do for everyone, she makes him a citizen, a man.

In Arthur Herman, *How the Scots Invented the Modern World* (2001)

Capitalism is about turning luxuries into necessities.

Carnegie maxim

Concentration is my motto—first honesty, then industry, then concentration.

I am after the winner. If he can win the race, he is our racehorse. If not, he goes to the cart.

Put all your eggs in the one basket and—WATCH THAT BASKET.

[Twain took the line from Carnegie.]

There is no use whatever trying to help people who do not help themselves. You cannot push anyone up a ladder.

As I grow older I pay less attention to what men say. I just watch what they do.

A word, a look, an accent, may affect the destiny not only of individuals, but of nations. He is a bold man who calls anything a trifle.

The first man gets the oyster, the second man gets the shell.

Immense power is acquired by assuring yourself in your secret reveries that you were born to control affairs.

Here lies a man who was able to surround himself with men far cleverer than himself.

[Epitaph.]

As a youngster, your compiler read a dozen biographies of great leaders to distill their common traits. They are: (1) a sense of destiny in life, (2) extraordinary energy, (3) risk-taking pluck, (4) high intelligence, and (5) a preference for strong colleagues. Otherwise, great leaders differ. Some are shy, some gregarious; some are detail-oriented, some big-picture types; some are vain, some self-effacing; some decide quickly, some agonize.

Peter Drucker said great leaders are "tolerant of diversity, but fiendishly intolerant about performance and values."

MARK TWAIN
1835–1910

American, comic genius. Samuel Clemens took his pen name from his experience as a riverboat pilot. "Mark twain" meant "two fathoms," below which was hazardous—and thus a warning. On the day Twain died in 1910, Haley's Comet was visible, just as on the day of his birth in 1835.

Twain's novels were anecdotes strung together, as in his masterpieces The Adventures of Tom Sawyer (1876) and The Adventures of Huckleberry Finn (1884). Tom Sawyer delights with the whitewashing of Aunt Polly's fence, curing warts with a dead cat in a graveyard, courting Becky Thatcher, and attending his own funeral. Huck Finn tells lies "merely to keep in practice."

Ernest Hemingway said of the Adventures of Huckleberry Finn, "It's the best book we've had. All American writing comes from it. There was nothing before. There's been nothing so good since." Huck is an illiterate twelve-year-old boy conflicted with the obligation of a corrupt society to turn in Jim, an escaped slave, and his desire to save his friend. The novel savagely satirizes the morals of a racist South. But many literal-minded and confused liberals ban the book from public and school libraries for its use of the N-word.

> Mark Twain walked 130 miles to Virginia City, Nevada to get a job as a reporter. The editor told him never to state as a fact anything he had not verified. His first story read: "A woman giving the name of Mrs. James Jones, who is reported to be one of the society leaders of the city, is said to have given what may be described as a party yesterday to a number of alleged ladies. The hostess claims to be the wife of a reputed attorney."
>
> *The Little Brown Book of Anecdotes* (1985),
> Clifton Fadiman, general editor

> Riding a train after a fishing trip in Maine during the off-season, Twain bragged to a stranger about the fish he had iced-down in the baggage car. Twain asked the suddenly agitated man who he was. The reply was, "I am a game warden, who are you?" Twain replied, "I'm the biggest damn liar in the whole United States."
>
> Ibid.

The calm confidence of a Christian with four aces.
> *Letter to the Golden Era* (May 22, 1864)

Travel is fatal to prejudice.
> *The Innocents Abroad* (1869)

Persons attempting to find a motive in this narrative will be prosecuted; persons attempting to find a moral in it will be banished; persons attempting to find a plot in it will be shot.
> *The Adventures of Huckleberry Finn* (1885)

That book was made by Mr. Mark Twain, and he told the truth, mainly. There was things which he stretched, but mainly he told the truth.
> Ibid., ch. 24

The difference between the right word and the almost right word is the difference between lightning and a lightning bug.
> "The Art of Composition" (1890), *Life As I Find It*, ed. Charles Neider (1961)

Familiarity breeds contempt—and children.
> *Mark Twain's Notebook* (c. 1894), ed. A. B. Paine (1935)

October. This is one of the peculiarly dangerous months to speculate in stocks. The others are July, January, September, April, November, May, March, June, December, August and February.
> *Pudd'nhead Wilson* (1894), ch. 13 (epigraph)

If you pick up a starving dog and make him prosperous, he will not bite you. This is the principal difference between a dog and a man.
> Ibid., ch. 16

In Boston they ask, How much does he know? In New York, How much is he worth? In Philadelphia, Who were his parents?
> "What Paul Bourget Thinks of Us", *North American Review* (January 1895)

To be good is noble; but to show others how to be good is nobler and no trouble.
Following the Equator (1897), Epigraph

[On Cecil Rhodes:]
I admire him, I frankly confess it; and when his time comes I shall buy a piece of the rope for a keepsake.
Ibid., ch. 2

Truth is the most valuable thing we have. Let us economize it.
Ibid., ch. 7

"Classic," A book which people praise and don't read.
Ibid., ch. 25

There are several good protections against temptations, but the surest is cowardice.
Ibid., ch. 36

Everyone is a moon and has a dark side which he never shows to anybody.
Ibid., ch. 66

A successful book is not made of what is in it, but what is left out of it.
Letter to William Dean Howells
(February 23, 1897)

The reports of my death are greatly exaggerated.
Cable to the Associated Press
(June 2, 1897)

Against the assault of laughter nothing can stand.
The Mysterious Stranger (1922), ch. 10

Wagner's music is better than it sounds.
Quoting Bill Nye in Autobiography (1924)

Thunder is good, thunder is impressive; but it is the lightning that does the work.
Letter (August 28, 1908)

Let us endeavor so to live that when we come to die even the undertaker will be sorry.

Everybody wants to have read the great books, but nobody wants to read them.

Few sinners are saved after the first twenty minutes of a sermon.

When we remember we are all mad, the mysteries disappear and life stands explained.

One man is as good as another, or maybe a little better.

There was worlds of reputation in it but no money.

Clothes make the man. Naked people have little or no influence in society.

Good sportsmen do not pick up lost golf balls while they are still rolling.

The man who does not read good books has no advantage over the man who can't read them.
My mother had a great deal of trouble with me, but I think she enjoyed it.

Too much good bourbon is barely enough.

It is better to have second hand diamonds than none at all.

I have never let my schooling interfere with my education.

Twins amount to a permanent riot. And there ain't no real difference between triplets and an insurrection.

Here and there a touch of good grammar for picturesqueness.

SIR WILLIAM GILBERT
1836–1911

English, comic opera librettist, who became so estranged from composer Sir Arthur Sullivan that they communicated only through an agent.

Things are seldom what they seem;
  Skim milk masquerades as cream.
           H.M.S. Pinafore (1878)

I always voted at my party's call,
And I never thought of thinking for myself at all.
                      Ibid.

You must stir it and stump it,
And blow your own trumpet,
Or trust me, you haven't a chance.
            Ruddigore (1887)

When every one is somebodee,
Then no one's anybody.
      The Gondoliers (1889), act 2

As some day it may happen that a vic-
    tim must be found,
I've got a little list—I've got a little list.
Of Society offenders who might well be
    underground,
And who never would be missed-—
    who never would be missed…
    The Mikado (1885). Song of Ko-Ko, the
              Lord High Executioner

The task of filling up the blanks I'd
    rather leave to you.
But it really doesn't matter whom you
    put upon the list,
For they'd none of 'em be missed—
They'd none of 'em be missed!
                    Ibid.

The threatened cloud has passed away,
And brightly shines the dawning day;
What though the night may come too
    soon,
We've years and years of afternoon!
   Ibid., Song of Nanki-Poo and Yum-Yum.

Sir, Saturday morning, although recur-
ring at regular and well-foreseen inter-
vals, always seems to take this railway by
surprise.
    [Letter complaining to a station-
    master.]

You have no idea what a poor opinion I
have of myself, and how little I deserve it.

JOHN PIERPONT MORGAN
1837–1913

American, banker, called "Jupiter," who sold $4 billion in bonds in Europe to build railroads in America. He merged large industrial companies, such as GE, AT&T, and U.S. Steel.

    A hard currency (gold) advocate, he kept the free silver populists at bay. Acting as a de facto reserve bank, he raised funds from U.S. banks to stop the panics of 1893 and 1907. His art collection became the New York Metropolitan Museum of Art. When Morgan died, John D. Rockefeller read that his net worth was only $80 million. Rock-efeller said, "And to think he wasn't even a rich man."

It will fluctuate.
[About the stock market.]
Quoted in *Time* (August 19, 1966)

Remember, my son, that any man who is a bear on the future of this country will go broke.
Quoted by his son, Chicago Club (December 10, 1908)

A man always has two reasons for what he does, a good one and the real one.
In Owen Wister, *Roosevelt: The Story of a Friendship* (1930)

Any man who has to ask about the annual upkeep of a yacht can't afford one.
In Bennett Cerf, *Laughing Stock* (1945)

[A man said he could not sleep at night from worrying about his stocks and asked what he should do. Morgan replied:]
Sell down to the sleeping point.
In L. R. Frank, *Quotationary* (1999)

You can do business with anyone, but you can only sail a boat with a gentleman.
In Harold Evans, *The American Century* (1999)

[Asked if credit were not based on collateral, Morgan replied] No. The first thing is character. A man I do not trust could not get money from me on all the bonds in Christendom.
In John S. Gordon, *An Empire of Wealth* (2004)

[When Theodore Roosevelt's government said it would sue the Northern Securities Corporation for antitrust violations, Morgan told Roosevelt:]

If we have done anything wrong, send your man to my man and they can fix it up.
Ibid.

I don't want a lawyer to tell me what I cannot do; I hire him to tell me how to do what I want to do.

I'm not interested in return *on* capital. I'm interested in return *of* capital.

HENRY BROOKS ADAMS
1838–1918

American, historian, Boston Brahmin, grandson of John Quincy Adams, and a man of letters, who despised egalitarianism. His autobiography, *The Education of Henry Adams* (1907), regretted he was educated in Greek and Latin when he needed mathematics. His biography tells readers about his conclusions about life, especially his fear that man may be overwhelmed by his inventions. He believes the multiplication of mechanical forces will lead to the degeneration of relationships between people as they lose their morals in money grubbing.

Politics, as a practice, whatever its professions, has always been the systematic organization of hatreds.
The Education of Henry Adams (1907), ch. 1
A friend in power is a friend lost.
Ibid., ch. 7

Knowledge of human nature is the beginning and end of political education.
Ibid., ch. 12

A teacher affects eternity; he can never tell where his influence stops.
Ibid., ch. 20

One friend in a lifetime is much; two are many; three are hardly possible. Friendship needs a certain parallelism of life, a community of thought, a rivalry of aim.

> Ibid.

They know enough who know how to learn.

> Ibid., ch. 21

Man has mounted science, and is now run away with. I firmly believe that before many centuries more, science will be the master of man. The engines he will have invented will be beyond his strength to control. Some day science may have the existence of mankind in its power, and the human race commit suicide by blowing up the world.

> Letter to Charles Francis Adams
> (April 11, 1862)

Philosophy gives us unintelligible answers to insoluble problems.

JAMES J. HILL
1838–1916

American, one of the greatest railroad builders. He built the profitable Great Northern Pacific without subsidies.

> If you want to know whether you are destined to be a success or a failure in life, you can easily find out. The test is simple and is infallible. Are you able to save money?

> The lucky fellow is the plucky fellow who has been burning midnight oil and taking defeat after defeat with a smile.

MARGARET ELIZABETH SANGSTER
1838–1912

American, poet.

> It isn't the thing you do, dear,
> It's the thing you leave undone
> That gives you a bit of heartache
> At setting of the sun.
> The tender word forgotten,
> The letter you did not write,
> The flowers you did not send, dear,
> Are your haunting ghosts at night.
> > "The Sin of Omission," st. 1

JOHN D. ROCKEFELLER
1839–1937

American, industrialist. He rationalized the oil refinery industry by slashing the price of kerosene from a dollar a gallon to eight cents, so a poor person could light his house for one cent per hour. Lower oil prices made the economy sing, which gave jobs to millions and allowed them to rise into the middle class. He created three hundred new products out of oil wastes that had been dumped.

Ida Tarbell, a muckraker whose father went bankrupt in oil refining, lied in her *History of the Standard Oil Company* (1902) that Rockefeller temporarily lowered prices to bankrupt rivals and then raised them to gouge consumers. For three decades until Standard Oil Company was broken up by the U.S. Supreme Court, oil prices fell steadily by two-thirds. Afterward, oil prices rose.

The real Gilded Age monopolists were politicians who passed the fraudulent Sherman Antitrust Act and whose high tariffs let favored industries bilk the public. Most companies prosecuted for antitrust violations have been charged with having *lower* prices than their competitors. The government gets confused about what hurts competition and what hurts competitors. The government, in order to placate politically powerful corporations and unions, often loses sight of what is good for the economy and the consumer.

Thomas Sowell in *Basic Economics* (2004), "Monopoly is the enemy of efficiency, whether under capitalism or socialism. The difference between the two systems is that monopoly is the norm under socialism."

> We must remember we are refining oil for the poor man and he must have it cheap and good.
> [Compare with the son of the founder of Merck and Co., George Merck II: "We try never to forget that medicine is for the patient.... It is not for the profits. The profits follow, and if we have remembered that they have never failed to appear. The better we have remembered it, the larger they have been."]
>
> Letter to a partner (1885)

From the beginning, I was trained to work, to save and to give.

At sixteen, Rockefeller earned fifty cents a day from which he tithed 10 percent and saved 40 percent. Starting his own business in grain shipping at age nineteen, he had the confidence of those who dealt with him in his scrupulous honesty. He recruited as partners and employees only those who were devoutly religious.

We never deceived ourselves.
[How Standard Oil became the leader.]

I believe that every right implies a responsibility; every opportunity, an obligation; every possession a duty.

You know that great prejudice exists against all successful business enterprise—the more successful, the greater the prejudice.

Good management consists in showing average people how to do the work of superior people.

If you want to succeed you should strike out on new paths rather than travel the worn paths of accepted success.

The road to happiness lies in two simple principles: find what it is that interests you and that you can do well, and when you find it, put your whole soul into it—every bit of energy and ambition and natural ability you have.

The ability to deal with people is as purchasable a commodity as sugar or coffee. And I will pay more for that ability than for any other under the sun.

9
BOUNTIFUL BARONS

Entrepreneurs have doubled America's standard of living at least every forty years! In 1900, life expectancy was 47 years, and only 10 percent of Americans had a standard of living higher than the official poverty level in 2000. As late as 1945, one-third of Americans lacked running water; most had no telephone or refrigerator; half of the farmers had no electricity; and the average income was $1,450.

In 2005, of the 36 million Americans "living in poverty," 98 percent own a refrigerator; 97 percent own one or more color TVs; 77 percent own telephones, VCRs, and DVDs; 76 percent own air-conditioning; 75 percent own autos; 73 percent own microwave ovens; 62 percent own cable or dish TV, 46 percent own homes. They have food stamps, free medical care for children, and more housing than the Parisians. The *Economist* in 1988 wrote that less than 1 percent of those who finished high school, stayed married, and kept a job were poor.

We now know after Say, Schumpeter, Drucker, Solow, and Gilder that the key to economic growth is knowledge made productive by entrepreneurial risk-taking and managerial skill. For example, the Franklin stove reduced by 80 percent the fuel needed to heat a house. A pound of sand made into fiber optics today can now carry more telephone calls than tons of twisted copper wire! Thus, the cost of a three-minute telephone call from San Francisco to

New York fell from $12.66 in 1960 to $0.15 in 2002—or $0.03 in a 1960 dollar. Entrepreneurs by self-sacrifice and embracing risk have given us all necessities and many comforts.

Yet intellectuals vilify entrepreneurs by calling them "robber barons," a term originally used for German lords on the Rhine who charged a fee to pass their castles. Matthew Josephson wrote *The Robber Barons* in 1933 condemning America's best entrepreneurs while he campaigned for Communist politicians and lived luxuriously off of his family's banking fortune. But America had increased her manufacturing output from 1865 to 1914—the period covered by his book—by a factor of 33, which had more than quadrupled the standard of living. Note: Most Marxist intellectuals were heirs to fortunes or had rich fathers, for example, Karl Marx, Friedrich Engels, Rosa Luxemburg, Vladimir Lenin, Fidel Castro, and Herbert Marcuse.

Harvard professor Robert Nozick argued that intellectuals (the media, academia, and men-of-letters who mold public opinion) tend to be anti-entrepreneurial. They feel they are the best people because they got the highest grades in school. But free markets more highly value risk-taking and leadership, the rarer and more productive attributes. Thus denied the wealth and power that accrues to daring entrepreneurs, disgruntled intellectuals try to redistribute wealth and power through politics, a medium that utilizes their word-smithing skills.

Marxists are right that entrepreneurs seek monopoly pricing power, for example, copyrights, patents, new distribution channels, etc.—the new paradigms that enrich us. But, all private monopolies are temporary, unless protected by government. Every new monopolist is threatened by future competition, unless there is a legal barrier to new entrants.

Monopolies are only problems if created or sustained by coercion, as are all of the government-protected monopolies, as for example, the U.S. Postal Service. Public monopolies go on forever. The most backward U.S. monopoly with over an 80% market share is k–12 public education, a $450 billion industry largely controlled by teacher unions.

> It is a grotesque distortion of the true state of affairs… to speak of *private cartels* instead of *government made cartels*. [Author's emphasis.]
> Ludwig von Mises, *Human Action* (1949)

Burton Folsom's *Myth of the Robber Barons* (1991) showed that "political entrepreneurs" bilk the public through government coercion: quotas, tariffs, monopolies, and the like.

ALFRED T. MAHAN
1840–1914

American, admiral, who wrote that the nation that controls the sea controls the world. Mahan's strategy required coaling stations, but not colonies.

The world has never seen a more impressive demonstration of the influence of sea power upon its history. Those far distant, storm-beaten ships, upon which the Grand Army never looked, stood between it and the dominion of the world. [Of the effectiveness of sea power in thwarting Napoleon's invasion of England.]

> *The Influence of Sea Power Upon History,
> 1660–1783* (1892) , vol. II

CLAUDE MONET
1840–1926

French, painter, whose view of the Le Havre harbor entitled *Impression: Sunrise* gave the name "impressionist" to a new school that began in France in the 1870s including Degas, Renoir, Pissarro, and Sisley. They captured spontaneous impressions and they broke with tradition by going outside their studios to paint. That was made practical by paints in tubes. Also, photography had made realism less important than capturing a mood.

> [Clemenceau wrote to Monet:] "I love you because… you taught me to understand light."

AUGUSTE RODIN
1840–1917

French, sculptor: *The Thinker, The Kiss,* and *Adam and Eve.*

> Civilization is, after all, but a coat of paint that washes away when the rain falls.

> I invent nothing. I rediscover.

WILLIAM GRAHAM SUMNER
1840–1910

American, laissez-faire economist, and disciple of Herbert Spencer. He castigated both corporate leaders and union officials who conspired with the government to enact tariffs and other protections from competition. He and Schumpeter agreed that free trade obviates any need for colonialism. Logically, capitalism is anti-imperialist.

> It is the greatest folly of which a man can be capable to sit down with a slate and pencil to plan out a new social world.
>
> In Harold Evans, *The American Century* (1999)

> The Forgotten Man…delving away in patient industry, supporting his family, paying his taxes, casting his vote, supporting the church and the school…but he is the only one for whom there is no provision in the big divide….his chief business in life is to pay.
>
> Speech, "The Forgotten Man" (1883)

> If we look back for comparison to anything of which human history gives us a type of experiment, we see that the modern free system of industry offers to every living human being chances of happiness indescribably in excess of what former generations have possessed.
>
> Jim Powell, *The Triumph of Liberty* (2000)

EMILE ZOLA
1840–1936

French, anticlerical novelist, and socialist, whose masterpiece *Germinal* (1885), features the mechanic Étienne Lantier as the hero leading a strike against a coal company.

> I accuse.
>
> ["J'accuse." Title of an open letter to the president of the French Republic regarding the Dreyfus Affair.]
>
> *L'Aurore* (January 13, 1898)

GEORGES CLEMENCEAU
1841–1929

French, socialist prime minister during World War I, and presiding officer at the Versailles Peace Conference, where he treated Germany harshly, which led to Hitler's empowerment and World War II. The Versailles Treaty violated Machiavelli's principle; it should have either been lenient, or crippled Germany beyond any possibility of recovery. It was said that Clemenceau had one illusion, France, and one disillusion, the French.

> War is too serious a business to be left to the generals.
>
> Attributed to him and others

> President Wilson had Fourteen Points when the Lord Himself only had ten.

> The United States has gone from barbarism to decadence without achieving any civilization in between.

EDWARD VII
1841–1910

English, king, who succeeded Victoria in 1901. A gluttonous hedonist, he spent his life in foreign spars. Typical of the effete elite, Edward accepted the socialists' pamphlets as truth. Happily, the middle class had more backbone than their royals.

We are all socialists nowadays.

Speech (1895)

Oliver Wendell Holmes, Jr.
1841–1935

American, associate justice (1902–32), a misanthropic Boston Brahmin, called the "great dissenter" and the "Yankee from Olympus." He revolted against natural law, the Hebrew and Roman legal theory espoused by virtually all of America's founders that basic moral principles are discernible through reason. A corollary to natural law is natural rights. Holmes subscribed to the theory of Positive Law, to wit, the law is whatever the Constitution, legislature, or precedence says it is. If the law endorses slavery, we should obey it.

When ninety-two and nearly blind, a friend volunteered to read to him and Holmes selected Plato's *Symposium*. When asked why so heavy a book, Holmes replied: "To improve my mind."

> The life of the law has not been logic: it has been experience. The felt necessities of the time, the prevalent moral and political theories, intuitions of public policy, avowed or unconscious, even the prejudices which judges share with their fellow-men, have had a good deal more to do than the syllogism in determining the rules by which men should be governed. The law embodies the story of a nation's development though many centuries, and it cannot be dealt with as if it contained only the axioms and corollaries of a book of mathematics....
> "The Common Law" (1881), lecture 1

I think that, as life is action and passion, it is required of a man that he should share the passion and action of his time at peril of being judged not to have lived.

Memorial Day Address (May 30, 1884)

We pause...to recall what our country has done for each of us, and to ask ourselves what we can do for our country.

Speech (May 30, 1884)

The prophecies of what the courts will do in fact, and nothing more pretentious, are what I mean by the law.

The Path of the Law (1897)

Certainty generally is illusion, and repose is not the destiny of man.

Ibid.

Taxes are what we pay for civilized society.
Compania de Tabacos v. Collector, 275 U.S. 87, (1904)

Great cases like hard cases make bad law.
Northern Securities Co. v. United States (1904)

Life is a romantic business. It is painting a picture, not doing a sum—but you have to make romance. And it will come to the question how much fire you have in your belly.

In L R. Frank, *Quotationary* (1999)

The only prize much cared for by the powerful is power. The prize of the general is not a bigger tent, but command.

"Law and the Court" speech (February 15, 1913)

I recognize without hesitation that judges do and must legislate, but they can do so only interstitially; they are confined from molar to molecular motions.
Southern Pacific Co. v. Jensen, 244 U. S. 205, 221 (1917)

The common law is not a brooding omnipresence in the sky but the articulate voice of some sovereign or quasi-sovereign that can be identified.

Ibid.

Certitude is not the test of certainty. We have been cock-sure of many things that were no so.

Natural Law (1918)

...the ultimate good desired is better reached by free trade in ideas—that the best test of truth is the power of the thought to get itself accepted in the competition of the market, and that truth is the only ground upon which their wishes safely can be carried out. That at any rate is the theory of our Constitution. It is an experiment, as all life is an experiment.

Abrams v. United States, 250 U.S. 616, 630 (1919) (dissent)

The most stringent protection of free speech would not protect a man in falsely shouting fire in a crowded theater.... The question in every case is whether the words are of such a nature as to create a clear and present danger that they will bring about substantive evils that Congress has a right to prevent. It is a question of proximity and degree.

[Holmes sustained Shenck's conviction for distributing leaflets soliciting men to disobey peaceably the military draft.]

Shenck vs. U.S., 249 U.S. 47 (1919)

It is said that this manifesto is more than a theory, that it was an incitement. Every idea is an incitement.

Gitlow v. New York, 268 U.S. 652, 673 (1925)

Upon this point a page of history is worth a volume of logic.

New York Trust Co. v. Eisner, 256 U.S. 345, 349 (1921)

It is better for all the world, if instead of waiting to execute degenerate offspring for crime, or let them starve for their imbecility, society can prevent those who are manifestly unfit from continuing their kind. The principle that sustains compulsory vaccination is broad enough to cover cutting the Fallopian tubes.... Three generations of imbeciles are enough.

Buck v. Bell, 274 U.S. 200, 207 (1927)

If there is any principle of the Constitution that more imperatively calls for attachment than any other it is the principle of free thought—not free thought for those who agree with us but freedom for the thought that we hate.

United States v. Schwimmer, 279 U.S. 644, 653 (1928)

The power to tax is not the power to destroy while this court sits.

Panhandle Oil Co. v. Mississippi (1930)

A policeman may have a constitutional right to talk politics, but he has no constitutional right to be a policeman.

Supreme Judicial Court of Massachusetts

...we need education in the obvious more than investigation of the obscure...

Every year we have to wager our salvation upon some prophecy based on imperfect knowledge.

It is revolting to have no better reason for a rule of law than that so it was laid down in the time of Henry IV. It is still more revolting if the grounds upon which it was laid down have vanished long since, and the rule simply persists from blind imitation of the past.

Oh, to be seventy again!
　　[When eighty-seven and seeing a pretty woman.]

If you want to hit a bird on the wing you must have all your will in focus, you must not be thinking about yourself and, equally, you must not be thinking about your neighbor: you must be living in your eye on that bird. Every achievement is a bird on the wing.

It is not well for soldiers to think much about wounds. Sooner or later we shall fall, but meantime it is for us to fix our eyes upon the point to be stormed and to get there if we can.
　　[He was wounded three times in the army.]

AMBROSE GWINETT BIERCE
1842–1914

American, journalist. His *Devil's Dictionary* (1911) was a retitle of *Cynic's Word Book* (1906).

"Acquaintance": A person whom we know well enough to borrow from, but not well enough to lend to.

"Bigot": One who is obstinately and zealously attached to an opinion that you do not entertain.

"Circumlocution": A literary trick whereby the writer who has nothing to say breaks it gently to the reader.

"Cynic": A blackguard whose faulty vision sees things as they are, not as they ought to be.

"Education": That which discloses to the wise and disguises from the foolish their lack of understanding.

"Egotist": A man of low taste more interested in himself than in me.

"Fashion": A despot whom the wise ridicule and obey.

"Heathen": A benighted creature who has the folly to worship something that he can see and feel.

"Hospitality": The virtue which makes us feed and lodge certain persons not in need of food or lodging.

"Lawyer": One skilled in circumvention of the law.

"Love": A temporary insanity curable by marriage.

"Revolution": An abrupt change in the form of misgovernment.

"Tariff": Taxes on imports designed to protect the domestic producer against the greed of his consumer.

"War": God's way of teaching geography.

The covers of this book are too far apart.
　　[A complete book review.]
　　　In C. H. Grattan, *Bitter Bierce* (1929)

WILLIAM JAMES
1842–1910

American, Harvard professor of philosophy and psychology, and brother of Henry James. He labeled his radical empiricism "pragmatism," a word coined by C. S. Pierce. There is no absolute truth and no transcendent principles. Something is true only if it is useful—the ultimate moral relativism. His *The Varieties of Religious Experience* (1902) held any faith to be "true" if it satisfied. In *The Meaning of Truth* (1909), he held "the ultimate test for us of what a truth means is the conduct it dictates or inspires." But G. K Chesterton rightly concluded that pragmatism never works because it supplies only the means and never the destination.

> The deepest principle of human nature is the craving to be appreciated.
>
> Letter (April 6, 1896)

> There is very little difference between one man and another; but what little there is, is very important.
>
> Ibid.

> The moral flabbiness born of the exclusive worship of the bitch-goddess SUCCESS.
>
> Letter to H. G. Wells
> (September 11, 1906)

> First, you know, a new theory is attacked as absurd; then it is admitted to be true, but obvious and insignificant; finally it is seen to be so important that its adversaries claim that they themselves discovered it.
>
> Pragmatism (1907), Lecture 6

> Hogamus higamus,
> Man is polygamous.

> Higamus, hogamus,
> Woman is monogamous.
>
> In *The Oxford Book of Marriage* (1990)

> The greatest revolution of our generation is the discovery that human beings, by changing the inner attitudes of their minds, can change the outer aspects of their lives.

> Nothing is so fatiguing as the eternal hanging on of an uncompleted task.

ALFRED MARSHALL
1842–1924

English, the world's greatest economist next to Adam Smith, according to Milton Friedman. He was the first to understand that "knowledge is our most powerful engine of production; it enables us to subdue nature and force her to satisfy our wants." He developed the theories of supply and demand curves and marginal utility (elasticity of supply and demand). "Time" is the key for determining value. In the short run, the value of any good, like diamonds, turns on existing demand and supply. An increase in demand will bid up the price, so over time new mines will be opened and then the price will fall as supply increases. If enough new supply is added, the higher-cost mines will be closed. For a seminal layman's treatment of marginal utility, see Jude Wanniski, *The Way the World Works* (1978).

> We might as reasonably dispute whether it is the upper or the under blade of a pair of scissors that cuts a piece of paper, as whether value is governed by utility or cost of production.
>
> *Principles of Economics* (1890)

GEORGE WASHINGTON PLUNKITT
1842–1924

American, Tammany Hall Democrat, who made millions self-dealing with public information.

> I seen my opportunities and I took 'em. [Referring to Tammany Hall's "honest graft," for example, to buy private property knowing about public improvements to come.]

HENRY JAMES
1843–1916

English (American-born), brother of William James. He wrote novels about the rich, and contrasted American parochialism and innocence with Europe's sophistication and corruption.

> Live all you can; it's a mistake not to. It doesn't so much matter what you do in particular, so long as you have your life. If you haven't had that what have you had?
> *The Ambassadors* (1903), bk. 5, ch. 2

> Summer afternoon—summer afternoon; to me those have always been the two most beautiful words in the English language.
> In Edith Wharton, *A Backward Glance* (1934), ch. 10

ANATOLE FRANCE
1844–1924

French, novelist, anti-clerical rationalist, and 1921 winner of the Nobel Prize in Literature.

> People who have no faults are terrible; there is no way of taking advantage of them.
> *The Crime of Sylvestre Bonnard* (1881), tr. Lafcadio Hearn (1890)

> They [the poor] have to labor in the face of the majestic equality of the law, which forbids the rich as well as the poor to sleep under bridges, to beg in the streets, and to steal bread.
> Le Lys Rouse (1894), ch.7

> Only men who are not interested in women are interested in women's clothes; men who like women never notice what they wear.

FRIEDRICH WILHELM NIETZSCHE
1844–1900

German, atheist, antidemocrat, existentialist, and self-styled "anti-Christ." He echoes Gibbon that Christian morality enervates the strong and Proudhon that the majority exploits the strong.

Whatever accords with human nature is moral, and our task in life is to fulfill our instincts, not to inhibit them. There have been two moral systems throughout history: one of the elite and one of the ruled. He favored the morality of the conquerors, under the banner that might makes right. Once Christianity is rejected, the morality that makes masters slaves and slaves masters will go. Christianity is "a declaration of war against life."

Nietzsche's philosophy is the foundation of modernism. He said, "There are no facts, only interpretations." Moral relativism is fundamental to both Nietzsche and modernism—anything is permitted to the powerful. To Nietzsche, ultimate truth is death, so we need poetry to tell us lies. "We possess art lest we should perish of the truth."

The greatest ideas are the greatest events.

Gott ist tot. God is dead.
> [Nietzsche observes that the intellectuals' belief in God is dead, so it will be replaced with faith in governments, that is, "barbaric nationalistic brotherhoods." This will cause great wars in the twentieth century and worse later in the "the total eclipse of all values."]
>> *The Gay Science* (1882) bk. 1, sec. 108, tr. Walter Kaufmann (1974)

Morality is the herd instinct in the individual.
> Ibid., bk. 3, sec. 116

One will rarely err if extreme actions be ascribed to vanity, ordinary actions to habit, and mean actions to fear.
> *Human, All Too Human* (1878), tr. Marion Faber (1984)

Where there is neither love nor hatred in the game, woman's play is mediocre.
> *Beyond Good and Evil* (1884) pt. IV, ch. 72

It is not the strength but the duration of great sentiments that makes great men.
> Ibid.

He who fights with monsters must take care lest he thereby become a monster. And if you gaze for long into an abyss, the abyss gazes also into you.
> Ibid. ch. 146.

The thought of suicide is a great source

of comfort: with it a calm passage is to be made across many a bad night.
> Ibid., ch. 157

It was subtle of God to learn Greek when he wished to become an author and not to learn it better.
> Ibid.

The blond beast of prey. (Blonde Bestie).
> *Genealogy of Morals* (1887), Essay 1

The sick are the greatest danger for the healthy; it is not from the strongest that harm comes to the strong, but from the weakest.
> Ibid., Essay 3

Whatever does not destroy me makes me stronger.
> *The Twilight of the Idols* (1888), tr. R. J. Hollingdale, "Maxims and Arrows"

It is my ambition to say in ten sentences what everyone else says in a whole book —what everyone else does not say in a whole book.
> Ibid., "Expeditions of an Untimely Man"

The Persian Zarathustra (Zoroaster) posited virtues opposite of the Christian's "slave morality." Man must use his will to surpass himself, to become "Übermensch" or "Overman" [not "superman"]. He must rise above ordinary men to love action and take pride in his creativity. Overman overcomes through his "Will to Power" the two great obstacles: "fear and custom." All institutions compel us to be normal; but we must resist and become creators. Übermensch can follow as well as lead; his only need for mastery is a self-mastery. All are animated by the Will to Power, even the weak, who collectively exploit the strong, live by evoking pity, and disguise their will to power as "social justice."

One must have chaos in oneself to be able to give birth to a dancing star.
Thus Spake Zarathustra (1883 – 91), tr. R. J. Hollingdale (1961), Prologue

Mistrust all in whom the urge to punish is powerful.
Ibid., "Of the Tarantulas"

Wherever I found a living creature, there I found the will to power.
Ibid., "Of Overcoming"

My time has not yet come either; some are born posthumously.
The Anti-Christ (1895), Foreword

Even a thought, even a possibility, can shatter us and transform us.
Ibid.

The weak and defective shall perish; and they shall be given assistance: that is the first principle of the Dionysian charity.
Ibid., "Aphorism 2"

Having stripped myself of all illusions, I have gone mad.
[Written in an asylum.]
In L. R. Frank, *Quotationary* (1999)

Unspoken truths become poisonous.
In L. R. Frank, *Wisdom* (2003)

Without music life would be a mistake.

During the journey we commonly forget its goal. Almost every profession is chosen and commenced as a means to an end but continued as an end in itself.

Forgetting our objectives is the most frequent of all acts of stupidity.

There surely exists for everyone a bait he cannot help taking. Thus to win many people over to a cause one needs only to put on it a gloss of philanthropy, nobility, charitableness, self-sacrifice—and on the what cause can one not put it? These are the dainties for their soul.

In certain cases it is indecent to go on living. To continue to vegetate in a state of cowardly dependence upon doctors, once the meaning of life has been lost, ought to be regarded with the greatest contempt.

The state tells lies in all the languages of good and evil; and whatever it says it lies—and whatever it has it has stolen.

Man is for woman the means; the end is always the child.

Two different things wanteth the true man: danger and diversion. Therefore wanteth he woman, as the most dangerous plaything. Man shall be trained for war, and woman for the recreation of the warrior; all else is folly.

Woman understands children better than man does, but man is the more childlike.

Thus spake the old woman: "Thou goest to women? Do not forget thy whip!"

He who has a why to live for can bear almost any *how*.

Self-respect depends on being able to make reprisals.

DANIEL HUDSON BURNHAM
1846–1912

American, architect, who pioneered the skyscraper in 1903 with his Flatiron Building (twenty-six stories) on a triangular lot on Broadway in New York City. He designed the Chicago's World's Fair and revised Pierre Charles L'Enfant's plans for Washington, D.C., by permitting only neo-classical buildings on the mall.

Note: The Otis Brothers built the first elevator, in 1889, in the Demarest Building in New York.

Make no little plans; they have no magic to stir men's blood.

ALEXANDER GRAHAM BELL
1847–1922

American (Scottish-born), inventor of the telephone. Western Union rejected Bell's offer to sell the rights to his telephone for $100,000.

Mr. Watson, come here; I want you.
[First words over a telephone, March 1876.]

THOMAS ALVA EDISON
1847–1931

American, inventor, and dyslexic thought to be retarded. He invented the telegraph receiver and transmitter, incandescent lamp (3,000 experiments over fourteen years), storage battery, gramophone, motion picture projector, and the carbon transmitter that made Bell's telephone practical. He founded the predecessor company to General Electric and built the first power plant in 1882 to electrify 85 houses in lower Manhattan. Most important, he invented the research laboratory. He said, "I find out what the world needs and proceed to invent it." Of Edison's 1069 patents, only 13 made money. Note: only one of 300 patents applied for makes money.

Genius is one per cent inspiration and ninety-nine per cent perspiration.
Harpers Monthly (September 1932)

The reason a lot of people do not recognize opportunity is because it usually goes around wearing overalls looking like hard work.

I am glad that the eight-hour day had not been invented when I was a young man. If my life had been made up of eight-hour-days I do not believe I could have accomplished a great deal.

Many of life's failures are men who did not realize how close they were to success when they gave up.

There is a way to do it better. Find it.

There is far more danger in public than in private monopoly, for when government goes into business it can always shift its losses to the taxpayers.

I am more of a sponge than an inventor. I absorb ideas from every source. I take half-matured schemes for mechanical development and make them practical. I am a sort of a middleman between the long-haired and impractical inventor and the hard-headed business man who measures all things in terms of dollars and cents. My principal business is giving commercial value to others' brilliant but misdirected ideas.

I start where the last man left off.

[Asked about the results of his attempts to develop a storage battery, Edison replied:] Results? Why, I have gotten a lot of results. I know fifty thousand things that won't work.

I have friends in overalls whose friendship I would not swap for the favor of all the kings of the world.

There ain't no rules around here! We're trying to accomplish something!

I am long on ideas, but short on time.
     [Said at 82; he died at 84.]

JOEL CHANDLER HARRIS
1848–1908

American, fabulist who compiled 185 African American folktales that are comparable in insight to Aesop's Fables. Today most schools ban them because they are written in black dialect and the narrator, Uncle Remus, was a happy old slave.

Watch out when you're getting all you want. A fat hog ain't in luck.
     Uncle Remus, His Songs and His Sayings
     (1880), "Plantation Proverbs"

Ef you don't lemme loose, I'll knock you agin', sez Brer Rabbit, sezee, en wid dat he fotch 'er a wipe wid de udder hen', en dat stuck. Tar-Baby ain't sayin' nuthin,' en Brer Fox, he lay low…
     Ibid., "The Tar-Baby Story"

"Howdy, Brer Rabbit," sez Brer Fox, sezee. "You look sorter stuck up dis mawnin," sezee, en den he rolled on de groun', en laughed twel he couldn't laugh no mo. "I speck you'll take dinner wid me dis time, Brer Rabbit. I done laid in some calamus root, en I ain't gwineter take no skuse," sez Brer Fox, sezee…
     Ibid.

"I don't keer w'at you do wid me, Brer Fox," sezee, "Roas'me, Brer Fox," sezee, "but don't fling me in dat briar-patch… "'Bred en bawn in a briar-patch, Brer Fox—bred en bawn in a briar-patch!" en wid dat he skip out des ez lively ez a cricket in de embers.

ELLEN KEY
1849–1926

Swedish, writer, and feminist.

The socially pernicious and soul-withering consequences of the working of mothers outside the home must cease.
     The Renaissance of Motherhood, pt. III, ch. 2

WILLIAM ERNEST HENLEY
1849–1903

English, poet and critic.

In the fell clutch of circumstance
I have not winced nor cried aloud.
Under the bludgeonings of chance
My head is bloody, but unbowed.
     [Invictus means unconquerable.]
     "Invictus," st. 2. (1875), *Poems* (1898)

It matters not how strait the gate,
How charged with punishments the scroll,

I am the master of my fate:
I am the captain of my soul.
                                        Ibid., st. 3

EMMA LAZARUS
1849–87

American, poet.

"Keep, ancient lands, your storied
    pomp!" cries she
With silent lips. "Give me your tired,
    your poor,
Your huddled masses yearning to
    breathe free,
The wretched refuse of your teeming shore,
Send these, the homeless, tem-
    pest-tossed, to me:
I lift my lamp beside the golden door!"
            "The New Colossus" (1883), st. 2

This poem demonstrates a poet's power. The Statue of Liberty was not designed by French sculptor Bartholdi to honor Europe's wretched refuse seeking shelter. It honored the heroic Anglo-Saxons who had left comfortable homes in the most advanced nation to tame a wilderness and win independence by force of arms from the world's greatest military power.

IVAN PETROVICH PAVLOV
1849–1936

Russian, physiologist, who discovered a dog would salivate on hearing a bell, if it were followed by food, a "conditioned reflex" to a stimulus. To Communists, this meant that human nature could be reshaped. American psychologist B. F. Skinner advanced Pavlov's work into "behavioral psychology": You can fix people by fixing their environment. Today there are few behaviorists.

SAMUEL GOMPERS
1850–1924

American (English-born), American Federation of Labor (AFL) founder. Unlike European unions, the AFL opposed socialism, so it would be free to organize far more strikes against private employers.

What does labor want? We want more schoolhouses and less jails; more books and less arsenals; more learning and less vice; more leisure and less greed; more justice and less revenge; in fact, more of the opportunities to cultivate our better natures, to make manhood more noble, womanhood more beautiful, and childhood more happy and bright. "More! More! More!"
[Speech given repeatedly for years.]

As one voice labor must speak—to reward its friends and punish its enemies.
    In *Labor* (Railroad Brotherhoods' weekly)

The worst crime against working people is a company which fails to operate at a profit.

When the union's inspiration through
    the worker's blood shall run,
There can be no power greater anywhere
    beneath the sun.
Yet what force on earth is weaker than
    the feeble strength of one?
But the union makes us strong.
            "Solidarity Forever" (1915), st. 1

Is there aught we hold in common with
    the greedy parasite,
Who would lash us into serfdom and
    would crush us with his might?

They have taken untold millions that
   they never toiled to earn,
But without our brain and muscle not a
   single wheel could turn.

Ibid., st. 2

LABOR UNIONS

Labor unions raise members' pay and
benefits by excluding competing workers,
promoting trade protection, restricting
work rules, and so forth.

   Under British and American common law,
both union and corporate restraints on trade
were illegal. Morgan Reynolds's *Making
America Poorer: The Cost of Labor Law* (1987)
argues that unions increase union wages
by about 15 percent. But those benefits are
achieved at the cost of reducing the national
rate of economic growth some 30 percent.

ROBERT LOUIS STEVENSON
1850–94

Scottish, novelist, poet, and essayist known
for *Treasure Island* (1881), *Kidnapped* (1886),
and *Dr. Jekyll and Mr. Hyde* (1886). Dr. Jekyll,
a physician, discovers a drug to give different physical bodies to his two personalities: one sympathetic and the other evil. As
the demonic Mr. Hyde, he commits dark
acts. Jekyll tries to protect Mr. Hyde, as a
loving father would a rebellious son. Mr.
Hyde commits a murder and resists being
transformed back into Jekyll. Jekyll commits suicide to end the evil.

If a man knows he will sooner or later
be robbed upon a journey, he will have a
bottle of the best in every inn, and look
upon all his extravagances as so much

gained upon the thieves.
   [Argument against death taxes.]

An Inland Voyage (1878)

The cruelest lies are often told in silence.

Virginibus Puerisque (1881), "Truth of
Intercourse"

Old or young, we are all on our last cruise.

Ibid., "Crabbed Age and Youth"

Give me the young man who has brains
enough to make a fool of himself.

Ibid.

Books are good enough in their own way,
but they are a mighty bloodless substitute for life.

Ibid., "An Apology for Idlers"

There is no duty we so much underrate as
the duty of being happy.

Ibid.

To travel hopefully is better than to
arrive, and the true success is to labour.

Ibid., "Eldorado"

We are in such haste to be doing, to be
writing, to be gathering gear, to make
our voice audible a moment in the deri-
sive silence of eternity, that we forget
that one thing, of which these are but the
parts—namely, to live.

Ibid., "Walking Tours"

To be what we are, and to become what
we are capable of becoming, is the only
end of life.

Familiar Studies of Men and Books (1882)

Fifteen men on the Dead Man's Chest
Yo-ho-ho and a bottle of rum.

Treasure Island (1883)

Under the wide and starry sky,
Dig the grave and let me lie.
Glad did I live and gladly die,
And I laid me down with a will.
  "Requiem," *Underwoods* (1887), bk. 1., st. 1

This be the verse you grave for me:
Here he lies where he longed to be;
Home is the sailor, home from sea,
And the hunter home from the hill.
                              Ibid., st. 2

These are my politics: to change what
we can; to better what we can; but still
to bear in mind that man is but a devil
weakly fettered by some generous beliefs
and impositions; and for no word however noble sounding, and no cause however just and pious, to relax the stricture
of these bonds.
  More New Arabian Nights: The Dynamiter
    (1885), "Epilogue of the Cigar Divan"

You, too, my mother, read my rhymes
For love of unforgotten times.
And you may chance to hear once more
The little feet along the floor.
      A Child's Garden of Verses (1885)

When I am grown to man's estate
I shall be very proud and great,
And tell the other girls and boys
Not to meddle with my toys.
              Ibid., "Looking Forward"

A child should always say what's true,
And speak when he is spoken to,
And behave mannerly at table;
At least as far as he is able.
          Ibid., "Whole Duty of Children"

Must we to bed indeed? Well then,
Let us arise and go like men,

And face with an undaunted tread
The long black passage up to bed.
  Ibid., "North-West Passage, Goodnight" st. 3

Still obscurely fighting the lost fight of
virtue, still clinging, in the brothel or on
the scaffold, to some rag of honour, the
poor jewel of their souls!
    Across the Plains (1892), "Lay Morals"

So long as we love we serve; so long as
we are loved by others, I would almost
say that we are indispensable; and no
man is useless while he has a friend.
                              Ibid.

If your morals make you dreary, depend
upon it, they are wrong. I do not say give
them up, for they may be all you have,
but conceal them like a vice lest they
should spoil the lives of better and simpler people.
                              Ibid.

Everyone lives by selling something,
whatever be his right to it.
                    Ibid., " Beggars"

Here lies one who meant well, tried a little,
failed much;—surely that may be his epitaph of which he need not be ashamed.
              Ibid., "A Christmas Sermon"

You cannot run away from a weakness;
you must some time fight it out or perish; and if that be so, why not now, and
where you stand?
          Ibid., "The Amateur Emigrant"

But all that I could think of, in the
    darkness and the cold,
Was that I was leaving home and my
    folks were growing old.
  "Christmas at Sea," st. 11, *Ballads* (1894)

Give us grace and strength to forbear and to persevere…. Give us courage and gaiety and the quiet mind. Spare to us our friends, soften to us our enemies. Bless us, if it may be, in all our innocent endeavors. If it may not, give us the strength to encounter that which is to come, that we be brave in peril, constant in tribulation, temperate in wrath, and in all changes of fortune, and down to the gates of death, loyal and loving one to another.

Go, little book, and wish to all
Flowers in the garden, meat in the hall,
A bin of wine, a spice of wit,
A house with lawns enclosing it,
A living river by the door,
A nightingale in the sycamore!

Successful is the person who has lived well, laughed often and loved much, who has gained the respect of children, who leaves the world better than he found it, who has never lacked appreciation for the earth's beauty, who never fails to look for the best in others or give the best of himself.

A man must not deny his manifest abilities, for that is to evade his obligation.

If a man love the labor of any trade, apart from any question of success or fame, the gods have called him.

ELLA WHEELER WILCOX
1850–1919

American, poet.

One ship drives east and another drives west

With the selfsame winds that blow.
'Tis the set of the sails and not the gales
Which tells us the way to go.
   "Winds of Fate," *Poems of Passion* (1883)

Laugh and the world laughs with you,
Weep, and you weep alone;
For the sad old earth must borrow its
   mirth,
But has trouble enough of its own.
   Ibid., "Solitude," st. 1 (partial)

Feast, and your halls are crowded;
Fast, and the world goes by.
   Ibid., st. 3 (partial)

There is no chance, no destiny, no fate,
Can circumvent or hinder or control
The firm resolve of a determined soul.
Gifts count for nothing; will alone is great;
All things give way before it, soon or late.
   Ibid., "Will," st. 1. (partial)

Each well-born soul must win what it
   deserves.
Let the fool prate of luck. The fortunate
Is he whose earnest purpose never
   swerves,
Whose slightest action or inaction serves
The one great aim. Why, even Death
   stands still,
And waits an hour sometimes for such
   a will.
   Ibid., st. 2

It is easy enough to be pleasant,
When life flows by like a song,
But the man worth while is one who
   will smile,
When everything goes dead wrong.
For the test of the heart is trouble,
And it always comes with the years,.
And the smile that is worth the praises
   of earth

Is the one that shines through tears.
        Ibid., "Worth While," st. 1

We flatter those we scarcely know,
We please the fleeting guest,
And deal full many a thoughtless blow
To those who love us best.
        Ibid., "Life's Scars," st. 3

FERDINAND FOCH
1851–1929

French, marshal and Allied commander in
World War I.

[A guest at a dinner given in honor of
Marshal Foch said that there was nothing but wind in French politeness. Marshal Foch retorted:] "Neither is there
anything but wind in a pneumatic tire,
yet it eases wonderfully the jolts along
life's highway."

This is not a peace treaty, it is an armistice for twenty years.
    [Treaty of Versailles, 1919.]
            In P. Reynaud, *Memoires* (1963)

My center is giving way, my right is
in retreat; situation excellent. I am
attacking.
    [At the Battle of the Marne, Sep-
    tember 1914.]

EDWIN MARKHAM
1852–1940

American, poet.

Why build these cities glorious
If man unbuilded goes?

In vain we build the world, unless
The builder also grows.
                "Man-Making"

Bowed by the weight of centuries he leans
Upon his hoe and gazes on the ground,
The emptiness of ages in his face,
And on his back the burden of the world.
Who made him dead to rapture and
        despair,
A thing that grieves not and that never
        hopes,
Stolid and stunned, a brother to the ox?
Who loosened and let down this brutal
        jaw?
Whose was the hand that slanted back
        this brow?
Whose breath blew out the light within
        this brain?
    [Of Millet's painting.]
        "The Man with the Hoe" (1899)," st. 1

When whirlwinds of rebellion shake all
        shores?
How will it be with kingdoms and with
        kings-
With those who shaped him to the
        thing he is-
When this dumb Terror shall rise to
        judge the world,
After the silence of the centuries?
                Ibid., st. 5 (partial)

Once where a prophet in the palm
        shade basked
A traveler chanced at noon to rest his
        mules.
"What sort of people may they be," he
        asked,
"In this proud city on the plains
        o'spread?"
"Well friend, what sort of people
        whence you came?"
"What sort?" the packman scowled;

"Why knaves and fools."
"You'll find the people here the same,"
    the wise man said.
"The Right Kind of People," st. 1

Another stranger in the dusk drew near,
And pausing, cried "What sort of
    people here
In your bright city where yon towers
    arise?"
"Well, friend, what sort of people
    whence you came?"
"What sort?" the pilgrim smiled, "Good,
    true and wise.
"You'll find the people here the same,"
    the wise man said.
Ibid., st. 2

He drew a circle that shut me out–
Heretic, rebel, a thing to flout.
But Love and I had the wit to win:
We drew a circle that took him in.
"Outwitted"

GEORGE A. MOORE
1852–1933

Irish, novelist.

A man travels the world over in search of what he needs and returns home to find it.
The Brook Kerith (1916), ch. 11

The substance of our lives is women. All other things are irrelevancies, hypocrisies, subterfuges. We sit talking of sports and politics, and all the while our hearts are filled with memories of women and the capture of women.
Confessions of a Young Man (1888)

VINCENT VAN GOGH
1853–90

Dutch, a failed Calvinist minister and a painter who sold only one painting. He was supported by his brother Theo. At first his paintings were dark and the subject matter peasants, à la Millet, but he developed a postimpressionist style of brilliant colors after meeting Pissarro, Degas, and Gauguin in Paris. He painted for only ten years, and some of his finest works were painted while in a mental institution near Arles, France, where he settled. An intense man, he cut off one ear to send to a prostitute. In 1990, Van Gogh's *Portrait of Dr. Gachet* sold for $82.5 million, then a world record.

It is no more easy to make a good picture than it is to find a diamond or a pearl. It means trouble and you risk your life for it.
Letter to his brother Theo (October 1888). In *Chambers Dictionary of Quotations* (1998)

I cannot help it that my paintings do not sell. The time will come when people will see that they are worth more than the price of the paint.
Ibid.

EDGAR WATSON HOWE
1853–1937

American, novelist.

There is nothing so well known as that we should not expect something for nothing—but we all do and call it Hope.
Country Town Sayings (1911)

There is always a type of man who says he loves his fellow men, and expects to make a living at it.

Ventures in Common Sense (1919), ch. 2

CECIL RHODES
1853–1902

South African, diamond miner and imperialist. He established scholarships to Oxford for male scholar-athletes from Britain's colonies, Germany, and the United States.

So little done—so much to do.

In Lewis Michell, *The Life and Times of the Right Honourable Cecil John Rhodes* (1910), ch. 2

OSCAR WILDE
1854–1900

Irish, poet, playwright, a genius of paradox, and a homosexual who wore a velvet jacket, silk stockings, and lavender gloves. He attacked hypocrisy, as in his comic masterpiece *The Importance of Being Earnest* (1895), which parodied the Victorians' pretense of "earnestness." As Gwendolyn summed it up, "In matters of grave importance, style, not sincerity, is the vital thing."

Over the piano was printed a notice: "Please do not shoot the pianist. He is doing his best."

Impressions of America: Leadville (1883)

The world is a stage, but the play is badly cast.

"Lord Arthur Savile's Crime" (1887)

An idea that is not dangerous is unworthy of being called an idea at all.

"The Critic as Artist" *Intentions* (1891), ch. 2

We are all in the gutter, but some of us are looking at the stars.

Lady Windermere's Fan (1892) act 3

Cecil Graham: What is a cynic?
Lord Darlington: A man who knows the price of everything and the value of nothing.

Ibid.

In this world there are only two tragedies. One is not getting what one wants, and the other is getting it.

Ibid.

[On *Lady Windermere's Fan*:]
The play was a great success, but the audience was a disaster.

Attributed

The English country gentleman galloping after a fox—the unspeakable in full pursuit of the uneatable.

A Woman of No Importance (1893), act 1

Children begin by loving their parents; as they grow older they judge them; sometimes they forgive them.

Ibid., act 2

To lose one parent, Mr. Worthing, may be regarded as a misfortune; to lose both looks like carelessness.

The Importance of Being Earnest (1895), act 1

I hope you have not been leading a double life, pretending to be wicked and being really good all the time. That would be hypocrisy.

Ibid., act 2

The good ended happily, and the bad unhappily. That is what fiction means.

Ibid.

When the gods choose to punish us, they answer our prayers.

An Ideal Husband (1895), act 2

Private information is practically the source of every large modern fortune.

Ibid.

And all men kill the thing they love,
By all let this be heard
Some do it with a bitter look,
Some with a flattering word,
The coward does it with a kiss,
The brave man with a sword.
   "The Ballad of Reading Gaol" (1898), st. 2

And so he who would lead a Christ-like life is he who is perfectly and absolutely himself. He may be a great poet or a great man of science…or a fisherman who throws his nets into the sea. It does not matter what he is, as long as he realizes the perfection of the soul that is within him. …to the claims of conformity no man may yield and remain free at all.

In Harold Bloom, Genius (2002)

A gentleman never hurts anyone's feelings unintentionally.

In L. R. Frank, *Wit and Humor Quotationary*

[Customs inspector] "Have you anything to declare?" Nothing. Nothing, but my genius!

Ibid.

Philosophy teaches us to bear with equanimity the misfortunes of others.

Ibid.

I live constantly in the fear of not being misunderstood.

It is only an auctioneer who can equally and impartially admire all schools of art.

One can always recognize women who trust their husbands. They look so thoroughly unhappy.

I like men who have a future and women who have a past.

> [When Wilde was requested to make some changes in one of his plays, he responded:]

Who am I to tamper with a masterpiece?

One should never listen. To listen is a sign of indifference to one's hearers.

LOUIS D. BRANDEIS
1856–1941

American, associate justice (1916–39) and a "trustbuster." He failed to understand that dynamic capitalism leads to monopoly profits for innovative firms, but such monopolies always fall by the wayside unless the firm continues to innovate or unless the government protects the monopoly.

Referring to chain stores, Brandeis said, "I have considered and do consider that the proposition that mere bigness cannot be an offense against society is false, because I believe that our society, which rests upon democracy, cannot endure under such conditions." A rich man, Brandeis attacked chain stores that sold food cheaply. But he supported New Deal organized cartels and monopolies. His "Brandeis brief" marshaled nonjudicial evidence in order to legislate from the bench.

> Fear of serious injury cannot alone justify suppression of free speech and assembly. Men feared witches and burned women.
> *Whitney v. California*, 274 U.S. 357, 375 (1927)

> Experience should teach us to be most on our guard to protect liberty when the government's purposes are beneficent. Men born to freedom are naturally alert to repel invasion of their liberty by evil-minded rulers. The greater dangers to liberty lurk in insidious encroachment by men of zeal, well-meaning but without understanding.
> In dissent, *Olmstead v. United States*, 277 U. S. 438, 479 (1928)

> Our government is the potent, the omnipresent teacher. For good or for ill, it teaches the whole people by its example. Crime is contagious. If the government becomes a lawbreaker, it breeds contempt for the law.
> Ibid.

> Sunlight is said to be the best of disinfectants.

10
MODERNISM TO POSTMODERNISM
(1900–1980)

"Modernism" (1900–1980) reacted against the Victorians' optimism, their belief in progress and traditional values, and their machine age. While modernists attached themselves to conflicting creeds, they all joined in believing society had found wrong answers to the major questions. Equality was their central value and nihilism was their central belief, that is, the view that there is no truth outside of science. Nietzsche declared that god was dead, so life had no meaning, and there was no distinction between good and evil. People could do whatever they wished. Freedom became the absence of limits, which ushered in a future of infinite possibilities. Into this vacuum poured the urban, avant-garde movements that ripped apart Victorian culture. Freud undermined morality by denying individual responsibility. William James turned Nietzsche's "There are no facts, only interpretations" into "pragmatism" and moral relativism, where nothing can be taken as a certainty. Franz Boaz morphed moral relativism into multiculturalism, that is, all cultures are equal and above criticism, except Western culture due to its intolerance. Marshall Berman said of modernism:

> To be modern is to find ourselves in an environment that promises us adventure, power, joy, growth, transformation of ourselves and the world—and, at the same time, that threatens to destroy everything we have, everything we know, everything we are.

Modernists discarded the uplifting paintings of Renoir and Degas for grotesque anti-Western art. Picasso said, "Art is not to decorate apartments. Art is a weapon of revolution." Picasso's ugly *Des Demoiselles d'Avignon* (five naked whores) and Tristan Tzara's dadaism degraded art. Charles Murray wrote:

> …where artists do not have coherent ideals of beauty, the work tends to be sterile, and where they do not have coherent ideals of the good, the work tends to be vulgar…. I am writing off some huge proportion of twentieth-century art, literature, and music as sterile, vulgar, and shallow.

Jacques Barzun sees modernism as the final stage of Romantism's "abandonment of rules, overstepping of limits, and ridicule of conventions." Tom Wolfe said modernist writers "attacked the bourgeoisie in a general assault on the respectable, resulting in a perverse triumph for a stigma-free society," where "there was no reward for excellence and no consequences for failure."

World War I completed the undermining of faith in progress. Le Corbusier's

1929 urban manifesto, *The City of Tomorrow*, read: "Our world, like a charnelhouse, is strewn with the detritus of dead epochs...." Amid the ruins of Victorian order and progress, modernists believed that technocrats could plan a utopian world. Communism and fascism quickly filled the vacuum opened by modernism's assault on Victorian virtue.

Modernism had five characteristics. First, it was self-referential. By discovering his self, the writer helps the reader to do the same. This contrasted with the Victorian, whose purpose had been to tell a story with a moral. Being subjective, the modernist is difficult to understand—try Joyce! Modernist poetry lacks moral content and is obscure.

Second, modernists were urbanites, who lived on the "left banks" of Paris, Vienna, Berlin, New York, and London. They were never rustics.

Third, modernists were elitists who wanted no limitations on government power. They were mostly socialists who believed an elite vanguard should order the future according to their systems.

Fourth, modernists rebelled against Victorian ethics and natural law, which is fundamental to Judeo-Christianity. Modernists were secularists and moral relativists, that is, there is no truth per se. Values are artificial constructs to serve the powerful. Modernists jettisoned the Victorian sexual restraints protecting the nuclear family. Peggy Guggenheim claimed a thousand lovers— more than Lord Byron!

Fifth, they opposed capitalism and sought subsidies for themselves and the use of coercion to enforce their visions of social justice. Rather than the rule of law, they wanted the government to benefit preferred citizens. Roscoe Pound said the left's "legal realism" had legitimized the Soviet and Nazi terrors as well as the New Deal.

Modernist pragmatists saw no themes to history, while the Communist/Nazi modernists believed history would work out according to their plan. Some modernists drifted between the two schools, such as the hapless Jean-Paul Sartre.

"Postmodernism" was coined in the 1980s to identify our era. Jacques Barzun says it includes representational art and poetry that is more easily understood and an abandonment of dictatorial political faiths. Your compiler speculates its great intellectual force will be complexity science, which teaches that progress comes best from decentralized systems. Top-down controls ring false in a dynamic, unpredictable world far too complex to reward government industrial policies or even long-term corporate planning. Because the centrifugal forces released by complexity science can only be contained by transcendent values at the core, traditional Western virtues will be revived.

To understand oscillations between the epochs of the Enlightenment, Romanticism, Victorianism, modernism, and postmodernism, think of Nietzsche's cyclical swings between Apollonian and Dionysian values. Apollo, god of rationality and freedom, vies with Dionysus, god of nature and instinct. Apollonian meritocracy and a strict moral code reigned in checkerboard fashion during the Enlightenment and Victorian Age and it should triumph in postmodernism. Similarly, Dionysian values (equality and utopianism) surged during the intervening Romantic and modernist ages.

SIGMUND FREUD
1856–1939

Austrian, neurologist, whose seminal work was *The Interpretation of Dreams* (1899), which undermined the notion of humans as rational beings. Freud argued that repressing sexual drives submerges them in the unconscious, which leads to neurosis or psychosis. We can only regain our free will by exposing these repressed sexual drives to the conscious mind. Dreams are wish fulfillments that reveal repressed desires. Because civilization represses sexuality, more civilization means more neurosis/psychosis, with more unhappy people taking refuge in drink, drugs, and religion.

Freud's conceptions lacked scientific discipline; they were merely a body of lore and imagery, for example, the psychic agencies (id, ego, and superego), the death wish, infantile sexuality, developmental immaturity caused by domineering or withholding mothers, Oedipus and Electra complexes, penis envy, and the "talking cure." Little remains of Freud's conceptions other than a civil war within the psyche. Psychoanalysis, like phrenology, contains a few nuggets of truth, but it is generally false. Karl Popper rightly called Freud a charlatan.

Paul Johnson said, Freudianism, like Marxism, "posits one big, simple cause of human behavior that is loosely defined and vague enough that all events, especially malign ones, can be fitted into the theory. Where Marxism used class warfare, Freud used infantile experience…in the unconscious."

Freud derailed the consensus in 1900 that schizophrenia and depression were organically based. Thus, Freud, like Galen, hampered serious medical research. We now know depression and schizophrenia are caused by biochemistry, not by poor potty training or sexual repression.

Freud attacked Western morality by arguing that man was not responsible for his actions because he was controlled by his unconscious. Freud sought to dispel personal guilt; we are not guilty individually but collectively. He saw religion as an "obsessional neurosis," a regressive longing for a parent's protection, and prayer as a crying out for a parent's intercession. A megalomaniac, he regarded dissent to his views as "denial" and a mental illness. He did not recognize women as colleagues and he only talked to his wife about household matters.

Freud's purpose was to displace the old reliance on religion to cure emotional stress. Research shows that one can better relieve traumas with a stiff upper lip and the support of friends than with the talking cure. See *One Nation under Therapy: How the Helping Culture is Eroding Self-Reliance*, Christina Sommers and Sally Satel, (2005).

Norman Cantor, in *The American Century* (1997) wrote, "Psychoanalysis unquestionably lay at the core of the modernist movement." In fact, most psychologists are leftists.

> The dream is the [disguised] fulfillment of a [repressed] wish.
>> *The Interpretation of Dreams* (1900), ch. 4, tr. A. A. Brill (1938)

> [George Santayana observed:]
> Nothing could be madder, more irresponsible, more dangerous than this guidance of men by dreams.
>> In L. R. Frank, *Quotationary* (1999)

The principal task of civilization, its actual raison d'être, is to defend us against nature.

A General Introduction to Psychoanalysis
(1916–17)

The little human being is frequently a finished product in his fourth or fifth year, and only gradually reveals in later years what lies buried in him.

Ibid.

By words one can give to another the greatest happiness or bring about utter despair....

Ibid.

Sublimation of instinct is a conspicuous feature of cultural evolution.... It is impossible to ignore the extent to which civilization is built up on renunciation of instinctual gratifications…

Civilization and Its Discontents (1930)

Women represent the interest of the family and sexual life; the work of civilization has become more and more men's business; it confronts them with ever harder tasks, compels them to sublimations of instinct which women are not easily able to achieve.

Ibid.

When making a decision of minor importance, I have always found it advantageous to consider all the pros and cons. In vital matters, however, such as the choice of a mate or a profession, the decision should come from the unconscious, from somewhere within ourselves.

Sometimes a cigar is just a cigar.

I could not point to any need in childhood as strong as that for a father's protection.

ELBERT HUBBARD
1856–1915

American, epigramist.

One machine can do the work of fifty ordinary men. No machine can do the work of one extraordinary man.

Thousand and One Epigrams (1911)

Little minds are interested in the extraordinary; great minds in the commonplace.

Ibid.

The probable fact is that we are descended not only from monkeys but from monks.

The Roycroft Dictionary and Book of Epigrams (1923)

God will not look you over for medals, degrees or diplomas, but for scars.

We are not punished for our sins, but by them.

HENRI PHILIPPE PÉTAIN
1856–1951

French, marshal, who halted Germany in World War I at Verdun, where 800,000 died. Germany bled France knowing Verdun could not be surrendered. In World War II, Pétain headed the pro-Nazi Vichy government of occupied France and was convicted of treason. De Gaulle commuted his death sentence.

Ils ne passeront pas!
They shall not pass!
   [At Verdun, February 26, 1916.]

GEORGE BERNARD SHAW
1856–1950

Irish, comic playwright, and winner of the 1935 Nobel Prize for literature. In his masterpiece *Pygmalion* (1913), taken from Ovid's poem, the phonetician Henry Higgins bets Colonel Pickering he can change a Cockney flower girl, Eliza Doolittle, into a lady who can pass in high society. The play, made into the film *My Fair Lady* (your compiler's favorite), endorses the liberal view that education can make a new person. Fabian socialism, started by Shaw and Sidney Webb, evolved into the British Labor Party.

The liar's punishment is, not in the least that he is not believed, but that he cannot believe any one else.
   The Quintessence of Ibsenism (1891), ch. 4

The fickleness of the women I love is only equaled by the infernal constancy of the women who love me.
   The Philanderer (1893), act 2

People are always blaming their circumstances for what they are. I don't believe in circumstances. The people who get on in this world are the people who get up and look for the circumstances they want, and, if they can't find them, make them.
   Mrs. Warren's Profession (1893), act 2

We have no more right to consume happiness without producing it than to consume wealth without producing it.
   Candida (1895), act 1

The worst sin towards our fellow creatures is not to hate them, but to be indifferent to them: that's the essence of inhumanity.
   The Devil's Disciple (1897), act 2

Martyrdom...the only way in which a man can become famous without ability.
   Ibid., act 3

This is the true joy in life, the being used for a purpose recognized by yourself as a mighty one; the being thoroughly worn out before you are thrown on the scrap heap; the being a force of nature instead of a feverish, selfish, little clod of ailments and grievances complaining that the world will not devote itself to making you happy.
   Man and Superman (1903), "Epistle Dedicatory"

The more things a man is ashamed of, the more respectable he is.
   Ibid., act 1

He who can, does. He who cannot, teaches.
   Ibid., act 4

Marriage is popular because it combines the maximum of temptation with the maximum of opportunity.
   Ibid.

Liberty means responsibility. That is why most men dread it.
   Man and Superman (1903), "Maxims"

The reasonable man adapts himself to the world: the unreasonable one persists in trying to adapt the world to himself. Therefore all progress depends on the unreasonable man.

Ibid.

The true artist will let his wife starve, his children go barefoot, his mother drudge for his living at seventy, sooner than work at anything but his art.

Ibid.

He knows nothing; and he thinks he knows everything. That points to a political career.

Major Barbara (1907), act 3

Like all young men, you greatly exaggerate the difference between one young woman and another.

Ibid.

All progress means war with society.

Getting Married (1908), preface

All professions are conspiracies against the laity.

The Doctor's Dilemma (1911), act 1

The great secret, Eliza, is not having bad manners or good manners...but having the same manners for all human souls...

Pygmalion (1913), act 5

Every drunken skipper trusts to Providence. But one of the ways of Providence with drunken skippers is to run them on the rocks.

Heartbreak House (1919)

You see things and you say why, but I dream of things that never were and say why not.

Back to Methuselah (1921), pt. 1, act 1

A government which robs Peter to pay Paul can always depend on the support of Paul.

Everybody's Political What's What? (1944)

Literature is like any other trade; you will never sell anything unless you go to the right shop.

New York Herald Tribune (May 4, 1955)

[Dancing is] a perpendicular expression of a horizontal desire.

New Statesman (March 23, 1962)

The trouble, Mr. Goldwyn, is that you are only interested in art and I am only interested in money.

[Why he turned down Goldwyn's offer to purchase the movie rights to his plays.]

In Alva Johnson, *The Great Goldwyn* (1937), ch. 3

I am pleased with the spirit of those who are now advocating war for its own sake as a tonic. Let those who believe in it repair to Salisbury Plain and blaze away at one another until the survivors (if any) feel that their characters are up to the mark.

In Jacques Barzun, *From Dawn to Decadence* (2000)

[Following the first performance of his *Arms and the Man* (1894), the applause was overwhelming, except for the hissing of the literary agent, Bright. At curtain call for the author, Shaw bowed to Bright and said:]
I quite agree with you, sir, but what can two do against so many?

Little Brown Book of Anecdotes (1985), Clifton Fadiman, ed.

Shaw sent Winston Churchill two tickets to the opening of his newest play with the note: "Bring a friend, if you have one." Churchill returned the tickets with the note that he was engaged that evening, but that he would like to have tickets for the second performance, "if there is one."

                                        Ibid.

[A lady at a dinner party replied she would sleep with Shaw for a million pounds. He then asked if she would for a fiver? Taking offense, she said, "What kind of woman do you think I am?" Shaw said,] "I thought we had established that. Now we are merely haggling over the price."

                                        Ibid.

Critics, like other people, see what they look for, not what is actually before them.

                In L. R. Frank, *Wit and Humor*
                                Quotationary

A perpetual holiday is a good working definition of hell.

                                        Ibid.

The roulette table pays nobody except him that keeps it. Nevertheless, a passion for gambling is common, though a passion for keeping roulette tables is unknown.

Mrs. Patrick Campbell, a friend of Shaw, said, "It doesn't matter what you do in the bedroom as long as you don't do it in the street and scare the horses."

What Englishman will give his mind to politics as long as he can afford to keep a motor car?

If you must hold yourself up to your children, hold youself up as an object lesson and not as an example.

BOOKER T. WASHINGTON
1856–1915

American, former slave, scientist, and founder of Tuskegee Institute, a college for Negroes. He worked in salt mines during the day and went to school at night to raise himself up—his formula for all Negroes. He was the "great accomodationist," who in 1885 joined "the Atlanta Compromise," accepting racial separation until Negroes acquired the attitudes and skills for economic independence. His *Up from Slavery* (1901) argued that taking personal responsibility would lift the Negro. He said, "Brains, property, and character for the Negro will settle the question of civil rights." And he added, "Merit, no matter under what skin, is in the long run recognized and rewarded...."

Washington was opposed by W. E. B. Du Bois (1868–1963), a Communist whose *Souls of Black Folk* (1903) argued that Washington allowed whites to "shift the burden of the Negro problem to the Negro's shoulders...when the burden belongs to the nation." He urged protesting to coerce reform. His Niagara Movement became the National Asso. for the Advancement of Colored People (NAACP).

The Washington-Du Bois debate continues even today, as the debate between Bill Cosby and Jesse Jackson.

The Negro should not be deprived by unfair means of the franchise, but political agitation alone will not save him.

Back of the ballot, he must have property, industry, skill, economy, intelligence and character. No race without these elements can permanently succeed.... We have a right to enter our complaints, but we shall make a fatal error if we yield to the temptation of believing that mere opposition to our wrongs will take the place of progressive constructive action....

Up from Slavery, Penguin Books (1986)

Think about it: we went into slavery pagans; we came out Christians. We went into slavery pieces of property; we came out American citizens. We went into slavery with chains clanking about our wrists; we came out with the American ballot in our hands....

Ibid.

No race can prosper till it learns that there is as much dignity in tilling a field as in writing a poem.

Ibid., ch. 14

I have learned that success is to be measured not so much by the position that one has reached in life as by the obstacles which he has overcome while trying to succeed.

Ibid.

In all things that are purely social we can be as separate as the fingers, yet one as the hand in all things essential to mutual progress.

"The Atlanta Exposition Address" (1895)

There is a class of colored people who make a business of keeping the troubles, the wrongs and the hardships of the Negro race before the public. Having learned that they are able to make a living out of their troubles, they have grown into the settled habit of advertising their wrongs—partly because they want sympathy and partly because it pays. [Some] do not want the Negro to lose his grievances, because they do not want to lose their jobs.

In Walter Williams, "Scholastic Expectations," *Washington Times* (November 18, 2000)

Few things help an individual more than to place responsibility upon him and to let him know that you trust him.

When a Negro boy learns to groom horses... or to practice medicine, as well or better than some one else, he will be rewarded regardless of race or color. In the long run, the world is going to have the best, and any difference in race, religion, or previous history will not long keep the world from what it wants.

Note: Botanist George Washington Carver conducted research at Tuskegee. He discovered hundreds of new uses for legume crops, such as peanuts, which restore nitrogen to the soil. This changed the South's single crop system, which had depleted the soil by growing only cotton or corn.

Woodrow Wilson
1856–1924

American, twenty-eighth president (1913–1921), the first Southern president after the Civil War, and the only one with a doctorate. Wilson changed the Democratic Party from its Jeffersonian origins as a pro-states' rights and issolationist party into a big-government and imperialist party. He passed constitutional amendments for woman's suffrage, prohibition, and a graduated income tax. He federalized: 1) banks via the Federal Reserve Act, 2) commerce via the Federal Trade Commission and Clayton Antitrust Acts, and, 3) agriculture via the farm loan program.

A disciple of Herbert Croly, progressive editor of the *New Republic*, Wilson concentrated power in the executive branch so that "experts" could manage the economy. Wilson, Franklin Roosevelt, and Lyndon Johnson were the superactivist presidents in expanding the central government. Prior to Wilson, Democrats believed in a small federal government. Grover Cleveland said:

> I do not believe that the power and duty of the general government ought to be extended to the relief of individual suffering, which is in no manner properly related to the public service or benefit.... The lesson should constantly be enforced that though the people support the government, government should not support the people.
>
> Cleveland's veto of the Texas Seed Bill
> (February 17, 1887)

Wilson, who abhorred Thomas Jefferson, adopted the populist and progressive programs. For populists, the enemies were big corporations and banks, "the money power." They demanded state ownership of railways and utilities, progressive taxation, power to the labor unions, and easy credit. The progressives, scions of the old money, supported trust busting, industry regulation, wilderness protection, and control of urban sprawl. Unlike European socialists, American progressives did not seek to own industry, but to socialize the benefits of private industry through regulations.

Under Wilson, the left hijacked the word "liberal," which had meant liberating individuals by abolishing monarchical privileges for the preferred. But "progressive" was associated with Teddy Roosevelt and "populist" with Southern agrarianism, so the left chose "liberal," which now stands for more government economic intervention to spread the wealth. Overseas, "liberalism" still stands for less government intervention.

Wilson won reelection in 1916 by charging that Republicans would enter the European war. Yet Wilson's bellicose policies forced Germany into unrestricted submarine warfare, causing America's entry, just as Secretary of State Bryan had forecast. After the war started, Wilson passed the Espionage and Sedition Acts making it illegal to utter "disloyal, profane, scurrilous or abusive" words about government officials.

Wilson believed in waging war to promote U.S. ideals. He intervened in World War I, Mexico, Haiti, the Dominican Republic, and Russia. Today, Wilsonians want to fight idealistic wars, as in Bosnia and Iraq, while realpolitikers prefer stability to war, unless vital U.S. interests are threatened, as for example, Afghanistan.

> A little group of willful men, representative of no opinion but their own, have rendered the great government of the United States helpless and contemptible.
> [Regarding a filibuster of Wilson's bill to arm U.S. merchantmen.]

He Kept Us Out Of War.
> [A month after inauguration, Wilson asked Congress to declare war on Germany.]
>
> Wilson's 1916 election campaign slogan

The world must be made safe for democracy.
> [Asking Congress for war, April 2, 1917.]
>
> John Dos Passos rejoined, "Wilson made the world safe for hypocrisy."

If I am to speak for ten minutes, I need a week for preparation;...if half an hour, two days, if an hour, I am ready now.
> From Josephus Daniels, *The Wilson Era: Years of War and After* (1946)

If you want your memoranda read, put them on one page.
> In L. R. Frank, *Quotationary* (1999)

To get French support for a League of Nations, Wilson abandoned his "peace without victory" and his Fourteen Points, which had inspired an undefeated Germany to agree to an armistice. An eighth of Germany was given away under the guise of self-determination, but no colony of the Allies was given self-determination. Article 231 of the Versailles Treaty said that Germany bore the war guilt for which reparations of $32 billion were due—three times her gross domestic product. That debt spurred hyperinflation and opened the way for Hitler. Lloyd George, the British prime minister, forecast that Germany's loss of territory to Poland would cause the next world war—it did. Keynes referred to Wilson as a "blind and deaf Don Quixote" who had imposed a "Carthaginian peace."

Senator Lodge, Republican leader, demanded the League contain a reservation that the U.S. retain for itself the right to declare war, so it would not automatically be drawn into wars to preserve all international borders under Article 10. Wilson refused, so America did not join. Lodge charged that the League was a "covenant without a sword" that would give a "fictitious sense of security." Lodge favored a NATO-type European alliance.

General Smuts understood the League's weakness: "What was everybody's business in the end proved to be nobody's business. Each one looked to the other to take the lead, and the aggressors got away with it."

BARON ROBERT S. SMYTH BADEN-POWELL
1857–1941

British, founded the Boy Scouts in 1908.

> On my honor I will do my best: To do my duty to God and my country, and to obey the Scout Law; To help other people at all times; To keep myself physically strong, mentally awake, and morally straight.
>
> Boy Scout Oath

JOSEPH CONRAD
1857–1924

English (born a Polish noble), a writer of pessimistic sea stories: *Lord Jim* (1900), *Nostromo* (1904), and *Heart of Darkness* (1902). He told H. G. Wells, "You don't care for humanity but think they are to be improved. I love humanity but know they are not."

[The artist] speaks to our capacity for delight and wonder, to the sense of mystery surrounding our lives; to our sense of pity, and beauty, and pain.

The Nigger of the Narcissus (1898), Preface

Going up that river was like traveling back to the earliest beginning of the world.... An empty stream, a great silence.... And this stillness of life did not in the least resemble peace. It was the stillness of an implacable force brooding over an inscrutable intention.

Heart of Darkness (1902)

[Of Kurtz on his deathbed:]
He cried in a whisper at some image, at some vision—he cried out twice, a cry that was not more than a breath: "The horror! The horror!"

Ibid. ch. 2

Heart of Darkness is the most Hobbesian book. A trading company sends Marlow into central Africa to search for its agent, Kurtz. The scenes are hellish with piles of skulls and blood caked on everything. Kurtz had gone to the Belgian Congo on a mission to civilize the natives, but he had became utterly depraved. Although ambiguous, Kurtz's evilness is usually interpreted as Everyman's capacity for evil, or as the evil of European colonialism, which Conrad condemned. But the Nigerian novelist Chinua Achebe called Conrad a "bloody racist" for dehumanizing blacks as the source of evil that had corrupted Kurtz.

The scrupulous and the just, the noble, humane, and devoted natures, the unselfish and the intelligent may begin a movement—but it passes away from them.

They are not the leaders of a revolution. They are its victims.

Under Western Eyes (1911), pt. 2, ch. 3

Every age is fed on illusions, lest man should renounce life early and the human race come to an end.

Victory (1915)

I could see the man's very soul writhing in his body like an impaled worm.

The last thing a woman will consent to discover in a man whom she loves, or on whom she simply depends, is want of courage.

The belief in a supernatural source of evil is not necessary; men alone are quite capable of every wickedness.

CLARENCE DARROW
1857–1938

American, labor lawyer, who in 1925 defended John T. Scopes, a Tennessee science teacher, for teaching the theory of evolution. Scopes was convicted. The case was a sham organized by town fathers to increase tourism and by the ACLU to promote secularism. Scopes had never taught evolution and only agreed not to deny the charge if he did not have to testify and if his fine was paid.

The first half of our lives is ruined by our parents and the second half by our children.

I owe everything to hard work. As a boy my father sent me to the field to dig potatoes. I decided to become a lawyer.

Whenever I hear people advocating birth control, I always remember that I was the fifth child.

I have suffered from being misunderstood, but I would have suffered a hell of a lot more if I had been understood.

I have never killed anyone, but I have read some obituary notices with great satisfaction.

FRANZ BOAS
1858–1942

American (German-born), anthropologist and Stalinist. Boas, Nietzsche, and Freud were the architects of nonjudgmental multiculturalism.

Boas accepted Darwin's "biological evolution," but rejected "cultural evolution," the notion that civilizations evolve. Boas argued in *The Mind of the Primitive Man* (1911): "No one culture's way of life is better than another; people live differently and that is all." Differences in civilizations are merely cultural adaptations, so all civilizations are equal. Boas with Eskimos and his student Mead in Samoa argued that their civilizations were equal to West's. Human sacrifice, female foot binding, cannibalism, and suttee should not be criticized or discouraged.

Cultural relativism, a variant of pragmatism, never works for the same reason pragmatism never works, to wit, it never supplies a goal, an ideal. Plato recognized the emptiness of the Sophists' relativism: With no absolute truths, there is no basis for concluding that one thing is better than another.

The French anthropologist Claude Levi-Strauss said, "The dogma of cultural relativism is challenged by the very people for whose moral benefit the anthropologists established it in the first place. The complaint the underdeveloped countries advance is not that they are being westernized, but that the westernization is proceeding too slowly."

MULTICULTURALISM

Multiculturalism, a by-product of cultural relativism, has captured America's schools. It does not stand for students learning about non-Western cultures. Per Suzanne Fields, "Multiculturalism has become the prevailing euphemism for discounting Western values and celebrating every ideology and mindset with an anti-American core." Courses in multiculturalism take the place of Western history, philosophy, and literature.

Western, Judeo-Christian philosophy gave dignity to every man and taught that virtue was the path to fulfillment. This led to an ordered liberty that integrated democracy, science, and capitalism, the propellers of Western prosperity. The West created most of the world's valuables (petroleum had no value until made into kerosene), and the West gave the world the "master idea of progress."

MAX PLANCK
1858–1947

German, physicist, Nobel laureate (1918) who discovered quantum mechanics.

> Scientific discovery and scientific knowledge have been achieved only by those who have gone in pursuit of them without any practical purpose whatsoever in view.
> *Where is Science Going?* (1932), pt. 4, tr.
> James Murphy

A new scientific truth does not triumph by convincing its opponents and making them see the light, but rather because its opponents eventually die, and a new generation grows up that is familiar with it.

A Scientific Autobiography (1949),
tr. F. Gaynor

THEODORE ROOSEVELT
1858–1919

American, twenty-sixth president (1901–1909) who was a historian, spoke four languages, read a book daily, and used the presidency as his "bully pulpit." He said the historian "must remember that unless he writes vividly, he cannot write truthfully."

In 1898 he resigned as McKinley's assistant secretary of the navy to lead the Rough Riders in the Spanish-American War. He led a charge up Kettle Hill, where an excited Confederate general Roosevelt had brought along, yelled, "We've got the Yankees on the run!" Secretary of State John Hay wrote, "It has been a splendid little war." Finley Peter Dunne said Teddy's book on the expedition should have been titled *Alone in Cuba*.

Roosevelt clamored for colonies, especially the Philippines. Historian Charles Beard concluded that imperialism sprang, not from business interests, but from nationalistic politicians, such as Roosevelt.

Vice President Roosevelt succeeded to the presidency after McKinley's assassination. He built the Panama Canal and set aside the acreage for most of America's national parks. The "Roosevelt Corollary to the Monroe Doctrine" held that the U.S. would intervene militarily to make Latin American nations repay their foreign creditors. He broke up business trusts, supported a progressive income tax and aid to agriculture, and denounced the "great malefactors of wealth." He forced Howard Taft on his party as his successor, but split the Republicans in 1912 by running on the Progressive or Bull Moose ticket, which gave the election to Wilson, with 42 percent; Roosevelt had 27 percent; and Taft 23 percent.

The best prize that life offers is the chance to work hard at work worth doing.

I wish to preach, not the doctrine of ignoble ease, but the doctrine of the strenuous life.

Speech, Chicago (April 10, 1899)

…if we shrink from the hard contests where men must win at the hazard of their lives and at the risk of all they hold dear, then bolder and stronger peoples will pass us by.…

Ibid.

Far better it is to dare mighty things, to win glorious triumphs, even though checkered by failure, than to take rank with those poor spirits who neither enjoy much nor suffer much, because they live in the gray twilight that knows not victory nor defeat.

Ibid.

The first requisite of a good citizen in this republic of ours is that he shall be able and willing to pull his weight.

Speech in New York City
(November 11, 1902)

Speak softly and carry a big stick; you will go far.

Speech, April 3, 1903, quoting an old maxim

It was my good fortune at Santiago to serve beside colored troops. A man who is good enough to shed his blood for his country is good enough to be given a square deal afterwards.

> Speech, Springfield, Illinois, July 4, 1903,
> in L. R. Frank, *Quotationary* (1999)

When I say I believe in a square deal I do not mean to give every man the best hand. If the cards do not come to any man, or if they do come and he has not the power to play them, that is his affair. All I mean is there shall be no crookedness in the dealing.

> Speech, Dallas, Texas (April 5, 1905)

It is not the critic who counts, not the man who points out how the strong man stumbled, or where the doer of deeds could have done them better. The credit belongs to the man who is actually in the arena; whose face is marred by dust and sweat and blood; who strives valiantly; who errs and comes short again and again, because there is no effort without error and shortcoming; but who does actually strive to do the deed; who knows the great enthusiasms, the great devotions, and spends himself in a worthy cause; who, at best, knows in the end the triumph of high achievement; and who at the worst, if he fails, at least fails while daring greatly, so that his place shall never be with those cold and timid souls who know neither victory nor defeat.

> Speech, the Sorbonne (April 23, 1910)

Do not hit at all if it can be avoided, but never hit softly.

> *Theodore Roosevelt: An Autobiography*
> (1913)

There is no room in this country for hyphenated Americanism.... The one absolutely certain way of bringing this nation to ruin, of preventing all possibility of its continuing to be a nation at all, would be to permit it to become a tangle of squabbling nationalities.

> Speech, New York (October 12, 1915)

[Hearing a big game hunter was in town, Roosevelt invited him to the Oval Office for an hour's animated conversation. When the befuddled big game hunter emerged, he was asked what he had told the president. He replied, "My name."]

[T]here are no words that can tell the hidden spirit of the wilderness, that can reveal its mystery, its melancholy, and its charm. There is delight in the hardy life of the open, in long rides rifle in hand, in the thrill of the fight with dangerous game. Apart from this, yet mingled with it, is the strong attraction of the silent places, of the large tropic moon, and the splendor of the new stars; where the wanderer sees the awful glory of sunrise and sunset in the wide waste spaces of the earth, unworn of man, and changed only by the slow change of the ages through time everlasting.

[Roosevelt wrote that he did not want his sons to:]
...shine over much in athletics in college because it takes too much time...

McKinley has no more backbone than a chocolate éclair.

The best executive is the one who has sense enough to pick good men to do what he wants done, and self-restraint enough to keep from meddling with them while they do it.

In any moment of decision, the best thing you can do is the right thing, the next best thing is the wrong thing, and the worst thing you can do is nothing.

To educate a person in mind and not in morals is to educate a menace to society.

Nine-tenths of wisdom consists in being wise in time.

There is only one quality worse than hardness of heart and that is softness of head.

The only one indispensable requirement of both an individual and a nation is character.

[When a cowboy employee suggested he put Roosevelt's brand on someone else's steer, Roosevelt fired him on the spot, saying:] A man who will steal for me will steal from me.

Predicaris alive or Raszuli dead.
　　[Telegram to the Sultan of Morocco refusing to pay the ransom demands of the bandit Raszuli, who had kidnapped the American consul, Predicaris. The Sultan paid Raszuli who returned Predicaris.]

Our first duty is to war against dishonesty…war against it in public life, and…war against it in business life. Corruption in every form is the arch enemy of this Republic, the arch enemy of free institutions and of government by the people, an even more dangerous enemy than the open lawlessness of violence, because it

works in a hidden and furtive fashion. The most important single ingredient in the formula of success is knowing how to get along with people.

Do what you can, with what you have, where you are.

　　[Alice Roosevelt Longworth (1884–1980) said:]
If you can't say something good about anyone, sit right here by me.
　　In L. R. Frank, *Quotationary* (1999)

I can do either one of two things. I can be president of this country, or I can control Alice. I cannot possibly do both.

HENRI BERGSON
1859–1941

French, philosopher, who opposed materialism with a nonreligious mysticism. A "life-force" with a purpose had caused man to evolve and was leading man to perfection. Man is distinguished from the other animals by an *élan vital,* or striving or purposeness given to him by the life-force. But this life-force has no morals or mind—it is a tame God that does not intervene in human affairs or make demands on man's behavior. However, the life-force created man with free will so that he would evolve into a Godlike being.

　　There is no happiness without security….This assurance is to be found either in the mastering of things, or in the mastering of self which makes one independent of things.
　　In L. R. Frank, *Quotationary* (1999)

Allow me to furnish the interior of my head as I please, and I shall put up with a hat like everybody else's.

Ibid.

...the essential function of the universe...is [being] a machine for the making of gods.

Ibid.

God needs us, just as we need God. Why should He need us unless to love us?

Ibid.

JOHN DEWEY
1859–1952

American, socialist founder of "progressive education" who praised the USSR's educational methodologies and dismissed its mass murders as a transitional phase. His *Impressions of Soviet Russia* (1929) admired the Soviets teaching children to act "collectively," not "individualistically," like the capitalists who focused on "the egotistic and private ideals inculcated by the institution of private property, profit, and acquisitive possession." He said, "You can't make Socialists out of individualists—children who know how to think for themselves spoil the harmony of the collective society which is coming, where everyone is interdependent." Lenin echoed, "Give me your four-year-olds, and in a generation I will build a Socialist state." Hitler agreed, "Let me control the textbooks and I will control the state."

The humanists are firmly convinced that [the] existing acquisitive and profit motivated society has shown itself to be inadequate and that a radical change in methods, controls, and motives must be instituted. A socialized and cooperative economic order must be established to the end that the equitable distribution of the means of life be possible.

Humanist Manifesto, para. 14, (1933),
which Dewey helped draft and
which he signed.

ARTHUR CONAN DOYLE
1859–1930

Scottish, the greatest modern storyteller whose master detective Sherlock Holmes is perhaps the world's most popular fictional hero, along with his befuddled sidekick and foil, Dr. Watson, and his evil archenemy, Professor Moriarty.

It's a capital mistake to theorize before you have all the evidence.

A Study in Scarlet (1888), ch. 3

How often have I said to you that when you have eliminated the impossible, whatever remains, however, improbable, must be the truth?

The Sign of Four (1890), ch. 6

It is quite a three-pipe problem, and I beg that you won't speak to me for fifty minutes.

The Red-Headed League (1892)

You know my method. It is founded upon the observance of trifles.

The Boscombe Valley Mystery (1892)

You see, but you do not observe.

Scandal in Bohemia (1892)

"Excellent!" I cried.
"Elementary," said he.

The Crooked Man (1894)

Come, Watson, come! The game is afoot.
The Adventure of the Abbey Grange (1904)

Inspector: "Is there any other point to which you would wish to draw my attention?"
Holmes: "To the curious incident of the dog in the night-time."
Inspector: "The dog did nothing in the night time."
Holmes: "That was the curious incident."
Silver Blaze (1894)

DYSLEXIA

The above illustrates "right-brain" or "holistic" thinking based on intuition and an ability to detect small anomalies in patterns. Intensive intuitive thinking is found in 5 percent of the population and is associated with dyslexics and artists. Most people are "left-brained," that is, logical, linear, quantitative, and analytical, and most problems are best solved by the left brain. The right brain is best for a few professons, such as art, design, and investing.

Most dyslexics have higher-than-average IQs. The right side of their brain is so extra powerful that it interferes with the left side's control of reading. With remedial training by phonics, dyslexics often progress from being the weakest students in their class to the strongest. Dyslexics seldom learn to read well unless they are taught by phonics.

Prominent dyslexics include Churchill, Edison, John Kennedy, Newton, Pasteur, Patton, Poe, da Vinci, Yeats, and Charles Schwab. One study found that self-made millionaires are four times more likely to be dyslexic! They are weak at rote tasks and at deductive "if-then" type reasoning. But when relying on contextual reasoning,

they can be inspired visionaries who pick out meaningful trends from a mass of data and think far into the future.

HAVELOCK ELLIS
1859–1939

English, psychologist.

Nature records the male but a secondary and comparatively humble place in the home, the breeding-place of the race; he may compensate himself if he will, by seeking adventure or renown in the world outside. The mother is the child's supreme parent....
Studies in the Psychology of Sex (1897–1928), vol. IV, pt. I "The Mother and Her Child" (1910)

The place where optimism most flourishes is the lunatic asylum.
The Dance of Life (1923), ch. 3

All civilization has from time to time become a thin crust over a volcano of revolution.
Ibid.

The Promised Land always lies on the other side of a wilderness.
Ibid., ch. 5

Charm is a woman's strength, just as strength is a man's charm.
The Task of Social Hygiene (1912), ch. 3

WILHELM II
1859–1941

German, bellicose Kaiser. Hearing of Chinese Boxer atrocities, he told German soldiers being sent to Peking that they should "fight like Huns," an unfortunate choice of words. Tragically, in 1890 he dismissed Bismarck as chancellor, whose polestar had been to remain friendly with Britain.

> No one can dispute with us the place in the sun that is our due.
> Speech, Hamburg (August 27, 1901)

> Remember, the German people are the chosen of God. On me the German emperor, the spirit of God has descended. I am his sword, his weapon, his vice-regent.
> August 4, 1914

> *Kinder, Kirche, Kuche.*
> Children, Church, Kitchen.
> [The roles of women.]

J. M. BARRIE
1860–1937

Scot, playwright, and novelist.

> The life of every man is a diary in which he means to write one story, and writes another; and his humblest hour is when he compares the volume as it is with what he vowed to make it.
> *The Little Minister* (1891), vol. 1, ch. 1

> His lordship may compel us to be equal upstairs, but there will never be equality in the servant's hall.
> *The Admirable Crichton* (1902), act 1

> I am not young enough to know everything.
> Ibid.

> Charm…it's a sort of bloom on a woman. If you have it, you don't need to have anything else; and if you don't have it, it doesn't much matter what else you have.
> *What Every Woman Knows* (1908), act 1

> Every time a child says 'I don't believe in fairies' there is a little fairy somewhere that falls down dead.
> *Peter Pan, The Boy Who Wouldn't Grow Up* (1904), act 1

> Do you believe in fairies? Say quick that you believe! If you believe, clap your hands!
> Ibid., act 4

Peter Pan led the Lost Boys in Never-Never Land, where children never grew up. Searching for his lost shadow in the real world, he finds Wendy, Michael, and John, whom he teaches to fly and takes to Never-Never Land. After many adventures with the pirate Captain Hook and the fairy Tinker Bell, he brings the children home. After *Peter Pan*'s opening, children hurt themselves by trying to fly. Barrie changed the script so only children sprinkled with fairy dust could fly.

> God gave us our memories so that we might have roses in December.

> We are all failures—at least, all the best of us are.

WILLIAM JENNINGS BRYAN
1860–1925

American, "the Great Commoner," who at thirty-six years of age gave an impassioned speech at the 1896 Democratic National Convention that won the presidential nomination. He led the Democratic Party toward populism by adopting platforms favoring the graduated income tax and "free silver." He was committed to states' rights and pacifism; he reigned from Wilson's cabinet over World War I.

> You shall not press down upon the brow of labor this crown of thorns. You shall not crucify mankind upon a cross of gold.
> Speech at the Democratic Convention (1896)

> The people of Nebraska are for free silver and I am for free silver. I will look up the arguments later.

ANTON CHEKHOV
1860–1904

Russian, playwright who wrote loving elegies about the passing of the Russian aristocracy in *The Three Sisters* (1901) and *The Cherry Orchard* (1904). Seeing the rise of nihilism and socialism, Chekhov forecast, "Under the banner of learning, art, and persecuted freedom of thought, Russia will one day be ruled by such toads and crocodiles as were unknown even in Spain under the Inquisition."

In *The Cherry Orchard*, due to an inability to adapt to new conditions, the Ranevskys are about to lose their estate. A decent entrepreneur, Lopakhim, suggests they chop down the orchard and develop houses on it. The Ranevskys refuse to defile the center of their idyllic life. The play ends after the sale of the estate to Lopakhim: The Ranevskys hear axes chopping the cherry trees as they leave.

> Man is what he believes.

> If many cures are suggested for a disease, it is incurable.
> *The Cherry Orchard* (1904), act 1

> When I read books I am not concerned with how the authors loved or played cards. I see only their marvelous works.
> Notebooks

WILLIAM RALPH INGE
1860–1954

English, dean of St. Paul's Cathedral, and classicist who, like Leo Strauss, noted that evolution produces change, but not always advancement, so new ideas are not necessarily better than old ones.

> It is useless for the sheep to pass resolutions in favor of vegetarianism while the wolf remains of a different opinion.
> "Patriotism" *Outspoken Essays, First Series* (1919)

> The nations which have put mankind and posterity most in their debt have been small states—Israel, Athens, Florence, and England.
> "State Visible and Invisible" *Outspoken Essays*, Second Series (1922)

HALFORD MACKINDER
1861–1947

British, professor who warned the West against a likely Russian-German alliance, which occurred.

> Who rules Eastern Europe, commands the Heartland;
> Who rules the Heartland, commands the World-island;
> Who rules the World-island, commands the World.

RABINDRANATH TAGORE
1861–1941

Indian (Bengali), poet, playwright, philosopher, and the first Asian Nobel laureate for literature for *Gitanjali* (1912). He tried to lead India between the Scylla of traditionalism without machines and the Charybdis of abandoning Indian culture. Gandhi reviled him for trying to take the best from the West and East. Tagore rejected Gandhi's primitive industries. To Tagore, the objectives were freedom and strength; the pitfalls were weakness and utopian escapism. He told about the goat kid who complains to God that the other beasts try to devour him and asks for help. God replied, "What can I do, my child? When I look at you, I myself am so tempted." [For an essay on the development dilemma, see Isaiah Berlin, "Rabindranath Tagore and the Consciousness of Nationality" *The Sense of Reality* (1996). Note: Japan's solution was "Western science, Japanese spirit."

> The only real gift is the gift of strength; all other offerings are vain.
> > Toward Universal Man (1961)

> A mind all logic is like a knife all blade. It makes the hand bleed that uses it.

FREDERICK JACKSON TURNER
1861–1932

American, frontier historian, who argued that free land on America's frontier made Americans independent, risk-accepting, and democratic.

The result is that to the frontier the American intellect owes its striking characteristics. The coarseness and strength combined with acuteness and inquisitiveness; that practical inventive turn of mind, quick to find expedients; that masterful grasp of material things, lacking in the artistic but powerful to effect great ends; that restless, nervous energy; that dominant individualism, working for good and for evil, and with all that buoyancy and exuberance which comes from freedom—these are traits of the frontier.
> > *The Significance of the Frontier in American History* (1894)

ALFRED NORTH WHITEHEAD
1861–1947

British, mathematician and philosopher.

> A clash of doctrines is not a disaster—it is an opportunity.
> > *Science and the Modern World* (1925), ch. 12

> In formal logic, a contradiction is the signal of defeat: but in the evolution of real knowledge it marks the first step in progress toward a victory.
> > Ibid.

> Seek simplicity, and distrust it.
> > Ibid.

> The safest general characterization of the European philosophical tradition is that it consists of a series of footnotes to Plato.
> > *Process and Reality* (1929), pt. 2, ch. 1

> A race preserves its vigor so long as it is nerved by the vigor to adventure beyond

the safeties of the past. Without adventure civilization is in full decay.

Adventures of Ideas (1933), ch. 19

There are no whole truths; all truths are half-truths. It is trying to treat them as whole truths that plays the devil.

Dialogues of Alfred North Whitehead (1953)

Shakespeare wrote better poetry for not knowing too much; Milton, I think, knew too much finally for the good of his poetry.

Ibid.

It must be admitted that there is a degree of instability which is inconsistent with civilization. But, on the whole, the great ages have been unstable ages.

The major advances in civilization are processes which all but wreck the societies in which they occur.

WILLIAM SYDNEY PORTER (O. HENRY)
1862–1910

American, short story writer from Texas, who picked up many plots from his three years' incarceration in prison for embezzlement.

She plucked from my lapel the invisible strand of lint (the universal act of woman to proclaim ownership).

Strictly Business (1910)

May his liver turn to water, and the bones of him crack in the cold of his heart. May dog fennel grow upon his ancestors' graves, and the grandsons of his children be born without eyes. May whiskey turn to clabber in his mouth, and every time

he sneezes may he blister the soles of his feet. And the smoke of his pipe—may it make his eyes water, and the drops fall on the grass that his cows eat and poison the butter that he spreads on his bread.

Sixes and Sevens (1911)

In the Big City a man will disappear with the suddenness and completeness of the flame of a candle that is blown out.

Ibid., "The Sleuths"

O' Henry's short stories are famous for their ending twists. The *Gift of the Magi* tells the story of a poor young couple on Christmas Eve. The wife, Della, sells her proudest possession, her beautiful long hair, to buy a platinum watch chain for her husband Jim. Jim's only possession of value is his gold watch, descended from grandfather and father. Jim sells his gold watch to buy Della a set of tortoiseshell hair combs.

In *The Cop and the Anthem,* Soapy, a New York City bum, decides to get himself arrested so he can enjoy a warm cell during the approaching winter. To no avail, he tries many things to get arrested, such as stealing an umbrella, but the victim does not press charges because he had snitched it earlier. Distraught, Soapy stands on a corner next to a church where he hears an anthem, which brings back memories of childhood dreams. As Soapy strides off to ask an old family friend for a job, a cop hauls him to jail for vagrancy.

HENRY FORD
1863–1947

American, founder of Ford Motor Company, who lacked a high school education.

His Model T ("Tin Lizzie") sold for $850 in 1909 when 17,771 cars were assembled and for $260 in 1926 (with an automatic starter) when 1.8 million cars were assembled. The meatpackers' moving disassembly line inspired him to cut the assembly time of a car from 12.5 to 1.5 hours. His five-day workweek and starting wage of $5 per day began in 1914, when U.S. wages averaged $11 for six days. That saved money by eliminating the annual labor turnover of 600 percent. Before the Model T, most Americans never traveled more than twenty miles from home.

Karl Bentz invented the automobile in 1885; Ford invented the automotive industry by dropping the price to expand the market, and making up the thinner margin through volume and spare parts. Ford said, "Get the prices down to the buying power." He intuited the experience curve (later refined by Bruce Henderson of Boston Consulting) by which unit costs drop 20 to 30 percent with every doubling of accumulated output. Yet GM leapfrogged Ford in the 1920s by segmenting the market into a ladder of cars in price and quality—from Chevy to Olds to Buick to Cadillac, while Ford stuck with one model.

The key to mass production and to the moving assembly line was the interchangeability of parts made possible by advances in machine tools able to work prehardened metals. Interchangeable parts assembled by semiskilled workers performing repetitive tasks created "mass production." In the old "craft production," skilled craftsmen used their arts to fit parts together. Mass production gave way in the 1970s to Japan's "lean production," the substitution of technology and management skills for semiskilled labor. Information technol-ogies are now displacing most remaining semiskilled labor and middle management in manufacturing.

I will build a motor car for the great multitude. It will be large enough for the family but small enough for the individual to run and care for. It will be constructed of the best materials by the best men to be hired, after the simplest designs that modern engineering can devise. But it will be so low in price that no man making a good salary will be unable to own one—and enjoy with his family the blessing of hours of pleasure in God's great open spaces.

Any color—so long as it's black.
[The choice of colors offered for cars.]
My Life and Work (1922), ch. 4

There are always two kinds of people in the world—those who pioneer and those who plod. The plodders always attack the pioneers. They say that the pioneers have gobbled up all the opportunity, when, as a plain matter of fact, the plodders would have nowhere to plod had not the pioneers first cleared the way.
In L. R. Frank, *Quotationary* (1999)

There is no happiness except in the realization that we have accomplished something.

There is no place in civilization for the idler. None of us has any right to ease.

Whether you think you can or can't—you are right.

Before everything else, getting ready is the secret of success.

Chop your own wood, and it will warm you twice.

From time waste there can be no salvage.

Profit is a by-product of work; happiness is its chief product.

Old men are always advising young men to save money. That is bad advice. Don't save every nickel. Invest in yourself. I never saved a dollar until I was forty years old.

Failure is only the opportunity more intelligently to begin again.

If you think of standardization as the best that you know today, but which is to be improved tomorrow—you get somewhere.

EDITH WHARTON
1862–1937

American, novelist of the social elite.

Mrs. Ballinger is one of the ladies who pursue Culture in bands, as though it were dangerous to meet it alone.
Xingu and Other Stories (1916), "Xingu"

There are two ways of spreading light: be the candle or the mirror that reflects it.
Vesalius in Zante

DAVID LLOYD GEORGE
1863–1945

English, prime minister, 1916–1922.

A New Deal for everyone.
Election slogan (1919)

He's no failure. He's not dead yet.

WILLIAM RANDOLPH HEARST
1863–1951

American, publisher of a newspaper empire that pioneered banner headlines and "yellow journalism," that is, sensational, half-true stories. When artist Frederic Remington cabled from Cuba that there would be no war, Hearst cabled back, "Please remain. You furnish the pictures and I'll furnish the war." Hearst was immortalized in Orson Welles' film *Citizen Kane* (1941).

GEORGE SANTAYANA
1863–1952

American (Spanish-born, who settled in Rome), philosopher, who rejected organized religion, but believed in the necessity of faith. Like Montaigne, Santayana was an atheistic Catholic.

Fanaticism consists in redoubling your efforts when you have forgotten your aim.
The Life of Reason (1905), Introduction

Progress, far from consisting of change, depends on retentiveness. When experience is not retained, as among savages, infancy is perpetual. Those who cannot remember the past are condemned to repeat it.
Ibid., vol. 1, ch. 12

...when men and women agree, it is only in their conclusions; their reasons are always different.

Ibid.

There is no cure for birth and death save to enjoy the interval.

Soliloquies in England and Later Soliloquies
(1922), "War Shrines"

Perchance when Carnival is done,
And sun and moon go out on one
Christ will be God, and I the one
That in my youth I used to be.
    [Written at mid-age. Yet when he was dying, he still could not believe.]

"Eastern Hymn"

History is a pack of lies about events that never happened told by people who weren't there.

MARGOT ASQUITH
1864–1945

Scottish, writer, and wife of Herbert Asquith, prime minister.

To marry a man out of pity is folly; and, if you think you are going to influence the kind of fellow who has "never had a chance, poor devil," you are profoundly mistaken. One can only influence the strong characters in life, not the weak...

The Autobiography of Margot Asquith
(1922), vol. I, ch. 6

The t is silent, as in Harlow.
    [Response to Harlow who couldn't pronounce Margot.]

ANDREW PATERSON
1864–1941

Australian, poet known for *The Man from Snowy River* (1895).

Once a jolly swagman camped by a
    billy-bong,
Under the shade of a Coolibar tree,
And he sang as he sat and waited for his
    billy-boil,
You'll come a-waltzing Matilda with me.

"A-Waltzing Matilda," *The Bulletin*,
(April 1885), st. 1

A-waltzing Matilda, a-waltzing Matilda,
You'll come a-waltzing Matilda with me.
And he sang as he sat and waited for his
    billy-boil,
You'll come a-waltzing Matilda with me.

Chorus

A "swagman" is a hobo, a "billy-bong" is a pond, "billy-boil" is coffee, and "A-Waltzing Matilda" means walking with a bouncing hobo bundle. This unofficial anthem is about a hobo who steals a jumbuck (sheep) and drowns in a pond. It celebrates Australia's spirit of equality where everyone is, or should be, a "mate."

MIGUEL DE UNAMUNO
1864–1936

Spanish (Basque), rector, University of Salamanca.

It is not usually our ideas that make us optimistic or pessimistic, but it is our optimism or pessimism...that makes our ideas.

The Tragic Sense of Life (1913)

Faith is in its essence simply a matter of will, not of reason, and to believe is to wish to believe, and to believe in God is, before all and above all, to wish that there may be a God.

Ibid., ch. VI

May God deny you peace, but give you glory!

Ibid.

We never know, believe me, when we have succeeded best.

In *Chambers Dictionary of Quotations*
(1996), ed. Alison Jones

These terrible sociologists are the astrologers and alchemists of our twentieth century.

Fanatical Skepticism

MAX WEBER
1864–1920

German, political sociologist. Weber argued that Protestants believed that prospering and improving the world through their "calling" was the ideal life because their success could bring others to Christ. But Catholics believed the ideal life was the renunciation of the world, as in being a monk. Protestants must use every minute to work hard, be frugal, and keep their wealth invested at risk—idle wealth is a sin. Also Protestants, unlike Catholics, were not idle on the one-hundred-plus saints' days. Due to this ethic, Protestants became disproportionately the leading industrialists, professionals, and scientists. David Landes in *The Wealth and Poverty of Nations* (1998), verified Weber's thesis.

A glance at the occupation statistics of any country of mixed religious composition brings to light with remarkable frequency…the fact that business leaders and owners of capital, as well as the higher grades of skilled labour, and even more the higher technically and commercially trained personnel of modern enterprises, are overwhelmingly Protestant.

The Protestant Ethic and the Spirit of Capitalism (1904), tr. Talcott Parson, (1930)

The impulse to acquisition of the greatest possible amount of money has in itself nothing to do with capitalism. This impulse exists among waiters, physicians, coachmen, artists, prostitutes, dishonest officials, soldiers, nobles, crusaders, gamblers, and beggars.

Ibid.

Ideas come when we do not expect them, and not when we are brooding and searching at our desks. Yet ideas would certainly not come to mind had we not brooded at our desks…

In L. R. Frank, *Quotationary* (1999)

ISRAEL ZANGWILL
1864–1926

English, Zionist who wrote about ghettos.

America is God's Crucible, the great Melting Pot where all the races of Europe are melting and reforming… God is making the American. The real American has not yet arrived. He is only in the Crucible. …he will be the fusion of all the races, the coming superman.

The Melting Pot (1908), act 1

WARREN G. HARDING
1865–1923

American, twenty-ninth president (1921–1923). Harding released Eugene Debs and six thousand foreigners not already deported under Wilson's Espionage and Sedition Acts, and he commuted the Wobblies' death sentences. But he was deconstructed as a crook by an anticapitalist press, led by Bruce Bliven, chief propagandist for the Communist-led Popular Front and editor of the *New Republic*.

> We must have a citizenship less concerned about what the government can do for it and more anxious about what it can do for the nation.
>
>   Republican National Convention, Chicago
> (June 7, 1916)

> America's present need is not heroics but healing; not nostrums but normalcy; not revolution but restoration.
>
>   Speech, Boston (June 1920)

> I can take care of my enemies all right. But my damned friends, my God-damn friends, they're the ones who keep me walking the floors nights.
>
>   In Paul Johnson, *A History of the American People* (1999)

RUDYARD KIPLING
1865–1936

English, poet and novelist, 1917 Nobel Prize for literature. The people, T. S. Eliot, and Harold Bloom loved him. He said, "To be born an Englishman is to win God's first prize in the lottery of life."

Evelyn Waugh (1903–66) said, "Kipling believed civilization to be something laboriously achieved, which was only precariously defended. He wanted to see the defenses fully manned and he hated the liberals because he thought them gullible and feeble, believing in the easy perfectibility of man and ready to abandon the work of centuries for sentimental qualms."

> I have eaten your bread and salt,
> I have drunk your water and wine.
> The deaths ye died I have watched
>   beside
> And the lives ye led were mine.
>   *Departmental Ditties*, "Prelude" (1886), st. 1

> I have written the tale of our life
> For a sheltered people's mirth,
> In jesting guise—but ye are wise,
> And ye know what the jest is worth.
>   Ibid., st. 3

> Open the old cigar-box—let me consider anew-
> Old friends, and who is Maggie that I
>   should abandon you?
>   "The Betrothed" (1886), st. 24

> A million surplus Maggies are willing to
>   bear the yoke;
> And a woman is only a woman, but a
>   good Cigar is a Smoke.
>   Ibid., st. 25

> More men are killed by overwork than the importance of the world justifies.
>   *The Phantom Rickshaw* (1888)

> We're poor little lambs who've lost our
>   way,
> Baa! Baa! Baa!
> We're little black sheep who've gone
>   astray,

Baa-aa-aa!
Gentlemen-rankers out on the spree,
Damned from here to eternity
God ha' mercy on such as we,
Baa! Yah! Bah!
Yale "Whiffenpoof Song" (1889)

Oh, East is East, and West is West,
   and never the twain shall meet,
Till earth and sky stand presently at
   at God's great Judgment seat;
But there is neither East nor West,
Border, nor Breed, nor Birth,
When two strong men stand face to
   face,
tho' they come from the ends of the
   earth.
"The Ballad of East and West"
(1889), last st.

Though I've belted you and flayed you,
By the livin' Gawd that made you,
You're a better man than I am, Gunga
   Din!
"Gunga Din" (1890)

If I were damned of body and soul,
I know whose prayers would make me
   whole,
Mother o'mine, O mother o'mine.
"The Light That Failed" (1891)

And the end of the fight is a tombstone
   white, with the names of the late
   deceased,
And the epitaph drear: "A fool lies here
   who tried to hustle the East."
The Naulahka (1892), ch. 5

It's Tommy this, an' Tommy that, an'
"Chuck 'im out, the brute!"
But it's "Saviour of 'is country,"
when the guns begin to shoot.
"Tommy" (1892), st. 5

I've a neater, sweeter maiden in a cleaner,
greener land.
"Mandalay" (1893), st. 5

He wrapped himself in quotations as a
beggar would enfold himself in the purple of Emperors.
The Finest Story in the World (1893), "Many
Inventions"

God of our fathers, known of old,
Lord of our far-flung battle-line,
Beneath whose awful Hand we hold
Dominion over palm and pine-
Lord God of Hosts, be with us yet,
Lest we forget—lest we forget!
    [The *Recessional* urged humility for
    Victoria's Diamond Jubilee. The
    royals did not receive it well, but it
    was prophetic.]
"Recessional" (1897), st. 1

Far-called, our navies melt away
On dune and headland sinks the fire
Lo, all our pomp of yesterday
Is one with Niveveh and Tyre!
Judge of Nations, spare us yet,
Lest we forget—lest we forget!
Ibid., st. 3

A fool there was and he made his prayer
(As you and I!)
To a rag and a bone and a hank of hair.
(We called her the woman who did not
   care.)
But the fool he called her his lady fair-
(Even as you or I!)
"The Vampire" (1897), st. 1

Take up the White Man's burden-
Send forth the best ye breed-
Go, bind your sons to exile
To serve your captives' need.
    [Paternalism was one motivation

for imperialism. Today corporations invest in inner cities sometimes as a charitable act.]
"The White Man's Burden" (1899), st. 1

If you can keep your head when all
    about you
Are losing theirs and blaming it on you,
If you can trust yourself when all men
    doubt you,
But make allowance for their doubting
    too....
    "If," *Rewards and Fairies* (1910), st. 1

If you can dream—and not make
    dreams your master;
If you can think—and not make
    thoughts your aim;
If you can meet with Triumph and
    Disaster
And treat those two impostors just the
    same....
    Ibid., st. 2

....If you can force your heart and nerve
    and sinew
To serve your turn long after they are gone,
And so hold on when there is nothing
    in you
Except the Will which says to them:
    "Hold on!"
    Ibid., st. 3

If you can talk with crowds and keep
    your virtue,
Or walk with Kings—nor lose the com-
    mon touch....
If you can fill the unforgiving minute
With sixty seconds' worth of distance run,
Yours is the Earth and everything that's
    in it,
And—which is more—you'll be a Man,
    my son!
    Ibid., st. 4

One man in a thousand, Solomon says,
Will stick more close than a brother
And it's worth while seeking him half
    your days
If you find him before the other.
Nine hundred and ninety-nine depend
On what the world sees in you,
But the Thousandth Man will stand
    your friend
With the whole round world agin you.
    "The Thousandth Man," *Rewards and
    Fairies* (1910)

If once you have paid him the Danegeld
You never get rid of the Dane.
    "Danegeld" (1911), st. 4

"Have you news of my boy Jack?'
Not this tide.
"When d'you think that he'll come back?"
Not with this wind blowing, and this tide.
[Kipling's only son was killed in action.]
    "My Boy Jack" (1918), st. 1

"Oh dear, what comfort can I find?'
None this tide, Nor any tide,
Except he did not shame his kind—
Not even with that wind blowing, and
    that tide.
    Ibid., st. 3

My son was killed while laughing at
    some jest. I would I knew
What it was, and it might serve me in a
    time when jests are few.
    "A Son" (1918)

I have slain none except my Mother. She
(Blessing her slayer) died of grief for me.
    "An Only Son" (1918)

If any mourn us in the workshop, say
We died because the shift kept holiday.
    "Batteries Out of Ammunition" (1918)

When the Himalayan peasant meets the
he-bear in his pride,
He shouts to scare the monster, who will
often turn aside.
But the she-bear thus accosted rends the
peasant tooth and nail.
For the female of the species is more
deadly than the male.
　　"The Female of the Species" (1919), st. 1

Words are the most powerful drug used
by mankind.
　　　　　　　Speech (February 14, 1923),
　　　　　　　　　　　　　A Book of Words

The flying bullet down the Pass,
That whistles clear: "All flesh is grass."
　　"Arithmetic on the Frontier," st. 1 (partial)

If you hit a pony over the nose at the
outset of your acquaintance, he may not
love you, but he will take a deep interest
in your movements ever afterwards.
　　　　　　　Plain Tales from the Hills

The married man must sink or swim
An'—'e can't afford to sink!
　　　　　　　　　　　"The Married Man"

I keep six honest serving men,
They taught me all I knew,
Their names are what and why and when
And how and where and who.

　　[An autograph hunter mailed
　　Kipling a dollar, noting that Kipling
　　earned a dollar a word, and he asked
　　for a sample. Kipling sent back an
　　unsigned postcard with the word:]
"Thanks."
　　Little, Brown Book of Anecdotes (1985),
　　　　　　　　　Clifton Fadiman, ed.

BARONESS E. ORCZY
1865–1947

English (Hungarian-born), novelist.

We seek him here, we seek him there,
Those Frenchies seek him everywhere,
Is he in heaven?—Is he in Hell?
That demmed, elusive Pimpernel?
　[The daring Sir Percy Blakeney.]
　　The Scarlet Pimpernel (1905), ch. 12

JEAN SIBELIUS
1865–1957

Finn, composer, known for *Finlandria*
(1899).

No statue has ever been put up for a
critic.

WILLIAM BUTLER YEATS
1865–1939

Irish, poet, playwright, and 1923 Nobel
Prize for literature. He was a table-tap-
ping occultist who married a medium and
entertained spirits for poetic inspiration.
Yeats and T. S. Eliot are generally deemed
to be the greatest poets of the twentieth
century. A modernist, he saw chaos in his
time, but he saw a cyclical pattern of disorder leading to rebirth. He believed science
could not answer great questions, so poets
needed to do that in simple language.

The Land of Faery,
Where nobody gets old and godly and
　　grave,
Where nobody gets old and crafty and
　　wise,

Where nobody gets old and bitter of
    tongue.
    "The Land of Heart's Desire" (1894), l. 48

Better go down upon your
    marrow-bones
And scrub a kitchen pavement or break
    stones
Like an old pauper, in all kinds of
    weather;
For to articulate sweet sounds together
Is to work harder than all these.
    In the Seven Woods (1903), "Adams' Curse"

All changed, changed utterly:
A terrible beauty is born.
    "Easter 1916"

I know that I shall meet my fate
Somewhere among the clouds above;
Those that I fight I do not hate,
Those that I guard I do not love.
    The Wild Swans at Coole (1918), "An Irish
    Airman Foresees His Death" l. 1–4

Turning and turning in the widening
    gyre
The falcon cannot hear the falconer;
Things fall apart; the center cannot hold;
Mere anarchy is loosed upon the world,
The blood-dimmed tide is loosed, and
    everywhere
The ceremony of innocence is drowned;
The best lack all conviction, while the
    worst
Are full of passionate intensity.
Surely some revelation is at hand;
Surely the Second Coming is at hand.
    "The Second Coming" (1921), st. 1

And what rough beast, its hour come
    round at last,
Slouches toward Bethlehem to be born?
    Ibid., st. 2 (partial)

An aged man is but a paltry thing,
A tattered coat upon a stick, unless
Soul clap its hands and sing, and louder
    sing
For every tatter in its mortal dress...
    The Tower (1928), "Sailing to
    Byzantium," st. 2

Only God, my dear,
Could love you for yourself alone
And not your yellow hair.
    The Winding Stair (1933), "For Anne
    Gregory," l. 16–18

Think where man's glory most begins
    and ends,
And say my glory was I had such friends.
    Last Poems (1936–39), "The Municipal
    Gallery Revisited," st. 7

All empty souls tend to extreme opinion.
It is only in those who have built up a
rich world of memories and habits of
thought that extreme opinions affront
the sense of probability. Propositions, for
instance, which set all the truth upon one
side can only enter rich minds to dislo-
cate and strain, if they can enter at all,
and sooner or later the mind expels them
by instinct.
    Dramatis Personae (Autobiography) (1936)

We poets would die of loneliness but for
women, and we choose our men friends
that we may have somebody to talk about
women with.
    Letter to Olivia Shakespeare (1936)

Happiness is neither virtue nor pleasure, nor this thing nor that, but simply
growth.
    In L. R. Frank, *Quotationary* (1999)

The Government does not intend these things to happen....but in legislation intention is nothing, and the letter of the law everything, and no government has the right...to forge an instrument of tyranny and say that it will never be used.

> Speech to the Irish Senate on a bill giving excessive power to the Minister of Justice.

Education is not the filling of a pail but the lighting of a fire.

I have certainly known more men destroyed by the desire to have a wife and child and to keep them in comfort than I have seen destroyed by drink and harlots.

GEORGE ADE
1866–1944

American, humorist.

He had been kicked in the head by a mule when young and believed everything he read in the Sunday papers.

> *Fables in Slang* (1899)

'Whom are you?' said he, for he had attended business college.

> "The Steel Box," *Chicago Record*
> (March 16, 1898)

LINCOLN STEFFENS
1866–1936

American, muckraking socialist journalist.

I have been over into the future, and it works.

> [Conversation with Bernard Baruch after visiting the U.S.S.R.]

SUN YAT-SEN
1866–1925

Chinese, revolutionist, who overthrew the Manchu Ch'ing dynasty in 1911 with the slogan "Nationalism, democracy, and guaranteed work." His Kuomintang (National People's Party) controlled China by 1930 under the leadership of Chiang Kai-shek, but it lost a civil war to the Communist Party in 1949.

> The Chinese people have only family and clan solidarity; they do not have national spirit they are just a heap of loose sand.
> "China As A Heap Of Loose Sand"
> (1924)

HERBERT GEORGE (H. G.) WELLS
1866–1946

English, historian, science fiction novelist.

The materialist determinism of H. G. Wells's *Outline of History* (1920) had a profound impact. It argued that humanity was inexorably progressing toward perfection. This determinism attacked the prevalent Victorian philosophy that man has the capacity for good and evil, so our future depends on our choices. Considering the peoples' support for Hitler, Stalin, and Osama bin Laden, Wells's optimism is suspect.

In his *The Time Machine* (1895), humans in the year 802,701 devolve into two species: the effete, vegetarian Eloi and the brutal Morlocks, who eat the Eloi. In *The War of the Worlds* (1898), Martians invade Earth. Orson Welles caused a panic using this theme in a realistic radio broadcast in 1938.

Human history becomes more and more a race between education and catastrophe.
The Outline of History (1920), vol. 2., ch. 41

Leaders should lead as far as they can and then vanish. Their ashes should not choke the fire they have lit.
In L. R. Frank, *Quotationary* (1999)

The great trouble with you Americans is that you are still under the influence of that third rate mind, Karl Marx.
[To Sinclair Lewis, 1935.]

Human history is, in essence, a history of ideas.

Marie Curie
1867–1934

French (Polish-born), first person to win Nobel prizes in two sciences: 1903 in physics and 1911 in chemistry. She discovered that polonium and radium rocks constantly poured out extraordinary energy (radioactivity), which Einstein later proved was a conversion of mass into energy. She died of radiation poisoning; her papers are too hot to hold.

You cannot hope to build a better world without improving the individual. To that end each of us must work for his own improvement, and at the same time share a general responsibility for all humanity, our particular duty being to aid those to whom we think we can be most useful.
Pierre Curie (1923), ch.1

[A reporter calling on the Curies was met by a dowdy woman. She said "yes" when he asked if she were the housekeeper. He asked if she could give any confidential information about her mistress. Marie Curie replied:] Madame Curie has only one message that she likes to be given to reporters. That is: be less curious about people and more curious about ideas.
In Clifton Fadiman, ed., *The Little Brown Book of Anecdotes* (1985)

Life is not easy for any of us. But what of that? We must have perseverance and, above all, confidence in ourselves. We must believe that we are gifted for something, and that this thing, at whatever cost, must be attained.

Ernest Dowson
1867–1900

English, a "decadent" poet. He spent his short, drug-addicted life pining over a twelve-year-old girl, Cynara, much as Dante and Petrarch did.

I have forgot much, Cynara! gone with
    the wind...
I have been faithful to thee, Cynara! in
    my fashion.
"Cynara" (1896)

They are not long, the weeping and the
    laughter,
Love and desire and hate;
I think they have no portion in us after
We pass the gate.
"Vitae Summa Brevis" (1896), st. 1

They are not long, the days of wine and
    roses;
Out of a misty dream
Our path emerges for a while, then closes
Within a dream.
Ibid., st. 3

FINLEY PETER DUNNE (MR. DOOLEY)
1867–1936

American, humorist, with an Irish brogue who said, "Politics ain't beanbag!"

No matther whether the' constitution follows the' flag or not, the' supreme coort follows the 'iliction returns.'
> *Mr. Dooley's Opinions* (1900), "The Supreme Court's Decisions"

The dimmycratic party ain't on speakin' terms with itsilt.
> Ibid., "Mr. Dooley Discusses Party Politics"

Thrust ivrybody—but cut the' ca-ards.
> Ibid., "Mr. Dooley's Philosophy"

A fanatic is a man that does what he thinks the Lord would do, if he knew the facts of the case.
> Ibid., "Casual Observations"

A man th'd expict to thrain lobsters to fly in a year is called a loonytic; but a man that thinks men can be tu-rned into angels be an iliction is called a rayformer an' remains at large.
> Ibid.

EDITH HAMILTON
1867–1963

American (Greek-born), classical scholar.

The fundamental fact about the Greek was that he had to use his mind. The ancient priests had said, "Thus far and no farther. We set the limits of thought." The Greeks said, "All things are to be examined and called into question. There are no limits set on thought."
> *The Greek Way* (1930), ch. 1

To be able to be caught up into the world of thought—that is being educated.

JÓZEF PIŁSUDSKI
1867–1935

Polish, general and statesman, whose Polish Republic in 1918 and 1921 defeated Soviet armies seeking to support a Communist revolution in Germany. If instead of cutting a deal with Lenin, Pilsudski had supported the White Russian armies advancing toward Moscow, Lenin might have been overthrown. However, another Pole, Lech Walesa, did help topple the Soviet Union with his Solidarity trade union. That convinced Mikhail Gorbachev to experiment with perestroika in Poland—leading to perestroika in the Soviet Union and its dissolution.

To be defeated, but not to surrender, that is victory.

HENRY L. STIMPSON
1867–1950

American, secretary of war (1940–45).

Gentlemen do not read other people's mail.
> In Walter Isaacson, *Kissinger* (1992)

HARVEY S. FIRESTONE
1868–1938

American, who improved Dunlop's 1888 invention of the pneumatic tire.

> A man with a surplus can control circumstances, but a man without a surplus is controlled by them, and often he has no opportunity to exercise judgment.

MIKHAIL POKROVSKY
1868–1932

Russian, Marxist historian.

> History is politics projected into the past.
> Quoted by Hugh Thomas in *Armed Truce*

EDMOND ROSTAND
1868–1918

French, playwright.

> What's that you say? Hopeless? Why, very well!
> But a man does not fight merely to win!
> No-no-better to know one fights in vain!
> You there-who are you? A hundred against one-
> I know them now, my ancient enemies
> Falsehood—Prejudice—Compromise—
> Cowardice...Ah, you too Vanity.
> *Cyrano de Bergerac* (1897), act 5

> [Final scene: Cyrano deliriously slashes his sword and dies in Roxanne's arms.]

There was a real Cyrano De Bergerac (1619–55), a boisterous soldier and duelist with an enormous nose. The real Cyrano was also a playwright, in whose *History of the Moon's States and Empires* (1657) the laws are made by the young, who are revered by the old; chastity is condemned; and suicide and large noses are praised.

NEVILLE CHAMBERLAIN
1869–1940

English, prime minister (1937–1940) who was popular for appeasing Hitler at Munich. After Munich, Chamberlain received a cable from President Franklin Roosevelt saying, "Good man."

> How horrible, fantastic, incredible it is that we should be digging trenches and trying on gas-masks here because of a quarrel in a far away country between people of whom we know nothing.
> September 27, 1938, before the Munich Treaty

> My good friends, this is the second time in our history, a British Prime Minister has returned from Germany bringing peace with honor. I believe it is peace for our time...Go home and get a nice quiet sleep.
> September 30, 1938, after the Munich Treaty

> In spite of the hardness and ruthlessness I thought I saw in his [Adolph Hitler's] face, I got the impression that here was a man who could be relied upon when he had given his word.
> Ibid.

MOHANDAS K. GANDHI
1869–1948

Indian, British attorney, and Indian states-man, who perfected nonviolent political protest to wrest India's independence from Britain. A key to any strategy is knowing both one's enemy and oneself. He knew the British thought of themselves as liberal and civilized. While they would ruthlessly crush a violent uprising, their self-image would not allow them to use force against passive resistance. Gandhi perfected the "passive-aggressive" strategy.

The British granted India dominion sta-tus in 1947, due to Gandhi's strategy and due to the belated realization that colonies were financial rat-holes. Although he was revered as the *Mahatma* or "Great Soul," a Hindu nationalist assassinated him for partitioning Pakistan after independence.

> I was a believer in the politics of peti-tions, deputations, and friendly nego-tiations. But all these have gone to the dogs. I know that these are not the ways to bring this Government round. Sedi-tion has become my religion. Ours is a nonviolent war.

> The moment the slave resolves that he will no longer be a slave, his fetters fall. Freedom and slavery are mental states.
> *Non-Violence in Peace and War* (1949),
> vol. 2., ch. 5

> [To "What do you think of Western civilization?"]
> I think it would be a good idea.

INDIA

Gandhi's economic program was "village self-sufficiency," a formula for a Dark Ages economy. India's first prime minister, Jawa-harlal Nehru, a Brahmin contemptuous of capitalism, adopted a socialist and closed-door regime. Thus, China has received forty times more foreign direct investment than India. In 1950 the per capita incomes of India and South Korea were the same, but by 2005 South Korea's was $20,000 ver-sus $3,000 for India. Prior to 1991, India's economic growth rate was 3.2 percent, but her population increase was 2.3 percent so per capita income rose less than 1 percent per annum. In 1938, India's share of world trade was 3 percent, but fell to 0.5 percent in 1980. In 1991, Finance Minister Manmo-han Singh, who admired Thatcher, began to deregulate, cut tariffs, privatize state industries, foster export-led growth, and promote sound money, so India's economy is now growing 7 percent per annum. Dr. Singh as prime minister in 2005 abandoned nonalignment for allegiance to "those who defend the values of liberal democracy and secularism."

EDWARD ARLINGTON ROBINSON
1869–1935

American, impoverished poet, whose gifts were recognized late in life.

> Miniver Cheevy, child of scorn,
> Grew lean while he assailed the seasons;
> He wept that he was ever born,
> And he had reasons.
> "Miniver Cheevy" (1910), st. 1

Miniver loved the days of old
When swords were bright and steeds
   were prancing.
The vision of a warrior bold
Would set him dancing.

Ibid., st. 2

Miniver cursed the commonplace
And eyed a khaki suit with loathing;
He missed the medieval grace
Of iron clothing.

Ibid., st. 6

Miniver Cheevy, born too late,
Scratched his head and kept on
   thinking;
Miniver coughed, and called it fate,
And kept on drinking.

Ibid., st. 8

WILLIAM STRUNK JR.
1869–1946

American, authority on English writing style.

The surest way to arouse and hold the attention of the reader is by being specific, definite, and concrete. The greatest writers—Homer, Dante, Shakespeare—are effective largely because they deal in particulars and report the details that matter. Their words call up pictures.

The Elements of Style (1918), ch. 2, sec. 11

Vigorous writing is concise. A sentence should contain no unnecessary words, a paragraph no unnecessary sentences, for the same reason that a drawing should have no unnecessary lines and a machine no unnecessary parts. This requires not that the writer make all his sentences short, or that he avoid all detail and treat his subjects only in outline, but that every word tell.

Ibid., sec 13

FRANK LLOYD WRIGHT
1869–1959

American, architect, who developed the "prairie style" house with low horizontal lines and the main rooms flowing together without walls. His "organic architecture" meant harmony with the environment. In 1936, he sketched in three hours his most famous house, "Falling Water" in Bear Run, Pennsylvania.

Wright was most productive in his seventies due to his third wife, Olga, who organized a revolving group of young architects to pay tuition to work at Wright's homes: "Taliesin" in Wisconsin and "Taliesin West" near Phoenix, Arizona.

After Le Corbusier said "a house is a machine for living in," Wright replied that our houses need not look like machines. His Imperial Hotel (1920) was one of the rare major structures in Tokyo to survive intact a major earthquake in 1923.

The physician can bury his mistakes, but the architect can only advise his client to plant vines—so they should go as far as possible from home to build their first buildings.

New York Times (October 4, 1951)

Ugliness is a sin.

Interview (1955)

Early in life I had to choose between honest arrogance and hypocritical humility.

Attributed

Form and function are one.
    [This responds to Louis Henri
    Sullivan's "Form follows function."
    Sullivan had pioneered metal frame
    buildings on which walls were
    hung—the precursor to skyscrapers.
    More perceptive is Henry Petroski's
    "Form follows failure." Ludwig
    Mies van der Rohe (1886–1969)
    pioneered glass skyscrapers out of
    his minimalist architecture, saying,
    "Less is more."]
    In Clifton Fadiman, *An American Treasury*
                                (1955)

No house should ever be
On any hill or on anything.
It should be of the hill,
Belonging to it, so hill and
House could live together
Each the happier for the other.

BERNARD MANNES BARUCH
1870–1965

American, investor, shunned as a Jewish
alarmist by FDR. Baruch persuaded Congress to pass the Neutrality Act in 1939,
which enabled Britain to buy war supplies,
and he persuaded FDR to support Lend-
Lease, which supplied $50 billion of war
materials to Britain and the USSR.

During my eighty-seven years I have
witnessed a whole succession of technological revolutions. But none of them has
done away with the need for character in
the individual or the ability to think.
                    My Own Story (1957)

Every man has a right to his opinion, but
no man has a right to be wrong in his
facts.

Always do one thing less than you think
you can do.

Buy straw hats in the winter. Summer
will surely come.

Buy something people use and throw away.

When the outlook is steeped in pessimism, I remind myself, "Two and two
still make four, and you can't keep mankind down for long."

    [On the day the Dow Jones Industri-
    als hit its bottom of 41.33 in 1932, an
    investor remarked to Baruch that it had
    been a tough day. Baruch replied:]
Not for the buyers.

As with most financial panics, the stage
had been set in advance by extravagant
hopes and talk of a "New Era."

    [When asked what book he would
    choose if stranded on an island, he
    replied:]
"A practical guide to boat building."

HILAIRE BELLOC
1870–1953

British, poet and essayist, who teamed
with Chesterton as Catholic apologists
against socialism.

Whatever happens, we have got
The Maxim gun, and they have not.
    [Kitchener lost 48 while killing 10,000.]
        The Modern Traveler (1898), ch. 6

Matilda told such dreadful lies,
It made one gasp and stretch one's eyes;
Her aunt, who, from her earliest youth,

Had kept a strict regard for truth,
Attempted to believe Matilda;
The effort very nearly killed her.
"Matilda," Cautionary Tales (1907)

When I am dead, I hope it may be said:
"His sins were scarlet, but his books
    were read."
On Everything (1909)

We've had quite enough
Of this horrible stuff
And we don't want to hear any more.
Cautionary Verses (1941)

How odd of God to choose the Jews?

The control of the production of wealth
is control of human life itself.

BENJAMIN N. CARDOZO
1870–1938

American, associate justice.

A trustee is held to something stricter
than the morals of the marketplace.
Not honesty alone, but the punctilio of
an honor the most sensitive, is then the
standard of behavior.
Mein Hard v. Saltnon, 249 N.Y. 458, 464
(1928)

VLADIMIR LENIN
1870–1924

Russian, socialist, who overthrew the Russian Republic in 1917. He turned a nation exporting 40 percent of its food into a food importer. He garnered support from Western fellow travelers, whom he labeled "useful idiots." Gorbachev said: "I can only say that cruelty was the main problem with Lenin." Robert Service's *Lenin: A Biography* (2000) shows that Lenin organized all the tools for mass murder, and he murdered 4,017,000 innocents. As Lenin said, "Violence is the midwife of history."

R. J. Rummel's *Death by Government* (1996) estimates that in the twentieth century, socialists murdered about 126 million people, to wit, the USSR 62 million, Mao 35 million, Hitler 21 million, Pol Pot 2.4 million, Vietnam 1.6 million, and others 4 million. *The Black Book of Communism* (1999) estimates that 85 to 100 million were so murdered. Both assume that only 20 million Chinese were murdered in Mao's political famine of 1958–61, but some argue that in fact 80 million Chinese were starved to death. In the *Black Book of Communism*, a leftist intellectual explained, "Agreed, both Nazis and Communists killed. But while the Nazis killed from hatred of humanity, the Communists killed from love."

It doesn't matter a jot if three-fourths of mankind perish! The only thing that matters is that, in the end, the remaining fourth should become communist.
In L. R. Frank, Quotationary (1999)

Without a revolutionary theory there can be no revolutionary movement.
What Is To Be Done (1902)

A scientific interpretation of dictatorship means nothing else but a government unlimited by any laws, and absolutely unhampered by any rules and relying directly on force.
V. I. Lenin, *Works*, XXV,

While the State exists, there can be no freedom.
State and Revolution (1919), ch. 5

[In November 1917] we knew that our victory will be a lasting victory only when our undertaking will conquer the whole world, because we have launched it exclusively counting on world revolution.

Polnoe sobraniesochinenii, vol. 42, 1

Lenin launched a Soviet attack in 1919 against Germany, but it was defeated by Poland. He decided to wait until another great European war so weakened Europe that Soviet armies could overrun it. This was the master plan bequeathed to Stalin.

Why should any man be allowed to buy a printing press and disseminate pernicious opinions calculated to embarrass the government?

Moscow speech (1920)

Communism is Soviet state power plus the electrification of the whole country.

Report to Congress (1920)

[In 1880 the Russian Alexander Herzen, anticipating tyrants would use technology, said:]
I fear most Genghis Khan with the telegraph.

If you strike steel, pull back; if you strike mush, keep going.

In L. R. Frank, *Quotationary* (1999)

Speaking the truth is a petty-bourgeois prejudice. A lie, on the other hand, is often justified by the end.

Ibid.

If we go, we shall slam the door on an empty house.

In Malcolm Muggeridge, *Diary*

The heart on fire, the brain on ice.

Maxim of Lenin

Of all the arts, the cinema is the most important.

It is true that liberty is precious—so precious that it must be rationed.

The whole of society will have become a single office and a single factory with equality of work and equality of pay. (1917) [See also Leon Trotsky:] "Where the sole employer is the State, opposition means death by starvation...he who does not obey shall not eat" (1937).

Anti-Semitism is the socialism of fools.

The way to crush the bourgeoisie is to grind them between millstones of taxation and inflation.

The worst enemies of the new radicals are the old liberals.

In principle we have never renounced terror and cannot renounce it.

We are not carrying out war against individuals. We are exterminating the bourgeoisie as a class. We are not looking for evidence or witnesses to reveal deed or words against the Soviet power. The first question we ask is—to what class does he belong, what are his origins, upbringing, education or profession? These questions define the fate of the accused. This is the essence of the Red Terror.

When I put a question to [Lenin] about socialism in agriculture, he explained with glee how he had incited the poorer peasants against the richer ones, "and they soon hanged them from the nearest tree—ha! ha! ha!" His guffaw at the thought of those massacred made my blood run cold.

> Bertrand Russell on a 1920 interview in Moscow, "Eminent Men I Have Known," *Unpopular Essays* (1950)

Alexander Kerensky, a socialist lawyer, won acquittals for Lenin's lieutenants against charges of treason. Those acquitted helped to liquidate 62 million people—such was Communism, which Lenin said was, "socialism in a hurry."

MARIA MONTESSORI
1870–1952

Italian, educator, and Italy's first female MD. Her system for teaching preschool children emphasized their natural desire to learn and freedom to explore in a sensory-rich environment with hands-on learning experiences. Montessori schools lost favor after it was proven that intelligence was not a product of childhood exploration but was largely genetically determined.

> Education is not acquired by listening to words, but by experiences in the environment.
> In Norman Davies, *Europe: A History* (1996)

HECTOR H. MUNRO
(SAKI)
1870–1916

Scottish, short story writer and journalist, killed in World War I.

The cook was a good cook, as cooks go, and as cooks go she went.

> *Reginald* (1904), "Reginald on Besetting Sins"

Every reformation must have its victims. You can't expect the fatted calf to share the enthusiasm of the angels over the prodigal's return.

> Ibid., "Reginald on the Academy"

A little inaccuracy sometimes saves tons of explanation.

> *The Square Egg* (1924), "The Comments of Moung Ka"

In "The Open Window," a man goes to a village on doctor's orders to avoid excitement. He calls on a lady to whom he had been given a letter of introduction and a young girl says she is to entertain him until her aunt is free. The girl notes the sitting room's roaring fire and its open window-door on a cold winter day, which she says results from a great tragedy. Years ago her aunt's husband went hunting and never returned. Her aunt always leaves the door open in the belief her husband will return. The aunt on entering the room tells the stranger the door is left open for her husband, who will soon return from hunting. The girl gives a knowing look to the stranger. After awhile, the little girl turns pale as the husband and his pack of hunting dogs come walking toward the open window-door. When the stranger sees this, he grasps at his heart and bolts out of the house. When her aunt and uncle express amazement at the stranger's behavior, the girl explains that the stranger's wife and child had been killed in India by a pack of wild dogs.

STEPHEN CRANE
1871–1900

American, who never served in the military, but who at age twenty-four wrote a psychological portrayal of fear in combat. *The Red Badge of Courage* (1895) focuses on Henry Fleming, who is not motivated by patriotism in his first battle in the Civil War, but by his fear of showing fear and by his cowardice. He deserts under fire. In the rear, he mixes with the wounded, and he too wishes for a wound (red badge) to symbolize a courage he has not shown. Shamed, he returns to his unit and fights courageously. The moral is that in the terror of combat one can alternate between being a coward and a hero.

> A man said to the universe:
> "Sir, I exist!"
> "However," replied the universe,
> "The fact has not created in me
> A sense of obligation."
> "A Man Said to the Universe" (1899)

MARCEL PROUST
1871–1922

French, novelist, known for *Remembrance of Things Past* (1913–26), an unending novel. Its stream of consciousness style lacks plot and timeline. Marcel, the narrator, does nothing in life but dote on memories, like memories of his mother not kissing him one night and his eating a *petite Madeleine* [small cake]. All scheme to rise socially as they all deteriorate from age and die. Intellectuals account Proust, a neurotic hypochondriac, and Gide, a narcissistic pro-Communist, as the best French writers of their period, rather than the heroic conservatives Paul Valéry and Charles Péguy.

> Our heart changes, and this is the greatest cause of suffering in life.
> "Swann's Way," *Remembrance of Things Past*
> (1913), vol. 1

> Everything great in the world comes from neurotics. They alone have founded our religions, and composed our masterpieces. Never will the world know all it owes to them nor all that they have suffered to enrich us.
> Ibid., vol. 3, "The Guermantes Way"

> We love only what we do not completely possess.
> Ibid., vol. 5, "The Captive"

> All of our resolutions are made in a state of mind that is not going to last.

ERNEST RUTHERFORD
1871–1937

British (New Zealand born), 1908 Nobel Prize in chemistry. He made the Cavendish Laboratory at Cambridge the first world-class scientific laboratory by assembling brilliant scientists who discovered the constitution of the atom. He gave his scientists objectives but no supervision. If they failed to achieve their objectives, he fired them. He first split an atom—a nitrogen atom—that he transmuted into oxygen and hydrogen, thereby achieving the goal of the alchemists. His invention of sonar for submarines saved Britain from starvation in World War I. His lab also improved radar—key to winning the Battle of Britain in 1940, which saved the West.

Note: Henry Cavendish (1731–1810), a brilliant chemist and physicist, was so shy he rarely talked to anyone. His maid communicated with him by letter. Those who had to talk to him would walk near him and "speak out as it were into vacancy," and there might be a hushed reply into vacancy. Cavendish anticipated: the law of the conservation of energy, Ohm's law, Dalton's Law of Partial Pressures, Richter's Law of Reciprocal Proportions, Charles's Law of Gases, and the principles of electrical conductivity.

We cannot control atomic energy to an extent which would be of any value commercially, and I believe we are not likely ever to be able to do so.

> Speech (1933)

PAUL VALÉRY
1871–1945

French, essayist, poet, and philosopher.

Collect all the facts that can be collected about the life of Racine and you will never learn from them the art of his verse.

> Introduction to *The Method of Leonardo da Vinci* (1895), tr. Thomas McGreevy

Two dangers constantly threaten the world: order and disorder.

> *The Nation* (January 5, 1957)

A poem is never really finished, only abandoned.

> In W. H. Auden, "Writing," *A Certain World* (1971)

At times I think and at times I am.

> *The New Yorker* (November 28, 1977)

To enter one's own self, it is necessary to go armed to the teeth.

> *Quelques Pensées de M. Teste*

The future is not what it used to be.

> In Joseph Epstein, *Ambition: The Secret Passion* (1980), Introduction

Nothing is more "original," northing more "oneself" than to feed on others. But one has to digest them. A lion is made of assimilated sheep.

> In Harold Bloom, *Genius* (2002)

The value of men's work is not in the works themselves but in their later development by others, in other circumstances.

> Ibid.

We say that an author is original when we cannot trace the hidden transformations that others underwent in his mind…

> Ibid.

An artist wants to inspire jealousy till the end of time.

> Ibid.

A man who is "of sound mind" keeps the inner madman under lock and key.

> In L. R. Frank, *Wit and Humor Quotationary*

CALVIN COOLIDGE
1872–1933

American, thirtieth president (1923–1929), and the only world leader in his era who did not expand the role of the state. He had been elected governor of Massachusetts after refusing to reinstate Boston police, who had gone on strike illegally. His telegram to AFL president Samuel Gompers read, "There is no right to strike against the public safety by anybody, anywhere, any time." Coolidge became the vice presidential nominee on Harding's 1920 "Return to Normalcy" ticket.

Coolidge, like Queen Elizabeth I, used a strategy of masterful inactivity and achieved similar results. He cut the top tax rate from 70 percent to 24 percent, and he also cut the national debt in half. During his term, the unemployment rate averaged only 3.6 percent, per capita income rose from $522 to $716, and real growth averaged 4.0 percent per annum. The Coolidge prosperity was real, widespread, and not a "drunken fiesta" as Edmund Wilson called it.

"Silent Cal" gave a press conference every two weeks in office—he spoke more to the press than any other president! Mencken said Coolidge was the best writer of America's presidents. The themes of his speeches were self-reliance, the dignity of work, and an economical government. A cum laude graduate of Amherst, he read Cicero in the original.

Coolidge did not run for a second term, perhaps because of grief over his youngest son dying of blood poisoning resulting from a blister contracted during a tennis match.

Coolidge viewed Hoover's succession with apprehension: "That man has offered me unsolicited advice for six years, all of it bad."

Nothing in the world can take the place of persistence. Talent will not: nothing is more common than unsuccessful men with talent. Genius will not; unrewarded genius is almost a proverb. Education will not; the world is full of educated derelicts. Persistence and determination alone are omnipotent. The slogan "Press On," has solved and always will solve the problems of the human race.

> Printed on Coolidge's Memorial Service Program (1933)

It is more important to kill bad bills than to pass good ones....

> Letter to his father 1910. In Peter Hannaford, *The Quotable Calvin Coolidge* (2001)

Do the day's work. If it be to protect the rights of the weak, whoever objects, do it. If it be to help a powerful corporation better to serve the people, whatever the opposition, do that. Expect to be called a standpatter, but don't be a standpatter. Expect to be called a demagogue but don't be a demagogue. Don't hesitate to be as revolutionary as science. Don't hesitate to be as reactionary as the multiplication table. Don't expect to build up the weak by pulling down the strong. Don't hurry to legislate. Give the administration a chance to catch up with legislation.

> His entire inauguration speech as President of the Massachusetts Senate (January 7, 1914)

Good government cannot be found at the bargain counter.... We cannot curtail the usual appropriations or the care of mothers with dependent children or the support of the poor, the insane, and the infirm....

> Campaign for Lieutenant-Governorship (August 28, 1916)

There is no greater service that we can render the oppressed of the earth than to maintain inviolate the freedom of our own citizens.

> Gubernatorial candidate (November 2, 1918)

Civilization and profits go hand-in-hand.
Speech, New York (November 27, 1920)

Inflation is repudiation.
Speech, Chicago (1922)

After order and liberty, economy is one of the highest essentials of a free government.
Speech as vice president in 1923

I agree perfectly with those who wish to relieve the small taxpayer by getting the largest possible contribution from the people with large incomes. But if the rates on large incomes are so high that they disappear, the small taxpayer will be left to bear the entire burden. If, on the other hand, the rates are placed where they will get the most revenue from large incomes, then the small taxpayer will be relieved.
Speech (February 12, 1924) to National Republican Club in New York

Doubters do not achieve; skeptics do not contribute; cynics do not create. Faith is the great motive power, and no man reaches his full possibilities unless he has the deep conviction that life is eternally important, and that his work, well done, is part of an unending plan.
Speech (July 24, 1924) to the Boy Scouts

The Constitution is the sole source and guarantee of national freedom.
Nomination acceptance speech (August 4, 1924)

Liberty is not collective, it is personal. All liberty is individual.
Speech (September 21, 1924), in Peter Hannaford, *The Quotable Calvin Coolidge* (2001)

The government of the United States is a device for maintaining in perpetuity the rights of the people, with the ultimate extinction of all privileged classes.
Speech, Philadelphia (September 1924)

The chief business of the American people is business. They are profoundly concerned with buying, selling, investing and prospering in the world.
Speech (January 17, 1925), Society of Newspaper Editors

I favor the policy of economy, not because I wish to save money, but because I wish to save people. The men and women of this country who toil are the ones who bear the cost of the government. Every dollar we carelessly waste means that their life will be so much more the meager....Economy is idealism in its most practical form.
Inaugural Address (March 4, 1925)

We live in an age of science and abounding accumulation of material things. These did not create our Declaration. Our Declaration created them. The things of the spirit come first.
Speech (July 4, 1926)

When I pick out a man to do a job, I don't generally instruct him, but if you wish instructions, you draw them up and I'll sign them.
Letter to Henry L. Stimson. In Peter Hannaford, *The Quotable Calvin Coolidge* (2001)

Perhaps one of the most important accomplishments of my administration has been minding my own business.
Ibid.

It is a great advantage to a president, and a major source of safety to the country, for him to know that he is not a great man.

Autobiography (1929)

[When asked what the minister had preached about sin]: He said he was against it.

Coolidge Wit and Wisdom (1933)

Collecting more taxes than is absolutely necessary is legalized robbery.

New York Times (March 6, 1955)

The man who builds a factory, builds a temple.

In Harold Evans, *The American Century* (1999)

America recognizes no aristocracy save those who work.

Nine-tenths of a president's callers at the White House want something they ought not to have. If you keep dead still they will run out in three or four minutes.

[When on a train, a companion remarked that the sheep in a field they were passing had just been sheared. Coolidge replied:] Well, on this side anyway.

[Walter Lippmann said of Coolidge:] Mr. Coolidge's genius for inactivity is developed to a very high point. It is far from being an indolent activity. It is a grim, determined, alert inactivity... Mr. Coolidge's inactivity is not merely the absence of activity. It is, on the contrary, a steady application to the task of neutralizing and thwarting political activity wherever there are signs of life. [When a matron said she bet she could get more than two words out of him, Coolidge replied:] You lose.

Calvin Coolidge in a Memorial Day speech in 1931 noted the sacrifices of the Great War's dead. He concluded by saying, "No nation can live which cannot command that kind of service."

Mrs. Coolidge asked a farmer how often a rooster did his duty, and the farmer replied "Many times." She asked the farmer to tell Mr. Coolidge. Mr. Coolidge asked if the rooster did his duty with only one hen, and the farmer said "No, with all the hens." He asked the farmer to tell Mrs. Coolidge.

> The people cannot look to legislation generally for success. Industry, thrift, and character are not conferred by act or resolve. Government cannot relieve from toil. It can, of course, provide for the defective...but the normal must care for themselves. Self-government means self-support.
>
> Address to Massachusetts Senate

LEARNED HAND
1872–1961

American, the most respected federal court of appeals judge (1924–1951). His opinions made the Second Circuit so prestigious that its opinions took precedence over those of other circuit courts.

> Anyone may arrange his affairs so that his taxes may be as low as possible; he is not bound to choose the pattern which will best pay the Treasury.
>
> *Helvering v. Gregory* (1934)

The spirit of liberty is the spirit which is not too sure that it is right; the spirit of liberty is the spirit which seeks to understand the minds of other men and women; the spirit of liberty is the spirit which weighs their interests alongside its own without bias...

Speech, "The Spirit of Liberty," New York City (May 21, 1944)

Liberty lies in the hearts of men and women; when it dies there, no constitution, no law, no court can save it.

Ibid.

If we are to keep our democracy, there must be one commandment: Thou shalt not ration justice.

Speech, New York Legal Aid Society (February 16, 1951)

John McCrae
1872–1918

Canadian, lieutenant colonel and poet.

In Flanders fields the poppies blow
Between the crosses, row on row,
That mark our place; and in the sky
The larks, still bravely singing, fly
Scarce heard amid the guns below.

"In Flanders' Fields" (1915), st. 1

We are the Dead. Short days ago
We lived, felt dawn, saw sunset glow,
Loved and were loved, and now we lie
In Flanders fields.

Ibid., st. 2

Take up our quarrel with the foe!
To you from failing hands we throw
The torch; be yours to hold it high.
If ye break faith with us who die

We shall not sleep, though poppies grow
In Flanders' fields.

Ibid., st. 3

Bertrand Russell
1872–1970

Welsh, Nobel laureate, leftist philosopher, mathematician, and pacifist, who urged the West to surrender to the Soviet Union rather than risk war.

Throughout history power has been the vice of the ascetic.

In L. R. Frank, *Quotationary* (1999)

You mustn't exaggerate, young man. That's always a sign that your argument is weak.

In L. R. Frank, *Quotationary* (1999)

The most savage controversies are those about matters as to which there is no good evidence either way.

In Bart Kosko, *Fuzzy Thinking* (1993)

Everything is vague to a degree you do not realize till you have tried to make it precise.

Ibid.

The megalomaniac differs from the narcissist by the fact that he wishes to be powerful rather than charming, and seeks to be feared rather than loved. To this type belong many lunatics and most of the great men in history.

In L. R. Frank, *Wit and Humor Quotationary*

In art nothing worth doing can be done without genius; in science even a very moderate capacity can contribute to a supreme achievement.

HARLAN FISKE STONE
1872–1946

American, chief justice (1925–41).

> While unconstitutional exercise of power by the executive and legislative branches is subject to judicial restraint, the only check upon our own exercise of power is our own sense of self-restraint.

CHARLES PÉGUY
1873–1914

French, Catholic poet, and essayist.

> Homer is new and fresh this morning, and nothing, perhaps, is as old and tired as today's newspaper.
> *Note sur M. Bergson et la Philosophie Bergsonienne* (1914)

> Freedom is a system based on courage.
> From Halevy, *Life of Charles Péguy*

EMILY POST
1873–1960

American, one of two great authorities on etiquette, who wrote *Etiquette* (1922). The other authority, Amy Vanderbilt (1908–1974) said in *Amy Vanderbilt's Compete Book of Etiquette* (1954): "Breakfast is the one meal at which it is perfectly good manners to read the paper."

> Nothing is less important than which fork you use.

WILLA CATHER
1873–1947

American, poet, and novelist, admired for her trilogy: *O Pioneers!* (1913), *The Song of the Lark* (1915), and *My Antonia* (1918). She portrayed the honor and self-denial of frontier families.

> No one can build his security upon the nobleness of another person.
> *Alexander's Bridge* (1912), ch. 8

> The universal human yearning for something permanent, enduring, without shadow of change.
> *Death Comes for the Arch-bishop* (1927), bk. III, ch. 3

G. K. CHESTERTON
1874–1936

English, poet, essayist, and a Catholic convert who wrote about Christianity for the young, as in the Father Brown mysteries. Chesterton said the "greatest challenge to society is to agree, not on what is wrong, but on what is right." This calls for relying on artists, not censors. He noted that when there aren't enough hats to go around, the problem isn't solved by lopping off some heads.

> The Christian ideal has not been tried and found wanting. It has been found difficult; and left untried.
> *What's Wrong with the World* (1910), pt. 1, ch. 5

> When men stop believing in God, they don't believe in nothing. They believe in anything.

For the great Gaels of Ireland
Are the men that God made mad,
For all their wars are merry,
And all their songs are sad.
>> "The Ballad of the White Horse"
>> (1911), bk. II

Democracy means government by the uneducated, while aristocracy means government by the badly educated.
>> *New York Times* (February 1, 1931)

[We don't need] a Church that is right when the world is right, but a Church that is right when the world is wrong.

[Tradition] is the democracy of the dead. Tradition refuses to submit to the small and arrogant oligarchy of those who merely happen to be walking about. All democrats object to men being disqualified by the accident of birth; tradition objects to their being disqualified by the accident of death.

All I desire for my funeral is not to be buried alive.

Poets have been mysteriously silent on the subject of cheese.

Tolerance is the virtue of people who do not believe in anything.

Merely having an open mind is nothing. The object of opening the mind, as of opening the mouth, is to shut it again on something solid.

Without education we are in a horrible and deadly danger of taking educated people seriously.

SIR WINSTON SPENCER CHURCHILL
1874–1965

English, prime minister 1940–45 and 1951–55, and Nobel Prize for literature (1953) for *The Second World War*. With words, Churchill infused 44 million Britons with the will to fight alone against Europe—united by Hitler's armies and his alliances with Stalin and Mussolini. He called on England not only to defend her island, but all of Western civilization. Edward R. Murrow said, "He mobilized the English language and sent it into battle to steady his fellow countrymen and hearten those Europeans upon whom the long dark night of tyranny had descended." William F. Buckley Jr. said the genius of Churchill's oratory was "his union of the affinities of the heart and of the mind. The total fusion of animal and spiritual energy."

When France surrendered and his war cabinet wanted to negotiate with Hitler, he rallied it with a heroic oration: "If this long island story of ours is to end at last, let it end only when each one of us lies choking in his own blood upon the ground."

All his life he had to fight prolonged fits of deep depression, which he called his "black dog." Because he was dyslexic, he had difficulty in high school and twice failed the entrance exam for Sandhurst. On his third try, candidates were told the examination would come from one of twenty-five maps. He gambled by concentrating his study time on only one map—it was the map on the test. Yet, he was graduated near the top of his class.

Perhaps Churchill's finest hour came in 1904 when he broke with the Conservatives to join the Liberals because he believed protectionism meant "dear food for the million, cheap labour for the millionaire." Or perhaps his finest hour came during the 1930s when he urged stopping Germany's rearmament and building a first-class air force. The Labor Party and liberal intellectuals opposed both. Another finest hour was in 1946 when his "Iron Curtain" speech in Fulton, Missouri, sounded the alarm on the Soviet threat to Western civilization. Or it may have been in the postwar period, when he warned that socialism would impoverish Britain.

History will bear me out, especially since I intend to write it.

Nothing in life is so exhilarating as to be shot at without result.
The Malakand Field Force (1898)

It is better to…be an actor rather than a critic.

Ibid.

You do not rise by the regulations, but in spite of them. Therefore in all matters of active service the subaltern must never take "No" for an answer. He should get to the front at all costs.
In Ian Hamilton's *March*

A terminological inexactitude.
    [A lie.]
Speech, House of Commons
(February 22, 1906)

Of all tyrannies in history, the Bolshevik tyranny is the worst, the most destructive, the most degrading.
Speech, London (April 11, 1919)

I decline utterly to be impartial as between the fire brigade and the fire.
    [Per his bias in editing a newspaper.]
Speech, House of Commons, 1926

By being so long in the lowest form [at Harrow] I gained an immense advantage over the cleverer boys…. I got into my bones the essential structure of the ordinary British sentence….
Roving Commission: My Early Life
(1930), ch. 2

It is a good thing for an uneducated man to read books of quotations. *Bartlett's Familiar Quotations* is an admirable work, and I studied it intently. The quotations when engraved upon the memory give you good thoughts. They also make you anxious to read the authors and look for more.
Ibid., ch. 9

Decided only to be undecided, resolved to be irresolute, adamant for drift, solid for fluidity, all-powerful to be impotent.
While England Slept (1936)

The belief that security can be obtained by throwing a small state to the wolves is a fatal delusion.
"On Czechoslovakia" (September 21,
1938)

An appeaser is one who feeds a crocodile—hoping it will eat him last.
Speech (October 2, 1938), referring to the
Munich Pact with Hitler

I cannot forecast to you the action of Russia. It is a riddle wrapped in a mystery inside an enigma….But, perhaps there is a key. That key is Russian national interest.
Broadcast (October 1, 1939)

Dictators ride to and fro upon tigers which they dare not dismount. And the tigers are getting hungry.
"Armistice or Peace" (November 11, 1937),
Step by Step (1939)

I have nothing to offer but blood, toil, tears and sweat.

> First speech as prime minister
> (May 13, 1940)

What is our policy?...to wage war against a monstrous tyranny, never surpassed in the dark, lamentable catalogue of human crime....What is our aim? ...Victory, victory at all costs, victory in spite of all terror; victory, however, long and hard the road may be; for without victory, there is no survival.

> Ibid.

We shall not flag or fail. We shall go on to the end. We shall fight in France, we shall fight on the seas and oceans, we shall fight with growing confidence and growing strength in the air, we shall defend our island, whatever the cost may be, we shall fight on the beaches, we shall fight on the landing grounds, we shall fight in the fields and in the streets, we shall fight in the hills; we shall never surrender.

> Speech after Dunkirk (June 4, 1940)

We must be very careful not to assign to this deliverance the attributes of a victory. Wars are not won by evacuations.

> On the Dunkirk evacuation

What General Weygand called the Battle of France is over. I expect that the Battle of Britain is about to begin. Upon this battle depends the survival of Christian civilization. Upon it depends our own British life, and the long continuity of our institutions and our Empire. The whole fury and might of the enemy must very soon be turned on us. Hitler knows that he will have to break us in this island or lose the war. If we stand up

to him, all Europe may be free and the life of the world may move forward into broad, sunlit uplands. But if we fail, then the whole world, including the United States, including all that we have known and cared for will sink into the abyss of a new dark age made more sinister, and perhaps more protracted, by the lights of perverted science. Let us therefore brace ourselves to our duties, and so bear ourselves that, if the British Empire and its Commonwealth last for a thousand years, men will still say, "This was their finest hour."

> Speech in Commons (June 18, 1940)

The only guide to a man is his conscience; the only shield to his memory is the rectitude and sincerity of his actions. It is very imprudent to walk through life without this shield, because we are so often mocked by the failure of our hopes and the upsetting of our calculations. But with this shield...however the fates may play, we march always in the ranks of Honor.

> Tribute to Neville Chamberlain (1940)

Never in the field of human conflict was so much owed by so many to so few.

> [Re: RAF pilots in the Battle of Britain.]
> Speech (August 20, 1940)

[Broadcast to the people of France] The story is not yet finished.... Have hope and faith, for all will come out right. Good night, then. Sleep to gather strength for the morning. For the morning will come. Brightly will it shine on the brave and true, kindly upon all who suffer for the cause, glorious upon the tombs of heroes.

> Speech (October 21, 1940)

...all the great struggles of history have been won by superior will-power wresting victory in the teeth of odds or upon the narrowest of margins.

[During the Battle of the Atlantic.]
In Robert Conquest, *Reflections on a Ravaged Century* (2000)

We are waiting for the long-promised invasion. So are the fishes.

Ibid.

Give us the tools and we will finish the job.

Speech on radio (February 9, 1941)

The destiny of mankind is not decided by material computation. When great causes are on the move in the world...we learn that we are spirits, not animals....

BBC Broadcast to America
(June 16, 1941)

I have only one purpose, the destruction of Hitler, and my life is much simplified thereby. If Hitler invaded Hell, I would make at least a favorable reference to the Devil in the House of Commons.

[June 21, 1941]
Grand Alliance (1950), ch.1

Never give in, never give in, never, never, never, never—in nothing, great or small, large or petty—never give in except to convictions of honor and good sense.

Speech at Harrow School
(October 29, 1941)

We have not journeyed all this way across the centuries, across the oceans, across the mountains, across the prairies, because we are made of sugar candy.

Speech to the Canadian Senate and House of Commons, (December 30, 1941)

When I warned them [France] that Britain would fight on alone whatever they did, their generals told their Prime Minister and his divided Cabinet, "In three weeks England will have her neck wrung like a chicken." Some chicken! Some neck!

Ibid.

...in all of her wars...Britain...always wins one battle—the last.

Ibid.

Now this is not the end. It is not even the beginning of the end. But it is perhaps, the end of the beginning.

[After El Alamein victory, November 10, 1942.]

There is no finer investment for any community than putting milk into babies. Healthy citizens are the greatest asset any country can have.

Speech, BBC (March 21, 1943)

The empires of the future are the empires of the mind.

Speech at Harvard (September 6, 1943)

In wartime, truth is so precious that she should always be attended by a bodyguard of lies.

[Remark to Joseph Stalin at Teheran, 1943.]
Closing the Ring (1951), ch. 4

[The Germans] combine in the most deadly manner the qualities of the warrior and the slave.

House of Commons (September 21, 1943)

There was a man who sold a hyena skin while the beast still lived and who was killed in hunting it.

House of Commons (August 2, 1944)

"Not in vain" may be the pride of those who have survived and the epitaph of those who fell.

House of Commons (September 28, 1944)

I think "No comment" is a splendid expression. I am using it again and again. I got it from Sumner Welles.

Washington (February 12, 1946)

From Stettin in the Baltic to Trieste in the Adriatic an iron curtain has descended across the continent.

Address at Westminster College, Fulton, Missouri (March 5, 1946)

We must never cease to proclaim in fearless tones the great principles of freedom and the rights of man which are the joint inheritance of the English-speaking world and which through Magna Carta, the Bill of Rights, the Habeas Corpus, trial by jury, and the English common law find their most famous expression in the American Declaration of Independence.

Ibid.

In War: Resolution. In Defeat: Defiance. In Victory: Magnanimity. In Peace: Good Will.

The Gathering Storm (1948)

Democracy is the worst form of Government except all those other forms that have been tried from time to time.

House of Commons (November 11, 1947)

When you have to kill a man it costs nothing to be polite.

The Grand Alliance (1950)

If you have an important point to make, don't try to be subtle or clever. Use a pile driver. Hit the point once. Then come back and hit it again. Then hit it a third time—a tremendous whack.

A King's Story (1951)

There is no worse mistake in public leadership than to hold out false hopes soon to be swept away.

The Hinge of Fate (1950)

Personally, I'm always ready to learn, although I do not always like being taught.

House of Commons (November 4, 1952)

I am not an orator. An orator is spontaneous. The written word—ah, that's different.

In L. R. Frank, *Quotationary* (1999)

To jaw-jaw is always better than to war-war.

White House (June 26, 1954)

A fanatic is one who can't change his mind and won't change the subject.

New York Times (July 5, 1954)

It was the nation and the race dwelling all round the globe that had the lion's heart. I had the luck to be called upon to give the roar.

London at Westminster Hall
(November 30, 1954)

In this century of storm and tragedy I contemplate with high satisfaction the constant factor of the interwoven and upward progress of our peoples. Our comradeship and our brotherhood in war were unexampled. We stood together, and because of that fact the free world now stands.

[Receiving Honorary U.S. Citizenship.]
White House, April 9, 1963

I am fond of pigs. Dogs look up to us. Cats look down on us. Pigs treat us as equals.

> In M. Gilbert, *Never Despair* (1988)

A sheep in sheep's clothing.
[Of the Labor leader, Clement Attlee.]

> In Lord Home, *The Way the Wind Blows* (1976), ch. 6

All I wanted was compliance with my wishes after reasonable discussion.

> In A. J. P. Taylor, *From the Boer War to the Cold War* (1995)

Socialism is the weakest of all bulwarks against Communism. Socialists lead people up the garden path to the brink of a precipice and then turn around and say, as they tumble over, "We are very sorry; we never meant to go so far."

On entering the men's room in the House of Commons, Churchill went to its opposite end, a long way away from Clement Attlee. Attlee said, "Feeling standoffish today, are we Winston?" Churchill replied, "That's right. Every time you see something big, you want to nationalize it."

Nazism and Communism, two peas, Tweedledum and Tweedledee.

Some Socialists see private enterprise as a tiger—a predatory animal to be shot. Others see it as an old cow to be milked. But we Conservatives see it as the sturdy horse that pulls along our economy.

It is a socialist idea that making profits is a vice. I consider the real vice is making losses.

This report, by its very length, defends itself against the risk of being read.

Short words are best and the old words when short are best of all.

This is the sort of impertinence up with which I will not put.
[Blue-penciling a dangling participle.]

Never hold discussions with the monkey when the organ grinder is in the room.
[Advising not to speak with Italy's foreign minister when Mussolini was present.]

Our inheritance of well-founded, slowly conceived codes of honor, morals and manners, the passionate convictions which so many hundreds of millions share together of the principles of freedom and justice, are far more precious to us than anything which scientific discoveries could bestow.

One cannot leap a chasm in two jumps.

The price of greatness is responsibility.

I get my exercise being a pallbearer for those of my friends who believe in running....

Nations which went down fighting rose again, but those which surrendered tamely were finished.

Bessie Braddock, M.P.: "Winston, you are drunk."
Churchill: "Bessie, you're ugly. And tomorrow morning I shall be sober."

Lady Astor: "Winston, if you were my husband, I should flavor your coffee with poison."

Churchill: "Madam, if I were your husband, I should drink it."

[Eleanor Roosevelt complained of the British treatment of the Indians. He replied:] Are we talking about the brown-skinned Indians in India who have multiplied under benevolent British rule, or are we speaking about the redskinned Indians in America, who, I understand, are now almost extinct?

[Churchill told of the man who heard his mother-in-law had died. He cabled:] Embalm, cremate, bury at sea, take no chances.

[When asked to critique a speech, Churchill said it has too many "passives." Asked what that meant, he replied:] What if I had said—instead of 'We shall fight on the beaches'—'Hostilities will be engaged with our adversary on the coastal perimeter.'"

I never worry about action, but only inaction.

[When asked to what he attributed his success, he replied:] Conservation of energy. Never stand up when you can sit down, and never sit down when you can lie down.

We are all worms. But I do believe that I am a glowworm.

Success is going from failure to failure without loss of enthusiasm.

When I am abroad, I always make it a rule never to criticize or attack the government of my own country. I make up for lost time when I come home.

It's not enough that we do our best; sometimes we have to do what's required.

[When asked about a dinner party, a young Churchill replied], It would have been splendid—if the wine had been as cold as the soup, the beef as rare as the service, the brandy as old as the fish, and the maid as willing as the Duchess.

There is only one thing worse than fighting with allies and that is fighting without them.

You can always count on the Americans to do the right thing, after having exhausted all the other possibilities.

I remember being taken to the celebrated Barnum's Circus, which contained an exhibition of freaks and monstrosities, but the exhibit on the program which I most desired to see was the one described as the "Boneless Wonder." My parents judged that the spectacle would be too revolting to my youthful eye, and I have waited fifty years to see the Boneless Wonder sitting on the Treasury Bench.

We shape our buildings and afterwards our buildings shape us.

The future, though imminent, is obscure.

This pudding has no theme.

Success is never found; Failure is never fatal; Courage is the only thing.

Upon retiring as prime minister in 1955, Churchill told his cabinet not to forget two things: "Man is spirit," and "Never be separated from the Americans."

ROBERT FROST
1874–1963

American, poet, who won four Pulitzer Prizes. He dropped out of Harvard, but read Latin and Greek. He wore his learning lightly as he wrote about common things, such as chopping wood, mowing grass, and putting in seed. From age 28 to 35 he raised a family as a subsistence farmer and led a tragic life, as his four children and wife died early. Ezra Pound plucked him from obscurity by finding him a publisher. Frost despised Franklin Roosevelt calling his "brain trust" the "guild of social planners." He also hated Communism, but accepted a cultural mission to the USSR, where his poetry that focused on the common man was loved.

Ah, when to the heart of man
Was it ever less than a treason
To go with the drift of things,
To yield with a grace to reason.
> "Reluctance" (1913), st. 4. In Everdell,
> *Robert Frost: Collected Poems, Prose, and
> Plays* (1995)

Something there is that doesn't love a wall.
> *North of Boston*, "Mending Wall" (1914)

My apple trees will never get across
And eat the cones under his pines, I tell
him.
He only says, "Good fences make good
neighbors."
> Ibid.

Nothing to look backward to with pride,
And nothing to look forward to with
hope.
> "The Death of a Hired Man" (1914),
> North of Boston

"Home is the place where, when you
have to go there,
They have to take you in."
> Ibid.

I shall be telling this with a sigh
Somewhere ages and ages hence:
Two roads diverged in a wood, and I -
I took the one less traveled by,
And that has made all the difference.
> "The Road Not Taken" (1916), st. 4

I'd like to go by climbing a birch tree,
And climb black branches up a snow-
white trunk
Toward heaven, till the tree could bear
no more,
But dipped its top and set me down again.
That would be good both going and
coming back.
One could do worse than be a swinger
of birches.
> "Birches" (1916)

Whose woods these are I think I know.
His house is in the village though;
He will not see me stopping here
To watch his woods fill up with snow.
> "Stopping by Woods on a Snowy Evening"
> (1923), st. 1

The woods are lovely, dark and deep.
But I have promises to keep,
And miles to go before I sleep.
And miles to go before I sleep.
> Ibid., st. 4

But yield who will to their separation,
My object in living is to unite
My avocation and my vocation
As my two eyes make one in sight.
Only where love and need are one,
And the work is play for mortal stakes,
Is the deed ever really done

For Heaven and the future's sakes.
"Two Tramps in Mud Time" (1936), st. 9

Writing free verse is like playing tennis with the net down.
Speech (May 17, 1935)

I hold it to be the inalienable right of anybody to go to hell in his own way.
Speech, Berkeley (1935)

No tears in the writer, no tears in the reader.
Collected Poems (1939), Preface

[Poetry] begins in delight and ends in wisdom…in a clarification of life—not necessarily a great clarification… but in a momentary stay against confusion.
Ibid.

I [am] so altruistically moral
I never take my own side in a quarrel.
A Witness Tree (1942)

I had a lover's quarrel with the world.
"The Lesson for Today" (1942)

The father is always a Republican toward his son, and his mother's always a Democrat.
Writers at Work (1963)

[After rising from a dinner party, Frost went out on the verandah with other guests, one of whom inquired if it were not a lovely sunset. Frost responded:] I never discuss business after dinner.
Little Brown Book of Anecdotes (1985), Clifton Fadiman, ed.

What brought the kindred spider to
   that height,
Then steered the white moth thither in
   the night?

What but design of darkness to appall?—
   [Re: the Christian argument of design.]

A jury consists of twelve persons chosen to decide who has a better lawyer.

The best things and best people rise out of their separateness; I'm against a homogenized society because I want the cream to rise.

Take care to sell your horse before he dies
The art of life is passing losses on.

I am not a teacher but an awakener.

How are we to write
The Russian novel in America
As long as life goes so unterribly?

Life is tons of discipline.

HERBERT CLARK HOOVER
1874–1964

American, thirty-first president (1929–33). A liberal in Wilson's cabinet, his nomination to Harding's cabinet was opposed by conservatives. He called himself an "independent progressive" until he ran for the Republican nomination.

Hoover signed the protectionist Smoot-Hawley Bill, which increased tariffs on average 59 percent, and he raised the top income tax rate from 24 percent to 63 percent. That, plus the Federal Reserve's slashing the money supply by one-third, turned a recession into the Great Depression. The market crashed on "Black Tuesday," October 29, 1929, the day after Democrat and Republican majorities announced support for Smoot-Hawley. On June 15, 1930, with the Dow at 230, Hoover said he would sign Smoot-Hawley, notwithstanding a petition of 1,028 economists. The economy contracted 27 percent between 1930 and 1933 and the Dow plummeted to 41 on July 8, 1932, from a 1929 high of 381. U.S. exports fell from $5.24 billion in 1929 to $1.16 billion in 1933. [See Jude Wannisky's *The Way the World Works* (1978).]

Treasury Secretary Andrews Mellon advised, "Liquidate labor, liquidate stocks, liquidate the farmers, liquidate real estate, and so purge the rottenness from the economy." That would have shifted resources to sound businesses and would have revived prosperity quickly. But, Hoover and FDR kept the terminally ill on artificial life support. That prolonged the depression for a decade! U.S. unemployment in 1940 was 11 million, the same as in 1933 when the New Deal began.

THE GREAT DEPRESSION

A more complete explanation of the causes of the Great Depression and its prolongation for ten years must take into account international trading and monetary conditions in the 1920s and the incompetence of the Federal Reserve, Herbert Hoover, and Franklin Roosevelt. After World War I, European industry was prostrate and the world owed the U.S. $11.9 billion. To pay its debts, Europe had to export to America, but America's market was partially closed by the protective Fordney-McCumber Tariff Act of 1922. As an alternative to accepting European imports, the Federal Reserve created a river of U.S. currency that enabled the world to roll over its U.S. debts, plus borrow an additional $11.8 billion between 1919 and 1929. The Fed's

irresponsible credit expansion created artificially low interest rates, which facilitated easy foreign loans as a substitute for free trade at the same time U.S. industries were protected by tariffs. In the 1920s, U.S. prices should have fallen 4 percent per annum due to a 4 percent annual rise in U.S. productivity. But prices remained stable because of the excessive creation of money. After Smoot-Hawley shut out foreign exports to America, the world retaliated and international trade collapsed. The Fed then slashed the money supply by 35 percent and raised interest rates to save its gold reserves, even as numerous businesses and banks were collapsing.

The Great Depression began on Hoover's watch due to his shutting down international trade with the Smoot-Hawley tariffs, followed by the Fed slashing the money supply and by Hoover raising the top federal tax rate from 24 percent to 63 percent in 1932. Roosevelt prolonged the Great Depression by raising income taxes to 79 percent and raising the death tax from 10 percent to 70 percent. FDR's executive order to tax incomes over $25,000 at 100 percent was repealed by Congress.

Only idiots take investment risks where federal and state income taxes seize 85 percent of profits, and one must give back 70 percent of the remainder at death! Under such conditions, rational people keep their assets in cash or gold. That happened, and that killed investment, which killed the economy. Roosevelt also killed investment with his National Recovery Administration (NRA), which cartelized business, with the biggest firms drafting the "codes of competition," which raised prices and wages that forced small competitors out of business.

The Great Depression was not a "crisis of heartless capitalism," it was a crisis of gross government mismanagement! The Federal Reserve whipsawed the economy between its loose money policy and its gold-hoarding; Congress was protectionist; Hoover bumbled; and Roosevelt went on a class-war tear. W. H. Hutt explains depressions in his *The Keynesian Episode*:

> To the Keynesian mind, depressions occur as a result of the unwillingness of people to buy goods, or the inability to sell goods, both of which may be brought under the idea of absence of markets. The truth is the contrary. Depressions occur as a result of an increasing unwillingness to sell things at prices consistent with the maintenance of noninflated money income and a consequent increasing inability to buy at the prices fixed. For the failure to buy all the valuable productive services potentially available cannot be due to the failure to demand them but to the failure to release them. The fact that they have value is proof that they are demanded; and they have value if they would be purchased at any price above zero. Failure to sell (that is, failure to price at market-clearing values) is frustration of the buyer, not the seller.
> *The Keynesian Episode* (1979)

For a lay analysis of the Great Depression, see Paul Johnson, *A History of the American People* (1998). For analysis by economists, see: Jude Wanniski, *The Way the World Works* (1978); Milton Friedman and Anna J. Swartz, *Monetary History of the United States, 1867–1960* (1963); Murray N. Rothbard, *America's Great Depression* (5th ed.); and W. H. Hutt, *The Keynesian Episode* (1979), Gene Smiley, *Rethinking the*

Great Depression: A New View of Its Causes and Consequences (2002), and Jim Powell's *FDR's Folly: How Franklin D. Roosevelt and His New Deal Prolonged the Great Depression* (2003). For an analysis friendly to Hoover and Roosevelt, see John Gordon's *An Empire of Wealth* (2004).

In the 1929 market crash, the S&P 500 fell 86 percent. That was partly offset by a 33 percent deflation, so in real terms the crash was 79 percent, which is close to the NASDAQ 76 percent crash in 2000-2002.

Hoover received a telegram before the 1932 election saying, "Please vote for Roosevelt so it will be unanimous."

SOMERSET MAUGHAM
1874–1965

Irish, cynical novelist, and physician whose autobiographical novel *Of Human Bondage* (1915) traced the agony of a maturing medical student.

> Like all weak men he laid an exaggerated stress on not changing one's mind.
> *Of Human Bondage* (1915), ch. 1

> Impropriety is the soul of wit.
> *The Moon and Sixpence* (1919), ch. 4

> It is not true that suffering ennobles the character; happiness does that sometimes, but suffering, for the most part, makes men petty and vindictive.
> Ibid., ch. 17

> From the earliest time the old have rubbed it into the young that they are wiser, and before the young had discovered what nonsense this was they were

old too, and it profited them to carry on the imposture.

Cakes and Ale (1930), ch. 11

The artist produces for the liberation of his soul. It is his nature to create as it is the nature of water to run down hill.

The Summing Up (1938)

The great tragedy of life is not that men perish, but that they cease to love.

In L. R. Frank, *Quotationary* (1999)

If a nation values anything more than freedom, it will lose its freedom. And the irony of it is that if it is comfort or money that it values more, it will lose that, too.

Strictly Personal (1941), ch. 31

Tolerance is only another name for indifference.

A Writer's Notebook (1949)

When you have loved as she has loved, you grow old beautifully.

The Circle

There are three rules for writing a novel. Unfortunately, no one knows what they are.

ROBERT W. SERVICE
1874–1958

Canadian, poet—the "Canadian Kipling."

A promise made is a debt unpaid,

"The Cremation of Sam McGee," st. 8

This is the law of the Yukon, and ever
    she makes it plain:
Send not your foolish and feeble; send
    me your strong and your sane....

Send me the best of your breeding, lend
    me your chosen ones;
Them will I take to my bosom, them
    will I call my sons....

"The Law of the Yukon," st. 1 (partial)

GERTRUDE STEIN
1874–1946

American, poet and novelist, who lived in Paris and ran the leading interwar salon. Clifton Fadiman called her "the mama of dada."

You are all a lost generation.

Letter to Ernest Hemingway (1926)

In America there is more space where nobody is than where anybody is—that is what makes America what it is.

The Geographical History of America (1936)

There is no there there.
    [Speaking of Oakland.]

Everybody's Autobiography (1937), ch. 4

CARL GUSTAV JUNG
1875–1961

German, analytic psychologist. Jung opposed Freud's psychoanalysis that held the libido to be only sexual energy. Jung held the libido to be generalized psychic energy. He believed the mind was divided into three parts: a conscious mind, a "personal unconscious," and a "collective unconscious," which is a human instinctive pattern of behavior. Religion and mythology are emanations from the collective unconscious—intuitive insights. The best introduction to Jung is his "Two Essays on Analytical Psychology."

The great decisions of human life have as a rule far more to do with the instincts and other mysterious unconscious factors than with conscious will and reasonableness.

Modern Man in Search of a Soul (1933)

The artist's life cannot be otherwise than full of conflicts, for two forces are at war within him—on the one hand the common human longing for happiness, satisfaction, and security in life, and on the other a ruthless passion for creation which may go so far as to override every personal desire.

Ibid., ch. 1

The creative force can drain the human impulses to such a degree that the personal ego must develop all sorts of bad qualities—ruthlessness, selfishness, and vanity (so-called "auto-eroticism") and even every kind of vice, in order to maintain the spark of life and to keep itself from being wholly bereft.

Ibid.

The conscious mind allows itself to be trained like a parrot, but the unconscious does not—which is why St. Augustine thanked God for not making him responsible for his dreams.

Psychology and Alchemy (1953)

Human beings should not overlook the danger of the evil lurking within them. It is unfortunately only too real, which is why psychology must insist on the reality of evil and must reject any definition that regards it as insignificant or actually nonexistent.

Aion

Every form of addiction is bad, no matter whether the narcotic be alcohol or morphine or idealism.

Memories, Dreams, Reflections, ch. 12

[In] the Christian reformation of the Jewish concept of the Deity, the morally ambiguous Yahweh became an exclusively good God, while everything evil was united in the devil…. The moral splitting of divinity into two halves.

"Psychological Aspects of the Mother Archetype," *The Archetypes and the Collective Unconscious* (1959), tr. R. F. C. Hull

A more or less superficial layer of the unconscious is undoubtedly personal. I call it the *personal unconscious*. But this personal unconscious rests upon a deeper layer, which does not derive from personal experience and is not a personal acquisition but is inborn. The deeper layer I call the *collective unconscious*. I have chosen the term *"collective"* because this part of the unconscious is not individual but universal; in contrast to the personal psyche, it has contents and modes of behavior that are more or less the same everywhere and in all individuals.

Ibid.

I could not say I believe, I know! I have had the experience of being gripped by something stronger than myself, something that people call God.

"The Old Wise Man," *Time* (February 14, 1955)

I regret many follies which spring from my obstinacy; but without that trait I would not have reached my goal.

In L. R. Frank *Quotationary* (1999)

Without freedom, there can be no morality.

In L. R. Frank, *Wisdom* (2003)

Vocatus atque non vocatus, Deus aderit—
Invoked or not invoked, God is present.
[Sign over entrance to Jung's home.]

Jung divided the human psyche into sixteen "personality types" based on four functions of the mind, each of which has an axis connecting two opposite poles for each function, and in each person, one pole dominates the other pole for that function. In each person, one function dominates the other three. One of the three lesser functions is second only to the dominating one. This was elaborated in the Myers-Briggs Type Indicator, the best test to help students choose a college major and/or career. Below, the four functions and eight poles:

1. Where you focus your attention:
Extroversion: Focus on the outer world of people and things; gain energy being with people.
Introversion: Focus on inner world of ideas; gain energy from solitary reflection.

2. How you take in information:
Sensing: Observe with senses; focus on the actual, the detailed, and practical; present oriented.
Intuition: Value the imaginative, the big picture; look for possibilities; future oriented.

3. How you make decisions:
Thinking: Value objective truth; logical, tough-minded, reasonable, fair.
Feeling: Place oneself in the situation of those involved; empathetic, compassionate.

4. How you organize your life:
Judging: A planned, orderly, systematic, scheduled life; time sensitive; want closure on issues.
Perceiving: Live in a flexible, spontaneous way; open to last-minute options; adaptable.

Everyone falls into one of the sixteen personality types. While the closest friendships of the same sex are identical types, married couples of exact opposite types are the least likely to divorce.

THOMAS MANN
1875–1955

German, novelist, Nobel laureate for literature in 1929, whose works dwell on decay and death. In *Buddenbrooks* (1901), a family of industrialists succumbs to gradual ruin over three generations. In *Death In Venice* (1912), a middle-aged artist, smitten with a young boy, dyes his hair and dies of plague sitting in a beach chair ogling the youth. In *The Magic Mountain* (1924), Castorp, a German engineer, visits a friend at a Swiss sanatorium, where he discovers he too has tuberculosis. After seven years of witnessing death and sickness, a recuperated Castorp is last seen in 1914 in a trench near a tremendous explosion of shrapnel.

To meet adverse conditions gracefully is more than a simple endurance; it is an act of aggression, a positive triumph.
Death in Venice (1912)

A man lives not only his personal life, as an individual, but also, consciously or unconsciously, the life of his epoch and his contemporaries.

The Magic Mountain (1924), ch. 2, tr. H. T.
Lowe-Porter (1927)

Order and simplification are the first steps toward the mastery of a subject.

Ibid., ch. 5

A man's dying is more the survivors' affair than his own.

Ibid.

ALBERT SCHWEITZER
1875–1965

German, theologian, surgeon, and missionary in French Equatorial Africa, 1952 Nobel Peace Prize. His guiding principle was: "Reverence for life."

Humanitarianism consists in never sacrificing a human being to a purpose.

The Philosophy of Civilization (1923)

The tragedy of man is what dies inside himself while he still lives.

Ibid.

ALFRED P. SLOAN, JR.
1875–1966

American, CEO of GM 1923–46. He created modern corporate management with an independent board of directors and with "divisional decentralization," that is, five independent divisions, each having a different price range of cars.

Take my assets—but leave me my organization and in five years I'll have it all back.

[Proven by Germany's and Japan's rapid recoveries after World War II.]

WILSON MIZNER
1876–1933

American, humorist.

A trip through a sewer in a glass-bottomed boat.

[Of visiting Hollywood]

In Alva Johnson, *The Legendary Mizners* (1953)

Be nice to people on your way up because you'll meet 'em on your way down.

Ibid.

If you steal from one author, it's plagiarism; if you steal from many, it's research.

Ibid.

I hate careless flattery, the kind that exhausts you in your effort to believe it.

To my embarrassment, I was born in bed with a lady.

JACK LONDON
1876–1916

American, seal hunter, Klondike gold miner, and novelist of intense adventure stories that made him at age twenty-nine America's most popular writer. In *The Call of the Wild* (1903), Buck, a St. Bernard mix, is stolen from a loving home, made into a sled dog, and is toughened by fights to the death. In *White Fang* (1907), a vicious fight-ing dog is tamed by human love. In *The Sea Wolf* (1904), Van Weyden is rescued from a shipwreck by the captain of the *Ghost*, Wolf Larsen, a skipper as evil as Iago.

In an anti-hubris short story, "To Build a Fire," "the Man" decides against the advice of an old-timer to walk alone several miles to another camp in temperature 75 degrees below zero. One foot breaks through ice into water so he must quickly build a fire to save his leg. Taking off his gloves he is able to build a fire, but the snow in the branches of the tree above melts and extin-guishes the fire. With frozen hands he fails to build another fire and dies.

> I would rather be ashes than dust! I would rather that my spark should burn out in a brilliant blaze than it should be stilled by dry-rot. I would rather be a superb meteor, every atom of me in magnificent glow, than a sleepy and per-manent planet. The proper function of man is to live, not to exist. I shall not waste my days in trying to prolong them. I shall use my time.
> In Joan London, *Jack London and His Times*

> If cash comes with fame, come fame; if cash comes without fame, come cash.
> In L. R. Frank, *Quotationary*

CHARLES F. KETTERING
1876–1958

American, automotive engineer, inventor, vice president of General Motors.

> If you want to kill any idea in the world today, get a committee working on it.

> It's easy to build a philosophy. It doesn't have to run.

> An inventor is an engineer who doesn't take his education too seriously.

> A problem well stated is a problem half solved.

JAMES TRUSTLOW ADAMS
1878–1949

American, a leading historian of America.

> The whole of the American Dream has been based on the chance to get ahead, for one's self or one's children. Would this country have ever reached the point it has if the individual had always been refused the rewards of his labors and dangers?

> Lincoln was not great because he was born in a log cabin, but because he got out of it.

DONALD R. P. MARQUIS
1878–1937

American, humorist and columnist, who wrote for the *Sun Dial*, the *New York Sun* (1913–22), and then the *New York Tribune*.
> Publishing a volume of verse is like dropping a rose-petal down the Grand Canyon and waiting for the echo.
> The *Sun Dial*

> An Idea isn't responsible for the people who believe in it.
> Ibid.

> If you want to get rich from writing,

write the sort of thing that's read by persons who move their lips when they're reading to themselves.

The successful people are the ones who can think up stuff for the rest of the world to keep busy at.

CARL SANDBURG
1878–1967

American, poet and biographer (*Life of Abraham Lincoln*, 1926–39). He celebrated the ordinary man and industrialization.

Hog Butcher for the World,
Tool Maker, Stacker of Wheat,
Player with Railroads and the Nation's
Freight Handler;
Stormy, husky, brawling,
City of the Big Shoulders
    "Chicago," *Chicago Poems* (1916)

The fog comes
on little cat feet.
It sits looking
over harbor and city
on silent haunches
and then moves on.
        Ibid., "Fog"

Pile the bodies high at Austerlitz and
    Waterloo
Shovel them under and let me work-
I am the grass; I cover all.
        Ibid., "Grass"

Sometime they'll give a war and nobody will come.
        "The People Yes" (1936)

This old anvil laughs at many broken hammers.

There are men who can't be bought.
        "The People Will Live On" (1936)

Why did the children put beans in their ears when the one thing we told the children they must not do was put beans in their ears?

SIR THOMAS BEECHAM
1879–1961

English, conductor, the Royal Philharmonic.

The function of music is to release us from the tyranny of conscious thought.
    In Harold Atkins and Archie Newman,
        Beecham Stories (1978)

Madam, you have between your legs an instrument capable of giving pleasure to thousands—and all you can do is scratch it.
    [To a cellist.]
    In Ian Crofton, *A Dictionary of Musical
        Quotations* (1985)

JAMES BYRNES
1879–1972

American, senator, governor, justice, and director of war mobilization. A member of Roosevelt's "brain trust," he opposed most New Deal programs. He resigned to protest Roosevelt's capitulation to the Soviets at Yalta. Truman recruited Byrnes to be secretary of state. Byrnes advised dropping the atomic bomb on Japan to dissuade the Soviets from overrunning Europe.

Power intoxicates men. When a man is intoxicated by alcohol he can recover, but when intoxicated by power he seldom recovers.

ALBERT EINSTEIN
1879–1955

American (German-born), physicist. Exploding the mechanistic world of Newton-ian physics, his special theory of relativity showed that energy and matter are different forms of the same thing, and that the conversion of matter into energy releases phenomenal forces. His general theory of relativity redefined gravity as curvature in space-time; space and time disappear if matter disappears. Space and time are as interactive as matter and energy. Time has a shape, is part of space, and is variable.

His general theory deduced that light would be bent by gravity from large objects—the observation of this phenomenon during a solar eclipse in West Africa on May 29, 1919, by Arthur Eddington proved Einstein's theory. Einstein also deduced that the universe must expand or contract. But he believed it to be static, so he added a constant, which he later called "the biggest blunder of my career."

Einstein believed in absolute truth and right and wrong. He argued "scientific relativity" had nothing to do with "moral relativity," which he abhorred.

Einstein alienated his professors by disputing their physics, so they blocked his graduation and his applications to teach science at both a university and high school. He became an examiner in the Swiss patent office, which gave him the time to invent the hearing aid and turn physics upside down. He was an anti-totalitarian, but he never understood that Communism was totalitarian. He did not believe in a personal God intervening in the world, but he believed in a designing creator.

$E = mc^2$.
> [Discovery in 1905 where E is the energy, m the mass, and c the velocity of light.]

The only really valuable thing is intuition.
> *Essays on Science* (1934)

The most beautiful and most profound emotion we can experience is the mysterious. It is the dower of all true science.
> *What I Believe* (1930)

I am not only a pacifist but a militant pacifist. I am willing to fight for peace.
> [Said in January 1931, yet on August 2, 1939, his letter to President Roosevelt advised that the U.S. build an atomic bomb.]

Science without religion is lame; religion without science is blind.
> *Science, Philosophy and Religion: A Symposium* (1941), ch. 13

The unleashed power of the atom has changed everything save our thinking and we thus drift toward unparalleled catastrophe.
> *Telegram to prominent Americans* (May 24, 1946)

Most of the fundamental ideas of science are essentially simple, and may, as a rule, be expressed in a language comprehensible to anyone.
> *The Evolution of Physics* (1938)

I lived in solitude in the country and noticed how the monotony of a quiet life stimulates the creative mind.
> *Out of My Later Years* (1950)

Everything that is really great and inspiring is created by the individual who can labor in freedom.

Ibid.

Perfection of means and confusion of goals seem—in my opinion—to characterize our age.

Ibid.

Everything should be made as simple as possible, but not more so.

Reader's Digest (October 1977)

There is no empirical method without speculative concepts and systems; and there is no speculative thinking whose concepts do not reveal, on closer investigation, the empirical material from which they stem. To put into contrast the empirical and the deductive is misleading.

Foreword to *Galileo's Dialogue*

How can it be that mathematics, being after all a product of human thought independent of experience, is so admirably adapted to the objects of reality?
[Mathematics does not involve observation or experimentation, but Carl Gauss called mathematics the "queen of the sciences" because it is the logic that governs the universe, although it is totally independent from matter.]

How do I work? I grope.

[N]ot everything that can be counted counts, and not everything that counts can be counted.

I simply ignored a maxim.

The greatest mathematical discovery of all time.
[Compounding interest.]

...the distinction between past, present and future is only an illusion, even if a stubborn one.

The deep emotional conviction of the presence of a superior reasoning power, which is revealed in the incomprehensible universe, forms my idea of God.

Science can only ascertain what is, but not what *should be,* and outside of its domain value judgments of all kinds remain necessary.

The hardest thing in the world to understand is the income tax.

Equations are more important for me than politics because politics are for the present, equations for eternity.
[Ulugh-Beg, Tamerlane's grandson, wrote on his astronomical observatory: "The religions disperse, kingdoms fall apart, but works of science remain for all ages."]

[When a student in advanced physics said the questions on the exam were the same as on the prior semester's exam, Einstein replied:]
That's all right because the answers are different."

There exists a passion for comprehension, just as there exists a passion for music. That passion is rather common in children, but gets lost in most people later on.

Joe Hill
1879–1915

(Joel Hagglund), American, organizer for the Industrial Workers of the World (IWW), or "Wobblies," a radical socialist labor union.

> Long-haired preachers come out ev'ry
>   night,
> Try to tell you what's wrong and what's
>   right,
> But when asked how 'bout something
>   to eat
> They will answer with voices so sweet
>   "The Preacher and the Slave" (1911), st. 1

> You will eat bye and bye,
> In that glorious land above the sky;
> Work and pray, live on hay,
> You'll get pie in the sky when you die.
>   Ibid., chorus

> Don't waste any time mourning—
> organize.
>   [Written before his execution for
>   killing two policemen while robbing
>   a store.]

Will Rogers
1879–1935

American, humorist, known as the "Cowboy Philosopher."

> Don't gamble. Take all your savings and buy some good stock. Hold it till it goes up—then sell it. If it doesn't go up, don't buy it.
>   *Autobiography of Will Rogers* (1949), ed.
>   Donald Day

Everybody is ignorant, only on different subjects.
   "Defending My Soup Plate Position," *The Illiterate Digest* (1924)

You can't say civilization don't advance, however, for in every war they kill you in a new way.
   New York Times (April 29, 1930)

More men have been elected between sundown and sunup than ever were elected between sunup and sundown.
   In L. R. Frank, *Wit and Humor Quotationary*

There is no credit to being a comedian, when you have the whole government working for you. All you have to do is report the facts.
                              Ibid.

All I know is what I read in the papers.

I am not a member of any organized party—I am a Democrat.

Thank heavens we don't get all the government we pay for.

My forefathers didn't come over on the *Mayflower*, but they met the boat.
   [Rogers was part Cherokee.]

America is the first country where people go to the poor house in their car.

In the early days of the Indian Territory, there were no such things as birth certificates. Your being there was certificate enough.

We can't all be heroes because somebody has to sit on the curb and clap as they go by.

I joked about every prominent man in my lifetime, but I never met one I didn't like.

[Compare with the statement of defensive tackle Lyle Alzado: "I never met a man I didn't want to fight."]

MARGARET H. SANGER
1883–1966

American, socialist, who founded Planned Parenthood in 1942 to form a better race. She subscribed to eugenics, the notion that humanity could be "improved" by selective breeding. Her slogan was "More children from the fit, less from the unfit." Sanger led the eugenics movement in America and succeeded in getting twenty-seven states to pass laws leading to the sterilization of sixty thousand persons. That was part of the eugenics effort, to eradicate continuously the "lower tenth" of the population until a pure race was achieved. Sanger, the leader of Planned Parenthood, described blacks as "human weeds" who were a "menace to civilization." [See Dinesh D'Souza, *The End of Racism* (1995).]

The pseudoscience of eugenics (widely endorsed by liberal intellectuals, major universities, and the Carnegie Foundation) was the foundation for Nazi racism, which led to the extermination of millions of Jews, Gypsies, homosexuals, Poles, Russians, and feeble-minded Germans.

Birth control appeals to the advanced radical because it is calculated to undermine the authority of the Christian churches. I look forward to seeing humanity free someday of the tyranny of Christianity no less than capitalism.

In Walter Adolphe Roberts, "Birth Control and the Revolution," *Birth Control Review* (June 1917)

[Abortion is useful for] weeding out the unfit; for preventing the birth of defectives, or of those who will become defectives.

Woman and the New Race (1920)

No woman can call herself free who does not own and control her own body. No woman can call herself free until she can choose consciously whether she will or will not be a mother.

Ibid., ch. 8

The most merciful thing a large family can do to one of its infant members is to kill it.

In George Grant, *Grand Illusions* (1988)

JOSEPH STALIN
1879–1953

Georgian, socialist, who reintroduced slavery into Europe. Economic growth under Stalin fell sharply from the 6 percent annual rate under the tsars in 1890–1914, despite the Soviets working to death tens of millions in slave labor camps and reducing Russians to subsistence-level incomes. Stalin did not industrialize Russia. Russia was the fourth-most-industrialized nation when Lenin seized power, and the Soviet economy at its best in the 1930s grew only at 3.5 percent per annum, even though it was exploiting slave labor, high-grading its natural resources, and despoiling its environment. In 1991, after seventy-two years of socialism, the USSR's per capita income was 1/20th the United States' versus 1/5th in 1917. Stalin's economy epitomized "value subtraction"; it turned raw materials into finished goods worth less than the raw materials. Stalin equated below-plan numbers with sabotage. Unsuccessful innovators were shot. Thus, as a Soviet premier said, Soviet managers shied away from innovation "as the devil shies away from incense." In 1980, the 2 percent of land privately owned produced 30 percent of the USSR's agricultural output.

R. J. Rummel in *Lethal Politics* estimates that the Soviet Communists between 1917 and 1987 killed between 28,326,000 and 126,891,000, so his prudent estimate was 61,911,000. There are other estimates. Roman Krutsyk, chairman of the Kiev Memorial, calculated the Soviets murdered 130 million people in the Gulag alone. Stalin died just before he could send 6 million Jews into the Gulag, some 800 camps where 80 percent of inmates perished.

Note: Mao killed 115 million (80 million in a political famine). Hitler killed 21 million Poles, Gypsies, Ukrainians, Balts, Russians, homosexuals, retarded, and Jews (six million of the 21 million).

New York Times' correspondent Walter Duranty told his friends after his 1934 visit to the USSR that millions had starved. But he lied in the *New York Times* that the stories of famine were "malignant propaganda." He was awarded the Pulitzer Prize for his "dispassionate" reporting on the USSR.

A single death is a tragedy, a million deaths is a statistic.
Anne Fremantle, "Unwritten Pages as the End of a Diary," *New York Times Book Review* (September 28, 1958)

The dictatorship of the proletariat is the domination of the proletariat over the bourgeoisie, unrestrained by the law and based on violence....
Speech (April 24, 1924), International Publisher, New York (1934)

[When Lady Astor in 1931 asked Stalin "How long are you going to go on killing people?" Stalin replied:]
As long as it's necessary.

Education is a weapon, whose effect depends on who holds it in his hands and at whom it is aimed.
Interview, H. G. Wells (July 23, 1934)

Lenin realized that a Communist revolution could not succeed in Western Europe, so he planned to communize it by provoking war between Germany and the West and attacking them both after they were exhausted. Following Lenin's plan, Stalin ordered the German Communist Party to concentrate its attacks on the Social Democrats, the principal opposition to the Nazis. The plan was to assist the Nazis to power because only the Nazis would start a European war. Trotsky said, "Without Stalin there would have been no Hitler...." The Politburo meeting August 19, 1939, stated:

...in time of peace the Communist movement in Europe has no chance of being strong enough to seize power. The dictatorship of the Communist party may be envisaged only as a result of a great war.

Four months after invading the USSR on June 22, 1941, Germany's 4,170 tanks and 3,613 aircraft had destroyed 22,000 Soviet tanks and 25,000 aircraft. That Soviet collapse was due to the concentration of its forces in tightly packed columns ready to attack Germany after Germany got bogged down in invading Britain. Stalin's light blitzkrieg tanks had been designed for Germany's autobahn. Stalin had more planes, tanks, and artillery than Germany, France, Britain, Japan, and the U.S. combined. Had the Soviets struck Germany first, they might have won. Hitler had to abandon "Operation Sea Lion" against Britain because he realized the threat of an imminent Soviet attack. [See James B. Edwards, *Hitler: Stalin's Stooge* (2004).]

To ensure that the West would declare war only on Germany and not on the USSR, Stalin broke his treaty with Hitler to attack Poland *simultaneously* in September 1939. Stalin pleaded inability to attack.

> The Pope! How many divisions has he got?
> [Said at the Yalta Conference when the rights of Catholics in Poland came up.]
> W. S. Churchill, *The Gathering Storm* (1948)

When Stalin's armies entered Germany in World War II, his general orders held that no Russian would be responsible for any offense against any German, soldier or civilian, adult or child, man or woman. Millions of unarmed Germans were murdered, often after being raped and tortured.

> [Ilya Ehrenburg published a novel in the Soviet Union in 1934 that justified the slaying of millions of rich peasants:]
> Not one of them was guilty of anything; but they belonged to a class that was guilty of everything.
> In Robert Conquest, *Reflections of a Ravaged Century (2000)*

Stalin's German-born spy in Japan, Richard Sorge, informed Stalin of the date the Japanese would attack Pearl Harbor (December 7, 1941). Stalin did not pass that to Roosevelt. Sorge learned that Japan would attack South Asia and not the USSR on discovering a button manufacturing plant that had switched from making winter to tropical buttons.

George Orwell said no normal person believed Stalin, only Western intellectuals.

> It's not the people who vote that count; it's the people who count the votes.

> When we hang the capitalists, they will sell us the rope we use.

> Quantity has a quality all of its own.

Stalin's five basic rules of propaganda:

1. Simplify: reduce all to a confrontation between good and evil.
2. Smear the opposition.
3. Manipulate the central values of the target audience to one's own purpose.
4. Use star performers to present one's view as the right thinking.
5. Repeat—endlessly repeat—the same message in different variations.
> In Norman Davies, *Europe: A History* (1996)

A Jewish engineer, Naftaly Frenkel, designed and organized the Soviet's 800 camp Gulag. He convinced Stalin that to maximize profits, inmates should be worked to death by investing nothing in health care and little in food, clothing and shelter. The entrance sign to the camps read: "With an Iron Fist, We will

Lead Humanity to Happiness." Hitler copied Frenkel's death camp design, but changed the sign to *Arbeit macht frei* (Work Liberates).

11
PERPETUAL CONFLICT

In the twentieth century, we repelled the Nazi and Communist counterrevolutions against liberty. That was one more chapter in the perpetual conflict between freedom and social control—a conflict that raged in 600 B.C. when the Athenian mob cried for Solon to redistribute the wealth. This conflict will still be alive in A.D. 6000. Political opportunists will always seek power by stealing from the wealth creators to pander to the majority.

In their vain attempts to found kingdoms of love and plenty, collectivists have spilled oceans of blood and destroyed mountains of treasure. As Von Mises observed in *Human Action*, "Every socialist is a disguised dictator," because "no socialist ever gave a thought to the possibility that the state, which he wants to vest with unlimited power, could act in a way of which he himself disapproves...."

Alan Kors, professor of history at the University of Pennsylvania, argues that Marxism, fascism, Nazism, and other socialisms always attract those who are morally the worst. "No cause, ever, in the history of all mankind," writes Mr. Kors, "has produced more cold-blooded tyrants, more slaughtered innocents, and more orphans than socialism with power."

The Communist-Nazi military alliance of 1939 was rooted in shared values. Both ideologies were blends of social-ism and nationalism. Communists were called "Red Nazis" and Nazis were called "Brown Communists." Both promised a "new order" once the bourgeoisie or Jews were eliminated. The Nazis copied from the Communists the one-party system, and the execution or imprisonment of political adversaries (concentration camps). Power was concentrated in: Stalin, the Vozhd; Hitler, the Fuehrer; Mussolini, the Duce; Mao, the Great Helmsman. Both weakened the family with state nurseries, youth movements, badges, parades, uniforms, flags, and rituals. In both, the state maintained a monopoly over information. Both registered and then confiscated firearms. At their cores stood nihilism: belief in scientific social engineering. The Nazi believed that eugenics could engineer a purified "master race." The Soviets saw the "laws" of historical development necessitating the victory of the proletariat, who would engineer a collectivist "new Soviet man" by education. [See Norman Davies, *Europe: A History* (1996) and Richard Overy, *The Dictators* (2004).]

In May 1940, when the Nazis invaded France, French Communists sabotaged the French army and then collaborated with the Nazis in fighting the republican French resistance and in rounding up France's Jews. Only after Hitler invaded the USSR in June 1941 did the French Communists resist the Nazis.

Great heroes defended the West. Winston Churchill braced Britain to stand alone after the Communist-Nazi alliance overran Europe. *Harry Truman* stopped the Soviets from overrunning Europe and Asia. Richard Nixon split the Sino-Soviet alliance. Ludwig von Mises and Friedrich von Hayek proved that socialism has an inherent tendency to become totalitarian. William F. Buckley Jr. popularized conservative ideas in his National Review. Peter Drucker (management) and Milton Friedman (economics) helped free societies outproduce socialist ones. William Shockley's transistor empowered free enterprise. Ronald Reagan and Lady Thatcher collapsed the will of the "evil empire." Another hero was Everyman, seen in Private Martin Treptow's letter home:

> America must win this war. Therefore, I will work, I will save, I will sacrifice, I will endure, I will fight cheerfully and do my utmost, as if the issue of the whole struggle depended on me alone.

America has long been blessed with heroes. Out of ammunition at Bunker Hill, Gen. Joseph Warren's unit fought only with bayonets to the last man to cover the retreat. General Warren had said:

> Our country is in danger now, but not to be despaired of. On you depend the fortunes of America. You are to decide the important questions upon which rest the happiness and the liberty of millions not yet born. Act worthy of yourselves.

Socialism is not dead, but it has metamorphosed into "cultural marxism" because it can no longer be justified by economic efficiency. Cultural Marxism remains constant to socialism's first principle, to wit, subordinate life to politics. Every future generation will need its Warrens and Treptows.

LEON TROTSKY
1879–1940

Russian, socialist, and war commissar. He was Lenin's heir apparent until outmaneuvered by Stalin, who purged the four Jews (Trotsky, Zinovyev, Kamenev, and Bukharin) from the seven-man Politburo, the USSR's ruling body. Trotsky favored "continuing international revolutions" while Stalin took the line of "socialism in one country." On Stalin's order, the exiled Trotsky was murdered in Mexico in 1940. Trotsky forecast that Soviet leaders would one day sell to themselves the property they had confiscated from the bourgeoisie.

> In a country where the sole employer is the state, opposition means death by slow starvation…. The old principle, "Who does not work shall not eat," has been replaced by a new one: "Who does not obey shall not eat."
>
> *The Revolution Betrayed* (1937)

> The dictatorship of the Communist Party is maintained by recourse to every form of violence.
>
> *Terrorism and Communism* (1924)

> Not believing in force is the same as not believing in gravity.
>
> *What Next?*

> Stalinism and fascism, in spite of a deep difference in social foundations, are symmetrical phenomena. In many of their features they show a deadly similarity.

[In a collectivist state] Man will become immeasurably stronger, wiser and subtler.... The average human type will rise to the heights of an Aristotle, a Goethe, or a Marx.

> Closing words, *Literature and Revolution* (1960), tr. Rose Strunsky

Old age is the most unexpected of all the things that can happen to a man.

> *Diary In Exile* (1958)

You may not be interested in war, but war is interested in you.

> In George F. Will, *With a Happy Eye* (2002)

W. C. FIELDS
1880–1946

American, actor and humorist. A friend said, "He had the greatest reverence for his colleagues, with the usual reservations and suspicions."

> [When accosted by a lady who recommended that he drink water, not whiskey, he replied],
> Madame, I never drink water. Fish f--- in water.

Women are like elephants to me. I like to look at them, but I wouldn't want to own one.

A woman drove me to drink and I never even had the courtesy to thank her.

Somebody put pineapple juice in my pineapple juice!
> [He claimed his thermos had pineapple juice, but it was martinis so he got mad when someone put pineapple juice in it.]

I always keep a supply of stimulant handy in case I see a snake—which I also keep handy.

B. C. FORBES
1880–1954

American, founder of *Forbes.*

If a pig could pray, it would pray for swill. What do you pray for?

I played golf with John D. Rockefeller [and] Charles M. Schwab.... Both played exactly the same. Neither overreached or tried to do more than he was capable of....

Many of the most successful men I have known have never grown up. They have retained bubbling-over boyishness. They have relished wit, they have indulged in humor.... Resist growing up!

Cultivate cheerfulness. The importance of developing a cheerful attitude impresses me more and more with every passing decade.
> [His last editorial.]

HELEN A. KELLER
1880–1968

American, lecturer. When nineteen months old she lost her sight, hearing, and ability to speak, but later regained the ability to speak. When Helen was six years old, Anne Sullivan Macy splashed her and spelled in her hand "water," a word she remembered from when she was nineteen months old. This Rosetta key to the alphabet helped her understand language. With Anne's tutorship, Helen was graduated cum laude from Radcliff College.

Keller, an atheist and admirer of Communism, overcame her handicaps only because she was raised by Christians in a capitalist nation.

> Security is mostly superstition. It does not exist in nature . . . Life is either a daring adventure or nothing.
> *The Open Door* (1957)

No pessimist ever discovered the secrets of the stars, or sailed to an uncharted land, or opened a new heaven to the human spirit.

Although the world is full of suffering, it is also full of the overcoming of it.

It gives me a deep, comforting sense that things seen are temporal and things unseen are eternal.

DOUGLAS MACARTHUR
1880–1964

American, general, first in his class at West Point and who commanded the U.S. armed forces in the Pacific in World War II. He was the most decorated American officer in World War I and was recommended for a Congressional Medal of Honor, but Pershing did not want his generals exposed to fire. In Japan he is revered because as director of the Allied occupation he introduced a practical democratic constitution and he did not try the emperor for war crimes. The emperor, in turn, commanded the Japanese to obey MacArthur.

[Ordered to take Chationnne with his Rainbow Division or publish a list of five thousand casualties, he replied:]
My name will be at the top of the list.

The unfailing formula for production of morale is patriotism, discipline, and self-confidence within a military unit, joined with fair treatment and merited appreciation from without. It cannot be produced by pampering or coddling an army, and is not necessarily destroyed by hardship, danger, or even calamity. Though it can survive and develop in adversity that comes as an inescapable incident of service, it will quickly wither and die if soldiers come to believe themselves the victims of indifference or injustice on the part of their government, or of ignorance, personal ambition, or ineptitude on the part of their military leaders.
> Annual Report of the Chief of Staff, U.S. Army (1933)

Generals become famous for the orders they refuse to obey.
> [He refused an order to charge prepared defenses without an artillery barrage.]

I came through and I shall return.
> [Promise to the Philippines on arriving in Australia after having evacuated Corregidor Island on March 11, 1942.]

[In war] there is no alternative than to apply every available means to bring it to a swift end. War's very object is victory, not prolonged indecision. In war there is no substitute for victory.
> Speech to Congress after being relieved from duty by President Truman (April 19, 1951)

Wars are caused by undefended wealth.
NY Daily News (November 18, 1945)

Old soldiers never die, they just fade away. And like the soldier in that ballad, I now close my military career and just fade away, an old soldier who tried to do his duty as God gave him the sight to see that duty.

Ibid.

It is fatal to enter any war without the will to win it.

Speech to Republican Convention (1952)

The history of failure in war can be summed up in two words: Too Late.

In L. R. Frank, *Quotationary* (1999)

[In 1933, as chief of staff, MacArthur offered to resign to FDR to protest unpreparedness.]
I felt it my duty to take up the cudgels. The country's safety was at stake, and I said so bluntly. The President turned the full vials of his sarcasm upon me.... I spoke recklessly and said something to the general effect that when we lost the next war, and an American boy, lying in the mud with an enemy bayonet through his belly and an enemy foot on his dying throat, spat out his last curse, I wanted the name not to be MacArthur, but Roosevelt."

Reminiscences (1964)

SPEECH AT WEST POINT ON MAY 12, 1962 (EXCERPTS)

Duty, honor, country—those three hallowed words reverently dictate what you want to be, what you can be, what you will be. They are your rallying point to build courage when courage seems to fail, to regain faith when there seems to be little cause for faith, to create hope when hope becomes forlorn.

The unbelievers will say they are words, but a slogan, but a flamboyant phrase. Every pedant, every demagogue, every cynic, every hypocrite, every troublemaker will try to downgrade them even to the extent of mockery and ridicule.

But these are some of the things they build. They build your basic character. They mold you for your future roles as the custodians of the nation's defense. They make you strong enough to know when you are weak, and brave enough to face yourself when you are afraid.

They teach you to be proud and unbending in honest failure, but humble and gentle in success; not to substitute words for action; not to seek the path of comfort, but to face the stress and spur of difficulty and challenge; to learn to stand up in the storm, but to have compassion on those who fall; to master yourself before you seek to master others; to have a heart that is clean, a goal that is high; to learn to laugh, yet never forget how to weep; to reach into the future, yet never neglect the past; to be serious, yet never take yourself too seriously; to be modest so that you will remember the simplicity of true greatness; the open mind of true wisdom, the meekness of true strength.

And through this welter of change and development your mission remains fixed, determined, inviolable. It is to win our wars.

Yours is the profession of arms, the will to win the sure knowledge that in war there is no substitute for victory....

This does not mean that you are warmongers. On the contrary, the soldier above all other people, prays for peace for he must suffer and bear the deepest wounds and scars of the war. But always in our ears ring the ominous words of Plato: "Only the dead have seen the end of war."

In my dreams I hear again the crash of guns, the rattle of musketry, the strange, mournful mutter of the battlefield. But in the evening of my memory I come back to West Point. Always there echoes and re-echoes: duty, honor, country.

Today marks my final roll call with you. But I want you to know that when I cross the river, my last conscious thoughts will be of the corps, and the corps, and the corps. I bid you farewell.

Truman relieved MacArthur as commander of the United Nations' forces in Korea for insisting on threatening to use atomic weapons against North Korea. Most U.S. casualties came after MacArthur was relieved. President Eisenhower later secured an armistice by threatening to use atomic weapons.

> The little bastard had the guts to fire me and I like him.
> [Of President Truman.]

> Listen, Oh, Listen.
> [MacArthur motto.]

Twelve generals sat on the court-martial of Gen. "Billy" Mitchell for insulting the secretary of the war department by permitting unqualified pilots to fly. Only MacArthur voted for acquittal. Voting against the secretary of war and eleven senior generals epitomized moral courage.

H. L. (HENRY LOUIS) MENCKEN
1880–1956

American, influential twentieth century journalist and magazine editor/publisher (*Smart Set* and *American Mercury*), who was called the "sage of Baltimore." A fierce libertarian and iconoclast, he gored the middle class as the "booboisie" or "boobus Americanus," the "Bible Belt" (his term), the South as "the land of Coca-Cola, hookworm, and Holy Rollers," and government as "the enemy of all well-disposed, decent, and industrious men."

Mencken called journalism a "craft to be mastered in four days and abandoned at the first sight of a better job." Parenthetically, Dr. Johnson said that the only two qualities "absolutely necessary to journalism are contempt of shame and indifference to truth."

Mencken, self-styled "Fool Killer" who at the end of life wrote, "So far as I can recall I have never thrown a dead cat at a single honest and intelligent man. My sneers and objurgations have been reserved for braggarts and mountebanks, quacks and swindlers, fools and knaves."

The left rejoiced in his hedonistic denunciation of Puritanism, and the right rejoiced in his praise of individualism and condemnation of collectivism. Like Nietzsche, he thought Overman was important, not the herd. He rarely supported positive visions or programs; he mostly used his incredible facility with caustic invective to ridicule.

Mencken could cut deeply. He called Veblen's thesis of the conspicuous consumption of the leisure class "one percent platitude and ninety-nine percent nonsense." The only president he could abide was Coolidge because Coolidge "had no ideas and was not a nuisance." He said belief in the Gospels "is now confined to ecclesiastical reactionaries, pious old ladies, and men about to be hanged." He attacked novelists, like Upton Sinclair, whose passion for politics killed their art, for "beginning as artists and ending as mad mullahs." He criticized the hoggishness of businessmen, who "raised the boobery in revolt." He criticized Joyce's *Ulysses* as "deliberately mystifying…"

He also turned his wit on himself. He said his secret ambition was to "write a book weighing at least five pounds." Dressed at his best, he said he looked "like a plumber got up for church."

Mencken's only positive cause was his crusade to persuade Franklin Roosevelt to admit all the Jewish refugees from Germany to save them from slaughter. Yet many believe Mencken was an anti-Semite, a strange charge against one who always had Jewish partners. But being of German descent, he was an isolationist during both world wars.

Mencken's time passed in the 1930s when the world wrestled with the Great Depression and totalitarianism. His forte was to wage *ad hominem* attacks against those identified with the Bible Belt, Prohibition, and Babbittry. He thus became in the 1930s a superannuated curmudgeon.

No sane man objects to palpable lies about him; what he objects to is damaging facts.

In Terry Teachout, *The Skeptic* (2002)

The whole policy of Roosevelt II…was founded upon the fanning of hatreds—the first and last resort of unconscionable demagogues…This fanning, of course, was done to the tune of loud demands for tolerance.

Ibid.

Q. If you find so much that is unworthy of reverence in the United States, then why do you live here?
A. Why do men go to zoos?

Ibid.

Conscience is the inner voice which warns us somebody may be looking.
A Little Book in C Major (1916), ch. 4

A gentleman is one who never strikes a woman without provocation.

Ibid., ch. 6

The great artists of the world are never Puritans, and seldom even ordinarily respectable.
Prejudices First Series (1919)

One of the crying needs of the time is for a suitable burial service for the admittedly damned.

Ibid.

Injustice is relatively easy to bear, what stings is justice.
Prejudices Third Series (1922), ch. 3

The prophesying business is like writing fugues; it is fatal to every one save the man of absolute genius.
Prejudices Fourth Series (1924)

When A annoys or injures B on the pretense of improving B, A is a scoundrel.
Newspaper Days: 1899–1906 (1941)

Women hate revolutions and revolutionists. They like men who are docile, and well regarded at the bank, and never late at meals.

Prejudices Firth Series (1925)

I am against all efforts to make men virtuous by law. I believe that the government, practically considered, is simply a camorra [Mafia] of incompetent and mainly dishonest men, transiently licensed to live by the labor of the rest of us. I am thus in favor of limiting its owners as much as possible, even at the cost of a considerable inconvenience....

American Mercury (September 1927)

When women kiss, it always reminds
   me of prizefighters shaking hands.

The Vintage Mencken (1955), ed.
Alistair Cooke

Self-Respect—The secure feeling that no one, as yet, is suspicious.

Ibid.

Adultery is the application of democracy to love.

Ibid.

I believe in only one thing: liberty; but I do not believe in liberty enough to want to force it upon anyone.

In L. R. Frank, *Freedom* (2003)

Some people read too much: the bibliobibuli...who are constantly drunk on books, as other men are drunk on whiskey...

The older I get the more I admire and crave competence, just simple competence, in any field from adultery to zoology.

The whole aim of practical politics is to keep the populace alarmed (and hence clamorous to be led to safety) by menacing it with an endless series of hobgoblins, all of them imaginary.

A pessimist is one who, when he smells flowers, looks around for a funeral.

It's impossible to imagine the universe run by a wise, just and omnipotent God, but it is quite easy to imagine it run by a board of gods.

The one permanent emotion of the inferior man is fear—fear of the unknown, the complex, the inexplicable. What he wants beyond everything else is safety.

Government is a broker in pillage, and every election is a sort of advance auction sale of stolen goods.

The urge to save humanity is almost always only a false-face for the urge to rule it.

GRANTLAND RICE
1880–1954

American, sportswriter.

Outlined against a blue-gray October sky, the Four Horsemen rode again. In dramatic lore they were known as Famine, Pestilence, Destruction, and Death. These are only aliases. Their real names are Stuhldreher, Miller, Crowley, and Layden.
   [The undefeated Four Horsemen weighed on average only 160 pounds.]

Of Notre Dame's football team, *New York Tribune* (October 19, 1924)

For when the One Great Scorer comes
   to mark against your name,
He writes—not that you won or lost—
   but how you played the Game.

                "Alumnus Football"

He won without arrogance and he lost
without alibis.

       Eulogy for Knute Rockne, head coach of
                Notre Dame (1916–28)

OSWALD SPENGLER
1880–1936

German, historian who theorized that
cultures pass though four phases of a life
cycle and then die. His *The Decline of the
West* (1918), forecast the doom of the West
(U.K., U.S., and France) and the rise of the
Germans because they were collectivists,
not individualists. In the early 1920s, he
forecast Prussianism and socialism would
combine in a "German National Socialism"
as a bulwark against Soviet Bolshevism.
Spengler inspired Dietrich Eckart, founder
of the Nazi Party, although Spengler hated
Nazism and anti-Semitism.

The influence of a genuine educator lies in
what he is rather than in what he says.

          In L. R. Frank, *Quotationary* (1999)

Optimism is cowardice.

              Statement in the 1930s

KEMAL ATATÜRK
1881–1938

Turk, called *Atatürk* (father of Turkey), for
repelling the 1922 Greek invasion. His "six
arrows" were: nationalism, secularism,

republicanism, popularism, statism, and
reformism. He sought a homogeneous
state by expelling the Greeks and Arme-
nians. He disestablished Islam as a state
religion, "cut out the tumor of the Middle
Ages"—the Caliphate—and outlawed
wearing the red fez, an Ottoman symbol.
He changed from Arabic to Roman script,
isolating Muslim libraries, and he shut
down religious schools. He gave women
the vote and made Turkey the only democratic nation of fifty-four Islamic nations.
He replaced religious courts with an independent judiciary interpreting Western
commercial codes. His rapid transformation of Turkey is comparable to Peter the
Great's nation-building in Russia and to
Japan's Meiji Restoration.

[As an officer in the Sultan's army,
Atatürk spurned proffered booty
from a raid, saying:]
Do you want to be a man of today or a
man of tomorrow?

      In Lord Kinross, *Atatürk: A Biography*
                    (1964)

I don't order you to attack, I order you to
die. In the time it takes us to die, other
troops and commanders can come and
take our places.

    [Without any authority, his orders
    at Gallipoli saved Turkey.]

                      Ibid.

It is for today that our mothers gave
birth to us.

    [Rallying troops against invading
    Greeks.]

                      Ibid.

[To the women he said] Win for us the
battle of education and you will do yet

more for your country than we have been able to do. [To the men he said:] If henceforward the women do not share in the social life of the nation, we shall never attain to our full development. We shall remain irremediably backward....

Ibid.

Let us recognize our own limits.
  [In discarding the Ottoman possessions.]

Ibid.

Atatürk told Douglas MacArthur in 1934 that Hitler would start a war in 1940 and overrun all Europe, except Britain and Russia. When America entered, Hitler would be defeated, but the real victor would be the Bolsheviks. As president, he listened to Mussolini's ambassador claim part of Turkey. He excused himself and changed from civilian dress to his marshal's uniform. Returning he said, "Now go ahead, please." The ambassador was speechless.

His Gallipoli monument honored all who fell so that British "Tommies" and Australian "Johnnies" would lie with Turkey's "Alis and Mehmets."

LUDWIG VON MISES
1881–1973

Austrian, economist and social philosopher, who was in the 1930s the principal intellectual opponent of Western socialists and Keynesians. He argued that free markets create great wealth and socialism cannot because it lacks price signals.

Mises' *Human Action* (1949), the libertarian Bible, elaborates a theory of "subjective valuation," that is, a value-free view opposed by traditional conservatives who endorse free markets but seek to balance individualism and social responsibility with a philosophy of objective truth. Libertarianism is not necessarily morally relativist. Libertarians may believe in absolute values and still not want the police to enforce them.

Unemployment as a mass phenomenon is the outcome of allegedly "pro-labor" policies of the governments and of labor union pressure and compulsion.

Bureaucracy (1944)

To Mises, all inflations and depressions originate in government mismanagement of the monetary and labor systems. In depressions, unemployment can only fall after sellers accept lower prices and workers accept lower wages, that is, after they face economic reality. He said the New Deal's attempt to raise prices and wages artificially would prolong the Great Depression. It did! Unemployment in 1940 was 11 million, the same as in 1933!

Our whole civilization rests on the fact that men have always succeeded in beating off the attack of the redistributors.... If we wish to save the world from barbarism we have to refute Socialism...

In the course of social events there prevails a regularity of phenomena to which man must adjust his actions if he wishes to succeed.

Human Action: A Treatise on Economics
(1949), 3rd rev. ed., (1966)

Everybody thinks of economics whether

he is aware of it or not. In joining a political party and in casting his ballot, the citizen implicitly takes a stand upon essential economic theories.

Ibid.

What is commonly called the "industrial revolution" was an offspring of the ideological revolution brought about by the doctrines of the [British economists.] [They] exploded the old tenets: that it is unfair and unjust to outdo a competitor by producing better and cheaper goods; that it is inequitable to deviate from the traditional methods of production; that machines are evil because they bring about unemployment; that it is one of the tasks of civil government to prevent efficient businessmen from getting rich and to protect the less efficient against the competition of the more efficient.

Ibid.

What is wrong is precisely the widespread ignorance of the role which these policies of economic freedom played in the technological evolution of the last two hundred years. People fell prey to the fallacy that the improvement of production was contemporaneous with the policy of laissez-faire only by accident.

Ibid.

Hegel pretended to know that Geist [the spirit of history] wanted to bring about the Prussian monarchy of Frederick William III. But Marx was better informed about Geist's plans…. There was still the main obstacle to overcome: the devastating criticism of the economists. Marx had a solution at hand. [The bourgeois mind is incapable of judging socialism, but] by a special privilege, the logic of certain elect bourgeoisie is not

tainted with the sin of being bourgeois. Karl Marx, son of a wealthy lawyer, married to the daughter of a Prussian noble, and Frederick Engels, a wealthy manufacturer, never doubted that they were above [this] law…

Ibid.

The teachings of utilitarian philosophy and classical economics have nothing at all to do with the doctrine of natural right. With them the only point that matters is social utility. They recommend popular government, private property, tolerance, and freedom not because they are natural and just, but because they are beneficial. The core of Ricardo's philosophy is the demonstration that social cooperation and division of labor between men who are in every regard superior and more efficient and men who are in every regard inferior and less efficient is beneficial to both groups.

Ibid.

It is a serious blunder to believe that the fall in commodity prices is caused by this striving after greater cash holding. The causation is the other way around. Prices of the factors of production—both material and human—had reached an excessive height in the boom period. They must come down before business can become profitable again. The entrepreneurs enlarge their cash holding because they abstain from buying goods and hiring workers as long as the structure of prices and wages is not adjusted to the real state of the market data. Thus any attempt of the government or the labor unions to prevent or to delay this adjustment merely prolongs the stagnation…. If commodities cannot be sold and workers cannot find jobs, the reason can only be that the prices or wages asked are too high.

Ibid.

Economic nationalism is incompatible with durable peace. Yet economic nationalism is unavoidable where there is government interference with business.... [There] free trade even in the short run would frustrate the aims sought by the various interventionist measures.

Ibid.

Keynes did not add any new idea to the body of inflationist fallacies, a thousand times refuted by economists. His teachings were even more contradictory and inconsistent than those of his predecessors who, like Silvio Gesell, were dismissed as monetary cranks. He merely knew how to cloak the pleas for inflation and credit expansion in the sophisticated terminology of mathematical economics.

Ibid.

The rich, the owners of the already operating plants, have no particular class interest in the maintenance of free competition. They are opposed to confiscation and expropriation of their fortunes, but their vested interests are rather in favor of measures preventing newcomers from challenging their position.

Ibid.

It is impossible to substitute other people's work for that of the creators. If Dante and Beethoven had not existed, one would not have been in a position to produce the *Divina Comedia* or the Ninth Symphony by assigning other men to those tasks.

Ibid.

It is...wrong to assume that there prevails within a market economy, not hampered and sabotaged by government interference, a general tendency toward the formation of monopoly. It is a grotesque distortion of the true state of affairs to speak of monopoly capitalism instead of monopoly interventionism and of private cartels instead of government made cartels.

There are no economic causes for armed aggression within a world of free trade and free enterprise. In such a world, no individual citizen can possibly derive any advantage from the conquest of a province or a colony. But in a world of totalitarian states, many citizens may come to believe in an improvement of their material well-being from the annexation of a territory rich in resources. The wars of the twentieth century...have not been caused by capitalism, as the socialists would have us believe. They are wars caused by governments aiming at complete political and economic omnipotence....

Lecture, Orange County, California, in
October 1944

If you increase capital, you increase the marginal productivity of labor, and the effect will be that real wages will rise.

PABLO RUIZ Y PICASSO
1881–1973

Spanish, a Stalinist and predator of women. He became the twentieth century's most renowned artist and a billionaire. He painted his most famous work, *Guernica*, after arranging to inspire himself by having two mistresses beat each other bloody. See Paul Johnson, *Creators* (2006).

His styles changed from representational ("blue period" 1901–4 and "rose period" 1904–6), to cubism (founded in 1908 with his *Les Demoiselles d'Avignon),* to surrealism, to extreme abstract expressionism. Picasso set the objective of becoming "the most shocking painter," which he achieved in cubism's distorted shapes inspired by primitive art. Between representational and abstract art came cubism, which was invented by Picasso and Braque. Paul Johnson said the essence of his art "was to move away from nature into the interior of his mind." Johnson claims Picasso's paintings without his signature have little intrinsic value.

> The refined people, the rich, the idlers seek the new, the extraordinary, the extravagant, the scandalous. I have contented these people with all the many bizarre things that come into my head. And the less they understand, the more they admire it. By amusing myself with all these games, all this nonsense, all these picture puzzles, I became famous.... I am only a public entertainer who has understood his time.
>
> In L. R. Frank, *Quotationary* (1999)

We all know that art is not truth; it is a lie that leads us to the truth.
> From Dore Aston, *Picasso on Art* (1972)

Art is not to decorate apartments. Art is a weapon of revolution.

Computers are useless. They can only give you answers.

A painter paints to unload himself of feelings and visions.

[At an exhibition of children's drawings, he said:]
When I was their age, I could draw like Raphael, but it took me a lifetime to learn to draw like them.

Painting can't be taught, it can only be found.

What I want is that my picture should evoke nothing but emotion.

People don't buy my pictures, they buy my signature.

Success is dangerous. One begins to copy oneself, and to copy oneself is more dangerous than to copy others. It leads to sterility.

I am always doing that which I cannot do, in order that I may learn how to do it.

God is really only another artist. He invented the giraffe, the elephant, and the cat. He has no real style; He just goes on trying other things.

FINE ART

Paul Johnson's *Art: A New History* (2003) refers to the twentieth-century as a century in which fine art was in ignominious retreat. Fine art, a combination of skill and novelty, becomes "fashion" art when the ratio of novelty and skill is changed radically in favor of novelty. Fashion art requires little skill so it is easily duplicated, thus the constant need for fresh novelties. Picasso, like Salvador Dalí (surrealism) and Andy Warhol (pop art), were fashion art con men. Cubism was followed by new schools of "stiff and awkward, anatomically incorrect, and clumsily painted" works of artists, many of whom were on ideological tears.

The weird degenerated into Marcel Duchamp's urinal bolted to a wall (ready-made art) and the emptying of a wastebasket into a glass container (dustbin art). Per Thomas Fleming, modernists were about "warping our sense of beauty with free verse, abstract painting, and Bauhaus architecture." As Andy Warhol put it, "Art is whatever you can get away with."

Paul Johnson says the twentieth century's great artists were representational artists, like Frederick Church, Albert Bierstadt, Norman Rockwell, Grant Wood, Edward Hopper, and Andrew Wyeth. But galleries and professional art critics slighted them so they could make a killing by churning art fashions, just as brokers churned stocks and designers churned dress fashions.

Paul Johnson praises true abstract art, which is pure geometrical form and design, not attempts to abstract nature, as in cubism. Like the wonderful Islamic mosaic designs, pure abstract art will live forever in the work of such artists as Henry Moore, Jackson Pollock, and Paul Klee.

John Barrymore
1882–1942

American, actor.

A man is not old until regrets take the place of dreams.

Love is the delightful interval between meeting a beautiful girl and discovering that she looks like a haddock.

Felix Frankfurter
1882–1965

American (born-Austrian), associate justice (1939–62).

[T]he ultimate touchstone of constitutionality is the Constitution itself and not what we have said about it.
> *Graves v. New York*, 306 U.S. 466 (1939)

If the function of this Court is to be essentially no different from that of a legislature, if the considerations governing constitutional construction are to be substantially those that underlie legislation, then indeed judges should not have life tenure and they should be made directly responsible to the electorate.
> Ibid.

It is a wise man who said that there is no greater inequality than the equal treatment of unequals.
> Dissenting opinion, *Dennis v. United States* (1949)

The [Supreme] Court's authority—possessed neither of the purse nor the sword—ultimately rests on sustained public confidence in its moral sanction. Such feeling must be nourished by the Court's complete detachment in fact and appearance, from political entanglements and by abstention from injecting itself into the clash of political forces and political settlements.
> In Earl Hatcher, *Earl Warren: A Political Biography* (1967)

SAMUEL GOLDWYN
1882–1974

American, film producer, famous for his malapropisms or "Goldwynisms."

Pictures are for entertainment; messages should be delivered by Western Union.
In L. R. Frank, *Quotationary* (1999)

What we want is a story that starts with an earthquake and works its way up to a climax.
In Leslie Halliwell, *Halliwell's Filmgoer's and Video Viewer's Companion*, 9th ed. (1989)

The most important thing in acting is honesty. Once you've learned to fake that, you're in.

I don't want any yes-men around me. I want everyone to tell me the truth, even if it costs him his job.

You can't judge Hollywood by superficial impressions. After you get past the artificial tinsel you get down to the real tinsel.

Note: In motion pictures, the "grip" builds the sets and rigs the lights, the "best boy" is the grip's assistant, and the "gaffer" is the head electrician.

JAMES JOYCE
1882–1941

Irish, modernist novelist, who believed real life is too chaotic to be understood. His labyrinthine prose fixates on his inner feelings. Joyce rejects plot and writes forty-five pages of impenetrable "stream of consciousness" in his masterpiece, *Ulysses* (1922), which made him world famous. It recounts one day in the lives of two Dublin men. A salesman named Leopold Bloom is a hedonist who dotes on his inner life, in contrast with the mythical hero Ulysses. A young artist named Stephen Dedalus has lost his muse. Using these two antiheroes, Joyce condemns the simple patriotism that led men to be cannon fodder in the Great War. Bloom and Dedalus are losers who fail in their search for spiritual values and are satisfied only by their daydreams. Joyce attacks capitalism because it inhibits doting on one's inner self. Joyce savaged popular fiction.

He was an outcast from life's feast.
Dubliners (1916)

Ireland is the old sow that eats her farrow.
A Portrait of the Artist as a Young Man (1916), ch. 5

He kissed the plump mellow yellow smellow melons of her rump, on each plump melonous hemisphere, in the mellow yellow furrow, with obscure prolonged provocative melon-smellious osculation.
Ulysses (1922)

A. A. MILNE
1882–1956

English, failed novelist and playwright, but the public loved the stories he wrote for his son, Christopher Robin: *When We Were Very Young* (1924), *Winnie-the Pooh* (1926), *Now We Are Six* (1927), and *The House at Pooh Corner* (1928).

James James
Morrison Morrison
Weatherby George Dupree
Took great care of his Mother
Though he was only three.
James James said to his Mother,
"Mother," he said, said he,
"You must never go down to the end of
    the town
if you don't go down with me."
> *When We Were Very Young* (1924)

I am a Bear of Very Little Brain, and
    long words Bother me.
> *Winnie-the-Pooh* (1926), ch. 4

SAMUEL TALIAFERRO RAYBURN
1882–1961

American, Democratic speaker of the
house 1940–47, 1949–53, and 1955–61—the
longest tenure of any speaker.

To get along, go along.
> In Neil MacNeil, *Forge of Democracy*
> (1963), ch. 6

Anyone who can't drink their booze, eat
their food, and take their money, and
then vote against them the next day
doesn't belong in politics.

Any jackass can kick a barn down, but it
takes a carpenter to build one.

A whore's vote is just as good as a
debutante's.

FRANKLIN DELANO ROOSEVELT
1882–1945

American, thirty-second president (1933–
45). He helped save the world from National
Socialism by maneuvering a reluctant U.S.
into World War II against opposition by
Republicans and Democrats.

FDR spun the biggest myth of the twentieth-century, that is, free markets caused
the Great Depression. He blamed it on
the "rulers of the exchange of mankind's
goods" (free markets). His prescription
was "to raise the prices of agricultural
products and with this the power to purchase the output of our cities." Even though
malnutrition was a serious problem, he
destroyed millions of gallons of milk, bull-
dozed 6 million hog carcasses, and took
other measures to raise food prices. But,
people lacked the money to buy food at the
artificially increased prices.

FDR's industrial policies mirrored his
agricultural policies. The National Industrial Recovery Act of 1933 created 700 cartels to fix above-market wages and prices.
That lowered output and prolonged the
Depression. The 1935 National Labor Relations Act also reduced output and increased
unemployment, just as his minimum wage
priced low-productivity workers out of
jobs. To see the economic carnage wrought
by FDR's hatred of markets see Jim Powell's outstanding *FDR's Folly: How Franklin
D. Roosevelt and His New Deal Prolonged the
Great Depression* (2003).

Roosevelt, a lifelong recipient of enormous inherited income, had no experience
in creating wealth. He intentionally set out
to reduce private investment in his 1932
campaign speech:

A mere builder of more industrial plants...is as likely to be a danger as a help...Our task now is not...necessarily producing more goods. It is the business of administering plants already in hand...of adjusting production to consumption...

The Great Depression continued for eight years after FDR entered office. In 1939, unemployment was 17.2 percent, more than the 16 percent when he took office in 1933. The Great Depression was the New Dealers' source of power—they needed the emergency to become a permanant crisis in order to increase government economic controls and maintain a majority coalition of dependent constituencies: union members, minorities, farmers, retirees, and so forth. In 1940 Wendell Willkie called on Roosevelt to "give up this vested interest you have in depression" as the justification for a "philosophy of distributed scarcity."

Roosevelt's Marxist thesis was that capitalism led to "underconsumption" because profits in the 1920s were too high, which made the poor too poor to buy the goods they produced. New Deal programs were schemes to deal with "underconsumption," when the real problems were the Federal Reserve's tight money policies, high taxes that prevented investment, protectionism that killed trade, and regulations that choked industry.

Roosevelt's misdiagnosis of the economy was predictable. He was a poor student at Groton, a C- student at Harvard, and he flunked out of Columbia Law School. He rarely read books. Oliver W. Holmes Jr. called him a "second class intellect," and Raymond Morley, a "brain truster,"

wrote in his diary, "I was impressed as never before by the utter lack of logic of the man, the scantiness of his knowledge of things that he was talking about, by the gross inaccuracies in his statements...." [See Burton Folsom Jr., "Franklin Roosevelt and the Greatest Economic Myth of the Twentieth Century," *Ideas on Liberty*, (November 2002).]

To deal with "underconsumption," Roosevelt experimented tactically with a smorgasbord of programs, but his strategy never changed, to wit, increase government control over the economy. To his credit, FDR did mitigate the harsh impact of his policies on the poor with welfare programs. It may be said of FDR what Alexander Pope said of a patron of the arts, "He helped to bury whom he helped to starve."

[Hoover] is certainly a wonder, and I wish we could make him President of the U.S.
FDR's Letter to Hugh Gibson (1920)

The country needs and, unless I mistake its temper, the country demands bold, persistent experimentation. It is common sense to take a method and try it; if it fails, admit it frankly and try another. But above all, try something.
Speech, Oglethorpe University (May 22, 1932)

I pledge you, I pledge myself, to a new deal for the American people.
Nomination acceptance speech (1932)

...the only thing we have to fear is fear itself—nameless, unreasoning, unjustified terror which paralyzes needed efforts to convert retreat into advance...
First Inaugural Address (March 4, 1933)

[Businessmen are] unanimous in their hate for me—and I welcome their hatred....

Campaign speech (1936)

[The concentration of wealth and power in ever larger corporations] has been a menace to the social system as well as to the economic system which we call American democracy.

(October 14, 1936)

To some generations much is given. Of others much is expected. This generation of Americans has a rendezvous with destiny.

Presidential nomination acceptance speech (1936)

[Businessmen] are economic royalists... the privileged princes of these new economic dynasties, thirsting for power.... They created a new despotism... a new industrial dictatorship.

Ibid.

He may be a son of a bitch, but he's our son of a bitch.

[Of Anastasia Somoza of Nicaragua.]

Here is one-third of a nation ill nourished, ill clad, ill housed—now!

The above came from Roosevelt's 1937 speech seeking to pack the Supreme Court with six new justices. Democratic senator Burton K. Wheeler said it was "the most demagogic speech I had ever heard," and it was terrifying that it was "coming from the President of the United States." The committee rejecting FDR's bill wrote, "This is a measure which should be so emphatically rejected that its parallel will never again be presented to the free representatives of the free people of America."

The liberal party insists that the Government has the definite duty to use all its power and resources to meet new social problems with new social controls.

Introduction to Public Paper (1938)

When you see a rattlesnake poised to strike, you do not wait until he has struck before you crush him.

Fireside Chat (September 11, 1941)

In 1942, against the protest of the General Staff and J. Edgar Hoover, and without a crumb of evidence of disloyalty, FDR put 110,000 Japanese Americans in concentration camps. Without any judicial hearings, his Executive Order 9066 put 30,000 Italian and German resident aliens in prisons and restricted the jobs and places of residence for another 600,000 Italian and German resident aliens, including Joe DiMaggio's parents. Many naturalized citizens lost their citizenship and were deported or jailed. FDR also gave the FBI power to censor all communications. Seventy newspapers were banned, and it was illegal to broadcast a long list of casualties or to criticize the equipment or the morale of the U.S. Army or its allies, or to say anything that brought aid and comfort to the enemy.

[After Neville Chamberlain appeased Hitler in Munich in 1938 with the Sudetenland, FDR telegraphed Chamberlain:] "Good man."

Nicholas John Cull, *Selling War: The British Propaganda Campaign against American 'Neutrality' in World War II* (1995)

And while I am talking to you mothers and fathers, I give you one more assurance. I have said this before, but I shall say it again and again and again: Your boys are not going to be sent into any foreign wars.

> Campaign speech in Boston
> (October 30, 1940)

We must be the great arsenal of democracy.

> Post-election speech (December 29, 1940)

Yesterday, December 7, 1941—a date which will live in infamy—the United States of America was suddenly and deliberately attacked by naval and air forces of the Empire of Japan.

> War Message to Congress
> (December 8, 1941)

At the Yalta Conference, against Churchill's protest, FDR agreed to the USSR incorporating the Baltic States and half of Poland—on condition it be kept a secret until after the 1944 U.S. elections. A war to preserve Poland's independence enslaved Poland, eight other East European states, and a third of Germany. FDR told Ambassador William Bullitt, "I think if I give Stalin everything I possibly can and ask nothing in return, noblesse oblige, he won't try to annex anything and will work with me for a world of peace and democracy." No wonder President G. W. Bush on May 7, 2005, said, "The agreement at Yalta followed in the unjust tradition of Munich and the Molotov-Ribbentrop Pact."

FDR made grave strategic mistakes. He fired Admiral Richardson when he refused in 1940 to move the fleet to Hawaii, where it would be vulnerable to a Japanese sneak attack. He purged all the anticommunists from the State Department's Russian Department. FDR refused Churchill's plea to accept Germany's conditional surrender. Anti-Nazi officers would have killed Hit-

ler, ending the war two years earlier and saving tens of millions of lives and Eastern Europe from Soviet rule. FDR erred because he saw the war as Allies versus Axis, not democracies versus Axis versus Communists. FDR was more suspicious of Churchill than of Stalin.

At Yalta, FDR agreed to Operation Keelhaul to repatriate to the USSR a million Russian civilian émigrés: men, women, and children and millions of prisoners of war. None survived. Most were shot just across the border, and the rest were sent into the Gulag. President Eisenhower refused to repatriate North Korean and Chinese prisoners who did not want to return.

Churchill did not attend Roosevelt's funeral.

> [FDR's first VP, Jack Garner, said
> the vice presidency was:]
> "not worth a pitcher of piss."
> [The sanitized version is "saucer of
> spit."]
> In O. C. Fisher, *Cactus Jack* (1978), ch. 11

Happy days are here again,
The skies above are clear again:
Let us sing a song of cheer again,
Happy days are here again.

> [Jack Yellen's 1929 "Happy Days
> Are Here Again" was used by FDR
> in the 1932 election. Hoover was
> associated with E. Y. Harburg's
> "Brother, Can You Spare a Dime,"
> from the *New Americana* (1932).]

VIRGINIA WOOLF
1882–1941

English, novelist, and feminist, known for *To the Lighthouse* (1927) and the essay "A

Room of One's Own" (1929). She organized a salon for liberal Cambridge intellectuals, the Bloomsbury Group.

To The Lighthouse advanced her thesis,
like that of Coleridge, that great minds are
androgynous. A masculine Dr. Ramsay,
a logical metaphysician, is an unsympathetic, distant father. A feminine Mrs. Ramsay is a loving mother, but hopeless in the
world. Their houseguest, Lily Briscoe, is
an artist who succeeds after she combines
her rational (masculine) and imaginative
(feminine) attributes.

> A woman must have money and a room
> of her own if she is to write fiction.
>> *A Room of One's Own* (1929), ch. 1

> Things have dropped from me. I have
> outlived certain desires; I have lost
> friends, some by death, others through
> sheer inability to cross the street.
>> *The Wave* (1931)

> This is an important book, the critic
> assumes because it deals with war.
> This is an insignificant book because it
> deals with the feelings of women in a
> drawing-room.
>> Ibid., ch. 4

KAHLIL GIBRAN
1883–1931

American (Syrian-born), poet, painter, and
mystic, whose *The Prophet* is one of the
most popular books of poetry.

> Your children are not your children.
> They are the sons and daughters of
>   Life's longing for itself.
> They came through you but not from you

> And though they are with you yet they
>   belong not to you.
> You may give them your love but not
>   your thoughts.
> You may house their bodies, but not
>   their souls,
> For their souls dwell in the house of
>   tomorrow, which you cannot visit,
>   not even in your dreams.
>> The Prophet (1923), "On Children"

> It is when you give of yourself that you
> truly give.
>> Ibid., "On Giving"

> The lust for comfort, that stealthy thing
> that enters the house a guest and then
> becomes a host, and then a master.
>> Ibid., "On Houses"

> Let there be spaces in your togetherness.
>> Ibid., "On Marriage"

> Work is love made visible. And if you
> cannot work with love but only with
> distaste, it is better that you should leave
> your work and sit at the gate of the
> temple and take alms of those who work
> with joy.
>> Ibid., "On Work"

FRANZ KAFKA
1883–1924

Czech, novelist of helplessness and spiritual despair, whose protagonists face the
ultimate reality of life that we are ines-
capably alone. He is the master of simple,
haunting ideas best told in short stories:
"The Hunter Gracchus," "In the Penal
Colony," and "The Hunger Artist," and
in the novella, *The Metamorphosis* (1915).

His novels are about nightmarish worlds where one is confronted with cruel, nameless authorities or forces.

The Trial (1914) begins "Someone must have been telling lies about Joseph K for without having done anything wrong he was arrested one fine morning." Mr. K, a totally conventional man, never learns why he is sentenced to death. In his never completed masterpiece, *The Castle* (1926), Mr. K, a stranger in town, has an appointment at a castle, but he cannot get past the village where the castle's functionaries insist he has no appointment. Everyone lies to Mr. K and there is no way to get admitted to the castle. Mr. K is an existential outsider, like Meursault in Camus' *The Stranger*. Unexplained forces sweep both Mr. K.'s along.

> I think we ought to read only the kind of books that wound and stab us…. A book must be the ax for the frozen sea inside us.
>
> Letter to Oska Pollak (January 27, 1904)

> When Gregor Samsa awoke one morning from uneasy dreams he found himself transformed in his bed into a gigantic insect.
>> [Gregor's parents thereafter kept him in his room, and they are relieved by his death because his sister was ready to find a husband. Becoming an insect is symbolic of any family embarrassment.]
>
> The Metamorphosis (1915), ch. 1

As a flood spreads wider and wider, the water becomes shallower and dirtier. The Revolution evaporates, leaving behind only the slime of a new bureaucracy. The chains of tormented mankind are made out of red tape.

> In Gustav Janouch, *Conversations with Kafka*, tr. Goronwy Rees (1953)

JOHN MAYNARD KEYNES
1883–1946

English, economist, whose main idea was that a free market economy is inherently unstable, but government can stabilize it with counter cyclical fiscal policies, that is, run deficits in bad times and surpluses in good times. Classical economists argued that market economies fluctuate due to credit and technology cycles, and that government interventions only extenuate these swings and lower output. In the Great Depression, Keynes's program made some sense, but Keyesians claimed it to be applicable at all times. But as Ronald Reagan said, "The closest thing to immortality on this earth is a federal government program."

In practice, Keynesianism meant ever ratcheting up government spending as a percent of gross national product, which made the economy ever more cyclical and inefficient. Keynes failed to appreciate Schumpeter's insight that capitalist economies are in perpetual disequilibrium: Some industries wax and some wane, otherwise we would be awash in buggy whips and vacuum tubes.

Keynes was soft on inflation since he believed unions would not permit wages to fall far enough to eliminate unemployment. Thus, government should inflate the currency to make real wages fall even though nominal wages remained the same.

Keynes ignored supply; he assumed it was a function of demand. He failed to understand in the Great Depression that 79 percent federal income tax rates, high state income taxes, mandated wage increases, laws against producing, and a collapsed money supply killed investment, that is, killed the willingness to create supply. Capital sought refuge in gold and cash, which made a recession a Great Depression.

Keynes' demand-side economics is illustrated by a passage from his *The General Theory of Employment, Interest and Money* (1936): "To dig holes in the ground, paid out of savings, will increase, not only employment, but the real national dividend of useful goods and services." Keynes also shared with Karl Marx a philosophical antipathy to thrift. Keynes said, "…that those walk most truly in the paths of virtue and sane wisdom who take least thought for tomorrow." Keynes also adopted the bogus "Income Effect Theory," that is, higher tax rates make people work harder to maintain their standard of living.

Milton Friedman exposed Keynes's errors, which have misled most academicians for two generations. One key to Keynesian theory was his idea that as societies get richer, they spend less of their income, resulting in oversaving, which limits demand, which stalls investment, which causes recession. To reduce saving, Keynes proposed high taxes on the rich and income transfers to the poor. Those policies had been standard socialism for one hundred years. Friedman's "A Theory of the Consumption Function" (1957) proved that Keynesianism was wrong, that is, societies do not spend a smaller part of income as they get richer. Friedman also proved in his *Monetary History of the United States* (1963) that the Great Depression resulted not from any failure of capitalism, but from government overexpanding and

overcontracting the money supply. For a brilliant one-chapter exposé of Keynes, see George Gilder, *Wealth and Poverty* (1981), chapter 4, "The Supply Side."

A corollary to the Keynesian demand-side heresy is the "Phillips curve," which argues that government must trade off between unemployment and inflation, that is, higher inflation promotes more rapid growth and lower unemployment. That notion is anathema to classical economists. Historically, inflation falls as the growth rate rises, and inflation rises as the growth rate falls—the opposite of the Phillips curve! Rapid U.S. economic growth from 1982 to 2006 while inflation fell from 13.5 percent per annum to 2 percent p.a. supports the classical economists' view.

Contrary to Keynes, high tax rates discourage both work and investment; saving is good; inflation is bad; and the Federal Reserve should focus on maintaining price stability. It is generally wrong to use monetary policy to slow down an economy or to pump up an economy that is underperforming due to nonmonetary factors. The Fed caused stagflation in the 1970s by keeping interest rates artificially low to compensate for the economic drag caused by high taxes and misregulation.

Keynes's *General Theory of Employment, Interest and Money* was not written in language understandable to educated laymen. Hayek charged Keynes deliberately obfuscated his text with jargon to hide that it was warmed-over inflationist theory that had been long rejected by classical economists.

Keynes, a brilliant man, was sometimes right. He argued that capitalist economies are driven by "animal spirits," the greed prompting entrepreneurs to assume huge risks. As for stock picking, he observed that to pick the winner of a beauty contest, one should study the judges more than the beauties. He intuited the Laffer Curve before Arthur Laffer:

> Nor shall the argument seem strange, that taxation could be so high as to defeat its object and that given sufficient time to gather the fruits, a reduction of taxation will run a better chance than an increase of balancing the budget. To take the opposite view is to resemble a manufacturer who, running at a loss, decides to raise his price. And when his declining sales increase the loss, wrapping himself in the rectitude of plain arithmetic, decides that prudence requires him to raise the price still more.

> Lenin was right. There is no subtler, no surer means of overturning the existing basis of society than to debauch the currency. The process engages all the hidden forces of economic law on the side of destruction, and does it in a manner which not one man in a million is able to diagnose.
>> *Economic Consequences of the Peace* (1919)

[The] long run is a misleading guide to current affairs. In the long run we are all dead.
> *A Tract on Monetary Reform* (1924)

A "sound" banker, alas, is not one who sees danger and avoids it but one who, when he is ruined, is ruined in a conventional and orthodox way along with his fellows, so that no one can really blame him.
> "The Consequences to the Banks
> of the Collapse of Money Values,"
> *Essays in Persuasion* (1931)

The economic problem may be solved …within a hundred years.
> [Said in 1931.]

Words ought to be a little wild for they are the assault of thoughts on the unthinking.
> "National Self-sufficiency" *New Statesman*
> (July 15, 1933)

The ideas of economists and political philosophers, both when they are right and when they are wrong, are more powerful than is commonly understood. Indeed, the world is ruled by little else. Practical men, who believe themselves to be quite exempt from any intellectual influences, are usually the slaves of some defunct economist. Madmen in authority, who hear voices in the air, are distilling their frenzy from some academic scribbler of a few years back.
> General Theory of Employment, Interest,
> and Money (1936)

To suppose that safety-first consists in having a small gamble in a large number of different [companies] compared with a substantial stake in a company where one's information is adequate, strikes me as a travesty of investment policy.
> In Peter Bernstein, *Capital Ideas* (1992), ch. 2

Nothing is more suicidal than a rational investment policy in an irrational world…. Markets can remain irrational longer than you can remain solvent.

That barbarous relic [gold].

I evidently knew more about economics than my examiners.
> [Why he almost failed the civil service economics examination.]

The difficulty lies not in the new ideas but in escaping from the old ones.

[Investment] is the one sphere of life where victory, security, and success is always to the minority and never to the majority. When I can persuade the Board of my insurance company to buy a share, that, I am learning from experience, is the right moment for selling it.

I think that Capitalism, wisely managed, can probably be made more efficient for attaining economic ends than any alternate system yet in sight, but that in itself is in many ways extremely objectionable.

End of Laissez-Faire, pt. 5

BENITO MUSSOLINI
1883–1945

Italian, socialist, and self-declared *Il Duce* (the leader) (1922–43). He founded the Italian Fascist Party after he failed to seize control of the Italian Socialist Party, where he had edited *Avanti*, its newspaper. Fascism began as "syndicalism": Each company is owned by its employees. Conflicts between companies led to socializing the whole economy by regulation, though not by government ownership. Fascism, a nationalistic socialism, retained socialism's cult of violence. "Fascist" came from *fasces*, ancient Rome's bundle of rods with a protruding ax-head symbolizing total state power.

Mussolini, like Teddy Roosevelt, was an intellectual and an environmentalist who spoke four languages, wrote forty-four books, and read philosophy. Like Caesar and Napoleon, he was never committed to anything other than power. Like Hitler, he

had been a corporal and a wounded war hero in World War I, but he was not a racist. He called fascism "organized centralized, state democracy."

War alone brings to its highest tension all human energy and puts the stamp of nobility upon the peoples who have the courage to face it.

"Peace Is an Illusion," *New York Times* (January 11, 1935)

Fascism accepts the individual only insofar as his interest coincides with the state's.

In *Encyclopedia Italiana*

JOSÉ ORTEGA Y GASSET
1883–1955

Spanish, elitist philosopher, whose *Revolt of the Masses* (1930) warned that democracy combined with science and mass culture threatened to create alienated, bloodthirsty, and tyrannical majorities of "homogenized blanks." Society advances only when its creative minority governs. But the masses refuse to accept their proper roles. In Europe, the masses are crushing everything that is excellent. The noble man is one who identifies a vital task to give his life meaning.

There is no culture where there are no principles of legality to which to appeal.... Barbarism is the absence of standards to which appeal can be made.

Revolt of the Masses (1932)

The will to be oneself is heroism.

Ibid.

Man's real treasure is the treasure of his mistakes, piled up stone by stone through thousands of years....

Toward a Philosophy of History (1941)

An age cannot be completely understood if all the others are not also. The song of history can only be sung as a whole.

Life cannot wait until the sciences may have explained the universe scientifically. We cannot put off living until we are ready.

JOSEPH SCHUMPETER
1883–1950

American, economist, who identified risk-taking entrepreneurs as the key to capitalism because they promote innovation. Unlike Marx, who saw capitalism moving toward a final crisis, Schumpeter saw periodic crises as the cost of progress. Keynes sought "equilibrium," but Schumpeter saw the real economy as a "moving disequilibrium" caused by "creative destruction" as new products and processes replace old ones.

In his *Capitalism, Socialism, and Democracy* (1942), Schumpeter argued that only capitalism could realize the human potential for wealth creation. Yet, he believed that socialism would triumph because rich societies would no longer accept the painful "gales of creative destruction" required for rapid growth. Schumpeter identified the naturally risk-averse intellectuals as grave diggers of capitalism, augmented by "administrators" who were replacing "entrepreneurs" in big corporations.

Intense internal opposition to capitalism does not come from falling standards of living of the masses, but from the downward social mobility of those who do not keep pace with the rapid changes.

Schumpeter believed economies grow rapidly, if and only if, they provide secure property rights, the rule of law, and modest taxation and regulation. Authoritarian market economies grow faster than democratic ones because in democracies interest groups, like labor unions and trade associations, restrain trade. The fastest growing economies have been Meiji Japan, Imperial Germany, Imperial Russia, the Asian Tigers, and China since 1978.

Schumpeter noted that great technology cycles lead to economic booms and busts. At the inception of new technologies, investors overestimate returns and over invest, leading to economic booms and stock market bubbles and busts. Usually, manias occur in nations at the height of their influence.

> The capitalist achievement does not typically consist in providing more silk stocking for queens but in bringing them within the reach of factory girls in return for a steadily decreasing amount of effort.
>
> *Capitalism, Socialism and Democracy* (1942)

> Innovation is the outstanding fact in the economic history of capitalist society.
>
> *Business Cycles*

> [An inheritance tax] always involves a conversion of capital into income, hence an act of economic waste which is damaging to all.

> There are three entrepreneurial motives more powerful than money: (1) The will to found a dynasty; (2) the will to con-

quer, to succeed, not for the fruits of success, but for success itself; and (3) the joy of creativity, of exercising one's energy and ingenuity.

OTHER FACTS

Sir John Cowperthwaite ran Hong Kong from 1961 to 1971 when its GDP grew 13.8 percent per annum. When implored to subsidize water, he responded, "I see no reason why someone content with a quick cold shower should subsidize another luxuriating in a deep hot bath." He also said, "In the long run, the aggregate of decisions of individual businessmen, exercising individual judgment in a free economy, even if often mistaken, is less likely to do harm than the centralized decisions of a government, and certainly the harm is likely to be counteracted faster." Per capita income in Hong Kong in 1949 was $100; by 1997 it had risen to $25,000!

ELEANOR ROOSEVELT
1884–1962

American, First Lady (1933–45), whose father made a fortune selling illegal opium in China.

> We have reached a point today where labor saving devices are good only when they do not throw the worker out of his job.
> [This Luddite thesis was the heart of the New Deal and why it prolonged the Great Depression! Our standard of living is increased by rises in productivity that destroy low-skilled jobs and subsequently create high-skilled jobs. When most Americans

were farmers, we were desperately poor compared to today, when only 2 percent of Americans farm. To maximize jobs one can substitute spoons for bulldozers, but doing so will also maximize poverty.]
> See Henry Hazlitt, *Economics in One Lesson* (1979)

> You gain strength, courage, and confidence by every experience in which you really stop to look fear in the face....You must do the thing which you think you cannot do.
> *You Can Learn by Living* (1960)

DAMON RUNYON
1884–1946

American, humorist, known for stories about New York. His "The Idyll of Miss Sarah Brown" was the basis for the musical *Guys and Dolls*.

> One of these days in your travels a guy is going to come up to you and show you a nice brand-new deck of cards on which the seal is not yet broken, and this guy is going to offer to bet you that the can make the jack of spades jump out of the deck and squirt cider in your ear. But, son, do not bet this man, for as sure as you stand there, you are going to wind up with an earful of cider.
> *Guys and Dolls* (1931)

> You are snatching a hard guy when you snatch Bookie Bob. A very hard guy, indeed. In fact, I hear the softest thing about him is his front teeth.
> *Blue Plate Special* (1933), "Snatching of Bookie Bob"

Life is tough, and it's really tough if you're stupid.

It may be that the race is not always to the swift, nor the battle to the strong— but that's the way to bet.

HARRY S. TRUMAN
1884–1972

American, thirty-third president (1945–53). By dropping atomic bombs on Japan, Truman may have saved a million Americans and millions of Japanese. He blocked Soviet expansion in Europe by showing a willingness to use atomic bombs and by sponsoring aid to Greece and Turkey, and with the Marshall Plan, the Berlin Airlift, NATO, and Point Four. He organized the UN repulse of North Korea's invasion of South Korea. The Truman Doctrine (March 1947) read "I believe it must be the policy of the United States to support free peoples who are resisting attempted subjugation by armed minorities or by outside pressure."

Truman expelled thousands of Communists from sensitive U.S. government posts, but to protect the New Deal he concealed that Soviet spies had penetrated the most sensitive U. S. government posts. The Venona Tapes (released July 11, 1995) showed 350 Soviet spies in FDR's administration and in the U.S. press, like the journalist I. F. Stone.

The Marshall Plan poured billions into Western Europe to jump-start their economies. George Marshall's original plan included generous grants to the Soviet Union and to its satellite states in Eastern Europe. After Stalin turned down the offer, Marshall actively opposed the Marshall Plan.

Truman initiated the civil rights movement in 1947 by an executive order integrating the armed forces, and he was largely responsible for creating Israel in 1948—only Reagan was as pro-Zionist.

Any six year old's hindsight is better than the smartest president's foresight.

If we see that Germany is winning we ought to help Russia, and if we see Russia is winning, we ought to help Germany.
U.S. Week (June 5, 1941)

The greatest epitaph in the country is in Tombstone, Arizona. It says, 'Here lies Jack Williams. He done his damndest.' That's the greatest epitaph a man can have.
Speech, Winslow, Arizona (June 13, 1948)

If you can't stand the heat, get out of the kitchen.
"The Presidency," *Time* (April 28, 1952)

I have found the best way to give advice to your children is to find out what they want and then advise them to do it.
CBS "Person to Person" Interview
(May 27, 1955)

I never did give anybody hell. I just told the truth and they thought it was hell.
Look (April 3, 1956)

This was a police action, a limited war, whatever you want to call it to stop aggression and to prevent a big war. And that's all it ever was.
[Speaking of the Korean War.]
Ibid.

I was in search of a one-armed economist so that the guy could never make a statement and then say, "On the other hand…"

Time (January 30, 1989)

The buck stops here.
[Sign on Truman's desk.]
In William Safire, *New Political Dictionary* (1993)

There is no limit to what a man can do or where he can go if he doesn't mind who gets the credit.
In David McCullough, *Truman* (1992)

Poor Ike; when he was a general, he gave an order and it was carried out. Now he is going to sit in that big office and he'll give an order and not a damn thing is going to happen.
In Peter Drucker, *The Essential Drucker* (2002)

If you want a friend in Washington, get a dog.

NIELS BOHR
1885–1962

Danish, father of quantum physics, winner of the 1922 Nobel Prize. Bohr united chemistry and physics, which Einstein said was one of the greatest discoveries. Max Planck had discovered that light is a form of electromagnetic radiation released in particles or "quanta" (bundles of energy and momentum) called photons. Bohr showed that the chemical properties of atoms came from their number of electrons and their distribution in orbital shells, whereas their radioactivity came from the nucleus. This showed how atomic structure related to Mendelejeff's Periodic Table of Elements.

Quantum mechanics reopened the ancient question of what is the smallest bit of matter. Today's paradigm holds protons and neutrons are made up of six types of quarks, and leptons consist of even lighter particles: muons, electrons, neutrinos, and gauge bosons, which are created out of nothing and exist only trillionths of a second. Given the wave-particle duality of matter, Pythagoras was right that the reality is numbers, that is, statistical probability fields. As Werner Heisenberg said, "Time and space are really only statistical concepts…."

If you aren't confused by quantum physics, then you haven't really understood it.

[Asked if he believed a horseshoe over his door would bring good luck], Of course not but I am told it works even if you don't believe in it.

Every sentence I utter must be understood not as an affirmation, but as a question.

The opposite of a trivial truth is plainly false. The opposite of a great truth is also true.
New York Times (October 20, 1957)

Prediction is very difficult, especially about the future.

QUANTUM MECHANICS

Quantum mechanics holds that matter and radiation possess both particle-like and wave-like properties. One cannot measure the position, momentum, mass, and spin of a subatomic particle because light used to illuminate it changes all that. One can only make predictions. This is not just a matter of lacking noninvasive instruments. In a real sense, uncertainty about a particle's position, momentum, mass, and spin is a deep principle of nature. Subatomic particles move by chance, not by cause. Heisenberg called this the "uncertainty or indeterminacy principle." Einstein objected, "God does not play dice with the universe." Neils Bohr responded, "Nor is it our business to prescribe to God how He should run the world."

Quantum mechanics reinforces J. B. Haldane's thought: "The universe is not only queerer than we suppose, but queerer than we can suppose...." J. B. Bell said all particles are connected, so "space is seamless." If a particle is split apart and its halves propelled at the speed of light in opposite directions, if you reverse the polarization of one, the polarization of the other changes simultaneously.

The rules of quantum mechanics, which deal with subatomic particles, do not square with the rules of gravity (General Theory of Relativity), which deal with big things, like Earth. Einstein and physicists ever since have searched for a grand unified theory. One contending theory is "string theory," that is, all so-called particles, from quarks to electrons, are actually strings of energy with different types of vibrations or harmonics. String theory makes gravity inevitable, whereas before it was impossible. But string theory introduces vast complexity, such as multiple new dimensions and parallel universes.

WILL & ARIEL DURANT
1885–1981 & 1889–1981

Americans, husband and wife historians.

Caesar and Christ met in the arena, and Christ won.
The Story of Civilization (1944), vol. 3

Rome had completed the fatal cycle known to Plato: monarchy, aristocracy, oligarchic exploitation, democracy, revolutionary chaos, dictatorship. Once more, in the great systole and diastole of history, an age of freedom ended and an age of discipline began.
Caesar and Christ (1944)

A great civilization is not conquered from without until it has destroyed itself within. The essential causes of Rome's decline lay in her morals, her class struggle, her failing trade, her bureaucratic despotism, her stifling taxes, her consuming wars.

Ibid., Epilogue

Rome was conquered...by barbarian multiplication from within... rapidly breeding Orientals were mostly of a mind to destroy that culture; the Romans possessing it, sacrificed it to the comforts of sterility.

Ibid.

Grow strong my comrade that you may stand
Unshaken when I fall; that I may know
The shattered fragments of my song will come
At last to a finer melody in you.
"To my Wife," Dedication in *The Story of Philosophy* (1926)

Philosophy is the front trench in the siege of truth. Science is the captured territory... Science tells us how to heal and how to kill.... Only wisdom can tell us when to heal and when to kill.

Ibid.

[Mankind] wrote the plays of Shakespeare, the music of Bach and Handel, the odes of Keats, the *Republic* of Plato, the *Principia* of Newton, and the *Ethics* of Spinoza; it built the Parthenon and painted the ceiling of the Sistine Chapel; it conceived and cherished, even if it crucified, Christ. Man did all this; let him never despair.
>   *The Age of Louis XIV* (1963)

A nation is born Stoic, dies Epicurean.
>   In L. R. Frank, *Quotationary* (1999)

Political and economic liberty decays for the same reason…that moral laxity increases: because the family and the church have ceased to function adequately as sources of social order, and legal compulsion insinuates itself into the growing gaps in natural restraint.
>   In L. R. Frank, *Freedom* (2003)

Every cultural flourishing finds root and nourishment in an expansion of commerce and industry…. For society, as well as for an individual, eating must come before philosophy, wealth before art.

History is mostly guessing; the rest is prejudice.

A proletarian dictatorship is never proletarian.

It is good that a philosopher should remind himself, now and then, that he is a particle pontificating on infinity.

He had the northern hunger for truth rather than the southern hunger for beauty.
[Of Spinoza.]

When liberty destroys order, the hunger for order will destroy liberty.

Sinclair Lewis
1885–1951

American, socialist, and first American to win a Nobel Prize for literature (1930). His fiction was semi-disguised essays caricaturing the bourgeoisie for both creating wealth and for not sharing it. In *Babbitt* (1922), George Babbitt is a real estate agent who is crass, thinks only about money, and speaks in clichés. Lewis excoriates Babbitt for his intolerance and his "ready-made opinions derived from the Elks."

His name was George F. Babbitt. He… made nothing in particular, neither butter, nor shoes…but was nimble in the calling of selling houses for more than people could afford to pay.
>   *Babbitt* (1922), ch. 1

Every compulsion is put upon writers to become safe, polite, obedient, and sterile.
[In declining the Pulitzer Prize for *Arrowhead Smith* (1926).]

George S. Patton Jr.
1885–1945

American, lieutenant general, a dyslexic who barely passed at West Point, but became America's greatest field general in World War II. He reinvigorated a dispirited army in North Africa, captured Sicily, and commanded the Third Army, which spearheaded the capture of Western Europe by driving his tanks at full speed while protecting his flanks with only the Eighth Air Force.

After Sicily, Franklin Roosevelt relieved Patton of command for slapping a soldier and appointed Mark Clark commander for the invasion of Italy. Clark got thousands of Americans killed unnecessarily by invading Italy from the bottom of its boot to fight up a mountain chain—no invader in history had ever tried that. He then got trapped on Anzio Beach by digging in and waiting below the mountains when no Germans were within seventy-five miles.

Patton was the best Allied general in minimizing his casualties relative to those of the enemy and the ground captured. Yet he had been passed over for promotion in the 1930s by a fitness report stating, "This officer is a disruptive influence on the peacetime army." But as Patton said, "War is very simple, direct, and ruthless. It takes a simple, direct, and ruthless man to wage war."

Patton led his army from the front, where he was exposed to direct enemy fire. He had been raised on the stories of the heroism of past generations of Pattons. His great fear was that he would disgrace his ancestor warriors, whom he saw in visions.

A man of diffident manner will never inspire confidence. A cold reserve cannot beget enthusiasm, and so with the others there must be an outward and visible sign of the inward and spiritual grace.
The Cavalry Journal, "Success in War,"
(1931)

The history of war is the history of warriors; few in number, mighty in influence. Alexander, not Macedonia, conquered the world. Scipio, not Rome, destroyed Carthage. Marlborough, not the Allies, defeated France. Cromwell, not the

Roundheads, dethroned Charles.
The Infantry Journal Reader, "Success in War," (1931)

Wars may be fought with weapons, but they are won by men. It is the spirit of the men who follow and of the man who leads that gains the victory.
Cavalry Journal (1933)

I pray daily to do my duty, retain my self confidence and accomplish my destiny.
Diary entry (June 20, 1943)

My men don't dig foxholes.... Keep moving. And don't give the enemy time to dig one either.... We are advancing constantly and we are not interested in holding onto anything, except the enemy's balls. Our basic plan of operation is to advance and to keep on advancing regardless of whether we have to go over, under or through the enemy.
Speech, England (June 5, 1944)

We don't want yellow cowards in this Army. They should be killed off like rats. If not, they will go home and breed more cowards.
Ibid.

A pint of sweat will save a gallon of blood.
Ibid.

You can thank God that twenty years from now when you're sitting by the fire-side with your grandson on your knee, and he asks you what you did in the war, you won't have to shift him to the other knee, cough and say, "I shoveled shit in Louisiana."
Ibid.

The most vital quality a soldier can possess is self confidence, utter, complete, and bumptious.
                    Letter to son (June 6, 1944)

To be a successful soldier, you must know history.
                    Ibid.

You are always on parade.
                    Ibid.

Fatigue makes cowards of us all.
          In L. R. Frank, *Quotationary* (1999)

A good plan violently executed *now* is better than a perfect plan next week.
                    War as I Knew It (1947)

Some officers require urging, others require suggestions, very few have to be restrained.
                    Ibid.

There is a great deal of talk about loyalty from the bottom to the top. Loyalty from the top down is even more necessary and much less prevalent.
                    Ibid.

Generals must never show doubt, discouragement, or fatigue.
          In L. R. Frank, *Quotationary* (1999)

Plans must be simple and flexible.... They should be made by the people who are going to execute them.
                    Ibid.

No son of a bitch ever won a war by dying for his country. He won it by making the other poor son of a bitch die for his country.
          James M. Gavin, "Two Fighting Generals"
                    Atlantic (June 1965)

Motto: Hard in training, easy in battle.
          Patton: A Study in Command (1974)

I don't need a brilliant staff, I want a loyal one.
                    Ibid.

Issuing orders is worth about 10 percent. The remaining 90 percent consists in assuring proper and vigorous execution of the order.
          In Robert Fitton, *Quotations from the World's Greatest Motivators* (1997)

If you can't get them to salute when they should salute and wear the clothes you tell them to wear, how are you going to get them to die for their country?
                    Ibid.

An experienced officer can tell, by a very cursory administrative inspection of any unit, the caliber of its commanding officer.
                    Ibid.

An officer must be the last man to take shelter from fire, and the first to move forward. He must be the last man to look after his own comfort at the close of a march. The officer must constantly interest himself in the welfare of his men and their rations. He should know his men so well that any sign of sickness or nervous strain will be apparent to him. He must look after his men's feet and see that they have properly fitting shoes in good condition; that their socks fit, for loose or tight socks make sore feet. He must anticipate change of weather and see that proper clothing and footgear are asked for and obtained.
                    Ibid.

If you want an army to fight and risk death, you've got to get up there and lead it. An army is like spaghetti. You can't push a piece of spaghetti, you've got to pull it.

> Ibid.

Practically everyone but myself is a pusillanimous son of a bitch.

Pacifists would do well to study the Siegfried and Maginot Lines, remembering that these defenses were forced; that Troy fell; that the walls of Hadrian succumbed; that the Great Wall of China was futile…In war, the only sure defense is offense, and the efficiency of offense depends on the warlike souls of those conducting it.

I'm getting as tactful as Hell. If you treat a skunk nicely, he will not piss on you as often.

Success is how high you bounce when you hit bottom.

EZRA POUND
1885–1972

American, fascist, and Modernist poet, who decried America's crass capitalism. T. S. Eliot dedicated "The Waste land" "To Ezra Pound, *il miglior fabbro*" (the better smith). Pound wrote his epic, the *Cantos*, a song of himself as an artist recording the history of his time. In World War II he broadcast in Italy supporting fascism. Instead of being tried for treason, he was confined in a U.S. mental hospital due to the support of many poets, especially Robert Frost and T. S. Eliot, for whom he had been highly effective in promoting their work.

Poetry must be as well written as prose.

Winter is icummen in,
Lhude sing Goddamm.
Raineth droop and staineth slop,
And how the wind doth ramm!
Sing: Goddamm.

> "Ancient Music" (1917)
> Parody of the "Cuckoo Song"(c. 1250)

I was
And I no more exist;
Here drifted
An hedonist.
    [About World War I.]
> "Hugh Selwyn Mauberley" (1920), pt. I

Some quick to arm,
some for adventure,
some from fear of weakness,
some from fear of censure,
some for love of slaughter, in
    imagination…
walked eye-deep in hell
believing in old men's lies, the
    unbelieving
came home, home to a lie.

> Ibid., pt. IV

There died a myriad,
And of the best, among them,
For an old bitch gone in the teeth,
For a botched civilization.

> Ibid., pt. V

What thou lov'st well remains, the rest
    is dross
What thou lov'st well shall not be reft
    from thee
What thou lov'st well is thy true
    heritage…

> *Contra Naturam*, LXXXI

Great literature is simply language charged with meaning to the utmost possible degree.

ABCs of Reading (1934), ch. 1

Real education must ultimately be limited to men who insist on knowing, the rest is mere sheep-herding.

Ibid., ch. 8

A slave is one who waits for someone else to come free him.

"Gists," *Impact: Essays on Ignorance and the Decline of American Civilization* (1960)

You can spot a bad critic when he starts by discussing the poet and not the poem.

In L. R. Frank, *Quotationary* (1999)

KENNETH ROBERTS
1885–1957

American, novelist, known for *Rabble In Arms* (1933). He is a wonderful author for inspiring boys!

On every side of us are men who hunt perpetually for their personal Northwest Passage, too often sacrificing health, strength, and life itself to the search; and who shall say they are not happier in their vain but hopeful quest than wiser, duller folks who sit at home, venturing nothing and, with sour laughs, deriding the seekers for the fabled thoroughfare?

Northwest Passage, Foreword

DAVID BEN-GURION
1886–1973

Israeli, prime minister 1948–53, 1955–63.

In Israel, in order to be a realist you must believe in miracles.

TV interview (October 5, 1956)

HUGO BLACK
1886–1971

American, associate justice (1937–71), former member of the KKK, who became the Supreme Court's foremost protector of freedom of speech.

An unconditional right to say what one pleases about public affairs is what I consider to be the minimum guarantee of the First Amendment.

New York Times Company v. Sullivan, 376 U. S. 254 (1964)

Without deviation, without exception, without any ifs, buts, or whereas, freedom of speech means you shall not do something to people for views they have, express, speak, or write.

In Alison Jones, ed., *Chambers Dictionary of Quotations* (1998)

When I was 40, my doctor advised me that a man in his forties shouldn't play tennis. I heeded his advice carefully and could hardly wait until I reached 50 to start again.

JOYCE KILMER
1886–1918

American, poet who was killed in action (KIA) in World War I.

> I think that I shall never see
> A poem lovely as a tree....
> Poems are made by fools like me,
> But only God can make a tree.
>> "Trees," *Trees and Other Poems* (1914)

> I am sorry you are wiser
> I'm sorry you are taller;
> I liked you better foolish,
> And I liked you better smaller.
>> "For the Birthday of a Middle-Aged
>> Child" st. 1

GEORGE L. MALLORY
1886–1924

English, mountain climber.

> Because it's there.
>> [Response to why he wanted to climb Mount Everest. His body was found in 1999 near the summit. He pioneered the North Face route, which Sir Edmund Hillary used in 1953 to reach the summit first.]
>> *New York Times* (March 18, 1923)

SIEGFRIED SASSOON
1886–1967

English, pacifist poet, who described the horrors of World War I.

> You smug-faced crowds with kindling eye
> Who cheer when soldier lads march by,
> Sneak home and pray you'll never know
> The hell where youth and laughter go.
>> *The War Poems* (1983), "Suicide in the
>> Trenches," st. 3

> Who will remember, passing through
>   this Gate,
> The unheroic Dead who fed the guns?
> Who shall absolve the foulness of their
>   fate,—
> Those doomed, conscripted, unvictori-
>   ous ones?
>   [Brussels' gate, with 54,889 engraved
>   names.]
>> Ibid., "On Passing the New Menin
>> Gate," st. 1

> Lord God of cruelties incomprehensible
> And randomized damnations
>   indefensible,
> Perfect in us thy tyrannous technique
> For torturing the innocent and weak.
>> Ibid., "Asking for It," st. 2

> "Good morning; good morning!" the
>   General said
> When we met him last week on our
>   way to the line.
> Now the soldiers he smiled at are most
>   of 'em dead,
> And we're cursing his staff for incompe-
>   tent swine.
> "He's a cheery old card," grunted Harry
>   to Jack
> As they slugged up to Arras with rifle
>   and pack.
> But he did for them both with his plan
>   of attack!
>> Ibid., "The General" (1917)

RUPERT BROOKE
1887–1915

English, poet, killed in action in World War I. Like other Europeans who welcomed the Great War, Brooke saw war as being as healthful "as swimmers into cleanness leaping." His idealism contrasts with later cynical poetry. See Siegfried Sassoon above.

> If I should die, think only this of me;
> That there's some corner of a foreign field
> That is forever England.
> "The Soldier" (1914)

JULIAN HUXLEY
1887–1975

English, biologist, philosopher, writer, and grandson of T. H. Huxley

> In general, the more elaborate social life is, the more it tends to shield individuals from the action of natural selection; and when this occurs…harmful mutations accumulate instead of being weeded out….
> Quoted in *New York Times* obituary
(February 15, 1975)

LE CORBUSIER
1887–1965

Swiss, architect, who disregarded aesthetics for mass efficiency. He designed housing for workers to be constructed in three days. His disciples built Brasilia, Brazil's vacant capital.

> A house is a machine for living in.
> *Vers Une Architecture* (1923)

BERNARD MONTGOMERY
1887–1967

British, field marshal, who defeated Rommel at El Alamein in 1942.

> I was well beaten myself, and I am the better for it.
> [About school.]
> News reports of November 8, 1955

> When all is said and done the greatest quality required in a commander is "decision"; he must be able to issue clear orders and have the drive to get things done. Indecision and hesitation are fatal in any officer; in a C-in-C they are criminal.
> *Memoirs* (1958)

> The leader must have infectious optimism…. The final test of a leader is the feeling you have when you leave his presence after a conference. Have you a feeling of uplift and confidence? Are you clear as to what is to be done, and what is your part of the task? Are you determined to pull your weight in achieving the object?
> *The Path to Leadership* (1961), ch. 1

> Rule 1, on page 1 of the book of war is: "Do not march on Moscow"…[Rule 2] is: "Do not go fighting with your land armies in China."
> Speech in the House of Lords
(May 30, 1962)

> The morale of the foot soldier is the greatest single factor in winning a war.

ARTHUR RUBINSTEIN
1887–1982

American (Polish-born), pianist. When judging a student piano competition, Rubinstein was given scorecards with potential scores from zero to twenty-one. He awarded two twenties and the rest zeros on the grounds that "either they can play the piano or they cannot."

ALEXANDER WOOLLCOTT
1887–1943

American, author and critic, with biting humor.

> She was so odd a blend of Little Nell and Lady Macbeth.
> [Of Dorothy Parker.]
> "Our Mrs. Parker," *While Rome Burns*
> (1934)

> My doctor forbids me to play, unless I win.

> The scenery was beautiful but the actors got in front of it.

> Doctors want to keep you alive. I want to live.

DALE CARNEGIE
1888–1955

American, necktie salesman who advised how to sell and speak publicly. *How to Win Friends and Influence People* (1938), which sold millions of copies, was a parcel of techniques for flattering:

1. Be genuinely interested in other people.
2. Smile.
3. Remember a man's name is to him the sweetest and most important sound.
4. Be a good listener. Encourage others to talk about themselves.
5. Talk in terms of the other man's interests.
6. Make the other person feel important—and do it sincerely.

JOHN FOSTER DULLES
1888–1959

American, secretary of state under President Eisenhower, 1953–59. He read Stalin's *The Problems of Leninism*, which convinced him that the Soviet Union was bent on global conquest.

> You have to take chances for peace, just as you must take chances in war.... The ability to get to the verge without getting into the war is the necessary art. If you cannot master it, you inevitably get into war. If you try to run away from it, if you are scared to go to the brink, you are lost.
> James Shepley, *Life* (January 16, 1956)

> If only we are faithful to our past, we shall not have to fear our future.

> The broad goal of our foreign policy is to enable the people of the United States to enjoy in peace the blessings of liberty.

T. S. ELIOT
1888–1965

English (American-born), playwright, critic, and perhaps the greatest poet since Shakespeare. In 1948 he won the Nobel Prize in literature for his *Four Quartets*. His poetry is religious and erudite with multiple allusions. A conservative, he called himself "a classicist in literature, a royalist in politics, and an Anglo-Catholic in religion."

Eliot's essay "Tradition and the Individual Talent" (1919) held that poetry should explore the universal and avoid self-absorption. The artist should remain separate from his creation, that is, "the more perfect the artist, the more completely separate in him will be the man who suffers and the mind which creates." And, the artist must know history, that is, have "a perception, not only of the pastness of the past, but of its presence."

Eliot's *The Waste Land*, perhaps the most important poem of the twentieth century, sums up the utter despair of the survivors of the Great War's desolation in the opening line, "April is the cruelest month," when April had always been held by poets as the month of new birth and hope. Eliot was contrasting a nightmarish present to a more humane past when the world was centered on religion. While writing during the middle of the modernist era, Eliot was an antimodernist because the essence of modernism is that nothing is sacred. Max Weber called *The Waste Land* "disenchantment," that is, sadness over the loss of Western purpose and vitality. Eliot's career was capped by the *Four Quartets* (1943), four poems on moods brought to mind by four places. His early *J. Alfred Prufrock* (1917) describes a timid, ineffectual man.

Let us go then, you and I,
When the evening is spread out against the sky
Like a patient etherized upon a table;
....
And time yet for a hundred indecisions,
And for a hundred visions and revisions,
Before the taking of a toast and tea.
....
In the room the women come and go
Talking of Michelangelo.
....
Should I, after tea and cakes and ices,
Have the strength to force the moment to its crisis?
....
I am no prophet—and here's no great matter;
I have seen the moment of my greatness flicker,
And I have seen the eternal Footman hold my coat, and snicker,
And in short, I was afraid.
....
No! I am not Prince Hamlet, nor was meant to be;
Am an attendant lord, one that will do
To swell a progress, start a scene or two,
Advise the prince; no doubt, an easy tool,
Deferential, glad to be of use,
Politic, cautious, and meticulous;
Full of high sentence, but a bit obtuse;
At times, indeed, almost ridiculous—
Almost, at times, the Fool.
....
Do I dare
Disturb the universe?
....
Shall I part my hair behind? Do I dare to eat a peach?
I shall wear white flannel trousers, and walk upon the beach....
"The Love Song of J. Alfred Prufrock"
(1917)

Webster was much possessed by death-
And saw the skull beneath the skin.
      "Whispers of Immortality" (1919)

Uncorseted, her friendly bust
Gives promise of pneumatic bliss.
                 Ibid.

Immature poets imitate; mature poets
steal; bad poets deface what they take,
and good poets make it into something
better, or at least something different.
  "Philip Massinger," *The Sacred Wood* (1920)

April is the cruelest month, breeding
Lilacs out of the dead land, mixing
Memory and desire, stirring
Dull roots with spring rain.
     The Waste Land (1922), opening lines,
           "The Burial of the Dead"

Between the idea
And the reality
Between the motion
And the act
Falls the shadow.
          "The Hollow Men" (1925)

This is the way the world ends
This is the way the world ends
This is the way the world ends
Not with a bang but a whimper.
            Ibid., closing lines

We know too much, and are convinced
  of too little.
    A Dialogue on Dramatic Poetry (1928)

If we take the widest and wisest view of
a Cause, there is no such thing as a Lost
Cause, because there is no such thing as
a Gained Cause. We fight for lost causes
because we know that our defeat and
dismay may be the preface to our suc-
cessors' victory, though that victory itself
will be temporary; we fight rather to
keep something alive than in the expectation it will triumph.
    For Lancelot Andrews (1928), "Essay on
            Francis Herbert Bradley"

Genuine poetry can communicate before
it is understood.
              Dante (1929)

Birth, and copulation, and death.
That's all the facts when you come to
brass tacks.
  "Fragment of an Agon," *Sweeney Agonistes*
                  (1932)

Where is the Life we have lost in living?
Where is the wisdom we have lost in
  knowledge?
Where is the knowledge we have lost in
  information?
          The Rock (1934), pt. 1

Do you need to be told that even such
  modest attainments
As you can boast in the way of polite
  society
Will hardly survive the Faith to which
  they owe their significance?
             Ibid., pt. VI

The last temptation is the greatest
  treason:
To do the right deed for the wrong
  reason.
     Murder in the Cathedral (1935), pt. 1

Human kind cannot bear very much
  reality.
     "Burnt Norton," *Four Quartets* (1936)

In my beginning is my end.
     Ibid., "East Coker," pt. 1 (1940)

The only wisdom we can hope to acquire
Is the wisdom of humility: humility is
    endless.
Ibid., pt. 2

There is only the fight to recover what
    has been lost
And found and lost again and again:
    and now,
under conditions
That seem unpropitious. But perhaps
    neither gain nor loss.
For us, there is only the trying. The rest
    is not our business.
Ibid., pt. 5

Only undefeated
Because we have gone on trying;
Ibid., "The Dry Salvages" (1941)

We shall not cease from exploration
And the end of all our exploring
Will be to arrive where we started
And know the place for the first time.
Ibid., "Little Gidding," pt. 4 (1942)

What we call the beginning is often the
    end
And to make an end is to make a
    beginning.
The end is where we start from.
Ibid., pt. 5

Culture may even be described simply as
that which makes life worth living.
Notes Towards a Definition of Culture,
ch. 1, (1948)

Half of the harm that is done in this world
is due to people who want to feel important. They don't mean to do harm—but
the harm does not interest them. Or they
do not see it, or they justify it because
they are absorbed in the endless struggle
to think well of themselves.
The Cocktail Party (1950)

What is hell?
Hell is oneself
Hell is alone, the other figures in it
Merely projections. There is nothing to
    escape from.
And nothing to escape to. One is always
    alone.
Ibid., act 1, sc. 3

Most editors are failed writers—but so
    are most writers.
In Robert Giroux, *The Education of an*
Editor (1982)

If Christianity goes, the whole of our
culture goes. Then you must start painfully again, and you cannot put on a new
culture ready-made.... You must pass
through many centuries of barbarism.
We should not live to see the new culture, nor would our great-great-great-
grandchildren; and if we did, not one of
us would be happy in it.
Christianity and Culture (1967)

The term "democracy," as I have said again
and again, does not contain enough positive content to stand alone against the
forces you dislike—it can easily be transformed by them. If you will not have God
(and He is a jealous God), you should pay
your respects to Hitler and Stalin.
Ibid.

As political philosophy derives its sanction from ethics, and ethics from the
truth of religion, it is only by returning
to the eternal source of truth that we can
hope for any social organization which

will not, to its ultimate destruction, ignore some essential aspect of reality.

Ibid.

A people without religion will in the end find that it has nothing to live for.

Russell Kirk, *Eliot and His Age* (1971)

Our literature is a substitute for religion, and so is our religion.

I am seldom interested in what he [Ezra Pound] is saying, but only in the way he says it.

Much of Eliot's early popularity may have been built upon a ludicrous vulgar misunderstanding of his intention: a feeling, especially among the rootless and aimless arising generation, that Eliot stood for the futility and fatuity of the modern era, all whimper and no bang: a kind of Anglo-American nihilist. But Eliot's real function has been that of conservator and restorer: merciless portrayer of the Waste land, but guide to recovered personal hope and public integrity…. Like Virgil in a similar era, Eliot has shown the way back to the permanent things.

Russell Kirk, *The Conservative Mind* (1953)

EUGENE O'NEILL
1888–1953

American, playwright, winner of the Nobel Prize in literature in 1936. His psychological dramas are grim family tragedies filled with incest, abortion, insanity, alcoholism, and other unwholesomeness. His greatest play is *The Iceman Cometh* (1946), whose theme is that man can survive life's horrors only by nourishing fantasies that give a false

illusion of hope. The "Iceman" is death.

For de little stealin' dey gits you in jail soon or late. For de big stealin' dey makes you Emperor and puts you in de Hall O' Fame when you croaks.

The Emperor Jones (1921), act 1

KNUTE ROCKNE
1888–1931

American, football coach. Notre Dame was unknown until Knute Rockne became the head football coach in 1918. Over thirteen years he won 105 games, lost 12, tied 5, and won 3 national championships. His 0.881 winning percentage was the best ever. Being innovative, he won with small players—his "Four Horsemen" averaged less than 160 pounds. He realized the potential of the forward pass; he invented the shifting offense and the platooning of offensive and defensive teams. In 1928 at halftime in the Army game, when losing 6 to 0, he implored his team to "win one for the Gipper." George Gipp, a football star who died of pneumonia in 1920, had said, "Some day, when things look real tough for Notre Dame, ask the boys to go out there and win one for the Gipper." Notre Dame won the "Gipp Game" 12 to 6.

I try to make every player on my team feel he's the spark keeping our machine in motion. On him depends our successes.

ALAN SEEGER
1888–1916

American, poet, who died fighting at the Somme in the French Foreign Legion.

I have a rendezvous with Death
At some disputed barricade.
When spring comes back with rustling
    shade
And apple blossoms fill the air;
        "I Have a Rendezvous With Death"
        (1916). In *North American Review*
        (October 1916), st. 1 (partial)

ROBERT BENCHLEY
1889–1945

American, humorist, and drama critic for *Life* and the *New Yorker*.

STREETS FLOODED. PLEASE ADVISE.
    [Telegram sent on arriving in Venice.]
    In R. E. Drennan, ed., *Wits End* (1973)

At Harvard, Benchley persuaded a friend to join him in a prank. They knocked on a door of a private residence and told the maid they had come to pick up the davenport. She allowed them to walk out with it, and they carried it across the square where they told a maid in another house that they had brought the davenport, which they placed in the sitting room and then left.
        Little Brown Book of Anecdotes
        (1985) Clifton Fadiman, ed.

CHARLIE CHAPLIN
1889–1977

English, comedian ("Little Tramp"), and movie director. He entered a Charlie Chaplin look-alike contest in Monte Carlo and won third prize.

All I need to make a comedy is a park, a policeman, and a pretty girl.
        My Autobiography, ch. 10

[When complimented at a party on his singing, Chaplin replied:]
"I can't sing at all. I was only imitating Caruso."
        Ibid.

JEAN COCTEAU
1889–1963

French, poet, novelist, and playwright.

Victor Hugo was a madman who thought he was Victor Hugo.
        Opium (1930)

ADOLF HITLER
1889–1945

German, socialist, who, compared to Stalin and Mao, was a piker in killing innocents. Hitler, a vegetarian, teetotaler, and anticigarette zealot, was voted into power in 1933. The Enabling Act made him dictator. Hitler won the election by a plurality because Stalin ordered the German Communist Party (KPD) not to join an anti-Nazi united front. Its slogan was *"Nach Hitler, Kommen wir"* ("After Hitler, Communists will take power.") Stalin, like Lenin, believed the only way to communize Europe was for the Nazis to win the election and start a war against France and Britain. The Soviets planned to invade and communize a Europe exhausted by prolonged war between Germany and the West.

Hitler had written *Mein Kampf (My Struggle)* to seize control of the Nazi Party. Its white-hot anger was directed at the party's democratic structure. After *Mein Kampf*'s publication, the party accepted Hitler's *führerprinzip* (leadership principle), just as the Bolsheviks had accepted Lenin's dictatorship under the oxymoron "democratic centralism."

Hitler could have been easily stopped when he remilitarized the Rhineland on March 7, 1936—his generals planned a coup to commence upon French resistance. He might have been stopped without a war before Czechoslovakia's thirty-five divisions and fortresses were handed to him at Munich.

Socialists aided Hitler. The British Labor Party in 1933 voted to abolish the Royal Air Force, and in 1938 it voted against conscription when Hitler was taking over the Sudetenland. On August 23, 1939, Stalin signed a military alliance with Hitler. When Hitler invaded France in 1940, French Communists sabotaged the French army, and America's Communist-controlled CIO unions called strikes to stop the shipment of arms to England and France. The Nazi-Soviet alliance called for both to invade Poland simultaneously. Nazism and Communism were not philosophical enemies but rival gangs.

"Nazi" is from "National," in National Socialist German Workers' Party or *Nationalsozialistische Deutsche Arbeiterpartei*.

[Hitler's boyhood friend Kubizek said:] Hitler would sometimes be taken by a certain mood and begin to change everything he saw. That house there was in a wrong position; it would have to be demolished....That street needed a correction in order to give it a more compact impression. Away with this horrible, completely bungled tenement block!...

This inclination to be dissatisfied with things as they were...was ineradicable in him.

Why need we trouble to socialize banks and factories? We socialize human beings.

In Norman Davies, *Europe: A History* (1996)

The moment the Nazi Party disappears, there will be another 10 million Communist votes in Germany.

In Paul Johnson, *Modern Times* (1991), ch. 10

The art of leadership...consists in consolidating the attention of the people against a single adversary and taking care that nothing will split up that attention.

Mein Kampf (1926), vol. 1, tr. Ralph Mannheim (1943)

All propaganda has to be popular and has to adapt its spiritual level to the perception of the least intelligent of those towards whom it intends to direct itself.

Ibid., ch. 6

In view of the primitive simplicity of their minds, the broad mass of a nation...will more easily fall victim to a big lie than to a small one.

Ibid., ch. 10

Those who see in National Socialism nothing more than a political movement know scarcely anything about it. It is more even than a religion: it is the will to create mankind anew.

In L. R. Frank, *Quotationary* (1999)

We must exterminate the idea that it is the judge's function to let the law prevail...That is pure madness. It should be the other way around: the primary task is to secure what is socially just!

> In Balint Vazsonyi, *The 30 Years War*
> (1998)

The annihilation of the Jews will be my first and foremost task.

> (1922)

Anyone who paints a sky green and pastures blue ought to be sterilized.

> [A German soldier in Holland was a member of an execution squad ordered to shoot hostages. When he refused to participate, immediately he was placed with the hostages and shot.]
> In L. R. Frank, *Quotationary* (1999)

The Catholic Church opposed Hitler more than the Protestants did. The Vatican on sixty occasions denounced Nazi behavior and required all German priests to read those denunciations. Israel planted 800,000 trees in Jerusalem to commemorate the 800,000 Jews Pope Pius XII saved from Hitler—no trees were planted for any Protestant bishops.

The Nazis were pagans. The OSS published in 1945 "The Nazi Master Plan: The Persecution of the Christian Churches," Hitler's plan to eliminate Christianity after exterminating the Jews.

WALTER LIPPMANN
1889–1974

American, socialist journalist, and a founder of the *New Republic*. He denounced the "containment" of the USSR and labeled

Churchill's "Iron Curtain" speech a "catastrophic blunder."

> A pleasant man who, without any important qualifications for the office, would very much like to be president."
> [Of Franklin Roosevelt in the 1920s]

The assumption of reformers from Theodore Roosevelt through Woodrow Wilson to Franklin Roosevelt was that the poor could be raised up only by a redistribution of wealth.

> Speech (1964)

ARNOLD J. TOYNBEE
1889–1975

English, historian, who argued that a civilization flourishes when its elite organizes it to respond to challenges better than competing civilizations. Toynbee said, "Civilizations die from suicide, not by murder" Thus, "Of the 22 civilizations that have appeared in history, 19 of them collapsed when they reached the moral state America is in today." To Toynbee, civilizations had no fixed life cycles; they collapsed whenever they slipped into decadence.

Civilizations advance rapidly when sub-units develop independently but remain close enough to imitate successes and avoid failures. Civilizations are moved by spiritual causes. Christianity gives the West an impulse to act on behalf of all humanity; that may save the world from annihilation.

> The things that make good headlines attract our attention because they are on the surface of the stream of life and they

distract our attention from the slower, impalpable, imponderable movements that work below the surface and penetrate to the depths. But, of course, it is really these deeper, slower movements that, in the end, make history....

> *Civilization on Trial* (1948) ch. 1

Civilizations, I believe, come to birth and proceed to grow by successfully responding to successive challenges. They break down and go to pieces if and when a challenge confronts them which they fail to meet.

> Ibid., ch. 4

Religion, after all, is the serious business of the human race.

> Ibid., closing words

America is a large, friendly dog in a very small room. Every time it wags its tail, it knocks over a chair.

> BBC news summary (July 14, 1954)

Our age will be well remembered not for its horrifying crimes nor its astonishing inventions but because it is the first generation since the dawn of history in which mankind dared to believe it practical to make the benefits of civilization available to the whole human race.

LUDWIG J. J. WITTGENSTEIN
1889–1951

English (Austrian-born), founder of logical positivism and the twentieth-century's most influential philosopher. His *Tractatus Logico-philosophicus* (1919) held that knowledge could be found only through empiricism. His *Philosophical Investigations* (1953) held that philosophical problems arise

from linguistic confusion, so language analysis is the principal work of philosophers. Anything that cannot be verified has no meaning. Ethics cannot be verified any more than religion, metaphysics, and art, so none can be addressed by philosophy.

Wittgenstein used empiricism to show the limits of empiricism with his metaphor of a fly in a bottle. The glass walls define the limits of the fly's senses. Wittigenstein believes that beyond the glass wall there is more, but he cannot prove it.

> To believe in God means to see that life has a meaning.
>
> > In L. R. Frank, *Quotationary* (1999)

> Of all that matters in life, we must be silent.

> It is not how things are in the world that is mystical, but that it exists.

DWIGHT D. EISENHOWER
1890–1969

American, thirty-fourth president (1953–61) and Supreme Commander, Allied Expeditionary Forces in World War II. As president he wore the mask of a kind, grinning uncle who used the slogan "I like Ike" to get elected. But in fact he was a ruthless realist. He ended the Korean War by doing what MacArthur wanted to do, to wit, threaten China with atomic bombs. Just as realistically, he refused to rescue the Hungarian uprising in 1956 and the French in Vietnam. He also stopped the French, British, and Israelis from attacking Egypt to keep the Suez Canal. At home, he held social spending in check, rearmed the military (Polaris submarine), paid down the debt, and built the interstate highway system. But Republicans lost ground during his two terms due to three recessions. He resisted Republican proffered tax cuts, but his democratic successor, John Kennedy, cut taxes and the economy boomed.

Humility must always be the portion of any man who receives acclaim earned in the blood of his followers and the sacrifices of his friends.
  Speech, Guildhall, London (July 12, 1945)

Every gun that is made, every warship launched, every rocket fired signifies, in the final sense, a theft from those who hunger and are not fed, those who are cold and not clothed.
                    Speech (April 16, 1953)

In the councils of government, we must guard against the acquisition of influence, whether sought or unsought, by the military-industrial complex.
  [It is rarely cited that this speech warned against the dangers of the federal funding of scientific research: "The prospect of domination of the nation's scholars by federal employment and project allocations…is gravely to be regarded."]
       Farewell broadcast (January 17, 1961)

Never lose your temper, except intentionally.
       In L. R. Frank, *Quotationary* (1999)

You have a row of dominoes all set up, you knock over the first one and what will happen to the last one is a certainty.
  [Re: resisting Communist conquests.]

Plans are worthless; planning is priceless.

CHARLES DE GAULLE
1890–1970

French, general and president of the Fifth Republic (1958–69).

There can be no prestige without mystery, for familiarity breeds contempt.
       In L. R. Frank, *Quotationary* (1999)

Politics is too serious a matter to be left to politicians.
       In Clement Attlee, *A Prime Minister Remembers* (1961), ch. 4

The French will only be united under the threat of danger. How else govern a country that has two hundred and forty-six kinds of cheese?
  "Gaulism? Never Heard of It," *Newsweek* (October 1, 1962)

Treaties are like girls and roses: they last while they last.
       Speech, Elysée Palace (July 2, 1963)

I respect only those who resist me, but I cannot tolerate them.
       In *New York Times* (May 12, 1966)

Old age is a shipwreck.

To be great is to be wedded to a great quarrel.

The graveyards are full of indispensable men.

CHRISTOPHER MORLEY
1890–1957

American, journalist and novelist.

There is only one success—to be able to spend your life in your own way.
>> Where the Blue Begins (1922), ch. 22

The courage of the poet is to keep ajar the door that leads to madness.
>> Inward Ho (1923)

When Abraham Lincoln was murdered, the one thing that interested Matthew Arnold was that the assassin shouted in Latin as he leaped from the stage. This convinced Matthew there was still hope for America.

BORIS PASTERNAK
1890–1960

Russian, author.

Art is unthinkable without risk and spiritual self-sacrifice.
>> Speech at Writers' Conference (1936)

Revolutions are made by fanatical men of action with one-track minds, geniuses in their ability to confine themselves to a limited field.
>> Doctor Zhivago (1957), ch. 14, tr. Max Hayward and Manya Harari (1958)

EDWARD V. RICKENBACKER
1890–1973

American, who was refused entry into the air service in World War I because he was 28-years-old. Having been America's greatest racing driver, he was assigned to drive for Col. Billy Mitchell, whom he badgered into letting him fly. He became America's top ace with 26 kills and won the Medal of Honor.

Most dogfights lasted less than a minute—the issue was often decided on the first turn. The greatest World War II ace, Luftwaffe Col. Erich Hartmann (358 kills), fled any offer of combat in which the other pilot had an advantage.

If a thing is old, it is a sign that it was fit to live. Old families' old customs, old styles survive because they are fit to survive.

CASEY STENGEL
1890–1975

American, managed the New York Yankees for 12 seasons, won 10 pennants and 7 World Series.

Knowing how to do something and doing it are two different things.

I know I'm a better manager when Joe DiMaggio is in center field.

Managing is getting paid for home runs someone else hits.

Good pitching will always stop good hitting and vice-versa.

Most games are lost, not won.

MICHAEL POLANYI
1891–1976

British (born-Hungarian), science philosopher, who said scientists are not purely rational but think intuitively, like historians. As science develops, it will lead man back to religion.

[Scientific advances] often have the character of a gestalt, as when people suddenly "see" something that had been meaningless before.

Science, Faith and Society (1946), ch. 1

It is not so much new facts that advance science but new interpretations of known facts, or the discovery of new mechanisms or systems that account for known facts.

Ibid.

It is pathetic to watch the endless efforts—equipped with microscopy and chemistry, with mathematics and electronics—to reproduce a single violin of the kind the half-literate Stradivarius turned out as a matter of routine more than two hundred years ago.

Personal Knowledge (1958)

EARL WARREN
1891–1974

American, chief justice (1953–69), the most activist U.S. justice in finding in the Constitution novel rights and burdens for different citizens.

To separate [black children] from others of similar age and qualifications solely because of their race generates a feeling of inferiority as to their status in the community that may affect their hearts and minds in a way unlikely ever to be undone…. In the field of public education the doctrine of "separate but equal" has no place. Separate educational facilities are inherently unequal.

Brown v. Board of Education of Topeka (1954)

CIVIL RIGHTS

The Supreme Court in *Brown v. Board of Education of Topeka*, 347 U.S. 483 (1954) overruled *Plessy v. Ferguson*, 163 U.S. 537 (1896), a decision that racially "separate but equal" facilities were constitutionally acceptable. But, the *Brown* Court did not hold that the equal protection clause of the Fourteenth Amendment prohibited invidious classification of citizens by race. Instead, the Court relied on the *Coleman Report* of 1953, a study that concluded blacks would be better educated in integrated schools (segregated schools injured the self-esteem of black students and thereby limited their ability to learn). Note: *Brown*'s reasoning has been undermined by David Armor's study that shows that the racial composition of student bodies does not effect black achievement.

Brown's lack of a color-blind standard enabled the court to expand "affirmative action" beyond enforcing nondiscrimination laws and reaching out to increase the pool of eligible minority candidates to remedy the effects of past discrimination. The court now promotes "benign discrimination" for favored races, even though Title VII of the Civil Rights Act of 1964 banned *any* discrimination due to race. Quotas and set-asides for favored races are not racist, but standardized tests deemed to be are *per se* racist, if a favored race is "statistically" disadvantaged. This reverts to the monarchical principle that, "If you tell me who you are, I will tell you how you will be judged."

Justice O'Connor's opinion in *Grutter v. Bollinger*, 539 U.S. 306 (2003), held that although a racial classification would be subjected to strict scrutiny, the University of Michigan in admissions may discriminate against whites and Asians because student "diversity" is a "compelling state interest." A government free to discriminate by race to advance student diversity is logically consistent with *Plessy vs. Ferguson*, which permitted racial discrimination to preserve "a compelling state interest in public peace and good order."

The court should have heeded Thurgood Marshall's 1954 brief for the NAACP in *Brown*:

> Distinctions by race are so evil, so arbitrary and invidious that a state bound to defend the equal protection of the laws must not invoke them in any public sphere.

George Will wrote that the *Brown* decision "encouraged the abandonment of constitutional reasoning…. And it legitimized a legislative mentality among judges…. The premise is that 'unjust' and 'unconstitutional' are synonymous." Justice Stanley Reed forecast that *Brown* would lead to rule by judges.

A color-blind Constitution was endorsed by Justice Antonin Scalia, a founder of the Federalist Society, in *Adarand Constructors* (1995)

> To pursue the concept of racial entitlement even for the most admirable and benign of purposes is to reinforce and preserve for future mischief the way of thinking that produced race slavery, race privilege and race hatred. In the eyes of the government, we are just one race here. It is American.

J. PAUL GETTY
1892–1976

American, oil industrialist.

> My formula for success? Rise early, work late, strike oil.

> The able industrial leader who creates wealth and employment is more worthy of historical notice than politicians or soldiers.
>
> Michael Jackman, ed., *The MacMillan Book of Business Quotations* (1984)

> No one can possibly achieve any real and lasting success or "get rich" in business by being a conformist.
>
> Interview, *Paris Herald Tribune* (January 10, 1961)

> There are one hundred men seeking security to one able man who is willing to risk his fortune.
>
> Ibid.

> If you can actually count your money, then you're not really rich.
>
> In L. R. Frank, *Wit and Humor Quotationary* (2000)

ROBERT H. JACKSON
1892–1954

American, associate justice (1941–54) and chief counsel at the Nuremberg War Crimes Tribunal. To rebut the argument that the tribunal was outside the law, Jackson said, "Civilization asks whether law is so laggard as to be helpless to deal with crimes of this magnitude."

The very purpose of a Bill of Rights was to withdraw certain subjects from the vicissitudes of political controversy, to place them beyond the reach of majorities and officials and to establish them as legal principles to be applied by the courts. One's right to life, liberty and property, to free speech, a free press, freedom of worship and assembly, and other fundamental rights may not be submitted to vote; they depend on the outcome of no elections.

West Virginia State Board v. Barnette, 319 U. S. 642 (1943)

Freedom to differ is not limited to things that do not matter much. That would be a mere shadow of freedom. The test of its substance is the right to differ as to things that touch the heart of the existing order.

Ibid.

It is not the function of our Government to keep the citizen from falling into error; it is the function of the citizen to keep the Government from falling into error.

American Communications Assn. V. Douds, (1950)

The advocate can make no greater mistake than to ignore or attempt to conceal the weak points in his case. The most effective strategy is at an early stage of the argument to invite attention to your weakest point before the court has discovered it, then to meet it with the best answers at your disposal, to deal with all the remaining points with equal candor and to end with as powerful a presentation of your strongest point as you are capable of making.

In L. R. Frank, *Quotationary* (1999)

Reinhold Niebuhr
1892–1971

American, theologian at the Union Theological Seminary, critic of capitalism, a pacifist (except for fighting fascism), and a founder of both the Americans for Democratic Action and the Fellowship of Christian Socialists. He opposed saving China, South Korea, and South Vietnam from Communism. He denied the Virgin birth and Christ's resurrection. He opposed Karl Barth, who argued the church should preach the gospel and stay out of politics. Niebuhr spent most of his energy pursuing socialism in the here and now.

God, give us the serenity to accept what cannot be changed;
Give us the courage to change what should be changed
Give us the wisdom to distinguish one from the other.
[Often used by alcoholics in remission.]

"Serenity Prayer" (1951)

Nothing that is worth anything can be achieved in a lifetime.
Therefore we must be saved by hope.
Nothing true or beautiful makes complete sense in any context of history.
Therefore we must be saved by faith.
Nothing we do, no matter how virtuous, can be accomplished alone.
Therefore we are saved by love.

The Irony of American History (1952)

The final enigma of history is therefore not how the righteous will gain victory over the unrighteous, but how the unrighteousness of the righteous is to be overcome.

MARTIN NIEMOLLER
1892–1968

German, minister (Protestant).

When Hitler attacked the Jews I was not a Jew, therefore, I was not concerned. And when Hitler attacked the Catholics, I was not a Catholic, and therefore, I was not concerned. And when Hitler attacked the unions and the industrialists…I was not concerned. Then, Hitler attacked me and the Protestant church—and there was nobody left to be concerned.

Congressional Record (October 14, 1968)

J. R. R. TOLKIEN
1892–1973

British (South African-born), Oxford professor of Anglo-Saxon, and a devout Catholic whose trilogy, *The Lord of the Rings,* chronicles a mythological struggle between good and evil in a fantasy land of humans and creatures such as trolls, dwarves, goblins, barrow-wrights, elves, orcs, ents, and hobbits. It has sold 50 million copies, and many considered it the best fiction of the twentieth century.

The Ring Trilogy is an Arthurian-like saga of fellowship among a nine-member comitatus on a desperate quest to save the world from an evil demon. Its protagonist is the hobbit Frodo Baggins, whose mission is to transport the One Ring of overwhelming power to Mount Doom and destroy it in its fires. He cannot use its power because it deprives users of free will and makes them evil. Frodo is aided by Gandalf, a wizard, whom Tolkien said was an incarnate angel.

Tolkien said the trilogy was "a fundamentally religious and Catholic work; unconsciously so at first but consciously in the revision," and that it was for "the elucidation of truth, and the encouragement of good morals in this real world."

The Lord of the Rings and Philosophy (2003), edited by G. Bassham and E. Bronson, collects essays probing Tolkien's themes. For example, Tolkien agrees with St. Augustine that all evil comes from inordinate desires, especially the desire to dominate other people. Thus, evil comes from exercising free will. Only a hobbit could carry the One Ring because what a hobbit most desires is to live in a happy community, not power.

Tolkien's ring is like Socrates' story of Gyges, who finds a ring that makes him invisible. The ring's power corrupts Gyges. Chilton Williamson wrote that power is "the first and preeminent temptation."

One Ring to rule them all,
One Ring to find them
One Ring to bring them all
And in the darkness to bind them.
In the Land of Mordor where the
    Shadows lie.

The Fellowship of the Ring (1965), bk. 1, ch.
2. epigraph

This thing all things devour:
Birds, beasts, trees, flowers;
Gnaws iron, bites steel;
Grinds hard stones to meal;
Slays kings, ruins towns,
And beats high mountain down.
    [Riddle whose answer is "Time."]

The Hobbit, or There and Back Again
(1966), ch. 5

Alive without breath,
As cold as death;
Never thirsty, ever drinking,
All in mail, never clinking.
    [Answer is "Fish."]

Ibid.

Women of this country learned long ago that those without swords can die upon them. [Eowyn.]

The Two Towers, Peter Jackson's film (2002)

Sons of Gondor, Rohan, brothers... A day may come when the courage of men fails, when we forsake our friends and break all bonds of fellowship. But, it is not this day. An hour of wolves and shattered shields when the age of man comes crashing down, but it is not this day. This day we fight. By all you hold dear, I bid you stand, men of the West.
    [Aragon.]

The Return of the King, Peter Jackson's film (2003)

DAME REBECCA WEST
1892–1983

Irish, journalist, novelist, essayist, and feminist.

I myself have never been able to find out precisely what feminism is; I only know that people call me a feminist whenever I express sentiments that differentiate me from a doormat.

Clarion (November 14, 1913)

The trouble about man is twofold. He cannot learn truths that are too complicated; he forgets truths that are too simple.

JAMES BRYANT CONANT
1893–1978

American, president of Harvard 1933–53.

There is only one proved method of assisting the advancement of pure science—that of picking men of genius, backing them heavily, and leaving them to direct themselves.

Letter, *New York Times* (August 13, 1945)

Behold the turtle. He makes progress only when he sticks his neck out.

In James G. Hershberg, *James B. Conant* (1993)

HUEY P. LONG
1893–1935

American, Louisiana governor, and U.S. senator, whose slogan was "Share Our Wealth." Franklin Roosevelt tacked to the left in 1934 to preempt Long's anticipated primary challenge. Long published *Every Man a King* and his own newspaper.

[When asked what large contributors got, Long said:]
Access.
[When asked what noncontributors got, Long said:]
Good government.

ANITA LOOS
1893–1981

American, silent film star, and playwright known for *Gentlemen Prefer Blondes* (1953).

I'm furious about the Woman's Liberationists. They keep getting up on soapboxes and proclaiming that women are brighter than men. That's true, but it should be kept very quiet or it ruins the whole racket.

In *The Observer* (December 30, 1973)

MAO TSE TUNG
1893–1976

Chinese, socialist poet, who murdered more people than any other person in history! Mao saw in the 1917 Bolshevik Revolution a vehicle to emulate the Emperor Qin Shihuang, who united China in 221 B.C. Mao said, "Qin only buried alive 460 Confucian scholars. We buried 460 thousand Confucian scholars." Mao sought to reestablish power over the "Sinic Zone" of Korea and Vietnam, and over the "Inner Asian Zone" of non-Chinese: Manchus, Mongols, Uighurs, Turks, and Tibetans.

> How beautiful these mountains and rivers,
> Enticing countless heroes to war and
>   strife.
> Too bad that Emperors Qin Shihuang
>   and Han Wudi lacked culture
> And that Emperors Tang Taizong and
>   Song Taizu lacked romance.
> Genghis Khan was the pride of his time,
> Though he was only good at shooting
>   eagles with his bow.
> They all belong to a time gone by
> Only today is a True Hero present.
>   "White Snow" 1936

According to University of Texas Professor Gerald Scully, Mao murdered 36 million Chinese by liquidating landlords (owners of two acres or more) and political dissidents (as during the Great Proletarian Cultural Revolution 1966–69). A reliable source informed your compiler of a Chinese state secret, that is, that an additional 80 million Chinese (not 20 million) starved in 1958–61 during the political famine of Mao's Great Leap Forward. Khrushchev said, when "I look at Mao, I see Stalin, a perfect copy."

A revolution is not a dinner party, or writing an essay, or painting a picture, or doing embroidery.

Selected Works of Mao Tse-Tung, Foreign Languages Press edition (1965), vol. 1

The enemy advances: we retreat. The enemy halts: we harass. The enemy tires: we attack. The enemy retreats: we pursue.

Party Report (1928)

Our strategy is "pit one against ten," and our tactics are "pit ten against one."
    [Mao contributed to military theory the concept of the protracted war, that is, a more powerful enemy can be defeated if one endures until the enemy is frustrated.]
    "Problems of Strategy in China's Revolutionary War," ch. 5, December 1936, in *Selected Works of Mao Tse-Tung* (1965), Foreign Languages Press edition, vol. 1.

Political power grows out of the barrel of a gun.
    "Problems of War and Strategy" (1937)

Proper guerrilla policy will provide for unified strategy and independent activity.
    In L. R. Frank, *Quotationary* (1999)

Classes struggle, some classes triumph, others are eliminated.
    Quotations from Chairman Mao, ch. 2

Communism is not love. Communism is a hammer which we use to crush the enemy.

Time (December 18, 1950)

Let a hundred flowers bloom and let a hundred schools contend.

[Announcement of a short-lived liberalization during which wall posters critical of Communism appeared. A draconian anti-rightist purge followed.]

Speech on (February 27, 1957)

Reactionaries must be deprived of the right to voice their opinions; only the people have that right.

Classics In Political Science, Philosophical Library (1963)

Chaos under the heavens and all is right with the world.

[Mao's revolutionary slogan.]

[When asked what he thought was the historical significance of the French Revolution, Mao's deputy Zhou Enlai said:]

"It is too early to tell."

DOROTHY ROTHSCHILD PARKER
1893–1967

American, critic/humorist for *The New Yorker*.

Razors pain you
Rivers are damp;
Acids stain you;
And drugs cause cramp.
Guns aren't lawful;
Nooses give;

Gas smells awful;
You might as well live.

"Resume," *Not So Deep as a Well* (1937)

By the time you say you're his,
Shivering and sighting
And he vows his passion is
Infinite, undying-
Lady, make a note of this;
One of you is Lying.

Ibid., "Unfortunate Coincidence"

Men seldom make passes
At girls who wear glasses.

Ibid., "News Item"

[When told of Calvin Coolidge's death, Parker asked:]
How can they tell?

In John Keats, *You Might As Well Live* (1970)

[In a game, Parker made a sentence using the word "horticulture" by saying:]
"You can lead a horticulture, but you can't make her think."

Ibid.

[No one visited Parker in her downtown office so she had a sign painted on her door:]
GENTLEMEN.

Ibid.

This is not a novel to be tossed aside lightly. It should be thrown with great force.

Book review quoted by A. Johnston, "Legend of a Sport," in *The New Yorker*

That woman speaks eighteen languages and can't say "no" in any of them.

ANDRES SEGOVIA
1893–1987

Spanish, classical guitarist. He continued to play concerts until he was past the age of ninety. He explained, "I will have an eternity to rest."

ALBERT SZENT-GYORGYI
1893–1986

American (Hungarian-born), biochemist, Nobel Prize, 1937.

> Discovery is to see what everybody else has seen, and to think what nobody else has thought.
>> "Science Needs Freedom," *World Digest* (1943)

MAE WEST
1893–1980

American, vaudeville and film actress who wrote many screenplays.

> "Goodness what beautiful diamonds!"
> "Goodness had nothing to do with it."
>> *Night After Night* (1932)

> Why don't you come up and see me sometime.
>> *She Done Him Harm* (1933)

> When I'm good I'm very very good, but when I'm bad I'm better.
>> *I'm No Angel* (1933)

> It's better to be looked over than to be overlooked.
>> *Belle of the Nineties* (1934)

> Is that a pistol in your pocket, or are you just glad to see me?
>> *Peel Me a Grape* (1935)

> I used to be Snow White—but I drifted.
>> Ibid.

> Between two evils, I always pick the one I never tried before.
>> *Klondike Annie* (1936)

> I always say, keep a diary and some day it'll keep you.
>> *Every Day's a Holiday* (1937)

> Too much of a good thing can be wonderful.
>> Joseph Weintraub, ed., *The Wit and Wisdom of Mae West* (1967)

JACK BENNY
1894–1974

American, comedian, who won Emmys as a violin-playing miser. In one skit, when a holdup man said, "Your money or your life," Benny replied, "I'm thinking it over." In real life, he said of a proffered award, "I don't deserve this, but then, I have arthritis and I don't deserve that either."

E. E. CUMMINGS
1894–1962

American, poet who championed the underdog.

> I sing of Olaf glad and big
> whose warmest heart recoiled at war:
> a conscientious object-or
>> "I Sing of Olaf glad and big" (1931), st. 1

...[Olaf] responds, without getting annoyed
"I will not kiss your f.ing flag"

Ibid., st. 2 (partial)

...Olaf (upon what were once knees)
does almost ceaselessly repeat
"there is some s. I will not eat"

Ibid., st. 4 (partial)

Christ (of His mercy infinite)
i pray to see; and Olaf, too

Ibid., st. 5

Preponderantly because
unless statistics lie he was
more brave than me: more blond than you.

Ibid., st. 6

O sweet spontaneous earth
how often has
the naughty thumb of science
prodded thy beauty
thou answereth them
only with spring.

"Tulips and Chimneys" (1924)

THE DREYFUS AFFAIR
1894–1906

French. Jewish captain Alfred Dreyfus was convicted on forged evidence of selling secrets to Germany and was sentenced to Devil's Island. The army discovered unequivocal evidence of Dreyfus's innocence, but covered it up in order to cover up their prior fabrication of evidence. Émile Zola wrote an open letter entitled "I Accuse," which showed that Colonel Esterhazy was guilty, but Zola was convicted of slander. In 1906, Dreyfus and Zola were cleared and Esterhazy convicted. Ironically, the affair discredited the conservatives and elected a socialist government that bungled the Versailles Treaty, which brought Hitler to power and led to the Jewish Holocaust.

ALDOUS HUXLEY
1894–1963

English, essayist, novelist, and grandson of T. H. Huxley. Aldous distrusted twentieth-century technology, and he saw capitalism and socialism as both subscribing to the same materialistic philosophy. In contrast to Orwell's fear of hobnail boots in *1984*, Huxley's *Brave New World* (1932) featured a paternalistic government six hundred years in the future that used biological and behavioral conditioning to suppress emotions and acclimate humans to promiscuity, infantile games, and following the directions of the Controllers. The elite exercised their will to power by using science to satisfy the people's desire for material security.

There are few who would not rather be taken in adultery than in provincialism.

Anti Hay (1923), ch. 10

Several excuses are always less convincing than one.

Point Counter Point (1928), ch. 1

There is no substitute for talent. Industry and all the virtues are of no avail.

Ibid., ch. 13

Happiness is like coke—something you get as a by-product in the process of making something else.

Ibid., ch. 30

By comparison with a night-club, churches are positively gay.

Do What You Will (1929)

Experience is not what happens to a man; it is what a man does with what happens to him.

Texts and Pretexts (1932), Introduction

That men do not learn very much from the lessons of history is the most important of all the lessons history has to teach.

"A Case of Voluntary Ignorance" (1959)

The surest way to work up a crusade in favor of some good cause is to promise people that they will have a chance of maltreating someone.... To be able to destroy with good conscience, to be able to behave badly and call your bad behavior "righteous indignation"—this is the height of psychological luxury, the most delicious of moral treats.

Quoted in his obituaries
(November 23, 1963)

Idealism is the noble toga that political gentlemen drape over their will to power.

Quoted in *New York Herald Tribune* obituary (November 24, 1963)

Maybe this world is another planet's hell.

The more powerful and original a mind, the more it will incline towards solitude.

To his dog, every man is Napoleon; hence the constant popularity of dogs.

The course of every intellectual, if he pursues his journey long and unflinch-ingly enough, ends in the obvious, from which the non-intellectuals have never stirred.

An intellectual is a person who has discovered something more interesting than sex.

NIKITA S. KHRUSHCHEV
1894–1971

Russian, dictator, who denounced Stalin but who almost started wars with China and the United States.

Whether you like it or not, history is on our side. We will bury you.

Moscow (November 18, 1956)

The Soviet Union will consider any attempt on the part of the Western Hemisphere powers to extend their system to any portion of the Communist world as dangerous to our peace and safety.

"Khrushchev Doctrine," aka
the "Monrovsky Doctrine"
(November 11, 1962)

NORMAN ROCKWELL
1894–1978

American, artist, who produced 322 paintings, many for the cover of the *Saturday Evening Post*. Most were paintings, not "illustrations" of products. Rockwell is America's Michelangelo. He could tell complete stories without a word: *Freedom from Want, Shuffleton's Barber Shop, The Marriage License,* and *Let's Give Him Enough on Time.*

I unconsciously decided that, even if it wasn't an ideal world, it should be and so I painted only the ideal aspects of it—pictures in which there are no drunken slatterns or self-centered mothers…only foxy grandpas who played baseball with the kids, and boys who fished from logs and got up circuses in the backyard.

Washington Post (May 1972)

ELZIE C. SEGAR
1894–1938

American, cartoonist.

I yam Popeye,
The Sailor Man

"Song of Popeye"

I yam what I yam
'Cause tha's what I yam.

Ibid., st. 1 (partial)

I yam jus' a little feller,
But I hasn't any yeller.

Ibid., st. 2 (partial)

I yam strong at the finitch
'Cause I eats me spinitch.

Ibid., st. 8 (partial)

I will gladly pay you Tuesday for a hamburger today.

[Wimpy, c. 1933.]

I am no physicacist, but I know what matters.

[Popeye]

JAMES THURBER
1894–1961

American, humorist, cartoonist, and managing editor of the *New Yorker*. He created a befuddled Walter Mitty, who dreamed of being a hero.

Her own mother, lived the latter years of her life in the horrible suspicion that electricity was dripping invisibly all over the house. Her principal activity was checking the wall switches for empty sockets happy in the satisfaction that she had stopped not only a costly but a dangerous leakage.

My Life and Hard Times (1933), ch. 2

He who hesitates is sometimes saved.

"The Glass in the Field," *Fables for Our Time* (1940)

Then, with that faint fleeting smile playing about his lips, he faced the firing squad; erect and motionless, proud and disdainful, Walter Mitty, the undefeated, inscrutable to the last.

"The Secret Life of Walter Mitty," *My World—And Welcome to It* (1942)

She developed a persistent troubled frown which gave her the expression of someone who is trying to repair a watch with his gloves on.

The Beast In Me and Other Animals, "Look Homeward, Jeannie" (1948)

No Oyster ever profited from its pearl.

"The Philosopher and the Oyster," *Further Fables* (1956)

"JACK" DEMPSEY
1895–1983

American, heavyweight boxer who won the championship from Jess Willard in 1919 and lost to Gene Tunney in 1926 and 1927. When asked if he aimed for an opponent's chin or his nose, Dempsey replied, "Neither, I aim for the back of his head."

Honey I forgot to duck.
[Comment to his wife after losing the fight to Gene Tunney in 1926.]

A champion is one who gets up when he can't.
In L. R. Frank, *Quotationary* (1999)

BUCKMINSTER FULLER
1895–1983

American, architect, mathematician, and philosopher. He created the "geodesic dome," a sphere of connected tetrahedrons, the only practical large building with no supporting columns. Incredibly, its strength increases as a ratio of its size.

He believed that technology was the answer, not the problem, and that the universe was design, not matter. He believed "Spaceship Earth" was "regenerative," that is, knowledge is negatively entropic, so wealth can increase geometrically without depleting resources.

Either man is obsolete or war is.
New Yorker (January 8, 1966)

Change the environment; do not try to change man.
Design Science (1969)

The most important thing about Spaceship Earth: an instruction book didn't come with it.
Operating Manual for Spaceship Earth (1969), ch. 4

I am not a thing, a noun.
I seem to be a verb,
an evolutionary process—
an integral function of the universe.
[Fuller also said, "God is a verb."]
I Seem To Be a Verb (1970)

When the National Science Foundation asked the "breakthrough" scientists what they felt was the most favorable factor in their education, the answer was almost uniformly, "intimate association with a great, inspiring teacher."
Ibid.

Nature does not depend on us. We are not the only experiment.
Interview with the *Minneapolis Tribune* (April 30, 1978)

There is nothing in a caterpillar that tells you it's going to be a butterfly.

When I am working on a problem, I never think about beauty. I think only about how to solve the problem. But when I have finished, if the solution is not beautiful, I know it is wrong.

E. H. LIDDELL HART
1895–1970

English, great military historian of the First and Second World Wars.

Be very careful never to show your own bias to anyone who is giving you information, or passing it on to you. Once he sees that you have a particular inclination he will instinctively tend to tell you what he thinks will suit you, and enhance your opinion of him.

"Intelligence Problems," *This Expanding War* (1941)

Originality is the most vital of all military virtues.

Thoughts on War (1944)

Various fresh ideas gained acceptance... when they could be presented not as something radically new, but as the revival in modern terms of a time-honored principle or practice that had been forgotten.

Strategy (1954), Preface

GROUCHO MARX
1895–1977

American, one of the vaudeville Marx Brothers team with Harpo (silent), Chico, and Zeppo.

Remember, you're fighting for this woman's honor—which is probably more than she ever did.

Duck Soup (1933)

Who are you going to believe, me or your lying eyes?
[Chico]

Ibid.

PLEASE ACCEPT MY RESIGNATION. I DON'T WANT TO BELONG TO ANY CLUB THAT WILL ACCEPT ME AS A MEMBER.

Telegram to the Delany Club, *Groucho and Me* (1959), ch. 26

[A lady in a limousine saw Groucho in old clothes working in his garden. She asked how much the lady of the house paid him? Groucho responded:]
I don't get paid in dollars. The lady of the house just lets me sleep with her.

The Little Brown Book of Anecdotes (1985), Clifton Fadiman, ed.

I wasn't kissing her. I was whispering in her mouth.
[Chico caught kissing a chorus girl.]

[Pounding his fist on the table:]
I have principles! But, I have others.

LEWIS MUMFORD
1895–1990

American, socialist sociologist, whose *Technics and Civilization* (1934) portrayed man as a victim of capitalist technologies. In *The Conduct of Life* (1951), he spoke of "mass man" "incapable of choice" "governed mainly by conditioned reflexes" who was either the pawn of "advertising agencies" or of "totalitarian propaganda." His equating advertisers with Bolshevik commissars showed his contempt of free people making free choices.

Our national flower is the concrete cloverleaf.

The Culture of Cities (1938)

GEORGE HERMAN "BABE" RUTH
1895–1948

American, baseball player, six-feet two-inches, left-handed "Sultan of Swat," who in 1932 called his home run at Wrigley Field against the Chicago Cubs. His 1927 record of 60 home runs lasted until Roger Maris's 61 homers in 1961 (albeit with eight extra games played). When Ruth hit 54 home runs in 1920, the entire American League hit only 369 home runs. In 1997, 2,458 home runs were hit in the American League. Ruth also pitched a record 29.66 straight scoreless innings and had 94 wins versus 46 losses. When Ping Bodie was asked what it was like rooming with Ruth, who was famous for breaking curfew, Bodie replied, "I don't room with Ruth. I room with his suitcase."

> [Ruth refused in the Depression to take a cut in his $80,000 salary. When told he made $5,000 more than President Hoover, Ruth replied:]
> Why not. I had a better year than he did.
> > *Baseball*, PBS TV Series (1994)

> [Babe Ruth struck out 1,330 times, but also hit 714 home runs.]

A year after the Boston Red Sox won the World Series in 1918, the owner Harry Frazee sold Ruth to the New York Yankees for $100,000 to produce a play that bombed. The Red Sox did not win another World Series until 2004 due to the "curse of the Bambino."

BASEBALL RECORDS

Bob Gibson pitched an earned run average of 1.12 one season; Ted Williams batted .406 in 1941, the last .400+ season; Barry Bonds surpassed 760 home runs as a career record in 2007; Pete Rose had 4,256 hits; but

most amazing was Jolting Joe DiMaggio's (1914 – 1999) 56 consecutive-game hitting steak in 1941. The Yankee Clipper struck out only eight times more than he hit home runs in his career and was never thrown out stealing second or third base. He never harassed umpires. DiMaggio told Ted Williams, "You were the greatest hitter." Williams (the "Splendid Splinter") replied, "You were the greatest player." Williams gave away his secret for hitting: "Wait, wait, wait, then quick, quick, quick."

Home-runs are now cheap. Only 17 players hit 50 or more homers in a season from 1901 to 1989, but 16 players did from 1990 to 2001 due to: smaller ballparks, smaller strike zones, livelier balls and bats, dilution of pitching talent, and steroids.

Some believe Ty Cobb (1880 – 1961), the "Georgia Peach," was the greatest baseball player. In 1942, he was asked what he thought he would hit if he were still playing and he replied, "About .320." When asked why so low given his having hit over .400 in one season, he said, "You have to remember, I'm sixty-two years old."

GEORGE BURNS
1896–1996

American, comedian.

> Too bad that all the people who know how to run the country are busy driving taxicabs and cutting hair.
> > *Life* (December 1979)

> I've never looked better; I've never made love better; I've never lied better.

> I can't die; I'm booked.
> > [Hundredth birthday.]

F. Scott Fitzgerald
1896–1940

American, novelist of the Jazz Age. His masterpiece, *The Great Gatsby* (1925), tracks his own life. As a poor army officer, Fitzgerald fell in love with Zelda, a Southern belle who initially spurned him due to his poverty. Similarly, the penniless James Gatz is spurned by Daisy, a "poor little rich girl" who attaches herself to her social equal, Tom Buchanan, who lives aimlessly on his family's wealth. To win Daisy, Gatz transforms himself into Jay Gatsby and acquires wealth illegally. Gatsby is great in the sense of self-transformation, but foolish in chasing Daisy, who allows him to accept responsibility for her hit-and-run killing. In the end, Gatsby dies and is deserted by all except one friend.

> They were careless people, Tom and Daisy—they smashed up things and creatures and then retreated back into their money or their vast carelessness, or whatever it was that kept them together, and let other people clean up the mess they had made.
>
> *The Great Gatsby* (1925), ch. 9

In the spring of '27, something bright and alien flashed across the sky. A young Minnesotan… [Charles Lindbergh] did a heroic thing, and for a moment people set down their glasses in country clubs and speakeasies and thought of their old best dreams.

Joseph Jacobs
1896–1940

American, boxing manager.

> The successful men of action are not sufficiently self-observant to know exactly on what their success depends.

William Faulkner
1897–1962

American, novelist, Nobel Prize (1949) for novels based on the fictional town of Jefferson, Yoknapatawpha County, Mississippi, and the poor white trash Snopes. Faulkner specialized in self-absorbed, dysfunctional, and decaying aristocratic families with dark secrets. *The Sound and the Fury* (1929) and *As I Lay Dying* (1930), employ stream of consciousness, but he also experimented by mixing voices. His themes were loss, endurance, and the past: "The past is never dead. It's not even past."

The Sound and the Fury depicts the decline of the Compsons, an elite family whose children avoid engagement in life to become a dipsomaniac classicist and suicide, a small-town redneck, a slobbering idiot, and mother and daughter sluts. Like Ibsen in *Ghosts*, the theme of Faulkner's life work was "there is no such thing as *was*; if *was* existed there would be no grief or sorrow." The past defines the future; our good and evil live on.

Faulkner did not graduate from high school, but he read voraciously. Self-styled, "Count-no-count," he said he wrote to impress the women he loved at a time when America's Eastern literary elite were debasing their work with social realism.

… the young man or woman writing today has forgotten the problems of the human heart in conflict with itself. He must learn them again. He must teach himself that the basest of all things is to be afraid and…[to leave] no room in his workshop for anything but the old verities and truths of the heart, the old universal truths lacking which any story is ephemeral and doomed—love and honour and pity and compassion and sacrifice. Until he does so, he labors under a curse. He writes not of love but of lust, of defeats in which nobody loses anything of value, of victories without hope and, worst of all, without pity or compassion. His griefs grieve on no universal bones, leaving no scars. He writes not of the heart but of the glands.

"I Decline to Accept the End of Man,"
Excerpts from December 10, 1950 Nobel
Prize speech

I believe man will not merely endure, he will prevail. He is immortal, not because he, alone among creatures, has an inexhaustible voice but because he has a soul, a spirit capable of compassion and sacrifice and endurance. The poet's, the writer's duty is to write about these things. It is his privilege to help man endure by lifting his heart, by reminding him of the courage and pity and sacrifice which have been the glory of his past. The poet's voice need not merely be the record of man; it can be one of the props, the pillars to help him endure and prevail.

Ibid.

By artist I mean of course everyone who has tried to create something….

New York City Speech (January 25, 1955)

An artist is a creature driven by demons. He doesn't know why they choose him and he's usually too busy to wonder why.

Interview, *Writers' First Series* (1958)

Really the writer doesn't want success…. He knows he has a short span of life, that the day will come when he must pass through the wall of oblivion, and he wants to leave a scratch on that wall—Kilroy was here—that somebody a hundred, or a thousand years later will see.

Lecture (1959)

The writer's only responsibility is to his art. He will be completely ruthless if he is a good one. He has a dream. It anguishes him so much he must get rid of it. He has no peace until then. Everything goes by the board: honor, pride, decency, security, happiness, all, to get the book written. If a writer has to rob his mother, he will not hesitate; the "Ode on a Grecian Urn" is worth any number of old ladies.

In *Paris Review* (Spring 1959)

The ideal job: Landlord of a bordello! The company's good and the mornings are quiet, which is the best time to write.

Henry James was one of the nicest old ladies I ever met.

BERTOLT E. BRECHT
1898–1956

German, playwright, poet, and Communist. John Gay in 1728 wrote the *Beggars Opera* to show there was no difference in the morals of prisoners and aristocrats. Brecht updated it in 1928 as *The Threepenny Opera*. Brecht's "theater of the absurd" rejected realism. His dramas lacked plots, but they developed character to emphasize utter despair.

Andrea: Unhappy the land that has no
 heroes!
Galileo: No. Unhappy the land that
 needs heroes.
   Life of Galileo (1939), sc. 12. tr. Charles
          Laughton (1961)

As for them [Zinoviev, Kamenev, and other
purge victims], the more innocent they are,
the more they deserve to be shot.
    In Sidney Hook, *Out of Step* (1987)

Art is not a mirror held up to reality but
a hammer used to shape it.

WILLIAM O. DOUGLAS
1898–1980

American, associate justice (1939–80), a
liberal who had four wives and tried desperately to become FDR's vice president.
He found new rights and burdens in the
Constitution's "emanations."

It usually costs money to communicate
an idea to a large audience. But no one
would seriously contend that a limitation on the expenditure of money to
print a newspaper would not deprive the
publisher of freedom of the press. Nor
can the fact that it costs money to make
a speech—whether it be hiring a hall or
purchasing time on the air—make the
speech any the less an exercise of First
Amendment rights.

A people who extend civil liberties only
to preferred groups start down the path
either to a dictatorship of the right or the
left.
      In *New York Times* obituary
         (January 20, 1980)

C. S. LEWIS
1898–1963

English, professor, perhaps the most influential modern voice of Christianity. He
offered a proof of God in *Mere Christianity* (1952). There he argued that if there
were a God, He would have put in people
the desire to know Him. And, "If I find in
myself a desire which no experience in
this world can satisfy, the most probable
explanation is that I was made for another
world." And if there is a moral law, there
is a moral lawgiver. Dartmouth College
in 2000 prohibited alumni from distributing free copies of *Mere Christianity* to
students.

Lewis also wrote marvelous beautiful
children's books, such as *Chronicles of Nar-
nia* (1950–56). No other twentieth century
author rivals C. S. Lewis in having all of
his forty books still in print fifty years after
his death! Over 50 million copies have
been sold. George Will said Lewis, Solzhenitsyn, or Orwell was the most influential twentieth-century author.

The greatest evil is not now done in
those sordid "dens of crime" that Dickens loved to paint. It is not even done
in concentration camps and labor camps.
In those we see its final results. But it is
conceived and ordered in clean, carpeted,
warmed, and well lighted offices by quiet
men with white collars and cut finger-
nails and smooth-shaven cheeks who do
not need to raise their voices....
     The Screwtape Letters (1942)

She's the sort of woman who lives for
others—you can always tell the others by
their hunted expression.

[In his *The Screwtape Letters* (1940), an old demon, Screwtape, writes advice to his young associate, Wormwood, on snaring souls. To seduce, link good deeds with religion and get your prey to elevate their importance over religion:]

Once you have made the World an end and faith a means, you have almost won your man, and it makes very little difference what kind of worldly end he is pursuing.

Ibid.

Courage is not simply one of the virtues but the form of every virtue at the testing point.

In Cyril Connolly, *The Unquiet Grave* (1944), ch. 3

We make men without chests and expect of them virtue and enterprise. We laugh at honor and are shocked to find traitors in our midst. We castrate and then bid the geldings to be fruitful.

The Abolition of Man (1947)

To love at all is to be vulnerable. Love anything, and your heart will certainly be wrung and probably be broken. If you want to make sure of keeping it intact, you must give your heart to no one, not even to an animal. Wrap it carefully round with hobbies and little luxuries; avoid all entanglements; lock it up safe in the casket or coffin of your selfishness. But in that casket—safe, dark, motionless, airless—it will change. It will not be broken; it will become unbreakable, impenetrable, irredeemable. The alternative to tragedy, or at least to the risk of tragedy, is damnation. The only place outside Heaven where you can be per-

fectly safe from all the dangers and perturbations of love is Hell.

The Four Loves (1960), "Charity"

We are composite creatures, rational animals, akin on one side to the angels, on the other to tom-cats.

Ibid., "Eros"

Of all tyrannies, a tyranny exercised for the good of its victims may be the most oppressive. It may be better to live under robber barons than under omnipotent moral busybodies. The robber barons' cruelty may sometimes sleep, his cupidity may at some point be satiated; but those who torment us for our own good will torment us without end, for they do so with the approval of their own conscience.

In James B. Edwards, *Hitler: Stalin's Stooge* (2004)

Nations, cultures, arts, civilization—these are mortal, and their life is to ours as the life of a gnat.

Eunuchs boasting of their chastity!

HENRY R. LUCE
1898–1967

American, publisher, who called the twentieth century "the American century."

Business more than any other occupation is a continual dealing with the future; it is a continual calculation, an instinctive exercise in foresight.

Fortune (October 1960)

GOLDA MEIR
1898–1978

Israeli (Russian-born), a founder of Israel and her fourth prime minister (1969–74).

> Women's liberation is just a lot of foolishness. It's the men who are discriminated against. They can't bear children. And no one's likely to do anything about that.
> > Quoted in *Newsweek* (October 23, 1972)

> We Jews have a secret weapon in our struggle with the Arabs; we have no place to go.

> Don't be so humble, you're not that great.

> Not being beautiful forced me to develop my inner resources. The pretty girl has a handicap to overcome.

LEONARD READ
1898–1983

American, founder of Foundation for Economic Education (FEE), which publishes *The Freeman, Ideas on Liberty*, the best periodical on economics. It was founded in 1950 and initially edited by Henry Hazzlitt and John Chambers.

Read's "I, Pencil" has a pencil describe its genealogy. It took millions of people to make the pencil! Each component, such as Malaysian rubber and Ceylonese graphite, could only be made with machines, each of which had parts made of all materials processed by untold numbers of different chemicals. No mastermind directed the action to make a pencil. The private sector spontaneously organized itself worldwide to make the pencil through a complex order superior to any order state bureaucrats could design to make the pencil.

NOEL COWARD
1899–1973

English, actor, playwright, and composer.

> Mad dogs and Englishmen go out in the midday sun.
> > "Mad Dogs and Englishmen" (1931)

> Dear 338171 (May I call you 338?)
> > In L. R. Frank, *Wit and Humor Quotationary* (2000)

> Thousands of people have talent. The only thing that counts is: Do you have staying power?

FRIEDRICH A. HAYEK
1899–1992

British (Austrian-born), 1974 Nobel Prize for Economics, and, per Peter Drucker, "our time's preeminent social philosopher." Hayek taught that humans began as hunter-gatherers who relied on "instinctual solidarity for the tribe and predation for outsiders." Capitalism, which Hayek called "the extended order of human cooperation," is the most modern form of social organization with its culturally developed notions of private property and contract. Because capitalism produces for strangers rather than preys on them, it increases the specialization of labor exponentially, which increases productivity and wealth exponentially.

Hayek believed competition was the key to making an economy grow and that real competition could only exist under a free market system. His greatest insight was that only free markets could process efficiently the vast amount of information necessary to make the best use of scarce resources.

His *The Constitution of Liberty* (1960) reads, "Right law constitutes, defines, creates liberty—right law is liberty." And the law must be abstract, that is, based on universal principles and not preferring classes of citizens. "Social justice" is the primary threat to the law because it prevents treating people equally and because there is no way to adjudicate individual claims of "need" and "merit."

Like Adam Smith, David Hume, and Edmund Burke, Hayek saw that order arose spontaneously in human society through innumerable personal interactions to create economies, moralities, laws, and institutions, and these were more efficacious than the utopias planned by intellectuals. Hayek called socialist central planning the "fatal conceit."

Hayek's *The Road to Serfdom* (1944) argued that Nazism was not a capitalist perversion, but a product of the "progressive" ideas of Western intellectuals. Western socialists are "dangerous idealists" who "prepared the way for totalitarians." The reason is that the socialist central planning was fundamentally inconsistent with liberty. It led to totalitarian socialism—the modern form of serfdom.

Hayek refuted Keynes's thesis that inherent flaws in capitalist economies are the principal causes of recessions. Central banks are the principal causes due to their excessive credit expansions and contractions, aided by other government actions that impede the free adjustment of capitalist economies.

Few are ready to recognize that the rise of fascism and Nazism was not a reaction against the socialist trends of the preceding period but a necessary outcome of those tendencies....

The Road to Serfdom (1944)

...the planning against which all our criticism is directed is solely the planning...which is to be substituted for competition.

Ibid.

...competition is superior not only because it is in most circumstances the most efficient method known but even more because it is the only method by which our activities can be adjusted to each other without coercive or arbitrary intervention of authority.

Ibid., ch. 3

...the democratic statesman who sets out to plan economic life will soon be confronted with the alternative of either assuming dictatorial powers or abandoning his plans...

Ibid., ch. 10

...these [racist] ideas [in Hitler's Germany] came precisely from the socialist camp. It was certainly not through the bourgeoisie, but rather through the absence of a strong bourgeoisie, that they were helped to power.

Ibid., ch. 12

The power which a multiple millionaire, who may be my neighbor and perhaps my employer, has over me is very much less than that which the smallest fonctionnaire possesses who wields the coercive power of the state, and on whose discretion it depends whether and how I am to be allowed to live or to work.

Ibid.

The great aim of the struggle for liberty has been equality before the law.

The Constitution of Liberty (1960)

The chief guidance which prices offer is not [how hard to work] but *what to do.*

New Studies in Philosophy, Politics, Economics, and the History of Ideas (1978), ch. 12.

[Socialists] have discovered that redistribution through taxation and aimed financial benefits was an easier and quicker method of achieving their aims.

Ibid.

We are only beginning to understand on how subtle a communication system the functioning of an advanced industrial society is based—a communications system which we call the market and which turns out to be a more efficient mechanism for digesting dispersed information than any that man has deliberately designed.

The Pretense of Knowledge

[It is to Lord Maynard Keynes's] general theory of economics—to which we owe the unique world-wide inflation of the third quarter of our century and the inevitable consequence of severe unemployment that has followed it.

The Fatal Conceit:The Errors of Socialism (1988), ch. 4

Socialism constitutes a threat to the present and future welfare of the human race, in the sense that neither socialism nor any other known substitute for the market order could sustain the current population of the world.

Ibid., ch. 8

We may be able to assist the weak and disabled, the very young and old, but only if the sane and adult submit to the impersonal discipline which gives us means to do so.

Ibid., Appendix D

It cannot be said of democracy as Lord Acton said of liberty, that it…"is itself the highest political end."…Democracy is essentially a means, a utilitarian device for safeguarding internal peace and individual freedom. As such it is by no means infallible or certain.

We shall not grow wiser before we learn that much that we have done was very foolish.

Without a theory, the facts are silent.

ERNEST HEMINGWAY
1899–1961

American, Nobel Prize (1954). New York critics condemned him for his "reactionary" lack of interest in politics. He wrote without adjectives. Good writing leaves most things unsaid—one sees only the "tip of an iceberg." In *The Old Man and the Sea* (1952), on his eighty-fifth fishing trip without a catch, Santiago, an old fisherman, captures a giant marlin after two days of excruciating struggle. As he rows back to port, despite his heroic efforts, sharks eat the marlin. It is an allegory of man's inevitable loss in life; but man can struggle against it with nobility and grace. *The Sun Also Rises,* a novel of postwar disillusion, ends with the words, "Isn't it pretty to think so?" It is a melancholy expression after the war to end all wars.

...that is the great fallacy; the wisdom of old men. They do not grow wise. They grow careful.

A Farewell to Arms (1929)

Grace under pressure.
[When Dorothy Parker asked what "guts" meant.]

New Yorker (November 30, 1929)

All stories, if continued far enough, end in death....

Death in the Afternoon (1932), ch. 11

Forget your personal tragedy. We are all bitched from the start, and you especially have to be hurt like hell before you can write seriously.

Letter to F. Scott Fitzgerald (May 28, 1934)

But did thee feel the earth move?

For Whom the Bell Tolls (1940), ch. 13

A man can be destroyed but not defeated.

The Old Man and the Sea (1952)

No classic resembles any previous classic....

McCall's (May 1956)

The most essential gift for a good writer is a built-in, shock-proof shit detector.

Paris Review (Spring 1958)

Nobody ever fielded 1000 if they tried for the hard ones.

In L. R. Frank, *Wit and Humor Quotationary* (2000)

ROBERT M. HUTCHINS
1899–1977

American, president of the University of Chicago 1929–45 and advocate of the "great books" curriculum.

To destroy the Western tradition of independent thought it is not necessary to burn the books. All we have to do is to leave them unread for a couple of generations.

The Conflict in Education (1953)

It is not so important to be serious as it is to be serious about the important things. The monkey wears an expression of seriousness which would do credit to any college student, but the monkey is serious because he itches.

The object of education is to prepare the young to educate themselves throughout their lives.

The great books of ethics, political philosophy, economics, history, and literature do not yield up their secrets to the immature.

How can a man call himself educated who does not grasp the leading ideas that since the dawn of history have animated mankind?

A liberal education...frees a man from the prison-house of his class, race, time, place, background, family, and even his nation.

Education can be dangerous. It is very difficult to make it not dangerous. In fact, it is almost impossible.

Modern Forum, Los Angeles (1963)

CHICAGO CANON OF WESTERN CIVILIZATION'S 'THE GREAT BOOKS'

A literary canon answers one question: With my limited time, which books must I read? It makes literature more competitive. Contemporary authors must compete with Shakespeare and so forth.

The Great Books movement began in 1921 at Columbia University with Professor John Erskine's course in the Western classics. It flourished in the 1930s under Robert Hutchins, president of Chicago University, and included Mark Van Doren, Jacques Barzun, Clifton Fadiman, and Mortimer J. Adler. In 1948, President James Bryant Conant of Harvard University published *General Education in a Free Society*, recommending that great literature be integral to humanities courses. Everyone in the Chicago Canon is represented in *Great Quotations* except those marked with an asterisk, who are mostly scientists.

Homer	Plutarch	Calvin
Aeschylus	Tacitus	Montaigne
Sophocles	Nicomachus*	W. Gilbert
Herodotus	Epictetus	Cervantes
Euripides	Ptolemy	Bacon
Thucydides	M. Aurelius	Shakespeare
Hippocrates	Galen	Galileo
Aristophanes	St. Augustine	Kepler
Plato	St. Aquinas	W. Harvey
Aristotle	Dante	Hobbes
Epicurus	Chaucer	Descartes
Euclid	Machiavelli	Milton
Archimedes	Erasmus	Molière
Apollonius*	Copernicus	Pascal
Cicero	T. More	Huygens*
Lucretius	Luther	Spinoza
Virgil	Rabelais	Locke

Racine	Comte	Joseph Conrad
Newton	Balzac	Faulkner
Liebniz	de Tocqueville	D. H. Lawrence
Defoe	J. S. Mill	T. S. Eliot
Swift	Darwin	Kafka
Congreve	Dickens	Chekhov
Berkeley	C. Bernard*	O'Neill
Montesquieu	Kierkegaard	Henry James
Voltaire	Marx	Kipling
Fielding	George Eliot	J. Dewey
Johnson	Melville	A. N. Whitehead
Hume	Dostoevsky	B. Russell
Rousseau	Flaubert	Santayana
Sterne	Ibsen	E. Gibson
Adam Smith	Tolstoy	J. P. Sartre
Kant	Twain	Ortega y Gasset
Gibbon	J. W. Dedekind*	Max Planck
Boswell	W. James	Einstein
Lavoisier	Nietzsche	N. Bohr
Goethe	G. Cantor*	E. Schrodinger*
Dalton	Freud	J. H. Woodger*
Hegel	D. Hilbert*	Poincaré*
Austen	T. Veblen	Dobzhansky*
Clausewitz	Keynes	Sorel*
Stendhal	G. B. Shaw	Trotsky
Schopenhauer	James Joyce	W. G. Summer
Faraday	Proust	Max Weber
Lyell	T. Mann	R. H. Tawney

WILLIAM H. HUTT
1899–1988

South African, economist, who called capitalism the "great leveler" because it most benefits workers. Government favoritism in Keynesian interventionist schemes leads to huge inequalities of wealth in developing countries. Hutt attacked Keynesianism in *The Theory of Idle Resources* (1939), a book on the Great Depression.

[Unemployment results from governmental restraints] in defense of private interests, but ultimately appearing to be reasonable and just because it defends an existing and customary distribution.

The Theory of Idle Resources (1939), Forward

E. B. WHITE
1899–1955

American, humorist, essayist at the *New Yorker*, and author of children's books.

The whole duty of a writer is to please and satisfy himself, and the true writer always plays to an audience of one. Let him start sniffing the air, or glancing at the Trend Machine, and he is as good as dead, although he may make a nice living.

In William Strunk Jr., *The Elements of Style*
(1959), ch. 5

I sometimes doubt that a writer should refine or improve his workroom by so much as a dictionary; one thing leads to another and the first thing you know he has a stuffed chair and is fast asleep in it.

LEO STRAUSS
1899–1977

American (German-born), professor of political philosophy at the University of Chicago and the godfather of neoconservatism. He believed in the "natural right" philosophy of Plato and the ancient Romans and that its antithesis, the relativism of modern liberals, leads to nihilism. In *Natural Right and History* he wrote that relativism holds that there are no absolute standards independent of positive law (law made by legislators and judges). Thus, he concludes, "If principles are sufficiently

justified by the fact that they are accepted by a society, the principles of cannibalism are as defensible or sound as those of civilized life."`

Alan Bloom became Strauss's most celebrated academic successor with his *The Closing of the American Mind* (1987), which focused on the injuries to American education and culture by the belief that truth is relative. Another successor, Irving Kristol, became the father of neoconservatism.

ERICH FROMM
1900–1980

American (German-born), psychoanalyst who departed from Freud and developed a "humanist psychology."

The successful revolutionary is a statesman, the unsuccessful one a criminal.
[Book of how totalitarianism exploits loneliness, which is freedom's downside.]

Escape from Freedom (1941)

Man's main task in life is to give birth to himself, to become what he potentially is. The most important product of his effort is his own personality.

Man for Himself (1947)

Destructiveness is the outcome of an unlived life.

Ibid.

There is perhaps no phenomenon which contains so much destructive feeling as "moral indignation," which permits envy or hate to be acted out under the guise of virtue.

In L. R. Frank, *Quotationary* (1999)

The fanatic's pathology is similar to that of a depressed person who suffers…from the incapacity to feel anything. He then acts, thinks and feels in the name of his idol….

May Man Prevail (1961)

Once a doctrine, however irrational, has gained power in a society, millions of people will believe in it rather than feel ostracized and isolated.

Psychoanalysis and Religion (1950), ch. 3

If a society is not healthy, then the neurotic is healthier than those who adapt to the culture.

Free man is by necessity insecure; thinking man by necessity uncertain.

HELEN HAYES
1900–1993

American, actress and writer.

We rely upon the poets, the philosophers, and the playwrights to articulate what most of us can only feel, in joy or sorrow. They illuminate the thoughts for which we only grope; they give us the strength and balm we cannot find in ourselves. Whenever I feel my courage wavering I rush to them. They give me the wisdom of acceptance, the will and resilience to push on.

A Gift of Joy (1965), Introduction

MARGARET MITCHELL
1900–1949

American, *Atlanta Journal Sunday Magazine* roving reporter, who was sidelined by a broken ankle and arthritis. Her husband gave her a ream of paper and told her to write a book. *Gone With the Wind* (1936) has sold 30 million copies; 250 thousand are still sold annually. Adjusted for inflation, the movie has sold a worldwide record of $3.8 billion. Scarlett was first named "Pansy." This was Mitchell's only book.

I'm tired of saying "How wonderful you are!" to fool men who haven't got one-half the sense I've got and I'm tired of pretending I don't know anything, so men can tell me things and feel important while they're doing it….
[Scarlett O'Hara]

Land is the only thing in the world worth working for, worth fighting for, worth dying for, because it's the only thing that lasts. It will come to you, this love of the land.
[Gerald O'Hara to Scarlett]

You kin polish a mule's feets an' shine his hide an' put brass all over his harness an' hitch him ter a fine cah'ige. But he a mule jes' de same. He doan fool nobody.
[Mammy]

What gentlemen say and what they thinks is two different things.
[Mammy]

He isn't received.
[Of Rhett Butler]

I can shoot straight if I don't have to shoot too far.
[Scarlett]

Scarlett: There's nothing to keep us here.
Ashley: Nothing, except honor.
[Scarlett wants to elope to Mexico]

As God is my witness! They're not going to lick me. I'm going to live through this and when it's all over, I'll never be hungry again. No, nor any of my folk.
[Scarlett]

I've got to go to a political meeting.
[Frank Kennedy.]

Frankly, my dear, I don't give a damn.
[Rhett to Scarlett. David O. Selznik paid $5,000 to the Motion Picture Production Code to keep "damn" in the script.]

I can't think about that right now. If I do, I'll go crazy. I'll think about that tomorrow. I'll think of some way to get him back. After all, tomorrow is another day.
[Scarlett's closing words.]

ANTOINE DE SAINT-EXUPÉRY
1900–1944

French, aviator and novelist, who exalted in risk-taking. A World War II aviator, he was listed as missing in action in 1944.

Let a man in a garret but burn with enough intensity, and he will set fire to the world.
Wind, Sand, and Stars (1939)

Love does not consist in gazing at each other but in looking together in the same direction.
Terre des Hommes (1939)

Pure logic is the ruin of the spirit.
Flight to Arras (1942), ch. 2,
tr. Lewis Galantière

A smile is often the key thing. One is

paid with a smile. One is rewarded with a smile. One is brightened by a smile. And the quality of a smile can make one die.
Lettre à un Otage (1944)

A rock pile ceases to be a rock pile the moment a single man contemplates it, bearing within him the image of a cathedral.

R. J. RENIER
1900?

Dutch, historian.

Nationality exists only in the minds of men. Outside men's minds there can be no nationality, because nationality is a manner of looking at oneself not an entity. This awareness, this sense of nationality, this national sentiment, is more than a characteristic of the nation. It is nationhood itself.
"The Criterion of Dutch Nationhood," An
Inaugural Lecture of University College,
London (June 4, 1945)

ADLAI STEVENSON
1900–1965

American, senator, Democratic nominee for president in 1952 and 1956. When told by an admirer that all the thinking people had supported him for president, Stevenson replied, "Yes, but I needed to win a majority." After a speech, an admiring woman told him his speech was "superfluous." He thanked her. Then she inquired when he was going to publish an article he referred to in the speech. He replied, "Posthumously." She said, "Oh, I hope that will be soon."

Communism is the corruption of a dream of justice.

> [Liberals praise Communist ideals and only mildly regret its mass liquidations.]
>
> Speech in Urbana, Illinois (1951)

A liberal will hang you from a lower branch.

> In L. R. Frank, *Wit and Humor Quotationary*

Nixon is the kind of politician who would cut down a redwood tree, then mount the stump for a speech on conservation.

> Ibid.

WHITTAKER CHAMBERS
1901–61

American, editor of the *Daily Worker* and *Time* magazine and a former Communist who exposed Alger Hiss as a Soviet spy. The statute of limitations prevented Hiss from being tried for treason, so he was convicted of perjury in denying he knew Chambers. Chambers produced papers typed on Hiss's typewriter. Chambers had hidden the papers in a pumpkin. His *Witness* (1952), one of the great nonfiction books of the twentieth century, labeled Communism "the focus of concentrated evil of our time."

I know that I am leaving the winning side for the losing side, but it is better to die on the losing side than to live under Communism.

> Un-American Activities Committee
> (August 3, 1948)

[W]hen I took up my little sling and aimed at Communism, I also hit something else. What I hit was the forces of that great socialist revolution which, in the name of liberalism, spasmodically, incompletely, somewhat formlessly, but always in the name of direction, has been inching its ice cap over the nation for two decades.

> *Witness* (1952)

[Why a German Communist became an anti-Communist:] ...one night, in Moscow, he heard screams. That's all. Simply one night he heard screams.... What Communist has not heard those screams? They come from husbands torn forever from their wives in midnight arrests. They come, muffled, from the execution cellars of the secret police, from the torture chambers of the Lubianka, from all the citadels of terror now stretching from Berlin to Canton. They come from those freight cars loaded with men, women and children, the enemies of the Communist State, locked in, packed in, left on remote sidings to freeze to death at night in the Russian winter. They come from minds driven mad by the horrors of mass starvation ordered and enforced as a policy of the Communist state. They come from the starved skeletons, worked to death or flogged to death in the freezing filth of sub-arctic labor camps. They come from children whose parents are suddenly, inexplicably, taken away from them—parents they will never see again.

> Ibid.

HIROHITO
1901–89

Japanese, emperor. Historians differ over how much authority Hirohito had over Japan's decision to go to war. After the war, he repudiated the quasi-divine status of emperors. His posthumous name was Shöwa, or "Enlightened Peace." His son, Crown Prince Akihi, broke a fifteen-hundred-year tradition by marrying a commoner.

[The war] has developed not necessarily to Japan's advantage.... We have resolved to endure the unendurable and suffer what is insufferable.... Unite your total strength to be devoted to the construction for the future. Cultivate the ways of rectitude, nobility of spirit, and work with resolution so that you may enhance the innate glory of the Imperial State and keep pace with the progress of the world.
[Message on August 15, 1945, to the Japanese announcing Japan's surrender in World War II. Across Japan, the people wept and asked the emperor's forgiveness for their not trying hard enough.]

ENRICO FERMI
1901–54

American (Italian-born), physicist, who designed the first atomic reactor.

Whatever nature has in store for mankind, unpleasant as it may be, man must accept, for ignorance is never better than knowledge.
Atoms in the Family

MARGARET MEAD
1901–78

American, anthropologist, who wrote in *Coming of Age in Samoa* (1928) that young Samoans were promiscuous and not restrained by "monogamy, exclusiveness, jealousy and undeviating fidelity." She extolled Samoa's "vision of the infinite variety of sexual patterns and the enormous plasticity of human nature." But, Derek Freeman's *The Fateful Hoaxing of Margaret Mead* showed that the Samoan girls had told Mead whatever she wanted to hear to feed her bias that most gender differences are culturally derived. Free love was actually alien to Samoan culture. Most feminism feeds on Mead's erroneous conclusions that female fulfillment is unrelated to biological imperatives and that human nature is highly malleable. Mead's work was also part of the crusade of American anthropologist Franz Boas (1858–1942) to deny all significant genetic differences between the races.

No one is hurried along in life or punished harshly for slowness of development. Instead the gifted, the precocious, are held back, until the slowest among them have caught the pace.
Coming of Age in Samoa (1928), ch. 13

Never doubt that a small group of thoughtful, committed citizens can change the world; indeed, it's the only thing that ever has.
In L. R. Frank, *Quotationary* (1999)

WILLIE SUTTON
1901–80

American, bank robber, who stole more than $2 million from banks.

Why rob banks? Because that's where they keep the money.
[He denied making this statement.]

ERIC HOFFER
1902–83

American, San Francisco longshoreman, and autodidact philosopher, who plumbed the psychology of the leaders and followers of the Nazi and Communist mass movements in *The True Believer* (1951). He believed that people who are disappointed in their lives are tempted to submerge themselves into larger causes.

> All mass movements, however different in doctrine...appeal to the same types of mind...the true believer—the man of fanatical faith who is ready to sacrifice his life for a holy cause. The frustrated predominate among the early adherents of all mass movements.
>
> *The True Believer: Thoughts on the*
> *Nature of Mass Movements* (1951)

> The burning conviction that we have a holy duty toward others is often a way of attaching our drowning selves to a passing raft. What looks like giving a hand is often a holding on for dear life. Take away our holy duties and you leave our lives puny and meaningless.
>
> Ibid.

> Mass movements can rise and spread without belief in god, but never without belief in a devil....the genius of a great leader consists in concentrating all hatred on the ideal devil.
>
> Ibid.

> The less justified a man is in claiming excellence for his own self, the more ready he is to claim all excellence for his nation, his religion, his race or his holy cause.
>
> Ibid.

People who bite the hand that feeds them usually lick the boot that kicks them.

> Ibid.

> The fanatic cannot be weaned away from his cause by an appeal to his reason or moral sense.... He cannot be convinced, but only converted.
>
> In L. R. Frank, *Quotationary* (1999)

> It is not actual suffering but the taste of better things which excites people to revolt.
>
> Ibid.

> It is not the wickedness of the old regime [the masses] rise against but its weakness.
>
> Ibid.

> Our credulity is greatest concerning the things we know least about. And since we know least about ourselves, we are ready to believe all that is said about us. Hence the mysterious power of both flattery and calumny.
>
> *The Passionate State of Mind and*
> *Other Aphorisms* (1954)

> We probably have a greater love for those we support than for those who support us. Our vanity carries more weight than our self-interest.
>
> Ibid.

> Rudeness is the weak man's imitation of strength.
>
> Ibid.

> It is not love of self but hatred of self which is at the root of the troubles that afflict our world.
>
> Ibid.

The weakness of a soul is proportionate to the number of truths which must be kept from it.

> Ibid.

Power corrupts the few, while weakness corrupts the many.

> *The Ordeal of Courage* (1963)

To have a grievance is to have a purpose in life.

> Ibid.

To dispose a soul to action we must upset its equilibrium.

> *The Ordeal of Change* (1964)

Scratch an intellectual and you find a would-be aristocrat who loathes the sight, the sound, and the smell of common folk.

> *First Things, Last Things* (1970)

The hostility, in particular of the scribe, towards the merchant is as old as recorded history.

> In F. A. Hayek, *The Fatal Conceit* (1988)

It is easier to love humanity than to love your neighbor.

> Interview, Eric Sevareid, CBS, (November 14, 1967)

A nation without malcontents is orderly, peaceful, and pleasant, but perhaps without the seed of things to come.

A compilation of what outstanding people said or wrote at the age of twenty would make a collection of asinine pronouncements. The creative mind is the playful mind.

SYDNEY HOOK
1902–89

American, philosophy professor, a Marxist who became a conservative. His *Hero in History* defined two types of heroes. The "Eventful Hero" is like the Dutch boy who places his finger in the dike—anyone could do it. The "Event-Making Hero" is "someone who by extraordinary traits of character or intelligence…has largely shaped the viable alternatives of action between which he chooses, alternatives that but for him would probably not have emerged." Such heroes can be villains, such as Lenin, or freedom-loving, such as Reagan.

I was guilty of judging capitalism by its works and socialism by its literature.

> *Out of Step* (1987)

RAY KROC
1902–84

American, founder of McDonald's. At age fifty-four, while peddling Mix-Masters, he discovered the McDonald brothers' hamburger joint was always busy due to great french fries and quick service (limited menu wrapped in paper). He partnered with the McDonalds in 1955 and twenty years later had 4,000 restaurants (29,000 by 2001). Kroc concentrated on making food while his CFO Harry Sonneborn often rescued the company from bankruptcy and made an art of franchising. Franchises of simple businesses are more profitable than company-owned businesses. The best franchisees are working-class people without MBA degrees who mortgaged their limited assets to buy their initial franchises.

It's easy to have principles when you're rich. The important thing is to have principles when you're poor.

Grinding It Out: The Making of
McDonalds (1977)

OGDEN NASH
1902–71

American, humorous poet.

Candy is dandy
But liquor is quicker.
"Reflections on Ice-breaking," *Hard Lines*
(1931)

The turtle lives 'twixt plated decks
Which practically conceal its sex.
I think it clever of the turtle
In such a fix to be so fertile.
Ibid., "The Turtle"

A bit of talcum
Is always walcum.
"The Baby," *Free Wheeling* (1931)

The cow is of the bovine ilk;
One end is moo, the other, milk.
Ibid., "The Cow"

Duty, oh duty,
Why are thou not a
Sweetie or a cutie?
Untitled (1935)

The camel has a single hump;
The dromedary, two;
Or else the other way around,
I'm not sure. Are you?
"The Camel" (1936)

Dogs display reluctance and wrath
If you try to give them a bath.

They bury bones in hideaways
And half the time they trot sideaways.
"An Introduction to Dogs," *I'm a Stranger*
Here Myself (1938)

There was a young belle of old Natchez
Whose garments were always in patchez
When comment arose
On the state of her clothes,
She drawled, When Ah itches, Ah
scratches!
Ibid., "Requiem"

One day he missed his loving bride.
She had, the guide informed him later,
Been eaten by an alligator.
Professor Twist could not but smile.
'You mean,' he said, 'a crocodile.'
"The Purist," *The Face is Familiar* (1941)

The trouble with a kitten is THAT
Eventually it becomes a CAT.
Ibid., "The Kitten"

He tells you when you've got on too
much lipstick,
And helps you with your girdle when
your hips stick.
"The Perfect Husband," *Versus* (1947)

My garden will never make me famous,
I'm a horticultural ignoramus,
I can't tell a string bean from a soybean,
Or even a girl bean from a boy bean.
"He Digs, He Dug, He Has Dug"

The old men know when an old man
dies.
"Old Men"

How confusing the beams from memory's
lamp are;
One day a bachelor, the next a grandpa.

What is the secret of the trick?
How did I get so old so quick?
"Preface to the Past," *You Can't Get There
from Here* (1957)

People who work sitting down get paid
more than people who work standing up.

KARL R. POPPER
1902–94

British (Austrian-born), philosopher who
argued that a scientific hypothesis is only
validated by the "falsiability" criterion.
That is, to be scientific a theory must make
predictions concrete enough to be proved
wrong if the claim is, in fact, not true. He
rejected Marxism, astrology, and psychoanalysis as not being scientific. He favored
democracy because its trial and error
approach is more scientific than revolutionary change. Popper also propounded
the Law of Unintended Effects. Popper
said history is affected by the growth of
science, which cannot be predicted, so history cannot be predicted.

> Every scientific statement must remain
> tentative forever.
> In Chambers *Dictionary of Quotations*
> (1998)

In so far as a scientific statement speaks
about reality, it must be falsifiable: and in
so far as it is not falsifiable, it does not
speak about reality.
Ibid.

JOHN STEINBECK
1902–68

American, novelist, Nobel Prize for literature 1962. He was famous for poignant
stories about the poor, such as *Cannery
Row* (1944) and *East of Eden* (1952). In the
novella *Of Mice and Men* (1937), George
Milton protects his fellow migrant worker,
Lennie Small, a simpleton. After Lennie
accidentally kills a girl who is trying to
seduce him, George lovingly executes Lennie with a pistol to prevent a lynch mob
from taking him.

In his masterpiece *The Grapes of Wrath*
(1939), the quintessence of "proletarian
realism," Steinbeck fulfilled what he considered the writer's mission, to wit, "set
down his time as nearly as he can understand it" and "serve as the watchdog of
society… to satirize its silliness, to attack
its injustices, to stigmatize its faults." The
novel is an attack against capitalism as it
recounts the trek of the Joad family from
the Oklahoma Dust Bowl to the migrant
farmer camps of California, where they
can earn only subsistence wages. After
Rose's baby is born dead, she volunteers
her milk to a famished man, so Ma concludes, "Use' ta be the fambly was fust. It
ain't so now. It's anybody. Worse off we
get, the more we got to do." Tom Joad Jr.
must flee for killing a policeman who had
killed his mentor, Jim Casey. Before fleeing, Tom comforts Ma:

> Well, maybe like Casey says, a fellow
> ain't got a soul of his own, but on'y a
> piece of a big one—an then—…Then it
> don' matter. Then I'll be all aroun' in the
> dark. I'll be everywhere—wherever you
> look. Wherever they's a fight so hungry

people can eat, I'll be there. Wherever they's a cop beatin' up a guy, I'll be there. If Casey knowed, why, I'll be in the way guys yell when they're mad an'—I'll be in the way kids laugh when they're hungry an' they know supper's ready. An' when our folks eat the stuff they raise an' live in the houses they build—why, I'll be there. See?

Grapes of Wrath (1939), ch. 28

Unless the bastards have the courage to give you unqualified praise, I say ignore them.

[Comment about critics.]

In J. K. Galbraith, *The Affluent Society* (1977), Introduction

A sad soul can kill you quicker, far quicker, than a germ.

Travels with Charley (1962)

The profession of book-writing makes horse racing seem like a solid, stable business.

Accepting the Nobel Prize, *Newsweek* (December 24, 1962)

COUNT GALEAZZO CIANO
1903–44

Italian, Mussolini's foreign minister, who was executed by Hitler.

Victory has a hundred fathers, but defeat is an orphan.

Diary (September 9, 1942)

KENNETH CLARK
1903–83

English, art historian.

However complex and solid [civilization] seems, it is actually quite fragile. It can be destroyed. What are its enemies? Well, first of all fear—fear of war, fear of invasion, fear of plague and famine, that make it simply not worthwhile constructing things, or planting .... And then exhaustion, the feeling of hopelessness.... [Civilization] requires confidence—confidence in the society in which one lives, belief in its philosophy, belief in its laws.... Vigor, energy, vitality; all the great civilizations have had a weight of energy behind them. People sometimes think that civilization consists in fine sensibilities and good conversation and all that. They can be among the agreeable results of civilization, but they are not what make a civilization...

Civilization (1969)

[I]t is lack of confidence, more than anything else, that kills a civilization. We can destroy ourselves by cynicism and disillusion, just as effectively as by bombs.

Ibid.

CYRIL CONNOLLY
1903–74

English, critic, novelist, and founder of the book series *Horizon*.

Whom the gods wish to destroy they first call promising.

Enemies of Promise

In the sex-war, thoughtlessness is the weapon of the male, vindictiveness of the female.

The Unquiet Grave

The man who is master of his passions is Reason's slave.

LOU GEHRIG
1903–1941

American, baseball player, Hall of Fame.

I may have been given a bad break, but I have an awful lot to live for. With all this, I consider myself the luckiest man on the face of the earth.

[On retiring from the Yankees on Lou Gehrig's Appreciation Day, July 4, 1939, due to an illness—Lou Gehrig's Disease, which took his life two years later.]

CLARE BOOTHE LUCE
1903–1987

American, editor of *Vanity Fair*, playwright, congresswoman, and America's first female ambassador to a major country, Italy. A perceptive public policy analyst and polemicist, she helped put backbone in the American conservative movement. An illegitimate child whose mother was a prostitute, she used her brilliance, acerbic wit, "drenching beauty," and incredible will to raise herself from poverty to write a smash hit for Broadway, become editor of a major magazine, and marry one of the most powerful men in America.

I don't like older women who get a crush on girls....

[Resigning from the National Woman's Party in 1923.]

In Sylvia Jukes Morris, *Rage for Fame*,(1997)

When I came into the world it was the horse-and-buggy, wood-and-coal-burning, gas-lit, ice-chest, pump-handle, out-house and tin-bathtub era...The prevailing smells were wood smoke, coal dust, gas, horse manure and human waste.

Ibid.

When one's mother dies, one suddenly ceases to be a child.

Ibid.

When one becomes even such a minor public character as myself, one is beset on all sides by people who want to get at one for this, that, or the other thing. One must adopt a "high hat" air... or simply be nibbled away at like a piece of cheese by hundreds of hungry little mice...

Ibid.

No good deed goes unpunished.

Attributed by William Safire, *New York Times* (January 9, 1994)

Whenever a Republican leaves one side of the aisle and goes to the other, it raises the intelligence quotient of both parties.

In L. R. Frank, *Quotationary* 1999)

Courage is the ladder on which all the other virtues mount.

Ibid.

Widowhood is one of the fringe benefits of marriage.

MALCOLM MUGGERIDGE
1903–90

English, journalist, humorist, and editor of *Punch*. In 1932 as a young, quasi-communist, the *Manchester Guardian* sent him to Moscow. In six months he was sending anti-Communist dispatches detailing the Great Famine, the casual murder of thousands, and the cowardice of Western journalists not reporting the truth. The *Guardian* did not print his articles, so he resigned. He became a talking head on the BBC. Like T. S. Eliot, he felt Western culture would disintegrate if Christianity fell to the atheists or to the liberal Protestants.

> *Copulo, ergo sum.*
> > *Esquire* (December 1970)

> They flocked there in an unending procession, from the great ones like Shaw and Gide and Harold Laski and the Webbs, down to the poor little teachers, crazed clergymen and millionaires, and driveling dons; all utterly convinced that, under the aegis of the great Stalin, a new dawn was breaking in which the human race would at last be united in liberty, equality, and fraternity for evermore…. They were prepared to believe anything, however preposterous; to overlook anything, however villainous; to approve anything, however brutally authoritarian, in order to be able to preserve in tact the confident expectation that one of the most ruthless and bloody tyrannies ever to exist on earth could be relied on to champion human freedom, the brotherhood of man, and all the other good liberal causes to which they had dedicated their lives.
> > "The Great Liberal Death Wish" (1970)

Freud and Marx…undermined the whole basis of Western civilization…by promoting the notion of determinism, in the one case in morals, in the other in history, thereby relieving individual men and women of all responsibility for their personal and collective behavior.

> > Ibid.

> All that I can claim to have learnt from the years I have spent in this world is that the only happiness is love, and that the world itself only becomes the dear and habitable dwelling place it is when we who inhabit it know we are migrants, due when the time comes to fly away to other more commodious skies.
> > *The Green Stick*, ch. 1

Copulation without population is the liberal goal.

ANAÏS NIN
1903–77

American (French-born), feminist, novelist of erotica, and famous for her diaries.

> Life shrinks or expands in proportion to one's courage.
> > *The Diary of Anaïs Nin* (1966)

> We don't see things as they are, we see them as we are.

GEORGE ORWELL
1903–50

English, anti-utopian novelist who fought in Spain for a socialist militia, the POUM, but fled to avoid being shot by the Communists. His *Homage to Catalonia* charged that the Communists were liquidating their leftist rivals. Given the climate, few critics would review his book or stores sell it. George Will said that the century's most influential author was Orwell, C. S. Lewis, or Solzhenitsyn.

Orwell's masterpiece is *1984* (1949), which, like Hayek's *The Road to Serfdom*, argues that utopia cannot be put into practice without tyranny. Big Brother runs the one-party, murderous state of Oceania from London, which is in perpetual war with Eurasia and Eastasia. Public hate sessions are held to denounce the party heretic, Goldstein. Everything is opposite of what it seems: the Ministry of Peace wages war, the Ministry of Truth rewrites history, and the Ministry of Love tortures. The term "Orwellian" signifies a suffocating tyranny and pervasive social conformity.

An agent provocateur solicits Winston Smith to read a conspiratorial tract, which leads to his arrest and re-education by O'Brien. O'Brien says, "We are not content with negative obedience…. When finally you surrender to us, it must be of your own free will." Winston is placed in Room 101, a torture chamber where each prisoner faces his carefully ferreted out greatest fear (rats for Winston). Winston is not shot until he truly loves Big Brother.

Reminiscent of Stalin's show trials, in the cellars of the Ministry of Love a prisoner says:

"Of course I'm guilty!" cried Parsons with a servile glance at the telescreen. "You don't think the Party would arrest an innocent man, do you?… Between you and me, old man, I'm glad they got me before it went any further. Do you know what I'm going to say to them when I go up before the tribunal? I'm going to say,

'thank you for saving me before it was too late.'"

Orwell's *Animal Farm* (1945) is a savage satire of Stalin (the Berkshire boar) and the USSR. Many publishers rejected it because it attacked Stalin. New York's Dial Press rejected it (wink) on the grounds that animal stories would not sell. The animals at Manor Farm overthrow farmer Jones and promulgate a constitution establishing equality. But after the pigs take over, its seven articles are reduced to just one article, "All animals are equal, but some animals are more equal than others."

He was an embittered atheist (the sort of atheist who does not so much disbelieve in God as personally dislike Him)….
Down and Out in Paris (1933), ch. 30

The high-water mark of socialist literature is W. H. Auden, a sort of gutless Kipling.
The Road to Wigan Pier (1937), ch. 11

BIG BROTHER IS WATCHING YOU!
1984 (1949), pt. 1, ch. 1

War is peace. Freedom is slavery. Ignorance is strength.
[Slogans of the Ministry of Truth.]
Ibid.

Who controls the past controls the future; who controls the present controls the past.
Ibid., ch. 3

Don't you see that the whole aim of Newspeak is to narrow the range of thought? In the end we shall make thoughtcrime literally impossible, because there will be no words in which to express it.

Ibid., ch. 5

Do you know that Newspeak is the only language in the world whose vocabulary gets smaller every year?

Ibid.

Doublethink means the power to hold two contradictory beliefs in one's mind and accept both of them.

Ibid., pt 2., ch. 9

Power is not a means; it is an end. One does not establish a dictatorship in order to safeguard a revolution; one makes the revolution in order to establish the dictatorship. The object of persecution is persecution. The object of torture is torture. The object of power is power.

Ibid., pt. 3, ch. 3

If you want a picture of the future, imagine a boot stamping on a human face—forever.

Ibid.

He wears a mask, and his face grows to fit it.

In L. R. Frank, *Quotationary* (1999)

I'm fat, but I'm thin inside. Has it ever struck you that there's a thin man inside every fat man, just as they say there's a statue inside every block of stone?

Coming Up for Air (1939), pt. 1, ch. 3

By bringing the whole life under the control of the State, Socialism necessarily gives power to an inner ring of bureaucrats, who in almost every case will be men who want power for its own sake and will stick at nothing in order to retain it.

In L. R. Frank, *Quotationary* (1999)

One ought to be able to hold in one's head simultaneously the two facts that Dali is a good draughtsman and a disgusting human being. The one does not invalidate or, in a sense, affect the other.

In *Chambers Dictionary of Quotations* (1996)

When one sees highly educated men looking on indifferently at oppression and persecution, one wonders which to despise more, their cynicism or their shortsightedness.

"The Prevention of Literature"

The sin of nearly all left-wingers from 1933 onwards is that they have wanted to be anti-Fascist without being anti-totalitarian.

One effect of the ghastly history of the last twenty years has been to make a great deal of ancient literature seem much more modern….Tamerlane and Genghis Khan seem credible figures now, and Machiavelli seems a serious thinker, as they didn't in 1910.

We sleep safely in our beds because rough men stand ready in the night to visit violence on those who would do us harm.

We have now sunk to a depth at which restatement of the obvious is the first duty of intelligent man.

BENJAMIN SPOCK
1903–98

American, pediatrician, whose baby book has been translated into thirty languages.

> What good mothers and fathers instinctively feel like doing for their babies is best after all.
>> *The Common Sense Book of Baby and Child Care* (1946), ch. 1

> Perhaps a child who is fussed over gets a feeling of destiny, he thinks he is in the world for something important and it gives him drive and confidence.
>> *New York Sunday News* (May 11, 1958)

> Inhibition is not unnatural…civilizations are built on restraints.
>> *New York Times* (November 4, 1970)

> Biologically and temperamentally… women were made to be concerned first and foremost with child care, husband care, and home care.
>> In an article by Barbara Dickered, *Issues* (1979)

GEORGE BALANCHINE
1904–83

American (Georgian-born), founded the American School of Ballet in 1933, a chief choreographer of the New York City Ballet.

> I don't want people who want to dance. I want people who have to dance.

SALVADOR DALI
1904–89

Spanish, most prominent of the surrealists, who sought to paint the "greater reality" of man's subconscious mind over his reason. His paintings were dreamworlds in which commonplace objects were deformed or out of place, albeit painted realistically, such as his limp, melting watches in *The Persistence of Memory* (1931). He became a flamboyant and highly successful self-promoter.

> [Dali was asked if it were difficult to paint. He said:]
> No. It's either easy or impossible.

> [Dali's wife asked him to paint a screen being used to hide a radiator in their home. He painted a picture of a radiator on the screen.]
>> *The Little, Brown Book of Anecdotes* (1985), Clifton Fadiman, ed.

DENG XIAOPING
1904–97

Chinese, dominant statesman after Mao Tse-tung died in 1976. He introduced capitalism to China as "a socialist market economy."

> Yellow cat, black cat, as long as it catches mice, it is a good cat!
>> [Deng was purged for this capitalist speech. After Mao's death, Deng was rehabilitated and indirectly led the Communist Party. His Four Modernizations of 1978 enabled the economy to grow at 9 percent: rural incentives, private enterprise, slash central direction, and spark foreign direct investment.]
>> Speech (1962)

Let some people get rich first.

Communists had guaranteed subsistence income for all: "iron rice bowl." Deng realized that to raise China out of poverty there would have to be uneven development where some people, regions, and sectors got rich while others remained impoverished. The alternative was perpetual egalitarian stagnation in poverty.

China knows Communism is anachronistic, but democracy is alien to 2,500 years of Confucian culture. Also, Russia in 1991 became a democracy first, and it is having difficulties creating a market economy. China wants to create a market economy first, like Hong Kong, Taiwan, and South Korea, whose authoritarian politics guided free markets through the extreme social dislocations of industrialization. Henry Rowen of the Hoover Institute argues that nations become democratic only after per capita income reaches $6,000: Greece, South Korea, and Spain are examples.

> Not a single country in the world, no matter what its political system, has ever modernized with a closed-door policy.
> 1982 speech. Quoted by Lucian W. Pye in
> *Asian Power and Politics* (1985)

An American watching 200 Chinese build a dam with shovels, said one bulldozer could do the work faster. The Chinese host said that would create unemployment. The American responded, "Oh, if you want employment rather than a dam, take back their shovels and issue them spoons."

CLIFTON FADIMAN
1904–99

American, writer, critic, and chief executive officer of the Book-of-the-Month Club. His *American Treasury* (1955) contains wonderful anecdotes; many are included in *Great Quotations*.

> The mama of dada.
> [Of Gertrude Stein.]
> *Party of One* (1955)

> When you reread a classic you do not see more in the book than you did before: you see more in you than there was before.
> *Any Number Can Play* (1957)

> The German mind has a talent for making no mistakes but the very greatest.

CARY GRANT
1904–86

American (British-born), actor in seventy-two movies, including: *The Philadelphia Story*, *Bringing Up Baby*, and *North By Northwest*. He only won an oversight Oscar.

> I pretended to be somebody I wanted to be until finally I became that person. Or he became me. Everybody wants to be Cary Grant. Even I want to be Cary Grant.

> [Response to telegram "How old Cary Grant?"]
> Old Cary Grant fine. How you?

GEORGE F. KENNAN
1904–2005

American, U.S. minister in Moscow, whose "Long Telegram" warned that Soviet Communism was dedicated to destroying American democracy and was "impervious to the logic of reason." The telegram was condensed into a 1947 article in *Foreign Affairs*, signed "Mr. X." In it Kennan outlined a strategy of "containing" the USSR "by the adroit and vigilant application of counterforce at a series of constantly shifting geographical and political points, corresponding to the shifts and maneuvers of Soviet policy." But, he sought to use only moral force. He opposed: using military force, the Truman Doctrine (aid to resist Communist subversion), NATO, the Korean and Vietnam Wars, Pershing missiles in Europe, and antiballistic missiles. A Democrat, he endorsed "moderate socialism" and unilateral disarmament. Diplomats like Acheson, Dulles, Rusk, and Kissinger had the backbone to contain the USSR with military force.

J. ROBERT OPPENHEIMER
1904–67

American, suspected Soviet spy, physicist, and director of the Manhattan Project, which developed the atomic bomb at Los Alamos, New Mexico. He made an atomic bomb to combat fascism, but refused to make a hydrogen bomb to counter Communism. Seeing the first explosion, he recited:

> If the radiance of a thousand suns
> Were to burst at once in the sky

That would be the splendor of the
Mighty One.
I am become Death
The destroyer of worlds.

Bhagavad-Gita

THEODORE SEUSS GEISEL (DR. SEUSS)
1904–91

American, maybe the best writer/illustrator of children's books. He wrote *Green Eggs and Ham* (1960), a book using only fifty words. In America today, only the *Bible* is read more than Dr. Seuss.

> I meant what I said
> And I said what I meant…
> An elephant's faithful
> One hundred percent.
>
> *Horton Hatches the Egg* (1940)
> [Maisy, a bird, asked Horton, an elephant, to sit on her egg for a few minutes. Horton warms the egg all winter while Maisy flies south. When it hatches, the hatchling looks more like an elephant and it wants to stay with Horton—bad science, great story.]

> The day they decided that Sneetches are Sneetches
> And no kind of Sneetch is the best on the beaches.
> That day, all the Sneetches forgot about stars
> And whether they had one, or not, upon thars.
>
> *Sneetches* (1953), last stanza

> For I live by a rule
> That I learned as a boy back in South-Going School.

Never budge! That's my rule. *Never budge
in the least!*
*Not an inch to the West, not an inch to the
East.*
I'll stay here, not budging! I can and I
will
If it makes you and me and the whole
earth stand still!"
> [In 1661 in the Hague, when the
> French and Spanish ambassadors
> met on a narrow bridge, they stood
> face-to-face until the town council
> cut off the bridge's railings to allow
> them to pass on equal terms.]
> *The Zax* (1953), st. 6

I do not like green eggs and ham, I do
not like them, Sam-I-Am.
> *Green Eggs and Ham* (1960)

He snapped, "I'm the Lorax who speaks
for the trees
Which you seem to be chopping as fast
as you please."
> [The "Once-ler" cut the "Truffula"
> trees to make "Thneeds" in a pollut-
> ing factory that killed the fish and
> the "Bar-ba-loots."]
> *The Lorax* (1971)

Adults are obsolete children.
> *Time* (May 7, 1979)

You have brains in your head.
You have feet in your shoes.
You can steer yourself
Any direction you choose…
Congratulations!
Today is your day.
You're off to great places!
You're off and away!…
You'll be on your way up!
You'll be seeing great sights!

You'll join the high fliers
who soar to high heights…
And somehow you'll escape
any waiting and staying.
You'll find the bright places
where Boom Bands are playing.
> "Oh: The Places You'll Go"

Maybe Christmas, the Grinch thought,
doesn't come from a store.
> *The Grinch Who Stole Christmas*

B. F. SKINNER
1904–90

American, psychologist, who reportedly
raised one of his daughters in a box, was
a disciple of Pavlov. Skinner's mechanistic
"behaviorism" argues that environmental
rewards shape behavior. Curiously, the
most powerful reinforcers of behavior are
those that are inconsistent. Skinner's "pro-
grammed learning" still has a following
among progressive educators.

The real question is not whether machines
think, but whether men do.
> *Contingencies of Reinforcement* (1969)

RAYMOND ARON
1905–83

French, political scientist, and philosopher. He denounced intellectuals who
were "merciless toward the failings of the
democracies but ready to tolerate the worst
crimes as long as they are committed in the
name of the proper doctrines."

Marxism is the opiate of the intellectuals.
> Quoted in *Time* (July 9, 1979)

Political thought, in France, is retrospective or utopian.

L'opium Des Intellectuals (1955), ch. 1

ARTHUR KOESTLER
1905–83

British (Hungarian-born), a Communist who became an anti-Communist due to Stalin's purges in the 1930s. His *Darkness at Noon* (1940) and *Arrival and Departure* (1943) give the best descriptions of the totalitarian mind, and they trace the similarities between fascism and Communism. *Darkness at Noon* describes a show trial where a Bolshevik deviationist, Rubashov, is purged. The horror is that Rubashov confesses a fictional crime to the Grand Inquisitor *without having been tortured*.

Noting that leftists deny their gulags, Koestler said, "Clinging to the last shred of the torn illusion is typical of the intellectual cowardice that prevails on the left."

The definition of the individual was: a multitude of one million divided by one million.

Darkness at Noon (1940) "The Grammatical Fiction" pt. 2

A writer's ambition should be…to trade a hundred contemporary readers for ten readers in ten years' time and for one reader in a hundred years.

In *New York Times Book Review* (April 1, 1951)

Every creative act involves…a new innocence of perception, liberated from the cataract of accepted belief.

The Sleepwalkers (1959)

The principal mark of genius is not perfection but originality, the opening of new frontiers.

AYN RAND
1905–82

American (Russian-born), goddess of "heroism and achievement," libertarian whose "objectivism" glorifies unfettered capitalism as the most efficient and moral system because it is voluntary. Her *Capitalism: The Unknown Ideal* (1967) answers the charges against capitalism. Selfishness is good, but it means pursuing your welfare by rationalism, not by harming others. Happiness is pride in one's achievements as one plays by objective rules. She said that envy was socialism's taproot.

Civilization is the progress toward a society of privacy. The savage's whole existence is public, ruled by the laws of his tribe. Civilization is the process of setting man free from men.

The Fountainhead (1943)

But what is freedom? Freedom from what? There is nothing to take man's freedom away from him, save other men. To be free, a man must be free of his brothers.

Anthem (1946)

My happiness is not the means to any end. It is the end. It is its own goal. It is its own purpose. Neither am I the means to any end others may wish to accomplish. I am not a tool for their use.

Ibid.

Atlas Shrugged (1957) may be the most widely read novel by college students, although it is seldom found in a syllabus. It opens with the question, "Who is John Galt?" Hank Rearden, the steel industrialist hero, joins John Galt, an inventor, in a strike of talented entrepreneurs. That crashes the economy and eventually the socialist government. That happened in the Soviet Union where risk-takers were selected out of the economy so industry focused only on maintaining the status quo.

> We are on strike against the creed of unearned rewards and unrewarded duties. We are on strike against the dogma that the pursuit of one's happiness is evil. [Rearden.]
>
> *Atlas Shrugged* (1957)

> [A] trader is a man who earns what he gets and does not give or take the underserved. A trader does not ask to be paid for his failures, nor does he ask to be loved for his flaws. ...[T]he mystic parasites who have, throughout the ages, reviled the trader and held him in contempt, while honoring the beggars and the looters, have known the secret motive of the sneers: a trader is the entity they dread—a man of justice.
>
> Ibid., speech of John Galt

In *Atlas Shrugged*, a bureaucrat, Dr. Floyd Ferris, explains to Hank Rearden that government controls citizens with its proliferating laws.

> We are after power and we mean it. There is no way to rule innocent men. The only power any government has is the power to crack down on criminals. Well, when there aren't enough criminals, one makes them. One declares so many things to be a crime that it becomes impossible for men to live without breaking laws.

America's abundance was created not by public sacrifices to "the common good," but by the productive genius of free men.

Upper classes are a nation's past; the middle class is its future.

LIONEL TRILLING
1905–75

American, radical literary critic, who nevertheless criticized liberalism for lacking any defense against totalitarianism, which recognizes no authority but the state. Liberalism's materialism and relativism cannot resist totalitarianism's paganism without a "moral imagination," which he said could be found in T. S. Eliot's moral and cultural sensibilities. He also warned against the dangers of a progressive's righteousness.

> Some paradox of our natures leads us, when once we have made our fellow men the objects of our enlightened interest, to go on to make them the objects of our pity, then of our wisdom, ultimately of our coercion.
>
> "Manners, Morals, and the Novel" (1947), in *The Liberal Imagination* (1950)

> In the United States at this time liberalism is not only the dominant but even the sole intellectual tradition.
>
> *The Liberal Imagination* (1950)

JEAN-PAUL SARTRE
1905–80

French, Nobel Prize for literature in 1964. A pro-Stalinist Marxist, he claimed Communist terror could be the midwife of humanism. He identified the existing order as "institutionalized violence," which justified using violence to overthrow it. The 1975 Cambodian genocide was hatched by seven disciples of his doctrine of "necessary violence." He advised hushing-up about the gulag so that the French workers would remain Communists. He demonized the U.S. as "the enemy of mankind."

Sartre in *Being and Nothingness* (1943) held that there is no God, so there is no meaning to life. Humans create their own meaning by their decisions. One can be a democrat, Nazi, or Communist—all are equally valid. In *Saint Genet*, Sartre celebrated a thief who lived according to the moral code he had chosen, so he was a saint.

Existence comes before essence [meaning]. We are defined not by nature but by our choices, even though all of us are limited in our choices.

Life was "absurd," so he felt "angst" at the "human condition." The only certainty is we are free and responsible, so we should not act in "bad faith *(mauvaise foi)*," the self-deceptive motives by which people often try to elude responsibility."

> Man is nothing else but that which he makes of himself. That is the first principle of existentialism.
>
> *Existentialism and Humanism* (1948), tr.
> Philip Mairer

> Man is condemned to be free. Condemned, because he did not create himself, yet is nevertheless at liberty, and from the moment he is thrown into this world he is responsible for everything he does.
>
> Ibid.

> The rebel is careful to preserve the abuses from which he suffers so that he can go on rebelling against them.
>
> *Baudelaire* (1947)

> She believed in nothing; only her skepticism kept her from being an atheist.
>
> *Les Mots* (1964), "Lire"

ROBERT PENN WARREN
1905–89

American, poet and novelist. A Southern "fugitive poet," he cherished tradition, agrarianism, and courtly manners. His most popular novel, *All the Kings Men* (1946), was about Huey Long.

> The poem is not a thing we see—it is, rather, a light by which we may see—and what we see is life.
>
> *Saturday Review* (March 22, 1958)

> Poets are terribly sensitive people and one of the things they are most sensitive about is cash.

HANNAH ARENDT
1906–75

American (German-born), whose *The Origins of Totalitarianism* (1951) argued that Communism and Nazism were similar terrorist movements that massacred millions not for what they *did*, but for who they *were*—Jews or bourgeoisie. The political spectrum features Communists and Nazis on the far left with the same objective, "social justice," and democrats favoring limited government on the far right.

Stalin called Hitler a "fascist" to conceal that Hitler was just another breed of radical socialist.

Arendt's *The Life of the Mind* argues that most people are capable of evil and will commit atrocities. Adolph Eichmann, who deported Jews to the death camps, symbolized the "banality of evil." She feared that a modern terror state could achieve permanence by reeducating its citizens. But the 1956 Hungarian Revolution affirmed "that human nature is unchangeable." She said the appeal of Communism is due to "pervasive, public stupidity."

Evelyn Waugh in 1938 anticipated Arendt's thesis with, "Barbarism is never finally defeated; given propitious circumstances, men and women who seem quite orderly will commit every conceivable atrocity. We are all potential recruits for anarchy. Unremitting effort is needed to keep men living together at peace; there is only a margin of energy left over for experiments, however beneficent."

> The banality of evil.
> *Eichmann in Jerusalem*, (1963), ch. 15

> The deeds were monstrous, but the doer...was quite ordinary, commonplace, and neither demonic nor monstrous.
> *The Life of the Mind*

> The rootless are always violent.

MILGRAM EXPERIMENTS

Yale psychologist Stanley Milgram's 1963 Milgram Experiment supports Arendt's thesis. Fake doctors asked volunteer teachers to help fake students learn words by administering electrical shocks when stu-dents made errors in memory. After being advised by doctors to turn the voltage way up, 65 percent of teachers increased the voltage as students screamed out loud. Two-thirds of us, when ordered by an apparent authority, will commit atrocities.

In the 1950s in the Solomon Asch Experiment, eight people, seven of whom were plants, were asked which two lines of four lines on a screen were the same length. The plants deliberately chose a wrong combination. One-third of the volunteers eventually gave up their individual judgments and went along with the views of the seven plants.

SAMUEL BECKETT
1906–89

Irish, playwright, novelist, and poet of malaise who immortalized the "theater of the absurd" with *Waiting for Godot* (1955) and the even more intense *Endgame* (1958). In *Godot*, two tramps, Estragon and Vladimir, appear on an empty stage (a country road), although they are sometimes accompanied by Pozzo and Lucky. They assume they are there for a purpose and they decide it is to wait for Godot. A boy comes twice saying Godot will come tomorrow. But there is no evidence that Godot made an appointment or even that there is anyone named Godot. They consider hanging themselves but decide it would be more prudent to wait for Godot. One critic said that in the play, "Nothing happens twice."

In *Endgame*, the blind autocrat Hamm learns in his wheelchair from his servant, Clov, about the people dying about him in a savage, disintegrating world. In the novel *Murphy* (1938), Beckett describes the disposal of Murphy's ashes after they are scattered on a saloon floor from a paper sack:

By closing time the body, mind and soul of Murphy were freely distributed over the floor of the saloon; and before another day the earth had been swept away with the sand, the beer, the butts, the glass, the matches, the spits, the vomit.

We are not saints, but we have kept our appointment. How many people can boast as much?
Waiting for Godot (1955), act 2

We give birth astride of a grave; the light gleams an instant, then it's night again.
Ibid.

Try again. Fail again. Fail better.

SIR JOHN BETJEMAN
1906–84

English, poet laureate (1972) of melancholy and nostalgic verse.

Gracious Lord, oh bomb the Germans,
Spare their women for Thy Sake,
And if that is not too easy
We will pardon Thy Mistake.
But, gracious Lord, whatev'er shall be,
Don't let anyone bomb me.
"In Westminster Abbey," 1940

And is it true? And is it true,
This most tremendous tale of all,
Seen in a stained-glass window's hue,
A Baby in an ox's stall?
The Maker of the stars and sea
Become a Child on earth for me?
A Few Late Chrysanthemums (1954),
"Christmas," st. 1

SOICHIRO HONDA
1906–91

Japanese, founder of Honda Motor Company. He defied Japan's Ministry of International Trade and Investment (MITI), which wanted to limit Japan to three auto manufacturers. After World War II, Honda made stoves in his house while his wife bicycled into town to sell eggs. After he attached a motor to her bicycle, many neighbors wanted one—whence Honda Motor Company. When he had less than a dozen employees assembling motorbikes, each Saturday he exhorted them "Take pride in your work. We are building a global transportation company." He wrote to eighteen-thousand bicycle shops in Japan praising their founders' courage in starting their businesses. He challenged them to summon a similar courage to sell motorcycles.

Success can only be achieved through repeated failure and introspection. In fact, success represents the one percent of your work which results only from the 99 percent that is called failure.

JOHN HUSTON
1906–87

American, actor, director, and screenwriter of *The Maltese Falcon*, a 1941 film from a 1930 novel by Samuel Hammett, father of hard-boiled detective fiction, whose protagonist was Sam Spade.

That, sir, is a matter that calls for delicate judgment. In the heat of action, we may forget where our best interests lie.
Sidney Greenstreet in *The Maltese Falcon*

ARISTOTLE S. ONASSIS
1906–75

Greek, industrialist.

The secret in business is to know something that nobody else knows.

If women didn't exist, all the money in the world would have no meaning.

JACQUES BARZUN
1907

American (French-born), professor of history and dean at Columbia University who opposed early specialization in undergraduate education. He defined a "real book" as a book that one wants to reread. Insights from his *From Dawn to Decadence* (2000), a survey of the last five hundred years of Western civilization, are sprinkled liberally throughout *Great Quotations*. He called the West a "mongrel civilization par excellence" because it borrowed widely from others. Its distinctive feature is the rights enjoyed by every citizen and alien. He fears that Western pluralism may disintegrate into separatism.

Every teacher and prospective teacher should read Barzun's *Teacher in America* (1944).

> Science is…a faith as fanatical as any in history.
> *Science: The Glorious Entertainment* (1964)

> But when we speak of Socrates, Jesus, Buddha, and "other great teachers of humanity,"…the politician's power begins to look shrunken and mean.
> *Teacher in America* (1944)

> …the only thing worth teaching anybody is a principle. Naturally principles involve facts and so some facts must be learned bare…
> Ibid.

> Above the beginner's level, the important fact is that writing cannot be taught exclusively in a course called English Composition. Writing can only be taught by the united efforts of the entire teaching staff.
> Ibid.,

> All serious reading should be done pencil in hand, with a book whose ownership allows of its being marked up.
> Ibid.

> The blind boys tend to think their achievement so remarkable that they should earn Phi Beta Kappa with B's when others need A's…. The crippled, the one-lunged, the foreign-born with imperfect knowledge of English, must similarly be kept from warping, from indemnifying themselves at the expense of the very currency of praise or honor which they seek…. The bending of the rules must only affect practical details—an extension of time, a special examination, extra hours of tutoring—anything of this kind, and nothing that damages the prize worked for.
> Ibid.

> …the damning of consequences, upon which all really great success is built.
> Ibid.

> It is true that as a general rule, girls are less interested than boys in theory, in ideas, in the logic of things and events….

Girls are more conscientious and hardworking....

Ibid.

The criterion for awarding [scholarship] funds should be, not the need of the student for a college education, but the need of the college and the country for top-notch students.

Ibid.

[Needs of the artist:]
One of these is the absence of noise—hence intellectual work is best done at night and sleep during the day. Another is continuity of work when the fit is on. Hence regular meals are a nuisance. A third is the need of space, closely allied to keeping the workbench in *status quo* while work is in progress—hence the housekeeper's poking and tidying is a cause of war. Again, the need for long incubation is an inescapable fact—hence the princely use of leisure and the disinclination for "regular work" have a meaning. Whitman has told us of the long period of "loafing" that preceded the writing of *Leaves of Grass*. This necessity knows no law except that in producers, loafing is productive; and no creator, of whatever magnitude, has ever been able to skip that stage, any more than a mother can skip gestation.

Ibid.

[Classics] are books for the most part addressed to other men and not to experts.

Ibid.

AL CAPP
1907–79

American, cartoonist of L'il Abner and Daisy Mae in Dogpatch.

A product of the untalented, sold by the unprincipled to the utterly bewildered.
[On abstract art.]
National Observer (July 1, 1962)

RACHEL L. CARSON
1907–64

American, "mother of environmentalism." Her *The Silent Spring* (1962) blamed DDT as a toxic blight on birds and people. Yet there has never been a documented case of human illness from the accepted use of pesticides. Due to Carson making DDT taboo, 60 million have died from malaria. 300 million people suffer from malaria annually.

Over increasingly large areas of the United States, spring now comes unheralded by the return of the birds, and the early mornings are strangely silent where once they were filled with the beauty of bird song.
The Silent Spring (1962)

MARY COYNE CHASE
1907–81

American, dramatist, whose *Harvey* became a 1950 classic film about a "pooka," Harvey, which was a six-foot, three-inch invisible white rabbit friend of Elwood P. Dowd, a simpleton played by Jimmy Stewart. A pooka is an Irish spirit that is mischievous, but not malevolent.

My regards to you and to anyone else you run into.
[Elwood P. Dowd]

Harvey (1950), film

Miss Kelly, when you wear my flower, you make it beautiful.
[Elwood P. Dowd]

Ibid.

And as I talked to her, I would hold her soft white hand and she would say, "Poor thing, you poor, poor thing."
[The psychiatrist's wish was to lie on a couch and have a woman repeat the above.]

Ibid.

LEWIS F. POWELL, JR.
1907–98

American, associate justice (1972–78).

The guarantee of equal protection cannot mean one thing when applied to one individual and something else when applied to a person of another color. If both are not accorded the same protection, then it is not equal.

Regents of the University of California v. Bakke (June 28, 1978)

NATHAN MARCH PUSEY
1907–2001

American, educator, president of Harvard University (1953–71).

The best teacher is not life, but the crystallized and distilled experience of the most sensitive, reflective, and most observant of our human beings, and this

experience you will find preserved in our great books and nowhere else.

ROBERT ARDREY
1908–80

American, anthropologist, author of *The Territorial Imperative* (1966).

In most but not all territorial species the female is sexually unresponsive to an unpropertied male.

The principal cause of modern warfare arises from the failure of an intruding power correctly to estimate the defensive resources of a territorial defender. The enhancement of energy engendered in the defender acts to multiply the apparent resources of a defending nation.

P. McKellar showed that aggression grows greater if it does not draw retaliation.

The need for security must be greater in prey animals than in predators, in the female than in the male...in the unpropertied than in the propertied, in the Omega fish than in the Alpha, in the unstable society than in the stable.

SIMONE DE BEAUVOIR
1908–86

French, Marxist godmother of radical feminism, lesbian, and "life-companion" of existentialist Jean-Paul Sartre. She wrote *The Second Sex* (1949), which argues that many women find advantages in femininity and do not revolt because men imposed passivity on them in their childhood. For self-realization, women must transcend motherhood. Marriage has become "an obscene bourgeois institution." She wanted women to act like men: She exalted maleness in that "risking life" was superior to "giving life." She glorified working women and she wanted state institutions to raise all children.

Beauvoir preferred promiscuity to marriage and child rearing. She served John-Paul Sartre, not as a lover, but as a pimp of teenage girls, including her students. The ugly, five-foot-tall Sartre never gave Beauvoir any property and left all of his papers, including Beauvoir's letters to him, to his mistress.

One is not born a woman, but rather becomes one.

The Second Sex (1949)

Abortion brings woman into full humanity—the sex that kills is the one that is honored.

Ibid.

A free individual blames only himself for his failure; he assumes responsibility for them. But everything happens to women through the agency of others, and therefore these others are responsible for her woes.

[Beauvoir denies existentialism by denying that women are responsible for their choices. She wants the state to coerce women to make the choices that she prefers.]

Ibid.

No woman should be authorized to stay at home and raise her children. Society should be totally different. Women should not have that choice, precisely because if there is such a choice, too many women will make that one.

Interview with Betty Friedan, "Sex, Society, and the Female Dilemma," *Saturday Review* (June 14, 1975)

As long as the family and the myth of the family...have not been destroyed, women will still be oppressed.

JACOB BRONOWSKI
1908–74

English (Polish-born), mathematician, humanist, and BBC broadcaster

Man is a singular creature. He has a set of gifts which make him unique among animals; so that, unlike them, he is not a figure in the landscape—he is a shaper of the landscape.

The Ascent of Man (1973), ch. 1

Among the multitude of animals which scamper, fly, burrow and swim around us, man is the only one who is not locked into his environment. His imagination, his reason, his emotional subtlety and toughness, make it possible for him not to accept the environment but to change it. And that series of inventions, by which man from age to age has remade his environment, is a different kind of evolution—not biological, but cultural evolution. I call that brilliant sequence of cultural peaks the ascent of man.

Ibid.

The notion of discovering an underlying order in matter is man's basic concept for exploring nature. The architecture of things reveals a structure below the surface, a hidden grain which, when it is laid bare, makes it possible to take natural formations apart and assemble them in new arrangements.

Ibid., ch. 2

The modern problem is no longer to design a structure from the materials, but to design the materials for a structure.

Ibid.

The most powerful drive in the ascent of man is his pleasure in his own skill.

Ibid.

We come from the womb still as embryos.

Ibid., ch. 13

The longest childhood has been civilization.

Ibid.

...only a tiny fraction of all that talent that mankind produces is actually used.

Ibid.

Man masters nature not by force but by understanding.

"The Creative Mind," *Science and Human Values* (1956)

BETTE DAVIS
1908–89

American, actress.

Discipline is a symbol of caring to a child. He needs guidance. If there is love, there is no such thing as being too tough with a child.

The Lonely Life (1962), ch. 9

If you have never been hated by a child, you have never been a parent.

JOHN K. GALBRAITH
1908–2006

American, elitist economist, whose *The Affluent Society* (1958) argued that advertising led to too much private spending and too little government spending. He hated vulgar American dolts buying cars and moving to the suburbs rather than living in cities and using public transportation. He accused advertisers of creating "artificial needs." Paul Johnson said that was like criticizing Monet for creating an artificial need for impressionist paintings. He opined in 1984, "The Soviet system has made great economic progress because in contrast with the Western industrial economies it makes full use of its manpower."

When Galbraith awkwardly skied down a hill, William F. Buckley Jr. asked how long he had been skiing. Galbraith said thirty years. Buckley replied, "About as long as you've been an economist."

All successful revolutions are the kicking in of a rotten door.

The Age of Uncertainty (1977), ch. 3.

Very specific and personal misfortune awaits those who presume to believe that the future is revealed to them.

LYNDON BAINES JOHNSON
1908–73

American, thirty-sixth president (1963–69) called "Landslide Lyndon" for his congressional victory by 83 votes. After losing in the first count, in the recount 202 Johnson votes were found, and miraculously they had been cast in perfect alphabetical order. Like Wilson in 1916 and Roosevelt in 1940, Johnson campaigned in 1964 on a peace platform. His military strategy for Vietnam was "graduated response," that is, he "sent signals" to North Vietnam with slightly increasing intensity rather than use overwhelming force. SAM missiles killed U.S. pilots while Johnson's "rules of engagement" prohibited suppressing SAM missile sites for fear of hurting a Russian.

> We are not about to send American boys ten thousand miles away from home to do what Asian boys ought to be doing for themselves.
>
> > [*The Pentagon Papers* show that LBJ had approved plans to send four hundred thousand more soldiers to Vietnam when he was pledging not to send any more. Thus the saw, "They said that if I voted for Goldwater we would have a big war in Vietnam. I voted for Goldwater, and sure enough we had a big war in Vietnam."]
> >
> > Campaign speech (October 21, 1964)

LBJ's War on Poverty was inspired by Marxist Michael Harrington's *The Other America* (1961), which argues there is "an under-developed nation" in the U.S. resulting from poor housing and so on. Thus, those in it are not responsible. Johnson's Great Society was an attempt to complete the New Deal. But George Gilder in *Wealth and Poverty* (1981) summarized the failure of the Great Society:

> What actually happened since 1964 was a vast expansion of the welfare rolls that halted in its tracks an ongoing improvement in the lives of the poor, particularly blacks, and left behind...a wreckage of broken lives and families worse that the

aftermath of slavery....poverty is less a state of income than a state of mind and the government dole blights most of the people who come to depend on it.

> Better to have him inside the tent pissing out, than outside pissing in. [Of J. Edgar Hoover.]
>
> > In D. Halberstam, *The Best and the Brightest* (1971) ch. 21

> I can teach the earth as round or flat. [Response to a question on evolution when interviewing for a job as a teacher.]
>
> > In Tom Wicker, *One of Us* (1991)

> Being president is like being a jackass in a hailstorm: There's nothing to do but stand there and take it.
>
> > In L. R. Frank, *Wit and Humor Quotationary*

> If one morning I walked on top of the water across the Potomac River, the headline would read: PRESIDENT CAN'T SWIM.
>
> > Ibid.

> Doing what is right is easy. The problem is knowing what is right.

> I'm going home where they know when you're sick and care when you die.

In public, Lyndon Johnson loved to quote Isaiah 1:8: "Come now, let us reason together." In private, he may have quoted the rest of that passage: "But, if ye refuse and rebel, ye shall be devoured by the sword."

OTTO KERNER JR.
1908–76

American, educator.

> Our nation is moving toward two societies, one black, one white—separate and unequal.
>
> Report of the National Advisory Commission on Civil Disorders (1968) p. 1

ABRAHAM H. MASLOW
1908–70

American, psychologist. He said that man's needs are hierarchical, rising from physical needs, to safety needs, to social needs, to self-esteem, to self-actualization (accomplishing one's potential). As lower needs are satisfied, man turns toward higher needs. You motivate by offering to satisfy a person's next level of unmet needs.

> A musician must make music, an artist must paint, a poet must write, if he is to be ultimately at peace with himself. What a man can be, he must be.
>
> *Motivation and Personality* (1954)

> When your only tool is a hammer, every job looks like a nail.

> A first-rate soup is better than a second-rate painting.

JOSEPH RAYMOND McCARTHY
1908–57

American, senator. He had been a Democratic judge who voted four times for Roosevelt, but he ran for the Senate in 1946 as a pro civil rights, liberal Republican. Arthur Herman wrote the definitive work, *Joseph McCarthy* (2000), on which this analysis is based.

> In my opinion the State Department, which is one of the most important government departments, is thoroughly infested with Communists. I have here in my hand fifty-seven cases of individuals who would appear to be either card carrying members or certainly loyal to the Communist Party, but who nevertheless are still helping to shape our foreign policy.
>
> Speech, Wheeling, West Virginia (February 9, 1950)

Only 40 of the 57 were later proven to be Communists so McCarthyism became the byword for imprecise and unproved political charges.

EDWARD TELLER
1908–2003

American (Hungarian-born), nuclear physicist known as the "father of the hydrogen bomb."

> [When asked if President Reagan's "Star War's" antiballistic missile defense system would work, he responded:]
> I don't know. I do know if you work only on things you know will work you are going to get nowhere.
>
> *Forbes* (May 17, 1999)

SIR ISAIAH BERLIN
1909–97

English (Russian-born), historian at Oxford.

> Liberty is liberty, not equality or fairness or justice or human happiness or a quiet conscience.
>
> "Two Concepts of Liberty," note. In Alison Jones, ed., *Chambers Dictionary of Quotations* (1998)

> Certainly no society will be wholly secure, wholly safe on rocklike foundations, while philosophers are allowed to roam at large. But their suppression will kill liberty too. That is why all the enemies of freedom, like the Communists and Fascists, automatically round up intellectuals and make them their first victims...
>
> "Philosophy and Government Repression" in *The Sense of Reality* (1966)

> Those who believe that final truths may be reached, that there is some ideal order of life on earth which may be attained, that all that is necessary is to establish it, by whatever means, whether peaceful or violent—all those who believe that such finality, whether of life or of thought and feelings, is in principle attainable will, however benevolent their desires, however pure their hearts, however noble and disinterested their ideals, always end by repressing and destroying human beings in their march towards the Promised Land [whether they be "secular Utopians or theocratic bigots"].
>
> Ibid.

12

MANAGEMENT IN THE INFORMATION AGE

Management innovations have occurred all along the way, like the thirteenth-century Italian bill of exchange (birth of banking) and the fifteenth century inventions: double-entry bookkeeping (Venice) and the limited liability corporation (Florence). But only in the late nineteenth century did management become a "science" with Frederick Taylor's "time and motion" industrial engineering. His "scientific management" called for management and labor not to fight over shares, but to cooperate to increase the size of the pie. Taylor also said, "Working smarter is better than working harder."

By the twentieth century, corporations were organized top-down in pyramids, like the army. Managers planned the work, organized it, and controlled it through the hierarchy. They organized work into simple, repetitive tasks so workers on moving assembly lines using interchangeable parts generated huge productivity gains through "mass production" over the old "craft production," in which skilled workmen slowly fitted parts together.

In the 1970s, Japanese "lean production" substituted management and technology for mass production's control over semi-skilled workers. For example, shipping lumber in a container ship displaced 98.5 percent of the labor that had been needed to load and unload a freighter of lumber.

Americans responded to the new competition by increasing the speed of product innovation, which slashed product life cycles. Entrepreneurial firms rapidly innovated new product generations, which overwhelmed Japanese *kaizen* (the incremental improvements to existing products). Americans disassembled vertically integrated companies and conglomerates, slashed staffs, abandoned long-term planning, eliminated layers of management, and sold divisions not vital to core competencies. Between 1974 and 1998, the production of the one hundred largest companies fell from 36 percent to 17 percent of United States' GNP. George Gilder explained the decentralized paradigm made possible by new information technologies:

> Rather than pushing decisions up through the hierarchy, the power of microelectronics pulls them remorselessly down to the individual. This is the law of the microcosm.
>
> *Microcosm* (1989)

Information technology (IT) now drives globalization by mooting geography—a fax circles the globe in an eighth of a second. Many businesses must become globally competitive even if they operate only in local markets. E-commerce enlarges markets and increases competition. And, as Walter Wriston said, "Money and ideas" now travel around the world at the speed of light to "where they are welcome" and "stay where they are well treated."

A World Bank 2001 study noted that the twenty-four developing countries (3 billion people) that doubled the ratio of trade to GNP over the past two decades increased their per capita income by a whopping 5 percent per annum in the 1990s. But, in a nonglobalizing group of 2 billion people, per capita income fell 1 percent per annum in the 1990s. Contrary to the charge that globalization creates inequality, it is due to globalization that living standards are converging among globalized economies.

In the Information Age, the winning nations are open to global markets, minimize government overhead, maintain sound currencies, and maintain high educational standards, especially for bright students. Peter Drucker said, "There will be no more 'poor' countries, only 'ignorant' countries."

In an information economy, additional supply often costs less per unit, not more. For example, the first unit of software may cost millions and copies pennies. When costs fall as supply increases, products quickly become commodities, so one must increase innovation to stay profitable. Everything must be speeded up, so it must be decentralized. Innovative products need temporary monopoly pricing power, per Lawrence Summers:

> An information-based world is one in which more of the goods that are produced will have the character of pharmaceuticals or books or records, in that they involve very large fixed costs and much smaller marginal costs…. [This] means the only incentive to produce anything is the possession of temporary monopoly power—because without that power…the high initial fixed costs cannot be recouped.

THE INFORMATION ECONOMY

1. It is a biome with unpredictable avalanches of speciation and extinction. Organize for robustness, not for optimal returns under existing conditions.

2. Knowledge has replaced "land, labor, and capital" as the chief economic resource. Knowledge workers are capital. And what is decisive is not how much capital is invested, but its productivity.

3. Companies must focus, because superior information is the key to competitiveness, and one has superior information only where one is focused.

4. Vertical integration is obsolete. Knowledge is so expensive and specialized it cannot be afforded or kept current unless it is used constantly. Also, because the Internet has cut the cost of integrating processes, there is less need for vertical integration.

5. Follow-the-leader strategies are disastrous when product life cycles are short.

6. States with high wages and low unemployment have jobs with the shortest life spans. Governments that protect low-value-added jobs will maximize both their unemployment and their low-paying jobs.

7. In 1943, 40 percent of the U.S. workforce was in manufacturing. By 2002, it was 14 percent, yet the U.S. was far wealthier in 2002 than it was in 1943 when more workers were in manufacturing. Due to innovation, fewer workers can manufacture more.

8. U.S. per capita income in 1970 was 10 percent greater than in the other advanced industrial nations; by 2000 the gap was 22 percent.

9. None of the top fifty transformational inventions in the past century came from an industry leader; for example, IBM did not invent the personal computer.

10. Just as in the past, due to the economies of scale, most new technology companies will fail; a few category-dominating winners will reign.

In the twenty-first century the United States and China will vie for economic leadership. America's trumps are its individualistic culture and its risk-embracing immigrants, from its early Scottish pioneers to recent Indian engineers. China's Confucian culture, which stresses community and rule by the dictates of the wise (opposite of the rule of law), so hobbled the development of China that it was discovered by Portugal, not vice-versa. Yet, since 1978 a new Chinese blend of capitalism and community has fostered 9 percent per annum growth. In 2005 its economy was eight times larger than it was in 1978.

China is as aggressive as America in using technology—China plans to build sixty nuclear power plants! China, including Hong Kong, has the third-largest economy, albeit about the one-hundredth in terms of GDP per capita. In many Southeast Asian states, the Chinese are 3 percent of the population but own 60 percent of the wealth. Hong Kong, Singapore, and Taiwan are wealthy developed nations.

Jacques Barzun in *From Dawn to Decadence* (2000) argued that separatism is the strongest global trend: "The ideal of Pluralism had disintegrated into Separatism. One partisan of the new goal put it, 'Salad Bowl is better than melting pot.' " Today's 191 nations (up from 58 in 1950) may become 500 nations in the twenty-first century given the separatism trend; for example, Quebec, Chechnya, Bretons, Basques, and so on. Separatism is fueled by two forces: the fall in external security threats

due to there being more democracies, and economic globalization that allows small states, like Singapore, to be competitive. But, as Frank Ogden said, "As the planet globalizes, groups tribalize."

Peter F. Drucker
1909–2005

American (Austrian-born), the "father of management," who discovered that management is neither art nor science, but a practice that can be learned. His consulting for organizations was his laboratory where he gained the insights for his real work of writing forty books about management. He believed that highly skilled people are the most important resources. He discovered: "knowledge worker," "management by objectives," "flat organization," and "privatization." In 1945 his book on General Motors introduced the organizational principle of decentralization in contrast to command and control. He discovered the three essential business questions: "What is our business? Who is our customer? What does the customer consider valuable?" He said, "Management is about human beings. Its task is to make people capable of joint performance, to make their strengths effective and their weaknesses irrelevant."

Drucker's skill was distilling truth out of complexity and expressing it simply. For example, he asked the directors of a billion-dollar service company conglomerate what was their business? None of them knew that their business was training and developing semiskilled workers. He said, "I never see anything in the future. I look for things that have already happened, but have not yet been perceived." He believed management's most difficult task is to balance continuity with change.

The secret to Drucker's insights into society and management was his profound understanding of economics. He rejected Keynesianism, for example, "excess savings," "equilibrium," "aggregate demand," and the like.

> The economy is biological rather than mechanistic in nature. The innovator is the true subject of economics. Entrepreneurs that move resources from old and obsolescent to new and more productive employments are the very essence of economics and certainly of a modern economy....

> My greatest strength as a consultant is to be ignorant and to ask questions.

> Don't tell me what you are doing Rick, tell me what you stopped doing.

> Successful enterprises create the conditions to allow their employees to do their best work.

> Whenever you see a successful business, someone once made a courageous decision.

> There is only one valid definition of business purpose: to create a customer.
> *The Practice of Management* (1954)

> [Managers should ask:] What is our business? What will be our business? And, What should be our business?

> [A manager] sets objectives, organizes, motivates and communicates, measures, and develops people.
> Ibid.

1. Resources and results exist outside, not inside, the business.
2. Results come from exploiting opportunities, not from solving problems.
3. Results do not go to minor players in a given market, but to leaders.
4. Leadership is not likely to last [unless steered toward new opportunities].
5. What exists is getting old [everything must be re-thought periodically].
6. [10 percent of effort gives 90 percent of results; thus, reallocate resources.]
7. To achieve economic results, concentrate on decisive opportunities.
   Managing for Results (1964)

> Working on the right things is what makes knowledge work effective.
> *The Effective Executive* (1966), ch. 1

> The important and relevant outside events are often qualitative and not capable of quantification. They are not yet "facts." For a fact is an event somebody has defined, has classified and above all, has endowed with relevance. To be able to quantify, one has to have a concept first. The truly important events on the outside are not the trends. They are changes in the trends. These determine ultimately success or failure of an organization and its efforts. Such changes, however, have to be perceived; they cannot be counted, defined, or classified.
> Ibid.

> Effectiveness is a habit; that is, a complex of practices. And practices can always be learned.
> Ibid.

Five Habits of Effective Leadership:

1. Work systematically at managing time. Time is the limiting factor.
2. Focus on results.
3. Build on strengths, yours and those of your superiors, colleagues and subordinates.
4. Concentrate on the few areas where superior efforts will produce out-standing results.
5. Find the right general strategies, rather than concentrate on raz-zle-dazzle tactics.

Ibid.

In human affairs, the distance between the leaders and the average is a constant. If leadership performance is high, the average will go up.
[The four-minute mile, an age-old barrier, was broken in 1954 by Roger Bannister. In the next year, thirty-seven runners broke it.]

Ibid., ch. 4

It is the duty of the executive to remove ruthlessly anyone…who consistently fails to perform with high distinction. To let such a man stay on corrupts the others.

Ibid.

If there is any one "secret" of effective-ness, it is concentration. Effective execu-tives do first things first and they do one thing at a time.

Ibid., ch. 5

[The critical personnel questions are:]
1. What has the person done well?
2. What does he need to use his strengths?
3. Would I want my son or daughter to work for this person?

Ibid.

Efficiency is concerned with doing things right. Effectiveness is doing the right things.

Management, Tasks, Responsibilities, Practices (1974), ch. 2

Integrity is the one absolute requirement of managers.

Ibid., ch. 28

The understanding that underlies the right decision grows out of the clash and conflict of opinions and out of the serious consideration of competing alternatives.

Ibid., ch. 29

Even the most competent management bats, at best 0.300 in the innovation area, with one real success for every three tries.

Managing in Turbulent Times (1980)

But a time of turbulence is also one of great opportunity for those who can understand, accept and exploit the new realities.

Ibid.

In turbulent times, liquidity is more important than earnings.

Ibid.

Once 85 percent of national income goes to employees, the labor union has lost its original rationale: that of increasing the share of national income that goes to the "wage fund." All one labor union can do is increase the share of its members at the expense of other employees.

Ibid.

To blame a promotion that fails on the promoted person, as is usually done, is no more rational than to blame a capital investment that has gone sour on the money that was put into it.

Ibid.

The single minded ones, the monomaniacs, are the only true achievers.

Ibid.

The only things that evolve by themselves in an organization are disorder, friction, and malperformance.

Adventures of a Bystander (1978)

The last buggy whip factory was no doubt a model of efficiency.

Ibid.

For it is the willingness of people to give of themselves over and above the demands of the job that distinguishes the great from the merely adequate organization.

Ibid.

So much of what we call management consists in making it difficult for people to work.

Ibid.

Salvation by society failed the most where it promised the most, in the communist countries. But it also failed in the West. Practically no government program enacted since the 1950s in the Western world—or in the communist countries—has been successful.

The New Realities (1989), ch. 1

A manager's task is to make the strengths of people effective and their weaknesses irrelevant—and that applies fully as much to the manager's boss as it applies to the manager's subordinates.

Managing for the Future (1992)

But the need to raise the productivity of [semiskilled labor] may be even greater. Unless it is met, the developed world faces increasing social tensions, increasing polarization, increasing radicalization. It may ultimately face a new class war.

Ibid., ch. 13

Innovation depends on what we might call "organized abandonment."'... As long as the patient eliminates there is a chance. But once the bowels and the bladder stop, death does not take long.

Ibid., Afterword

Science-based innovation is actually less reliable, less predictable, and probably less likely to lead to company profits than almost any other sort.

Ibid.

The one unambiguous lesson of the last forty years is that increased participation in the world economy has become the key to domestic economic growth and prosperity.

Managing in a Time of Great Change (1995), ch. 13

The evidence is thus crystal-clear. Modern welfare destroys. It does not build competence; it creates dependence.... The one thing these corrupted and poisoned people have in common is that they are being financially rewarded for staying on welfare and financially penalized for getting off it.

Ibid., ch. 25

There can be no doubt anymore that Neo-Classics work as *economics*. In fact, they work like a wonder drug. As soon as an economy moves toward Free-Market policies—that is, cuts government spending and balances the budget; privatizes government-owned businesses; cuts back or eliminates government regulations and government controls of economic activity; opens its borders to imports and thereby allows competition; eliminates or at least cuts back government restrictions on the movement of money and capital, an economic boom gets going.

Ibid.

[Four parallel entrepreneurial activities:] One is the organized abandonment of products, services, processes, markets, distribution channels and so on that are no longer an optimal allocation of resources. Then any institution must organize for systematic, continuing improvement (what the Japanese call *kaizen*). Then it has to organize for systematic and continuous exploitation, especially of its successes. It has to build a different tomorrow on a proven today. And, finally, it has to organize systematic innovation, that is, to create the different tomorrow that makes obsolete and, to a large extent, replaces even the most successful products of today in any organization.

"Management's New Paradigms," *Forbes*
(October 5, 1998)

The main challenge to information technology in the next 30 years will be to organize the systematic supply of meaningful outside information.

Ibid.

The social and political consequences of the information revolution will greatly outweigh its economic and technological consequences.

Atlantic Monthly, (February 2000)

Not to innovate is the single largest reason for the decline of existing organizations. Not to know how to manage is the single largest reason for the failure of new ventures.

The Essential Drucker (2001)
[A summary of twenty-four management and societal books.]

None of our institutions exists by itself and is an end in itself. Every one is an organ of society and exists for the sake of society.... Business exists to supply goods and services to customers, rather than to supply jobs to workers and managers, or even dividends to stockholders.

Ibid.

If archangels...sat in directors' chairs, they would still have to be concerned with profitability.... The misunderstanding of the nature of profit in our society and deep-seated hostility to profit are among the most dangerous diseases of an industrial society. It is largely responsible for the worst mistakes of public policy.... Profit is a condition of survival. It is the cost of the future, the cost of staying in business.

Ibid.

Whoever is content to rise with the tide will also fall with it.

Ibid.

Objectives must be transformed into work. And work is always specific, always has clear unambiguous, measurable results, a deadline and a specific assignment of accountability.

Ibid.

The foundation of effective leadership is thinking through the organization's mission, defining it, and establishing it, clearly and visibly.... The leader's first task is to be the trumpet that sounds a clear sound.... The second require-ment is that the leader sees leadership as responsibility...[accepts personal respon-sibility for everything that happens or fails to happen. The third requirement is integrity, that is, that he means what he says.]

Ibid.

All effective innovations are breathtak-ingly simple. Indeed, the greatest praise an innovation can receive is for people to say, "This is obvious. Why didn't I think of it?"

Ibid.

Drucker writes in *Managing in the Next Society* (2002) that the challenge of the next century is to maintain the autonomy of institutions. The USSR collapsed for want of autonomy in its institutions. When FDR asked John L. Lewis to call off his coal miners' strike during World War II, Lewis replied, "The president of the United States is paid to look after the interests of the nation; I am paid to look after the inter-ests of the coal miners." That is an example of necessary autonomy.

Drucker said that Douglas McGregor in *The Human Side of Enterprise* (1960) was wrong in saying that there is one best way of managing, to wit, assume all people want to work and only need guidance. Rather, Abraham H. Maslow was right in that different people must be managed dif-ferently. For example, knowledge workers must be managed as associates, not as sub-ordinates. CEOs managing professional workers who are able to job-hop should read Drucker's *Managing The Non-Profit*

Organization (1992). Volunteer workers for nonprofits will quit unless they are given "challenging work" in a "pleasant environment."

Drucker also saw that a new technol-ogy could not replace an old one with its installed equipment, training, and custom-ers unless the new technology is ten times more cost-effective. And, competitors should not try to catch up, but should try to innovate new technologies at least ten times better.

Thirty years from now big universities will be relics. Universities won't survive.

Never promote on an employee's poten-tial, but only on his or her performance.

[Make a decision] no later than you need it, but as late as possible because you always have more information.

Julius J. and Philip G. Epstein and Howard Koch

Americans, screenwriters: *Casablanca*, a 1942 film.

Rick Blaine, American expatriate and proprietor of Cafe Americain—Humphrey Bogart.
Senor Ugarte, European expatriate who has the stolen letters of transit—Peter Lorre.
Capt. Louis Reynaud, senior Vichy Police Prefect in Casablanca—Claude Rains.
Ilsa Lund, wife of Victor Laslow, and former fiancée of Rick—Ingrid Bergman.
Sam, friend of Rick and piano player in

Cafe Americain—Dooley Wilson.
Victor Laslow, underground leader and
husband of Ilsa—Paul Henreid.
Ferrari, competitor night club owner—
Sydney Greenstreet.
Major Strasser, senior German officer in
Casablanca—Conrad Veidt.

Here's looking at you, kid.
[Rick to Ilsa.]

You're right Ugarte, I am a little more
impressed with you.
[Rick to Ugarte.]

How extravagant you are throwing away
women like that. Someday they may
become scarce.
[Louis to Rick.]

Play it, Sam. Play "As Time Goes By."
[Ilsa to Sam.]

Of all the gin joints in all the towns in all
the world, she walks into mine.
[Rick]

Excuse me Captain. Another visa
problem has come up.
[Sergeant]
Show her in.
[Louis]

I'm shocked, shocked to find that gambling is going on here.
[Louis to Rick.]

The problems of the world are not in
my department. I am a saloon keeper.
[Rick to Victor.]

If you don't help us, Victor Laslow will
die in Casablanca.
[Ilsa]

What of it? I'm going to die in Casablanca. It's a good spot for it.
[Rick]

Welcome back to the fight. This time I
know our side will win.
[Victor to Rick.]

Major Strasser has been shot. Round
up the usual suspects.
[Louis to a sergeant.]

Louis, I think this is the beginning of a
beautiful friendship.
[Rick to Louis.]

STANISLAW J. LEC
1909–66

Polish, poet.

Is it progress if a cannibal uses a knife
and fork?
> *Unkempt Thoughts* (1962), tr. Jacek
> Galazka

You will always find some Eskimos willing to instruct the Congolese on how to
cope with heat.
> Ibid.

"Oh to be old again," said a young
corpse.
> L.R. Frank, *Wit and Humor, Quotationary*
> (2000)

When smashing monuments, save the
pedestals—they always come in handy.
> Ibid.

NORTHCOTE PARKINSON
1909–93

English, historian, and author of *Parkinson's Law and Other Studies in Administration*, (1957):

> Parkinson's Law: Work expands so as to fill the time available for its completion.

> Second Law: Expenditure rises to meet income.

> Third Law: Time spent on any item of the agenda will be in inverse proportion to the sum involved.

> Fourth Law: Delay is the deadliest form of denial.

> Fifth Law: Perfection of a planned layout is achieved only in institutions on the point of collapse.

(DAVID) DEAN RUSK
1909–94

American, secretary of state. In 1966 when de Gaulle took France out of NATO and ordered U.S. troops off French soil, Secretary Rusk asked if that included the U.S. soldiers buried in Normandy. In 2003, Colin Powell replied to the charge of empire building in Iraq, "The only land we have ever asked for in return is enough to bury those that did not return."

> One of the best ways to persuade others is with your ears—by listening to them.

JEAN ANOUILH
1910–87

French, playwright known for *Antigone* (1944) and *Becket* (1959). He adapted classical stories.

> There will always be a lost dog somewhere that will prevent me from being happy.
>
> *La Sauvage* (1938), act 3

HAROLD GENEEN
1910–97

American, CEO of ITT who increased sales from $0.76 billion to $22.0 billion!

> In the business world, everyone is paid in two coins, cash and experience. Take the experience first; the cash will come later.
>
> *Managing 1984*, ch. 3, epigraph

MOTHER TERESA
1910–97

Albanian, Roman Catholic nun, founder of the Order of the Missionaries of Charity in Calcutta, India, and Nobel Peace Prize in 1979. Her order operates 280 centers worldwide to serve the aged, lepers, orphans, sick, and dying. She opined that at the Last Judgment our sins will not be enumerated, but the question will be whether we were loving.

> The biggest disease today is not leprosy or tuberculosis, but rather the feeling of being unwanted.

> I don't have to succeed, but I do have to do my duty.

The greatest misery of our time is the generalized abortion of children. It is poverty to decide that a child must die so that you may live as you wish.

PAUL (BEAR) BRYANT
1911–83

American, football coach at the University of Alabama, who won 13 SEC championships and six national championships in 25 years. A huge number of his assistant coaches became head coaches at major universities. Georgia Coach Vince Dooley said, "Coach Bryant has put a lot of people into coaching. But he's put a lot of them out of coaching." John Underwood's biography *Bear* (1974) should be required reading for all MBAs.

> Blanda said when Bryant walked into a room you wanted to stand up and applaud.
>
> *Bear* (1974)

> If you were to ask me if football is a coach's game I'd have to say it is. And always was. And if you were to ask me why some coaches are going to win more than others—why they get their players to win, and why a certain few win consistently, no matter where they coach. I wouldn't tell you if I knew. This is my book you're buying, not my blood. [He does tell!]
>
> Ibid.

> Surround yourself with good people.
>
> Ibid.

> [Bryant did not offer a scholarship to a highly touted prospect, who later failed elsewhere, because in his interview:]
> Not once did he mention anything about winning, about beating somebody.
>
> Ibid.

Bryant said his talent was not motivating players, but identifying motivated players. Yet he found many ways to motivate, such as saying, "Now they'll see what kind of mamas and papas we've got."

Alabamians loved Bryant for his unexcelled ability to "poor mouth." He would call an eleven-and-one season "fair," and even if Alabama was the prohibitive favorite in an impending game, he would just say how proud Alabama was to be there and he hoped Alabama could score.

> Five seconds of total effort, going all out, giving a hundred percent. You oughta be able to hold your hand in a fire that long.
>
> Ibid.

> Treat everybody alike. That's bull. Treat everybody fairly. Everybody is different. If you treat them all alike you won't reach them. Be fair with all of them and you have a chance. One you pat on the back and he'll jump out the window for you. Another you kick in the tail. A third you yell at and squeeze a little. But be fair.
>
> Ibid.

> [UCLA basketball Coach John Wooden said:]
> Don't treat players the same. Treat them the way they deserve to be treated.

> If anything goes bad, I did it.
> If anything goes semi-good, then we did it.

If anything goes real good, then you
did it.
That's all it takes to get people to win
football games.

Ibid.

A tie is like kissing your sister.

Be good or begone.
[Bear's slogan]

MILOVAN DJILAS
1911–95

Yugoslavian vice president, who became
an anti-Communist. Arguing against the
slogan "Better Red than Dead," he said
that if Communism triumphed, living
standards would collapse, which would
foment countless wars and revolutions.

> The strongest are those who renounce
> their own times and become a living part
> of those yet to come.

Land without Justice (1958)

RAYA DUNAYEVSKAYA
1911–87

American, Marxist writer.

> It is not "socialism" which acted as a cata-
> lyst for the Vietnam anti-war movement
> and, indeed, gave birth to a whole new
> generation of revolutionaries, but the
> black revolution which was both catalyst
> and reason….

"We Speak in Many Voices," *Notes on*
Women's Liberation (1970)

NOEL LANGLEY
1911–80

American, screenwriter, whose MGM film
The Wizard of Oz was based on *The Emerald
City of Oz* (1910) by Frank L. Baum (1856
– 1919). Dorothy Gale runs away to protect her dog Toto. Then she is taken by
a tornado to the land of the Munchkins
and Emerald City. Dorothy learns many
lessons, including that to find her heart's
desire, she needn't look any further than
her own back yard "because if it isn't there,
you never lost it in the first place."

> Toto, I've a feeling we're not in Kansas
> anymore.
> [Dorothy]

> Follow the yellow brick road.
> [Munchkins]

> As coroner, I must aver, I thoroughly
> examined her. And she's not only merely
> dead, she's really most sincerely dead.
> [Munchkin coroner]

> Begone, you have no power here.
> [Glinda, Good Witch of the North]

> Pay no attention to that man behind the
> curtain.
> [The Wizard]

> I'm a very good man. I'm just a bad
> wizard.
> [The Wizard]

> There's no place like home; there's no
> place like home.
> [Dorothy]

MARSHALL MCLUHAN
1911–80

Canadian, communications expert who believed information technology was as important as information itself and that technology is not neutral. He predicted television was best suited to politicians who were "cool" and used a "simple, folksy, sincere style of address." Ronald Reagan and Bill Clinton proved it.

The new electronic interdependence recreates the world in the image of a global village.
The Guttenberg Galaxy (1962)

The medium is the message.
Understanding Media (1964), ch. 1

Television brought the brutality of war into the comfort of the living room. Vietnam was lost in the living rooms of America—not on the battlefields of Vietnam.
[The *Wall Street Journal* denied the war was lost due to journalists. Rather it resulted from a loss of faith in a government whose war plans did not include winning.]

McLuhan claimed he missed nothing by reading only the right-hand pages of books.

DAVID M. OGILVY
1911–99

American, advertising executive, who said ads should have a big photo of the product, a long headline, and lots of text to tell consumers why they should buy the product. He said "Darling" had the highest impact of any word.

The consumer isn't a moron; she is your wife.
Confessions of an Advertising Man (1963)
ch. 5

It is the professional duty of the advertising agent to conceal his artifice. When Aeschines spoke, they said, "How well he speaks," but when Demosthenes spoke, they said "Let us march against Philip."
Ibid.

The best leaders are apt to be found among those executives who have a strong component of unorthodoxy in their character. Instead of resisting innovation, they symbolize it.
Ogilvy on Advertising (1983)

If each of us hires people smaller than we are, we shall become a company of dwarfs. But if each of us hires people who are bigger than we are, we shall become a company of giants.
Ibid.

RONALD WILSON REAGAN
1911–04

American, fortieth president (1981–89), the oldest elected president (sixty-nine). According to Dinesh D'Souza's *Reagan* (1997), "Remarkable events occurred during the 1980s: the restoration of economic growth, the curbing of inflation, the end of the gasoline crisis, the technological boom, the beginning of the collapse of Soviet communism, the spread of freedom and democracy around the world."

In the words of Lady Thatcher, Reagan was "the Great Liberator." In the five years before Reagan's inauguration, ten new pro-Soviet regimes were established on three continents. None were established after his inauguration. Reagan, Lady Thatcher, and Pope John Paul II lit the spark of freedom that doomed the Soviet Union. Mikhail Gorbachev, chairman of the Soviet Union's Communist Party, called Reagan a "great president...[who was] instrumental in bringing about the end of the Cold War." The West may have eventually won the Cold War without Reagan, but ending it sooner reduced the risk of a nuclear exchange, and its "peace dividend" has led to a global economic boom ever since.

Reagan transformed the world. When he entered office Communism was on the march worldwide. Democrats, like Samuelson, praised the Soviet economy. But Reagan forecast in 1981, "The West won't contain Communism. It will transcend Communism. It will dismiss it as some bizarre chapter in human history whose last pages are even now being written."

Domestically, Reagan got America back on its 1776 track of limited government and the rule of law. He changed the rules of politics. Since FDR, Democrats had played Santa Claus by initiating spending programs while Republicans had played Scrooge by raising taxes to pay for them. Instead, he supported Robert Mundell's "supply-side" tax cuts, which shifted capital from political beneficiaries to entrepreneurs. Reagan cut the top income tax rate from 70 percent to 28 percent and capped the federal budget at about 20 percent of GNP. Reagan also supported Friedman's hard-money "monetarist" policy, which

ended two decades of rising inflation, although at the cost of a severe recession, through which Reagan "stayed the course."

Under Reagan, the national debt rose by $1.4 trillion, but that debt paid astronomical dividends: It rearmed America, which ended the Cold War and the threat of nuclear annihilation; it reduced inflation from 12.8 percent to 4 percent; it cut mortgage interest rates from 21 percent to 8 percent; it created 16 million net new jobs as the economy grew 35 percent; and it increased U.S. net private assets from $17 to $33 trillion. Reagan quipped, "The best sign that our economic program is working is that they don't call it Reaganomics anymore." The "Misery Index" (inflation rate + unemployment rate) fell from 20 under Carter to 9 under Reagan.

Fifty-five nations followed Reagan's shift to lower taxes and less regulation, which reduced "Europessimism" and the "Eurocommunist" threat. As Reagan said in his farewell address, "We set out to change a country and wound up changing the world." Lady Thatcher said Reagan had "achieved the most difficult of political tasks, changing attitudes and perceptions about what is possible."

> There are no easy answers, but there are simple answers. Either we accept the responsibility for our own destiny, or we abandon the American Revolution and confess that an intellectual elite in a far distant capital can plan our lives for us better than we can plan them ourselves.
>
> TV address for Barry Goldwater
> (October 27, 1964)

Freedom is a fragile thing and is never more than one generation away from extinction. It is not ours by inheritance; it must be fought for and defended constantly by each generation....

First Inaugural, as governor of California (January 5, 1967)

I'm sure everyone feels sorry for the individual who has fallen by the wayside or who can't keep up in our competitive society, but my own compassion goes beyond that to those millions of unsung men and women who get up every morning, send the kids to school, go to work, try to keep up the payments on their house, pay exorbitant taxes to make possible compassion for the less fortunate, and as a result have to sacrifice many of their own desires and dreams.

Speech (1976)

[We need] a platform that is a banner of bold unmistakable colors with no pale pastel shades.

Republican Convention (1976)

Government exists to protect us from each other. Where government has gone beyond its limits is in deciding to protect us from ourselves.

New York Times (April 13, 1980)

I'm not running for the presidency because I believe that I can solve the problems we've discussed tonight. I believe the people of this country can.

Debate with President Carter (October 28, 1980)

Are you better off today than you were four years ago?

Campaign slogan (1980)

There you go again.

Debate with Walter Mondale (1984)

If we look to the answer as to why for so many years we achieved so much, prospered as no other people on earth, it was because here in this land we unleashed the energy and individual genius of man to a greater extent than has ever been done before.... We're not, as some would have us believe, doomed to an inevitable decline. I do not believe in a fate that will fall on us no matter what we do. I do believe in a fate that will fall on us if we do nothing.

First Inaugural address (January 20, 1981)

In this [economic] crisis, government is not the solution, it's the problem.

Ibid.

It is the Soviet Union that runs against the tide of history.... [It is] the march of freedom and democracy which will leave Marxism-Leninism on the ash heap of history as it has left other tyrannies which stifle the freedom and muzzle the self-expression of the people.

Speech to Britain's Parliament (1982)

Let us beware that while they [Soviet rulers] preach the supremacy of the state, declare its omnipotence over individual men, and predict its eventual domination over all the peoples of the earth, they are the focus of evil in the modern world.

Speech to the National Association of Evangelicals (March 8, 1983)

In the new economy, human invention increasingly makes physical resources obsolete.... In the beginning was the spirit, and it was from this spirit that the material abundance of creation issued forth.

Moscow State University. In George Gilder, *Microcosm* (1989)

Please tell me you're Republicans.
   [Comment to surgeons after the assassination attempt by John W. Hinckley, Jr. on March 30, 1981. As his gurney was pushed into the operating room, he saw White House staffers standing in the hall. He asked, "Who's minding the store?" Later he explained to Nancy how it happened: "Honey, I forgot to duck."]

We intend to keep the peace—we will also keep our freedom.
   State of the Union (January 26, 1982)

They didn't want it good, they wanted it Thursday.
   [Speaking about some movie producers.]
   TV interview (1982)

I urge you to beware the temptation to ignore the facts of history and the aggressive impulses of an evil empire, to simply call the arms race a giant misunderstanding and thereby remove yourself from the struggle between right and wrong and good and evil.
   Speech to Catholic Bishops
   (March 8, 1983)

I will not make age an issue.... I am not going to exploit for political purposes my opponent's youth and inexperience.
   [Reagan (73) in campaign debate against Walter Mondale (56), October 21, 1984.]
   In L. R. Frank, *Quotationary* (1999)

Nations do not mistrust each other because they are armed; they are armed because they mistrust each other.
   Speech, United Nations
   (September 22, 1986)

General Secretary Gorbachev, if you seek peace, if you seek prosperity for the Soviet Union and Eastern Europe, if you seek liberalization: Come here to this gate. Mr. Gorbachev, open this gate. Mr. Gorbachev, tear down this wall!
   [The State Department tried to cut this out of the speech as "Soviet bashing." Yet, 880 days later the wall fell, and two years later the USSR fell. The inspiration for these lines came from a Berlin waitress who said to Peter Robinson, Reagan's speechwriter, "If Gorbachev is serious about *glasnost* and *perestroika*, he can prove it by getting rid of this wall."]
   Speech at Brandenburg Gate
   (June 12,1987)

Reagan told the story of the carrier *Midway* sailing in the South China Sea during the time of the Vietnamese boat people. It came across "a leaky little boat" filled with refugees risking all on the slightest chance of reaching America. One refugee yelled in broken English, "Hello, American sailor. Hello, freedom man!"

If the schools are bad, how is paying bad teachers more money going to help?

A hungry child knows no politics.
   [Reagan sent food aid to Soviet Ethiopia.]

There's some good in everybody.
   [When Sandinistas shot at a U.S. press helicopter.]

I did turn 75 today—but, that's only 24 Celsius.

You can't hit a home run off a soft pitch.

The best minds are not in government. If any were, business would hire them away.

[When Democrats proposed dismantling two old weapons systems for each new one, Reagan quipped:] "How about for every new Democratic Congressman, we dismantle two old ones?"

[Reagan noted Gorbachev was a new-era Russian leader who weighed more than his wife.]

I won a nickname, "the Great Communicator." But I never thought it was my style or the words I used that made a difference: It was the content. I wasn't a great communicator, but I communicated great things.

Farewell address (January 11, 1989)

I hope we have once again reminded people that man is not free unless government is limited. There's a clear cause and effect here that is as neat and predictable as a law of physics: as government expands, liberty contracts.

Ibid.

A final word to the men and women of the Reagan Revolution. Well friends, we did it. We weren't just marking time, we made a difference. We made the city stronger, the city freer. So goodbye. God bless you and God bless America.

Ibid.

E. F. SCHUMACHER
1911–77

British (German-born), environmentalist guru and economist, who began as a Marxist. He glorified "Buddhist economics," that is, primitive economies that purify humanity by supplying only a paucity of goods. He wanted the state to prohibit citizens from acquiring too much property. Thus, he was the favorite economist of the malaise-monger and declinist, Jimmy Carter. Schumacher said, "Small is beautiful," but he would have helped the poor a heap more if he had said, "Liberty is beautiful."

Call a thing immoral or ugly, soul-destroying or a degradation of man, a peril to the peace of the world or to the well-being of future generations: as long as you have not shown it to be "uneconomic" you have not really questioned its right to exist, grow and prosper.

Small Is Beautiful (1973), pt. 1., ch. 3

Any organization has to strive continuously for the orderliness of order and the disorderliness of creative freedom. And the specific danger inherent in large-scale organization is that its natural bias and tendency favor order, at the expense of creative freedom.

Ibid., pt. 4, ch. 2

Our intentions tend to be much more real to us than our actions, and this can lead to a great deal of misunderstanding with other people, to whom our actions tend to be much more real than our intentions.

A Guide for the Perplexed (1977), ch. 8

JOHN A. WHEELER
1911

American, physicist.

There is nothing in the world except empty curved space. Matter, charge, electromagnetism, and other fields are only manifestations of the curvature of space.

> Quoted in *New Scientist*
> (September 26, 1974)

GEORGE J. STIGLER
1911–91

American, Chicago School economist, and winner of the Nobel Prize in 1982 for measuring the actual effects of laws and regulations on economies. He said most government regulation is not designed to benefit the public but the politically most powerful special interests. "As a rule, regulation is acquired by the industry and is designed and operated primarily for the industry's benefit." Regulations restrict competition and raise prices.

He challenged the dominant view monopoly power was a major element of a capitalist economy. Rather, competition quickly erodes the power of monopolies notwithstanding the industrial structure. Most antitrust legal actions are boons for inefficient enterprises and lawyers seeking triple damages.

Stigler's work led to abolishing the Interstate Commerce Commission and the Civil Aeronautics Board, and it spurred deregulation industrywide.

A useful and somewhat surprising lesson of historical scholarship is that widely accepted facts are often wrong.

> *Memoirs of an Unregulated Economist*
> (1988)

TENNESSEE (THOMAS LANIER) WILLIAMS
1911–83

Great American playwright, known for *The Glass Menagerie* (1944), *Camino Real* (1953), *Cat on a Hot Tin Roof* (1955), *Suddenly Last Summer* (1958), *Sweet Bird of Youth* (1959), and *The Night of the Iguana* (1962). His characters are unhappy and fail to reconcile, just as his life was tormented with divorced parents, an insane sister, depression, and drug and alcohol addiction. His violent dramas reflect his belief—typical of Southerners—that civilization is but veneer over simmering violence. Thus, good manners are a matter of survival.

While America can boast of a many great novelists, essayists, and poets, its great playwrights are sparse, that is, only Williams and Eugene O'Neil.

I have always depended on the kindness of strangers.
> [Exit line of Blanche Du Bois.]
> *A Streetcar Named Desire* (1947), sc. 11

There is a time for departure even when there's no certain place to go.
> *Camino Real* (1953), no. 8

We're all of us guinea pigs in the laboratory of God. Humanity is just a work in progress.
> Ibid., no. 12

Life is all memory, except for the present moment that goes by you so quick you hardly catch it going.

The Milk Train Doesn't Stop Here Anymore
(1963), sc. 3

Devils can be driven out of the heart by the touch of a hand on a hand.

WERNER VON BRAUN
1912–77

American (German-born), scientist. He developed Germany's V-2 rocket and America's Apollo moon rocket. When he was twelve years old, Werner's parents told their priest that Werner was failing math. The priest asked what he was doing with a toy rocket. He said he was learning to shoot a rocket to the moon. The priest replied, "Only learning math will let you shoot a rocket to the moon." Werner then got straight A's in math.

Our sun is one of 100 billion stars in our galaxy. Our galaxy is one of the billions of galaxies populating the universe. It would be the height of presumption to think that we are the only living things within that enormous immensity.

New York Times (April 29, 1960)

Basic research is what I am doing when I don't know what I am doing.

A Random Walk in Science (1973)

I have learned to use the word impossible with the greatest caution.

MILTON FRIEDMAN
1912-2006

American, libertarian, who won the Nobel Prize for Economics (1976). Leading the

"Monetarist" or "Chicago School" of economists, he held that the business cycle is primarily a function of the money supply and interest rates and not of fiscal policy, as Keynes wrongly claimed. His *Monetary History of the United States, 1867–1960* (1963) argued that government mismanagement caused the Great Depression: an incompetent Federal Reserve, high taxes, and cartelizing regulations. The U.S. boom (1983–2006), with only two mild recessions in 1991 and 2001, supports Friedman's thesis.

Friedman estimates that all levels of American government spend 40 percent of GNP and impose a regulatory cost of an additional 10 percent of GNP.

There is no such thing as a free lunch.

The great threat to freedom is the concentration of power.

Underlying most arguments against the free market is a lack of belief in freedom itself.

History speaks with a single voice on the relation between political freedom and a free market. I know of no example in time or place of a society that has been marked by a large measure of political freedom, and that has not also used something comparable to a free market to organize the bulk of economic activity.

In a free society there is one and only one social responsibility to business—to use its resources and engage in activities designed to increase profits so long as it says within the rules of the game, which is to say, engages in open and free competition without deception or fraud.

Capitalism and Freedom (1962)

Fundamentally, there are only two ways of coordinating the economic activities of millions. One is central direction involving the use of coercion—the technique of the army and of the modern totalitarian state. The other is voluntary cooperation of individuals—the technique of the market place.

Ibid.

The role of government [in a free society]…is to do something that the market cannot do for itself, namely to determine, arbitrate, and enforce the rules of the game.

Ibid., ch. 2

The Great Depression, like most other periods of severe unemployment, was produced by government mismanagement rather than by any inherent instability of the private economy.

Ibid., ch. 3

Most economic fallacies derive…from the tendency to assume that there is a fixed pie, that one party can gain only at the expense of another.

Free to Choose (1979)

Inflation occurs when the quantity of money rises appreciably more rapidly than output, and the more rapid the rise in the quantity of money per unit of output, the greater the rate of inflation. There is probably no other proposition in economics that is as well established as this one.

Ibid., ch. 9

Nowhere are the rich richer and the poor poorer, than in those societies that do not permit the free market to operate. That is true of medieval societies like India before independence, and much of modern South America, where inherited status determines position. It is equally true of centrally planned societies, like Russia or China or India since independence where access to government determines position. It is true even where central planning was introduced, as in all three of these countries, in the name of equality.

Ibid., p. 179

The FDA [Food and Drug Administration] has done enormous harm to the health of the American public by greatly increasing the costs of pharmaceutical research, thereby reducing the supply of new and effective drugs, and by delaying the approval of such drugs as survive the tortuous FDA process.

In Durk Pearson and Sandy Shaw, *Freedom of Informed Choice* (1993)

We could say to the world: We believe in freedom and intend to practice it. We cannot force you to be free. But we can offer full cooperation on equal terms to all. Our market is open to you without tariffs or other restriction. Sell here what you can and wish to. Buy whatever you can and wish to.

ALBERT CAMUS
1913–1960

French, Nobel Prize novelist (1957), and existentialist who thought that in a world where science had shattered religion, man had become an alien or stranger and life had become absurd. Man lives in a hostile universe without hope. However, life is still possible on these terms so man can avoid despair and, like Sisyphus, find the joy to fill his heart in futile struggles to ascend to the heights. The good is preserving dignity in life's hopelessness.

When he resigned from the Communist Party in 1952, he was denounced by Jean-Paul Sartre and he was thereafter shunned by the liberal clerisy.

The Stranger (1942) and *The Myth of Sisyphus* (1942) portray man's condition to be absurd because he is mortal and there is no divinity. Man should understand his cosmic meaninglessness and "revolt" against this condition by creating his own human meaning. In *The Plague* (1947), Camus asks what is man's responsibility for his fellow man in the face of this absurdity? Bubonic plague in Oran is a metaphor for the human condition because it merely speeds up the inevitable. Various characters react in different ways: defiance, acceptance, detachment, criminality, social commitment, and so on. The protagonist, Dr. Rieux, for whom the plague simply quickens his normal routine of losing out to disease, learns that human contact is important for everyone. When the plague seemed defeated and the populace rejoiced in the streets, Dr. Rieux:

> ...remembered...that the plague bacillus never dies or disappears for good... and [one day] it would rouse up its rats again and send them forth to die in a happy city.
>
> *The Plague* (1947)

Good intentions may do as much harm as malevolence, if they lack understanding.

Ibid.

The struggle itself towards the heights is enough to fill a human heart. One must imagine that Sisyphus is happy.

The Myth of Sisyphus (1942)

There is but one truly serious philosophical problem, and that is suicide. Judging whether life is or is not worth living amounts to answering the fundamental question of philosophy.

Ibid.

For the first time, I laid my heart open to the benign indifference of the universe. To feel it so like myself, indeed, so brotherly, made me realize that I'd been happy, and that I was happy still.

> [Meursault sees his pending execution as liberation. His killing someone was acceptable since he was willing to suffer the consequences.]
>
> *The Stranger* (1942), tr. Stuart Gilbert (1946)

We are killing to build a world in which no one will ever kill. We accept criminality for ourselves in order that the earth may at last be full of innocent people.

> [Satirical play of a Russian terrorist justifying an assassination plot.]
>
> "Les Justes"

To know oneself, one should assert oneself.

Notebooks (1935–42) published (1962)

All modern revolutions have ended in a reinforcement of the power of the state.

"Historical Rebellion: State Terrorism and Irrational Terror," *The Rebel* (1951), tr. A. Bower (1956)

The absurd is sin without God.

Ibid.

…the welfare of humanity is always the alibi of tyrants.

[Camus's Nazi friend argued that Nazism's nihilism was no worse than the logic of suicide implicit in existentialism's nihilism. Camus thereafter fought his way out of nihilism to absolute values. There are few real relativists. Most only want to discredit your virtues—try offering a cigarette to a relativist.]

WALT KELLY
1913–73

American, cartoonist and satirist. Besides Pogo (Possum), other regulars were Howland Owl, Albert the Alligator, and Churchy LaFemme, a turtle.

We have met the enemy and he is us.
[Pogo.]
[Speaking of environmental degradation.]

VINCENT T. LOMBARDI
1913–70

American, football coach who, in nine seasons (1959–69), led the moribund Green Bay Packers to five NFL championships and victory in the first two Super Bowls. In the 1967 "Ice Bowl" played at 13 degrees below zero (wind chill minus 40 degrees) on a sheet of ice, Bart Starr brought the Packers back on a four-minute drive to win in the final seconds the NFC Conference Championship 17 to 14 over the Dallas Cowboys. On a fourth down on the one-yard line, Starr followed his right guard,

Jerry Kramer, who blew out defensive tackle Jethro Pew. Biographer David Maraniss called Lombardy the "patron saint of American competition and success."

Football isn't a contact sport, it's a collision sport. Dancing is a contact sport.
James A Michener, *Sports in America* (1976), ch. 13

Build for your team a feeling of oneness, of dependence upon one another and of strength to be derived by unity.

[After a rookie back had celebrated in the end zone, Lombardi went up to him and said:]
The next time you get into the end zone, act like you're been there before.

[A former player said about Lombardi:]
When he said "Sit down!" I didn't even look for a chair.

The difference between a successful person and others is not a lack of strength, not a lack of knowledge, but rather a lack of will.

I've never known a man worth his salt who in the long run, deep down in his heart, didn't appreciate the grind, the discipline…. I firmly believe that any man's finest hour…is that moment when he has worked his heart out in a good cause and lies exhausted on the field of battle victorious.

Winning isn't everything—but the effort to win is.
["The effort to win" is pregnant with meaning. It means preparing oneself

as well as possible for the contest, which itself becomes almost anti-climactic. Lombardi regretted his initial formulation, "Winning isn't everything, it's the only thing." He later explained that that was not at all what he had meant to say.]

Robert Riger in *Esquire* (November 1962)

You can make a mistake on a player, and we're going to lose a couple games. But if you make a mistake on a quarterback, we're all going to get fired.

RICHARD MILHOUS NIXON
1913–1994

American, thirty-seventh president (1969–74), who resigned to avoid impeachment for obstruction of justice by covering up the breaking and entering by Republican operatives of the Democratic Party's headquarters in the Watergate Building in Washington, D.C.

Nixon declared "We're all Keynesians now" as he imposed the first peacetime wage and price controls and devalued the currency. He was as bad a president on the economy as Hoover and FDR. He supported national health insurance, income maintenance, higher taxation of investment income, and he created the alternative minimum tax. In Nixon's defense, he agreed to the Democratic economic agenda to earn the political capital to end the Vietnam War and split the Sino-Soviet alliance.

Nixon's finest hour came in 1960 when he declined to contest the elections in Illinois and Texas stolen by the Mafia, Mayor Daly, and Lyndon Johnson. [See Paul Johnson, *A History of the American People* (1997).]

When the president does it, that means that it is not illegal.... I gave them a sword and they stuck it in and twisted it with relish.

Interview with David Frost
(May 19, 1977)

In assembling a staff, the conservative leader faces a greater problem than does the liberal. In general, liberals want more government and hunger to be the ones running it. Conservatives want less government and want no part of it.... Liberals flock to government, conservatives have to be enticed and persuaded.

RED SKELTON
1913–97

American, vaudevillian, radio, movie, and TV comedian—as Freddie the Freeloader, the cross-eyed seagull Gertrude, and Clem Kadiddlehopper.

I have a sixth sense, but not the other five. If I wasn't making money, they'd put me away.

In "Thoughts on Business Life," *Forbes*,
(February 19, 1990)

That devout young lady is gentle, kind, and pure, but wherever she spits, grass never grows again.

RANDALL JARRELL
1914–65

American, poet.

From my mother's sleep I fell into the State,

And I hunched in its belly till my wet
    fur froze.
Six miles from earth, loosed from its
    dream of life
I woke to black flak and the nightmare
    fighters.
When I died they washed me out of the
    turret with a hose.
        "The Death of the Ball Turret Gunner"
                        (1944)

JOE LOUIS
1914–81

American, champion heavyweight boxer
for a record 12 years against 25 challengers.

He can run but he can't hide.
    [Title fight of June 19, 1946,
    with Billy Conn, who had fancy
    footwork.]
           My Life Story (1947), ch. 21

JONAS EDWARD SALK
1914–95

American, virologist, who discovered the
polio vaccine.

When something is suggested, the first
response [of scientific colleagues] is "It
can't possibly be true." And then, after
a bit the next response is, "Well, if it's
true, it's not very important." And then
the third response is, "Well, we've known
it all along."

DANIEL J. BOORSTIN
1914–2003

American, social historian, Librarian of

Congress, and author of the incomparable
The Discoverers (1983), *The Creators* (1992),
and *The Seekers* (1998), even though he is a
Keynesian.

A sign of a celebrity is often that his
name is worth more than his services.
              The Image (1961)

The greatest obstacle to discovery is
not ignorance—it is the illusion of
knowledge.

BUDD SCHULBERG
1914

American, novelist, journalist, and
scriptwriter.

I couda had class, I couda been somebody, I couda been a contender. I could
have been somebody—instead of a bum,
which is what I am.
    [Marlon Brando as Terry Malloy,
    who threw a fight in *On The Water-
    front*, a 1954 film.]

DYLAN THOMAS
1914–53

Welsh, surrealistic poet and playwright
who died young of alcohol abuse.

Do not go gentle into that good night,
Old age should burn and rage at close
    of day;
Rage, rage against the dying of the light.
    [Written when his father was
    dying.]
        "Do Not Go Gentle into That Good
                    Night" (1952)

Alone until she dies, Bessie Bighead...
picks a posy of daisies in Sunday Meadow
to put on the grave of Gomer Owen who
kissed her once by the pig-sty when she
wasn't looking and never kissed her again
although she was looking all the time.

Under Milk Wood (1954)

A good poem is a contribution to reality.
The world is never the same once a good
poem has been added to it.

"On Poetry," *Quite Early One Morning*
(1954)

HUGH TREVOR-ROPER
1914–2003

English, historian at Oxford, known for
The Last Days of Hitler (1947).

The function of genius is not to give new
answers, but to pose new questions which
time and mediocrity can resolve.

THOMAS J. WATSON JR.
1914–93

American, chairman of IBM, once the
world's largest computer company.

Solve it quickly, solve it right or wrong.
[How to deal with problems.]

Fortune (1977)

Within us all there are wells of thought
and dynamos of energy which are not
suspected until emergencies arise. Then
oftentimes we find that it is comparatively simple to double or treble our former capacities and to amaze ourselves by
the results achieved. Quotas, when set

up for us by others, are challenges which
goad us on to surpass ourselves. The outstanding leaders of every age are those
who set up their own quotas and constantly exceed them.

Forbes (October 11, 1982)

WORLD WAR I
1914–1918

After one hundred years of general peace
in Europe, war erupted in 1914. Thousands
of books have tried to identify the causes.
One was tension between the German, British, Russian, Austro-Hungarian, Ottoman,
and French empires. Imperialist states tend
to be hypernationalistic, and protectionist
ones are especially so. Protectionist states
are not export competitive, so they seek
economic self-sufficiency through annex-
ing neighboring lands or seizing colonies.
In 1914 it was believed that a state's power
was proportional to the amount of land
and number of people it controlled. Today
power is associated more with a state's
technologies than with its mass. Another
cause includes Germany's inept diplomacy that created an unnatural alliance
between Britain and France by challenging
Britain with a naval buildup and humiliat-
ing France over Morocco in 1911.

Another reason for the war was that
Germany expected it to last only forty-
two days, but it lasted four years because
barbed wire and machine guns eliminated
offensive maneuver. Also, transport trip-
wires left no time for diplomacy. Russia
had to begin mobilizing immediately due
to her primitive railroads, and Germany
believed it had to knock out France before
Russia could complete mobilizing.

The assassination of the Austrian archduke Ferdinand by a Serbian was the spark that set off the "Central Powers" of Germany, Austria-Hungary, and the Ottomans against the "Allies": Russia, France, Britain, Italy, Serbia, and Japan.

Germany's "von Schlieffen plan" was to hold the line on France's border while the bulk of its forces (sixteen corps) would wheel through Holland and Belgium in a giant envelopment. But, Army Chief Helmut von Moltke only invaded through Belgium, and not Holland, in an attempt to mollify the British so they would not join the French. This narrowed the invasion and delayed its envelopment. Further, only eleven of sixteen planned corps enveloped the French. Three extra corps were held in defense and two extra corps were detached to the Eastern Front.

Even so, Erich von Ludendorff might not have been stopped thirty-five miles from Paris had he not been cowed by the "straight front" doctrine that one should never create a salient. That doctrine required using reserves to attack fortified positions while holding back the advance at defensively weak spots. Allied generals also erred: The English were late to adopt the machine gun and to deploy tanks. Barbara Tuchman said in *Guns of August* (1962), "War is the unfolding of miscalculations."

Ten million soldiers perished—800,000 at Verdun. More deadly was the scarcely remembered Spanish influenza of 1918, which killed 20 million Europeans and perhaps 100 million worldwide.

Worse than the generals' miscalculations were those of the politicians. Clemenceau demanded a Carthaginian peace and a weak Wilson caved in to get his will-of-the-wisp League of Nations. The catastrophic Treaty of Versailles doomed the West to a repeat of the Great War. Indeed, the antiliberal forces causing World War I, nationalism and protectionism, were metastasized by World War I into Communism and Nazism. These represented a counterrevolution against the great achievements of the eighteenth and nineteenth centuries, to wit, the birth of classical liberalism.

OTHER FACTS

Germany in World War II used a variation of the von Schlieffen plan. Germany feinted along the Maginot Line while wheeling into Holland and Belgium to suck the British and French into Belgium, after which the Germans thrust through the Ardennes, the hinge between the Maginot Line and Belgium. That trapped the British and French at Dunkirk. The coordination by radio of massed tanks aided by dive-bombers acting as mobile artillery created blitzkrieg (lightning warfare). Unafraid of salients, Germany's massed tanks and motorized infantry enveloped France's far more numerous and higher quality tanks, which had been spread out thinly as defensive infantry support. As De Gaulle had warned, the German doctrine of concentrating its tanks trumped France's greater numbers of troops, artillery, and tanks.

AMERICAN ASSOCIATION OF UNIVERSITY PROFESSORS: DECLARATION ON ACADEMIC FREEDOM 1915

An inviolable refuge from tyranny should

be found in the university. It should be an *intellectual experience station,* where new ideas may germinate and where their fruit, though still distasteful to the community as a whole, may be allowed to ripen until finally, perchance, it may become part of the accepted food of the nation or of the world.

William Buckley in *Let Us Talk of Many Things* (1999) reminds us that academic freedom is sacred in the sense that we should be able to pursue knowledge without legal interference. But it does not mean that all ideas are equal or that teachers should not be guardians of our civilization. To believe that every student should "begin afresh, as if Plato and Aristotle and St. Augustine and St. Thomas had among them reached not one dependable conclusion, is to doubt the very structure of learning...."

LORD PETER T. BAUER
1915–2002

British (Hungarian-born), economist who fought the Keynesians who were selling developing countries a poisonous cocktail of government central planning, foreign aid, and expropriation of small farmers to subsidize state-owned industries. Bauer concluded that "official aid is more likely to retrard development than to promote it."

The excuse that poverty results from overpopulation ignores the fact that Hong Kong, with 247,500 people per square mile, is richer than China, with a population of 409 per square mile. As Bauer said, "Economic achievement and progress depend on people's conduct, not on their numbers."

...political action which deliberately aimed to minimize, or even remove, economic differences would entail such extensive coercion that the society would cease to be open and free. The successful pursuit of the unholy grail of economic equality would exchange the promised reduction or removal of differences in income and wealth for much greater actual inequality of power between rulers and subjects.

Equality, the Third World, and Economic Delusion (1981)

Far from the West having caused the poverty in the Third World, contact with the West has been the principal agent of material progress there. The materially more advanced societies and regions of the Third World are those with which the West established the most numerous, diversified and extensive contacts...

Ibid.

[T]he suspicion and antagonism of academics, clerics and intellectuals towards the market ...go hand in had with their disdain for the preferences and habits or ordinary people.

Reality and Rhetoric: Studies in the Economics of Development (1983), ch. 1

The market system provides no mechanism for its own survival. Attempts by firms or individuals to influence the climate of opinion or the overall political situation involve costs in time and money, and occasionally also in unpopularity. Most of these costs are certain and are incurred in the present. They are borne by firms and persons who can expect at best to secure only a small proportion of an uncertain and delayed benefit.

Ibid., ch. 2

[Foreign aid] has made it possible for [recipient] governments to pursue such policies as subsidized import substitution, forced collectivization, price policies which inhibit agricultural production, inflationary financial policies, and the maintenance of over-valued exchange rates.

Ibid., ch. 3

To support rulers [with foreign aid] on the basis of the poverty of their subjects does nothing to discourage policies of impoverishment.

Ibid.

It's not the quantity of investment, it's the quality of investment.

Economic achievement depends primarily on people's abilities and attitudes and also on their social and political institutions.

BRUCE HENDERSON
1915–1993

American, CEO, Boston Consulting Group, Inc.

It is a paradox that the greater the decentralization, the greater the need for both leadership and explicit policies from the top management.

Henderson on Corporate Strategy (1986)

ARTHUR MILLER
1915–2005

American, playwright, whose single great play, *Death of a Salesman* (1951), was a biography of his father, a manufacturer destroyed by the Great Depression. The play's genius is the recognition that a tragedy is not limited to noble Greeks, but can be found in the lives of everyday people. Miller never created another masterpiece. As he said, "The quickest route to failure is success." He became famous for marrying Marilyn Monroe and for not answering questions about his Communist ties. Miller was a lifelong Depression-era writer who ended as a left-wing apologist and screed writer.

I don't say he's a great man. Willy Loman never made a lot of money. His name was never in the paper. He's not the finest character that ever lived. But he's a human being, and a terrible thing is happening to him. So attention must be paid.

Death of A Salesman (1951), act 1

A good newspaper, I suppose, is a nation talking to itself.

In the *Observer* (November 26, 1962)

An era can be said to end when its basic illusions are exhausted.

PAUL A. SAMUELSON
1915

American, Nobel Prize (1970). His textbook *Economics* (1948) imbued two generations of students with Keynesian errors, until replaced in recent years in enlightened universities by Greg Matthew's text. Samuelson also followed the line of a flourishing Soviet economy. But the Soviet reality was very slow economic growth accompanied by horrific environmental degradation and subsistence-level incomes. *Economics*

(1985) read: "But it would be misleading to dwell on the [Soviet economy's] shortcomings....What counts is results, and there can be no doubt that the Soviet planning system has been a powerful engine for economic growth." *Economics* (1989) read: "Measured Soviet real GNP has grown more rapidly over the long run than have most of the major market economies." The Soviet economy collapsed the very next year.

The Soviets always inflated their economic statistics. In 1935 the coal miner Aleksei Stakhanov was made a Hero of Socialist Labor for extracting 102 tons of coal in one shift, fourteen times the quota. But, just as Marx had made up the critical statistics in *Das Capital*, the Soviet Union made up the statistics about Stakhanov and Soviet GNP. Samuelson accepted those statistics because they validated his erroneous Keynesian economics.

When the Soviets came to power in 1917, U.S. per capita income was five times that in Russia; when the Soviets lost power in 1991, per capita income in the U.S. was twenty times that in Russia.

> I don't care who writes a nation's laws—
> or crafts its advanced treaties—if I can
> write its economics textbooks.
> In L. R. Frank, *Quotationary* (1999)

> Wall Street indexes predicted nine out of
> the last five recessions.
> *Newsweek* (September 19, 1966)

No other American intellectual has wrecked as much economic havoc as Samuelson, the "Ptolemy of Economics" and "the backdoor to socialism." College students taking economics rarely get to read Von Mises, Friedman, or Hayek. They read

Samuelson's textbooks, economic history with Heilbroner's *The Worldly Philosophers*, and public finance with Musgrave's *The Theory of Public Finance*. These Keynesian texts argue that government should redistribute wealth and maintain high levels of taxation and government spending to stabilize the economy. Few students learn James Buchanan's "public choice theory," to wit, public officials are as self-interested as capitalists—they create public policies designed to enhance their own prospects for reelection, reappointment, or promotion.

Fortunately, two great universities teach classical economics: the University of Chicago and George Mason University in Fairfax, Virginia.

When Samuelson preceded the classical economist George Stigler on a dais, he said he knew what Stigler was going to say and that it was all wrong. When Stigler stood up, he said, "Two plus two equals four," and then sat down.

ORSON WELLES
1915–85

American, actor, screenwriter, producer, and creative film director. In 1938 he adapted for radio H. G. Wells's *War of the Worlds* as a simulated newscast about Martian spaceships invading earth and destroying American cities with ray guns.

> In Italy for thirty years under the Borgias they had warfare, terror, murder, bloodshed—they produced Michelangelo, Leonardo da Vinci and the Renaissance. In Switzerland they had brotherly love, five hundred years of democracy

and peace, and what did they produce?
The cuckoo clock.
[Harry Lime.]
The Third Man (1950), an RKO film.
Screenplay by Graham Greene and
Carol Reed

Harry Lime sells diluted penicillin on the black market in postwar Vienna, killing many. To avoid capture, he informs on his girlfriend, Anna Schmidt, who is put at risk of being deported to Russia. Despite Anna's knowledge of Harry's treachery and the human carnage he had wrought, she is held spellbound to the end by his evil charm.

Look down there. Would you really feel any pity if one of those dots stopped moving forever? If I said that you can have twenty thousand pounds for every dot that stops, would you really, old man, tell me to keep the money or would you calculate how many dots you could afford to spare.
[Harry to Holly Martin on a Ferris wheel.]
Ibid.
An artist is always out of step with the time. He has to be.
New York Times (August 7, 1966)

This is the biggest electric train set any boy ever had!
[Speaking of the RKO studio.]
Peter Noble, The Fabulous Orson Welles
(1956), ch. 7

SIR FRANCIS CRICK
1916

British, scientist, Nobel Prize with James D. Watson for the 1953 discovery of the struc-

ture of a DNA molecule at Cambridge's Cavendish Lab.

[The reason discoveries are difficult] is that you've got to take a series of steps, three or four steps, which if you don't make them you won't get there, and if you go wrong in any one of them you won't get there. It isn't a matter of one jump—that would be easy. You've got to make several successive jumps.
In Peter L. Bernstein, Capital Ideas (1992)

ROBERT S. MCNAMARA
1916

American, exemplar of the Peter Principle. As president of Ford Motor Company, he invested in the Edsel, the biggest turkey in auto history; and he blocked both Iacocca's inexpensive four-seat sports car (Mustang) and front-wheel-drive technology critical to downsizing of cars to compete with Japan.

After being fired from Ford, he became secretary of defense and he lost the first U.S. war following a grand strategy of "graduated response" rather than using overwhelming conventional force. For example, for years McNamara's rules of engagement prohibited U.S. pilots from suppressing North Vietnamese SAM missle sites for fear of hurting a Russian advisor. Worse, he refused to interdict NVA infiltration from North Vietnam, Laos, and Cambodia as Eisenhower had urged. Although he believed a U.S. defeat was inevitable given his constraints, he continued to conscript Americans.

After losing his job as secretary of defense, he was appointed president of the World Bank, which he made into the capitalist bank for socialist countries. According to the Heritage Foundation's "The World Bank and Economic Growth: Fifty Years of Failure" (1996), of 66 countries receiving World Bank aid for 25 or more years, only 24 are better off than when the aid began. Ignoring Lord Peter Bauer, who said that giving aid to developing countries was counterproductive unless they safeguarded private property, McNamara funded kleptocracies and socialists, which condemned Africa to regress to the Stone Age. For an opposite, laudatory opinion of McNamara, see *Colliers Encyclopedia* (1996).

ROBERT CONQUEST
1917

British, historian, who unveiled the horrors of Communist death camps. He argues that the greatest catastrophes have been inflicted by "idea addicts" who believed in constructing utopias by violence. His *The Harvest of Sorrows: Soviet Collectivization and the Terror-Famine* details how the Communists murdered 15 million to eliminate two enemies: Ukrainian nationalists and resisting Soviet peasants. The problem of leaving parentless children was solved by hanging the children.

Conquest's *The Dragons of Expectation* (2005) describes the error in the worldview of Western intellectuals who support egalitarian utopianism. Just as Eratosthenes' solar system lost out to Ptolemy's geocentric view for 1380 years, so it is possible for the American founders' political pluralism to lose out to utopian egalitarianism at incalculable costs.

It is not so much that "democracy" as such is incapable of aggression, as that only states which represent rather than repress internal variety, which are themselves based on consensuality, which tolerate divergent cultures and ideas, which are not themselves enslaved to unquestioned dogma, are likely to have a reasonably cooperative attitude on the international scene.

Reflections on a Ravaged Century (2000)

"Intelligentsia" is, of course, a Russian word. The condition of being an *intelligent* was defined not by intelligence, but by the acceptance of the Idea—so given, with the capital letter, and defined as the total destruction of the existing order and its replacement by a perfect society run by none other than the intelligentsia.

Ibid.

The delusion that problems are susceptible, in principle, to being solved by political decision has led many backward countries further and further into the grip of incompetent autocrats. Each time a solution imposed by force has, after all, failed to improve matters, it is thought that the fault is merely that insufficient power has been put behind it. If one more refractory social group is liquidated, if party discipline is tightened and all shirkers and compromisers adequately dealt with, then next time all will be well.

The Dragons of Expectation (2005)

JOHN F. KENNEDY
1917–63

American, thirty-fifth (1961–63) and first Catholic president. His weakness at the

Bay of Pigs tempted the USSR to install two hundred atomic ballistic missiles in Cuba. He got the Soviets to remove them by removing U.S. missiles from Turkey and promising Castro a free hand in Latin America and Africa. Against the advice of both MacArthur and Eisenhower, he entered the Vietnam War and, worse, permitted McNamara to wage war gently. He reduced taxes, which stimulated the economy.

Lee Oswald, a communist, assassinated Kennedy, but leftists want to pin it on the CIA. George Will wrote, "People determined to believe that a vast conspiracy assassinated President Kennedy believe that the absence of evidence of the conspiracy proves the vastness and cleverness of the conspiracy."

> "Don't buy a single vote more than necessary. I'll be damned if I'm going to pay for a landslide."
> [A telegram from his father in 1958.]

Should I become president...I will not risk American lives...by permitting any other nation to drag us into the wrong war...
> Campaign speech, *New York Times* (October 13, 1960)

My fellow Americans, ask not what your country can do for you, ask what you can do for your country....My fellow citizens of the world, ask not what America will do for you, but what together we can do for the freedom of man.
> Inaugural address (January 20, 1961)

[T]he torch has been passed to a new generation of Americans, born in this century, tempered by war, disciplined

by a hard and bitter peace, proud of our ancient heritage, and unwilling to witness or permit the slow undoing of those human rights to which this nation has always been committed, and to which we are committed today at home and around the world. Let every nation know, whether it wishes us well or ill, that we shall pay any price, bear any burden, meet any hardship, support any friend, oppose any foe to assure the survival and the success of liberty.
> Ibid.

There is always inequality in life. Some men are killed in a war and some men are wounded, and some men never leave the country.... Life is unfair.
> Press conference (March 21, 1962)

Ich bin ein Berliner.
I am a Berliner.
> ["Ein Berliner" is a jelly-filled doughnut. JFK should have said, *"Ich bin Berliner."*]
> Speech in West Berlin (June 26, 1963)

We must face [the] fact that the United States is neither omnipotent nor omniscient—that we are only six percent of the world's population...that we cannot right every wrong or reverse each adversity—and that therefore there cannot be an American solution to every world problem.
> Speech (1962)

It is a paradoxical truth that tax rates are too high and tax revenues too low, and the soundest way to raise revenues in the long run is to cut rates now.... An economy hampered by restrictive tax rates will never produce enough revenue to balance our budget, just as it will never produce enough jobs or enough profits.

New York (December 14, 1962)

You can't beat brains.

In L. R. Frank, *Quotationary* (1999)

We in this country...are—by destiny rather than by choice—the watchmen on the walls of world freedom.

[From a speech, not delivered on November 22, 1963.]

DADAISM
1918–1925

Dadaism was a post-World War I distorted genre of painting that was virulently anti-capitalist, antimilitary, and antireligion. Tristan Tzara called it "anti-art for anti-art's sake." Its leading practitioner was Marcel Duchamp, who invented "readymade art," which is art not made by an artist. For example, Duchamp bolted a commercial urinal to a wall in an art gallery.

RUSSEL A. KIRK
1918–94

American, political philosopher, and a founder of the *National Review*. His *The Conservative Mind* (1953) gave the lie to J. S. Mill's charge that conservatives were the stupid party. Today traditional conservatives are called "Kirkians" who recognize man's spiritual and social nature and thus emphasize community, natural law, and religion versus libertarians who emphasize individualism. He said "Traditions are the wisdom of the race...." that free us from T. S. Eliot's "provincialism of time." He said,

"The permanent things are derived from the experience of the species, the ancient usages of humanity..." Kirk called the U.S. "Constitution the most sagacious conservative document in political history." He taught that respect for one's noble ancestry and the desire to found a great family were the greatest forces in building individual character.

THE CONSERVATIVE MIND: FROM BURKE TO ELIOT, 1953

...the essence of social conservatism is preservation of the ancient moral traditions of humanity. Conservatives respect the wisdom of their ancestors...they are dubious of wholesale alterations...I think that there are six canons of conservative thought:

1. Belief in a transcendent order, or body of natural law, which rules society as well as conscience....
2. Affection for the proliferating variety and mystery of human existence, as opposed to the narrowing uniformity, egalitarianism, and utilitarian aims of most radical systems....
3. Conviction that civilized society requires orders and classes, as against the notion of a "classless society."
4. Persuasion that freedom and property are closely linked; separate property from private possession, and Leviathan becomes master of all.
5. Faith in prescription and distrust of "sophisters, calculators, and economists" who would reconstruct society upon abstract designs. Tradition, sound prejudice, and old

prescription are checks both upon man's anarchic impulse and upon the innovator's lust for power.

6. Recognition that change and reform are not identical, and that innovation is a devouring conflagration, more often than…progress.

The twentieth-century conservative is concerned, first of all, for the regeneration of spirit and character—with the perennial problem of the inner order of the soul, the restoration of the ethical understanding, and the religious sanction upon which any life worth living is founded.

Ibid., ch. V

The people under the influence of high principle sometimes may be elevated to sublimity; they may also shout for Hitler or Stalin or any man who wants to burn a witch. Without the power of those virtuous customs and laws that Tocqueville outlined, the people become Hamilton's 'great beast'; and to trust them in the abstract is an act of reckless faith far more credulous than medieval relic-veneration.

Ibid., ch. VI

All culture arises out of religion. When religious faith decays, culture must decline, though often seeming to flourish for a space after the religion which has nourished it has sunk into disbelief.

Eliot and His Age (1971)

ROBERT HALF
1918

American, author of *Robert Half on Hiring*:

There is something that is much more scarce, something rarer than ability. It is the ability to recognize ability.

The search for someone to blame is always successful.

One uncooperative employee can sabotage an entire organization because bad spirit is contagious.

Whoever created the name life insurance had to be the sales genius of all time.

ALEXANDER SOLZHENITSYN
1918

Russian, poet, Nobel Prize for literature in 1970. Interned for eight years in gulag labor camps, he wrote about them in *The First Circle* (1968), *Cancer Ward* (1968), and *The Gulag Archipelago* (1973–78). He delegitimized the Soviet Union by documenting how Communists ran tens of millions of men, women, and children through a "human sewage disposal system." Asked to explain his writing, he said, "When you've been pitched headfirst into Hell, you just write about it." Exiled in 1974 for *Gulag*, he returned in 1994. George Will said the most influential author of the twentieth century was Solzhenitsyn, Orwell, or C. S. Lewis.

You only have power over people as long as you don't take everything away from them. But when you've robbed a man of everything he's no longer in your power—he's free again.

The First Circle (1964), ch. 17,
tr. Michael Buybon

GULAG ARCHIPELAGO (1918–56)

[N]owhere on the planet, nowhere in history, was there a regime more vicious, more bloodthirsty than the Bolshevik, the self-styled Soviet regime.

Ibid.

In the fever of epidemic arrests, people leaving for work said farewell to their families every day, because they could not be certain they would return at night.... The Organs had no profound reasons for their choice of whom to arrest and whom not to arrest. They merely had assignments, quotas for a specific number of arrests. These quotas might be filled on an orderly basis or wholly arbitrarily. [For example, a woman who entered an NKVD office to solicit help for a child was arrested to fill a quota.]

Ibid.

Solzhenitsyn wrote about his experiences and those of 227 witnesses. However, he had no access to Soviet documents, so there is little aggregated data. He tells of persons being tortured or shot without knowing why. A woman was sentenced to ten years' hard labor for stealing a spool of thread, characterized as "a hundred meters of material." The gulag's 800 camps (250 major regions) held some 12 million inmates at any time, and 80 percent perished due to starvation, lack of medicines, the bitter cold (many camps were beyond the Arctic Circle), beatings, and hard labor in constructing canals, mines, and so forth. Camps in the Kolyma area had an annual death rate of 30 percent, but in their worst camps, the average life expectancy was only four months.

Tens of millions perished in the gulag in discrete waves of purges: Constitutional Democrats, social revolutionaries, Mensheviks, anarchists, Popular Socialists, Kulaks, Catholic priests, Catholics, Trotskyites, Old Communists, Soviet officers, limiters and wreckers, Koreans, Volga Germans, Russian prisoners of war, Soviet Greeks, Russian émigrés, and others. Soviet Jews scheduled for the next wave were saved by Stalin's death. Ironically, N. A. Frenkel, a Jew, organized the gulag (*Glanoe Upravlenie Lagerei*—Chief Administration of Camps), the model for Hitler's death camps.

Anything could be a crime against the state. Not working hard was "weakening the state"—five years in the gulag. Engineers who said the railroads could not stand loads over ten tons per axle were "limiters"—ten years; engineers who tore up the tracks by placing more than ten tons per axle were "wreckers"—twenty-five years. Owning a gun meant ten years for terrorism. A twelve-year-old farm girl caught "sniping" corn to feed her family got five years, but twenty-five years if she sniped corn with a friend because that was organized sabotage. No one survived twenty-five years in the gulag. Pavlik Morozov, a fourteen-year old "Pioneer," was made a "hero" after sending his family to the gulag for hoarding grain.

Western intellectuals shunned Solzhenitsyn on discovering he turned against Communism after converting to Christianity in the gulag.

Power is a poison well known for thousands of years. But to the human being who has faith in some force that holds dominion over all of us, and who is therefore conscious of his own limitations, power is not necessarily fatal. For those, however, who are unaware of any higher sphere, it is a deadly poison. For them there is no antidote.

Ibid.

To do evil a human being must first of all believe that what he's doing is good, or else that it's a well-considered act in conformity with natural law.... Ideology is what gives evildoing its long-sought justification and the evildoer the necessary steadfastness and determination.... That is how the agents of the Inquisition fortified their wills; by invoking Christianity... the Nazis, by race; and the Jacobins (early and late) by equality, brotherhood, and the happiness of future generations.

Ibid.

It has been explained to us that *the heart of the matter is not personal guilt, but social danger.* One can imprison an innocent person if he is socially hostile, and one can release a guilty man if he is socially friendly.

[Author's emphasis.]

Ibid.

I have spent my whole life under a Communist regime, and I will tell you that a society without any objective legal scale is a terrible one indeed.

Commencement address, Harvard University (1978)

The humanistic way of thinking did not admit the existence of intrinsic evil in man, nor did it see any task higher than the attainment of happiness on Earth. It started modern Western civilization on the dangerous trend of worshipping man and his material needs....

Ibid.

[In his review of *Gulag Archipelago* for the *Guardian*, W. L. Webb wrote:] "To live now and not to know this work is to be a kind of historical fool missing a crucial part of the consciousness of the age."

In Peter Watson, *The Modern Mind* (2001)

A people that no longer remembers has lost its history and its soul.

SOVIET REALISM
1918–89

The official artistic doctrine of the Soviet Union, formalized by a resolution of the Central Committee in 1932, required artists "to educate the toilers in the spirit of socialism." Artists should only create protagonists who were "positive heroes," that is, healthy men and women who sacrificed themselves to build Communism. Protagonists could not be "superfluous men" alienated from society and unable to fulfill a productive social role.

ROBERT S. STRAUSS
1918

American, lawyer, and chairman of the Democratic Party.

[Asked when he would quit as chairman of the party:]
It's a little like makin' love to a gorilla. You don't quit when you're tired—you quit when the gorilla's tired.

Chicago Tribune (February 5, 1978)

JAMES MCGILL BUCHANAN
1919

American, economist, Nobel Prize 1986, and professor at George Mason University. His Public Choice Theory holds that people in government pursue their personal interests as intensely as anyone in the private sector. They regulate to secure promotion or reelection. Public Choice compares actual markets with "rent-seeking" officials rather than compare actual markets with idealistic officials.

Public Choice identifies the asymmetrical incentives resulting from the concentration of benefits and the diffusion of burdens arising from government intervention in the economy. The beneficiaries from laws and regulations providing subsidies or limiting competition will handsomely reward public officials—aid their promotions and re-elections. Also, politicians are far less accountable than entrepreneurs, who have real competitors. The politician has a monopoly on his seat until the next election, and rarely do incumbents lose elections.

MALCOLM FORBES
1919–90

American, publisher of *Forbes,* son of B. C. Forbes and father of Steve Forbes.

> The only advice I can think of that's of any value to anybody that is eager to have success is to do what turns you on.
> Commencement address (1988)

> When the joy of the job's gone, when it's no fun trying anymore, quit before you're fired.

Reported in a recent *New York Times* piece was a passage describing today's youth as "loving luxury, hating authority, being bored, ill-mannered, and lacking respect for adults." That observation was ascribed to fourth century B.C. philosopher Socrates.

ROBERT GOHEEN
1919

American, educator, and past president of Princeton University.

> If you feel that you have both feet planted on level ground, then the university has failed you.
> Baccalaureate address, *Time* (June 23, 1961)

A previous president of Princeton, said, "Madame, we guarantee results—or we return the boy!"

LAURENCE J. PETER
1919–90

Canadian, educator.

> In a hierarchy every employee tends to rise to his level of incompetence.
> *The Peter Principle* (1969), ch. 1

> History teaches us the mistakes we are going to make.
> *Peter's Quotations* (1977)

> Lead, follow, or get out of the way.
> "Peter's Survival Principle," *Peter's People* (1979), ch. 8

The problem with success is that its formula is the same as the one for ulcers.

> In L. R. Frank, *Wit and Humor Quotationary*

Facts are stubborn things, but statistics are more pliable.

Prisons will not work until we start sending a better class of people there.

WALTER B. WRISTON
1919–2005

American, banker (Citicorp), who argued that in a global economy "money and ideas" would travel at the speed of light to "where they are welcome" and "stay where they are well treated." He propounded the thesis that governments and central banks will no longer be able to misbehave economically, because of instantaneous global price signals. He noted that speed is what changes still pictures into motion pictures.

A person with the skills to write a complex software program that can produce a billion dollars of revenue can walk past any customs officer in the world with nothing of "value" to declare.

> *Twilight of Sovereignty* (1992)

The global market weighs the fiscal and monetary policies of each government that issues currency and places a value on it that is instantly seen by traders in Hong Kong, London, Zurich and New York.

> Ibid.

Intellectual capital is becoming relatively more important than physical capital.

Indeed, the new source of wealth is not material, it is information, knowledge applied to work to create value. The pursuit of wealth is now largely the pursuit of information.

> Ibid.

The Doomsayers have always had their uses, since they trigger the coping mechanism that often prevents the events they forecast.

> *Risk and Other Four Letter Words* (1986)

We read…solemn words about "risky investments" and "risky loans" from writers who do not seem to realize that these phrases are redundant.

> Ibid.

FRANK HERBERT
1920–86

American, science fiction writer of the *Dune* books, a study of absolute power corrupting even the purest in heart. Paul, who sought power to do good, becomes evil, the Kwisatz Haderach.

Without change, something sleeps inside us. The sleeper must awaken.
[Duke Leto Atreides.]

> *Dune* (1965)

Father, father, the sleeper has awakened.
[Paul Atreides.]

> Ibid.

Fear is the mind-killer. Fear is the little death that brings total obliteration. I will face my fear. I will permit it to pass over me and through me. And when it has gone past, I will turn the inner eye to see its path. Where the fear has gone there will be nothing. Only I will remain.

Heretics of Dune (1988), ch. 1

Most deadly errors arise from obsolete assumptions.

Ibid.

Show me a completely smooth operation and I will show you someone covering mistakes. Real boats rock.

POPE JOHN PAUL II
1920–2005

Polish, born Karol Joseph Wojtyla. He became the 265th pope in 1978, the first non-Italian in 456 years. He inspired Polish resistance to Communism and Soviet domination, which facilitated the implosion of the Soviet Union.

The fundamental error of socialism is anthropological in nature. Socialism considers the individual person simply as an element, a molecule within the social organism, so that the good of the individual is completely subordinated to the functioning of the socio-economic mechanism. Socialism likewise maintains that the good of the individual can be realized without reference to his free choice, to the unique and exclusive responsibility, which he exercises in the face of good or evil... the concept of the person as the autonomous subject of moral decisions disappears.

Centesimus Annus

Where self-interest is suppressed, it is replaced by a burdensome system of bureaucratic control that dries up the wellsprings of initiative and creativity.

Ibid.

IRVING KRISTOL
1920

American, father of neoconservatism, editor, and economist. He saw the main problem with liberalism was that it was "woefully blind to human and political reality." This blindness led liberalism to aim for collectivism and moral anarchy. Instead of looking at man's greed, laziness, and so forth as the sources of his troubles, liberals blame external causes, like poverty and prejudice. The root of these assumptions is the mistaken principle of equality:

Rich men are fine, poor men are fine, so long as they are decent human beings. I do not like equality. I do not like it in sports, in the arts, or in economics. I just don't like it in this world.

"Spiritual Roots of Capitalism and Socialism" in Michael Novak (ed.), *Capitalism and Socialism* (1991)

Kristol's initial neoconservative targets were Communism and the consistent refusal of liberals to condemn Communism as the moral equivalent of Nazism. After the fall of the Berlin Wall, Kristol led neoconservatives to support the encouragement of democracy worldwide as part of a morality of opposing tyranny and safeguarding Western liberty. He criticizes conservatives for being so gloomy about an inevitable Western decline and social breakdown that they are not willing to fight. Richard Perle said neoconservatives are "closer to being revolutionaries than conservatives" given their proclivity to fight against cultural collapse.

Note: While neocons believe that America's security is inseparable from global security and thus favored the war on Iraq in 2003, Paul Wolfowitz noted the limits on achieving global democracy: "We cannot ignore the uncomfortable fact that economic and social conditions may better prepare some countries for democracy than others."

> [A neoconservative is] a liberal who has been mugged by reality.
> *Two Cheers for Capitalism*, Introduction
> (1978)

> History does not provide us with any instance of a society that repressed the economic liberties of the individual while being solicitous of his other liberties.
> Ibid.

> [To believe that] no one was ever corrupted by a book, play, or movie you almost have to believe that no one was ever improved by a book, play, or movie.
> *Reflections of a Neo-Conservative* (1983)

> [Multiculturalism is] as much a war against the West as Nazism and Stalinism ever were.

Timothy Leary
1920–96

American, Harvard professor, and psychedelic guru, who advocated using LSD.

> Turn On, Tune In, Drop Out.
> [1967 lecture recommending doing drugs.]

> Women who seek to be equal with men lack ambition.

Mario Puzo
1920–99

American, author, who wrote about the fictional Don Corleone family.

> He made him an offer he couldn't refuse. [A threat.]
> *The Godfather* (1969)

> A lawyer with his brief case can steal more than a hundred men with guns.
> Ibid.

> Keep your friends close, but keep your enemies closer.
> Ibid.

Thomas S. Szasz
1920

American (Hungarian-born), psychiatrist, and libertarian, who opposes confining mentally ill people unless they have committed crimes. He argues that disease causes mental illness.

> People are free in proportion as the state protects them from others; and are oppressed in proportion as the state protects them from themselves.
> In L. R. Frank, *Freedom* (2003)

> Traditionally, men used power to gain sex, and women used sex to gain power.
> In L. R. Frank, *Quotationary* (1999)

> The greatest analgesic, soporific, stimulant, tranquilizer, narcotic, and to some extent even antibiotic—in short the closest thing to a genuine panacea—known to medical science is work.

Sam More Walton
1920–1992

American, retailer (founder of Wal-Mart), who became the richest man on Earth.

People think we got big by putting big stores in small towns. Really, we got big by replacing inventory with information. [Point of sale databases are created by cash registers, which daily inform suppliers how much of each item to restock in each store, thereby assuring a full line of merchandise while minimizing inventory costs.]

There is only one boss. The customer. And he can fire everybody in the company, from the chairman on down, simply by spending his money somewhere else. [Walton denied that he put little shops out of business—the customers did that.]

I probably have walked into more variety stores than anybody in America. I am just trying to get ideas, any kind of ideas, that will help our company. Most of us don't invent ideas. We take the best ideas from someone else.

Betty Friedan
1921–2006

American, feminist, and founder of the National Organization for Women (1966). Her *The Feminine Mystique* (1963) "identified the problem that had no name": the soul-draining frustration of educated women who had to concentrate on "ring around the collar." Friedan described the suburban housewife as living in a "comfortable concentration camp." She believed that teaching the children of others was more rewarding than raising one's own.

Women, because they are not generally the principal breadwinners, can be perhaps most useful as the trail blazers, working along the by-paths, doing the unusual job that men cannot afford to gamble on.

The Feminine Mystique (1963)

The problem lay buried, unspoken, for many years in the minds of American women. It was a strange stirring, a sense of dissatisfaction, a yearning that women suffered in the middle of the twentieth century in the United States. Each suburban wife struggled with it alone. As she made the beds, shopped for groceries, matched slipcover material, ate peanut butter sandwiches with her children, chauffeured Cub Scouts and Brownies, lay beside her husband at night—she was afraid to ask even herself the silent question—"Is this all?"

Ibid., ch. 1

William (Bill) Mauldin
1921–2003

American, cartoonist of "Willie and Joe," two bedraggled "dogfaces" who fought in World War II.

I feel like a fugitive from the law of averages.

Up Front (1945)

He's right, Joe, when we ain't fightin' we should ack like sojers.

Ibid.

GENE RODDENBERRY
1921–91

American, film producer, TV series *Star Trek*.

These are the voyages of the starship Enterprise. Its five-year mission: to explore strange new worlds, to seek out new life and new civilizations, to boldly go where no man has gone before.

PETER USTINOV
1921–2004

English, (Russian-born), playwright, actor.

I do not believe that friends are necessarily the people you would like best, they are merely the people who got there first.

Dear Me (1977), ch. 5

The young need old men. They need men who are not ashamed of age, not pathetic imitations of themselves…. Parents are the bones on which children sharpen their teeth.

Ibid., ch. 18

MICHAEL CACOYANNIS
1922

Greek, screenwriter of *Zorba the Greek* (1964). Nikos Kazantzakis (1883–1957) wrote *Zorba the Greek* (1946). An old Greek, Zorba, a passionate type, teaches Basil, a weak, ineffectual British writer, how to dance and how to face the world.

I like you. Take me with you.
[Zorba.]

I don't want any trouble.
[Basil.]
To be alive is trouble.
[Zorba.]

Am I not a man? And is not a man stupid? I am a man, so I am married. Wife, children, house, the full catastrophe.
[Zorba.]

Make a pass. It's only polite.
[Zorba, advising Basil to make a pass at Madame Hortense.]

Boss you had better make up your mind. Are you or are you not a gosh-dern capitalist?
[Zorba.]

My brain is not the right weight. It gives me crazy ideas.
[Zorba.]

If a woman sleeps alone, it puts a shame on all men…God has a very big heart, but there is one sin he will not forgive. If a woman calls a man to her bed and he will not go. I know because a very wise old Turk told me.
[Zorba.]

Why do the good die young? Why does anyone die?
[Zorba.]
I don't know.
[Basil.]
What's the use of all your damn books if they don't tell you that? What do they tell you?
[Zorba.]
They tell me about the agony of men who can't answer questions like yours.
[Basil.]

You have everything but madness. A man needs a little madness or else he never dares to cut the rope and be free.
[Zorba.]

THOMAS KUHN
1922–96

American, MIT science historian. His *The Structure of Scientific Revolution* (1962) argues that science does not progress by measured steps but by periodic revolutions, "paradigm shifts," when the old systems can no longer reconcile new data. They cause research to be concentrated along a new single path, which hastens discovery on that path but blinds research to alternatives. Discoveries usually come from young scientists who are not indoctrinated in the discipline. Social paradigm shifts follow scientific paradigm shifts; for example, Social Darwinism followed Darwin's theory of evolution. Kuhn inspired the radical sociologists for whom "paradigm shifts" or holistic revolutions became the routes toward social justice.

CHARLES M. SCHULZ
1922–2000

American, cartoonist. He was famous for his "Peanuts" characters: Charlie Brown, the bland, round-faced kid who always loses—he never kisses the little red-haired girl or kicks the football; Snoopy, a beagle who makes his life meaningful with fantasies, like being a fighter pilot or Joe Cool; Sally, Charlie's little sister; the crabby and tyrannical Lucy; her younger brother, Linus, who carries a security blanket; plus Schroeder, Pigpen, Peppermint Patty, Marcie, and Woodstock.

Charlie Brown knew Lucy would pull the ball away at the last moment, but he persevered in trying to kick it. Charlie Brown is Everyman, who wants to be a champion but cannot, because only those gifted with rare talent can be champions.

Schulz's high school rejected his cartoons; his sweetheart married someone else; and, unable to afford college, he learned to draw through an art school correspondence course. Yet, eventually he was carried in 2,600 newspapers in 75 countries and read by 350 million people. Good grief!

Yesterday I was a dog. Today I am a dog. Tomorrow I'll probably still be a dog.
[Snoopy]

"It was a dark and stormy night. Suddenly a scream pierced the air…." Good writing takes enormous concentration.
[Snoopy]
Peanuts (1988)

I love mankind. It's people I can't stand.
In L. R. Frank, *Wit and Humor Quotationary*

There's no heavier burden than a great potential.
[Linus]
Ibid.

JOSEPH HELLER
1923–99

American, writer.

Orr would be crazy to fly more missions and sane if he didn't, but if he was sane he had to fly them. If he flew them, he was crazy and didn't have to; but if he didn't want to he was sane and had to.

Catch 22 (1961)

Colonel Cathcart had courage and never hesitated to volunteer his men for any target available.

Ibid.

He was a long-limbed farmer, a God-fearing, freedom-loving, law-abiding rugged individualist who held that federal aid to anyone but farmers was creeping socialism.

In L. R. Frank, Wit and Humor
Quotationary (2000)

CHARLTON HESTON
1923

American, movie star, and past president, National Rifle Association (NRA).

It is America's first freedom, the one that protects all the others.... It alone offers the absolute capacity to live without fear.

Speech at the National Press Club, Wash-
ington (September 1, 1997)

From my cold dead hands!
[Holding a Revolutionary War musket over his head, he defied those threatening the constitutional right to keep and bear arms.]

RIGHT TO BEAR FIREARMS

A well regulated Militia, being necessary to the security of a free State, the right of the people to keep and bear Arms, shall not be infringed.

Article II of the Amendments of the
Constitution

The right to self-protection is ancient. Jesus in Luke 22:36 said, "And let him who has no sword sell his mantle and buy one." Man is morally obligated to protect his family, himself, and all innocents. To do this, a weapon is absolutely necessary to enable weakness to cope with strength.

America's Founders as readers of history knew that the citizens of Greece's democratic city-states had been armed. Aristotle said that tyrants "mistrust the people and therefore deprive them of their arms." He also noted that the confiscations of arms by Pisistratus and the Thirty had empowered those Greek tyrannies. The Founders also knew that republican Rome became a tyranny only after its citizen soldiers had been disarmed.

More immediately, the Founders knew English history. The Treaty of Limerick in 1691 disarmed the Irish while guaranteeing full civil, religious, and property rights. After disarmament, Irish Catholics were not permitted to vote, be educated, hold public office, work in a profession, purchase/lease land, or own a horse, and Irish life expectancy went from the highest in the Western world to the lowest. When the English disarmed the Highlanders, they made it criminal for Scots to own a bagpipe or wear a kilt. The American Revolution began not when Britain imposed taxes, but when Britain tried to seize the colonists' armories in Lexington and Concord. Patrick Henry's "give me liberty or give me death" speech responded to the threat by the British to seize privately owned arms. John Dickerson's Farmer's Letters in 1767 charged that Britain planned to reduce the colonies to the status of Ireland by depriving American citizens of their right to bear arms.

America's rebellion was instigated precisely by threats of being disarmed.

Most of America's Bill of Rights confers rights on citizens, but the First and Second Amendments do *not*! Freedom of speech, press, religion, assembly and to bear arms are not conferred by the Constitution but are deemed to be preexisting inalienable rights.

The Founders wanted citizens to be armed not to shoot game or burglars, but to fight a tyrant's soldiers and police. *Federalist 47* decried European government that were "afraid to trust the people with arms." Noah Webster said, "The supreme power in America cannot enforce unjust laws by the sword, because the whole body of the people are armed, and constitute a force superior to any band of regular troops."

The Second Amendment is a doomsday article designed to remove tyrants by force during times when courts do not protect constitutional rights.

> *Washington:* "Firearms stand next in importance to the Constitution itself. They are the American people's liberty teeth and keystone under independence."

> *Mason:* "Who are the militia? They consist of the whole people."

> *Jefferson:* "No man shall ever be debarred the use of arms. The strongest reason for the people to retain the right to keep and bear arms is, as a last resort, to protect themselves against tyranny in government."

> *Madison:* "The Constitution preserves the advantage of being armed which Ameri-cans possess over the people of almost every other nation…[where] governments are afraid to trust the people with arms."

> *Hamilton:* [If the government were to] "form an army of any magnitude, that army can never be formidable to the liberties of the people while there is a large body of citizens, little if at all inferior to them in discipline and the use of arms who stand ready to defend their rights…"
>
> *Federalist No. 29*

> *Henry Lee:* "To preserve liberty it is essential that the whole body of the people always possess arms…"

> *Justice Joseph Story:* "The right of a citizen to keep and bear arms has justly been considered the palladium of the liberties of the republic, since it offers a strong moral check against the usurpation and arbitrary power of rulers…"

The argument that the Second Amendment merely guarantees the states a militia is bogus. It refers to "the rights of the people." The Constitution grants "rights" only to people; it never grants "rights" to a state. To states it grants "powers" or "authorities." Also, a canon of constitutional construction holds a preamble does not limit a broad rights clause. Last, the preamble's militia did not mean an army but the right (in some states the duty) of all households to possess arms. Guaranteeing to each individual the right to bear arms guaranted the material of a militia. Note: A federal law still says every able-bodied American man from 17 to 44 is a member of the United States militia.

Let's keep our powder dry, barrels swabbed and then: breathe, relax, aim, slack, squeeze!

ARTHUR JENSEN
1923

American, professor of Educational Psychology at the University of California, Berkeley. The American Psychological Association in 1995 concluded that there are substantial gender, age, and racial differences in Intelligence Quotient (IQ) and that the IQ tests that measured those differentials are not biased. Jensen's *The g Factor: The Science of Mental Ability* (1998) argues that the principal cause of these differences is genetic. He demolishes all alternative hypotheses. Educators who ignore Jensen will likely injure their students through inappropriate expectations.

HENRY KISSINGER
1923

American, secretary of state under President Nixon and Nobel Peace Prize in 1973 for negotiating the end of the Vietnam War. He noted that "even paranoids have enemies."

In guerrilla war, superior mobility and firepower lose their old relevance. Guerrillas need only join battle where they enjoy local superiority, but the defenders must be strong everywhere in anticipation of the unexpected. No longer is the ability to occupy territory decisive, for the real target has become the morale of the population and the system of the civil administration. If these can be undermined through protracted struggle, the insurgents will prevail no matter how many battles the defending forces have won.

In L. R. Frank, *Quotationary* (1999)

Power is the great aphrodisiac.

New York Times (January 19, 1971)

High office teaches decision-making, not substance. It consumes intellectual capital; it does not create it. Most high officials leave office with the perceptions and insights with which they entered.

White House Years (1979)

While I hold strong opinions, I have always felt it essential to test them against men and women of intelligence and character; those who stood up to me earned my respect and often became my closest associates.

Ibid., ch. 2

One cannot combine the benefits of every course of action. And if one goes down a certain road, at some point one has to face the consequences that this road implies.

Newsweek (December 10, 1990)

Any people who have been persecuted for 2,000 years must be doing something wrong.

In Walter Isaacson, *Kissinger* (1992)

[The Treaty of Westphalia initiated a] doctrine of sovereignty, which declared a state's domestic conduct and institutions to be beyond the reach of other states. These principles were an expression of the conviction that domestic rulers were less likely to be arbitrary than crusading foreign armies bent on conversion.... Noninterference in the domestic affairs of other states has been abandoned in favor of a concept of universal humanitarian intervention....

Does America Need a Foreign Policy (2000)

The successful conduct of foreign policy demands, above all, the intuitive ability to sense the future and thereby to master it. ...most great statesmen were less distinguished by their detailed knowledge...than by an ability to discern amidst the myriad of impressions that impinge on consciousness those most likely to shape the future.... The study of history and philosophy [are] the disciplines most relevant to perfecting the art of statesmanship....

Ibid.

The road to empire leads to domestic decay because, in time, the claims of omnipotence erode domestic restraints. No empire has avoided the road to Caesarism.... A deliberate quest for hegemony is the surest way to destroy the values that made the United States great.... America's ultimate challenge is to transform its power into moral consensus, promoting its values not by imposition, but by their willing acceptance...

Ibid.

Nobody will ever win the battle of the sexes. There's just too much fraternizing with the enemy.

Ninety percent of the politicians give the other ten percent a bad reputation.

L.R. Frank, *Wit and Humor Quotationary* (2000)

An expert is someone who is capable of articulating the interest of people with power.

Ibid.

GEORGE H. W. BUSH
1924

American, forty-first president (1989–93). After running on Reagan's record, he fired the Reaganauts and abandoned Reagan's policies. Bush admitted he lacked "the vision thing." Paul Johnson called him an "Eastern Wasp in a Stetson" who was "at his best when he had a more resolute foreign ally to stiffen his resolve..." Yet Bush assembled an international alliance to thwart Iraq's invasion of Kuwait and obtained Senate authorization for war by a margin of only two votes, and against the opposition of *every* Democratic House and Senate officer and 80 percent of the Democratic members.

The Congress will push me to raise taxes, and I'll say no, and they'll push, and I'll say no, and they'll push again. And all I can say to them is read my lips: No New Taxes.

[Bush broke his pledge and therefore lost the 1992 election.]

Republican National Convention (August 18, 1988)

I do not like broccoli, and I haven't liked it since I was a little kid. I am President of the United States, and I am not going to eat it anymore.

In L. R. Frank, *Wit and Humor Quotationary* (2000)

JAMES CLAVELL
1924

American (English-born), historical novelist: *King Rat* (1962), *Tai-Pan* (1966), *Shögun* (1975), *Noble House* (1981), and *Gai-Jin* (1993).

> It's all so simple. Just change your view of the world.
> [Mariko to Blackthorn]
> *Shogun* (1975)

> Blackthorn: It's too bad not to be able to trust anyone.
> Mariko: It's not too bad; it's just one of life's more important rules.
> Ibid.

LEE IACOCCA
1924

American, who saved Ford (responsible for the Mustang and front-wheel drive), and saved Chrysler (acquired Jeep and introduced the minivan).

> If I had to sum up in one word what makes a good manager, I'd say decisiveness.

> So what do we do? Anything. Something. So long as we just don't sit there. If we screw it up, start over. Try something else. If we wait until we've satisfied all the uncertainties, it may be too late.... I have always found that if I move with 75 percent or more of the facts I usually never regret it. It's the guys who wait to have everything perfect that drive you crazy.

> A major reason capable people fail to advance is that they don't work well with their colleagues.

DAVID S. LANDES
1924

American, Harvard professor emeritus of economics and history.

> In this world, the optimists have it, not because they are always right, but because they are positive. Even when wrong, they are positive and that is the way of achievement, correction, improvement, and success. Educated, eyes-open optimism pays; pessimism can only offer the empty consolation of being right.
> *The Wealth and Poverty of Nations* (1998)

> If we learn anything from the history of economic development, it is that culture makes all the difference. (Here Max Weber was right on.) Witness the enterprise of expatriate minorities—the Chinese in East and Southeast Asia, Indians in East Africa, Lebanese in West Africa, Jews and Calvinists throughout much of Europe, and on and on.
> Ibid.

JEAN-FRANCOIS REVEL
1924–2006

French, humanist, and secularist philosopher. In the 1960s he led many French intellectuals out of Marxism. His *How Democracies Perish* (1988) claimed that democracies underrated the Communist expansionist threat and were too eager to negotiate.

> Ordinarily we think of utopian philosophers as harmless dreamers, the only flaw of whose generous idealism is that it is unrealistic.... But all the utopian

authors factor repressive totalitarianism into their blueprints for society. Tyranny is the very essence of their thinking, not a consequence of the difficulty of putting it into practice.

Democracy Against Itself (1993),
tr. Roger Kaplan

DANIEL SELIGMAN
1924

American, scientist, who believes that stereotypes are usually truthful statistical approximations and can be positive, as in "Asian-Americans are smart and industrious."

> The idea that humans are equal in ability implies that the manifest inequalities observable in everyday life are unfair— also that they are reversible. For some, this lively faith is combined with a more politicized thought: that the nurtural side of the argument is the "progressive side".... In the Stalin era, many scholars were shot for positing that human differences might have some genetic basis.
>
> *A Question of Intelligence* (1992)

Seligman concludes the average Intelligence Quotient (IQ) of whites, East Asians, and Jews are 100, 106, and 112 respectively. Jews constitute only 2.5 percent of the U.S. population, but they constitute a third each of America's Nobel laureates and the Forbes' 400 wealthiest list. Asian IQs are concentrated around the mean, while white IQs are more variable. At very high and low IQ levels, Caucasians outnumber Asians, which explains why America leads Japan in high technology. Male IQs are more variable than female IQs. With

age, IQ falls, so a scientist making a major discovery at fifty years of age is about as likely as someone playing linebacker in the NFL at fifty.

YOGI (LAWRENCE P.) BERRA
1925

American, New York Yankees catcher and manager who was selected to the All-Star team every year from 1948 to 1962. See his quotations in *The Yogi Book: "I Really Didn't Say Everything I Said"* (1998).

> No one goes there nowadays; it's too crowded.
>
> Robert Lipsyte, *New York Times*
> (October 25, 1963)

> It ain't over till it's over.
> [Baseball is not limited by a clock.]

> Baseball is ninety percent mental. The other half is physical.

> You can observe a lot by watching.

> It was déjà vu all over again.

> How can you think and hit at the same time?

WILLIAM F. BUCKLEY JR.
1925

American, political philosopher, author of 4,000 columns and 47 books, and founder in 1955 of the *National Review*, a magazine championing Edmund Burke's traditional values and Adam Smith's limited government and free markets. *NR*,

Human Events (founded in 1944 by libertarians, like Frank Frank Chodorov), and the *Freeman* (founded in 1950 by Leonard Read) carried the conservative torch for two decades while all other journals were liberal to socialist. Seeing a flood tide of statism in the West, *NR's* inaugural issue claimed it would "stand athwart history, yelling 'Stop!' " It became the recognized voice of American conservatism by withdrawing conservatives to defensible positions through purging the anti-Semites and abandoning isolationism and attempts to repeal Social Security.

NR's hardest task was reconciling the two principal warring conservative factions: anti-government libertarians who only prize individual freedom and traditionalists who want government to support virtue and community. Buckley was the unifying figure who welded together the traditionalist, individualist, libertarian, skeptical, Straussian, Burkean, and Voegelinian factions. He did that by supporting Frank Meyer's "fusion doctrine" that is, freedom is insecure unless society is grounded in a moral order, and paternalism carried too far corrupts society. Buckley taught the virture of prudence and the necessity of historical knowledge as a guide to public policy. As Jeffrey Hart, an *NR* editor said, "Without a deep knowledge of history, policy analysis is feckless." In elections, *NR* supported Buckley's formulation, "the most rightward electable candidate." See Jeffrey Hart, *The Making of the American Conservative Mind* (2005), for a history of the *NR* and its times.

Buckley also addressed the role of religion in conservative politics. Some conservatives, like George Santayana and David Hume, have been atheists or skeptics, even though Christianity has been at the center of Western civilization. Buckley resolved this issue with the formulation: "A conservative need not be religious, but a conservative cannot despise religion."

Like Horatius at the bridge, Buckley and his tiny crew checked the socialists of all stripes with his rapier wit and courtly manners until other small circulation conservative journals entered the lists, such as the *American Spectator*. Eventually it became possible for conservative books to be published and sold on Amazon, and Fox News began to broadcast both sides of political debates. George Will called *NR* "the most consequential journal of opinion ever." David Brooks said, "No Buckley, no conservative movement; no conservative movement, no Ronald Reagan. You fill in the rest."

> Truth does not carry within itself an antitoxin to falsehood. The cause of truth must be championed, and it must be championed dynamically.
>
> *God and Man at Yale* (1951)

> How can the modern relativist exercise tolerance if he doesn't believe in anything to begin with? It is not hard to exhibit toleration toward a point of view if you have no point of view of your own with which that point of view conflicts.
>
> *Up From Liberalism* (1984)

> Socialize the individual's surplus and you socialize his spirit and creativeness....
>
> Ibid.

> Without [the state] we have anarchy, and the lawlessness of anarchy is counter to the natural law; so we abjure all political theories which view the state

as inherently and necessarily evil. But it is the state which has been in history the principal instrument of abuse of the people and so it is central to the conservatives' program to keep the state from accumulating any but the most necessary powers.

The Catholic World (March 1961)

I should live in a society governed by the first two thousand names in the Boston telephone directory than in a society governed by the two thousand faculty members of Harvard University.

Rumbles Left and Right (1963)

Mr. G. D. H. Cole lectured the Fabian Society on the necessity to recognize that outright ownership is merely a technicality. What he asked, is the purpose of government ownership if, instead, the government can with far greater convenience control corporations by indirect means?

"On the Right" (December 17, 1964)

Democracy has no eschatology, no vision, no point of arrival. Neither does academic freedom. Both are merely instruments, the one supposed to induce a harmonious society, the second supposed to advance knowledge. But let me say that I, for one, would not willingly die for "democracy," any more than I would willing die for "academic freedom." I do understand the disposition to die for the kind of society democracy sometimes ushers in; and I do understand the disposition to die in behalf of some of the truths academic freedom may have been instrumental in apprehending.

"Should Liberalism be Repudiated?"
(1959) in *Let Us Talk of Many Things*
(Speeches, 1999)

Harvard, like so many other great universities, has become an engine for the imposition of secular and collectivist values. One out of two Protestants who go through Harvard lose their faith.... seven-tenths have changed either "from conservative to liberal" or "from liberal to more liberal."

Ibid., "The Aimlessness of American Education" (1966)

If we cannot hold up the Bill of Rights over against the Communist Manifesto and declare the one a benchmark of civilization, the other of modern atavism, then learning is really of little use....

Ibid., "Democracy and the Pursuit of Happiness" (1984)

The survival of everything we cherish depends on the survival of the culture of liberty; and that this hangs on our willingness to defend this extraordinary country of ours, so awfully mixed up, so much of the time; so schizophrenic in its understanding of itself and its purposes; so crazily indulgent of its legion of wildly ungovernable miscreants—to defend it at all costs. With it all, this idealistic republic is the finest bloom of nationhood in all recorded time, and save only that God may decide that the land of the free and the home of the brave has outrun its license on history, we Americans must contend, struggle, and if necessary fight for America's survival.

Ibid., "The Genesis of Blackford Oakes"
(1984)

[Those of us who live in the Free World] are left with the numbing, benumbing thought that we owe nothing to Plato and Aristotle, nothing to the prophets who wrote the Bible, nothing to the generations who fought for freedoms, activated in the Bill of Rights…. We need a rebirth of gratitude for those who have cared for us, living and, mostly, dead. The high moments of our way of life are their gifts to us.

Ibid., "Toward a Recovery of Gratitude" (1998)

[Buckley told the story of a Yale classmate, Roaring Henry, who was called to the dean's office for missing the first day of classes. Henry explained, "I spent the summer studying the Middle Ages, and I became so engrossed in the subject I completely forgot about the Gregorian calendar change." The scholarly dean deftly brushed that excuse aside saying, "In that event, you would have arrived in New Haven a week early."]

Ibid., "A Distinctive Gentility" (1990)

[Buckley reflecting on his years at Yale, concluded its greatest gifts were having been taught:] something about the scales of human achievement and having met most of my friends.

Ibid.

Buckley argues Russia needs a much freer economy than the U.S., which subsidizes many groups. Russia cannot afford to do that.

The Jewish community will never let the world forget about the Holocaust. Understandably so. Every living German is aware of that holocaust, most of them unborn when it happened. By contrast, not one in five hundred Westerners could answer the question, How many Ukrainians were starved to death by Sta-

lin from 1930 to 1933? Not one in one thousand would know that that figure is higher than the figure for all those killed during the Holocaust.

Ibid., "We Won. What Now?" (1991)

The man who pushes an old lady into the path of an oncoming truck and the man who pushes an old lady out of the path of an oncoming truck are not to be denounced even handedly as men who push old ladies.

[Comparing the Soviet Union and the U.S.]

Ibid., "Preserving the Heritage" (1999)

He is a man of his most recent word.

[Of Lyndon B. Johnson.]

In L. R. Frank, *Wit and Humor Quotationary*, 2000

[When a reporter in 1965 inquired what he would do if he won the election for mayor of New York as the Conservative Party's candidate, Buckley replied:]

I'd demand a recount.

BARBARA PIERCE BUSH
1925

American, first lady (1989–93).

Somewhere out in this audience may even be someone who will one day follow in my footsteps, and preside over the White House as the President's spouse. I wish him well!

Address at Wellesley College (June 1, 1990)

JOHN EHRLICHMAN
1925–1999

American, President Nixon's chief of staff.

We ought to let him hang there. Let him turn and twist slowly in the wind.
[Referring to Patrick Gray III's nomination to head the FBI, which Congress held up.]

HENRY HAZLITT
1925–93

American, economist. His *Economics In One Lesson* (1946) and *The Failure of the New Economics* (1959) describe the fallacies of Marxism and Keynesianism, which fallacies usually get obscured by special interest pleading. The slight beneficial effects of Keynesianism are immediate and visible, while its crippling of incentives to work and invest, though massive, is gradual and invisible. He noted that full employment is easy to organize. Primitive cultures have full employment; what they lack are high living standards.

ECONOMICS IN ONE LESSON
(1979)

The art of economics consists in looking not merely at the immediate but at the longer effects of any act or policy; it consists in tracing the consequences of that policy not merely for one group but for all groups.

1. [Any job created by government investment requires taxation or borrowing that destroys another job. Make-work wastes.]

2. [Government credit programs shift capital from the credit worthy to the non-credit worthy and promote favoritism and graft.]

3. [Better machines create jobs over time, but promote job insecurity in the short term. Countries with advanced technologies have the lowest unemployment (3-12 percent), and the least technologically developed countries have the highest unemployment (40-80 percent).]

4. [Spread-the-work impoverishes. If two are hired to do the work of one, then the second worker cannot be hired to create real value.]

5. [Our goal is to maximize production, which will maximize employment. If we seek to maximize employment, we will not have full production. "Nothing is easier to achieve than full employment, if divorced from the goal of full production."]

6. [Tariffs deflect labor and capital from what they do efficiently. Tariffs raise wages and profits in protected industries at the expense of other industries and workers, especially export industries. In the long run exports and imports must equal. To reduce imports is to reduce exports; subsidies to increase exports increase imports.]

7. [The Marxist "production-for-use-and-not-for-profit" argues business should not stop making products when it is no longer profitable if more can be produced. But you can only expand production of one product by stopping the equivalent production of other products.]

8. [Stabilizing commodity prices builds up inventories that depress prices.]

9. [Price-fixing increases shortages. Rationing limits demand without sending a price signal to produce more. Worst is price-fixing to combat inflation, because it does not cure the cause, a surplus of money. Rent control deters the sharing of space.]

10. [Total wages are determined, not by unions, but by productivity. U.S. wages are higher than those in Germany, whose unions are stronger. Unions cause unionized industries to pay higher wages to the detriment of other workers and capital formation.]

11. [Marxists and Keynesians argue that the only wages that can prevent depressions are wages high enough to enable labor "to buy back the product it creates." But only by investing profits have we risen from starving hunter-gatherers.]

12. [Inflation causes over-expansion in some industries at the expense of others. It distorts the wage-price structure, inhibiting incentives to invest or produce and causing recessions or depressions.]

13. [Keynes accepted the old canard that saving is a sin and dissaving is a virtue because money not spent results in unemployment. But saving is spending. If invested, it is spent directly, and if put into savings, it is loaned to others who spend it.]

14. [Artificially low interest rates reduce the incentive to save so there can be less investment.]

15. [Destruction of property is a negative even though it creates jobs to rebuild. Capital and labor used to rebuild would have been used to produce other useful goods.]

THEODORE LEVITT
1925–2006

American, Harvard Business School professor, who tied Peter Drucker for most articles in *HBR*.

Good managers have strong colleagues. Those that don't are not good. In a very short time it will show.
Thinking About Management (1991)

We decline in energy as we advance in age; also in decisiveness and daring. All people finally wear out.
Ibid.

Not everything that can be learned can be taught…. The paradox is that the less teachable something is, the rarer and therefore more valuable it is.
Ibid.

Leaders produce consent, others seek consensus. Consent is given to the confident and composed, those with firm and persuasive convictions. Only people who believe in themselves generate believers.
Ibid.

The effective manager develops the ability to hear what others are not saying.
Ibid.

Nothing characterizes the successful organization so much as its willingness to abandon what has been long successful.
Ibid.

It is not so much the accurately forecasted future we need as quick response to the forces shaping today's events and environment…. In this age of fast history, equivocation is more harmful than prediction is helpful.

Ibid.

If you don't market, something terrible happens—nothing.

Ibid.

Advertising works because the familiar is safer than the unfamiliar.... It matters not why this is so, only that in all societies (even, indeed, in the animal kingdom), it has always been so. Strangers are avoided if not actually suspected or attacked, the familiar tolerated if not necessarily welcomed or embraced, the known always preferred to the unknown. Familiarity breeds.

Ibid.

By far the greatest flow of newness is not innovation at all. Rather, it is imitation.

Harvard Business Review (September/October 1966)

MARGARET H. R. THATCHER
1925

English, Conservative Prime Minister (1979–90) "Iron Lady of the Western World." She was Europe's first female Prime Minister and Britain's longest-serving Prime Minister since 1827. She cut the top tax rate from 83 percent to 40 percent and the basic rate from 33 percent to 25 percent. She privatized nationalized companies, which got loss-makers off the dole, raised cash, and created taxpayers. She cured the "British disease" of interminable strikes by breaking the coal miners' union. Britain's unemployment rate went from the highest to the lowest in Europe.

William F. Buckley Jr. said of her, "She is blessed also by a singular capacity to combine absolute firmness with sweetness of manner, attributes that have made her the formidable historical figure she is."

Victorian values...were the values when our country became great.

I owe nothing to Women's Lib.

The Observer (December 1, 1974)

Let our children grow tall, and some taller than others, if they have it in them to do so.

Speech (October 1975)

To those who wait with bated breath for that favorite media catch phrase, the U-turn, I have only this to say. You turn if you want to. The lady's not for turning.

Speech to Conservative Party conference (1980)

If we are safe today, it is because America has stood with us. If we are to remain safe tomorrow, it will be because America remains powerful and self-confident. When, therefore, the Americans face difficulties, we need to say to them more clearly: "We are with you..."

Speech to the Pilgrims Society (January 30. 1981)

No one would remember the Good Samaritan if he'd only had good intentions; he had money, too.

London Times (January 12, 1986)

Ronald Reagan won the Cold War without firing a shot.

Heritage Foundation, 1991

The Declaration of Independence is a world declaration.

> Speech to the London Institute of U.S. Studies (September 21, 1996)

The very essence of Western culture… was recognition of the unique value of the individual human being.

> Statecraft (2002)

[The Western model of liberty's] most important defining feature is that it is based upon truth—about the nature of Man, about his aspirations, and about the world he can hope to create.

> Ibid.

America is more than a nation or a state or a superpower; it is an idea—and one that has transformed and continues to transform us all.

> Ibid.

Five Conditions Necessary for Capitalism:
1. Private Property.
2. Rule of law, as per Roger Scruton's definition: "The form of government in which no power can be exercised except according to procedures, principles and constraints contained in the law, and in which any citizen can find redress against any other, however powerfully placed, and against the officers of the state itself, for any act which involves a breach of the law."
3. Culture promoting invention, such as curiosity, risk acceptance, belief in free will, and the value of the individual.
4. A diversity of states and competition between them.
5. An encouraging tax, monetary and regulatory regime.

> Ibid.

In order to practice liberty successfully, a nation needs first to have a critical mass of individuals who truly understand it.

> Ibid.

During my lifetime, all of the problems have come from mainland Europe; and all of the solutions have come from English-speaking nations that have kept law-abiding liberty alive for the future.

George, this is no time to go wobbly.
   [When Bush wavered on Kuwait.]

[Dennis Thatcher, husband of Margaret Thatcher, was asked who wore the pants in his house. He answered:]
I do, and I also wash and iron them.

JEANNE KIRKPATRICK
1926–2006

American, neoconservative political scientist, U.S. ambassador to the United Nations (1981–85), and a Humphrey Democrat who became a Republican. She noted the tendency of the left "to blame America first and most, and to extend to others understanding and tolerance denied the United States." She added, "We did not doubt that American society could be improved but we believed it first had to be preserved."

When Marxist dictators shoot their way into power in Central America, the San Francisco Democrats don't blame the guerrillas and their Soviet allies, they blame United States policies of one hundred years ago, but then they always blame America first.

> Republican Convention (1984)

ALAN GREENSPAN
1926

American, chairman of the Federal Reserve under George Bush, Bill Clinton, and W. Bush.

It is precisely the greed of the business-man, or, more appropriately, his profit seeking, which is the unexcelled protec-tor of the consumer.

In Michael Lewis, "Beyond Economics, Beyond Politics, Beyond Accountability," *Worth* (May 1995)

ROBERT HERON BORK
1927

American, federal appellate judge. He is the supreme intellectual opponent of judi-cial activism, which Sen. Sam Ervin defined as "a judge who interprets the Constitu-tion to mean what it would have said if he, instead of the Founding Fathers, had writ-ten it." As Justice Antonin Scalia said, "Day by day, case by case, [the Court] is busy designing a Constitution for a country I do not recognize." Bork sees judicial activism undermining the separation of powers as the Supreme Court relegates to itself pow-ers the Constitution placed in the federal, legislative, and executive branches, and in the states.

The judge's authority derives entirely from the fact that he is applying the law and not his personal values. That is why the American public accepts the decisions of its courts, accepts even decisions that nullify the laws a majority of the elector-ate or their representatives voted for.

Statement at a hearing to become associate justice of the Supreme Court (1987)

When a judge goes beyond [his proper judicial function] and reads entirely new values into the Constitution, values the framers and ratifiers did not put there, he deprives the people of their liberty.

Ibid.

The defining characteristics of mod-ern liberalism are radical egalitarianism (the equality of outcomes rather than of opportunities) and radical individualism (the drastic reduction of limits to per-sonal gratification).

Slouching Towards Gomorrah (1996), Introduction

Politics is a lagging indicator. Culture eventually makes politics.

Ibid.

It is arguable that the American judi-ciary—the Supreme Court, abetted by the lower federal courts and many state courts—is the single most powerful force shaping our culture.

Ibid., ch. 6

Multiculturalism is a lie, or rather a series of lies, the lie that European-American culture is uniquely oppressive...the lie that other cultures are equal to the cul-ture of the West.

Ibid., ch. 15

Originalism simply means that the judge must discern from the relevant materi-als...the principles the ratifiers under-stood themselves to be enacting. The remainder of the task is to apply those principles to unforeseen circumstances, a task that law performs all the time. Any philosophy that does not confine judges to the original understanding makes the

Constitution the plaything of willful judges.

Wall Street Journal (October 19, 2005)

MIDGE DECTER
1927

American, editor and social commentator.

We allowed you (the children) a charade of trivial freedoms in order to avoid making those impositions on you that are in the end both the training ground and proving ground for true independence. We pronounced you strong when you were still weak in order to avoid the struggles with you that would have fed your true strength. Thus, it was no small anomaly of your growing up that while you were the most indulged generation, you were also the most abandoned to your own meager devices by those into whose safe-keeping you had been given.

Liberal Parents/Radical Children (1975) ch. 1

SAMUEL P. HUNTINGTON
1927

American, political science professor at Harvard University. His *The Clash of Civilizations and the Remaking of World Order* (1996) describes the new geopolitical global reality in the post-Cold War world as truly as George F. Kennan's "Mr. X" article did in 1947. The cultures of the seven major civilizations, not political ideologies, will shape the conflicts in the twenty-first century. Those seven are: Sinic, Japanese, Hindu, Islamic, Orthodox, Western, and Latin American.

Contrary to the prevailing point of view, Westernization is not producing a universal civilization, although most of the world is modernizing. Westernization and modernization are different things. For example, the democratization of non-Western nations gives rise to anti-Western governments. Huntington said democracy is "inherently a parochializing not a cosmopolitanizing process." Another illustration of the difference was Richard Nixon's statement in 1994, "Today China's economic power makes U.S. lectures about human rights imprudent.... Within two decades it will make them laughable." Only in nations where Western Christianity obtains have multiparty democratic transitions occurred.

The West is declining in relative power as Asia rises and as Islam explodes demographically. Nations sharing cultural affinities will tend to cooperate with each other. The survival of the West depends on Americans reaffirming their Western identity and in accepting that their civilization is unique and not universal, that is, not appropriate for other cultures. Avoidance of global war will require nations to maintain the multicivilizational shape of global politics. Also, the stability of any nation will depend on its adhering to a single culture; all multicultural nations splinter.

The defining characteristics of Western civilization include: 1) the classical legacy of Greek philosophy and Roman law; 2) Catholicism and Protestantism; 3) separation of spiritual and temporal authority; 4) the rule of law; 5) social pluralism in autonomous organizations; 6) representative bodies; and, 7) the central distinguishing mark is *individualism*.

Huntington believes civilizations decline when those that control the economic surplus use it for nonproductive purposes. Risk-averse decadence is preceded by a decline in morals, including family decay, illegitimacy, loss of the work ethic, and decreased commitment to learning. Decadence depresses living standards and leads to a reluctance to fight for the society. As in Rome, this will result in civil wars.

Western civilization is under assault by multiculturalist intellectuals who want to destroy the West's creed of liberty, rule of law, constitutionalism, and private property. They seek a country of many cultures, but no such country has endured for long.

> The principal responsibility of Western leaders is not to attempt to reshape other civilizations in the image of the West, which is beyond their declining power, but to preserve, protect, and renew the unique qualities of Western civilization.
> *Clash of Civilizations* (1996)

> Islam has bloody borders.
> Ibid.

> Confucians, Buddhists, Hindus, Western Christians, and Orthodox Christians have less difficulty adapting to and living with each other than any one of them has in adapting to and living with Muslims.
> Ibid.

ABBY MANN
1927

American, scriptwriter for *Judgment at Nuremberg*, a 1961 film. The 1945–46 International War Crimes Trials for aggressive warfare and genocide were held in Nuremberg.

> Ernst Janning (German jurist):
> I did not know it would come to that.
> [Millions of state directed-murders.]

Robert Jackson (American justice):
It came to that the first time you sentenced to death a man you knew to be innocent.

DANIEL PATRICK MOYNIHAN
1927–2003

American, Democratic senator.

> A community that allows a large number of young men (and women) to grow up in broken families, dominated by women, never acquiring any stable relationship to male authority, never acquiring any set of rational expectations about the future, that community asks for and gets chaos.
> *The Negro Family: The Case for National Action* (1965)

> The central conservative truth is that it is culture, not politics, that determines the success of a society. The central liberal truth is that politics can change a culture and save it from itself.

> Everyone is entitled to his own opinion but not his own facts.

ANDY WARHOL
1927–87

American, commercial artist, who gulled the public into buying prints of Campbell soup cans, Brillo boxes, and repetitive silkscreen portraits in garish colors. Pioneer of "mechanized art," he employed legions of workers in his "factory sites." When asked what he was going to do with a mess of canvas and paints, he replied, "I'm starting pop art because I hate abstract expressionism." Modern art had been harshly critical of popular culture, but pop art cheerfully celebrated it!

In the future everybody will be world famous for fifteen minutes.

Andy Warhol (1968)

PAUL JOHNSON
1928

English, great historian. His *Modern Times* (1991) best depicts the twentieth century, and his *History of the American People* (1998), proves that foreigners have the most penetrating insights into the American experiment.

Once the rule of law is humbled, all else that is valuable in a civilized society will vanish, usually with terrifying speed.

Enemies of Society (1977)

It is sobering to find huge and frightening errors constantly repeated; lessons painfully learnt forgotten in the space of a generation; and the accumulated wisdom of the past heedlessly ignored in every society, and at all times.

The Recovery of Freedom (1980)

...by cutting the umbilical cord with God, our source of ethical vitality would be gone...For the truth is that we humans are all Jekyll and Hyde creatures, and the monster within each of us is always striving to take over.... The history of the twentieth-century proves the view that as the vision of God fades, we first become mere clever monkeys; then we exterminate one another.

Readers Digest (June 1985)

Those who pillory capitalism for "creating artificial needs" strike me as timid and dismal souls. You might just as well denounce Monet for creating an "artificial need" for Impressionism.

The Pick of Paul Johnson (1985)

The more I study history, the more convinced I am that what happens is influenced as much by the will power of key individuals as by the underlying pressure of collective forces.

American Spectator (July 1988)

...social engineering has been the salient delusion and the greatest curse of the modern age.... In the twentieth century it has killed scores of millions of innocent people in Soviet Russia, Nazi Germany, Communist China....

Intellectuals (1988)

Intellectuals reveals Johnson's philosophy, that an intellectual is "someone who thinks ideas are more important than people." His book unveils the chasm between the professed ideals of intellectuals and their actual effect on people.

It is a commonplace that men are excessively ruthless and cruel not as a rule out of avowed malice but from outraged righteousness.

Modern Times (1991)

As Churchill correctly noted, the horrors he listed were perpetrated by the "mighty educated States"... The destructive capacity of the individual, however, vicious, is small—of the state, however well-intentioned, almost limitless.

Ibid.

Nietzsche [in 1886 saw that] the decline and ultimately the collapse of the religious impulse would leave a huge vacuum…. [which would] produce a new kind of messiah, uninhibited by any religious sanctions whatever, and with an unappeasable appetite for controlling mankind. The end of the old order, with an unguided world adrift in a relativistic universe, was a summons to such gangster statesmen to emerge. They were not slow to make their appearance.

Ibid.

Lenin abolished the idea of personal guilt and started to exterminate whole classes…. There is no essential difference between class-warfare and race-warfare.

Ibid., ch. 2

The hideous crimes committed in Cambodia from April 1975 onwards, which involved the deaths of between a fifth and a third of the population, were organized by a group of Francophone middle-class intellectuals… Of its eight leaders, five were teachers, one a university professor, one a civil servant and one an economist.

Ibid.

Totalitarianism of the Left bred totalitarianism of the Right…it was Stalinism which made possible the Nazi Leviathan.

Ibid.

Hitler was not in the business of liberation. Like Stalin, he was in the business of slavery. The accident of race made them opponents, and pitted their regimes against each other. But in essential respects they were fellow-ideologues,

pursuing Utopias based on a fundamental division of mankind into elites and helots.

Ibid.

The outstanding event of modern times was the failure of religious belief to disappear.

Ibid.

In Latin America, every would-be plunderer or ambitious bandit now called himself a "liberator'"; murderers killed for freedom, thieves stole for the people.

The Birth of the Modern (1991)

The study of history is a powerful antidote to contemporary arrogance. It is humbling to discover how many of our glib assumptions, which seen to us novel and plausible, have been tested before, not once but many times and in innumerable guises; and discovered to be, at great human cost, wholly false.

The Quotable Paul Johnson (1994)

This book is dedicated to the people of America—strong, outspoken, intense in their convictions, sometimes wrong-headed but always generous and brave, with a passion for justice no nation has ever matched.

A History of the American People (1997), Dedication

STANLEY KUBRICK
1928–99

American, film director in 1968 of *2001: A Space Odyssey*, in which Hal, a spacecraft's computer, malfunctions. Having a personality, Hal was more advanced than computers in 2006, but being room-sized he was also ancient history.

Gentlemen, you can't fight in here. This is the war room.

Dr. Strangelove (1973), film

In *Dr. Strangelove*, the maniacal Gen. Jack D. Ripper believes the "Rooskies" are poisoning his "precious bodily fluids" with fluoridated water, so he sends Capt. Lionel Mandrake on a Stratofortress to nuke Russia.

The great nations have always acted like gangsters, and the small nations like prostitutes.

Guardian (June 5, 1963)

TOM LEHRER
1928

American, educator.

It is sobering to consider that when Mozart was my age he had already been dead for a year.

An Encyclopedia of Quotations about Music
(1978)

Plagiarize, plagiarize, why do you think the good Lord made your eyes?

T. BOONE PICKENS
1928

American, founder of Mesa Petroleum Company.

Be willing to make decisions. That's the most important quality in a good leader. Don't fall victim to what I call the "ready-aim-aim-aim syndrome." You must be willing to fire.

Interview in the *New York Times*
(June 11, 1995)

Keep things informal. Talking is a natural way to do business. Writing is great for keeping records, but talk generates ideas.

ALVIN & HEIDI TOFFLER
1928

American, futurists, who say companies need a long-term strategy and the agility to change instantly.

We believe that the most basic of all changes in human social organization have been the result of three processes. Starting 8,000 to 10,000 years ago, agriculture was invented in the Middle East. That's the First Wave. Roughly 250 years ago, the Industrial Revolution triggered a Second Wave of change. Brute-force technologies amplified human and animal muscle power and gave rise to an urban, factory-centered way of life. Sometime after World War II, a gigantic Third Wave began transforming the planet, based on tools that amplify mind rather than muscle. The Third Wave is bigger, deeper and faster than the other two. This is the civilization of the computer, the satellite, and the Internet.

Interview with Claudia Dreifus, *New York Times* (June 11, 1995)

Future shock…the shattering stress and disorientation that we induce in individuals by subjecting them to too much change in too short a time.

Future Shock (1970), Introduction

In *Powershift* (1990), Toffler said the three most important sources of power are violence, wealth, and knowledge; and knowledge has risen exponentially as a power source. As Toffler said:

Knowledge has gone from being an adjunct of money power and muscle power, to being their very essence. It is, in fact, the ultimate amplifier. This is the key to the powershift that lies ahead.... It is the truly revolutionary characteristic of knowledge that the weak and the poor can grasp it as well. Knowledge is the most democratic source of power.

Ibid.

WARREN T. BROOKS
1929–90

American, business journalist, and the 1980s' most perceptive forecaster of the U.S. economy. While Keynesians had forecast Reagan's economic policies would cause hyperinflation and depression, Brooks forecast that they would end inflation and stimulate rapid economic growth. He advised buying forty year zero coupon Treasuries at 14 percent and stocks when the Dow was under 800.

In any free society, through invention, creativity, and enterprise, a comparatively small part of the population still contributes the major share of economic growth. In this largest and richest of all industrial democracies, it is still safe to say that 80 percent-90 percent of the new jobs and economic growth is contributed by the efforts, imagination, energy, and initiative of 5 percent-10 percent of all individuals, through whose creativity the great wealth of this country still "trickles down" to the economy.

The Economy in Mind (1982)

Trickle-down is really the natural order of things, not merely in economics and business, but in nearly every other facet of life as well. We are all blessed by the genius of relatively few.... The world's greatest music is still the work of a handful of great composers, and most of the world's great art is the product of a few hundred brilliant talents.

Ibid.

ANNE FRANK
1929-45

Dutch, Jewish victim of the Nazis in the Bergen-Belsen concentration camp.

In spite of everything I still believe that people are really good at heart.
The Diary of a Young Girl (1952)
(Entry of March 7, 1944)

MARTIN LUTHER KING JR.
1929–68

American, civil rights leader, and Nobel Peace Prize (1964). A Baptist minister, he founded the Southern Christian Leadership Conference in 1957 to mobilize passive resistance against segregation, culminating on August 28, 1963, in the 200,000 person "March on Washington." His electrifying speech at the Lincoln Memorial sped the passage of the Civil Rights Act of 1964. When Dr. King supported a sanitation workers' strike in Memphis, Tennessee, he was assassinated by James Earl Ray.

Five score years ago a great American in whose symbolic shadow we stand, signed the Emancipation Proclamation. But one hundred years later, we must face the tragic fact that the Negro is still not free.... There will be neither rest nor tranquility in America until the Negro is granted his citizenship rights.

Keynote Speech at the "March on
Washington" (August 28, 1963)

I have a dream my four little children will one day live in a nation where they will not be judged by the color of their skin but by the content of their character.

Ibid.

When we let freedom ring, when we let it ring from every village and every hamlet, from every state and every city, we will be able to speed up that day when all of God's children, black men and white men, Jews and Gentiles, Protestants and Catholics, will be able to join hands and sing in the words of that old Negro spiritual, "Free at last! Free at last! Thank God Almighty, we are free at last!"

Ibid.

I submit to you that if a man hasn't discovered something he will die for, he isn't fit to live.

Speech in Detroit (June 23, 1963)

I would agree with St. Augustine that "an unjust law is no law at all."...An unjust law is a code that is out of harmony with the moral law.... All segregation laws are unjust because segregation distorts the soul and damages the personality.... One who breaks an unjust law must do so openly, lovingly, and with a willingness to accept the penalty.... An individual who breaks a law that conscience tells him is unjust, and willingly accepts the penalty by staying in jail to arouse the conscience of the community over its injustice, is in reality expressing the very highest respect for law.... We should never forget that everything Hitler did in Germany was "legal" and everything the Hungarian freedom fighters did in Hungary was "illegal."

A civil disobedience "Letter from Birmingham City Jail" (Easter, 1963)

The modern civil disobedience movement against American racial segregation began with Rosa Parks, a civil rights activist in Montgomery, Alabama, who refused on December 1, 1955, to move to the back of the bus when so ordered by the driver. Her arrest, conviction, and fine of ten dollars led to a 381-day African-American boycott of the Montgomery bus system led by Dr. King, pastor of a Montgomery Baptist church. Montgomery's white establishment eliminated segregated seating, which signaled that white establishments could be turned by peaceful demonstrations. Dr. King seized that opportunity and transformed American culture. The civil rights movement, which initially championed equality under the law, later went off the track by resurrecting its slain enemy, to wit, by putting racial preferences (affirmative action) back into the law.

I've been to the mountaintop...and I've looked over and I've seen the Promised Land. I may not get there with you.

April 3, 1968.

[The next day Dr. King was assassinated.]

NICHOLAS VON HOFFMAN
1929

American, columnist.

[Of the Democratic Party:] To its committed members it was still the party of heart, humanity, and justice, but to those removed a few paces it looked like Captain Hook's crew—ambulance chasing lawyers, rapacious public grants persons, civil rights gamesmen, dizzy brained movie stars, fat-assed civil servant desk squatters, recovering alcoholics, recovering drug addicts, recovering wife beaters, recovering child buggers—a grotesque lineup of ill-mannered, self-pitying, caterwauling freeloaders banging their tin cups on the pavement demanding handouts.

William Safire
1929

American, Pulitzer Prize journalist who wrote speeches for President Nixon.

> Appeasement does not always lead to war; sometimes it leads to surrender.
> > In L. R. Frank, *Wit and Humor Quotationary*

> I'm a right wing Republican.... The big moment of my year comes in October when daylight savings ends, and you can actually turn back the clock.
> > Ibid.

> Never use a long word when a diminutive one will do.
> > Ibid.

Edward O. Wilson
1929

American, whose *Sociobiology* (1975) studied the biological basis of social behavior. Sociobiology threatens the core left tenet that there is no inherent human nature, that

is, given the right environment, humans can be taught to live collectively. Rather, sociobiology holds that human institutions and customs must conform to a reasonable extent to humanity's biological realities in order to thrive.

The left attacks Wilson as racist, sexist, and capitalist. A corollary of sociobiology is that by nature men are more aggressive and risk-taking and women more nurturing and prudent. Realistic feminists accept this thesis and seek liberation not by creating androgynous beings but from each sex being free to express its inherent nature

Neil Armstrong
1930

American, astronaut who landed on the moon on July 20, 1969, with "Buzz" Aldrin on *Apollo XI*.

> That's one small step for a man, one giant leap for mankind.
> > [On first stepping on the moon.]

> Houston, Tranquility Base here. The Eagle has landed.
> > [Spoken by Buzz Aldrin.]

Jeffrey Hart
1930

American, senior editor of the *National Review* and English professor, Dartmouth College. His *The American Conservative Mind: Where We Are Now* (2005) offers an updated synthesis of conservatism as seen by the *NR*:

1) Opposition to the "hard utopianism" of Communism and National Socialism, which "tried to build versions of the Perfect Society." In Gerhart Niemeyer's words, *NR* opposes "the thought systems around utopian fantasies with which to manipulate human beings into false hopes."

2) Opposition to "soft utopianism," that is, beliefs in benevolent illusions, "such as all goals are reconciablable, as in such dreams as the Family of man, World Peace, multiculturalism, pacifism, and Wilsonian global democracy." Without divine intervention, the lion will eat the lamb if they lie down together, and it is suicide to think otherwise.

3) The nation is not a passing nuisance, but the palladium of civilization and individual freedom.

4) A strong national defense is necessary to preserve the nation. Given man's nature, weakness often invites aggression.

5) Constitutional government that aims not to govern by majorities alone, but by consensus for major changes. This is achieved by mechanisms that delay change and require supra-majorities. Because legislation is more easily reversed than court rulings, judicial restraint is critical.

6) Free market economics has replaced socialism as the world's tacit orthodoxy to the great benefit of most people. However, free markets should not always override all other values.

7) Beauty is a nonquantifiable need of civilization that Burke called the "unbought grace of life." While some conversatives, like T. R. Roosevelt, have preserved the wild lands, liberals have taken the lead in the preservation movement. Conservatives need to catch up here.

8) Religion is integral to the distinctive identity of Western civilization. *NR* supports Protestant, Catholic, and Jewish religions, which are "traditional, or intellectually and institutionally developed, not dependent upon spasms of emotion."

10) Abortion is condemned by *NR*, even to defending the "right to life" of a single-cell embryo. Hart differs from *NR* on the grounds that women will not surrender control of their reproductive capacities. To resist feminism here is imprudent.

11) Wilsonianism, which has been adopted by the Bush Republican Party, "derives from the Lockean and Rousseauian belief in the fundamental goodness of mankind and hence in a convergence of interest." This ignores the intractability of culture and thus is not conservative.

12) The Republican Party has been considered by *NR* as the conservative party. But as Machiavelli observed, institutions can retain the same outward aspect while transforming their substance entirely.

Hart concludes by saying that conservatives rely on prudence and a healthy practical skepticism. And, "Without a deep knowledge of history, policy analysis is feckless."

ALAN BLOOM
1930–92

American, professor of political science at the University of Chicago. To Bloom, most students are unified in their belief in moral relativism. To them, the great sin is intolerance.

> The liberally educated person is one who is able to resist the easy and preferred

answers, not because he is obstinate but because he knows others worthy of consideration

> *The Closing of the American Mind* (1987), Preface

The same people who struggle to save the snail-darter...defend abortion.

> Ibid., pt. 2

Zelig is a man who literally becomes whoever or whatever is expected of him—a Republican when with the rich; a gangster when with Mafioso; black, Chinese or female, when with blacks, Chinese or females. He is nothing in himself, just a collection of roles prescribed by others.

[Commenting on Woody Allen's film.]

> Ibid.

HAROLD BLOOM
1930

American, one of the foremost twentieth-century literary critics. He champions the aesthetic value of literature, as against the "school of resentment," as exemplified by Derrida, who values literature only to the extent it endorses his views on race, class, gender, and so forth. Bloom says that the best students are forsaking literature due to the loss of standards caused by the feminists, Marxists, Afrocentrists, deconstructors, and new historicists, who have seized the academy to promote their idea of social justice. It is worse in primary and secondary education, in which political correctness reigns supreme.

Bloom's *The Western Canon* (1994) answers the question, "Given what little time we have, what should we read?" He surveys his favorite authors and offers his canonical list. What makes a work canonical is its "beauty" and "originality."

Bloom's pantheon of the greatest authors since ancient times comprise Dante, Chaucer, Cervantes, Montaigne, Shakespeare, Goethe, Wordsworth, Dickens, Tolstoy, Joyce, and Proust. His two greatest authors of all time are Shakespeare and Yahwist or J, author of the Hebrew Bible. His greatest English writers are Shakespeare and Chaucer, and his greatest wisdom writers are Shakespeare, Cervantes, and Montaigne. William Faulkner is his greatest American writer in the twentieth century, especially *As I lay Dying* (1930), and his greatest living American writer is Cormac McCarthy for his *Blood Meridian* (1985).

Bloom argues that one cannot defend the canon on the grounds that it inspires virtuous behavior. Great writers are subversives. For example, Homer teaches butchery. Thus, reading the canon will not necessarily make us better citizens. "All that the Western Canon can bring one is the proper use of one's own solitude, that solitude whose final form is one's confrontation with one's own mortality."

> ...the fashion in our schools and colleges, where all aesthetic and most intellectual standards are being abandoned in the name of social harmony and the remedying of historical injustice. Pragmatically, the "expansion of the Canon" has meant the destruction of the Canon....
>
> *The Western Canon* (1994), Preface

[Of Shakespeare] He perceived more than any other writer, thought more profoundly and originally than any other, and had an almost effortless mastery of language, far surpassing everyone, including Dante.... Shakespeare is almost as free of ideology as are his heroic wits: Hamlet, Rosalind, and Falstaff. He has no theology, no metaphysics, no ethics, and rather less political theory than is brought to him by his current critics.

Ibid.

Marxism, famously a cry of pain rather than a science...

Ibid.

...how can *Paradise Lost* or *Faust, Part two* ever lend themselves to universal access? The strongest poetry is cognitively and imaginatively too difficult to be read deeply by more than a relative few of any social class, gender, race, or ethic origin.

Ibid.

RICHARD HERRNSTEIN
1930–95

American, psychologist. Charles Murray's coauthor of *The Bell Curve* (1995).

Greater health, wealth, freedom, fairness, and educational opportunity are not going to give us the egalitarian society of our philosophical heritage. It will instead give us a society sharply graduated, with ever greater innate separation between the top and bottom, and ever more uniformity within families as far as inherited abilities are concerned...making the social ladder even steeper for those left at the bottom.

The Bell Curve (1995)

H. ROSS PEROT
1930

American, industrialist, founder of Electronic Data Systems Corporation (EDS), and independent candidate for the presidency in 1992 who enabled Bill Clinton to win by a plurality.

Ready, fire, aim.

Eagles don't flock.

The first EDSer to see a snake kills it. At GM, the first thing you do is organize a committee on snakes. Then you bring in a consultant who knows a lot about snakes....

In Tom Peters, *Thriving on Chaos* (1987)

Brains and wit will beat capital spending ten times out of ten.

STEPHEN SONDHEIM
1930

American, composer and lyricist.

Dear kindly Sergeant Krupkie, you
    gotta understand
It's just our bringing upke that gets us
    out of hand.
Our mothers are all junkies, our fathers
    all are drunks
Golly Moses, naturally we're punks.
"Gee Officer Krupkie," *West Side Story*
(1957 musical), st. 1 (partial)

Yes, Officer Krupkie, he shouldn't be here.
He doesn't need a couch, he needs a
    useful career.
Society has played him a terrible trick,
Unh, sociologically, he's sick.
Ibid., st. 3 (partial)

THOMAS SOWELL
1930

American, classical economist. Reading his *Basic Economics* (2004) ought to be a qualification for voting. His plain English without math explains all the economic issues that politicians argue about.

Sowell says politicians who oppose "trickle down" investment policies are ignorant. Before there are any profits, the first money of an investment is paid as wages for those who design, build, and operate the new investment. Profits, if any, come later, that is, the profits trickle down.

Sowell says profits are not extra costs that raise prices. Pushing for profits reduces costs, and those profits fund the creation of new generations of better and cheaper products. In the U.S. for thirty years to 1998, average corporate after-tax profits were 6 percent to 9 percent, albeit in the 2002 recession, the Fortune 500 companies averaged only 1 percent after-tax profits.

> Economics is the study of the use of scarce resources which have alternative uses.
> [Lionel Robbins's classic definition of economics.]
> *Basic Economics* (2004)

What is called "capitalism" might more accurately be called consumerism. It is the consumers who call the tune, and those capitalists who want to remain capitalists have to learn to dance to it.
> Ibid.

There have been various calculations of how much of a rise in national income saves how many lives. Whatever the correct figure may be—X million dollars to save one life—anything that prevents national income from rising that much has, in effect, cost a life. If some particular safety law, policy, or device costs 5X million dollars, either directly or in its inhibiting effect on economic growth, then it can no longer be said to be worth it "if it saves just one human life" because it does so at the cost of 5 other human lives. There is no escaping trade-offs, so long as resources are scarce and have alternative uses.
> Ibid.

TOM WOLFE
1931

American, novelist and cultural reporter who coined the terms "the me decade," "radical chic," and "the right stuff." Unlike most authors, who write about what they know, he investigates unknown milieus. *Bonfire of the Vanities* (1987) is about stockbrokers, and *A Man in Full* (1998) is about real estate developers. Proof of Wolfe's genius is that his books were panned by the men-of-malaise: John Irving, Norman Mailer, and John Updike.

> [Referring to the intellectuals' fixation on: anomie, alienation, mass man, and the lonely crowd:]
> This victim of modern times has always been a most appealing figure to intellectuals, artists.... The poor devil so obviously needs us to be his Engineers of the Soul, to use a term popular in the Soviet Union in the 1920s.... But once the dreary little bastards started getting money in the 1940s, they did an astonishing thing—they took their money and ran!
> "The Purple Decades" (1982), in Peter Watson, *The Modern Mind* (2001)

You have reached the pinnacle of success as soon as you become uninterested in money, compliments, or publicity.

UMBERTO ECO
1932

Italian, novelist and philosopher best known for *The Name of the Rose* (1981).

Superstition brings bad luck.
Foucault's Pendulum (1988)

ROBERT A. MUNDELL
1932

Canadian, Columbia University professor, Nobel laureate economics (1999), and "godfather of Supply-Side Economics." The Keynesian view in the 1960s was that inflation was a fiscal phenomenon, not monetary. Thus, Presidents Johnson and Nixon "fought" inflation by raising taxes and devaluing the dollar, policies that Mundel said would increase inflation and kill growth, which they did. Mundell convinced a few economists (Jude Wanniski, Arthur Laffer, Robert Bartley, Jack Kemp, Paul Craig Roberts, Norman Ture, and Bruce Bartlett) that: a hard currency would reduce inflation while lower marginal tax rates would stimulate growth, increase employment, and propel the stock market, all of which they did!

MANCUR OLSON
1932–96

American, economist, who believed societies lose the ability to grow rapidly due to the rise of "distributional coalitions" which reduce competition, as by passing protective tariffs, establishing minimum fees for attorneys, giving labor unions monopolistic powers, and so forth. Free trade breaks up distributional coalitions—in fact, that is the principal value of free trade. Without free trade, economic sclerosis caused by distributional coalitions becomes so endemic that the economy can only be reformed after the shock of a revolution or a defeat in war.

Values reflect what used to pay.

It takes an enormous amount of stupid policies or bad or unstable institutions *to prevent* economic development. Unfortunately, growth-retarding regimes, policies and institutions are the rule rather than the exception, and the majority of the world's population lives in poverty.
The Rise and Decline of Nations: Economic Growth, Stagflation, and Social Rigidity (1982)

SYLVIA PLATH
1932–63

American, poet, canonized as a feminist martyr for committing suicide after losing the struggle to escape an overbearing father, a weak husband, masculine institutions, and confining sexual roles. Her "Daddy" is perhaps the world's bitterest poem. Rejoicing in killing her father and husband, it ends: "Daddy, daddy, you bastard, I'm through."

I saw my life branching out before me like the green fig tree in the story. From the tip of every branch, like a fat purple fig, a wonderful future beckoned and winked. One fig was a husband and a happy home and children, and another fig was a famous poet...I saw myself sitting in the crotch of this fig-tree, starving to death, just because I couldn't make up my mind which of the figs I would choose. I wanted each and every one of them, but choosing one meant losing all the rest, and, as I sat there, unable to decide, the figs began to wrinkle and go black, and one by one, they plopped to the ground at my feet.

The Bell Jar (1963), ch. 7

DONALD H. RUMSFELD
1932

American, businessman, and secretary of defense to presidents Ford and George W. Bush.

Success tends to go not to the person who is error-free, because he also tends to be risk-averse. Rather it goes to the person who recognizes that life is pretty much a percentage business.

JULIAN L. SIMON
1932–98

American, economist, whose *A Resourceful Earth* (1984) took on the Club of Rome, which had forecast in *Global 2000* (1980) that in 2000 the world would be poorer. Contrarywise, Simon said natural resources were becoming more abundant, the environment was improving, and world incomes were rising. In 1980, Simon bet Paul Ehrlich that the real price of any combination of five metals Ehrlich would pick would fall by 1990. Simon won. Ben Wattenberg said, "Simon's central point was natural resources are not finite in any seri-

ous way; they are created by the intellect of man, an always renewable resource."

The Club of Rome forecast that the world would run out of oil by 2000, but in 2006 the world has proven reserves for another 40 years, or for 150 years if you assume $100 per barrel oil, which would make oil shale economically viable. Most likely, by 2020 coal gasification will lead to the production of methane gas that will sell for as little as $5 per million Btu. Chinese and U.S. coal could supply the world's energy for hundreds of years.

We ride the greatest trend of all, the drive to create a bit more than we use, and to leave the world a little better than we entered it.

"The Five Greatest Years for Humanity," *Wired* (January 1998)

Human beings are not just more mouths to feed, but are productive and inventive minds that help find creative solutions to man's problems, thus leaving us better off over the long run.... Every time a calf is born, the per capita GDP of a nation rises. Every time a human baby is born, the per capita GDP falls?

THE MATH OF NATURAL RESOURCES

Paul Romer in "Endogenous Technological Change" (1990) used mathematics to explain the inexhaustibility of the earth's natural resources. Since the beginning of time there have been 10 to the 18th power number of seconds; a pack of cards offers possible combinations of 10 to the 68th power (if you shuffle a pack of cards it is highly probable that particular combination has never occurred before and never will again); the number of elementary particles in the universe equals 10 to the 88th power; and the possible combinations of 1 and 0 in a 1.4 megabyte floppy disc equals 10 to the 3,500,000th power. Yet the latter number pales into insignificance in relation to the combinations one can make out of the earth's resources.

JOHN BOORMAN
1933

American, director and screenwriter (with Rospo Pallenberg) of *Excalibur* (1981), a film based on Mallory's *Le Morte D 'Arthur*.

> Remember all, this time well, for it is the doom of men that they forget.
>   [Merlin.]

> *Arthur*: Which is the greatest quality of knighthood? Courage? Compassion? Loyalty? Humility?
> *Merlin*: Truth, that's it. Yes. It must be truth above all. When a man lies he murders some part of the world.

> *Arthur*: My laws must bind everyone high and low, or there are no laws at all.
> *Guinevere*: You are my husband.
> *Arthur*: I must be king first.
> *Guinevere*: Before husband?
> *Arthur*: If need be.

SUSAN SONTAG
1933–2004

American, radical feminist, who labeled American culture "dead, coercive, and authoritarian," so America "deserves" to have its wealth "taken away" by the Third World.

> The white race is the cancer of history. It is the white race and it alone—its ideologies and inventions—which eradicates autonomous civilizations wherever it spreads, which has upset the ecological balance of the planet, which now threatens the very existence of life itself.
>   In *Partisan Review* (Winter 1967)

GLORIA STEINEM
1934

American, chair of the Democratic Socialists of America, and radical feminist who founded *Ms Magazine* in 1971. The sexual revolution was driven by Steinem, Susan Sontag, Andrea Dworkin, Betty Friedan, Carolyn Heibrun, Adrienne Rich, Naomi Wolfe, and Valerie Solanas, who founded SCUM (Society for Cutting Up Men).

> A liberated woman is one who has sex before marriage and a job after.
>   *Newsweek* (March 28, 1960)

> Some of us are becoming the men we wanted to marry.
>   Speech, Yale University (September 1981)

> A woman needs a man like a fish needs a bicycle.

> I can't mate in captivity.

> Rich people plan for four generations. Poor people plan for Saturday night.

COLIN WELLAND
1934

Scottish, Academy Award–winning screenwriter.

Examine yourself. Let each of you discover where your true chance for greatness lies. Seize this chance. Rejoice in it and let no power or persuasion deter you in your task.
[The headmaster greets a new class.]
Chariots of Fire (1981), film

I believe God made me for a purpose, but he also made me fast, and when I run, I feel God's pleasure....To give up running would be to hold Him in contempt.
[When Olympian Eric Liddell's sprinting event was rescheduled for the Sabbath, he refused to run it, though he was favored to win gold. Later he won gold for 1,000 meters, for which he had never trained. Before that race, a stranger handed him a paper with Samuel 2:30 written on it: "He who honors Me, I will honor."]
Ibid.

WOODY ALLEN
1935

American, comedian.

My one regret in life is that I am not someone else.
In Eric Lax, *Woody Allen and his Comedy* (1975)

I don't want to achieve immortality through my work.... I want to achieve it through not dying.
Ibid.

Eighty percent of success is showing up.
In T. J. Peters and R. H. Waterman, *In Search of Excellence* (1982), ch. 5

Halley: I wanted to give you this love letter back.
Clifford: It's my one love letter.
Halley: It's beautiful. I'm just the wrong person.
Clifford: It's just as well. I plagiarized most of it from James Joyce. You probably wondered about all the references to Dublin.
Crimes and Misdemeanors (1989), film

Bisexuality immediately doubles your chances for a date on Saturday night.
In L. R. Frank, *Wit and Humor Quotationary* (2000)

You're the opposite of a paranoid: you go around with the insane delusion that people like you.
Ibid.

[As a child in the movie *Annie Hall*, he refused to do homework because in 5 billion years the sun would explode, "so what's the use?"]

He cheated on his metaphysics exam by looking into the soul of the student sitting next to him.

I took a speed-reading course and read *War and Peace* in twenty minutes. It involves Russia.

Now that I'm famous, I'm striking out with a higher class of women.

Norman R. Augustine
1935

American, industrialist, whose *Augustine's Laws* (1986) is full of wisdom.

> The ability to balance risks and potential gains is the very essence of decision-making in business—and, for that matter in private life as well.
>
> *Augustine's Laws* (1986)

> Bulls do not win bullfights; people do. People do not win people fights; lawyers do.
>
> Ibid., 10th Law

> If a sufficient number of management layers are superimposed on top of each other, it can be assumed that disaster is not left to chance.
>
> Ibid., 26th Law

> It is better to be the reorganizer than the reorganizee.
>
> Ibid., 28th Law

> The early worm gets eaten.
>
> Ibid., 38th Law

> It is sagacious to eschew obfuscation.
>
> Ibid., 65th Law

> The foremost distinguishing feature of effective managers seems to be their ability to recognize talent and to surround themselves with able colleagues.

> Teamwork is the fabric of effective business organizations.

> [One must not] reward poor performance or neglect outstanding performance....

> Centralize goal setting, policy formulation and resource allocation, and decentralize execution.

Jack (John Francis) Welch
1935

American. When named CEO of GE in 1981, its capitalization was $14 billion. When Welch retired in 2000, GE's capitalization was $500 billion, the world's highest (a 23 percent compounded growth rate). He tells how he did it in his *Jack: Straight from the Gut* (2001) (with John B. Byrne) and in *Winning* (2005) (with Suzy Welch). *Winning* is the "how to" manual for implementing Jack's philosophy. He culled the headquarters staff, sold 71 businesses, and fired 81,000 people, whence his moniker "Neutron Jack." He required every business to be first or second in world market share.

His grand strategy was "commoditization is evil and people are everything." GE exited commodity businesses and entered large-scale innovative ones, from jet engines to venture capital. He said, "Nothing matters more in winning than getting the right people on the field."

He reinvented GE with lessons learned from his Irish mother: *integrity* was the number one *value*; *facing reality* was a close second; the third was *self-confidence*, font of the courage to accept risks; and the fourth was *differentiation* or rewarding the best people and weeding out the less effective.

Welch made "people" GE's core competency by expending 75 percent of his energy in recruiting, training, developing, and rewarding the smartest, most creative, and most competitive people, and providing fora in which they exchanged ideas.

The "relentless sharing of ideas" included "work-out" sessions between bosses and employees, who suggested unnecessary work to cut out; annual training for 5,000 managers; and, meetings for his top 500 managers. Welch said his job was being a "teacher who fostered a learning meritocracy."

Welch distrusted elaborate strategies. Like Clausewitz, he responded rapidly to changes in the environment. Within months of Three Mile Island, GE stopped manufacturing nuclear plants and started a profitable service for existing nuclear plants.

Welch had *Four Initiatives* for all businesses: *Globalization:* leverage existing assets over more geography and hire more brilliant people; *Services*: leverage by adding complementary services, for example, maintaining jet engines; *Six sigma quality* reducing errors (this works for repetitive internal processes and complex new product designs, but not for creative activities or one-off transactions); and *E-business*, where big, old companies leverage their existing investments in brands, and so forth.

Differentiation was his way to get the right people on the field: offer double the rewards to the top 20 percent of the managers in each business (the "A players") as to the 70 percent of the middle performers ("B players"), and removing annually the bottom 10 percent ("C players"). GE, like a professional basketball team, annually cuts its weaker players to make room for new prospects.

Welch demanded that his managers have *Integrity*: (tell the truth and take responsibility for mistakes) and *Intelligence*: a breath of knowledge so he can lead other smart people. Managers also must have the *Four Es*: high *Energy* level; *Energize* others; *Edge*, or the courage to make tough,

quick decisions; and, consistent *Execution*. More C players were removed for failing in integrity or values than for not making their numbers. Another value was *Boundarylessness:* search for the best ideas and practices no matter the source, including no barriers between layers of employees, the functions (sales, finance, etc.), or geographic areas. GE's internal slogan was "Find a Better Way Every Day." GE worked "informally," as in a "corner grocery."

The heart of *Jack* is looking for leaders aching to "kick ass and break glass." Welch's style is "being brutally honest and outspoken." He advocates motivating by "alternately hugging and kicking" people and relentlessly checking on their performance. In *Winning*, he calls "lack of candor the biggest dirty little secret in business." Lack of frankness blocks smart ideas and fast action, especially in getting the right people in the right positions. But in second-rate companies, candor is called abrasiveness and will get you fired.

Peter Drucker attributes part of Welch's success to making GE's chief financial officer and chief human-resources officer almost equals to the CEO and excluding them from succession to CEO.

> I wanted to create a company "where people dare to try new things—where people feel assured in knowing that only the limits of their creativity and drive, their own standards of personal excellence will be the ceiling on how far and how fast they move."
>
> *Jack* (2001)

> GE, the greatest people factory in the world, a learning enterprise, with a boundaryless culture.
>
> Ibid.

You build strong teams by treating individuals differently.... Everybody's got to feel they have a stake in the game. But that doesn't mean everyone of the team [is] treated the same way.

Ibid.

One of the real advantages of a big company is the ability to take on big projects with huge potential. The quickest way to neutralize that advantage is to go after the scalps of those who dare to dream and reach—but fail. That just reinforces a risk-averse culture.

Ibid.

Eventually I learned that I was looking for people who were filled with passion and a desire to get things done. A résumé didn't tell me about that inner hunger. I had to "feel" it.

Ibid.

I've never seen a business ruined because it reduced its costs too much or too fast. When good times come again, I've always seen business teams mobilize quickly and take advantage of the situation.

Ibid.

Removing people will always be the hardest decision a leader faces. Anyone who "enjoys doing it" shouldn't be on the payroll, and neither should anyone who "can't do it."

Ibid.

Change doesn't come from a slogan or speech. It happens because you put the right people in place to make it happen. People first. Strategy and everything else next.

Ibid.

You can't waste time on the C player, although we do spend resources on their redeployment elsewhere.

Ibid.

Almost every good thing that has happened in the company can be traced to the liberation of some business, some team, or an individual.

Ibid.

Social responsibility begins with a strong, competitive company.

Ibid.

Never allow anyone to get between you and your customers or your suppliers.

Ibid.

The true test of self-confidence is the courage to be open—to welcome change and new ideas regardless of their source. Self-confident people aren't afraid to have their ideas challenged. How to you find them? By seeking out people who are comfortable in their own skin....

Ibid.

Welch said, "Never become a victim in your company." If you cannot sell your idea to management, resign and sell it to another company. However, as a junior executive he did not "tilt at windmills" by criticizing GE's bureaucracy.

When the rate of change inside an institution becomes slower than the rate of change outside, the end is in sight.

Ibid.

The capitalist genie is almost out of the bottle in China.... For those of you sitting in conference rooms drawing pie charts of the competitive landscape, leave half of the pie open for the Chinese.

Ibid.

Compensation for individuals and businesses is not linked to performance against budget. It is linked primarily to performance against the prior year and against the competition, and takes real strategic opportunities and obstacles into account.

Winning (2005)

[Get promoted by:] at every opportunity expand your job beyond its official boundaries.

Ibid.

Quotas undermine meritocracies. They artificially push some people ahead, independent of qualifications.

Ibid.

One of the things about leadership is that you cannot be a moderate, balanced, careful articulator of policy. You've got to be on the lunatic fringe.

Lawyers insulate. They slow things down. They garble.

Václav Havel
1936

Czech, playwright, and in 1993 the first president of the Czech Republic.

The worst thing is that we live in a contaminated moral environment. We fell morally ill because we became used to saying something different from what we thought.

First speech as Czechoslovakian president
(January 1, 1993)

Mario Vargas Llosa
1936

Peruvian, novelist, essayist, and satirist who began as a Marxist and became a free market conservative. He believes one of the duties of a writer is to aid society by helping to identify the cultural values and political doctrines necessary to maintain a just and prosperous society.

The culture within which we live and act in Latin America is neither liberal nor is it altogether democratic. We have democratic governments, but our institutions, our reflexes and our *mentalidades* are very far from being democratic. They remain populist and oligarchic, or absolutist, collectivistic or dogmatic, flawed by social and racial prejudices, immensely intolerant with respect to political adversaries....

In Claudio Veils, *The New World of the Gothic Fox*

Balint Vazsonyi
1936–2003

American (born-Hungarian), political theorist who fled Hungary in 1956. He was distressed that American education was not instilling the principles that had led to America's success. His *America's Thirty Years War* (2000) saw the same hostility to freedom among members of the U.S. liberal media and academia that he had seen in Hungary under both the Nazis and the Communists.

Not until we realize that our economic success is a function of our legal system, and not until we understand that

socialism in all its forms aims to eradicate that legal system will we fully comprehend the agenda and the bahavior of
socialists from Pierre Proudhon to Karl
Marx, from Lenin to Adolf Hitler, from
Martin Heidegger to Hillary Clinton.

Washington Times (November 21, 2000)

SPANISH CIVIL WAR
1936–1939

In 1931, a leftist republican government
disestablished the state church and began
to expropriate its land. A center right government elected in 1933 slowed down
those reforms. In 1936 the left organized
a Popular Front (Communists, anarchists, tradeunionists, socialists) that narrowly defeated the parties representing
the bourgeoisie, landowners, Catholics,
monarchists, and Falangists. To secure
enough votes for its agenda, the Popular
Front began to assassinate conservative
legislators. Leftists also burned churches
and executed priests, nuns, landowners,
and the bourgeoisie. Reacting to the left's
terror, Gen. Francisco Franco (Il Caudal)
revolted. Communists-socialists-anarchists
were called "Republicans" or "Loyalists" because they controlled the central
government. The right was called the
"Nationalists." German Nazis and Italian
Fascists supplied the Nationalists and the
Soviet Union supplied the Loyalists. Three
thousand Americans (60 percent of whom
were Communists) fought in the Abraham
Lincoln Brigade for the Loyalists. The war
killed 500,000 to 1 million.

The Communist Dolores Ibárruri (La
Pasionaria) popularized the slogan, "It is
better to die on your feet than to live on

your knees!" Taking a train to Paris, she
left her followers to die on their feet while
they sang, "We shall overcome."

Leading four columns to Madrid, General Mola boasted that he had a "fifth column" inside Madrid.

Ironically, in World War II Franco
refused Hitler passage to attack Gibraltar,
which controlled access to the Mediterranean. That doomed Hitler.

PATRICK J. BUCHANAN
1938

American, conservative pundit, and presidential candidate in 1992 and 1996. His *The
Death of the West* (2002) argues that democracy is threatened by Cultural Marxism or
the Frankfurt School of Communism led
by Antonio Gramsci and Herbert Marcuse.
This school realized that capitalism was
not impoverishing workers so they would
not revolt while capitalism's immune system, Western culture, remained strong.
Thus, Cultural Marxism organizes the elite
media and academia to criticize Western
heroes with charges of racism, sexism,
homophobia, and fascism to induce deep
"cultural pessimism," that is, nothing
Western is worth loving or defending.

Per Samuel Francis, Cultural Marxism
leads to "Anarcho-tyranny." Here the state
fails to enforce protective laws, but enforces
laws that criminalize the law-abiding middle class. For example, the state ignores the
violence of the underclass and aliens while
oppressing the middle class with unfair
taxes, speed traps, hate crime and antigun
laws, and so forth. An elite and its apparat-
chiks seek power by allying with the lower
classes to exploit the middle class.

Cultural Marxism is waxing. Hollywood and the three major television networks are left wing, and 90 percent of newspaper reporters vote Democrat. At Swarthmore College only 2 of 160 professors are registered Republicans. The ratio of registered Democrat to Republican professors are: Santa Barbara University 72 to 1; Cornell 27 to 1; Harvard 21 to 1, and so on. As Eric Hoffer said, "Nowhere is there such a measureless loathing of their country by educated people as in America."

John Hayes Pritchard, Jr.
1938

American, English professor, novelist, and poet. His *Junior Ray* (2005) is a *massively politically incorrect* story of the Mississippi Delta's folkways and dialect in the 1950s. No other book contains such language; no other book paints as true a picture of the deep South in the 1950s. It is pious and hilarious, profane and God-drenched: "I am desperate to believe the unbelievable."

Pritchard's poem "Ghosts" was written at a reunion of the 1956 high school class of Sewanee Military Academy, which was closed by the University of the South during the Vietnam War's anti-military hysteria. At reunions, diminishing lines of gray-haired classmates reenact with drummers the traditional Sunday parade from Quintard Hall to All Saints Chapel. In their youth, their battalion in dress gray had paraded smartly with flags and pennants flying and their band trumpeting "Onward Christian Soldiers." "Ghosts" anticipates their final march to chapel.

It was evening on the mountain,
And ghosts were gathered there;
Some have said that ghosts are bred
Upon that mountain's air
> "Ghosts" (1992), st. 1

Down from Quintard once again
To All Saints' open door,
They will march for one last time
And then shall march no more.
> Ibid., st. 8

They will not come with muffled drums
On aging, shuffling feet,
But as they were within their time
To take their final seat;
> Ibid., st. 9

For on that last parade to chapel,
No trumpet sounds retreat...
And until the last man marches in,
There'll be ghosts upon the street.
> Ibid., st. 10

Absence is the core of my charm.

13
TURBO SCIENCE IN HYPER-DRIVE

Can we ring the bells backward? Can we unlearn the arts that pretend to civilize and then burn the world? There is a march of science; but who shall beat the drums for its retreat?

Charles Lamb

After man invented settled agriculture around 9000 B.C., it took 6,000 years to learn how to write and 4,500 more years to learn how to print with movable type. But only 66 years after Orville and Wilbur Wright flew the *Flyer* six hundred feet near Kitty Hawk, North Carolina, man walked on the moon. Free markets and science have given us "autocatalysis," perpetual self-accelerating advancement—the single most important fact for both good and ill in the world today.

Accumulated knowledge has doubled every ten years since TRADIC put eight hundred transistors on a chip in 1955. Soon a chip will host a billion transistors. We are in the third information revolution (after the writing and printing revolutions). Chips double in power in 18 to 24 months (Moore's Law), and a network's value grows as the square of the power of all the computers attached to it (Law of the Telecosm).

Thirty more years of Moore's Law will produce computers a million times more powerful than today's. That will super-charge nanotechnology, genetics, and robotics, which will lead to self-replicating machines and a biological revolution able to redesign any organism—limited only by our imagination. Biologist E. O. Wilson said we are entering "a new epoch of life" where we can "change the essence of our humanity." Dinesh D'Souza said, we are nearing the "post-human era." Indeed, in George Orwell's *1984*, party boss O'Brien defined ultimate power as the ability to "tear human minds to pieces and put them together again in new shapes of your own choosing."

Man's task in the twenty-first century will be to manage this extraordinary science that will eliminate poverty and disease, but also create untold dangers. Heretofore, evil men could wreak global havoc only if, like Hitler or Lenin, they controlled a large nation. Now a lone man might kill billions of people by releasing a virus, just as a Filipino student destroyed billions of dollars by releasing the Love Bug computer virus.

Science will cure our chronic diseases, protect the environment, and realize Aristotle's dream of machines liberating mankind from most menial labor. But while science extends our abilities, the dark side of human nature lies hard by. Jung said "psychology must insist on the reality of evil and must reject any definition that regards it as insignificant or actually non-existent." In addition to the threats from our evil nature, we are also imperiled by the unintended consequences of our new technologies.

The knee-jerk reaction to threatening science is regulation. Yet, overregulation can be counterproductive. Outlawing DDT condemned tens of millions to death by mosquito-borne diseases. More people may have been killed by environmental regulations than saved by them. Outlawing all bioengineered foods would condemn countless millions to starvation.

There are two reasons to tilt toward freedom for innovation. First, the most serious threats will come from terrorists, who will not be deterred by regulations, but regulations could prevent finding defenses against terrorists. Second, some serious threats are natural ones, such as pandemics and asteroids. Only freedom to innovate can generate the knowledge necessary to protect us.

The Information Age will eliminate many of the evils of industrialization, like mind-numbing jobs that, in the words of Adam Smith, make man "as stupid and ignorant as it is possible for a human creature to become." It will unite families through telecommunications. Also, one can join worldwide communities over the Internet, such as chess and gardening clubs.

But technology will not make people better. Without a footing in the spiritual world, Western civilization may be shattered by an explosive mix of superscience and the belief that "everything is permissible." Nietzsche forecast that the weakening of Christianity would cause great wars in the twentieth-century and that the twenty-first century would be worse as Christian values ran out in a "total eclipse of all values." Today's wholesale abortions presage grave danger for all inconvenient people who are powerless.

Peter Singer, Princeton's chair of the Center for Human Values, believes parents should have twenty-eight days after birth to kill disabled infants. He argued, "The notion that human life is sacred just because it's human life is medieval." That is reminiscent of Alfred Hoche, a Nazi professor who said, "A new age will come which, from the standpoint of higher morality, will no longer heed an overestimation of the value of life as such." William F. Buckley Jr. saw the full implications of Singer-Hoche's relativist values:

> The infrastructure of our governing assumption—that human beings are equal—derives from our conviction that they are singularly creatures of God. If they are less than that—mere evolutionary oddments—we will need to busy ourselves mightily to construct rationales for treating alike disparate elements of humanity which anthropological research might persuasively claim to be unequal.
>
> *Let Us Talk of Many Things* (1999)

Let us leave the final word on science to Will Durant from his first chapter on *The Reformation* (1957):

> Science gives man ever greater powers but ever less significance; it improves his tools and neglects his purposes; it is silent on ultimate origins, values, and aims; it gives life and history no meaning or worth that is not canceled by death.

CHESS AND COMPUTERS

A Chinese emperor was so pleased with chess that he offered its inventor one wish. The inventor said he wanted one grain of rice on the first of the sixty-four squares, two grains on the second, four on the third, and so forth. The emperor acceded. But 2 to the 64th power is 18 million trillion. The emperor could have satisfied the wish through 2 to the 32nd power—a mere 4 billion grains. But after 2 to the 32nd power, each new doubling meant something big! By about 2006, computing power had increased by 2 to the 32nd power since the invention of the ENIAC. Now, each doubling of computer power every 18 to 24 months portends something really big.

GEORGE F. GILDER
1939

American, supply-side futurist who was the most quoted living author by President Ronald Reagan. His books broke critical ground in explaining the causes of poverty, the inherent morality of capitalism, and the promise of digital technologies. As editor of the *Gilder Technology Report*, he has correctly predicted the paths of many new technologies, usually against the weight of "informed" opinion. His *Microcosm* (1989) forecast that government and business bureaucracies would lose power to the "capital of the human mind."

Real poverty is less a state of income than a state of mind.
Wealth and Poverty (1981)

The welfare culture tells the man he is not a necessary part of the family; he feels dispensable, his wife knows he is dispensable, his children sense it.
Ibid.

No nation can grow and adapt to change except to the extent that it is capitalistic, except to the extent, in other words, that its productive wealth is diversely controlled and can be freely risked in new causes, flexibly applied to new purposes, steadily transformed into new shapes and systems.
Ibid.

Capitalism begins with giving.
[The gifts are investments where returns are problematical. Providing incentives for investment is not "trickle-down economics" because the first payments are wages for those who design and build the investment—profits may or may not follow.]
Ibid.

Socialism is an insurance policy bought by all the members of a national economy to shield them from risk. But the result is to shield them from knowledge of the real dangers and opportunities.... The entire economy absorbs the much greater risk of remaining static in a dynamic world.
Ibid.

...the crucial role of the rich in a capitalist economy is... to invest; to provide unencumbered and unbureaucratized cash.
Ibid.

...liberals force lower middle-class families, who love their children to dispatch them to ghetto schools dominated by gangs of fatherless boys bearing knives.

Ibid.

For the upper classes to accept lower-class behavior is to…assign them to permanent poverty, erode the requirements of growth and opportunity, and foster processes of cultural and economic deterioration. Only people who have already made it can afford the self-indulgent styles of lower-class life.

Ibid.

A successful economy depends on the proliferation of the rich, on creating a large class of risk-taking men who are willing to shun the easy channels of a comfortable life in order to create new enterprise, win huge profits, and invest them again.

Ibid.

[The capitalist] is not chiefly a tool of markets but a maker of markets; not a scout of opportunities but a developer of opportunity; not an optimizer of resources but an inventor of them; not a respondent to existing demands but an innovator who evokes demand; not chiefly a user of technology but a producer of it…. In their most inventive and beneficial role, capitalists seek monopoly: the unique product, the startling new fashion, the marketing breakthrough, the novel design.

The Spirit of Enterprise (1984)

When the capitalists are thwarted, deflected, or dispossessed, the generals and politicians,… and socialist intellectuals, are always amazed at how quickly the great physical means of production—the contested tokens of wealth

and resources of nature—dissolve into so much scrap, ruined concrete, snarled wire, and wilderness.

Ibid.

[Successful] projects that entrepreneurs initiated and carried through had one essential quality. All had been thoroughly contemplated by the regnant experts and dominant companies, with their large research staffs and financial resources, and had been judged too difficult, untimely, risky, expensive and unprofitable.

Ibid.

A democratic society that is unwilling to bar *Hustler* on public newsstands or ban billboards from beautiful views cannot justly blame capitalism for these offenses. It is up to the political, judicial, and religious institutions of the society, not other businesses, to eliminate such opportunities for ugly profit… The tragedy of the commons bears the compelling truth that capitalism without a moral and legal context is self-destructive.

Ibid.

The key to growth is quite simple: creative men with money. The cause of stagnation is similarly clear: depriving creative individuals of financial power.

Ibid.

The key role of entrepreneurs, like the most crucial role of scientists, is not to fill in the gaps in an existing market or theory, but to generate entirely new markets or theories…. They stand before a canvas as empty as any painter's; a page as blank as any poet's.

Ibid.

The world of the business school, like the world of the economist, assumes what needs most to be explained: the existence of products and markets where there was only poverty and stagnation before.

Ibid.

In the entrepreneur's contrarian domains, he needs most of all a willingness to accept failure, learn from it, and act boldly in the shadows of doubt. He inhabits a realm where the last become first, where supply creates demand, where belief precedes knowledge.

[Gilder notes a high rate of business failures in an economy indicates rapid economic growth.]

Ibid.

The central event of the twentieth century is the overthrow of matter. In technology, economics, and the politics of nations, wealth in the form of physical resources is steadily declining in value and significance. The power of mind is everywhere ascendant over the brute force of things.... Today, the ascendant nations and corporations are masters not of land and material resources but of ideas and technologies.

Microcosm (1989)

Rather than pushing decisions up through the hierarchy, the power of microelectronics pulls them remorselessly down to the individual. This is the law of the microcosm.

Ibid.

Watching the Soviet Union gain control over one after another Third World backwater...many American observers believe that the Communists are winning

the Cold War. But the Soviet strategy is obsolete. The Soviet Union could capture the entire Third World without in any way gaining military or economic power. In fact, each new conquest swerves only as a new drain on the Soviet economy

Ibid.

This is the age of the individual and family. Governments cannot take power by taking control or raising taxes, by mobilizing men or heaping up trade surpluses, by seizing territory or stealing technology. By imperialism, protectionism, and mercantilism, nations eventually wither and weaken into Third Worldly stagnation. In the modern world, slaves are useless; they enslave their owners to systems of poverty and decline.

Ibid.

The key fact of knowledge is that it is anti-entropic, it accumulates and compounds as it is used.... The materialist superstition succumbs to an increasing recognition that the measures of production in capitalism are not chiefly land, labor, and machines, present in all systems, but emancipated human intelligence...the driving force of its growth is innovation and discovery.

Ibid.

The telecosm...will make communication universal, instantaneous, unlimited in capacity, and at the margins free.... The information power of the electromagnetic spectrum...is...essentially infinite.

[Higher frequencies mean less interference, more bandwidth, and less power required. But, they cannot penetrate buildings.]

Telecosm (2000)

Unpredictability dictates openness as a prime prerequisite of growth, and it requires flexibility as a key to successful planning.

Ibid.

Today the ascendant technology is optics and the canonical abundance is bandwidth.

Ibid.

[The telecosm] distributes power out of companies to their customers. It gives every customer the ability to survey the entire global marketplace and make optimal purchases...

Ibid.

The Internet saves the customer's time. Because many experts continue to see the customer's time as an externality, outside of productivity data, they miss the profound impact of this technology.

Ibid.

Any nihilistic culture will destroy itself in the end by undermining the willingness of people to make sacrifices and endure privations in its perpetuation and defense.

Forbes ASAP (December 1996)

The key to paradigm shifts is the collapse of formerly pivotal scarcities, the rise of new forms of abundance, and the onset of new scarcities. Successful innovators use the new forms of abundance to redress the emergent shortages. For example, the Industrial Revolution saw an abundance of watts, plummeting in price, used to overcome shortages of labor and natural resources.

Forbes ASAP (February 1997)

Don't solve problems. When you solve problems, you end up subsidizing your weaknesses, starving your strengths, and achieving expensive mediocrity....

CATO Policy Report (September 1997)

Activity and creativity almost always flow to the least regulated arena.

Experts usually reflect obsolescent expertise, derived from the mastery of legacy systems and installed bases.

Entrepreneurs, in accepting risk, achieve security for all. In embracing change, they ensure social and economic stability.

Capitalism offers nothing but frustrations and rebuffs to those who wish—because of claimed superiority of intelligence, birth, credentials, or ideals—to get without giving, to take without risking, to profit without sacrifice, to be exalted without humbling themselves to understand others and meet their needs.

STUART KAUFFMAN
1939

American, biologist at the Santa Fe Institute, which investigates Complexity Science. He posits that a "spontaneous order" arises in all complex systems, that is, snowflakes always exhibit a sixfold symmetry. Further, complex systems "self-organize," that is, atoms naturally group into molecules, molecules to cells, cells to organisms, and organisms to ecosystems. Groups self-organize by feedback from individual members relating to shared goals, that is, flocks of birds respond to bits of information discovered by any of their members as to food, danger, and so on.

Complexity theory holds that our economy and culture are also biomes where decentralized, organic development will outperform centrally managed development because decentralized systems make use of the information available to every individual. A czar of a centralized system (state planning board) cannot possibly acquire the aggregate information known to society.

> ...the emerging sciences of complexity offer fresh support for the idea of a pluralistic democratic society, providing evidence that it is not merely a human creation but part of the natural order of things.
>
> *At Home in the Universe* (1995)

> Not we the accidental, but we the expected.
>
> Ibid.

> Coevolving species in ecosystems generate small and large avalanches of extinction and speciation.
>
> Ibid.

> Order, vast and generative, arises naturally.
>
> Ibid.

> Upon hearing a theory by a younger colleague, Wolfgang Pauli is said to have responded, "It's crazy, but not crazy enough."
>
> Ibid.

> ...flatter, decentralized organizations may function well: contrary to intuition, breaking an organization into "patches" where each patch attempts to optimize for its own selfish benefit, even if that is harmful to the whole, can lead, as if by an invisible hand, to the welfare of the whole organization.
>
> Ibid.

Everyone pursuing happiness in his own way optimizes social progress. In "disorganized systems" productivity is higher because there are more experiments prompted by competition, so there are more successes to be emulated. This insight underlies: (1) Adam Smith's view of an invisible hand producing the greatest common good as individuals seek their own advantage, (2) the Physiocrats' Laissez-faire, (3) Burke's preference for evolved social traditions over reason, (4) Toynbee's belief that civilizations advance most when subunits are free to develop independently, (5) Hayek's insight that civilization evolves from tribal control to individual autonomy, (6) capitalism's eclipse of socialism, and (7) management's flattening of organizations and unwinding of conglomerates. In capitalism, what appears to be chaotic competition is order, and government control that appears orderly leads to stasis and convulsion.

> We live on a self-organized sand pile that sheds avalanches down the critical slopes with each footstep. We have hardly a clue what will unfold.
> [Per Bak's sand pile.]
>
> Ibid.

Piling grains of sand on top of a pile has no effect on its base until one grain causes an avalanche (tipping behavior), unlike the linear world where a car goes a little faster if you slightly press down on the gas pedal. The economy and the stock market are more like the sand pile than like the car. Events that should have a tendency to produce X result, seem to have no effect until suddenly X "tips," and radical change occurs.

Complexity or chaos also makes forecasting difficult because small changes in a chaotic system can have outsize amplifying effects—the "butterfly effect." For investors, this places a premium on portfolio diversification. For business, this places a premium on having strong balance sheets and experimenting ceaselessly with new business models. Difficulty in forecasting means, in the words of Sir Karl Popper in *Conjectures and Refutations* (1963), "Our aim must be to make our successive mistakes as quickly as possible."

Religion and Science

After Copernicus removed the earth from the center of the universe and after Darwin posited that humanity evolved from random biological mechanisms, many intellectuals lost faith in God. For example, the scientist Jacques Monod said, "Man knows at last that he is alone in the universe's unfeeling immensity, out of which he emerged only by chance." Bertrand Russell concluded humanity was "a curious accident in a backwater." Thus the eternal tension between the *physici* of Athens, who rely on the five senses (empiricism), and the *theologi* of Jerusalem, who argue there is something beyond what we sense.

Modern science should give pause to atheists. Most scientists agree with Edwin Hubble's 1927 theory that the universe was created in a "big bang," an event that violates all laws of physics—it is *supernatural* that *everything* came from *nothing*. Jeffrey Hart said, "Philosophical materialism was dead and the universe had a beginning. Yet, *something cannot come from nothing.*" What's beyond the wall?"

More profoundly, according to the "anthropic principle" of cosmologist Brandon Carter, for the universe to support life it had to have been constructed with twenty mathematical constants (such as gravity) being exactly as they are (not a trillionth off on any one of them). The odds of that are like a "typhoon blowing through a junkyard and constructing a Boeing 747," per cosmologist Fred Hoyle. A. S. Eddington gave much higher odds, that is, "like a monkey randomly typing all the books in the British Museum." Graham Cairns-Smith said 140 operations had to be created *simultaneously* for the formation of DNA. The odds against that are one in ten to the 109th power, a greater number than all the electrons in the universe! No biblical miracle is near as improbable as the miracle of life.

To rescue randomness, physicist Leonard Susskind invented "string theory" that posits an infinity of "parallel universes," and we exist on the one universe with life. But string theory abandons the idea that nature follows one set of laws, the principle upon which modern science was founded. Atheists deny random forces can build a watch, but see random forces constructing a life-sustaining universe—that makes a leap of faith against incredible odds (10 to the power of 500) in order to exclude a designing creator.

Nobel physicist Charles Townes believes in a designing creator. He notes that science, like religion, is based on faith, that is, postulates, or things that cannot be proven. Newton's classical mechanics is wrong, as shown by quantum mechanics, which itself cannot be squared with reality. Townes says we should use all our resources: instincts, intuition, logic, observation, experimentation, postulates, and revelation.

Polls in 2005 of 1,646 research scientists by Elaine Ecklund at Rice University and of 2000 medical doctors by the University of Chicago show that only one-third of each do not believe in God.

MONKEYS AND SHAKESPEARE

T. H. Huxley said that if enough monkeys typed long enough, one would type the complete works of Shakespeare. But Dean Overton in *A Case Against Accident and Self-Organization* (1997) notes the probability of typing at random twelve-lines of *Macbeth* would be 26 to the 379th power. Mathematician Paul Davies said that anything with a probability greater than 10 to the 60th power is virtually impossible; it is like hitting a one-inch target with a random rifle shot from a distance of 20 billion light years.

PAUL CRAIG ROBERTS
1939

American, supply-side economist.

> Tariffs protect ill-considered government policies, such as costly regulations and high taxes on labor and capital that make our goods uncompetitive in international markets. Tariffs also protect coercive and self-serving union policies, and they protect fat corporate bureaucracies. A government that has erected a tariff wall can squeeze businesses with taxes and mandates and workers with payroll taxes without fear that the companies will fail due to foreign competition.
> "Tariffs Protect Big Government,"
> *Washington Times* (October 13, 1997)

Roberts countered the protectionist argument that America grew rapidly with protective tariffs in the nineteenth-century with facts: nineteenth century tariffs (excepting the 1828 Tariff of Abominations—repealed in 1833) were revenue tariffs with low rates (20 percent ad valorum) designed to maximize tax revenues, not to reduce imports. By 1846, U.S. tariffs were so low that the U.S. led the world as a free-trading nation.

Per Leonard Read, the primary case for free trade is moral: If two people voluntarily agree to exchange goods, no one else has a right to disrupt it. The case is also practical and it extends to unilateral free trade: When a nation lowers its trade barriers, it benefits the most. Its consumers get better and cheaper products and its producers are forced by foreign competition to be innovative.

TOM BETHELL
1940

American (British-born), whose *The Noblest Triumph* (1998) concludes that prosperity inevitably follows laws that provide widespread, secure, and transferable ownership interests in property. That laws determine a nation's modes of production is diametrically opposite to Marx's view that modes of production determine the laws. Bethell's *The Politically Incorrect Guide to Science* (2005) is the seminal work on the politicization of modern science.

> When property is privatized and the rule of law is established in such a way that all including the rulers themselves are subject to the same law, economies will

prosper and civilization will blossom.

The Noblest Triumph (1998)

...the Industrial Revolution came to England first because the rule of law came there first...

Ibid.

[Marx was clearheaded. He] understood that if private property were to be dispensed with, human nature would have to change. Marx believed that it was in fact changing.... Today, very few people believe that human nature is changing.

Ibid.

By the late nineteenth century, many socialists were aware of the [free riding] problem of communes. So they began to conceive of life organized in a very different way: controlled from the center.... Free riding would no longer be possible because it would be forbidden. The shortage of virtue that had disabled communes would be remedied by force.

Ibid.

The great blessing of private property, then, is that people can benefit from their own industry and insulate themselves from the negative effects of others' actions. It is like a set of invisible mirrors that surround individuals, households or firms, reflecting back on them the consequences of their acts. The industrious will reap the benefits of their industry, the frugal the consequences of their frugality; the improvident and the profligate likewise. They receive their due, which is to say they experience justice as a matter of routine. *Private property institutionalizes justice.*

[Author's emphasis.]

Ibid.

...competition in a free-market economy is so unrelenting that good habits, or their corresponding vices, will before too long overpower the lotteries of inheritance...

Ibid.

The great difference between the developed and the underdeveloped economies is not that the former have markets and the latter do not. The difference is one of scale, and of legal protection.... It was this great difference in the range and elaboration of the law that the economists for a long time overlooked.

Ibid.

In the period when the great shift in the balance of power [between the West and other civilizations] occurred, the notion of rights generally, and property rights in particular, emerged in the Western world. The result was a tremendous increase in material prosperity.

Ibid.

In the later twentieth century a reversal is underway. Legal privileges associated with group membership have been restored, threatening to undermine the greatest triumph of Western law: the emergence of a single class of citizens, equal before the law.

Ibid.

HERNANDO DE SOTO
1941

Peruvian, economist, and president of the Institute for Liberty and Democracy in Lima, Peru, which *The Economist* called one of the two most important think tanks in the world. His thesis is that capitalism fails outside of the West not for lack of wise macroeconomic policies, but for the lack of a unified legal property system. That is, the poor in developing countries often have substantial assets, like shacks and informal businesses. What they lack is property rights to their assets so they can improve them, sell them, and/or mortgage them, that is, turn them into capital.

De Soto found that in Peru it took: 289 days to obtain the permits to establish a small garment shop; six years and seven months to get the 207 permits necessary to build a house on state-owned land; and 728 steps to get a taxi license. Thus, most small industry operates extralegally, which means they cannot get credit, insurance, or utility services, and they are not taken seriously as contracting partners. Also, they must pay extra-high tax rates in the form of bribes.

In Latin America, 85 percent of new jobs are in extralegal sectors. For example, 70 percent of Brazil's new construction is extralegal. Until there is a formal property system in developing countries, capitalism's motor, the division of labor will be clogged-up and most assets will be dead capital. For details, see Hernando de Soto's *The Mystery of Capital: Why Capitalism Triumphs in the West and Fails Everywhere Else* (2000).

GEORGE WILL
1941

American, the Shakespeare of columnists, and a rich source of quotations not found in any quotation book. Will's keys to life are "a flourishing family, hearty friends, and a strong bullpen." His self-described writing style is one that is as "spare and pointed as an ice pick."

There can be no reasonable right to live on sidewalks. Society needs order, and hence has a right to a minimally civilized ambience in public spaces. Regarding the homeless, this is not merely for aesthetic reasons because the anesthetic is not merely unappealing. It presents a spectacle of disorder and decay that becomes a contagion.

In L. R. Frank, *Quotationary* (1999)

The Cold War is over and the University of Chicago won it.

Column (December 9, 1991)

Modern politics is a compassion contest.

ABC TV (May 5, 1996)

Clinton is not the worst president the republic has had, but he is the worst person ever to have been president.

Column (January 11, 2001)

What turns out to be a lifetime job—very steady work—is conservatism's task of keeping government where it belongs, which is on a short constitutional leash, and politics in its place, which is at the margins of life.

Column (May 3, 2001)

[Cultural relativism] licenses the envy of the untalented, giving rise to what has been called the revenge of failure: Those who cannot paint destroy the canons of painting; those who cannot write reject canonical literature.

"The Great Refutation" (September 12, 2002)

Ideas have consequences—indeed, only ideas have large and lasting consequences—so history is, at bottom, the history of mind.

Ibid.

Tolerance is a virtue only when it is difficult—when it involves keeping strong beliefs on a short leash. Tolerance that reflects the absence of strong beliefs is a symptom of a distinctively contemporary form of decadence....

With a Happy Eye (2002)

In [writing columns], literary and historical allusions are not just pretty filigrees, they are practical necessities. They enable us to make a large point with a small reference. They help us to save time and words by triggering a response from the readership's reservoir of shared understandings.

Ibid.

Unlike virtues, *everyone* has *lots* of values; *everyone* has as many as he or she chooses, Hitler had *scads* of values. George Washington had *virtues*.

Ibid.

The purpose of higher education for citizens in a democracy should be to help them identify excellence in its various realms and to understand what virtues make it so.

Ibid.

Society flourishes when and only when its molecular unit, the family, flourishes. We know that lasting improvement comes only in the small increments produced by individuals adhering to the simple rules of life.... The most important business of one generation is the raising of the next generation. Nothing else you do in life will be as deeply satisfying...

Ibid.

One radical free spirit nonconformist is pretty much like another.

The Democrat's dominant ideology is victimology.

[Will noted that sometimes newspapers err, as shown in the following retraction by a newspaper:]
Instead of being arrested, as we stated, for kicking his wife down the stairs and hurling a lighted kerosene lamp after her, the Rev. James P. Wellman died unmarried four years ago.

[Will told about two liberals who see a man who has been viciously beaten. They angrily exclaim: "We have to find the man who did this—he desperately needs our help."]

[Will wrote, "Little things mean a lot." He told of the actress Margaret Anglin leaving another actress a note: "Margaret Anglin says Mrs. Fiske is the best actress in America." The note was returned: "Margaret Anglin, says Mrs. Fiske, is the best actress in America."

Extra-marital sex is frowned on, but extra marital sex is applauded.

Column (May 21, 2004)

Democracy is more than a mechanism for picking leaders; it is institutions of pluralism and attitudes of majority forbearance and minority acceptance.

Column (February 1, 2005)

He was not, shall we say, all polish. He once lost a ground ball in the sun.

Reality is strange: solid objects are mostly space; the experience of time is a function of speed; gravity bends light. The inevitably of progress is a myth, hence the certainty that mankind is wiser today than yesterday is chimeric.

STEPHEN HAWKING
1942

English, theoretical physicist of black holes.

If we find the answer to that [why the universe exists], it would be the ultimate triumph of human reason—for then we would know the mind of God.

A Brief History of Time (1988), ch. 12

I am confident we will discover [the Theory of Everything] by the end of the twenty-first century and probably much sooner. [Probably within twenty years starting now.]

Address at the White House
(September 7, 1997)

GARRISON E. KEILOR
1942

American, humorist.

That's the news from Lake Wobegon, where all the women are strong, all the men are good looking, and all the children are above average.

A Prairie Home Companion (radio series)

Government, as a profession, tends to attract people who have a lot of time to kill.

TOM PETERS
1942

American, management consultant.

If a manger is really willing to listen, he or she will find that the average employee is loaded with ideas, most of which the manager can allow the person to try.

In Supervisory Management
(February 1984)

We need impassioned champions by the thousands. Yet the impassioned champion is anathema to every thing that civil, organized corporate endeavor stands for. But we must hire him, even though he will alienate some good people, irritate almost every one, and in the end fail anyway more often than not.

Thriving on Chaos (1987)

The best leaders...almost without exception and at every level are master users of stories and symbols.

Ibid.

Today's successful business leaders will be those who are most flexible of mind. An ability to embrace new ideas, routinely challenge old ones, and live with paradox will be the effective leader's premier trait.

Ibid.

Obsession doesn't guarantee success, but a lack of obsession guarantees failure.

CHARLES MURRAY
1943

American, political scientist, whose *The Bell Curve* (1995, with Richard Herrnstein) argues IQ is 40 percent to 80 percent genetic, and IQ is the best single predictor of divorce, socioeconomic status, and so forth. He opined that the "cognitive elite" is becoming the economic elite, because using new technologies requires higher intelligence. He forecast that social problems will be correlated with specific genes, such as low IQ, short time-horizons, and impulsiveness. His *Losing Ground* (1984) inspired welfare reform by showing that a self-perpetuating urban underclass had been fostered by U.S. social policies.

> We tried to provide more for the poor and produced more poor instead. We tried to remove the barriers to escape poverty, and inadvertently built a trap.
>
> *Losing Ground* (1984)

> ...illegitimacy is the single most important social problem of our time—more important than crime, drugs, poverty, illiteracy, welfare, or homelessness because it drives everything else.
> > [In 1960, illegitimacy was 2 percent for whites and 22 percent for blacks. In 1991, after introducing sex education in schools, white illegitimacy rose to 22 percent and black illegitimacy rose above 70 percent.]
> >
> > "The Coming White Underclass," *Wall Street Journal* (October 29, 1993)

GEORGE LUCAS
1944

American, film director, and screenwriter, famous for the *Star Wars* trilogy.

> Mind what you have learned. Save you it can.
> [Yoda's advice to Luke Skywalker.]
> *The Empire Strikes Back*, film

> Do or do not. There is no "try."
> Ibid.

GEORGE W. BUSH
1946

American, forty-third U.S. president, and son of George H. W. Bush, forty-first U. S. president.

> The gravest danger to freedom lies at the perilous crossroads of radicalism and technology.... Enemies in the past needed great armies and great industrial capabilities to endanger the American people and our nation. The attacks of September the 11th required a few hundred thousand dollars in the hands of a few dozen evil and deluded men.... [I]f we wait for threats to fully materialize, we will have waited too long.... Our security will require all Americans to be ready for preemptive action when necessary to defend our liberty and to defend our lives.
>
> Speech to West Point Cadets (September 11, 2002)

JAMES DALE DAVIDSON
1947

American, investment adviser. In *The Great Reckoning* (1989), Davidson and Lord William Rees-Mog (editor, *The Times*), update Edward C. Banfield's *The Unheavenly City* (1968). That book argued that programs to upgrade skills in the inner cities miss the point. What is lacking is not skills but qualities, such as "reliability, motivation to learn, and adaptability to the demands of the work."

> The tendency to assign rewards according to status rather than through competition is a common characteristic of

closed societies.

The Great Reckoning (1989)

The day before an earthquake, the great city gleams in the sun, with scarcely a hint that beneath the surface, pressures are building along the fault lines.

Ibid.

When one nation enjoys cheap military predominance, along with disproportionate shares of manufacturing output and financial power, the world tends to enjoy free trade and monetary stability and thus prosperity.

Ibid.

Poverty is not the cause but the consequence of perverse values and antisocial behavior.

Ibid.

One of the fond illusions of people shielded from life's realities is that power no longer matters. It is an illusion that arises in a secure environment where order is established and taken for granted. Those who live closer to the normal dangers of human life, such as the underclass of a big city like New York, know better.

Blood in the Streets (1987)

Persons without sufficient means to protect and support themselves may become economically superfluous. Indeed, they could become even more useless than the slaves of ancient times, who at the darkest moments of bad luck could at least command the means to survive so long as hard labor was in demand. Someday, technology may antiquate even that security.

Ibid.

MITCHELL WALDROP
1947

American, science writer.

As we begin to understand complex systems, we begin to understand that we're part of an ever-changing, interlocking, nonlinear, kaleidoscopic world. So the question is how you maneuver in a world like that. And the answer is that you want to keep as many options open as possible. You go for viability, something that's workable, rather than what's "optimal."… What you're trying to do is maximize robustness, or survivability, in the face of an ill-defined future…. You observe the world very, very carefully and you don't expect circumstances to last.

Complexity: The Emerging Science at the Edge of Order and Chaos (1992)

Some highlights from *Complexity:* From lipids and nucleic acids to flocks of birds to men acting in an economy, all are systems that spontaneously self-organize. These systems are "adaptive," not like leaves blown by the wind, but like a plant that turns toward the sun.

Self-organizing systems create "increasing returns," not "diminishing returns." Once a system gets a lead, it becomes a commanding lead, such as VHS over Beta. This principle is "positive feedback," or self-reinforcement, a tendency for small effects to become magnified. Even suboptimal systems, such as "QWERY," a typing system invented in 1873 by Christopher Scholes to slow down the machine to prevent jamming, remain the standard. "Increasing returns" result in "winner take all results."

JAMES K. GLASSMAN
1947

American, senior economist at J. P. Morgan, and one of today's best stock market journalists.

> Entrepreneurship is the last refuge of the troublemaking individual.

ROBERT H. WATERMAN JR.
1948

American, management consultant.

> Renewing organizations *have made curiosity an institutional attribute.* They listen to their customers, of course. They also listen to competitors, first-line employees, suppliers, consultants, outside directors, politicians, and just about anyone else who can reflect a different view of who they are.... They seek a *different mirror*, something that tells them that the world has changed and that, in the harsh light of the new reality, they aren't as beautiful as they once were.
>
> *The Renewal Factor* (1987)

BILL BRYSON
1951

American, popularizer of science, whose *A Short History of Nearly Everything* (2003) starts with the Big Bang and surveys up to the present: astronomy, biology, chemistry, genetics, geology, meteorology, oceanography, paleontology, physics, taxonomy, and zoology. For each science, he lays out the earliest theories and then tracks all the major discoveries. His language is easy to understand and is full of witty anecdotes. He teaches that the world is a cauldron of violent change. But change occurs over geologic time, so man can defend against most threats. Some tidbits from *A Short History* are:

Space does not exist within an emptiness; only space exists. Space and all in it were created out of nothing. There is neither an edge nor a center to the universe; it is boundless, but finite.

In our Milky Way Galaxy, there are up to 400 billion stars, and there are 140 billion galaxies. Yet, 90 percent to 99 percent of matter is "dark matter," that is, something other than stars, planets, asteroids, gases and so on. Using conservative estimates, Dr. Frank Drake figures there are now millions of advanced civilizations in our Milky Way.

James Hutton created the science of geology in the late eighteenth century by explaining why marine fossils were found on mountaintops—heat within the earth pushed up mountains. Most startling, this required the earth to be many millions of years old. Archbishop James Ussher in 1664 had stated that the earth had been created at midday on October 23, 4004 B.C. To date, the oldest fossils found are 3.85 billion years old.

An atom is mostly empty space—its nucleus is only one millionth of a billionth of its volume. There are some 150 to 250 types of subatomic particles within the nucleus. Thus, Enrico Fermi said, "If I could remember the names of these particles, I would have been a botanist." Some particles appear and disappear within a 0.0000000000000000000000001 of a second. Some physicists believe in Superstring

Theory, that is, many things thought of as particles have no mass and are vibrating strings of energy that oscillate in eleven dimensions. Perhaps Karl Popper is right—there is no ultimate theory of physics, but only "an infinite chain of more and more fundamental principles."

Each atom in you has passed through several stars and been part of millions of living organisms. In you are at least a billion atoms that were once part of Shakespeare.

Wolfgang Pauli Exclusion Principle: subatomic particles in certain pairs when separated by vast distances instantly react to changes in the spin in the other. Thus, some things travel far, far faster than the speed of light.

Annually, a billion asteroids crisscross our Solar System at 66 thousand miles an hour. One the size of a house could destroy New York City. Since 1991 two medium sized asteroids missed the earth by 106,000 and 90,000 miles. A medium asteroid hitting earth would trigger earthquakes, volcanoes, and tsunamis. A billion people would die the first day, and most would starve because dust would blot out the sun for years.

Yellowstone Park is the world's largest volcano with a crater 40 miles in diameter. Most of the Earth's crust under the continents is 25 miles thick, but Yellowstone's crust is only 8 miles above its magma, which has lifted it up 1,700 feet for 300 miles. It has erupted about 100 times, once every 600,000 years, and the last time was 630,000 years ago. One of its eruptions was up to 8,000 times greater than of Mt. St. Helen—it buried New York under 67 feet of ash.

Without the moon, earth would wobble in its rotation causing catastrophic climatic effects. The moon moves away an inch annually, so in a billion years earth will shake chaotically.

Decaying vegetation and volcanoes excrete thirty times more carbon dioxide into the atmosphere than does modern man.

Given food, the *Clostridium perfrigens* bacteria, which causes gangrene, reproduces in nine minutes, so in two days theoretically it can produce more offspring than there are protons in the universe. Bacteria can live at least 250 million years. If you totaled all the biomass on earth, at least 80 percent of it would be microbes.

Earth has produced 30 billion species of creatures and 99.99 percent of them are extinct. Only one species in ten thousand has made it in the fossil record. For species of complex organisms, the average life span is 4 million years. Besides many smaller episodes, there have been five major extinction episodes in each of which up to 96 percent of species became extinct: Ordovician (440 million years ago); Devonian (365 million years ago); Permian (240 million years ago); Triassic (210 million years ago), and Cretaceous (65 million years ago). Potential culprits include global cooling and/or warming, epidemics, meteor impacts, volcanoes, and solar flares.

Per the Human Genome Project, 97 percent of human DNA is non-coding junk, so there are 35,000 to 40,000 coding genes, the same as in grass. But these are merely a parts list that tells us nothing about how the genes work. To learn about that we must crack the "human proteome," that is, understand proteins. But proteins are vastly more complicated: There are as many as a hundred million proteins in each cell of your body, and they come in extravagant varieties.

The prevailing scientific theory of human evolution is that *Homo sapiens* evolved from *Homo erectus* in Africa, and then *Homo sapiens* left Africa to spread around the world. The "multiregional hypothesis" holds that the Chinese *Homo sapiens* evolved from the *Homo erectus* living in China, the European *Homo sapiens* from the *Homo erectus* living in Europe, the African *Homo sapiens* from the *Homo erectus* living in Africa, and so forth. But, the *Multiregional Hypothesis* is condemned because it is not politically correct, to wit, it implies there are greater differences between the races than does the *Homo Sapiens Out of Africa Hypothesis*.

RUSH LIMBAUGH
1951

American, conservative talk show host with the largest U.S. audience: 20 million listeners.

> Poverty and suffering are not due to the unequal distribution of goods and resources, but to the unequal distribution of capitalism.
>
> *Policy Review* (Summer 1992)

> I prefer to call the most obnoxious feminists what they really are: feminazis.
>
> *The Way Things Ought To Be*

FRANCIS FUKUYAMA
1952

American, who wrote in the *National Interest* quarterly in 1989 that liberal democracy marks the "end of history" in the sense that Hegel thought history was an evolution toward some final form of government that would free man.

> A remarkable consensus concerning the legitimacy of liberal democracy as a system of government had emerged throughout the world over the past few years, as it conquered rival ideologies like hereditary monarchy, fascism, and most recently communism…. [L]iberal democracy may constitute the "end point of mankind's ideological evolution" and the "final form of human government," and as such constitutes the "end of history." …liberal democracy was arguably free from fundamental internal contradictions.
>
> *The End of History and the Last Man* (1992)

This thesis that democratic capitalism will sweep the globe is challenged by Samuel Huntington's *Clash of Civilizations* (1996). Huntington denies that Western civilization can be a universal civilization. Other civilizations have different values so there will be conflicts along the fault lines between civilizations. Allan Bloom argued there will be a jingoistic return to national myths (fascism) to resist being homogenized in a global stew. Even Fukuyama worries that neuropharmacology and genetic engineering may so alter human nature that despotism may replace democratic capitalism.

Fukuyama's *State-Building* (2004) concludes that the most critical step in converting a developing nation into an advanced industrial democracy is to create institutions that support the rule of law. For example, Russia's privatization of industry after 1991 in the absence of the rule of law tainted free markets.

In states with strong governments, the Reagan formula of reducing the scope of state activities is the right first step. But in others it must be building core rule of law functions. As Fukuyama wrote: "From the standpoint of long-term economic growth, it is best to have a state that is restrained in scope, focusing on the provision of necessary public goods, but strong in its ability to enforce a rule of law."

[Relativism] fires indiscriminately, shooting out the legs of not only the absolutism, dogmas, and certainties of the Western tradition, but that tradition's emphasis on tolerance, diversity, and freedom of thought as well.

Ibid.

JAMES GLEICK
1954

American, science author.

[Believers in chaos] feel that they are turning back a trend in science toward reductionism, the analysis of systems in terms of their constituent parts: quarks, chromosomes, or neurons. They believe that they are looking for a whole.

Chaos-Making a New Science (1987), Prologue

[Most science works as follows:] Given the approximate knowledge of a system's initial conditions and an understanding of natural law, one can calculate the approximate behavior of the system…you don't have to take into account the falling of a leaf on some planet in another galaxy when you're trying to account for the motion of a billiard ball on a pool table on earth. Very small influences can be neglected. [Thus, a belief in "approxi-

mation" and "convergence." But natural systems subject to "chaos" are highly sensitive to the smallest variation in initial conditions, so long-range forecasting is fruitless unless one can know exactly all initial conditions, which is impossible.]

[Some natural systems never repeat themselves exactly; they are "aperiodic" and thus unpredictable.]

Ibid. ch. 1

CHARLES SYKES
1954

American, writer.

What then is the nature of the danger facing higher education? It is that it is in the Western tradition that we find the origins of democratic society, of the focus on individual worth and human dignity, and of aspirations for human freedom…. To lose that legacy through a curriculum of enforced cultural amnesia is to deconstruct an entire civilization.

The Hollow Men: Politics in Higher Education (1990)

BILL H. GATES
1955

American, founder in 1974 of Microsoft, the world's largest corporation by capitalization.

Success is a lousy teacher. It seduces smart people into thinking they can't lose. And it's an unreliable guide to the future.

The Road Ahead (1995), ch. 3

The network will draw us together, if that's what we choose, or let us scatter ourselves into a million mediated communities. Above all, and in countless new ways, the information highway will give us choices.

Ibid., ch. 12

Obsolete Our Own Products.
[Microsoft's motto.]

Microsoft has two hiring requirements: brilliance, and the ability to adapt to constant revolutions in technologies and business practices. Interviewees must solve puzzles, such as answering the following in five minutes: Four people together on one side of a bridge at night with one flashlight must all cross to the other side in seventeen minutes, but the bridge can hold only two people at a time. A flashlight is needed for crossing to avoid holes in the bridge. One person can cross the bridge in one minute; another can cross it in two minutes; another in five minutes; and the fourth in ten minutes. There is a proper logistical answer; there is no trick.

Bill Gates advised graduating high school students that "feel-good" teaching is harmful:

1. The world only cares about your accomplishments, not your self-esteem. Real life wants to know who was in the top 15 percent.

2. In life you don't get summers off, and few employers are interested in helping you find yourself.

3. If you think your teacher is tough, wait till you get a boss who doesn't have tenure.

4. Be nice to nerds. Chances are you will work for one.

5. Flipping burgers is not beneath your dignity. You grandparents called it opportunity.

Note: these rules are included in Charles Sykes' *50 Rules Kids Won't Learn in School* (2007).

JIM COLLINS
1958

American, management consultant, who organized a team that devoted fifteen thousand hours over five years to determine what makes a good company great. His *Good to Great* (2001) explains their empirically derived conclusions, many of which are counter-intuitive:

(1) Celebrity leaders from the outside are negatively correlated with making a company great.

(2) There is no linkage between greatness and executive compensation systems.

(3) Strategy *per se* did not separate good to great companies.

(4) Great companies focus most on what not to do and what to stop doing.

(5) Technology and acquisitions can accelerate a transformation to greatness, but cannot cause it.

(6) Great companies pay scant attention to motivating their employees, but they only hire the motivated.

(7) Great companies are found in terrible industries as well as in good ones.

The first step in going from good to great is not finding a strategy, but getting wrong people out of the company and right people in. "Great vision without great people is irrelevant." Disciplined, motivated people do not have to be tightly managed or motivated. A culture of discipline avoids bureaucracy and hierarchy. Also, character attributes are more important than skills. Nucor teaches hardworking farmers in small towns how to make steel, rather than teach a work ethic to skilled unionized steelworkers.

Great leaders credit others for company successes and blame themselves for its failures. They are fearless and ferocious in their resolve to advance company interests, for example, they are utterly intolerant of mediocrity. Collins believes there is no dearth of great leaders, but they are naturally selected out of top management.

Third, great companies continually realign their strategy with the brutal facts of reality. Everyone on the management team speaks his mind exactly, including searing criticism of the CEO. Charismatic leaders are often a liability because many filter the brutal facts from them.

Fourth, great companies are hedgehogs: They concentrate on only what they can be the best in the world at. As Warren Buffett said, "Find your circle of competence and stay in it."

DINESH D'SOUZA
1962

American (Indian-born), AEI scholar. His *The Virtue of Prosperity* (2000) outlines how capitalists created the first affluent nations, after centuries of failure by bishops, soldiers, and intellectuals who talked about redistributing wealth but mostly arrogated power to themselves.

Most American universities have diluted or displaced their "core curriculum" in the great works of Western civilization to make room for new course requirements stressing non-Western cultures, Afro-American Studies, and Women's Studies.

Illiberal Education (1991), ch. 1

[Universities teach] that individual rights are a red flag signaling social privilege, and should be subordinated to the claims of group interest; that all knowledge can be reduced to politics...that double standards are acceptable as long as they are enforced to the benefit of minority victims....

Ibid., ch. 8

What was distinctively Western was not slavery but the moral crusade to end slavery.

The End of Racism (1995), Preface

Remarkable events occurred during the 1980s: the restoration of economic growth, the curbing of inflation, the end of the gasoline crisis, the technological boom, the beginning of the collapse of Soviet communism, the spread of freedom and democracy around the world.

Ronald Reagan (1997), ch. 10

[States ought not equalize opportunities] because it undermines the scope of parents to invest in their children's betterment that is an essential part of their exercise of freedom. What the government can guarantee is not equality of outcomes, not even equality of opportunity, only equality of rights.

The Virtue of Prosperity (2000)

The capitalist has this over the politician and the clergyman; he has in practice done more to raise the standard of living of the poor than all the government and church programs in history....Monsanto and the Archer Daniels Midland Company have fed more hungry people than all the...soup kitchens combined.

Ibid.

DOUGLAS MURRAY
1979

British, "practicing Anglican," and Eton and Oxford educated neoconservative. Irving Kristol defined a neocon as being a liberal mugged by reality. Murray says he was mugged by Europe's willingness to allow genocide in Kosovo and by the "self-blame reaction" of the multiculturalists to 9/11. He faults liberals for not seeing the world as it is and conservatives who only offer defensive isolation strategies to Islamic jihad because to stay on the defensive is to commit suicide.

Because the status quo is no longer conservative, conservatives must seek to change the status quo. In so doing they must become new conservatives, radical conservatives—revolutionary conservatives. They should become neoconservatives.

Neoconservatism (2006)

Black culture, as it is currently presented, is a cesspit of degradation, violence, and nihilism. Tolerance of it demonstrates relativism's awful appeal....Until a stand is made against a culture that glorifies and encourages rape, murder, gun crime, hate crimes, and grotesquely unchecked materialism, that culture will continue

to cause palpable and visible damage to American society.

Ibid.

Islamic extremism is today the most explicit enemy of our society. It is the declared intention of Islamic extremists to undermine the traditions of America and replace them with subservience to the *dar el-Islam*.

Ibid.

[Western students] may know very little about their country, but they know that to appear clever they should be cynical, critical, and hostile to the past they don't know....They have arrived in an endplace of sorts, but because they have not themselves done the intellectual journeying, they have neither sympathy nor understanding. What they have instead is an increased sense of rage and indignation. Young people who demonstrate against wars with countries they cannot find on a map are useless citizens...

Ibid.

VIETNAM WAR

In the Vietnam War, as in the Korean War and in the nuclear standoff in Europe, the U.S. was following both George Kennan's 1947 grand strategy of containing Communism and the Truman Doctrine of supporting "free peoples who are resisting attempted subjugation by armed minorities or by outside pressure." Americans died in Vietnam to stop a Communist holocaust that had murdered some 170 million people and enslaved 2 billion. As it turned out, Vietnam was Communism's last hurrah, so the West's defeat there was not critical, but that was unknown then.

President Eisenhower decided not to commit infantry in Vietnam. He told President Kennedy that if he intervened, he would have to cordon off the Ho Chi Minh Trail through Laos so the NVA could not resupply the Viet Cong. But a Democratic Congress favored Defense Secretary McNamara's strategy of fighting an Asian ground war of attrition without crossing borders or using overwhelming conventional force.

Despite the repeated protests of the Joint Chiefs of Staff and the CIA, McNamara followed a "gradualist" strategy. America's anti-war movement went ballistic when President Nixon temporarily inserted forces into Cambodia's Parrot's Beak to stop the resupply of the VC. America then decided that quitting was better than fighting with no-win political constraints.

PART 2
QUOTATIONS ORGANIZED THEMATICALLY

Part 1 traces chronologically grand themes in Western civilization by featuring prominent authorities addressing the ideas that led the West to liberty, democracy, science, capitalism, and a blossoming of all literary forms.

Part 2 features a potpourri of quotations on specialized subjects, such as Armed Forces, proverbs, humor, the Bible, and historical nuggets of special use to writers and speakers. Also, most Part 2 quotations are either anonymous or by people who are not famous. For example:

Good parents ask each of their children, "Have I told you *today* how much I adore you?"

Anon.

May you give your children roots and wings.
[Wedding toast.]

Anon.

Proof of his farsightedness is that none of his predictions have yet come true.

Anon.

When you see a Hungarian, kick him. He'll know why.

Austrian proverb

Before setting out on revenge, dig two graves.

Chinese proverb

"First Law on Wing-Walking": Don't leave hold of what you've got till you've got hold of something else.

Anon.

14
SHORT THEMES

ARMED FORCES

Choosing to die resisting, rather than to live submitting, they fled only from dishonor, but met danger face to face.

> Pericles, Funeral Oration, 431 B.C.

[R]emember that this greatness [of Athens] was won by men with courage, with knowledge of their duty, and with a sense of honor in action…. For you now, it remains to rival what they have done and knowing the secret of happiness to be freedom and the secret of freedom a brave heart, not idly to stand aside from the enemy's onset.

> Ibid.

We will never bring disgrace on this
  our City by an act of dishonesty or
  cowardice.
We will fight for the ideals and Sacred
  Things of the City both alone and
  with many.
Thus, in all these ways we will trans-
  mit this City, not only not less, but
  greater and more beautiful than it
  was transmitted to us.

> Athenian oath for seventeen-
> year-old males

Fight on, my men, says Sir Andrew
  Bartton,

I am hurt, but I am not slain;
I'll lie me down and bleed a while,
And then I'll rise and fight again.

> "Ballad of Sir Andrew Bartton"

He that fights and runs away,
May turn and fight another day;
But he that is in battle slain,
Will never rise to fight again.

> James Ray, "History of the Rebellion"

Lord! Thou knowest how busy I must
  be this day,
If I forget thee, do not thou forget me.

> Jacob Astley, Prayer before the Battle of
> Edgehill, October 23, 1642

[At Tsar Nicholas I's coronation in 1825, a mob and three thousand rebellious soldiers gathered at one end of Moscow's main square. An officer saluted the tsar and said] "Give the order to clear the square with cannon fire, or abdicate."

No plan survives the first five minutes of encounter with the enemy.

> Helmuth von Moltke

We have met the enemy, and they are ours.

> Battle of Lake Erie, September 10, 1813
> Oliver Perry

The lamps are going out all over Europe; we shall not see them lit again in our lifetime.

Lord Grey, August 3, 1914

Lafayette, we are here.
[Address in Paris at the Tomb of Lafayette on July 4, 1917.]

Col. Charles E. Stanton

Enlisted men are ignorant, but they are shrewd. They bear watching at all times.

U. S. Navy Officer's Manual, c. 1940

A Marine on duty has no friends.

Marine Corps Officer's Guide, 1967

No better friend, no worse enemy.

Gen. James N. Mattis, USMC

Hi diddle diddle, right up the middle!

Marine war cry

It's a grand and glorious day to be alive and in the Marine Corps, where every day is a holiday and every meal a banquet.

Marine saying

The road to Hell is paved with the bleached bones of commanders who failed to provide for all-around security.

Marine saying

Fire without maneuver is ineffective; maneuver without fire is disastrous.

Marine saying

Uncommon valor was a common virtue.
[Of the Iwo Jima Marines.]

Chester Nimitz, Commander, Pacific Fleet

Retreat Hell! We're attacking in the other direction!
[At Chosin Reservoir in Korea, in December 1950, fighting its way out of a trap, the 1st Marine Division so mauled seven Chinese divisions that they were decommissioned.]

Gen. Oliver P. Smith

Combat is hours of boredom broken by a few moments of sheer terror.
[American (part Sioux), Flying Tiger and later Marine ace (28 kills) who commanded the Black Sheep Squadron in World War II.]

"Pappy" Boyington

When this war is over, the only place where they will speak Japanese will be in Hell.
[On seeing a destroyed Pearl Harbor.]

Adm. William F. (Bull) Halsey

Tell them when the war is over and who won.
[What to tell the press.]

Ernest Joseph King, Chief of Naval Operations

When you get in trouble, you send for the sonsabitches.

Ibid.

The difficult we do immediately, the impossible takes a little longer.

Seabees saying

Nuts!
[Reply to demand to surrender Bastogne.]

Gen. Anthony C. McAuliffe

The second highest ground is no good.

Mountain warfare maxim

There are old pilots and there are bold pilots, but there are no old, bold pilots.

Aviator saying

Because Charles Lindbergh had been against the war prior to Pearl Harbor, FDR refused to reinstate his commission. Without FDR's knowledge, Lindbergh as a contractor modified the P-38's engines, which doubled their range to eighteen hundred miles, which made possible MacArthur's island hopping strategy. He also surreptitiously flew combat missions.

Claire Chennault's Flying Tigers (AVG or American Volunteer Group) at Rangoon shot down 296 Japanese planes and destroyed 200 on the ground while losing only 14. Having only 36 pilots, Chennault's strategy was to dive steeply in a single pass through a Japanese air formation and then break away without engaging in individual dogfights. Chennault copied this tactic from the Red Baron's World War I Flying Circus.

The Curse of Not Invented Here: In World War II American bomber losses over Germany within fighter cover averaged 3.6 percent per mission, but 16.0 percent when beyond fighter cover. When Americans brought bombers to Great Britain in 1942, they brought the P-51 Mustang, an excellent fighter, but its Packard engine could not rise to high altitude to protect the bombers. Not until May 1944 did the Americans install British Rolls Royce Merlin engines, which enabled the P-51 to rise high enough to protect the bombers deep in Germany. Herman Goering said, "When I saw the fighters over Berlin, I knew the war was over."

In the Korean War, Col. John Boyd noted that American pilots won nine of ten dogfights even though Migs were superior in speed, climb, and turning ability. But American hydraulics allowed a faster transition from one maneuver to another. Boyd saw that dogfights involved repeated cycles of observation, orientation, decision, and action. Americans changed maneuvers quicker and "got inside the opponent's decision loop" until the enemy's actions became inappropriate. The "Boyd-Cycle" applies generally to any competition.

A congressman told a colonel that for the cost of one B-1 bomber, the U.S. could triple its Fulbright scholars. The colonel explained that Fulbright scholars don't do a damn thing if you drop them on a bridge from twenty thousand feet.

The second best air force is as good as the second best poker hand.

Gen. H. H. (Hap) Arnold

French Foreign Legionnaires were never defeated; they were only killed.

A maximum of caution, combined with supreme dash at the right moment.

Rommel's maxim

Rommel in the attack never worried about his own flanks: a punch protects itself.

Correlli Barnett

If it moves, salute it; if it doesn't move, pick it up; and if you can't pick it up, paint it.

British army proverb

The smallest amount of vanity is fatal in airplane fighting. Self-distrust is the quality to which many a pilot owes his protracted existence.

> Baron Manfred von Richthofen

The first essential of a general is the quality of robustness, the ability to stand the shocks of war.

> Field Marshal Sir Archibald P. Wavell

Intelligence, while generally necessary, is not a sufficient means to victory…in combat willpower always counts for more than foreknowledge.

> John Keegan, *Intelligence in War* (2002)

There are no examples in military history of a state weaker in force than its enemy achieving victory in a protracted conflict.

> Ibid.

North Koreans tortured to death a Turkish squad leader, futilely attempting to elicit information. Then they tortured to death the assistant squad leader without learning anything. When the Koreans asked who was next in command, the three Turkish corporals began to quarrel, each claiming to be the senior.

I have slipped the surly bonds of Earth… Put out my hand, and touched the face of God.

> John G. Magee (1922–41), "High Flight"

The nation that will insist upon drawing a broad line of demarcation between the fighting man and the thinking man is liable to find its fighting done by fools and its thinking by cowards.

> Sir William Francis Butler

Going to war without France is like going deer hunting without your accordion.

> Norman Schwartzkopf

To rally the morale of B-17 crews in 1942, Colonel Wray invented the "Order of the Rigid Digit," a silver medal of a clenched hand with a raised middle finger. Inspiration came from the RAF's fictional epitome of ineptitude—Pilot Officer Percival Algernon Prune, who destroyed twenty-three British aircraft in as many different ways during training. The medal's inscription read, "In gross disregard for his own safety and that of his passengers and bringing great shame and discredit to the military service, this medal is awarded to…" Soon, everyone wanted one, including General Doolittle. (Marion H. Havelaar, *The Ragged Irregulars of Bassingbourn*.)

It is the Soldier, not the reporter,
Who gave us Freedom of the Press.
It is the Soldier, not the poet,
Who gave us Freedom of Speech.
It is the Soldier, not the campus organizer,
Who gave us Freedom of Assembly.
It is the Soldier, not the lawyer,
Who gave us the right to a fair trial…

> Charles M. Province

Motto: Duty, Honor, and Country.

> U. S. Military Academy at West Point

Honor Code: The cadet will not lie, cheat, or steal, nor tolerate those who do.

> Ibid.

Korean War Memorial: "Freedom is not free."

I pledge allegiance to the flag of the United States of America and to the republic for which it stands, one nation, under God, indivisible, with liberty and justice for all.

> ["Under God" was added by Congress in 1954.]

Francis Bellamy (1892)

Let's roll. Jesus help me!

Todd Beamer on Flight 93

Respect for the Flag of the United States:

1. When the flag passes on parade or during the playing of the National Anthem or during the recital of the Pledge of Allegiance, face the flag, stand at attention, and (unless in uniform) place your right hand over your heart.

2. Display the flag outdoors only from sunrise to sunset, unless it is illuminated.

3. Hoist the flag briskly; lower it slowly.

4. Only display an "all-weather" flag in the rain or other precipitation.

5. The flag is placed in the center of other flags and held higher.

6. The flag is displayed with the stars down only as a signal of danger or distress.

7. When the flag is torn or soiled, burn it.

BUSINESS WISDOM

Growth for growth's sake is the ideology of the cancer cell.

Edward Abbey

The creative person is more primitive and more cultivated, more destructive and more constructive, a lot madder and a lot saner, than the average person.

Frank Barron

Every organization has a Siberia.

Warren G. Bennis

Only intuition can protect you against the most dangerous individual of all, the articulate incompetent.

Robert Bernstein

A desk is a dangerous place from which to view the world.

John Le Carre

Always remember that this whole thing was started by a mouse.

Walt Disney

All business proceeds on beliefs, or judgments of probabilities, and not on certainties.

Charles William Eliot

Few great men could pass Personnel.

Paul Goodman

Find a need and fill it.

Henry J. Kaiser

It is a paradox that the greater the decentralization, the greater the need for leadership.

Bruce Henderson

Choose an occupation in which you can win praise. Most things depend upon the satisfaction of others.

Baltasar Gracián

Avoid victories over superiors.

Ibid.

Great men are rarely isolated mountain peaks; they are the summits of ranges.

Thomas Higginson

Experience is a hard teacher because she gives the test first, the lesson afterwards.

Vernon Law

People are rarely fired for incompetence; it's almost always for not getting along.

Stuart Margulies

Patience: the beggar's virtue.

Philip Massinger

The price you pay for precision is inability to deal with real-world problems.

Douglas North

The difference between insanity and genius is success.

Jonathan Price

I cannot give you the formula for success, but I can give you the formula for failure: Try to please everybody.

Herbert Swope

What actually is true of journalism is true of a number of other professions. Outsiders tend always to overrate the malice and underrate the incompetence.

Louis Rukeyeser

Where work is ceaseless and progress is zero.

Tycoon: I need a man who can say "No" when I talk nonsense. Are you that man? Job applicant: "No."

Continue the flogging until morale improves.

On Columbus's map, the Atlantic Ocean was inscribed, "Here be dragons."

Career advice: Enter a field that others find difficult and you find easy. Play in the major leagues. Ride to the sound of the guns. Seek early responsibility. Develop a unique skill. Get paid.

Two ways to be independent: be a virgin or a prostitute.

Two laborers at a construction site were asked what they were doing. One said, "I'm digging a ditch." The other said, "I am building a great cathedral."

Cap'n says to John Henry,
"Gonna bring me a steam drill 'round,
Gonna take dat steam drill out on de job,
Gonna whop dat steel on down,
Lawd, Lawd, gonna whop dat steel on down."

"The Ballad of John Henry," st. 4

John Henry was hammerin' on de
   mountain,
An' his hammer was strikin' fire,
He drove so hard till he broke his pore
   heart,
An' he lied down his hammer an' he died,
Lawd, Lawd, he lied down his hammer
   an' he died.
                                Ibid., st. 15

There was a thirty-five minute contest between a steam drill and John Henry on the Big Bend Tunnel for the Chesapeake and Ohio road in West Virginia in the 1870s. John Henry, a 225-pound railroad worker celebrated for his skill and strength, won the contest. He drilled two holes, each seven feet deep with a twenty-pound hammer, while the steam hammer drilled one nine-foot hole. He won the hundred-dollar prize but lost his life from a brain hemorrhage triggered by the contest. John Henry epitomizes the tragedy of a man's skills pitted against new technology, but he is a testimonial to man's pride in his work

EPITAPHS

All the brothers were valiant,
  and all the sisters virtuous.
        Tomb of Duchess of Newcastle in
                Westminster Abbey.

Warm summer sun shine kindly here;
Warm southern wind blow softly here;
Green sod above lie light, lie light,
Good night, dear heart, good night,
  good night.
   Tombstone of Susy Clemens, daughter of
                Mark Twain

Underneath this tomb doth lie
As much beauty as could die;
Which in life did harbor give
To more virtue than doth live.
     Ben Jonson, "Epitaph on Elizabeth"

If there is another world, he lives in bliss;
If there is none, he made the best of this.
     Robert Burns, "Epitaph on William
         Muir," *Posthumous Pieces* (1799)

A tomb now suffices him for whom the whole world was not sufficient.
    Epitaph on Alexander the Great's tomb

If you would see his monument, look around.
   Tomb in St. Paul of London for the architect Sir Christopher Wren (1632–1723)

Let mortals rejoice that so great an ornament to the human race has existed.
        Sir Isaac Newton (1642–1727)

The end of the fight is a tombstone white,
with the name of the late deceased,
And an epitaph drear: "A fool lies here,
who tried to hustle the East."
     Kipling, *The Kaulahka* (1892), ch. 5

Here lies W. C. Fields. On the whole, I'd rather be living in Philadelphia.
      Suggested epitaph for himself in
          Vanity Fair (June 1925)

This is the grave of Mike O'Day
Who died maintaining his right of way.
His right was clear, his will was strong,
But he's just as dead as if he'd been
  wrong.
   Ogden Nash, "Lather as You Go" (1942)

It is so soon that I am done for.
I wonder what I was begun for.
Tombstone, Cheltenham churchyard

Excuse my dust.
Dorothy Parker

If after I depart this vale, you ever remember me and have some thought to please my ghost, forgive some sinner and wink your eye at a homely girl.
H. L. Mencken

Papa loved Momma, Momma loved men
Momma's in the graveyard, Papa's in the pen.
Carl Sandburg

Remember man that passeth by,
As thou art now so once was I;
And as I am so must thou be;
Prepare thyself to follow me
Tombstone in Linton, England (1825)

To follow you is not my intent,
Unless I know which way you went.
Inscription under the Linton tombstone

Liberty has been the key to our progress in the past and is the key to our progress in the future. If we can preserve liberty in all its essentials, there is no limit to the future of the American people.
Robert A. Taft memorial

My sire brought this on me.
Abu'l-'Ala al-Ma'ari, Arab poet (b. 1045)

If I did not accomplish great things, I died in their pursuit.
Cervantes [for Don Quixote]

The Body of B. Franklin, printer; Like the Cover of an old Book, Its contents torn out and stript of its Lettering and Gilding, Lies here, Food for Worms. But the Work shall not be wholly lost, For it will, as he believed, appear once more, In a new and more perfect Edition, Corrected and Amended By the Author.
Benjamin Franklin (written at age
twenty-two)

Here lies Frank Pixley—as usual.
Ambrose Bierce, epitaph for a deceased liar

Stoop, angels, hither from the skies!
There is no holier spot of ground
Than where defeated valor lies,
By mourning beauty crowned!
Henry Timrod (1828–67),
"Ode on Decorating the Graves of the
Confederate Dead"

And when he goes to heaven
To Saint Peter he will tell:
Another Marine reporting, sir;
I've served my time in hell!
Pfc. Cameron, USMC, Guadalcanal
(1942)

We have died only in vain if you believe so;
You must decide the wisdom of our choice
By the world that you shall build upon
    our headstones.
And the everlasting truths which have
    your voice.
Though dead, we are not heroes yet, nor
    can be,
'Til the living, by their lives that are the
    tools,
Carve us the epitaphs of wise men,
And give us not the epitaphs of fools.
Pfc. David Phillips, Bastogne (1944)

On fame's eternal camping ground,
Their silent tents are spread,
And glory guards—silent round
The bivouac of the dead.
[Inscribed at all national cemeteries.]
Theodore O'Hara, 1820 – 67, "The
Bivouac of the Dead," (1847),
Commemorating the Battle of
Buena Vista

Here Rests in Honored Glory an Amer-
ican Soldier Known but to God.
Tomb of the Unknown Soldier,
Arlington, Virginia

Not for fame or reward... not for place or
rank... not lured by amibtion or goaded
by necessity... but in simple obedience
to duty as they understood it, these men
suffered all, sacrificed all, dared all, and
died.
Arlington Cemetary

FORECASTING VISIONARIES

No railroad baron invested in the auto;
IBM did not invent the personal computer
nor did Sears invent Wal-Mart; Bell Labs
missed the chance to become Cisco, and on
and on. David keeps beating Goliath! As
Lord Melbourne said, "What all the wise
men promised has not happened, and
what all the damned fools said would happen has come to pass."

The learned German, Schedel, in 1493
wrote the *Nüremberg Chronicle,* which
said that the last age of man was drawing to a close. He left a few pages blank
to record anything of interest during the
final days.

What, sir, would you make a ship sail
against the wind and currents by lighting a bonfire under her deck? I pray you
excuse me. I have no time to listen to
such nonsense.
Napoleon to Robert Fulton, c. 1800

Rail travel at high speeds is not possible
because passengers, unable to breathe,
would die of asphyxia.
Dionysius Larder (1793–1859)

Otto Cossel said of his student, Johannes
Brahms (1833–97), "He might become a
good pianist, but he won't leave his compositions alone."

Charles Darwin's father scolded him:
"You care for nothing but shooting, dogs,
and rat-catching, and you will be a disgrace to yourself and all your family."

In 1859, Whitwell Elwin, Editor of Britain's *Quarterly Review,* refused to print
Darwin's *Origin of Species,* but did urge
Darwin to write a book about pigeons saying, "Everyone is interested in pigeons."

"They couldn't hit an elephant from
this dist--." Last words of Yankee general John Sedgwick during the Battle of
Spotsylvania in 1864, when he declined
a suggestion to duck as he walked past
an open parapet.

In 1874, fifteen years after Colonel Drake
drilled the first oil well in Pennsylvania,
the state's chief geologist opined that
the copious use of kerosene for lighting
would drain the U. S. petroleum reserves
by 1878.

In 1876 a Western Union memo advised against purchasing Bell's telephone patent for $100,000: "This telephone has too many short-comings to be seriously considered as a means of communication. The device is inherently of no value to us."

Sir William Preece, chief engineer, British Post Office, said in 1886, "Americans have need of the telephone, but we do not. We have plenty of messenger boys."

In 1895, Lord Kelvin, president of the Royal Society said, "Heavier-than-air machines are impossible."

In 1895, Roebuck sold out to Sears for $25,000; in 1906 Henry Ford's largest original investor sold out.

In 1899, Charles H. Duell, chief, U.S. Patent Office, recommended to President McKinley that it be closed because "everything which can be invented has already been invented."

Charles Schwab, CEO of Bethlehem Steel, refused to finance the experiments of the Wright brothers, calling their plans for an airplane a "harum-scarum stunt."

Maréchal Ferdinand Foch in 1912 said, "Airplanes are interesting toys but of no military value."

E. J. Smith, captain of *RMS Titanic*, said in 1912, "I cannot conceive of any condition which could cause this ship to founder."

In 1929, Irving Fisher, professor at Yale University, said, "Stocks have reached what looks like a permanently high plateau."

In 1934, Parker Brothers unanimously rejected the game of Monopoly saying, "It is too complicated, it takes too long to play, and people will not like to keep circling a board."

On hearing that Louis B. Mayer planned to make a film of *Gone With the Wind*, studio executive Irving Thalberg advised, "Louis forget it. No Civil War picture ever made a nickel."

About sinking a ship with a bomb, it just can't be done.
     RADM Clark Woodward, USN, 1939

In the 1940s Darryl F. Zanuck said, "[Television] won't be able to hold onto any market it captures after the first six months. People will get tired of staring at a plywood box every night."

Thomas Watson, chairman of IBM, predicted in 1943, "I think there is a world market for maybe five computers."

A Grand Ole Opry agent in 1955 said to Elvis Presley after hearing his first performance, "You ain't goin' nowhere with that, son. You ought to go back to drivin' a truck."

Soviet Communist Party chairman Nikita Khrushchev in 1955 said, "Those who wait for the USSR to reject Communism must wait until a shrimp learns to whistle." In 1956, speaking of the United States he said, "History is on our side. We will bury you."

In 1958, IBM passed up the chance to buy Xerography technology; in 1968, IBM dismissed minicomputers as too small to do serious computing; and in the 1970s, IBM let Microsoft develop IBM's operating system.

The managing director of the International Monetary Fund in 1959 said, "In all likelihood, inflation is over."

Decca Recordings in 1962 rejected the Beatles, saying: "Guitar music is on the way out."

In 1963 the *Journal of Geophysical Research* told Lawrence Morley it would not publish his Theory of Plate Tectonics because "such speculations make interesting cocktail talk, but it is not the sort of thing that ought to be published under serious scientific aegis."

In 1964 a studio rejected Ronald Reagan for the role of president in *The Best Man*, saying, "Reagan doesn't have the presidential look."

A Yale professor awarded a 'C' to Frederick Smith's senior thesis proposing a private overnight mail delivery service [Federal Express] because "The idea is not feasible."

Ken Olsen, president of Digital Equipment Corporation, said in 1977, "There is no reason for any individual to have a computer in their home."

In 1988, MIT's Charles Ferguson in the *Harvard Business Review* proposed a government industrial policy to save America's microchip and software industries from elimination by Japanese competition.

Joe Flaherty, CBS senior vice president for technology in 1989: "We'll have digital television the same day we have an antigravity machine."

Rush Limbaugh was fired seven times before he became the radio talk show host with the world's largest audience— 20 million listeners weekly.

Robert X. Cringely's rules on forecasing: (1) We overestimate change in the short term. (2) We underestimate change for the long term. (3) The more specific and shorter term a forecast, the greater probability of error. (4) The most reliable forecasts are based on the continuation of trends.

Peter Drucker said the most important thing is not trends, but changes in trends, and the most consequential changes in trends for your company will occur outside of your industry.

HUMOR

I married beneath me—all women do.
Nancy Astor

If I'd known I was gonna live this long, I'd have taken better care of myself.
[On one-hundredth birthday. He died within five days.]
Eubie Blake

There was a young lady named Bright, Whose speed was far faster than light; She set out one day in a relative way And returned on the previous night.
Arthur H. R. Buller, "Relativity"

I never saw a purple cow, I never hope to see one; But I can tell you, anyhow, I'd rather see than be one.
Gelett Burgess, "The Purple Cow" (1895)

I speak Spanish to God, Italian to women,
French to men, and German to my horse.

Charles V

"Why not" is a slogan for an interesting life.

Mason Cooley

The average man is more interested in a woman who is interested in him than he is in a woman—any woman—with beautiful legs.

Marlene Dietrich

Very, very, very few
People die at ninety-two.
I suppose that I shall be
Safer still at ninety-three.

Willard Espy

You know you're growing old when almost everything hurts, and what doesn't hurt doesn't work.

Hy Gardner in L. R. Frank, *Wit and Humor Quotationary* (2000)

Billy, in one of his nice new sashes,
Fell in the fire and was burnt to ashes;
Now, although the room grows chilly,
I haven't the heart to poke poor Billy.

Harry Graham, *Ruthless Rhymes for Heartless Homes* (1930), "Tender-Heartedness"

Weep not for little Leonie
Abducted by a French Marquis!
Though loss of honour was a wrench
Just think how it's improved her French.

Ibid., "Compensation"

Growing old is not for sissies.

John Grier

I keep forgetting. Am I in the groove, or in a rut?

Mal Hancock in L. R. Frank, *Wit and Humor Quotationary* (2000)

Fathers are what give daughters away to other men who aren't nearly good enough, so they can have grandchildren who are smarter than anybody's.

Paul Harvey

I am firm; you are obstinate; he is pig-headed.

Katherine Harvill

It's wonderful you could all be here for the forty-third anniversary of my thirty-ninth birthday.

Bob Hope in L. R. Frank, *Wit and Humor Quotationary* (2000)

Talk to him of Jacob's ladder, and he would ask the number of the steps.

Douglas Jerrold

As I was going up the stair
I met a man who wasn't there.
He wasn't there again today.
I wish, I wish he'd stay away.

Hughes Mearns

We may live without poetry, music and art;
We may live without conscience, and
    live without heart;
We may live without friends; we may
    live without books;
But civilized man cannot live without
    cooks.

Owen Meredith, "Lucille" (1860), pt. 1, canto 2., st. 19

All the world is queer save thee and me,
and even thou art a little queer.

> Robert Owen

I just hit the dry side of the ball.
[How to handle a spitball.]

> Stan Musial

Not drunk is he who from the floor
Can rise alone and still drink more;
But drunk is he, who prostrate lies,
Without the power to drink or rise.

> Thomas Love Peacock, *In The Misfortunes
> of Elphin* (1829), ch. 3

If once a man indulges himself in murder, very soon he comes to think little of robbing; and from robbing he next comes to drinking and Sabbath-breaking, and from that to incivility and procrastination.

> Thomas de Quincy, "Murder Considered
> as One of the Fine Arts" (1827)

Born with the gift of laughter and the sense that the world was mad, and that was his only patrimony.

> Rafael Sabatini, *Scaramouche* (1921), ch. 1

I told you 158 times I cannot stand notes on my pillow, "We are out of corn flakes, F. U." It took me three hours to figure out F. U. was Felix Unger.

> Neil Simon, *The Odd Couple* (1965)

The least thing upset him on the links. He missed short putts because of the uproar of the butterflies in an adjoining meadow.

> P. G. Wodehouse in L. R. Frank, *Wit and
> Humor Quotationary* (2000)

There were times when my pants were so thin, I could sit on a dime and know if it was heads or tails.

> Spencer Tracy in L. R. Frank, *Wit and
> Humor Quotationary* (2000)

Oh! Some where in this favored land
the sun is shining bright;
The band is playing somewhere, and
somewhere hearts are light;
And somewhere men are laughing and
somewhere children shout,
But there is no joy in Mudville—
mighty Casey has struck out.

> Ernest Lawrence Thayer, "Casey at Bat"
> (1888), st. 13

It is not enough to succeed. Others must fail.

> Gore Vidal

The tragedy of Wile E. Coyote isn't that he never caught the Road Runner but that he failed to understand that he never *could* catch him.

> *Wall Street Journal* editorial

Everybody denies I am a genius—but nobody ever called me one!

> Orson Welles

A Christian is a man who feels
Repentance on a Sunday
For what he did on Saturday
And is going to do on Monday

> Thomas R. Ybarro, "The Christian"

The word must be spoken that bids you
depart–
Though the effort to speak it should
shatter my heart–

Though in silence, with blighted
    affection, I pine,
Yet, the lips that touch liquor must
    never touch mine!
           George W. Young, "The Lips that
                      Touch Liquor"

From ghoulies and ghosties and
    long-leggety beasties
And things that go bump in the night,
    Good Lord, deliver us.
                      Scottish prayer

Say it ain't so Joe.
    [A little boy to Shoeless Joe Jackson
    regarding the Chicago "Black Sox"
    scandal, to wit, the throwing of the
    1919 World Series by the White
    Sox.]

There are two types of computers: proto-
types and the obsolete.

Why did God invent whiskey?
So the Irish would not conquer the
world.

Children seldom go around showing
snapshots of their grandparents.

At Oxford, it was decided by a majority
vote that the minority was always right.

Many pessimists got that way by lending
to optimists.

An optimist is not worried he cannot
pay his bills, but is happy because he is
not one of his creditors.

Ef you wants to see how much folks is
goin' to miss you, jest stick yo' finger in de
pond den pull it out an' look at de hole.

MacGregor won the Scottish lottery:
one dollar a year for a million years.

A scion of Charleston was asked why she
never traveled. She replied, "Why travel,
I'm already there."

Parents shouldn't give a child a name
they can't spell.

American Envy: "My neighbor has a
Chevy, God, I want a Cadillac.
Russian Envy: "My neighbor has a pig,
God, I hope it dies."

Pepsi's slogan, "Come alive with Pepsi,"
was translated in China as: "Pepsi brings
you back from the grave."

All dirt roads lead to Woodberry Forest.

Sign in Vail, Colorado: "Leave your kid
for the day—$30. You help—$60."

Except for bad luck, I wouldn't have any
luck at all.

A man who has taken your time recognizes no debt, yet it is the only debt he
can never repay.

Harlequin gave six reasons why his master could not accept a dinner invitation.
The fourth was that his master was dead.

Every time I hear the Ten Commandments, I am relieved that at least I never
made "any graven images."

He who whispers down a well
About the goods he has to sell,
Will never reap the golden dollars
Like him who shows them round and
    hollers.

"Where women cease from troubling and the wicked are at rest."

[Cut into stone at the New York Princeton Club, but removed after Princeton admitted coeds. For overnight guests, the Princeton Club only admitted members or wives. On hearing that a member had a woman who was not his wife in his room, a club official objected until he learned that she was the wife of another member.]

She was poor but she was honest,
And her parents was the same,
Till she met a city feller,
And she lost her honest name.

A teacher asked a kindergartner what he was drawing and he replied, "The face of God." The teacher said, "How are you going to do that? No one's seen it before." The child replied, "In a minute they will."

HUMOROUS ANIMALS

You can put lipstick on a pig and call her Monique, but she's still a pig.

Never try to teach a pig to sing. It wastes your time and it annoys the pig.

When you wrestle with a pig, you will both get dirty, but the pig will enjoy it.

Hog weighing at Auburn University: Put the hog at one end of a plank laying across a log and pile rocks at the other end until the plank balances. Then, guess how much the rocks weigh.

Major, born a dog, died a gentleman.

LOST DOG: 3 legged, blind in one eye, missing left ear, broken tail, castrated—answers to "Lucky."

He has all the attributes of a mongrel dog, except loyalty.

That dog won't hunt.

Reform is not like taking a bone from a dog—it's like taking a moose carcass from a pack of wolves.

Every time I come to town
The boys keep kicking my dawg around;
Makes no difference if he is a hound,
They've got to quit kicking my dawg
    around.

The deputy stud is sent in to see if the mare is receptive. If not, she kicks the hell out of him. If so, they pull him off and send in the prize stallion.

If your horse dies, we suggest you dismount.

You can pull and pull, but you can't milk a bull.

A freshman said, "Ah, there is one of Princeton's famous black squirrels." A wise junior rejoined, "For all we know, that may be *the* famous Princeton black squirrel." A seasoned senior said, "All we really know is that may be Princeton's famous squirrel that is black on one side."

Only dead fish always go with the flow.

If a veterinarian can't catch a patient, there's nothing much to worry about.

James Herriot

The Paris Peace Conference in 1919 was described as "A riot in a parrot house."

This bill is a hydra-headed, cloven hoofed, five fanged, forked-tail combination of polecat, mad-dog, and rattlesnake. It sounds the death-knell for our way of life in Georgia and it drives a stake through the heart of the American Constitution; all the while shedding alligator tears and laughing the hyena-like laugh of a mad man who has just wounded his dearest friend and now envisions his annihilation.
[Georgia congressman critiquing a bill.]

There ain't no such animal.
[Farmer at a state fair looking at a camel.]

MURPHY'S LAWS, ET AL.

Allen's Law:
Almost anything is easier to get into than out of.

Bonetti's Law:
The less you bet the more you lose when you win.

Capone's Belief:
You can get more with a kind word and a gun than with a kind word alone.

Ettore's Observation:
The other line moves faster.

First Law on Wing Walking:
Don't leave hold of what you've got till you've got hold of something else.

Getty's Reminder:
The meek shall inherit the Earth, but not its mineral rights.

Gordon's Law:
If a project isn't worth doing, it isn't worth doing well.

Jones' Declaration:
A Smith & Wesson beats four aces.

Joy's Law:
Most of the smartest people are not in your company.

Morton's Law:
If rats are experimented on, they will develop cancer.

Murphy's Law:
If something can go wrong, it will, and at the most inopportune time.

Philip's Corollary:
Murphy was an optimist.

Murphy's Law on Thermodynamics:
Things get worse under pressure.

Pareto's Law (80/20 Rule):
Twenty percent are responsible for eighty percent of results. [Also, 80 percent of the problems are caused by 20 percent of the people. In World War II, 11 percent of U. S. fighter pilots had 90 percent of the kills.]

Parkinson's Law:
Work expands to fill the time available for its completion.

Peter Principle:
In a hierarchy every employee tends to rise to his level of incompetence.

Herb Stein's Law:
If something cannot go on forever, it will stop.

Van Roy's Law:
An unbreakable toy breaks other toys.

Wriston's Law of Capital:
Capital will always go where it's welcome and stay where it's well treated.

DIGITAL LAWS

Metcalfe's Law :
The value of a network rises by the square of the nodes on the network.

Moore's Law:
Computer power doubles or its cost halves every eighteen to twenty-four months. [Digital stuff gets 40 percent cheaper annually at same performance point.]

Gilder's Law on Bandwidth:
Bandwidth grows at least three times faster than computer power.

Gilder's Law of the Microcosm:
Microelectronics pulls decisions remorselessly down to the individual.

Gilder's Law on Winner's Waste:
The best business models waste the era's cheapest resources in order to conserve the era's most expensive resources.

Law of Information Theory:
Every relay doubles the noise and cuts the information in half.

MIDDLETON FAMILY LAWS

Austin's Axiom:
Ninety-nine percent of lawyers give the rest a bad name.

Carl's Conclusion:
Moderate your moderation.

Ginny's Jest:
To solve the parking problem, buy a parked car.

Hueston's Hypothesis:
Eagles may soar, but weasels don't get sucked into jet engines.

Wade's Wisdom:
The sooner you fall behind, the more time you have to catch up.

POLITICS AND POLITICIANS

Know, my son, with how little wisdom the world is governed.
> Gustavus Adolphus [dying words]

We started off trying to set up a small anarchist community, but people wouldn't obey the rules.
> Alan Bennett

And this is good old Boston,
The home of the bean and the cod,
Where the Lowells talk to the Cabots,
And the Cabots talk only to God.
> John Bossidy

An honest politician is one who when he's bought stays bought.
> Simon Cameron

I don't believe you can find any evidence of the fact that I have changed government policy solely because of a contribution.
> William Jefferson Clinton

Never believe anything until it has been officially denied.

Claud Cockburn

Yesterday Senator _____ wrestled with his conscience. He won.

Elmer Davis, in L. R. Frank, *Wit and Humor Quotationary* (2000)

A billion dollars here, a billion dollars there, and pretty soon you're talking about real money.

Everett McKinley Dirkson

What is a Communist? One who hath yearnings
For equal division of unequal earnings.
Idler or bungler, or both, he is willing
To fork out his copper and pocket your shilling.

Ebenezer Elliott, "Epigram" (1846)

The whole duty of government is to keep the peace and stand outside the sunshine of the people.

President James Garfield

Above all, mankind needs a sense of smell.

Robert Ranke Graves, *I Claudius*

When I make a mistake, it's a beaut.

Fiorello La Guardia

A very weak-minded fellow I am afraid, and, like the feather pillow, bears the marks of the last person who has sat on him.

Douglas Haig [of 17th Earl of Derby.]

[Politics pits "equality" against "prudential order and the functional necessity of hierarchy."]

Martin Malia, Foreword, *The Black Book of Communism* (1999)

Treason doth never prosper, what's the reason?
For if it prosper, none dare call it treason.

John Harrington, *Epigrams* (1618)

Now and then an innocent man is sent to the legislature.

Frank Hubbard

Nobody ever forgets where he buried a hatchet.

Kin Hubbard

Why did men die of hunger for six thousand years? Why did they walk and carry goods and other men on their backs for six thousand years, and suddenly in one century, only on a sixth of this earth's surface, they make steamships, railroads, motors, and airplanes? Why did families live thousands of years in floorless hovels, without windows or chimneys, then in eighty years and only in these United States, they are taking floors, chimneys, glass windows for granted and regarding electric lights, porcelain toilets, and window screens as minimum necessities? The answer is liberty.

Rose Wilder Lane

The more I see of the representatives of the people, the more I admire my dogs. [Of the French Revolution.]

Larmartine

Never argue with people who buy ink by the barrel.

Tommy Lasorda

Politicians use statistics like drunks use lampposts—for support rather than illumination.

Andrew Lang

It is forbidden to forbid.
  Counterculture slogan on a Sorbonne wall

I never vote for the best man because he's never a candidate.

Norman Podhoretz in *Ex-Friends* (1999) observed a meeting of disheveled young American radicals. He concluded that everyone was a tragedy to some family.

Absolutism tempered by assassination.
  [Of Russian politics.]
    Count Ernest Von Munster

Always love your country, but never trust your government.
    Robert Novak

Taxation without representation is tyranny.
    James Otis

When war is declared, truth is the first casualty.
    Ponsonby

And thus Place…is the end of half the labors of human life; and is the cause of all the tumult and bustle, all the rapine and injustice which avarice and ambition have introduced into this world.
    Adam Smith

Tyrrellism—the technique of blackening an opponent's reputation by quoting him.
    R. Emmett Tyrrell, Jr.

Money is the mother's milk of politics.
    Jesse Unruh in L. R. Frank, *Wit and Humor Quotationary* (2000)

Socrates was a good man who went around giving wise advice. The state poisoned him.

Frothy eloquence neither convinces nor satisfies me. I am from Missouri. You have got to show me.
    Willard Vandiver, congressman

Gettysburg had a local ordinance forbidding the discharge of firearms.

I'm for sound money and plenty of it.

May the last of the kings be strangled with the guts of the last priest.
    Jacobin toast

Socialism: You have two cows—The government takes both and keeps the milk. *Communism*: You have two cows—The government takes both and shoots you. *New Dealism*: You have two cows—The government takes both—shoots one, milks the other, and throws the milk away. *Capitalism*: You have two cows—You trade one for a bull.

Claude Pepper is a known extrovert, a man who practiced celibacy before marriage and who now indulges in nepotism with his sister-in-law.

Don't tax you. Don't tax me. Tax that man behind the tree.

He held a worldview that Bo Peep would have considered to be hopelessly naïve.

A secret in a politician's sense: You may tell it to only one person at a time.

Everything changes except the avant-garde.

Lease a man a garden
And in time he will leave you
A patch of sand.
Make a man a full owner

Of a patch of sand
And in time he will grow there
A garden on the land.

PROFESSIONS

ACCOUNTANTS are the witch doctors of the modern world.

> J. Harman

Doing business without **ADVERTIS-ING** is like winking at a girl in the dark. You know what you're doing, but nobody else does.

> Stuart H. Britt

Nothing but the mint can make money without advertising.

> Thomas Macaulay

The best ad is a good product.

> Alan Meyer

Early to bed, early to rise, work like hell, and advertise.

> Ted Turner in L. R. Frank, *Wit and Humor Quotationary*

Half the money I spend on advertising is wasted, but I don't know which half.

> John Wanamaker

The ark was built by **AMATEURS,** the *Titanic* by professionals.

An **ARCHAEOLOGIST** is the best husband any woman can have; the older she gets, the more interested he is in her.

> Dame Agatha Christie

The **ARTIST** isn't particularly keen on getting a thing done, as you call it. He gets his pleasure out of doing it, playing with it, fooling with it, if you like. The mere completion of it is an incident.

> William McFee

Artists are like prostitutes…never off duty.

> Andrew Wyeth

What poor **ASTRONOMERS** they are That take women's eyes for stars!

A perfect **BUREAUCRAT** makes no decisions and escapes all responsibility.

> Brooks Atkinson

The Six Phases of a Successful Bureaucratic Program:
    Enthusiasm
    Disappointment
    Panic
    Search for the guilty
    Punishment of the innocent
    Increase in funding

Paul Hindemith, a modern **COMPOSER,** interrupted his orchestra's rehearsal at a particularly dissonant point, saying, "No, no gentlemen. Even though it sounds wrong, it's still not right."

Wars begin when **DIPLOMATS** tell lies to journalists and then believe what they read in the newspapers.

Diplomacy is to do and say
The nastiest thing in the nicest way.

> Isaac Goldberg

A diplomat is a person who can tell you to go to hell in such a way that you actually look forward to the trip.

> Caskie Stinnett in L. R. Frank, *Wit and Humor Quotationary* (2000)

Diplomacy is the art of saying "nice doggie" while you hunt for a bigger stick.

If you believe the **DOCTORS**, nothing is wholesome; if you believe the theologians, nothing is innocent; if you believe the soldiers, nothing is safe.

> Robert Gascoyne-Cecil

A good bedside manner is no substitute for the right diagnosis.

> Alfred Sloan

When I told my doctor I couldn't afford an operation, he offered to touch up my X rays.

> Henny Youngman

Politicians ask, "What do you want?" **ECONOMISTS** ask, "What do you want most?"

> Peter Jay

If a man marries his cook, the gross national product falls.

> Arthur Pigou

Two types of people **FORECAST:** Those who don't know and those who don't know they don't know.

> John Kenneth Galbraith

Proof of his farsightedness is that none of his predictions have yet come true.

Rules of forecasting: if you give a number, don't give a date; it you give a date, don't give a number. If you must forecast with numbers and dates, do it frequently.

Forecast what has happened, but stay at the cautious end.

You will get nowhere in economic forecasting until you throw out all econometric models. Electricity is no substitute for thought.

> Maxwell Newton

I only played **GOLF** to get the money to hunt and fish.

> Sam Snead

The easiest way to change history is to become a **HISTORIAN.**

> [If Khrushchev, not Kennedy, had been assassinated in 1963, what of history?] With history one can never be certain, but I think I can safely say that Aristotle Onassis would not have married Mrs. Khrushchev.
>
> Gore Vidal

INVESTMENT genius: One lucky enough to have used leverage in a bull market.

The market is like a beautiful woman— endlessly fascinating, endlessly complex, always changing, always mystifying.

> Edward C. Johnson III

He who sells what isn't his'n,
Buys it back or go to pris'n.

> Daniel Drew, [On short-selling]

My **LAW** firm: Dewey, Cheatum, and Howe.

If you don't have the facts, argue the law. If you don't have the law, argue the facts. If you don't have either the facts or the law, pound on the table.

I'm not a potted plant.
> [When told not to speak while defending Col. Oliver North in 1987 at the Iran-Contra hearings.]
>   Brendan Sullivan

Asked to define pornography, Chief Justice Potter Stewart said, "I know it when I see it."

To convict in capital cases, an Alabama jury must find that (1) the accused killed the deceased, and (2) the deceased did not need killing.

Legal pleas in the alternative: My client did not take a chicken. My client took his own chicken. If it were the plaintiff's chicken, he had given permission for my client to take it. My client won't do it again.

The United States wins its case when justice is done.
> [U. S. Solicitor General's Office.]

Equal Justice Under Law.
> [Entrance to the Supreme Court.]

Justice the guardian of liberty.
> [East Portico of Supreme Court.]

Don't tell me what the law is; tell me who the judge is.

For my friends, anything. For my enemies, the law.
> [Oscar R. Venavides, president of Peru.]

MATHEMATICIAN Merton Miller said, "Roberts and I run an average of five miles a day; Roberts runs ten."

When asked how he could sell rabbit sandwiches so cheaply, the merchant replied, "I put some horse meat in too, but I mix 'em up fifty-fifty: one horse for one rabbit.

I did poorly in math. Mrs. Henshaw took my answers literally.

There are only three kinds of people: Those who can count and those who can't.
>   Warren Buffett

A **METAPHYSICIAN** is a blind man who goes into a dark cellar at midnight without a light, looking for a black hat that is not there.
>   Lord Bowen

MUSICIAN. If I don't practice one day, I know it: two days, the critics know it: three days, the public knows it.
>   Jascha Heifetz in L. R. Frank, *Wit and Humor Quotationary* (2000)

PAINTER. There has never been a boy painter, nor can there be. The art requires a long apprenticeship, being mechanical as well as intellectual.

John Constable

[Degas saw one of his old paintings in an auction house sell for $100,000. He remarked to a friend:] "I feel as a horse must feel when the beautiful cup is given to the jockey."

A **PIONEER** is a man lying facedown in the dirt with arrows in his back.

PSYCHOANALYSTS reduce everything to sexual desires, except their occupation.

A neurotic is a man who builds a castle in the air. A psychotic is the man who lives in it. A **PSYCHIATRIST** is the man who collects the rent.

Jerome Lawrence

Two shoe **SALESMEN** traveled to a remote island. One cabled back, "No market here; no one wears shoes." The other cabled back, "Fantastic market here; no one has shoes."

I'm not selling experience, I'm selling talent.

The old maxim for **REPORTERS** was if your mother says she loves you, check it out.

In **SCIENCE** the credit goes to the man who convinces the world, not to the man to whom the idea first occurs.

Sir William Osler

SPEAKER: It's my job to speak and yours to listen. Let me know if you get through before I do.

Speakers need gray hair for the look of distinction and hemorrhoids for the look of concern.

It's easier to change audiences than to change speeches.

Speak carefully, if you speak at all; Carve every word before you let it fall. Speak with words that are soft and sweet. You never know which ones you may eat.

Any fact is better established by two or three good testimonies than by a thousand arguments.

Nathaniel Emmons

To **TEACH** without first inspiring the pupil to learn is hammering on cold iron.

Horace Mann

The mediocre teacher tells. The good teacher explains. The superior teacher demonstrates. The great teacher inspires.

William A. Ward

WRITER: I don't care what you say about me, as long as you say something about me, and as long as you spell my name right.

George M. Cohan in L. R. Frank, *Wit and Humor Quotationary* (2000)

The world may be full of fourth-rate writers, but it's also full of fourth-rate readers.

Stan Barstow

PROVERBS

If a man abandons his customs, he had better make certain he can replace them with something of value.

African proverb

The greatest risk is not taking one.

AIG motto

Where you're going is not as important as who you are going with.

Alabama proverb

The dogs bark, but the caravan moves on.

Arab proverb

To make God laugh, tell Him your plans for the future.

Arab proverb

My brother and I against my cousin; my cousin and I against the stranger.

Arab proverb

Victory is gained not by the number killed but by the number frightened.

Arab proverb

One cannot both feast and become rich.

Ashanti proverb

When you see a Hungarian, kick him; he'll know why.

Austrian proverb

The gods do not deduct from man's allotted span the hours spent in fishing.

Babylonian Proverb

Before seaking revenge, dig two graves.

Chinese proverb

It is the beautiful bird that gets caged.

Chinese proverb

One Chinese is a dragon; three Chinese are a worm.

Chinese proverb

One Japanese is a worm; three are a dragon.

Chinese proverb

The mountain is high and the emperor is far away.

Chinese proverb

Man must sit with mouth open for very long time before roast duck fly in.

Chinese proverb

Sticks can only break my bones, but words can shatter me.

Chinese proverb

On the subject of singing, the frog school and the lark school disagree.

Chinese proverb

A man without a smiling face must not open a shop.

Chinese proverb

Kill one, frighten ten thousand.

Chinese proverb

Who would be constant in happiness must often change.

Chinese proverb

A fish begins to rot at the head.

> Chinese proverb

The great man is a public misfortune.

> Chinese proverb

May you live in interesting times.

> Chinese curse

May the worst day of your past be better than the best day of your future.

> Chinese curse

You're still alive.

> Chinese greeting

The Kanji character for "crisis" combines "danger" and "opportunity."

> Chinese writing

I hear and I forget; I see and I remember; I do and I understand.

> Chinese saying

Extremes meet.

> Coleridge's favorite proverb

A smooth sea never made a skilled mariner.

> English proverb

A man is as old as his arteries.

> English proverb

There are more old drunkards than old doctors.

> French proverb

Only that which is provisional endures.

> French proverb

He who is born to be hanged shall never be drowned.

> French proverb

It's all very well in practice, but it will never work in theory.

> French proverb

He who licks, bites.

> French proverb

People count the faults of those who keep them waiting.

> French Proverb

Birds of prey do not sing.

> German proverb

What is the use of running when we are not on the right road?

> German proverb

They are not all cooks who carry long knives.

> German proverb

Wealth lost, something lost;
Honor lost, much lost;
Courage lost, all lost.

> German proverb

The ancient Greeks asked but one question of a man, "Does he have passion?"

> Greek saying

Above all, liberty.

> Greek proverb

Many trades, few blessings.

> Hebrew proverb

A wise man knows everything, a shrewd one, everybody.

> Hebrew proverb

God could not be everywhere, so he made mothers.

> Hebrew proverb

Send a fool to close the shutters and he'll close them all over town.

> Hebrew proverb

Clever people extricate themselves from situations that wise people avoid.

> Hebrew proverb

A wise man hears one word and understands two.

> Hebrew proverb

With money in your pocket, you are wise, handsome, and sing well, too.

> Hebrew proverb

Thy friend has a friend, and thy friend's friend has a friend; be discreet.

> Hebrew proverb

After crossing the mountain, more mountains.

> Indian proverb

If I am a gentleman and you are a gentleman, who will milk the cow?

> Irish proverb

Between two cowards, he has the advantage who first detects the other.

> Italian proverb

After victory, tighten your helmet cords.

> Japanese proverb

The nail that sticks up gets hammered down.

> Japanese proverb

Knowledge without wisdom is a load of books on the back of an ass.

> Japanese proverb

Time spent laughing is time spent with the gods.

> Japanese proverb

Life is lighter than a feather; duty is heavier than a mountain.

> Japanese proverb

Hear no evil, see no evil, speak no evil. "Three Wise Monkeys."

> Japanese legend

The Koreans don't know there is a finish line.

> About Koreans

One witness is no witness.

> Latin proverb

Before you trust a man, eat a peck of salt with him.

> Latin proverb

Live Free or Die.

> New Hampshire motto

If fortune turns against you, even jelly breaks your tooth.

> Persian proverb

An egg thief becomes a camel thief.

Persian proverb

Don't burn down your house to roast the pig.

Polish proverb

A slave who has three masters is a free man.

Roman proverb

From good to evil is only one quaver

Russian proverb

If you are not behind bars, it's not your merit; it means the system does not work properly.

Russian proverb

Under capitalism, man exploits man. Under Communism, it's the opposite.

Russian proverb

The tears of strangers are only water.

Russian proverb

Confide a secret to a dumb man and he will speak.

Russian proverb

It's enough to show a well-beaten dog the whip.

Russian proverb

Become a sheep and you'll soon meet a wolf.

Russian proverb

Severitas.
   [Be severe with yourself.]

Scottish virtue

Death to privilege.

Scottish motto

Fools look to tomorrow; wise men use tonight.

Scottish proverb

I don't do favors; I collect debts.

Sicilian proverb

You can do almost anything you want, so long as you know better.

Southern saying

Too poor to paint and too proud to whitewash.

Southern saying

He who has daughters is always a shepherd.

Spanish proverb

Big hat and no cattle.

Texas proverb

One riot, one Ranger.

Texas proverb

The infidel's wisdom comes too late.

Turkish proverb

He that would speak the truth must have one foot in a stirrup.

Turkish proverb

Wear it out, make it do, or do without.

Vermont proverb

SELF-IMPROVEMENT

If everything seems under control, you're not going fast enough.

Mario Andretti

Meet difficulties by altering them or by altering yourself to meet them.

Phyllis Bottome

It takes twenty years to become an over-night success.

Eddie Cantor

Success is going from failure to failure without losing your enthusiasm.

Winston Churchill

Zest is the secret of all beauty.

Christian Dior

If we don't discipline ourselves, the world will do it for us.

William Feather

A pound of pluck is worth a ton of luck.

James A. Garfield

In life as in football, fall forward when you fall.

Arthur Gutterman

Pack your own parachute.

T. L. Hakala

The act of writing is the act of discovering what you believe.

David Hare.

Ideas lose themselves as quickly as quail, and one must wing them the minute they rise out of the grass—or they are gone.

Thomas Kennedy

Never eat more than you can lift.

Jim Henson [Miss Piggy]

At one point in time every great man in history has said, "Damn the torpedoes."

David Murdock

He who would do some great thing in this short life must apply himself to work with such a concentration of his forces as, to idle spectators who live only to amuse themselves, looks like insanity.

Francis Parkman

Capitalize upon criticism. It's one of the hardest things in the world to accept criticism, especially when it's not presented in a constructive way, and turn it to your advantage.

James Cash (J. C.) Penney.

If you don't feel exploited, you're not working hard enough.

Mike Shapiro

To know your ruling passion, examine your castles in the air.

Richard Whately

Your attitude, not your aptitude, determines your altitude.

Zig Ziglar

Heroism is endurance for one moment more.

Caucasus Mountaineer saying

The answer to fear cannot always be to avoid the danger; sometimes it must lie in courage.

Use the talent you have. The woods would be quiet if only the best songbird sang.

If you are coasting, you're going downhill.

On the plains of hesitation bleach the bones of those who at the dawn of victory paused to rest, and in resting died.

Every man is enthusiastic at times. One man has enthusiasm for thirty minutes—another man has it for thirty days, but it is the man who has it for thirty years who makes a success in life.

You won't advance far within any organization, unless others want you to.

If at first you don't succeed, skydiving is not for you.

If you can say "no," you're better off than if you can speak Latin.

A diamond is only a hunk of coal that made good under pressure.

Adversity introduces a man to himself.

WEDDING TOASTS

May you understand that you are both angels with only one wing. You can only soar while embracing each other.

Luciana de Crescenzo

Á la famille!
    [Include both families in this Italian toast.]

Fathers are what give daughters away to other men who aren't nearly good enough, so they can have grandchildren who are smarter than anybody's.

Paul Harvey

May you grow old using the same pillow. May you give your children roots and wings.

Thalassio!
    [He was the Roman boy who carried away the most beautiful of the Sabine maidens.]

Virgil (70 B.C.)

WISDOM

Pay attention to your enemies, for they are the first to discover your mistakes.

Antisthenes

Perhaps humankind cannot bear too much reality, but neither can it bear too much unreality, too much abuse of the truth.

Saul Bellow

If you think education is expensive, try ignorance.

Derek Bok

Losing an illusion makes you wiser than finding a truth.

Ludwig Borne

[Montag in *Fahrenheit 451* (1963) exposes the emptiness of materialism by shouting at his wife's friend:]
Go home and think of your first husband divorced…and your third husband blowing his brains out, go home and think of the dozen abortions you've had…and of your children who hate your guts!

Ray Bradbury

But for the grace of God there goes John Bradford.

John Bradford

The optimist proclaims we live in the best of all possible worlds; and the pessimist fears this is true.

James Cabell

Change is certain. Progress is not.

Edward H. Carr

Tolerance: the virtue of those who don't believe in anything.

G. K. Chesterton

The heart of marriage is memories.

Bill Cosby

Wisdom consists in the anticipation of consequences.

Norman Cousins in L. R. Frank, *Wisdom* (2003)

When I see a bird that walks like a duck and swims like a duck and quacks like a duck, I call that bird a duck.

Cardinal Richard Cushing

What a poor life this, if full of care, We have no time to stand and stare?

W. H. Davies

My children didn't have my advantages: I was born into abject poverty.

Kirk Douglas in L. R. Frank, *Wit and Humor Quotationary* (2000)

Sweet Alice, whose hair was so brown;
Who wept with delight when you gave
   her a smile,
And trembl'd with fear at your frown!

Thomas English, "Ben Bolt"

A place to put down our roots and to leave our bones.

Thomas Fleming

I would remind you that extremism in the defense of liberty is no vice. And let me remind you also that moderation in the pursuit of justice is no virtue.

Barry M. Goldwater, in L. R. Frank, *Wisdom* (2003)

The kiss of the sun for pardon,
The song of the birds for mirth,
One is nearer God's Heart in a garden
Than anywhere else on earth.

Dorothy Frances Gurney, "God's Garden" (1913)

You're only here for a short visit. Don't hurry. Don't worry. And be sure to smell the flowers along the way.

Walter C. Hagen

I am only one,
But still I am one.
I cannot do everything,
But still I can do something;
And because I cannot do everything
I will not refuse to do the something
   that I can do.

Edward Everett Hale, "For the Lend-a-Hand Society"

And as the smart ship grew
In stature, grace and hue,
In shadowy silent distance grew the
   Iceberg too.
Alien they seemed to be:
No mortal eye could see
The intimate welding of their later
   history.

Thomas Hardy, "The Convergence of the Twain: Lines on the Loss of the Titanic"

The most important thing a father can do for his children is to love their mother.

Rev. Theodore Hesburgh

The ability to simplify means to eliminate the unnecessary so that the necessary may speak.

Hans Hofmann

This universe is not hostile, nor yet is it friendly. It is simply indifferent.

John H. Holmes

Never tell a young person that something cannot be done. God may have been waiting for centuries for somebody ignorant enough of the impossible to do that thing.

Ibid.

I slept and dreamed that life was beauty.
I woke—and found that life was duty.

Ellen Sturgis Hooper, "Beauty and Duty"
(1840)

And so it criticized each flower,
This supercilious seed;
Until it woke one summer hour,
And found itself a weed.

Mildred Howells, "The Difficult Seed," st. 5

Great books conserve time.

Holbrook Jackson

I'm tired of this nonsense about beauty being only skin-deep. Do you want an adorable pancreas?

Jean Kerr

Be bold and mighty forces will come to your aid.

Basil King

The harder I work, the luckier I get.

Stephen Leacock

Reciprocity is the fundamental law of social life.

Claude Lèvi-Strauss

The great geniuses of the past still rule over us from their graves; they still stalk or scurry about in the present, tripping up the living, confusing values in art and manners, a brilliant cohort of mortals determined not to die, in possession of the land.

Wyndham Lewis

All knowledge is sterile which does not lead to action and end in charity.

Desire-Joseph Cardinal Mercier

Be kind, for everyone you meet is fighting a great battle.

Philo of Alexandria

Freedom does not make people strong; rather it makes strength possible.

Leonard E. Read

Impartiality is either a delusion of the simple-minded, a banner of the opportunist, or the boast of the dishonest.

Gaetano Salvemini

No matter how old a mother is, she watches her middle-aged children for signs of improvement.

Florida Scott-Maxwell

"Men of sense are really but of one religion..." "Pray, my lord, what religion is that?" "Madam," says the earl immediately, "men of sense never tell it."

First Earl of Shaftesbury

Happiness is not in our circumstances but in ourselves. It is not something we see, like a rainbow, or feel, like the heat of a fire. Happiness is something we are.

> John B. Sheerin

I would willingly give up my whole career if I could have just one normal child.

> Beverly Sills

Woman's virtue is man's greatest invention.

> Cornelia Otis Skinner

People say that life is the thing, but I prefer reading.

> Logan Pearsall Smith

All reformers, however strict their social conscience, live in houses just as big as they can pay for.

> Ibid.

We see things as we are, not as they are.

> Jennifer Stone, in L. R. Frank, *Wisdom*

The saddest epitaph which can be carved in memory of a vanished liberty is that it was lost because its possessors failed to stretch forth a saving hand while yet there was time.

> Justice George Sutherland
> in L. R. Frank, *Freedom* (2003)

The hand that rocks the cradle is the hand that rules the world.

> William Wallace

All change in history, all advance, comes from the nonconformists. If there had been no troublemakers, no dissenters, we should still be living in caves.

> A. J. P. Taylor in L. R. Frank, *Freedom* (2003)

Strephon kissed me in the spring,
Robin in the fall,

But Colin only looked at me
And never kissed at all.

> Sarah Teasdale, "The Look," st. 1

Strephon's kiss was lost in jest,
Robin's lost in play,
But the kiss in Colin's eyes
Haunts me night and day.

> Ibid., st. 2

The rewards of genius go to society. The price of being a genius is paid by the genius alone.

> James Thorpe

I've never been poor, only broke. Being poor is a frame of mind. Being broke is a temporary situation.

> Mike Todd

…when we have made our fellow men the objects of our enlightened interest, to go on to make them the objects of our pity, then of our wisdom, ultimately of our coercion.

> Lionel Trilling

Ideas Have Consequences
> Richard Weaver [book title, 1948]

The best career advice to give the young is "Find out what you like doing best and get someone to pay you for doing it."

> Katharine Whitehorn in L. R. Frank, *Wit and Humor Quotationary* (2000)

There are no illegitimate children—only illegitimate parents.

> Leon Yankwich

The library's information is free; all you have to do is bring the container

You will lose most 50-50 bets.

There are knowns, known unknowns, and unknown unknowns.

When one bases his life on principle, 99 percent of his decisions are already made.

Most of us need someone who will not permit us to do less than our best.

Is it a good exchange to trade our dreams for wisdom?

He was only five feet, but measured from the chin up, he was a giant.

A transition period is that period which falls between two transition periods.

Epimenides the Cretan said, "All Cretans are liars." If Epimenides is telling the truth, then he must be lying.

Nothing in fine print is ever good news.

The enemy of my enemy is my friend.

Depend on the rabbit's foot if you will, but it didn't work for the rabbit!

The Quakers came to the New World to do good and ended up doing well.

The road to oblivion sometimes passes under a triumphal arch.

A half an hour after you've entered a poker game, if you haven't figured out who the fish is, you're it.

Friends come and go, but enemies accumulate.

You lose not only your youth, but the youth of your children, too.

We are getting old when we do more things for the last time and fewer things for the first time.

The rich can only stay healthy by abstention and physical labor, that is, by living like the poor.

Long life, by itself, gets you no more wisdom than riding an exercise bicycle five miles gets you to town.

More people commit suicide with a fork than a gun.

Old men plant trees whose shade they will never enjoy.

When his gardener objected to planting a tree because it would take a hundred years to mature, the French marshal replied, "In that case, there is no time to lose, plant it this afternoon."

Your ship is safe in the harbor, but what good is it there?

Two ways to be independent: be a virgin or a prostitute.

If it is hard to change yourself, how much harder will it be for you to change another?

One can present people with opportunities. One cannot make them equal to them.

What you measure will improve.

Man strives for glory, honor, fame,
That all the world may know his name,
Amasses wealth by brain and hand;
Becomes a power in the land.
But when he nears the end of life
And looks back o'er the years of strife,
He finds that happiness depends
On none of these, but love of friends.

There is a lady sweet and kind,
Was never face so pleased my mind;
I did but see her passing by,
And yet I love her till I die.

May the road rise with you
and the wind be ever at your back.
May the sun shine warm on you, and
the rain fall softly on your fields, and
Until we meet again, may the Lord hold
you in the palm of His hand.

Gaelic blessing

The will to prepare to win is more important than the will to win.

Coach Bobby Knight

Life is 10 percent what happens to me and 90 percent how I react to it.

Coach Lou Holt

15
INVESTMENT WISDOM

The market tries to inflict the maximum pain on the greatest number of investors.

Michael Santoli

Warren Buffett, "oracle of Omaha," is probably the best portfolio investor ever. He bought a fading textile maker, Berkshire Hathaway (BRK), and used its declining cash flow to reinvest in undervalued companies. An investment of $16 in 1964 for a share of (BRK) was worth $87,000 in 2004. From 1951 to 2004, Buffett earned an average annual return of 23 percent versus 11 percent for the S&P 500.

Buffett's investment lodestar is a company with a "durable competitive advantage": a company whose future earnings are highly predictable, as where: 1) the product changes slowly and is used up quickly, such as razor blades; 2) the business has a monopoly-like brand or franchise; and, 3) it can adjust prices to inflation. He avoids technology companies, which change too quickly to identify long-term winners. He requires: 1) projected earnings in two years can pay off all debt; 2) return on equity for ten years of at least 15 percent; 3) a minimum of 15 percent return on retained earnings; and 4) confidence in management's integrity and ability.

Buffett does not "time the market" by trading when pessimistic or optimistic about the market. But in May 1969 he liquidated his partnership and returned the investors' money because the prices of securities had risen too high. He wrote: "I am out of step with present conditions.... I will not abandon a previous approach whose logic I understand even though it may mean forgoing large, and apparently easy, profits to embrace an approach which I don't fully understand, have not practiced successfully, and which, possibly, could lead to substantial permanent loss of capital." While not a market timer, Buffett goes to cash if prices rise too high for him to follow his discipline.

Rule No. 1: Never lose money.
Rule No. 2: Never forget Rule No. 1.

My favorite holding period is forever.

Noah principle: Predicting rain doesn't count; building arks does.

Truly conservative investment arises from intelligent hypotheses, correct facts, and sound reasoning. These qualities may lead to conventional acts, but they also can lead to unorthodoxy. We derive no comfort because important people, vocal people, or great numbers of people agree with us. Nor do we derive comfort if they don't. A public opinion poll is no substitute for thought. When we really sit back with a smile on our face is when we run into a situation we can understand, where the facts are ascertainable and clear and the course of action obvious.

In that case—whether conventional or unconventional, whether others agree or disagree—we feel we are progressing in a conservative manner.

Stocks are simple. All you do is buy shares in a great business for less than the business is intrinsically worth, with managers of the highest integrity and ability. Then you own those shares forever.

An investor cannot obtain superior profits from stocks by simply committing to a specific investment category or style. He can earn them only by carefully evaluating facts and continuously exercising discipline.

I intensely observe business performance and managerial behavior.

The really important thing is to be in the right business.

> [The principal drivers of industry profitability are (1) buyer power, (2) supplier power, (3) threat of substitutes, (4) rivalry among existing players, and (5) threat of new entrants. Buffet's desired companies have "fortress business franchises," that is, they are unassailable by buyers, suppliers, or competitors.]

The primary test of managerial economic performance is the achievement of a high earnings rate on equity capital employed (without undue leverage, accounting gimmickry, etc.) and not the achievement of consistent gains in earnings per share.

Unless experiencing tremendous growth, outstanding businesses by definition generate large amounts of excess cash.

[He invests in businesses with] demonstrated, consistent earnings power (future projections are of little interest to us, nor are "turnaround" situations).

I read annual reports of the company I'm looking at and I read the annual reports of the competitors—that is the main source of material.

I have seen no trend toward value investing in the thirty-five years I've practiced it. There seems to be some perverse human characteristic that likes to make easy things difficult.

It's just so simple. It's like studying for the priesthood and finding out that the Ten Commandments were all you needed.

If the [value of a company] doesn't scream out at you, it's too close.

We don't want to stray from businesses that we understand. There may be all kinds of wonderful businesses out there that we don't understand. We can't jump seven feet, either. There are a lot of things that Charlie and I can't do that might be very profitable if we could do them. We can't knock out Mike Tyson, for example.

I am a better investor because I am a businessman, and a better businessman because I am an investor.

Sometimes earnings are worth less than their face amount due to the necessity of reinvesting them on pain of losing all. But sometimes earnings are worth more than 100 percent because they can be retained and produce an extraordinary rate of return.

A great investment opportunity occurs when a marvelous business encounters a one-time huge, but solvable, problem.

Our long-term goal…is to maximize the average annual rate of gain in intrinsic business value on a per share basis. We do not measure the economic significance of performance of Berkshire by its size; we measure by per-share progress.

We have no ability to forecast interest rates and believe no one else can.

[In runaway inflation] a diversified stock portfolio would almost surely suffer an enormous loss in real value. But bonds already outstanding would suffer far more. An all bond portfolio carries a small but unacceptable "wipeout" risk. Only when bond purchases appear decidedly superior to other business opportunities will we engage in them. Those occasions are likely to be few and far between.

Diversification is protection against ignorance, but if you don't feel ignorant, the need for it goes down drastically.

Charlie and I decided long ago that in an investment lifetime it's just too hard to make hundreds of smart decisions…. Therefore, we adopted a strategy that required our being smart—and not too smart at that—only a very few times. Indeed, we'll settle for one good idea a year. (Charlie says it's my turn.)

…the only value of stock forecasters is to make fortunetellers look good. Short-term market forecasts are poison and should be kept…away from children and grownups who behave in the market like children.

We don't know and we don't think about when something will happen. We think about what will happen.

We delegate to the point of abdication.

Don't ask your barber if you need a haircut.

If you feel you can dance in and out of securities in a way that defeats inflation and taxes, I would like to be your broker, but not your partner.

Beware of past performance proofs in finance. If history books were the key to success, the Forbes 400 would consist of librarians.

[Buffett said managers must overcome the four Institutional Imperatives:] 1.) …an institution will resist any change in its current direction; 2.) Corporate projects or acquisitions will materialize to soak up additional funds; 3.) Any business craving of the leader…will be quickly supported by detailed rate of return and strategic studies prepared by his troops [or outside advisers to justify his stance]; 4.) Behavior of peer companies…will be mindlessly imitated.]

In a difficult business, no sooner is one problem solved than another surfaces—never is there just one cockroach in the kitchen.

We believe that according the name "investors" to institutions that trade actively is like calling someone who repeatedly engages in one-night stands a romantic.

It's only when the tide goes out that you learn who's been swimming naked.

Unlike the Lord, the market does not forgive those who know not what they do.

If you invest a dollar and it doubles and you reinvest the proceeds for the next nineteen years and it doubles each year, it would become $1,048,576. But, if each year you paid a 35 percent tax on the gain, at the end of 20 years, you would have only $22,370.
[The reason for buying and holding.]

A contrarian approach is just as foolish as a follow-the-crowd strategy. What's required is thinking, rather than polling.

Lethargy bordering on sloth remains the cornerstone of our investment style.

If you want to pile up money, find your circle of competence and stay within it.

Observing correctly that the market was frequently efficient, [backers of efficient market theory] went on to conclude incorrectly that it was always efficient. The difference between these propositions is night and day.
[Buffett threatened to endow a university chair for the efficient market hypothesis to emasculate competing investors.]

To invest successfully, you need not understand beta, efficient markets, modern portfolio theory, option pricing or emerging markets. You may, in fact, be better off knowing nothing of these. That, of course, is not the prevailing view at most business schools.

We have embraced the twenty-first century by entering such cutting-edge industries as brick, carpet, insulation, and paint. Try to control your excitement.
  Berkshire Hathaway Annual Report (2001)

If you don't know jewelry, know your jeweler.

Buffett On Careers

Somebody once said that in looking for people to hire, you look for three qualities: integrity, intelligence, and energy. And if they don't have the first, the other two will kill you. You think about it; it's true. If you hire somebody without the first, you really want them to be dumb and lazy.

I go into business only with people whom I like, trust and admire. We have never succeeded in making a good deal with a bad person.

  Are you a monomaniac on a mission?
    [The question Buffett asks all job applicants]

    [Mr. Buffett gave written permission to publish those quotations above that are copyrighted. That permission does not extend hereby to any further publication.]

The great lesson in microeconomics is to discriminate between when technology is going to help you and when it's going to kill you.
  Charles Munger, Buffett's partner

Phillip A. Fisher and Benjamin Graham were the intellectual godfathers of Warren Buffett. Fisher sought companies through intense investigation of their competitors, employees, suppliers, and customers. His portfolio consisted of about six stocks that he held for an average of twenty years. His motto was, "Eternal vigilance with benign neglect."

> I have stressed management, but even so, I haven't stressed it enough. It is the most important ingredient.... It's not what industry you're in, it's what you're doing right that your rivals haven't yet figured out.... I want companies that welcome dissent, rather than stifle it, that don't penalize people who criticize what management is doing.... I don't like highly leveraged companies, even if they are well run.
>
> *Forbes* (September 23, 1996)

> Doing what everybody else is doing at the moment, and therefore what you have an almost irresistible urge to do, is often the wrong thing to do at all.
>
> *Common Stocks and Uncommon Profits* (1984), rev. ed.

> The average investor is not a specialist in the field of investment.... The result is that the typical investor has usually gathered a good deal of the half-truths, misconceptions, and just plain bunk that the general public has gradually accumulated about successful investing.
>
> Ibid.

Benjamin Graham, Buffett's other godfather, was the supreme "value investor" whose mantra was a "margin of safety." He only bought stocks for less than their working capital—Depression-era prices that are no longer available. But his principle remains valid: Only buy stocks at a large discount to true value. He asked investors to imagine they were partners

with Mr. Market, who was subject to wild mood swings. Every day he gave you three choices: at a stated price you could sell him your shares, buy his shares, or do nothing. You should sell to him when his mood was wildly optimistic and buy when he was so pessimistic you could buy with a margin of safety.

Graham said the worst enemy of investment performance was not fluctuating markets, but the inappropriate temperament of most investors. Their proclivity is short-term: to plunge into hot stocks or to cower in cash from fear. No blind bottom fisher, Graham believed that the worst losses came from investing in second tier companies during good times. He said, "Investing is most intelligent when it is most business-like."

> Though the stock market functions as a voting machine in the short term, it acts as a weighing machine in the long run.
>
> Ben Graham and David Dodd, *Security Analysis: Principles and Technique* (1932)

> The art of investment has one characteristic that is not generally appreciated. A creditable, if unspectacular, result can be achieved by the lay investor with a minimum of effort and capability; but to improve on this easily attainable goal by merely trying to bring just a little extra knowledge and cleverness to bear upon your investment program, instead of realizing a little better than normal results, you may well find that you have done worse.
>
> *The Intelligent Investor* (1949)

> Obvious prospects for physical growth in a business do not translate into obvious profits for investors.
>
> *The Intelligent Investor* (1973)

I have little confidence even in the ability of analysts, let alone untrained investors, to select common stocks that will give better than average results. Consequently, I feel that the standard portfolio should be to duplicate, more or less, the DJIA.

The Memoirs of the Dean of Wall Street
(1996)

Joel Greenblatt's *The Little Book That Beats the Market* (2006) provides a workable system for laymen to invest according to Warren Buffett's principles, that is, buy stocks of companies that have demonstrated an ability over a long term to generate a high return on equity without undue leverage, and buy them for substantially less than their intrinsic worth. Greenblatt and partners average over 30 percent per annum return using his system after tweaking it with sophisticated financial analysis. But without any analysis or forecasting, he believes lay investors should average returns of 15 percent or more per annum with less than average risk, if followed consistently over a long period. All one needs to implement Greenblatt's system is fourth-grade math and the online stock screens he references. This may be the best way for disciplined lay investors to invest.

Burton Malkiel wrote a pioneering investment book, *A Random Walk Down Wall Street* (1991): "Past movements of stock prices cannot be used to foretell future movements. The central proposition of charting, therefore, is absolutely false...." The market is "efficient" in that it reflects all that is known or thought. The market moves according to new information as it is revealed in the future, so it moves as if it were a "random walk." Thus "a blind-folded chimpanzee throwing darts" at

stock listings can pick stocks as well as the Wall Street professionals.

There are three versions of the random walk: 1) The Strong: "Nothing that is known or knowable about a company will benefit the fundamental analyst." 2) The Semi-Strong: "No published information will help the analyst to select undervalued securities." 3) The Weak: "Past movements of stock prices are no guide to future movements." Few believe the Strong or the Semi-Strong versions. Warren Buffett said there is a difference between the market being frequently efficient and being always efficient. Many believe the Weak version.

Malkiel himself noted one exception: "Efficient markets do not allow investors to earn above-average returns without accepting above-average risks." Malkiel also said, "The stock market is like a gambling casino with the odds in your favor. Over the long pull, it beats inflation by a great deal."

Peter L. Bernstein's *Capital Ideas* (1992) gives an overview of all the advanced theories on investing and risk, from the Efficient Market Theory to the Capital Asset Pricing Model.

Jeremy J. Siegel, professor of finance at the Wharton School, wrote two outstanding books for laymen who manage their investments: *Stocks for the Long Run* (1994) (*SLR*) and *The Future for Investors* (2005) (*FFI*). In the preface of *The Future for Investors,* Siegel states the single most important fact of portfolio investing:

...over extended periods of time, stock returns not only dominate the returns on fixed-income assets, but they do so with lower risk when inflation is taken into account.

SLR shows that $1 invested in 1801 in indexes of stocks, bonds, and bills would have provided a total real return by 2001: stocks: $599,505; bonds: $952; bills: $304. After-inflation, a diversified equity portfolio earns 6.5 percent to 7 percent, so its purchasing power "has doubled on average every decade over the last two centuries..." Other studies have shown that in no twenty-year period in U.S. history has the average annual return on diversified equities been less than 3 percent! The worst case was investing a lump sum in equities at the 1929 peak. The return on diversified equities for 25 years starting at the peak in 1929 was a 6 percent per annum. Of course, had one invested in equities at the 1929 peak and sold at the bottom on July 8, 1932, the loss would have been 85 percent. When investors abandon the safety of short-term, fixed-income assets, they can suffer great loss if forced to sell in depressed markets. *SLR*'s charts show the risk/reward trade offs for equities, bonds, and bills over different time periods.

SLR quotes *Triumph of the Optimists: 101 Years of Global Investment Return* by Elroy Dimson and Paul Marsh: "The US experience of equities outperforming bonds and bills has been mirrored in all sixteen countries examined...."

In *FFI*, Siegel explores the "growth trap," the belief that the fastest-growing companies, industries, and national economies make good investments. "The long-term return on a stock depends not on the actual growth of its earnings, but on the difference between its actual earning growth and the growth that investors expected."

Stated otherwise, "value" investing usually outperforms "growth" investing. The best stocks may be fast growers, but only if they can be purchased at reasonable valuations. He recommends considering a stock's PEG ratio, or price-to-earnings ratio divided by the estimated growth rate of earnings. Thus, a stock with a 10 PE ratio that grows earnings 20 percent p.a. = 10 divided by 20 or 0.5 PEG. Ideally, one would want a PEG ratio of 0.5 or less, but certainly a PEG ratio under 1.0, whereas the S&P 500 average PEG in 2005 is about 1.7.

The *persistence* of high earnings is critical. Most companies that grow earnings persistently have brands with a reputation for high quality. Siegel advises, "Be ready to pay up for good stocks (as you would for good wine), but there is no such thing as a 'buy at any price.' "

Many good investments are found in hapless industries, such as steel (Nucor) and airlines (Southwest). They are usually the lowest cost providers.

New technologies destroy industries. Billions were invested in fiber-optic lines assuming only one beam of light at a time could be sent down a fiber line. Multiplexing increased this by a factor of 1,000, which bankrupted many telecoms! Due to competition, 90 percent of new technology benefits go to consumers and only 10 percent to owners.

Capital investment is responsible for only a small percent of increases in productivity. Most gains come from innovative management changes. Be skeptical that new investments will pay dividends.

Siegel's "global solution" for the aging of the West and Japan and their inability to pay the pensions and Social Security benefits promised is for them to sell their assets to China and India, whose economies will grow rapidly for generations.

John C. Bogle is the founder of the Vanguard Group of Investment Companies, the world's second largest mutual fund company. It specializes in no-load, low-fee, domestic and international mutual funds that index major markets. *Bogle on Mutual Funds* (1994) is among the best investment books for average lay investors. It advises why one should invest in index funds and how to do it.

Sir John Templeton, father of global investing, told us when to sell: "When you have another investment opportunity that is significantly better." His "principle of maximum pessimism" was to invest in the worst looking foreign markets.

> If you search worldwide, you will find more bargains and better bargains than by studying only one nation.

> It takes a well-trained person to evaluate a corporation. And, even if one can do this, the information is not useful until thousands of other corporations have been studied.

> The best time to invest is when you have money.

> The four most expensive words in the English language are: "This time it's different."

> For long-term investors there is one objective: maximum total real return after taxes.

David Dreman likes large-cap stocks battered by a crisis, because investors overvalue the "best" and undervalue the "worst." Negative surprises kill overvalued stocks but have little effect on under-valued ones. Positive surprises propel the undervalued, but barely effect the overvalued. Buy stocks in the lowest quintile of price to earnings, book, cash flow, sales, and dividends.

> The human animal is apparently heavily influenced by the whims of the moment, rather than by the wisdom of the past.
> *Psychology and the Stock Market* (1977)

> The rational man—like the Loch Ness monster—is sighted often, but photographed rarely.
> *Contrarian Investment Strategies* (1998)

> A market can become a giant Rorschach test, allowing the investor to see any pattern he wishes. The market gives illusory correlations since half the time it goes up and one may have any particular explanation for it going up.

> In a configurative problem, the decision maker's interpretation of any single piece of information changes depending on how he evaluates many other inputs. Successful investors must be adept at configurative processing, integrating many diverse factors, since changes in any may require a revision of the total assessment. Most people are low level configurative processors.

> Initially change is numberless. The new numbers that measure the change will not be available for some time after the change has already occurred. Thus, to deal with change one has to rely on the intuitive mode. A portfolio manager needs to identify change early before it can be empirically measured by everyone.

John Train noted that none of the families of ancient Rome that had accumulated fortunes still retained them. He explained this phenomenon thus:

> The rest of society yearns to erase the claim on it represented by your capital, and pursues that objective unremittingly, through tax, inflation, regulation, labor demands, and other weapons. In this unending duel between the saver and society, society almost always wins in time.
>
> *The New Money Masters* (1990)

Trusts prevent rapid dissipation of inheritances. But bank trustees are terrible investors because they are risk-averse and expensive. To avoid nominal losses so they cannot be sued, they invest in "safe," assets so that after expenses, taxes, and inflation, their real returns are meager.

> No amount of Tanzanians can put a man on the moon. No amount of mediocre researchers can find you a great stock.
>
> *Preserving Capital and Making It Grow* (1983)

James O'Shaughnessy's *What Works on Wall Street* (1998) argues that we overvalue qualitative analysis and recent events over quantitative analysis and historical trends. Those tendencies cause valuation anomalies, such as value stocks usually outperforming growth stocks, especially if value is determined by a low price-to-sales ratio. Also, micro-cap stocks usually outperform small caps. Buy value stocks that also have "high relative strength," that is, stocks whose prices have appreciated recently. The worst strategies involve buying stocks with great stories and "low relative strength."

Peter Lynch likes to own small-cap growth stocks for one to two years. He likes local stocks that have not been discovered by Wall Street and whose prosaic products grow earnings at 20 to 25 percent per annum, and which have a PEG ratio not greater than 1.0 and preferably at less than half that.

Lynch wrote, "It isn't the head but the stomach that determines the fate of the stock-picker." He warns against selling securities due to macroeconomic/political fears. The market frequently falls by 10 percent or more due to fears. The greatest threat is being whipsawed in and out of the market.

> When it comes to predicting the market, the important skill here is not listening, it's snoring. The trick is not to learn to trust your gut feelings, but rather to discipline yourself to ignore them. Stand by your stocks as long as the fundamental story of the company hasn't changed.
>
> *One Up On Wall Street* (1989)

> All the math you need in the stock market you get in the fourth grade.
>
> Ibid.

> We can begin to separate gambling from investing not by the type of activity but by the skill, dedication, and enterprise of the participant. To a veteran handicapper with the discipline to stick to a system, betting on horses offers a relatively secure long-term return.
>
> Ibid.

> As a place to invest, I'll take a lousy industry over a [rapidly growing] industry anytime.
>
> *Beating the Street* (1993)

Over every twenty-year period, common stocks have been the best portfolio investment.

TV ad (2001)

Jude Wanniski, was an economist who sold Reagan on Mundell's "supply-side" economics, popularized it in the *Wall Street Journal*, and wrote *The Way the World Works* (1978), acclaimed by Professor Arthur Laffer as the best economics book. He believed only supply-side economics could save the world from poverty and war.

The most important information coming to the market is political news. War and peace, after all, can turn on the chemistry of a single mind. Political news is volatile, because it can instantly and dramatically alter the market's future income streams.

The Way the World Works: How Economies Fail—and Succeed (1978)

Elroy Dimson in his *Triumph of the Optimists* (2002) examines from 1900 to 2001 the markets of 16 countries (14 European, plus US and Japan). In the U.S., equities provided an annualized nominal return of 10.1 percent, or 6.7 percent after adjusting for 3.2 percent inflation, versus a nominal bond return of 4.8 percent, or 1.6 percent after inflation, and a nominal bill return of 4.1 percent, or 0.9 percent after inflation. In the European countries and Japan, the average real return on equities was only 5.2 percent, reflecting periodic wipeout losses from hyperinflation, war, and expropriation. But "the US experience of equities outperforming bonds and bills has been mirrored in all 16 countries examined...."

The "equity risk premium" (higher return for equities over bills) in the U.S. in the twentieth century of 5.8 percent may fall in the twenty-first century due to the lower perceived risks of a democratic and capitalistic world. If so, one will need a longer time to be confident that equities will outperform bonds.

FUTHER COMMENTS

The unpublished 1995 book, *Fire Your Stockbroker,* concluded that brilliant professional investors in equities can thrive using many different strategies. But for laymen who do not dedicate their lives to studying the market, there are three sensible equity investment strategies. The first and most consistent is to invest in exchange traded funds (ETFs) and/or in no-load, low-fee mutual funds that index diversified equity markets, such as Vanguard's Total Stock Market Index (VTSMX). [25 percent should be in foreign funds.] Diversified index funds/ETFs over 20 years should outperform before tax 80 percent of managed funds and after-tax 95 percent of managed funds. Over 20 years, diversified equity markets return about 10 percent p.a. nominally or 7 percent p.a. after inflation. A 10 percent return doubles principal in 7.2 years. Warren Buffett wrote, "Those index funds that are very low-cost (such as Vanguard's) are investor-friendly by definition and are the best selection for most of those who wish to own equities."

A second strategy is finding classes of equities that provide higher than average market returns over long periods, such as, "value stocks" that outperform "growth stocks," and "small cap" stocks that outperform "large cap" stocks, each on average by 2 percent p.a. That differential is huge because 2 percent doubles capital in

36 years (over 36 years a 12 percent rate of return will double your capital over a 10 percent rate of return). The downside of owing small-cap and value stocks is their higher volatility that will prompt undisciplined investors to panic and sell out near the bottom of markets. DFA Funds have outperformed the market by specializing in value and small-cap stocks. They also reduce risks by avoiding IPOs and companies in financial stress. DFA's (DFAVX) (U.S. small cap value fund) for ten years has ranked in the top 20 of 1700 diversified equity funds—the top 1.2 percent of such funds.

The third strategy is to imitate investors who have outperformed the market by wide margins for long periods. Bill Miller's Legg Mason Value Trust as of 2005 outperformed the S&P 500 for 15 straight years, and the Muhlenkamp Fund (all-cap value fund) for ten years has ranked in the 98 percentile. *The Prudent Speculator*, ranked first by Hulbert Financial Digest among investment newsletters for 20 years, has averaged returns over 20 percent per annum. A 20 percent return doubles your capital every 3.6 years. *Burrons* (January 9, 2006) listed 19 managed, funds that had outperformed the S&P 500 over 15 years to 2006. Over the past 40 years, rebalancing on each January 1 the Value Line 100 top ranked stocks for timeliness produced a compound 19 percent p.a. return. *Caveat*: All fantastic streaks come to an end sometime.

Also see Joel Greenblatt's investment system for disciplined laymen as described in his *The Little Book that Beats the Market* (2006).

Below are specific investment beliefs:

1) The greatest investment danger is to be whipsawed out of an equity portfolio for lack of a rock-solid belief in the validity of one's portfolio. One should be so committed to the design of a portfolio that one hopes that share prices will fall so that more shares can be bought at cheaper prices.

2) Politics is the greatest exogenous risk to a diversified equity portfolio. Bad monetary, fiscal, and trade policies can cause depressions and crash markets as in 1929 or flat-line a market for decades as in 1964–82. High taxes, protectionism, and inflation are the most common political risks.

3) Market timing (trading on market forecasts) is a loser's game. One should stay fully invested in equities, except 1) when prices rise so high that one cannot find sound equities, or 2) the threat of high taxes, protectionism, or inflation is great. Bubbles occur about once a generation. The U.S. approached a bubble when the market was capitalized at 109 percent of GDP in 1929, and it was in a bubble when it was capitalized at 190 percent of GDP in 2000. In 2000 the bubble lay mostly in dot-com/telecom/media stocks.

4) "Regression to the mean" is a powerful tendency among things that fall along a bell-shaped curve. Thus, children of tall parents tend to be shorter than their parents. Thus, groups that outperform the market eventually under perform, and vice-versa. But, radical changes in a system can shift a bell-shaped curve, as when earth's weather shifts from an ice-age to an interglacial period. The S&P 500's mean 17 PE ratio (1950 to 2003) may shift dramatically in the future as risks rise or fall.

Due to reversion to the mean, value stocks tend to outperform growth stocks. Michael O'Higgins "Dow Dog Theory" in *Beating the Dow* (1992) saw that if on the same date annually you select ten stocks from the 30 Dow Jones Industrials that have the highest dividend yields and hold them for one year and rebalance annually, you will outperform the Dow 30. For the 18.5 years (June 1973–June 1990) this strategy returned 1753 percent versus 559 percent for owning the Dow 30. By accepting a higher risk of picking only five Dow stocks rather than ten with the highest yield and rebalancing annually, the return was 2819 percent. Back-testing from 1931 to 2004 shows that selecting the five Dow stocks annually with the worst "percentage change in their prices" over the prior year provides a higher return than the Dow Dog Theory. *Caveat*: On average during 1973 to 1996 the Dow Dogs returned 17 percent versus 12 percent for the Dow, but in the ten year period to 2006, the Dow Dog Theory underperformed in six years.

5) Academic studies have not been kind to technicians/chartists. The general technical advice is to wait to buy stocks until they have risen past a resistance point and wait to sell them until after they have fallen below a support level—the opposite of buying low and selling high. Yet, most financial houses, except CitiGroup, sport technicians because they encourage customers to churn. But, because so many traders use technical analysis, well-known patterns, like island reversal tops, can temporarily overwhelm fundamentals. Technical analysis is a losing game, except for rare brilliant professionals, such as Ralph Bloch at Raymond James.

6) Rarely are stockbrokers qualified to advise on investing. They are salesmen who must turn over their clients' portfolios every two years to survive, and they are often compelled to sell awful products, like variable annuities and their house's funds. Frequent transactions in taxable accounts

impose prohibitive costs! Also bad are 3 percent "wrap" accounts and programs to manage an account for 1 percent p.a. (recommended for inactive accounts).

7) Equity portfolios should have at least 25 percent invested internationally. Stock prices in different countries are not highly correlated so an equity portfolio with 25 percent foreign stocks should be less volatile than a 100 percent U.S. equity portfolio. U.S. stocks represent 50 percent of the value of global markets in 2005, versus 66 percent in 1970. A few great international funds, such as Thornburg Intl. Value (TGVAX), may be more prudent than foreign index funds.

8) Investing in *managed* equity mutual funds—as distinguished from passive equity index funds—is foolish 96 percent of the time, according to David F. Swensen's *Unconventional Success* (2005). Over a fifteen-year term, only 4 percent of managed equity mutual funds beat Vanguard's 500 Index Fund after tax. The average managed fund trailed Vanguard by 4.8 percent p.a., and the 4 percent of managed funds that outperformed Vanguard only did so by 0.6 percent p.a. The problems with managed funds include: (1) amortization of a sales charge, (2) average annual expense ratio of about 1.4 percent of assets, (3) "phantom trading costs" of moving the market as it buys and sells huge quantities of stocks, and (4) the opportunity costs of holding 5 to 10 percent of assets in cash. Thus, the average managed mutual fund imposes annual costs of about 3 percent, versus only about 0.3 percent for owning a Vanguard index fund. In addition, because the average managed fund turns over its portfolio every ten months and index funds turn over only 5 percent of their portfolios

annually, managed funds over 15 years incur annual capital gains taxes of about 2 percent more p.a. than if the capital gains taxes were incurred by selling only at the end of the 15 years. Thus, the "all-in" additional annual cost of owning a managed equity fund in a taxable account is about 5 percent. That is gargantuan. The real long-term return on U.S. equities in the twentieth-century was 6.7 percent. But, managed equity mutual funds may make sense if the fund has outperformed the S&P 500 by 2 percent or more for at least ten years and/ or for international diversification.

Exchange traded funds, or ETFs, avoid paying capital gains taxes whereas index mutual funds pay capital gains taxes on their annual turn-over of about 5 percent of their portfolio. Generally, taxable accounts ought to prefer ETFs over indexed mutual funds.

INVESTMENT NUGGETS

I have looked at economic history back to the Babylonian era and there has never been a country that has prospered on the back of a weak currency.

Economist Stephen Roach

In the twentieth century, the average S&P 500 PE ratio was 14, although it was 17 in the second half of the twentieth century. Five arguments support the theory that the U.S. PE ratio in the twenty-first century will exceed 20: (1) the twentieth century's PE ratio of 14 was low due to two world wars, a global depression, and the threat of Communism. More free markets and democracies reduce those risks. (2) An information economy increases productivity. (3) Replacing Keynesianism with supply-side economics causes lower inflation and taxes. (4) We now know stocks are safer than bonds if held in diversified portfolios for the long term. (5) A 14 PE reflected a market dominated by heavy industrials that trade at lower PEs than digital stocks. Counterarguments include: war and terrorism remain threats. Socialism may now be a greater threat because illegal immigrants vote Democratic.

According to David F. Swensen's *Unconventional Success*, average investors do no better in investing in venture capital partnerships than in diversified equities. Top tier venture firms do not deal with new investors and returns from lower tier firms do not compensate for the risk.

Markets may not follow economies. Consider two back-to-back 17-year periods (1964 to the end of 1981 and 1982 to end of 1998): (1) The Dow only rose from 874 to 875 from the end of 1964 to the end of 1981, during which the U.S. GDP rose 373 percent. (2) The Dow rose from 875 to 9181 from the end of 1981 to the end of 1998, during which U.S. GDP rose only 177 percent. See Warren Buffett in December 10, 2001 *Fortune*.

The reasons are: a) the interest rate on the 30-year bond rose from 4.2 percent in 1964 to 13.65 percent in 1982, but then fell to 5.09 percent in 1998. The rise in interest rates from 1964 to 1982 reduced the present value of dollars to be received from investing. b) Expectations of profitability fell during high inflation. c) Falling valuations induced further falls.

These factors worked in reverse from 1982 to 1998 as interest rates fell. Interest rates have an overwhelming impact on valuing financial assets, and inflation has an overwhelming impact on interest rates.

From 1924 to 1995 stocks were on average valued around 50 percent of GDP and seldom above 70 percent of GDP except for a spike up to 109 percent of GDP in September 1929. But in March 2000, stocks peaked at 190 percent of GDP. Warren Buffet concluded from this analysis that the average investor will likely only do well buying stocks when the stock market is valued at or below 70 percent of GDP.

George Eliot wrote in *Silas Marner:* "The sense of security more frequently springs from habit than from conviction, and for this reason it often subsists after such a change in the conditions as might have been expected to suggest alarm. The lapse of time during which a given event has not happened is, in this logic of habit, constantly alleged as a reason why the event should never happened, even when the lapse of time is precisely the added condition which makes the event imminent."

Investors near retirement should own treasury bills on certificates of deposit equal to at least four years of living exenses in order to have the courage to ride-out inevitable bear markets in equities.

> Always own enough gold coins to bribe the border guards.

16
FOREIGN PHRASES

LATIN

A fortiori.
For the more compelling reason.

A posteriori.
Reasoning after study of the facts—inductive thinking.

A priori.
Reasoning based on assumptions—deductive thinking.

Abitt ad plures.
He's gone to join the majority.
    (The Dead.)
    [Petronius.]

Actus non facit reum, nisi mens sit rea.
The act is not criminal unless the intent is criminal.

Alter ego.
A close friend, a second self.

Amicus humani generis.
Friend of the human race.

Anno Domini (A.D.).
In the year of the Lord.
    [Christ was born not later than 4 B.C. and maybe as early as 20 B.C.]

Annuit Coeptis.
He (God) smiled on our Beginnings.
    [Reverse motto of Seal of the U.S.]

Annus horribilis.
A year of horrors or a horrible year.

Annus mirabilis.
A year of wonders or a wonderful year.

Argumentum ad hominem.
To shift an argument from the point at issue to the personality of the opponent.

Atque inter silvas academi quaerere verum.
Seek for truth even in the groves of academe.
    [Horace.]

Audentis fortuna invat.
Fortune helps those who dare. Or, Fortune favors the brave.
    [Virgil.]

Aut Caesar, aut nihil.
Either Caesar or nothing.
    [Cesare Borgia, 1476–1507.]

Aut non tentaris, aut perfice.
Either don't attempt it, or carry it through to the end.

Aut vincere aut mori.
Either to conquer or die.

Ave Caesar, morituri te salutant.
Hail Caesar, we who are about to die salute you.

Bellum omnium in omnia.
War of all against all.

Bona fide.
In good faith—without fraud.

Bonus intra melior exi.
Enter good, leave better.

Caput mundi.
Head of the world.
    [Imperial Rome then papal Rome.]

Carpe diem, quam minimum credula postero.
Seize the day, put no trust in the future.
    [Horace.]

Carpent tua poma nepotes.
Your descendants shall gather your fruits.
    [Virgil.]

Casus belli.
Event that is a reason or excuse for going to war.

Cato contra mundum.
Cato against the world.
    [Against any overriding power in a hopeless struggle.]

Cave ab homine unius libri.
Beware the man of one book.

Caveat emptor, quia ignorare non debuit quod jus alienum emit
Let the buyer beware, for he ought not be ignorant of the property he is buying.

Cave canem.
Beware of the dog.

Ceteris paribus.
Other things being equal.

Chi compra terra, compra guerra.
    [Italian.]
He who buys land, buys war.

Christianos ad leonem.
Christians to the lions.

Citius, Altius, Fortius.
Swifter, Higher, Stronger.
    [Olympic motto.]

Civis Romanus sum.
I am a Roman citizen.
    [A claim of inviolacy.]

Collegium lupanariorum.
Roman guild of brothel keepers.

Consensus gentium.
Unanimous opinion of mankind.

Corruptio optimi pessima.
The corruption of the best becomes the worst.

Cui bono?
Who stood to gain?
    [Cicero's question.]

Cygnea cantio.
Swan song.
    [To speak eloquently at the end of life, as swans are said to break into beautiful songs at the point of death.]

De facto.
From the fact.
    [What actually exists as distinguished from *De jure*, or according to the rule of law.]

De gustibus non disputandum est.
There is no arguing about tastes.

De minimis non curat lex.
The law is not concerned with trifles.

De mortuis nil nisi bonum.
About the dead, say something good or
nothing at all.

De nihilo nihilum.
Out of nothing naught.

Deos fortioribus adesse.
The gods are on the side of the
strongest.

Deus vult.
God wills it.
    [Motto of the Crusades.]

Dictum factum.
No sooner said than done.

Divide et impera.
Divide and Rule.

Dramatis personae.
Cast of characters.

Duce tempus eget.
The times require a leader.

Ducunt volentem, nolentem trahunt.
Draw those who are willing, drag those
who are not.
    [Motto of the Fates.]

Ecce homo.
Behold, the man.
    [Pontius Pilate introduces Christ to
    his accusers, John 19:5.]

E Pluribus Unum.
From many, one.
    [From thirteen colonies, one nation.
    This is one of three mottos on the

Great Seal of the United States.
The others are *Novus Ordo Seclorum* (A new order of the ages) and
Annuit Coeptis (Begun under divine
origins).]

Elephantus non capit murem.
Elephants don't catch mice.

*Est quadam prodire tenus, si non datur
ultra.*
All may make some progress, though it
be not allowed them to go beyond a certain point.

Ex cathedra.
From the chair. By the authority of an
office.

Facile largiri de alieno.
It is easy to be generous with other people's money.

Falsus in uno, falsus in omnibus.
Untrue in one thing, untrue in everything.

Fata obstant.
The Fates are against it.
    [Virgil.]

Felix qui potuit rerum cognoscere causas.
Happy is the man who is able to understand the causes of things.
    [Virgil.]

Festina lente.
Make haste slowly.
    [Augustus Caesar's motto.]

Fiat justitia ruat caelum.
Let justice be done though heaven
should fall.

Fortis In Arduis.
Strong in difficulties.
　　[Motto of Scottish Middletons.]

Furor scribendi.
Rage for writing.

Habeas corpus.
You must produce the person.

Hannibal ad portas!
Hannibal is at the gates!

Historia est magistra vitae.
History is the teacher of life.

Homo homini lupus.
Man is a wolf to man.

Homo sapiens.
Man the wise.

Homo sum, humani a me nil alienum pu to.
I am a man, and nothing human is foreign to me.
　　[Terrence]

Hostes humani generis.
Enemies of the human race.
　　[Legal doctrine providing jurisdiction over pirates since their crimes on the high seas were not subject to other criminal justice.]

Iniquum est aliquem rei sui esse judicem.
It is unjust that anyone should be judge in his own cause.
　　[Sir Edward Coke.]

Ignorantia juris neminem excusat.
Ignorance of the law excuses no one.

In loco parentis.
Acting in place of a parent; a guardian.

In te omnis domus inclinata recumbit.
On thee repose all the hopes of your family.
　　[Amata trying to dissuade her son Turnus from fighting Aeneas, who slew him.][Virgil.]

Inter arma silent leges.
In time of war, the laws are silent.

Kyrie, eleison. Christe, eleison.
Lord, have mercy. Christ, have mercy.

Laborare est Orare.
To work is to pray.
　　[John Calvin.]

Latet anguis in herba.
A snake lurks in the grass.

Laudator temporis acti.
One who praises past times.

Magnum opus.
The crowning work of one's life.

Mea culpa.
The fault is mine.

Mel in ore, verba lactis, fel in corde, fraus in factis.
A honeyed mouth with milky words hides a heart filled with gall and evil deeds.

Mendacem memorem esse oportere.
A liar should have a good memory.

Mens sana in corpore sano.
A healthy mind in a healthy body.
　　[Juvenal.]

Mobilitate vigemus.
In mobility lies our strength.
　　[Cavalry motto.]

Modus operandi.
Method of operation. (M.O.)

Modus vivendi.
A way of getting along temporarily.

Mutatis Mutandis.
With the necessary changes in detail—things are generally the same, but may need to be changed in points of detail.

Ne plus ultra.
Thus far and no further.
    [Inscribed on the Pillars of Hercules.]

Nec scire fas est omnia.
It is not permitted us to know all things.
    [Horace.]

Nemo me impune lacessit.
No one provokes me with impunity.
    [Motto of Scotland, the Order of the Thistle, and all Scottish regiments.]

Nemo solus satis sapit.
No man is sufficiently wise by himself.
    [Plautus.]

Nil carborundum illegetimi.
Don't let the bastards wear you down.

Nil credam et omnia cavebo.
Believe nothing and beware of everything.

Nil desperandum.
Never despair.

Nil repente..
Never repent.
[Machiavelli's maxim.]

Non faciat malum, ut inde veniat bonum.
You are not to do evil that good may come of it.

Non omnia possumus omnes.
We are not all capable of everything.
    [Virgil.]

Non sequitur.
The conclusion does not follow from the premise.

Novus Ordo Seclorum.
The New Order of the Ages.
    [Motto on U.S. Great Seal]
    [Virgil.]

Nullius In Verba.
Take nobody's word for it.
    [The Royal Society's motto.]

Nunc est bibendum!
Now is the time to drink!
    [Horace.]

Omnia fert aetas, animum quoque.
Time bears away all things, even the memory.
    [Virgil.]

Omnia mutantur nihil interit.
Everything changes; nothing dies.
    [Pythagoras.]

Omnia vincit amor, et nos ceda mus.
Love conquers all things. Let us too give in to love.
    [Virgil.]

Panem et circenses.
Bread and circuses.

Pari Passu.
With equal pace. Simultaneously, equally.

Pecunia non olet.
Money does not smell.

Pontifex maximus.
Chief priest.

Post hoc, ergo propter hoc.
After this, therefore because of this.
   [A logical fallacy.]

Primum est edere, deinde philosophari.
Eating must come before philosophy.

Primum non nocere.
Above all, do no harm.
   [Hippocrates' motto.]

Primus inter pares.
First among equals.

Pro bono publico.
For the public good, as in donated
services.

Qui desiderat pacem, praeparet bellum.
Let him who desires peace, prepare for
war.
   [Vegetius.]

Qui non improbat, approbat.
He who does not blame, approves.

Qui timide rogat, docet negare.
Who makes timid requests invites
denial.

Quid pro quo.
An equivalent exchange; tit for tat.

Quis custodiet ipso custodes?
Who shall guard the guardians?
   [Juvenal.]

Quod erat demonstrandum. [Q.E.D.]
Which was to be proved.
   [Euclid.]

Quod licet Jovi, non licet bovi.
What is okay for the gods to do is not
okay for the cows to do.

Quod principi placuit legis habet vigorem.
Whatever pleases the king is the law.

Quod vitae sectabor iter?
What path of life shall I follow?
   [Descartes' question.]

Reductio ad absurdum.
To take an argument to a ridiculous
extreme to show that it is false.

Requiescat In Pace Domini.
Rest in peace with God. [R. I. P.]

Res ipsa loquitur.
The thing speaks for itself.

Res tantum valet quantum vendi potest.
A thing is worth only what someone else
will pay.

Respice post te, hominem te memento.
Look behind you and remember you are
but mortal.
   [A slave stood behind a Roman
   general in his triumphal chariot and
   whispered these words in his ear.]

*Rex non debet esse sub homine, sed sub Deo
et lege.*
The king should not be under any man,
but under God and law.
   [The king must obey the law.]

Sapere Aude.
Dare to know.
   [Kant's motto.]

Semper Fidelis.
Always faithful.
   [U.S. Marine Corps motto.]

Semper Paratus.
Always be prepared.
 [Motto of the Coast Guard.]

Sic Semper Tyrannis.
Thus ever to tyrants.
 [State of Virginia motto.]

Sic transit gloria mundi.
Thus passes away the glory of this world.
 [Said at the coronation of popes.]

Silentium, stultorum virtus.
Silence is the virtue of fools.

Sine die.
Without a day.
 [To adjourn without setting a date for the next meeting; to adjourn indefinitely.]

Sine qua non.
A prerequisite condition for another thing to happen.

Status quo.
The existing order of things.

Status quo ante bellum.
Each side to revert to the position it held before the war.

Sui generis.
Unique; in a class by itself.

Summum bonum.
The greatest good.

Tempora mutantur.
Times change.

Tempus edax rerum.
Time, the devourer of everything.

Tempus fugit.
Time flies.
 [Vergil.]

Ubi libertas ibi patria.
Where liberty is, there is my country.

Ultra vires.
Above one's authority or jurisdiction.

Vae victis!
Woe to the conquered.

Videant consules ne quid respublica detrimenti capiat.
Let the consuls take care that the republic suffer no damage.
 [Formula by which the Senate conferred dictatorship during national emergencies.]

Vincit qui se vincit.
He conquers who first conquers himself.

Virtutum viva imago.
A living embodiment of the virtuous.
 [Said of Cato.]

Vox justiciae, vox Dei.
The voice of the magistrate is the voice of God.

Vox populi, vox Dei.
The voice of the people is the voice of God.
 [Alcuin to Charlemagne.]

Vox populi, vox Diaboli.
The voice of the people, the voice of the Devil.
 [Coleridge.]

FRENCH

Achete aux cannons, vendez aux clairons.
Buy at the sound of the canons, sell at
the sound of the trumphets.

Agent provocateur.
One who joins an organization to incite
it to do acts for which it will be punished
or vilified.

À propos.
To the purpose or to the point; pertinent.

Au courant.
To be well informed on current events.

Bête Noire.
Someone or something one hates.

Carte blanche.
Blank card; the license to do what one
wants.

Coup de foudre.
A stroke of lightning.

Dégringolade.
The rapid deterioration of a situation.

Déjà vu.
An illusion of having experienced something before.

De rigueur.
Required by custom or fashion.

Dieu et mon droit.
God and my rights.
    [Motto of Richard the Lion Hearted
    and later, the British royal house.]

Dirigisme (or) Étatisme.
Government-guided economy.

Droit du Seigneur.
Right of feudal lord to sleep with the
bride of a vassal on her wedding night.

Eminence grise.
Gray cardinal. The power behind a throne.
    [Cardinal Richelieu ran France for
    Louis XIII.]

En famille.
What any given family usually does
together.

Enfants perdus.
Lost children: soldiers sent to dangerous
posts.

Esprit de l'escalier.
Escalator spirit: a repartee thought of
too late.

Fait accompli.
Something done that cannot be reversed.

Fausse idée claire.
A terrific idea that doesn't work.

Faux pas.
False step; embarrassing social error.

Honi soi qui mal y pense.
Evil to him who thinks evil.
    [Motto of the Order of the Knights
    of the Garter 1348, by Edward III.]

Idée fixe.
A fixed idea or obsession.

Il ne faut pas être plus royaliste que le roi.
One need not be more royalist than the
king.

Joie de vivre.
Joy of living.

Laissez-faire.
Let one work.
[Noninterference by government.]

Lettres de cachet.
Right to arrest without a warrant and detain without trial.

Les envieux mourront, mais non jamais l'envie.
The envious will die, but envy never.
[Molière.]

Lèse-Majesté.
Crime against the sovereign; overstepping.

Merde en bas de soie.
You are shit in a silk stocking.
[Napoleon to Talleyrand.]

On s'éngage et puis on voit.
Engage and then see what happens.
[Napoleon.]

Pas d'emnemi a gauche.
No enemy to the left.

Pefide Albion.
Perfidious Albion (England).

Plus ça change, plus c'est la même chose.
The more it changes, the more it's the same.

Raison d'être.
Reason for being.

Reculer pour mieux sauter.
To draw back to make a better jump.

Regardez mon droit.
Watch out for my rights.

Revenons à nos moutons.
Let us return to our sheep: Let us get back to the subject.

Rien ne reussit comme le succes.
Nothing succeeds like success.

Sangfroid.
Cold blood.
[Composure in the face of difficulties.]

Savoir-faire.
Ease and dexterity in social situations.

Si jeunesse savait, si viellesse pouvait!
If youth only knew, if age only could.

Succès d'estime.
Success due to the sympathy of friends.

Surtout, Messieurs, point de zèle.
Above all, gentlemen, no zeal.
[Talleyrand.]

Tour de force.
A feat accomplished through great skill and ability.

Tout est perdu fors l'honneur.
All is lost save our honor.
[Francis I in 1525 after losing the battle of Pavia.]

GERMAN

Arbeit macht frei.
Work liberates.
[Sign on gate to Auschwitz death camp.]

Blut und Boden.
Blood and soil.
[German romanticism of Fichte.]

Ersatz.
Substitute material; shoddy.

Götterdämmerung.
Twilight of the Gods.
   [Final battle between good and
   evil.]

Ichschmerz.
Sorrow or dissatisfaction with the state
of one's condition.

Kinder, Kirche, Küche.
Children, church, kitchen.
      [The realm of women.]

Kulturkampf.
Conflict of beliefs or culture war.

Lebensraum [and] *Nahrungs freiheit.*
"Living space" and "Freedom from a
scarcity of food"
   [Both terms refer to the need to
   conquer territories rich in natural
   resources so that Germans could
   live with minimal reliance on foreign trade. This was one underlying cause of World Wars I and II.
   Socialists, whether fascist, Nazi, or
   Communist, must strive to become
   self-sufficient. They cannot earn
   enough foreign exchange because
   they cannot command foreigners
   to buy their shoddy goods; so they
   must steal foreign resources.]

Schlimmbesserung.
When your attempts to improve something worsen it.

Schadenfreude.
Delighting in the misery of others.

Uebermensch.
Superman.

Vernunft wird Unsinn/Wohltat, Plage.
Reason becomes nonsense/
Good deeds become afflictions.
   [Goethe's disenchantment with the
   French Revolution.]

Völkerwanderung.
Mass migration, such as the barbarian
migrations in Roman times or the 1835
Boer Great Trek.

Weltanschaaung.
One's worldview, one's philosophy.

Weltschmerz.
Sorrow or dissatisfaction over the state
of the world.

Wirtschaftswunder.
Economic miracle.
   [Applied to Germany in the 1950s.]

Zeitgeist.
The spirit of the times.

GREEK

Gnothi Sauton.
Know Thyself.
   [Socrates' motto, also engraved
   near the entrance to the temple at
   Delphi.]

Thumos.
   [Greek notion of spiritedness, or
   modern-day manliness.]

17

THE OLD TESTAMENT OF THE HOLY BIBLE
(HEBREW SCRIPTURES OF ANCIENT ISRAEL)
KING JAMES VERSION (1611)

The Hebrew Scriptures are divided into the Torah, the Prophets, and the Writings.

For perspective: Abraham lived around 1800 B.C.; the Israelites entered Egypt a century later; and the Exodus occurred around 1200 B.C. Thus, Moses lived during the Bronze Age at the time of the fall of Troy. David ruled over Judah and Israel from 1000 to 960 B.C. The Five Books of Moses, or Pentateuch (Genesis, Exodus, Leviticus, Numbers, and Deuteronomy), were written by the Yahwist, known as "J" around 900 B.C. Around 550 B.C., "R," an editor-writer, wrote the Hebrew Bible from Genesis to Kings by subsuming the work of J. The Torah is the scroll on which the Pentateuch is written.

GENESIS

In the beginning God created the heaven and the earth. And the earth was without form, and void; and darkness was upon the face of the deep. And the Spirit of God moved upon the face of the waters. And God said, Let there be light; and there was light.

I, 1–3

And God said, Let us make man in our image, after our likeness…

I, 26

Be fruitful and multiply and replenish the earth and subdue it, and have dominion over the fish of the sea and over the fowl of the air and over every living thing that moveth upon the earth.

I, 28

But of the tree of the knowledge of good and evil, thou shalt not eat of it; for in the day that thou eatest thereof thou shalt surely die.

II, 17

And the rib, which the Lord God had taken from man, made he a woman…

II, 22

Unto the woman he said, "I will greatly multiply thy sorrow and thy conception; in sorrow thou shall bring forth children; and thy desire shall be to thy husband, and he shall rule over thee."

III, 16

In the sweat of thy face shalt thou eat bread, till thou return unto the ground; for out of it wast thou taken: for dust thou art, and unto dust shalt thou return.

III, 19

Am I my brother's keeper?
[Cain, who slew Abel, became a vagabond in the land of Nod that is "east of Eden."]

IV, 9

His [Ishmael's] hand will be against every man, and every man's hand against him…

XVI, 12

Ishmael was the firstborn of Abraham, but his mother was Haggar, a servant sent by Sarah, Abraham's wife, to service Abraham, an aged man. After Sarah bore a son for Abraham, Sarah drove out Haggar and Ishmael, who became the patriarch of the Arab Nation.

EXODUS

Who made thee a prince and a judge over us?

II, 14

I have been a stranger in a strange land.

II, 22

And God said unto Moses, I AM THAT I AM [or Yahweh].
> [The voice from the flaming bush answers Moses' question as to God's name, which means that God is existence itself.]

III, 14

Let my people go that they may serve me.

1X, 13

And this day [Passover] shall be unto you for a memorial; and you shall keep it a feast to the Lord throughout your generations.

XII, 14

THE TEN COMMANDMENTS

1. Thou shalt have no other gods before me.
2. Thou shalt not make unto thee any graven image…. For I the Lord thy God am a jealous God, visiting the iniquity of the fathers upon the children unto the third and fourth generation of them that hate me.
3. Thou shalt not take the name of the Lord thy God in vain.
4. Remember the Sabbath day, to keep it holy.
5. Honor thy father and thy mother.
6. Thou shalt not kill.
7. Thou shalt not commit adultery.
8. Thou shalt not steal.
9. Thou shalt not bear false witness against thy neighbor.
10. Thou shalt not covet thy neighbor's house…

XX, 3–17

Sometimes the Sixth Commandment is mistranslated as "Thou shalt not kill." But the Hebrew word is *rasah*, which means, "murder." Proof of this is that Moses executed the three thousand Hebrews he discovered worshiping a golden calf when he brought down the tablets with the Ten Commandments from Mount Sinai.

He that smiteth a man, so that he die, shall be surely put to death.

XXI, 12

…eye for eye, tooth for tooth, hand for hand, foot for foot.

XXI, 24

And the Lord said unto Moses, "I have seen this people, and behold, it is a stiff-necked people."

XXXII, 9

Jacob and Esau were the sons of Isaac, the son of Abraham. As eldest, Esau should have inherited the covenant with God that Abraham had passed to Isaac, but Esau traded his birthright to Jacob for a mess of pottage when hungry. Jacob used deceit to gain his father's blessing, and he wrestled with God to get God's blessing. God named Jacob "Israel," or "One who has been strong against God."

DEUTERONOMY

The poor shall never cease out of the land.

XV, 11

I have set before you this day life and death, blessing and curse; therefore, choose life and live, you and your children.

XXX, 19

RUTH

Intreat me not to leave thee,
Or to return from following after thee:
For wither thou goest, I will go;
And where thou lodgest, I will lodge.
Thy people shall be my people,
And thy God my God.
Where thou diest, will I die,
And there will I be buried.

I, 16–17

After her husband died, Ruth left her country, Moab, to live with her Hebrew mother-in-law, Naomi, in Bethlehem, Judea. Ruth would not desert her elderly, widowed mother-in-law. In Judea, they gleaned the fields for food. A rich farmer, Boaz, fell in love with Ruth and married her. Ruth's great grandson was King David.

FIRST SAMUEL

For them that honor me, I will honor, and they that despise me shall be lightly esteemed.

II, 30

Be strong, and quit yourselves like men.

IV, 9

SECOND SAMUEL

King David sent the husband of the beautiful Bathsheba, Uriah the Hittite, to lead the assault on a city so he would be killed and David could marry her. Nathan the prophet confronted David with the story of a rich man with large herds of sheep who stole the one ewe of a poor man, to which David responded, "As the Lord liveth, the man that hath done this thing shall surely die…" Nathan responded, "Thou art the man." (XII, 5–7).

SECOND CHRONICLES

If my people, which are called by my name, shall humble themselves, and pray, and seek my face, and turn from their wicked ways; then will I hear from heaven, and will forgive their sin, and heal their land.

VII, 14.

ESTHER

Maimonides, the great twelfth-century Jewish theologian, thought the Book of Esther was the most important book in the Bible after the five books of Moses. Hitler outlawed the Book of Esther and closed all synagogues in Germany on each feast day of Esther, the Feast of Purim.

Mordecai raised Esther, an orphan and his great-niece. The king of Persia, Ahasuerus, summoned his queen to a royal feast, and when she refused to come, he put her away and then selected Esther, the most beautiful virgin in his kingdom, to be his queen. Mordecai advised her not to reveal that she was a Jew. Mordecai also discovered and revealed a plot among the harem's eunuchs to assassinate the king. Later, Haman, chief prince and adviser to the king and enemy of the Jews, persuaded the king to allow citizens throughout Persia on a given day to murder all of Persia's Jews and confiscate their property. Mordecai discovered the secret decree and urged Esther to rush to the king and persuade him to rescind it. She hesitated, because to go to the king without being summoned was a capital offense, unless he showed mercy. Esther's intervention led to a repeal of the degree and even to the hanging of Haman and his ten sons on the very gallows he had built to hang Mordecai.

> So will I go unto the king... and if I perish, I perish.
>
> IV, 16

JOB

Job, who lived in the land of Uz, was "perfect and upright" in his love and fear of God, so he enjoyed great wealth and ten children. Satan got God's permission to test Job's faith through adversity by killing Job's children, destroying his wealth, and covering his body with boils. The Book of Job explores how God, the all-knowing, all-powerful, and all-benevolent, permits the suffering of the innocent.

Harold Bloom accounts Job as the greatest aesthetic triumph of the Hebrew Bible and one of the world's greatest poems.

> Naked came I out of my mother's womb,
> And naked shall I return thither;
> The Lord gave, and the Lord hath taken away; blessed be the name of the Lord.
>
> I, 21

> Then said his wife unto him, Dost thou still retain thine integrity? curse God and die.
> [Job's "friends" assumed he must have sinned to be so tormented by God, so they advised him to repent. Only Job understood that God's plan does not have to make sense to man; that God does not always punish evil or reward righteousness.]
>
> II, 9

> There the wicked cease from troubling;
> And there the weary be at rest.
>
> III, 17

> The life of man upon earth is a warfare.
>
> VII, 1

> Man that is born of a woman
> Is of few days, and full of trouble.
> He cometh forth like a flower, and is cut down:
> He fleeth also as a shadow, and continueth not.
>
> XIV, 1

> But where shall wisdom be found? And where is the place of understanding?
> Man knoweth not the price thereof; neither is it found in the land of the living.

The depth saith, It is not in me: and the
sea saith, It is not with me.
It cannot be gotten for gold, neither
shall silver be weighted for the price
thereof....
And unto man he [God] said, Behold,
the fear of the Lord, that is wisdom; and to depart from evil is
understanding.
						XXVIII, 12–28

Who is this that darkeneth counsel by
words without knowledge?
						XXXVIII, 2

PSALMS

Thou shalt break them with a rod of
iron;
Thou shalt dash them in pieces like a
potter's vessel.
Be wise now therefore, O ye kings:
Be instructed, ye judges of the earth.
						II, 9 – 10

For thou hast made him [man] a little
lower than the angels…
Thou hast put all things under his feet…
						VIII, 5

Let the words of my mouth
And the meditation of my heart, be
acceptable in thy sight,
O Lord, my strength, and my redeemer.
						XIX, 14

The Lord is my shepherd; I shall not
want,
He maketh me to lie down in green
pastures;
He leadeth me beside the still waters.
He restoreth my soul;
He leadeth me in the paths of righ-
teousness for his name's sake.

Yea, though I walk through the valley of
the shadow of death,
I will fear no evil: for thou art with me;
Thy rod and thy staff they comfort me.
Thou preparest a table before me in the
presence of mine enemies;
Thou annointest my head with oil; my
cup runneth over.
Surely goodness and mercy shall follow
me all the days of my life;
And I will dwell in the house of the
Lord for ever.
						XXIII

The words of his mouth were smoother
than butter, but war was in his heart;
His words were softer than oil, yet were
they drawn swords.
						LV, 21

For a thousand years in thy sight
Are but as yesterday when it is past,
And as a watch in the night.
						XC, 4

The days of our years are threescore
years and ten;
And if by reason of strength they be
fourscore years,
Yet is their strength labor and sorrow;
For it is soon cut off, and we fly away.
						XC, 10

A thousand shall fall at thy side,
And ten thousand at thy right hand;
But it shall not come nigh thee.
						XCI, 7

Offer to God a sacrifice of thanksgiving
And make good your vows to the Most
High.
Call upon me in the day of trouble;
I will deliver you, and you shall honor me.
						C, 14–15

The stone which the builders refused
Is become the head stone of the corner.

CXVIII, 22

PROVERBS

My son, despise not the chastening of
    the Lord; Neither be weary of his
    correction.
For whom the Lord loveth he
    correcteth;
Even as a father the son in whom he
    delighteth.

III, 11–12

Wisdom is the principal thing; there-
    fore get wisdom:
And with all thy getting get
    understanding.

IV, 7

For the lips of a strange woman drop as
    a honeycomb,
And her mouth is smoother than oil;
But her end is bitter as wormwood;
Sharp as a two-edged sword.

V, 4–5

Go to the ant, thou sluggard;
Consider her ways, and be wise.

VI, 6

Yet a little sleep, a little slumber,
A little folding of the hands to sleep;
So shall thy poverty come as one that
    traveleth, And thy want as an armed
    man.

VI, 10–11

I love those who love me;
And those who seek me diligently find
    me.

VIII, 17

He that spareth the rod hateth his son;
But he that loveth him chasteneth him
    betimes.

XIII, 24

A soft answer turneth away wrath;
But grievous words stir up anger.

XV, 1

And before honor is humility.

XV, 33

Pride goeth before destruction,
And an haughty spirit before a fall.

XVI, 18

Children's children are the crown of old
    men; And the glory of children are
    their fathers.

XVII, 6

A word fitly spoken
Is like apples of gold in pitchers of
    silver.

XXV, 11

He that hath no rule over his own spirit
Is like a city that is broken down, and
    without walls.

XXV, 28

As a dog returneth to his vomit,
So a fool returneth to his folly.

XXVI, 11

Whoso diggeth a pit shall fall therein;
And he that rolleth a stone, it will
    return upon him.

XXVI, 27

The wicked flee when no man pursueth;
But the righteous are bold as a lion.

XXVIII, 1

A fool uttereth all his mind.

XXIX, 11

Where there is no vision, the people
perish.

XXIX, 18

Who can find a virtuous woman?
For her price is far above rubies.

XXXI, 10

ECCLESIASTES
THE PREACHER

Vanity of vanities; all is vanity.

I, 2

One generation passeth away, and
another generation cometh; but the earth
abideth for ever.

I, 4

The thing that hath been, it is that which
shall be; and that which is done is that
which shall be done: and there is no new
thing under the sun.

I, 9

For in much wisdom is much grief;
   and he that increaseth knowledge
   increaseth sorrow.

I, 18

To every thing there is a season, and
   a time to every purpose under the
   heaven.
A time to be born, and a time to die;
A time to plant and a time to pluck up
   what has been planted;
A time to kill and a time to heal;
A time to break down and a time to
   build up;
A time to weep, and a time to laugh;

A time to mourn, and a time to dance;
A time to cast away stones, and a time
   to gather stones together;
A time to embrace, and a time to refrain
   from embracing;
A time to get, and a time to lose;
A time to keep, and a time to cast away;
A time to rend, and a time to sew;
A time to keep silent and a time to
   speak;
A time to love, and a time to hate;
A time for war, and a time for peace.

III, 1–8

A threefold cord is not quickly broken.

IV, 12

A good name is better than precious
ointment; And the day of death than the
day of one's birth.

VII, 1

For there is not a just man upon earth,
that doeth good, and sinneth not.

VII, 20

Then I commended mirth, because a man
hath no better thing under the sun, than
to eat, and to drink, and to be merry; for
that shall abide with him of his labour
the days of his life, which God giveth
him under the sun.

VIII, 15

Whatsoever thy hand findeth to do, do
it with thy might; for there is no work,
nor device, nor knowledge, nor wisdom
in the grave, whither thou goest.

IX, 10

I returned, and saw under the sun, that
the race is not to the swift, nor the battle
to the strong, neither yet bread to the

wise, nor yet riches to men of understanding, nor yet favor to the men of skill; but
time and chance happeneth to them all.
For man also knoweth not his time: as the
fishes that are taken in an evil net, and as
the birds that are caught in the snare; so
are the sons of men snared in an evil time,
when it falleth suddenly upon them.

IX, 11–12

A wise man's heart inclineth him toward
the right; but a fool's heart toward the left.

X, 2

Of making many books there is no end;
And much study is a weariness of the flesh.

XII, 12

ISAIAH

Come now, let us reason together, saith
   the Lord…
But if ye refuse and rebel,
Ye shall be devoured by the sword….

I, 18–20

They shall beat their swords into
   plowshares, And their spears into
   pruning-hooks;
Nation shall not lift up sword against
   nation, Neither shall they learn war
   any more.

II, 4

Here am I; send me.

VI, 8

Behold, a virgin shall conceive, and
   bear a Son, And shall call his name
   Immanuel.

VII, 14

For unto us a child is born, unto us a
   Son is given;

And the government shall be upon his
   shoulder;
And his name shall be called Wonder-
   ful, Counselor, The mighty God,
The everlasting Father, The Prince of
   Peace.

IX, 6

The wolf also shall dwell with the lamb,
And the leopard shall lie down with the
   kid.

XI, 6

We have made a covenant with death;
And with hell are we at agreement.

XXVIII, 15

Their strength is to sit still.

XXX, 7

In returning and rest shall ye be saved;
In quietness and in confidence shall be
   your strength.

XXX, 15

The voice of him that crieth in the
   wilderness,
Prepare ye the way of the Lord,
Make straight in the desert a highway
   for our God.

XL, 3

Every valley shall be exalted,
And every mountain and hill shall be
   made low;
And the crooked shall be made straight,
And the rough places plain.

XL, 4

The voice said, Cry.
And he said, what shall I cry?
All flesh is grass…
The grass withereth and the flower
   fadeth;

But the word of our God shall stand
forever.

XL, 6

But they that wait upon the Lord shall
renew their strength;
They shall mount up with wings as
eagles;
They shall run, and not be weary; And
they shall walk, and not faint.

XLVII, 27–31

All we, like sheep, have gone astray;
We have turned every one to his own
way;

LIII, 6

For my thoughts are not your thoughts,
Neither are your ways my ways saith the
Lord.
For as the heavens are higher than the
earth,
So are my ways higher than your ways
And my thoughts than your thoughts.

LV, 8–9

JEREMIAH

Saying, peace, peace; when there is no
peace.

VI, 14

The harvest is past, the summer is ended,
and we are not saved

VIII, 20

Is there no balm in Gilead?
[God told Jeremiah he would spare
Jerusalem if Jeremiah could find
one righteous man: "Run to and fro
through the streets of Jerusalem,
look around and take note! Search

its squares and see if you can find
one person who acts justly and
seeks truth that I may pardon her."
Jeremiah could not find a single
just man, so his lament for Jerusalem cannot be comforted by any
balm in Gilead, a city known for its
medicines.]

VIII, 22

Thou art my hope in the day of evil.

XVII, 17

And you will seek me and find me when
you search for me with all of your heart.

XX1X, 13

EZEKIEL

And the word of the Lord came unto
me again, saying, What mean ye, that ye
use this proverb concerning the law of
Israel, saying, The fathers have eaten sour
grapes, and the children's teeth are set on
edge? As I live, saith the Lord God, ye
shall not have occasion any more to use
this proverb in Israel. Behold, all souls
are mine; as the soul of the father, so also
the soul of the son is mine: the soul that
sinneth, it shall die.

XVIII, 1–4

DANIEL

Shadrach, Meshach, and Abednego fell
down bound into the midst of the burning fiery furnace.

III, 23

King Nebuchadnezzar took the elite of
Judah as hostages in the "Babylonian cap-
tivity" to ensure loyalty. When Shadrach,
Meshach and Abednego refused to worship

a golden image, he threw them into a great furnace, where they stood unharmed. Amazed, Nebuchadnezzar promulgated a law against criticizing Jehovah.

Years later, Babylon was incorporated in the Persian empire of King Darius, for whom Daniel became an adviser. Other advisers jealous of Daniel prompted Darius to promulgate a law that for thirty days no one would pray to any god. Daniel continued to pray three times daily, so the advisers had Daniel thrown into a lion pit that was sealed by a stone. Missing Daniel, Darius went to the pit and unsealed it to see if Daniel's God had saved him. Daniel called up that an angel had protected him through the night. Darius pulled Daniel out of the pit and threw in the other advisers with their wives and children, who were all devoured.

MENE, MENE, TEKEL, UPHARSIN
[The writing on the wall forecasting the destruction of Babylon.]

V, 25

HOSEA

My people are destroyed for lack of knowledge.

IV, 6

They have sown the wind, and they shall reap the whirlwind.

VIII, 7

JOEL

And it shall come to pass afterward, that
I will pour out my spirit on all flesh;
Your sons and your daughters shall
prophesy, Your old men shall dream
dreams,

Your young men shall see visions.

II, 28

MICA

And what doth the Lord require of thee,
But to do justly, and to love mercy,
And to walk humbly with thy God?
[In Judaism as opposed to Christianity and Islam, faith is not necessary to salvation only the doing of God's will, essentially the Ten Commandments. Requiring faith for salvation makes Christianity and Islam messianic.]

VI, 8

HAGGAI

You have sown much, and bring in little.

I, 6

He that earnesth wages, earneth wages to put it into a bag with holes.

I, 6

SIRACH
C. SECOND CENTURY B.C.

The Lord sets a father in honor over his
children;
A mother's authority he confirms over
her sons.
He who honors his father atones for
sins;
He stores up riches who reveres his
mother.

ECCLESIASTICUS

Now let us praise famous men, and our fathers that begat us.

XLIV, 1

18

THE NEW TESTAMENT OF THE HOLY BIBLE
KING JAMES VERSION (1611)

This Bible is for the Government of the People, by the People, and for the People.
Wycliffe (1382), general prologue

THE GOSPEL ACCORDING TO MATTHEW

Behold, a virgin shall be with child, and shall bring forth a son, and they shall call his name Emmanuel, which being interpreted is, God with us.

I, 23

...Rachel weeping for her children, and would not be comforted, because they are not.

II, 18

It is written man shall not live by bread alone, but from every word that proceedeth out of the mouth of God.
[Jesus Christ]

IV, 4

Blessed are the poor in spirit: for theirs is the kingdom of heaven.
Blessed are they that mourn: for they shall be comforted,
Blessed are the meek: for they shall inherit the earth.
Blessed are they which do hunger and thirst after righteousness: for they shall be filled.
Blessed are the merciful: for they shall obtain mercy.
Blessed are the pure in heart: for they shall see God.
Blessed are the peacemakers: for they shall be called the children of God.
Blessed are those who are persecuted for righteousness' sake, for theirs is the kingdom of heaven.
Blessed are you when men revile you and persecute you and utter all manner of evil against you falsely for my sake.
Rejoice and be exceedingly glad for great is your reward in heaven: for so persecuted they the prophets which were before you.
[Jesus Christ]

V, 3–11

In the Sermon on the Mount, Jesus goes beyond the Ten Commandments to say that good behavior according to the law is not enough. Man needs a radical purification of being. Jesus said, "You have heard it said to the people long ago, 'Do not commit murder.' But I tell you that anyone who is angry with his brother will be subject to judgment." Jesus demands perfection of the soul, a far greater demand than obeying the law.

Ye are the light of the world. A city that is set on a hill cannot be hid.
[Jesus Christ]

V, 14

Let your light so shine before men,
that they may see your good works,
and glorify your Father which is in
heaven.
[Jesus Christ]

V, 16

Lay not up for yourselves treasures
upon earth where moth and rust doth
corrupt, and where thieves break
through and steal: but lay up for yourselves treasures in heaven where neither moth nor rust doth corrupt and
where thieves to not break through nor
steal: for where your treasure is, there
will your heart be also.
[Jesus Christ]

VI, 19–21

No man can serve two masters....Ye
cannot serve God and mammon.
[Jesus Christ]

VI, 24

Judge not, that ye be not judged.
[Jesus Christ]

VII, 1

Neither cast ye your pearls before swine,
lest they trample them under their feet,
and turn again and rend you.
[Jesus Christ]

VII, 6

Ask, and it shall be given you; seek,
and ye shall find; knock, and it shall be
opened unto you.
[Jesus Christ]

VII, 7

Wide is the gate, and broad is the way,
that leadeth to destruction, and many
there be which go in thereat: because
straight is the gate, and narrow is the way

which leadeth unto life, and few there be
that find it.
[Jesus Christ]

VII, 13

Beware of false prophets, which come
to you in sheep's clothing, but inwardly
they are ravening wolves.
[Jesus Christ]

VII, 15

And every one that heareth these sayings
of mine, and doeth them not, shall be
likened unto a foolish man, which built
his house upon the sand: and the rain
descended, and the floods came, and the
winds blew and beat upon that house:
and it fell: and great was the fall of it.
[Jesus Christ]

VII, 26–28

But the children of the kingdom shall be
cast out into outer darkness: there shall
be weeping and gnashing of teeth.
[Jesus Christ]

VIII, 12

Whosoever therefore shall confess me
before men, him will I confess also before
my Father which is in heaven. But whosoever shall deny me before men, him
will I also deny before my Father which
is in heaven.
[Jesus Christ]

X, 32–33

I came not to send peace, but a sword.
[Jesus Christ]

X, 34

For by thy words thou shalt be justified,
and by thy words thou shalt be condemned.
[Jesus Christ]
XII, 37

A prophet is not without honour, save in his own country and in his own house.
[Jesus Christ]

XIII, 57

If the blind lead the blind, both shall fall into the ditch.
[Jesus Christ]

XV, 14

Thou art the Christ, the Son of the living God.
[Simon Peter]

XVI, 16

Thou art Peter, and upon this rock I will build my church; and the gates of hell shall not prevail against it.
[Jesus Christ]

XVI, 18

For what is a man profited, if he shall gain the whole world and lose his own soul?
[Jesus Christ]

XVI, 26

For verily, I say unto you, if ye have faith as a grain of mustard seed, ye shall say unto this mountain, "Remove hence to yonder place," and it shall move; and nothing shall be impossible unto you.
[Jesus Christ]

XVII, 20

Except ye be converted, and become as little children, ye shall not enter into the kingdom of heaven.
[Jesus Christ]

XVIII, 3

What therefore God hath joined together, let not man put asunder.
[Jesus Christ]

XIX, 6

It is easier for a camel to go through the eye of a needle, than for a rich man to enter into the kingdom of God.
[Jesus Christ]

XIX, 24

For many are called, but few are chosen.
[Jesus Christ]

XXII, 14

Ye are like unto whited sepulchers, which indeed appear beautiful outward, but are within full of dead men's bones, and of all uncleanness.
[Jesus Christ]

XXIII, 27

Well done, thou good and faithful servant; thou hast been faithful over a few things, I will make thee ruler over many things.
[Jesus Christ]

XXV, 21

Unto every one that hath shall be given, and he shall have abundance; but from him that hath not shall be taken away even that which he hath.
[Jesus Christ]

XXV, 29

Cast ye the unprofitable servant into outer darkness; there men will weep and gnash their teeth.
[Jesus Christ]

XXV, 30

For ye have the poor always with you.
[Jesus Christ]

XXVI, 11

The spirit indeed is willing, but the flesh is weak.
[Jesus Christ]

XXVI, 41

Put upon again thy sword in its place; for all they that take the sword will perish with the sword.
[Jesus Christ]

XXVI, 52

The Gospel According to Mark

If a house be divided against itself, that house cannot stand.
[Jesus Christ]

III, 25

Lord, I believe, help thou mine unbelief.

IX, 24

Suffer the little children to come unto me, and forbid them not; for of such is the kingdom of God.
[Jesus Christ]

X, 14

Beware of the scribes, which love to go in long clothing, and love salutations in the marketplaces, and the chief seats in the synagogues, and the uppermost rooms at feasts: which devour widows' houses, and for a pretence make long prayers: these shall receive greater damnation.
[Jesus Christ]

XII, 38

Go into all the world and preach the good news to all creation.
[Jesus Christ]

XVI, 15

The Gospel According to Luke

Love your enemies, do good to them which hate you, bless them that curse you, and pray for them that despitefully use you. And unto him that smiteth thee on one cheek, offer also the other…
[Jesus Christ]

VI, 27 - 29

Her sins, which are many, are forgiven; for she loved much.
[Jesus Christ]

VII, 47

If any man would come after me, let him deny himself, and take up his cross daily, and follow me.
[Jesus Christ]

IX, 23

"You shall love the Lord your God with all your heart, and with all your soul, and with all your strength, and with all your mind; and your neighbor as yourself." And he said to him, "You have answered right; do this and you will live."
[A lawyer and Jesus Christ]

X, 27 – 28

Thou fool, this night thy soul shall be required of thee; then whose shall those things be, which thou hast provided? So is he who layeth up treasure for himself, and is not rich toward God.
[Jesus Christ]

XII, 20 – 21

For unto whomsoever much is given, of him shall be much required.
[Jesus Christ]

XII, 48

Which of you, intending to build a tower, sitteth not down first, and counteth the cost, whether he have sufficient to finish it?
[Jesus Christ]

XIV, 28

"Father, forgive them; for they know not what they do."
[Jesus Christ]

XXIII, 34

The Gospel According to John

In the beginning was the Word, and the Word was with God, and the Word was God.

I, 1

And the Word was made flesh and dwelt among us…

1, 14

When he had made a scourge of small cords, he drove them all out of the temple.

II, 15

Except a man be born again, he cannot see the kingdom of God.
[Jesus Christ]

III, 3

For God so loved the world, that he gave his only begotten Son, that whosoever believeth in him should not perish, but have everlasting life.
[Jesus Christ]

III, 16

God is spirit: and they that worship him must worship him in spirit and in truth.
[Jesus Christ]

IV, 24

He that is without sin among you, let him first cast a stone at her.
[Jesus Christ]

VIII, 7

If ye continue in my word…ye shall know the truth, and the truth shall make you free.
[Jesus Christ]

VIII, 31

The night cometh when no man can work.
[Jesus Christ]

IX, 4

I am come that they might have life, and that they might have it more abundantly.
[Jesus Christ]

X, 10

Other sheep I have, which are not of this fold: them also I must bring…
[Jesus Christ]

X, 16

I am the resurrection, and the life: he that believeth in me, though he were dead, yet shall he live: And whosoever liveth and believeth in me shall never die.
[Jesus Christ]

XI, 25–26

In my father's house are many mansions: if it were not so, I would have told you. I go to prepare a place for you. And if I go and prepare a place for you, I will come again, and receive you unto myself; that where I am, there ye may be also. And whither I go ye know, and the way ye know. Thomas saith unto him, Lord, we know not whither thou goest; and how can we know the way? Jesus saith unto him, I am the way, the truth, and the life; no man cometh unto the Father, but by me.
[Jesus Christ]

XIV, 2–7

Greater love hath no man than this, that a man lay down his life for his friends.
[Jesus Christ]

XV, 13

Except I shall see in his hands the print of the nails, and put my finger into the print of the nails, and thrust my hand into his side, I will not believe.
[Thomas]

XX, 25

Feed my sheep.
[Jesus Christ]

XXI, 16

THE LETTER OF PAUL TO THE ROMANS

For as many as have sinned without the law shall also perish without the law, and as many as have sinned in the law shall be judged by the law. For not the hearers of the law are just before God, but the doers of the law shall be justified. For when the Gentiles, which have not the law, do by nature the things contained in the law, these having not the law, are a law unto themselves...
[Paul]

II, 12–14

For all have sinned, and come short of the glory of God.
[Paul]

III, 23

For the good that I would, I do not; but the evil which I would not, that I do.
[Paul]

VII, 19

If God be for us, who can be against us?
[Paul]

VIII, 31

For I am persuaded that neither death, nor life, nor angels, nor principalities, nor powers, nor things present, nor things to come, nor height, nor depth, nor any other creature, shall be able to separate us from the love of God, which is Christ Jesus our Lord.
[Paul]

VIII, 38–39

Vengeance is mine; I will repay, saith the Lord.
[Paul]

XII, 19

THE FIRST LETTER OF PAUL TO THE CORINTHIANS

Be not deceived: neither fornicators, nor idolaters, nor adulterers, nor effeminate, nor abusers of themselves with mankind, nor thieves, nor covetous, nor drunkards, nor revilers, nor extortionists, shall inherit the kingdom of God. And such were some of you... but ye are justified in the name of the Lord Jesus.
[Paul]

VI, 9

It is better to marry than to burn.
[Paul]

VII, 9

If I speak with the tongues of men and of angels, but have not charity, I am become as sounding brass, or a tinkling cymbal. And though I have the gift of prophecy, and understand all mysteries and all knowledge; and though I have all faith, so that I could remove mountains, and have no charity, I am nothing. And though I bestow all my goods to feed the poor, and though I give my body to be burned, and

have not charity, it profiteth me nothing. Charity suffereth long, and is kind; charity envieth not; charity vaunteth not itself, is not puffed up, doth not behave itself unseemly, seeketh not her own, is not easily provoked, thinketh no evil; rejoiceth not in iniquity, but rejoiceth in the truth; beareth all things, believeth all things, hopeth all things, endureth all things. Charity never faileth: but where there be prophecies, they shall fail; where there be tongues, they shall cease; where there be knowledge, it shall vanish away. For we know in part, and we prophesy in part. But when that which is perfect is come, then that which is in part shall be done away. When I was child, I spake as a child, I understood as a child, I thought as a child: but when I became a man, I put away childish things. For now I know in part; but then shall I know even as also I am known. And now abideth faith, hope, charity, these three, but the greatest of these is charity.
[Paul]

XIII, 2–13

For if the trumpet give an uncertain sound, who shall prepare himself to the battle?
[Paul]

XIV, 8

THE SECOND LETTER OF PAUL TO THE CORINTHIANS

For the things which are seen are temporal; but the things which are not seen are eternal.

IV, 18

THE LETTER OF PAUL TO THE GALACIANS

Be not deceived; God is not mocked:
for whatsoever a man soweth, that
shall he also reap.
[Paul]

VI, 7

Let us not be weary in well doing; for in due season we shall reap, if we faint not.
[Paul]

VI, 9

THE LETTER OF PAUL TO THE EPHESIANS

For by grace ye are saved through faith; and not of yourselves: it is the gift of God: not of works, lest any man should boast.
[Paul]

II, 8 – 9

We wrestle not against flesh and blood, but against principalities, against powers, against the rulers of the darkness of this world, against spiritual wickedness in high places.
[Paul]

VI, 12

THE LETTER OF PAUL TO THE PHILIPPIANS

Work out your own salvation with fear and trembling.
[Paul]

II, 12

THE SECOND LETTER OF PAUL TO THE THESSALONIANS

Now we command you, brethren, in the name of our Lord Jesus Christ, that you keep away from any brother who is living in idleness…If any one will not work, let him not eat.
    [Paul]

III, 6–11

THE FIRST LETTER OF PAUL TO TIMOTHY

The is a faithful saying and worthy of full acceptance, that Christ Jesus came into the world to save sinners, of whom I am the chief.
    [Paul]

I, 15

A bishop then must be blameless, the husband of one wife, vigilant, sober, of good behavior, given to hospitality, apt to teach; not given to wine, no striker, not greedy of filthy lucre; but patient, not a brawler, not covetous; one that ruleth well his own house, having his children in subjection with all gravity; (for if a man know not how to rule his own house, how shall he take care of the church of God?)…Moreover he must have a good report of them which are without; lest he fall into reproach…
    [Paul]

III, 2

For the love of money is the root of all evil.
    [Paul]

VI, 10

THE SECOND LETTER OF PAUL TO TIMOTHY

I have fought a good fight, I have finished my course, I have kept the faith.
    [Paul]

IV, 7

THE LETTER TO THE HEBREWS

Now faith is the substance of things hoped for, the evidence of things not seen…. But without faith it is impossible to please Him: for he that cometh to God must believe that he is…
    [Paul]

XII, 6

THE LETTER OF JAMES

Was not Abraham our father justified by works, when he had offered Isaac his son upon the altar? Seest thou how faith wrought with his works, and by works was faith made perfect? And the scripture was fulfilled which saith, Abraham believed God, and it was imputed unto him for righteousness: and he was called the Friend of God. Ye see then how that by works a man is justified, and not by faith only…. For as the body without the spirit is dead, so faith without works is dead also.

II, 21–26

THE FIRST LETTER OF JOHN

And if any one does sin, we have an advocate with the Father, Jesus Christ the righteous; and he is the propitiation for our sins, and not for ours only but also for the sins of the whole world.
    [John]

II, 1–2

Beloved, let us love one another: for love is of God; and every one that loveth is born of God, and knowetht God. He that loveth not, knoweth not God; for God is love.

[John]

IV, 7– 8

THE THIRD LETTER OF JOHN

He that doeth good is of God: but he that doeth evil hath not seen God.

[John]

Verse 11

THE REVELATION OF SAINT JOHN THE DIVINE

I know thy works, that thou art neither cold not hot: I would thou wert cold or hot; So then because thou art lukewarm, and neither cold nor hot, I will spew thee out of my mouth.

[Jesus Christ]

III, 15–16

Behold a pale horse: and his name that sat on him was Death, and Hell followed with him.

[Saint John the Divine]

VI, 8

And I saw the dead, small and great, stand before God; and the books were opened: and another book was opened, which is the book of life: and the dead were judged out of those things which were written in the books, according to their works. And the sea gave up the dead which were in it; and death and hell delivered up the dead which were in

them: and they were judged every man according to their works. And death and hell were cast into the lake of fire. This is the second death. And whosoever was not found written in the book of life was cast into the lake of fire.

[Saint John the Divine]

XX, 12–15

And God shall wipe away all tears from their eyes; and there shall be no more death, neither sorrow, nor crying, neither shall there be any more pain: for the former things are passed away.

[Saint John the Divine]

XXI, 4

I am Alpha and Omega, the beginning and the end, the first and the last.

[Jesus Christ]

XXII

19
BOOK OF COMMON PRAYER, AVE MARIA, GRACE, AND HYMNS

A GENERAL CONFESSION

Almighty and most merciful Father; We have erred and strayed from thy ways like lost sheep. We have followed too much the devices and desires of our own hearts. We have offended against thy holy laws. We have left undone those things which we ought to have done; And we have done those things which we ought not to have done; And there is no health in us. But thou, O Lord, have mercy upon us, miserable offenders. Spare thou those, O God, who confess their faults. Restore thou those who are penitent; according to thy promises declared unto mankind In Christ Jesus our Lord. And grant, O most merciful Father, for his sake; That we may hereafter live a godly, righteous, and sober life, To the glory of thy holy Name. Amen.

A GENERAL THANKSGIVING

Almighty God, Father of all mercies, we, thine unworthy servants, do give thee most humble and hearty thanks for all thy goodness and loving-kindness to us and to all men. We bless thee for our creation, preservation, and all the blessings of this life; but above all, for thine inestimable love in the redemption of the world by our Lord Jesus Christ; for the means of grace, and for the hope of glory. And, we beseech thee, give us that due sense of all thy mercies, that our hearts may be unfeignedly thankful; and that we show forth thy praise, not only with our lips, but in our lives, by giving up ourselves to thy service, and by walking before thee in holiness and righteousness all our days; through Jesus Christ our Lord, to whom, with thee and the Holy Ghost, be all honour and glory, world without end. Amen.

THE LORD'S PRAYER

Our Father, who art in heaven, Hallowed be thy Name. Thy kingdom come. Thy will be done, On earth as it is in heaven. Give us this day our daily bread. And forgive us our trespasses, As we forgive those who trespass against us. And lead us not into temptation, But deliver us from evil. For thine is the kingdom, and the power, and the glory, for ever and ever. Amen.

APOSTLES' CREED

I believe in God the Father Almighty, Maker of heaven and earth; And in Jesus Christ his only Son our Lord: Who was conceived by the Holy Ghost, Born of the Virgin Mary: Suffered under Pontius Pilate, Was crucified, dead, and buried:

He descended into hell; The Third day he rose again from the dead: He ascended into heaven, And sitteth on the right hand of God the Father Almighty: From thence he shall come to judge the quick and the dead. I believe in the Holy Ghost: The holy Catholic Church; The communion of Saints: The Forgiveness of sins: The Resurrection of the body: and The life everlasting. Amen.

To Receive Holy Communion

Ye who do truly and earnestly repent you of your sins, and are in love and charity with your neighbours, and intend to lead a new life, following the commandments of God, and walking from henceforth in his holy ways; Draw near with faith and take this holy Sacrament to your comfort; and make your humble confession to Almighty God, devoutly kneeling.

The Body of our Lord Jesus Christ, which was given for thee, preserve thy body and soul unto everlasting life. Take and eat this in remembrance that Christ died for three, and feed on him in thy heart by faith with thanksgiving.

A Prayer for all Conditions of Men

O God, the Creator and Preserver of all mankind, we humbly beseech thee for all sorts and conditions of men; that thou wouldest be pleased to make thy ways known unto them, thy saving health unto all nations. More especially we pray for thy holy Church universal; that it may be so guided and governed by thy good Spirit, that all who profess and call themselves Christians may be led into the way of truth, and hold the faith in unity of spirit, in the bond of peace, and in righteousness of life. Finally, we commend to thy fatherly goodness all those who are any ways afflicted, or distressed in mind, body, or estate; that it may please thee to comfort and relieve them, according to their several necessities; giving them patience under their sufferings, and a happy issue out of all their afflictions. And this we beg for Jesus Christ's sake. Amen.

Solemnization of Matrimony— The Plighting of Troths

To have and to hold from this day forward, for better, for worse, for richer, for poorer, in sickness, and in health, to love and to cherish [to love, to cherish and to obey], till death us do part.

Burial of the Dead

Unto Almighty God we commend the soul of our *brother* departed, and we commit *his* body to the ground; earth to earth, ashes to ashes, dust to dust; in sure and certain hope of the Resurrection unto eternal life, though our Lord Jesus Christ.

Ave Maria, or Hail Mary
Eleventh century

Hail Mary, full of grace, the Lord is with Thee; Blessed art Thou among women, and blessed is the fruit of Thy Womb, Jesus. Holy Mary, Mother of God, pray for us sinners now and at the hour of our death.

GRACE
AT SEWANEE MILITARY ACADEMY

For all these mercies to us and to all
men, may God's Holy Name be praised.
Amen.

HYMNS

"Welcome, happy morning!" age to age
    shall say;
Hell today is vanquished, heaven is won
    today!
Lo! The dead is living, God for ever more!
Him their true Creator, all his works adore!
"Welcome, happy morning!" age to age
    shall say.
> Venantius Honorius Fortunatus (580), st.1

Jesus Christ is risen today, Al-le-lu-ia
Our triumphant holy day, Al-le-lu-ia
Who did once upon the cross,
    Al-le-lu-ia
Suffer to redeem our loss, Al-le-lu-ia
> Latin carol, fourteenth century

A mighty fortress is our God,
A bulwark never failing;
Our helper he amid the flood
Of mortal ills prevailing;
For still our ancient foe
Doth seek to work us woe;
His craft and power are great,
And, armed with cruel hate,
On earth is not his equal.
> Martin Luther (1529), st. 1

Jesus, Lover of my soul,
    Let me to thy bosom fly,
While the near waters roll,
    While the tempest still is high;
Hide me, O my Saviour, hide,
    Till the storm of life be past;

Safe into the haven guide,
    Receive my soul at last.
> Charles Wesley (1740), st. 1

O God, our help in ages past,
Our hope for years to come,
Our shelter from the stormy blast,
And our eternal home.
> Issac Watts (1674–1748), st. 1

A thousand ages in thy sight
Are like an evening gone,
Short as the watch that ends the night
Before the rising sun.
> Ibid., st. 4

Time, like an ever-rolling stream,
Bears all its sons away;
They fly, forgotten, as a dream
Dies at the opening day.
> Ibid., st. 5

O for a closer walk with God
A calm and heavenly frame,
A light to shine upon the road
That leads me to the Lamb!
> William Cowper (1731–1800), st. 1

Where is the blessedness I knew
When first I saw the Lord?
Where is the soul refreshing view
Of Jesus and his word?
> Ibid., st. 2

Return, O holy Dove return,
Sweet messenger of rest;
I hate the sins that made thee mourn,
And drove thee from my breast.
> Ibid., st. 3

The dearest idol I have known,
Whe'er that idol be,
 Help me to tear it from thy throne,
And worship only thee.
> Ibid., st. 4

So shall my walk be close with God,
Calm and serene my frame;
So purer light shall mark the road
That leads me to the Lamb.

> Ibid., st. 5

Rock of ages, cleft for me,
Let me hide myself in Thee;
Let the water and the blood,
From Thy riven side which flowed,
Be of sin the double cure,
Cleanse me from its guilt and power.

> Augustus Montague Toplady (1776), st. 1

Amazing grace! How sweet the sound
That saved a wretch like me!
I once was lost, but now am found
Was blind, but now I see.

> John Newton (1779), st. 1

'Twas grace that taught my heart to fear,
And grace my fears relieved;
How precious did that grace appear
The hour I first believed.

> Ibid., st. 2

Through many dangers, toils and snares,
I have already come;
'Tis grace hath brought me safe thus far,
And grace will lead me home.

> Ibid., st. 4

My country, 'tis of thee,
Sweet land of liberty,
Of thee I sing:
Land where my fathers died,
Land of the pilgrims' pride,
From every mountainside
Let freedom ring.

> Samuel Smith (1831), st. 1

Our fathers' God! To thee,
Author of liberty,
To Thee we sing.

Long may our land be bright
With freedom's holy light;
Protect us by thy might,
Great God our king.

> Ibid., st. 4

Silent night, holy night,
All is calm, all is bright
Round yon virgin mother and child.
Holy infant so tender and mild,
Sleep in heavenly peace,
Sleep in heavenly peace.

> Joseph Mohn (1792–1848), st. 1

"Fairest Lord Jesus"
Fair are the meadows, fairer still the
    woodlands
Robed in the blooming garb of spring;
Jesus is fairer, Jesus is purer,
Who makes the woeful heart to sing.

> Melody from *Schlesische Volkslieder* (1842),
> st. 2

Fair is the sunshine, fairer still the
    moonlight,
And all the twinkling, starry host;
Jesus shines brighter, Jesus shines purer,
Than all the angels heaven can boast.

> Ibid., st. 3

All things bright and beautiful,
All creatures great and small,
All thing wise and wonderful,
The Lord God made them all.

> Cecil Frances Alexander (1848), refrain

Faith of our fathers! Living still
In spite of dungeon, fire, and sword:
O how our hearts beat high with joy,
When e'er we hear that glorious word:
Faith of our fathers, holy faith,
We will be ture to thee till death.

> Frederick W. Faber (1848–63), st. 1

Eternal Father, Strong to Save,
Whose arm hath bound restless wave,
Who bidd'st the mighty ocean deep
Its own appointed limits keep,
O hear us when we cry to thee
For those in peril on the sea!

William Whiting (1860), st. 1,
"The Navy Hymn"

Shall we gather at the river,
Where bright and angel-feet have trod,
With its crystal tide forever
Flowing by the throne of God?

Robert Lowry (1865), st. 1

Yes, we'll gather at the river,
The beautiful, the beautiful river;
Gather with the saints at the river
That flows by the throne of God.

Ibid., chorus

The Church's One Foundation
Is Jesus Christ her Lord;
She is his new creation
By water and the word:
From heaven he came and sought her
To be his holy bride;
With his own blood he bought her,
And for her life he died.

Samuel John Stone (1839-1900)

We shall overcome,
We shall overcome some day.
Oh, deep in my heart I do believe,
We shall overcome some day.

Anon. pre-Civil War hymn, civil rights
song in 1946, and later favored by
Martin Luther King

Now the day is over,
Night is drawing nigh,
Shadows of the evening
Steal across the sky.

Sabine Baring-Gould (1865) st. 1

Jesus, give the weary
  Calm and sweet repose,
With thy tenderest blessing
  May our eyelids close.

Ibid., st. 2

Grant to little children
  Visions bright of thee;
Guard the sailors tossing
  On the deep, blue sea.

Ibid., st. 3

Comfort every sufferer
  Watching late in pain;
Those who plan some evil
  From their sin restrain.

Ibid., st. 4

Through the long night watches
  May thine angels spread
Their white wings above me,
  Watching round my bed.

Ibid., st. 5

When the morning wakens,
Then may I arise
Pure, and fresh, and sinless
In thy holy eyes. Amen

Ibid., st. 6

Conclusions

Great Quotations that Shaped the Western World following thoughts are good guides for our social and individual development.

Socrates is wisest for saying the only thing he was sure of was that seeking the truth was better than not seeking the truth. T. H. Huxley added that there can be no alleviation of suffering except for facing the world as it is. Facing reality is the key to good judgment, which is the key to everything. Kant said, "Dare to know! That is the slogan of the Enlightenment." Western progress has come from its openness to debate what is true and from its toleration of even odious speech.

Truth can be as harsh as cancer and as harsh as David Landes' insight about society: "Culture makes all the difference." Harsh but hopeful. We are not eternal children, so we can pursue the virtues touched upon here. Virtue leads to liberty, a loving community, and abundance; and, per Claire Booth Luce, courage is the ladder on which all virtues mount.

In all worthy civilizations, a critical mass of the people are virtuous, self-reliant, and educated. Cultures deficient in such cannot handle liberty. As Edmund Burke said, "The effect of liberty on individuals is that they may do what they please; we ought to see what it will please them to do, before we risk congratulations."

America, which is the castle-keep of Western civilization, is not a tribe but a sublime creed of liberty rooted in a constitutionally limited government. Its foundation is the Rule of Law, viz. law that is predictable because it is based on abstract principles that treat each citizen as an individual. The Rule of Law also requires that the Constitution and laws must be interpreted by their original intent, else we fall under the "rule of men." Jefferson said, "Our peculiar security is in the possession of a written Constitution. Let us not make it a blank paper by construction."

My surprising discovery—the Saul-en-route-to-Damascus type—is that complexity science endorses the conservative bias for decentralized systems. They develop more rapidly because they allow freedom and competition, which prompt more experiments and thus more innovation. Jean Monnet, architect of Europe's postwar economic miracle, said, "Avoid bureaucracy. Guide, do not dictate. Minimal rules." Conservatives from Hume to Buckley have sought to decentralize political power, while still insisting that an adequate moral political authority is essential to civil society.

The authors herein demonstrate the awesome power of words. As Petrarch said, "Gold, silver, gems, fine raiment, a marble palace...such things as these give one nothing more than a mute and superficial pleasure. Books delight us through and through, they converse with us, they give us good advice; they become living and lively companions to us." Great writers make us wiser and help us to speak and write with greater clarity and wit. Aristotle said man comes closest to the life of the gods when he is "active and contemplative."

As for finding happiness, one key is living a meaningful life by approaching the potential of our talents. Robert L. Stevenson said, "To become what we are capable of becoming is the only end of life." This agrees with Aristotle that living things have a "telos" or purpose, as for example, an acorn's telos is to become a tree.

Hugo said, "The supreme happiness of life is the conviction that we are loved." Thus, the importance of a loving family and hearty friends. Such connectedness can only be found in communities abiding by the moral law. Where perverse values dominate in individuals, families, communities, or nations, then poverty, crime, and despair are consequences. Thus, the Stoic Seneca correctly believed that virtue, not pleasure, is the way to happiness.

Great Quotations that Shaped the Western World celebrates the words of individuals, but Robert Bork opined that radical individualism can shred society. Jack Welch said winning organizations most value team players, and the poet Luciana De Crescenzo agreed.

> We are, each of us, angels with only one wing.
> We can only fly while embracing each other.

APPENDIX
COMPILERS LETTER TO HIS SONS

Grow strong my sons that you may stand
Unshaken when I fall; that I may know
The shattered fragments of my song will
   come
At last to a different and finer melody in
   you.

Adapted from Will Durant

Dear Wade, Hueston, and Austin,

Your mother asked me to use lessons from this book to write to you about life. But first, we are grateful for having had the opportunity to raise you. Life without any one of you would have been a mistake. We loved cheering at your sporting events, attending your shows, and laughing with your friends. Each of you enabled us to relive our youths more gloriously! And we have enjoyed your company more and more the older you have grown.

Advice? First, take good care of your mother. She never gave up on any of you, and you each needed saving more than once. Second, to be true to your Southern heritage, you must live honorably and suffer to do your duty. Third, discover and pursue your mission in life, and help your children to do the same. We have no right to self-fulfillment without first fulfilling our duties to our family.

To achieve your potential, you must understand the world as it is, learn who you are, and decide what you want to accomplish. All of that is difficult. To learn who you are you must sort through all your talents and interests to see what you do easily that others find difficult. And to soar, you must concentrate your energies into your one best field. As the headmaster in *Chariots of Fire* put it: "Let each of you discover where your true chance for greatness lies. Seize this chance. Rejoice in it and let no power or persuasion deter you in your task."

In pursuing our life's mission, we all have limited talents and options. As de Tocqueville said, "Around every man a fatal circle is traced beyond which he cannot pass; but within the wide verge of that circle he is powerful and free." Press against your boundaries by developing the following attitudes:

Integrity (truth-telling and promise-keeping). The U.S. Marine Corps ranks integrity as the key element of leadership. Warren Buffett only hires and partners with people of proven integrity.

Facing Reality is critical to good judgment, which is the key to everything. John D. Rockefeller ascribed Standard Oil's success to the fact that "We never deceived ourselves." One aspect of facing reality is keeping an open mind, because truth is so elusive. Humility keeps us open to counterintuitive truths and to truths from simple people and even from enemies. Another aspect of facing reality is to "grasp the hot irons of the truth"—deal with it! The greatest historian, Paul Johnson, said when he needed advice he turned not to "someone with first-class honors from a top university" but to someone who had "knocked about the world" and "developed the habit of asking questions of wise people and listening to their replies," as did Ronald Reagan.

Risk-acceptance (the hallmark of the knights of old and today's entrepreneurs). To soar you must have the courage to "find your own voice." Because you three are creative, you must assume extra risks to achieve your potential. To create is to experiment, which means failing most of the time. Thomas Edison failed some three thousand times before he discovered the right filament for an incandescent lightbulb. Society advances by replicating widely those few experiments that succeed. Most progress is attributable to the experimenters, who are called entrepreneurs, creators, artists, discovers, inventors, and so forth. But even if you show the greatest courage, act boldly and wisely, and persist tenaciously to the end, you may still fail utterly and become known as a failure. So be it.

Proactive bias: "Noah Principle": Predicting rain doesn't count; building arks does. Your judgments will always be based on inconclusive information, but nevertheless you must act decisively, sometimes with only the faintest light. Make mistakes quicker than your competitors, learn quicker, and adjust quicker. Ross Perot advised: "Ready, fire, aim." Thomas J. Watson Jr. said, "Solve it quickly, solve it right or wrong." Napoleon said, "One engages and then one looks."

On strategic thinking, per Peter Drucker:

(1) concentrate on marshaling your strengths, not on repairing your weaknesses; (2) associate with the strongest colleagues; (3) find the right general strategy before developing tactics; (4) pursue the few critical objectives that make a big difference; and (5) abandon quickly what no longer works well.

Diet and exercise to generate maximum energy. Great men all share one characteristic without exception: extraordinary energy levels.

Save and invest. Per James Hill, it is easy to predict who will be financially successful in life—the simple test is the ability to save. Be a fanatical saver! And, as Henry Ford observed, investing in developing your skills is the best investment. You may also need to be a good portfolio investor, per this book's investing insights.

In addition to the above, a cheerful, optimistic disposition is the first thing any prospective wife or partner will notice and value. Be sensitive; the only enemies you want are those you select. Care for your brothers, your nieces, nephews, cousins, and in-laws. Ecclesiastes informs us that a threefold cord is not easily broken. But never subsidize anyone's halfhearted performance.

My goal since my youth has been to reestablish our family. Perhaps my father thought the same, because he worked ceaselessly without benefit of college to finance my education. Grand projects, such as gothic cathedrals and first families, require generations to construct. It is enough in a lifetime to raise a wall; you don't have to build it all, so you should avoid rash risks. More important, founding first families has always been principally the work of great women. If you share my goal, beware of beauty and find a happy, loving wife smarter than you who values motherhood above everything else and who prefers murder to divorce. As the playwright Thomas Middleton said, "In the election of a wife, as in a project of war, to err but once is to be undone forever."

Here is my philosophy. Socrates was right to confine himself to examining ethics and politics, because ignorance prevented him from tackling metaphysics. Wittgenstein says that of all that matters in life, philosophers can have no answers. And as Will Durant said, "We are only particles pontificating on eternity." So we should remain awestruck, skeptical, and provisional. But, we must act decisively, so we should adopt Thomas Reid's "common sense." That is, cherry pick cogent rules of thumb, even if they do not constitute a consistent philosophical system. Our best hope is to be approximately right more often than not. Aristotle's Nicomachean Ethics called this becoming a *phronemos*, or "person of practical wisdom."

Happiness is found in developing your talents (realizing your telos) and enjoying loving, godly friends. T. S. Eliot wrote in *The Rock:*

> What life have you if you have not life
>   together?
> There is no life that is not in
>   community,
> And no community not lived in praise
>   of God…

Most important, St. Matthew XVI, 26, gave us the biggest picture in the words of Jesus Christ: "For what is a man profited, if he shall gain the whole world and lose his own soul?" Seek faith for eternity, but also for felicity and fortitude during life.

Index of Authors and Events

INDEX BY AUTHOR PROFESSION

Painters/Sculptors

Philosophers

Physicians

Playwrights

Compiler's Biography

Carl H. Middleton was born in 1938 and raised in Tuscumbia, Alabama. He received a B.A. from Princeton University's Woodrow Wilson School of Public and International Affairs, with a concentration in history and economics, and an L.L.B. from the University of Virginia Law School. After serving as a captain in the U. S. Marine Corps, he practiced law in Alabama, and then was president of a smelting company, a GS 15 civil servant in Washington, DC, the Washington Representative of an international consulting firm, and an investment adviser. He has given many presentations in the United States, Europe, and Japan on "The U.S. and Global Economies." He lives in Arlington, Virginia, and is married to the former Genevieve Marie Campbell. They have three adult sons.